Africa Yearbook

Africa Yearbook

Politics, Economy and Society South of the Sahara in 2016

VOLUME 13

Edited by

Jon Abbink
Sebastian Elischer
Andreas Mehler
Henning Melber

BRILL

LEIDEN | BOSTON

The Library of Congress Cataloging-in-Publication Data is available online at http://catalog.loc.gov

Typeface for the Latin, Greek, and Cyrillic scripts: "Brill". See and download: brill.com/brill-typeface.

ISSN 1871-2525
ISBN 978-90-04-35590-3 (paperback)
ISBN 978-90-04-35591-0 (e-book)

This book is printed on acid-free paper and produced in a sustainable manner.

Contents

Preface

In May 2003, the Africa-Europe Group of Interdisciplinary Studies (AEGIS) encouraged some of its member institutions to publish an *Africa Yearbook* with a wider international appeal. The African Studies Centre in Leiden (ASC), the Institute of African Affairs in Hamburg (IAA) and the Nordic Africa Institute in Uppsala (NAI) – all very active AEGIS centres with similar profiles – accepted this challenge and their joint efforts first bore fruit in the initial volume of the series in 2004. In 2007, the Dag Hammarskjöld Foundation in Uppsala (DHF) joined this international project, while the NAI ended its involvement with the fifth volume, published in 2009. As from 2014, the DHF ended its collaboration, and from the 11th volume the NAI re-joined the collaborating institutions, ensuring the *Yearbook*'s continued publication. In a subsequent further step towards strengthening the collaboration, the University of Florida also decided with this volume to join the network of institutions. We take this opportunity to thank Rolf Hofmeier for his solid support as one of the previous editors for many years; he remains a member of the team as a contributor.

As in previous volumes, the country-specific articles cover domestic politics, foreign affairs and socioeconomic developments in the states of SSA during the calendar year under review. While we recognise the impossibility of finding fully objective indicators for the relative importance of each of the states covered by the *Yearbook*, the length of the country-specific articles aims to reflect the approximate weight of each country. The four sub-regions are also introduced by means of an overview article. Further overviews summarise general continental developments and European-African relations.

The *Yearbook* is based on scholarly work, but is oriented towards a wider target readership, including students, politicians, diplomats, administrators, journalists, teachers, practitioners in the sphere of development cooperation and business people. Without forcing the individual contributions too much into a straitjacket, the volume is primarily concerned with providing factual (though not necessarily neutral) information. Each issue, in focusing almost exclusively on developments during a particular calendar year, provides a completely fresh annual overview of events and thereby adds to the cumulative record of on-going developments.

In November 2012, the *Yearbook* received the prestigious biennial Conover-Porter Award for outstanding Africa-related reference works from the African Studies Association and the Africana Librarians Council in the USA. This was an encouraging sign that the *Yearbook* has become a permanent and appreciated feature in Africanist publishing. The same year, thanks to a generous arrangement by Brill, the Africa Institute of South Africa joined as an African co-publisher, thereby greatly enhancing local distribution on the continent.

This is the thirteenth consecutive volume of the *Yearbook*, and we are proud to present a record of another year in African affairs in what we believe is a solid scholarly contribution towards a better understanding of and more knowledge about SSA countries. Brill has since 2016 taken the initiative to publish in addition some country-focused chronologies in compilations of *Yearbook* chapters. These testify to the value of information steadily accumulated over time, enhancing accessibility to readers with a main interest in one specific country.

Once again we wish to express our gratitude to all the contributors for their collaboration in this endeavour; to the partner institutions in AEGIS for encouraging us to embark on this ambitious project; to Carol Rowe for her meticulous language editing; to Bas van der Mije for his unfailing coordinating assistance; and to Brill Publishers for their continued commitment. And last but not least, we would once again like to thank our participating institutions for their on-going support.

The Editors
(Freiburg, Gainesville, Leiden and Uppsala, June 2017)

List of Abbreviations

ACP	African, Caribbean, and Pacific Group of Countries (Lomé/Cotonou Agreement)
AfDB	African Development Bank (Tunis)
AGOA	African Growth and Opportunity Act
AI	Amnesty International
APRM	African Peer Review Mechanism
AU	African Union (Addis Ababa)
BCEAO	Banque Centrale des Etats de l'Afrique de l'Ouest (Dakar)
BEAC	Banque des Etats de l'Afrique Centrale (Yaoundé)
CAR	Central African Republic
CBLT	Commission du Bassin du Lac Tchad (N'Djaména)
CEEAC	Communauté Economique des Etats de l'Afrique Centrale (Libreville) = ECCAS
CEMAC	Communauté Economique et Monétaire de l'Afrique Centrale
CEN-SAD	Community of Sahel-Saharan States (Tripoli)
CFAfr	Franc de la Communauté Financière Africaine (BCEAO; BEAC)
COMESA	Common Market for Eastern and Southern Africa (Lusaka)
CPLP	Comunidade dos Países de Língua Portuguesa
DDR	Disarmament, Demobilisation and Reintegration
DFID	Department for International Development (London)
DRC	Democratic Republic of the Congo
EAC	East African Community
ECA	Economic Commission for Africa (United Nations; Addis Ababa)
ECCAS	Economic Community of Central African States (Libreville)
ECF	Extended Credit Facility (IMF)
ECOWAS	Economic Community of West African States (Abuja)
EDF	European Development Fund (Brussels)
EIB	European Investment Bank (Luxemburg)
EITI	Extractive Industries Transparency Initiative.
EPA	Economic Partnership Agreement
EU	European Union (Brussels)
FAO	Food and Agricultural Organisation (Rome)
FDI	Foreign Direct Investment
GDP	Gross Domestic Product
HDI	Human Development Index (UNDP)
HIPC	Heavily Indebted Poor Countries
HRW	Human Rights Watch
ICC	International Criminal Court
ICGLR	International Conference on the Great Lakes Region

IDA	International Development Association (Washington)
IDP	Internally Displaced Person
IFAD	International Fund for Agricultural Development (Rome)
IFC	International Finance Corporation (Washington)
IGAD	Intergovernmental Authority on Development (Djibouti)
ILO	International Labour Organisation (Geneva)
IMF	International Monetary Fund (Washington)
IOC	Indian Ocean Commission (Quatre Bornes)
IORA	Indian Ocean Rim Association (Ebène/Mauritius)
MDGS	Millennium Development Goals
MRU	Mano River Union (Freetown)
NEPAD	New Partnership for Africa's Development
NGO	Non-Governmental Organisation
OAU	Organization of African Unity
ODA	Official Development Assistance
OECD	Organisation for Economic Cooperation and Development (Paris)
OIC	Organisation of the Islamic Conference (Jeddah)
OIF	L'Organisation Internationale de la Francophonie
OPEC	Organisation of Petroleum Exporting Countries (Vienna)
PPP	Purchasing Power Parity
SACU	Southern African Customs Union (Pretoria)
SADC	Southern African Development Community (Gaborone)
SDR	Special Drawing Right (IMF)
SSA	Sub-Saharan Africa
TI	Transparency International
UAE	United Arab Emirates
UEMOA	Union Économique et Monétaire Ouest-Africaine (Ouagadougou)
UN	United Nations (New York)
UNDP	United Nations Development Programme (New York)
UNESCO	United Nations Educational, Scientific and Cultural Organisation (Paris)
UNHCR	United Nations High Commissioner for Refugees (Geneva)
UNICEF	United Nations Children's Fund (New York)
UNSC	United Nations Security Council
USAID	United States Agency for International Development (Washington)
WFP	World Food Programme (Rome)
WHO	World Health Organisation (Geneva)
WTO	World Trade Organisation (Geneva)

Factual Overview (as of 31 December 2016)

West Africa

Country	Area (in sq km)	Population (in m)	Currency	HDI (2015)	Head of State	Prime Minister
Benin	112,622	10.8	CFA Franc	0.485	Patrice Talon	
Burkina Faso	274,122	19.0	CFA Franc	0.402	Roch Marc Christian Kaboré	Paul Kaba Thiéba
Cape Verde	4,033	0.5	Cape Verdean Escudo	0.648	Jorge Carlos Fonseca	Ulisses Correia e Silva
Côte d'Ivoire	322,462	23.9	CFA Franc	0.474	Alassane Ouattara	daniel Kablan Duncan
Gambia	11,295	2.1	Dalasi	0.452	Yahya Jammeh	
Ghana	238,500	28.2	Cedi	0.579	John Dramani Mahama	
Guinea	245,857	11.2	Guinean Franc	0.414	Alpha Condé	Mamady Youla
Guinea-Bissau	36,125	1.9	CFA Franc	0.424	José Mário Vaz	Umaro Sissoco Embaló
Liberia	111,370	4.6	Liberian Dollar	0.427	Ellen Johnson- Sirleaf	
Mali	1,240,000	17.3	CFA Franc	0.442	Ibrahim Boubacar Keïta	Modibo Keïta
Mauritania	1,030,700	4.2	Ouguiya	0.513	Mohamed Ould Abdel Aziz	Yahya Ould Hademine
Niger	1,267,000	19.7	CFA Franc	0.353	Mahamadou Issoufou	Brigi Rafini
Nigeria	923,768	186.5	Naira	0.527	Muhammadu Buhari	
Senegal	197,162	14.8	CFA Franc	0.494	Macky Sall	Mahammed Boun Abdallah Dionne
Sierra Leone	71,740	6.6	Leone	0.420	Ernest Bai Koroma	
Togo	56,785	7.5	CFA Franc	0.487	Faure Essozimna Gnassingbé	Komi Sélom Klassou

Central Africa

Country	Area (in sq km)	Population (in m)	Currency	HDI	Head of State	Prime Minister
Cameroon	475,442	24.4	CFA Franc BEAC	0.518	Paul Biya	Philémon Yang
Central African Republic	622,984	5.0	CFA Franc BEAC	0.352	Faustin Archange-Touadéra	Simplice Sarandji
Chad	1,284,000	14.5	CFA Franc BEAC	0.396	Idriss Déby Itno	Albert Pahimi Padacke
Congo	342,000	4.9	CFA Franc BEAC	0.592	Denis Sassou-Nguesso	Clément Mouamba
DR Congo	2,344,855	79.8	Congolese Franc	0.435	Joseph Kabila	Samy Badibanga
Equatorial Guinea	28,051	0.9	CFA Franc BEAC	0.592	Teodoro Obiang Nguema Mbasogo	Francisco Pascual Obama Asue
Gabon	267,667	1.8	CFA Franc BEAC	0.697	Ali Bongo Ondimba	Emmanuel Issoze-Ngondet
São Tomé and Príncipe	1,001	0.2	Dobra	0.574	Evaristo Carvalho	Patrice Trovoada

Eastern Africa

Country	Area (in sq km)	Population (in m)	Currency	HDI	Head of State	Prime Minister
Burundi	26,338	11.1	Burundi Franc	0.404	Pierre Nkurunziza	
Comoros	1,862	0.8	Comoran Franc	0.497	Azali Assoumani	
Djibouti	23,200	0.9	Djiboutian Franc	0.473	Ismail Omar Guelleh	Abdoulkader Kamil Mohamed
Eritrea	124,320	5.4	Nakfa	0.420	Isaias Afewerki	
Ethiopia	1,121,900	101.7	Birr	0.448	Mulatu Teshome	Hailemariam Desalegn
Kenya	569,259	45.4	Kenya Shilling	0.555	Uhuru Kenyatta	
Rwanda	26,338	11.9	Rwanda Franc	0.498	Paul Kagame	Anastase Murekezi
Seychelles	455	0.09	Seychelles Rupee	0.728	James Michel	
Somalia	637,600	11.1	Somali Shilling	n.a.	Hassan Sheikh Mohamud	Omar Abdirashid Ali Sharmarke
(Somaliland)	137,600	3.5	Somaliland Shilling	n.a.	Ahmed Mohamed Mahamoud 'Silanyo'	
Sudan	2,505,805	42.1	Sudanese Pound	0.490	Omar Hassan Ahmad al-Bashir	
South Sudan	619,745	12.7	South Sudanese Pound	0,418	Salva Kiir Mayardit	
Tanzania	945,087	54.2	Tanzania Shilling	0.531	John Magufuli	Majaliwa Kassim Majaliwa
Uganda	197,000	36.6	Uganda Shilling	0.493	Yoweri Kaguta Museveni	Ruhakana Rugunda

Southern Africa

Country	Area (in sq km)	Population (in m)	Currency	HDI	Head of State	Prime Minister
Angola	1,246,700	25.8	Kwanza	0.533	José Eduardo dos Santos	
Botswana	581,730	2.2	Pula	0.698	Seretse Khama Ian Khama	
Lesotho	30,344	2.2	Lesotho Loti	0.497	King Letsie III	Bethuel Pakalitha Mosisili
Madagascar	592,000	23.7	Malagasy Ariary	0.512	Hery Rajaonarimampianina	Olivier Mahafaly Solonandrasana
Malawi	118,484	17.2	Malawian Kwacha	0.476	Peter Mutharika	
Mauritius	2,040	1.3	Mauritian Rupee	0.781	Ameenah Gurib-Fakim	Pravind Kumar Jugnauth
Mozambique	799,380	27.2	Mozambiquen Métical	0.418	Filipe Nyusi	Carlos Agostinho do Rosário
Namibia	824,269	2.5	Namibian Dollar	0.640	Hage Gottfried Geingob	Saara Kuugongelwa-Amadhila
South Africa	1,219,090	55.7	Rand	0.666	Jacob Zuma	
Swaziland	17,364	1.3	Swazi Lilangeni	0.541	King Mswati III	Sibusiso Dlamini
Zambia	752,614	15.9	Zambian Kwacha	0.579	Edgar Lungu	
Zimbabwe	390,580	16.0	Zimbabwean Dollar	0.516	Robert Gabriel Mugabe	

(Population figures are for mid-2016 according to Stiftung Weltbevölkerung, www.weltbevölkerung.de)

List of Authors

Jon Abbink
Senior researcher at the African Studies Centre, Leiden University, and research professor at the Department of Anthropology at VU University, Amsterdam, abbink@ascleiden.nl

Alfred Babo
Assistant Professor of International Studies, Sociology & Anthropology Department, Fairfield University, Fairfield, CT, US, ababo@fairfield.edu

Jean-Nicolas Bach
PhD in Political Science, is currently the Coordinator of the French research institute in Khartoum (CEDEJ Khartoumand coordinator with Roland Marchal (CERI Sciences Po) of the Observatory of Eastern Africa/Observatoire de l'Afrique de l'Est, jeannicolas_bach@yahoo.fr.

Alice Bellagamba
Professor of Cultural and Social Anthropology, Department of Human Sciences for Education "Riccardo Massa", University of Milan-Bicocca, alice.bellagamba@unimib.it

Heinrich Bergstresser
Media Consultant, Freelance Research Associate of the Institute of African Affairs in Hamburg and Freelance Trainer of Deutsche Gesellschaft für Internationale Zusammenarbeit GIZ, Germany, heinrich.bergstresser@web.de

Mamadou Bodian
Ph.D. (2016) in political science, University of Florida, is a Project Coordinator for the Trans-Saharan Elections Programme (TSEP) and a member of the Sahel Research Group, mbodian79@ufl.edu

Yolande Bouka
Independent scholar and practitioner, Toronto, Ontario, ybouka@gmail.com

Jennifer C. Boylan
Ph.D. (2016) in Political Science, Managing Editor, Perspectives on Politics, jboylan@ufl.edu

Brett Logan Carter
Assistant Professor, School of International Relations, University of Southern California, blcarter@usc.edu

Clément Deshayes
PhD student, Department of Sociology and Anthropology, University Paris 8 Saint Denis, associate researcher at LAVUE and CEDEJ-Khartoum, deshayes.clement@gmail.com

George Dzimbiri
Lecturer at the Department of Business Administration, the Polytechnic, University of Malawi, gdzimbiri@poly.ac.mw

Lewis Dzimbiri
Professor of Public Administration, Chancellor College, University of Malawi, proflewisdzimbiri@gmail.com

Daniel Eizenga
Doctoral Candidate, Department of Political Science, University of Florida, USA, deizenga@ufl.edu

Sebastian Elischer
Ph.D. (2010) in Comparative Politics, Jacobs University Bremen, is assistant professor of comparative politics at the University of Florida, selischer@ufl.edu

Lansana Gberie
Academic and Writer, Ottawa, Canada, lagberie@yahoo.com

Dr Christine Hackenesch
Senior researcher, German Development Institute / Deutsches Institut für Entwicklungspolitik (DIE), Bonn, Germany, christine.hackenesch@die-gdi.de

Joseph Hanlon
Visiting Senior Fellow, Department of International Development, London School of Economics, UK and Visiting Senior Research Fellow at the Development Policy and Practice Centre of the Open University, UK, j.hanlon@open.ac.uk

Ketil Fred Hansen
Associate Professor in Modern African History, University of Stavanger, Norway. ketil.f.hansen@uis.no

Kurt Hirschler
Freelance Political Scientist, Hamburg, Germany, kurt_hirschler@web.de

Nicole Hirt
Freelance Research Associate, Institute of African Affairs, GIGA German Institute of Global and Area Studies, Hamburg, Germany, e-mail: nicole.hirt@giga-hamburg.de

Rolf Hofmeier
Former Director, Institute of African Affairs, GIGA German Institute of Global and Area Studies, Hamburg, Germany, rolf.hofmeier@giga-hamburg.de

Amin Kamete
Senior Lecturer, Urban Studies, School of Social and Political Sciences, University of Glasgow, Scotland, UK, amini.kamete@glasgow.ac.uk

Niels Keijzer
Researcher, German Development Institute / Deutsches Institut für Entwicklungspolitik (DIE), Bonn, Germany, niels.keijzer@die-gdi.de

Christoph Kohl
Researcher, Peace Research Institute Frankfurt, Frankfurt am Main, Germany, kohl@hsfk.de

Dirk Kohnert
Retired Deputy Director, Institute of African Affairs, GIGA German Institute of Global and Area Studies, Hamburg, Germany, Kohnert@giga-hamburg.de

Daniel Large
Assistant Professor at the School of Public Policy, Central European University, Budapest, and non-Resident Senior Fellow at the China Policy Institute, University of Nottingham, larged@spp.ceu.edu

Gabrielle Lynch
Professor of Comparative Politics, Department of Politics and International Studies, University of Warwick, UK, g.lynch@warwick.ac.uk

Joseph N. Mangarella
Lecturer at the Université de Panthéon-Assas (Paris 2), Ph.D candidate at the Africa Studies Center, Leiden, and at the Institut Français de Géopolitique, Université Paris 8, joseph.mangarella@gmail.com

Richard R. Marcus
Professor and Director, The Global Studies Institute and the International Studies Program, California State University, Long Beach, USA, richard.marcus@csulb.edu

Simon Massey
Senior lecturer and post-graduate course director in the School of Humanities, Coventry University, s.massey@coventry.ac.uk

Andreas Mehler
Director of the Arnold Bergstraesser Institute and professor of Political Science at the University of Freiburg, andreas.mehler@abi.uni-freiburg.de

Henning Melber
Senior Research Associate of The Nordic Africa Institute and Director emeritus of The Dag Hammarskjöld Foundation, both in Uppsala, Sweden Henning.Melber@nai.uu.se

Sanusha Naidu
Senior Research Associate, Institute for Global Dialogue, sanusha.naidu@gmail.com

Anthoni van Nieuwkerk
Professor in political science and Academic Director at the Wits School of Governance, University of the Witwatersrand, Johannesburg. Anthoni.vannieuwkerk@wits.ac.za

Helena Olsson
Political Scientist and Staff Member at the Department of Sociology, Uppsala University, Sweden, helena.olsson@soc.uu.se

Claes Olsson
Political Scientist and Editor at Global Publications Foundation, Uppsala, Sweden, claesolsson@globalpublications.org

Krijn Peters
Associate Professor in Armed Conflict & Post-war Reconstruction, Department of Political & Cultural Studies, Swansea University, UK, k.peters@swansea.ac.uk

Fanny Pigeaud
Journalist, France, Fanny.pigeaud@gmail.com

Marisha Ramdeen
Senior Programme Officer at the African Centre for the Constructive Resolution of Disputes (ACCORD) in Durban, South Africa. Marisha@accord.org.za

Edalina Rodrigues Sanches
Postdoctoral Research Fellow at the Institute of Social Sciences-University of Lisbon and the Portuguese Institute of International Relations-New University of Lisbon and Guest Assistant Professor at ISCTE-IUL ersanches@ics.ul.pt

Anita Schroven
Researcher at 'Integration and Conflict along the Upper Guinea Coast', Max Planck Institute for Social Anthropology, Halle/Saale, schroven@eth.mpg.de

Jon Schubert
Senior Research Fellow, 'War and State Formation', Global Studies Institute, University of Geneva, jonschubert@gmx.net

David Sebudubudu
Professor of Political Science and Dean of the Faculty of Social Sciences, University of Botswana, Sebudubu@mopipi.ub.bw

Gerhard Seibert
Associate professor at the Universidade da Integração Internacional da Lusofonia Afro-Brasileira (UNILAB), São Francisco do Conde, Bahia, Brazil, mailseibert@yahoo.com

Tor Sellström
Ph.D.hc (Uppsala 2011), researcher and writer. His latest book is Africa in the Indian Ocean: Islands in Ebb and Flow (Brill; 2015). tg.sellstrom@gmail.com

Claudia Simons
Policy Advisor and Deputy Head of the Africa Department, Heinrich-Boell-Foundation, Berlin, simons@boell.de

Roger Southall
Professor Emeritus, Department of Sociology, University of the Witwatersrand, and Research Associate in Political Studies, University of Cape Town, South Africa, Roger.Southall@wits.ac.za

Alexander Stroh
Assistant Professor of African Politics and Development Policy, University of Bayreuth, Germany, alexander.stroh@uni-bayreuth.de

Stef Vandeginste
Lecturer, Institute of Development Policy (IOB), University of Antwerp, Belgium, stef.vandeginste@uantwerpen.be

Klaas van Walraven
Researcher, African Studies Centre, Leiden, The Netherlands, walraven@ascleiden.nl

Volker Weyel
Consultant, Former Editor-in-chief 'Vereinte Nationen' (1977–2004), Bonn, Germany, volker.weyel@outlook.com

Bruce Whitehouse
Director, Global Studies Program, Associate Professor of Anthropology, Lehigh University, USA, bruce.whitehouse@lehigh.edu

Douglas Yates
Professor of Political Science at the American Graduate School in Paris, France, douglas.yates@ags.edu

PART 1

Sub-Saharan Africa

Jon Abbink, Sebastian Elischer, Andreas Mehler and Henning Melber

World market-related shocks, alongside domestic failures, were among the factors contributing to sluggish economic growth in most countries. Illicit capital outflows continued at a high level and illegal transfers of money added to the financial woes caused by generally low GDP growth. Climate change and related environmental degradation were other factors that had a mainly negative impact, exacerbating natural disasters and also contributing to ongoing migration. Terrorist activities and other violent conflicts, mainly in parts of West, Central and East Africa, contributed to the fragility of political situations and internal displacement. Peacekeeping missions in conflict zones continued with mixed results. Presidential elections were held in 17 countries and parliamentary elections in eight, resulting in some cases in a change of government and in others to power being retained by undemocratic means. A general trend towards erosion of the freedom of the media was visible, while the APRM was reactivated.

Africa in the Global Economy

African economies continued to grow, but at a much slower pace than in previous years: the continental *GDP average* increased by 1.5%. While caution should be exercised in accepting and interpreting the statistical data on African economies due to deficiencies in data-gathering and the pressure of state-prescribed targets in certain countries, some general trends were clear. Overall GDP growth was lower than expected, with only a moderate prospect of recovery in 2017 towards 2.5%–2.6%. Slackening global demand, structural deficiencies, lack of diversification, political uncertainties and governance problems (corruption, lack of property security and private sector support or participation) hampered overall development and institutional resilience. With a few exceptions, industrialisation policies were slow in developing. With an average of 5.3% growth, Eastern Africa was in the lead, well above North (3.3%), South (1.1%), Central (0.8%) and West Africa, which had the lowest (0.4%) according to the AfDB.

Nigeria recorded negative growth (-1.5%), partly due to the ongoing devastating Boko Haram conflict in the North-East and the stagnation in world oil prices, the latter revealing the weaknesses of a one-resource-dependent economy such as Nigeria. Like other mineral wealth economies, it still did not make serious headway with long-term planning for diversification, broad-based agrarian development or industrialisation, and it also had serious forex shortages. These deep problems in

 | DOI 10.1163/9789004355910_002

Africa's largest economy, with a basis in oil wealth and great human potential, continued to present a dilemma.

South Africa, the most industrialised country, also did not perform well, with a growth rate over the year of only 0.4%, a population growth of 1.6% and unemployment at about 27%. Many of the problems were related to continued political instability and investors' nervousness, along with some stagnation in mining and manufacturing. South Africa underwent a rather shocking credit downgrade, to one notch above 'junk status'. Like South Africa, *Angola* felt the adverse effects of the slump in commodity prices and a regional drought, but these were seen as temporary setbacks, with expectations of growth recovery in 2017. *Mauritius* continued to perform very well, despite its high dependence on developments in Europe, due to diversification away from the long-dominant sugar and tourism sectors. In some countries, corruption and elite greed continued to have a negative impact on economic development. In several countries, notably Nigeria and Angola, the poor policy environment for business growth was a brake on economic development.

The socio-economic trajectory of Africa over the year testified, however, to the continent's growing and irreversible *integration into the global economy*, although the pace varied between the sub-regions, being determined by local political regimes, conflict durability, institutional capacity and international investment preferences. In the World Bank's 'Doing Business 2017' report for 2016, Mauritius ranked top in Africa, at 49th out of 190 countries worldwide. Rwanda followed at 56th, then Morocco (at 68th), Botswana (at 71st) and South Africa (at 74th). At the lower end of the spectrum were Nigeria (169th) and, disappointingly, Angola at 182nd – squandering its once high potential and its (oil) wealth in an unclear and unproductive economic trajectory.

An important part of Eastern Africa's dynamics was continued *infrastructure investment*, including in railways, roads, green energy projects, and dams in Kenya and Ethiopia, but a general problem was, again, continued drought, which reduced agricultural production. This also affected wider socio-economic activity – including agro-pastoralism – in some countries, notably Kenya, Somalia and eastern Ethiopia, exacerbating local conflicts. Steady though moderate growth was seen in some countries, supported by tourism (Seychelles), infrastructure development and increasing private consumption (Comoros, Ethiopia). Most countries experienced problems with tight foreign exchange liquidity. With rising debt levels and an environment of tighter and more volatile financial conditions, many African countries faced the challenge of undertaking their much-needed development spending without jeopardising their debt sustainability. A durable problem across Eastern Africa was growing socio-economic *inequality*.

Central Africa – the Great Lakes area and the CAR – and parts of West Africa were hampered by *enduring conflict* and often crippling violence, preventing socio-economic progress, educational development and institution-building. In

West Africa, Senegal and Côte d'Ivoire were growth hot spots, with their CFA franc pegged to the euro (thus limiting currency instability), while for Ghana doubts arose over its debt sustainability. In Nigeria and adjacent countries, problems of violent conflict and terrorism caused much loss of life as well as political instability and economic damage. There were a growing number of violent clashes across the sub-region between sedentary farmers and Fulani herders, with many of the latter veering towards Islamist-jihadist discourse. Southern Africa, although with a more developed industrial base and more institutional stability, showed sluggish growth, an only modest increase in consumer demand, and underlying political insecurity (including in Zimbabwe, Mozambique and even South Africa).

As for *ODA*, in contrast to suggestions in the media, the US was still SSA's largest donor, providing close to $ 9 bn. But the election of President Donald Trump in November suggested a future change of course on the part of the US, with a more protectionist policy (revisiting AGOA and duty-free market access) and an ODA reduction. Some observers in Africa, however, saw this as a blessing in disguise that might force African countries and the AU to get their act together more, with or without China and other 'new donors' and partner countries, focusing on business investments. At the same time, Africa retained its place as a continent much affected by *illicit capital outflows*, estimated this year at some $ 55–60 bn, i.e., between 7.5% and 11.5% of its total trade value, leading to a tax revenue loss of about $ 14 bn. Only Russia and former Soviet republics, including in Eastern Europe, had higher figures. Registered *remittances* provided an inflow of about $ 33 bn (with Nigeria accounting for about $ 19 bn), but the real figure was estimated to be more than double that amount. Official remittances to SSA slumped by about 6%. Inflation rose slightly across Africa, but the average remained moderate, at around 7.5%, with the list topped by South Sudan (47%), Angola (33%), Nigeria (15.5%), Malawi and Ghana (19%) and Sudan (13.5%).

The AfDB estimated that 55% of SSA's economic activity was still in the *informal sector* – reflecting problems of inclusion, vocational training, education and employment growth, but also proving an opportunity to gradually 'formalise' the sector and add to GDP. Encouraging activity was seen in the *ICT sector*, with more emerging tech ventures, start-ups, innovation centres and inventive applications in the field of mobile money etc. Kenya and Nigeria were at the forefront, but Ghana and Rwanda also showed much dynamic innovation in this field.

An undiminished challenge amidst the stories of growth and possibilities was *environmental pressure and ecological decline*. While some areas in West Africa and elsewhere showed resilience, with a selective recovery of rainfall patterns, forest cover and pasture lands, the overall trend was towards impoverishment and drying out, with mounting dangers for soil fertility, water availability and regenerative capacity. Population pressure was a major factor here, and one hardly addressed in policy. Some countries were more serious in planning for a 'green economy', partly following up on the COP21 Paris process, but funding was as yet inadequate, and the issue was not prominent in policy forums or public debate. The COP22 meeting was held on 7–18 November in Marrakech (Morocco), focusing on the difficult issue of implementation of the climate change accords in Africa.

Some areas in Africa also retained persistent *high poverty rates*, even amidst good national GDP growth figures (such as in Eastern Africa), and the continent faced the ongoing challenge of making this growth more 'inclusive' – the often heard refrain on the level of the World Bank and NGOs and at the AU. The reforms that were needed to achieve that – improving institutions for private sector growth, developing local capital markets, respecting rights, enhancing the efficiency of utilities provision, improving the quantity and quality of public infrastructure, and increasing domestic resource mobilisation and allocation – were not in place and were usually defined too narrowly in a primary economic rather than political and socio-cultural framework.

The high-profile *World Economic Forum on Africa* was held on 11–13 May in Kigali (Rwanda) (after the 'removal' of street vendors, sex workers, beggars, homeless people and suspected petty criminals from the streets of the city). The central theme of the Forum was 'Connecting Africa's resources though digital transformation'. Some 1,500 delegates from more than 70 countries took part, with many prominent speakers, including a number of African leaders. Discussions were characterised by encouraging rhetoric and were on Africa's economic challenges amidst slowdown, reducing dependency on primary commodities exports, ICT for growth, youth employment programmes (pushed by the AfDB) and public-private partnerships. The Forum also celebrated five top female African business innovators. *Risks* to the economic outlook for many parts of Africa included, externally, a stronger-than expected tightening of global financing conditions and rising protectionist sentiment, and domestically, a slippage on reforms, increasing security threats and, in some countries, political uncertainty ahead of elections.

Significant *out-migration* from Eastern and West Africa continued, mainly to Europe and not always of refugees fleeing unrest and insecurity in conflict-ridden countries. There was as much of an exodus from relatively stable areas (including Senegal or Ghana) of labour migrants and those seeking a better life. Various routes via Libya, Morocco and Egypt were used and human trafficking flourished. EPAs with African countries to set up youth employment and entrepreneurship schemes were in progress but were not yet providing much of a panacea.

The AU and the APRM

The AU held its regular annual meetings and pursued its plans and activities in the domains of political coordination, diplomacy development initiatives such as

Agenda 2063, and various security missions via deployment in Darfur and in Somalia (AMISOM), and continued mediation efforts in crises such as that in Burundi. The *26th AU Summit* took place on 21–31 January in Addis Ababa (Ethiopia), where Chadian president Idriss Déby was elected chair of the AU for the coming year. The year's theme was 'African Year of Human Rights, with a particular focus on the rights of women'. But during the year the AU rarely spoke up about human rights abuses by certain regimes. Outgoing AU chairman Robert Mugabe gave a parting speech, again full of UN-bashing and anti-Western rhetoric. The speech was described as 'absurd' by Zimbabwean opposition parties and raised eyebrows within the AU amidst public applause on its delivery. During this summit, the 'Rules of Procedure' for the AU's African Governance Architecture (AGA) were legally adopted, giving the AGA a legal guide for its activities. Its goals – to strengthen 'good governance' and 'consolidate democracy' on the continent – were based on 23 preceding constitutive declarations and legal instruments, but quite far from being realised. Derivative organs such as the AGA Platform and African Governance Facility (AGF) were also available. The AGF, as the resource mobilisation framework of the AGA, was tasked with supporting Platform members' initiatives and programmes to promote good governance and democracy initiatives. These organs were, however, not clearly or strongly connected to the African Peace and Security Architecture (APSA), so practice remained significantly behind theory. Despite calls from Tanzania and Nigeria to send an AU delegation to Burundi to persuade the leadership to accept peacekeeping troops, the summit appeared to shelve the plans for sending such a force.

On 10–18 July, the *27th AU Summit* was held in Kigali, where a key decision was taken by the 35 heads of state and government present on the financing of the AU – through a new 0.2 % import levy, expected to yield up to $ 1.2 bn yearly for the AU. Other major issues discussed were AU passports for African citizens, the Continental Free Trade Area (CFTA), the Peace and Security Decisions on South Sudan, the situation in Burundi, the situation in Libya, terrorism, and the appointment of two judges to the African Court on Human and Peoples' Rights. Burundi was absent from both summits, which were characterised by plenty of uplifting rhetoric on Africa's potential and promise. Several leaders picked up the idea of African industrialisation. In the context of the July summit, NEPAD also held its 8th heads of state and government Orientation Committee meeting on 16 July, focused on "utilization of Africa's rich natural and human resources, as well as [...] technological advancement to enhance development in the continent".

Dozens of other meetings of the AU and its various sub-units and affiliated bodies were held during the year, not always with any clearly visible results apart from the production of inventive rhetoric on African development, employment creation, energy infrastructure building, and peace and security. An *AU Extraordinary Summit* of heads of state and government on 'Maritime Security and Safety and Development in Africa' took place on 15 October in Lomé (Togo). It addressed the issue of maritime space as a possible 'key driver of Africa's economic and social development' and established a roadmap on maritime security and stability in Africa (38 of 54 African states being coastal states). Experts and business leaders were also in attendance. A new Lomé Charter of Maritime Security and Safety was signed.

On the margins of this conference, the *ECOWAS heads of state and government* discussed the conclusions of the Conakry mediation for the Guinea-Bissau crisis, led by President Alpha Condé of the Republic of Guinea(-Conakry), the ECOWAS mediator for this crisis. A six-point roadmap, the 'Agreement on the Resolution of the Political Crisis in Guinea Bissau', was signed in Bissau on 10 September. Apart from this agreement, the AU had no major successes in mediating in the existing conflicts or achieving peace on the continent, as massive violence and civil strife continued in Somalia, the DRC, the CAR, South Sudan, Sudan, Burundi and Mali, among others. The AU leadership was conspicuously silent on the wave of domestic repression and killing of hundreds of demonstrators in Ethiopia. It was also remarkable that the AU chose 2016 to consider mass withdrawal from the ICC, as had been consistently suggested at previous AU summits. Here, South Africa, Burundi and the Gambia led the charge and announced their intention of withdrawal, while Namibia later considered doing the same. One of those facing charges at the ICC, Sudanese President Omar al Bashir, was again able to travel freely to various African countries without being arrested.

On 10 August, the African Day of Decentralisation and Local Development was celebrated across the continent, under the theme 'Gender, equity, and women's empowerment key for achieving African's Agenda 2063 and Sustainable Development Goals (SDGs)'.

Elaborating the AU's complex *APSA* to give it power to act went slowly ahead but without major breakthroughs. It had three key parts: the PSC (the 15-member Peace and Security Council as the standing organ of the AU for prevention, management and resolution of conflicts); the ASF (African Standby Force); and the ACIRC (African Capacity for Immediate Response to Crisis), which held a second summit on 9 November in Addis Ababa. It declared that ACIRC was "... ready to respond swiftly to crises and contribute to Peace Support Operations". But there were major doubts as to its deployment capacity.

The AU continued its mission in *Somalia* (AMISOM), now in its tenth year, and was present in the joint mission in Darfur, with the AU-UN Hybrid Operation in Darfur (UNAMID). AMISOM again suffered major casualties in indiscriminate terrorist 'suicide attacks' and ambushes by the Islamist *al-Shabaab* movement on their bases and checkpoints. AMISOM, in retaliatory actions, also inadvertently killed several dozen civilians and later apologised for such collateral loss of life, including in operations around Bulo Mareer (April), El Wareegow and Qoriooley villages (in December).

Relations with the EU continued to revolve around development partnerships, migration issues and security problems. On 7 April, the AU Commission (AUC) and European Commission met in Addis Ababa for the annual College-to-College meeting to address shared EU-Africa challenges (the seventh meeting). On 29 June, the AUC and the EU signed the third phase of the AU Support Programme (AUSP III), with a three-year programme funding of € 51 m (85% EU and 15% AUC). The Annual Joint Consultative meeting of the AU's PSC and the EU's Political and Security Committee took place on 25 October in Brussels. There was talk of reducing EU funding for the AU programme budget, but it still amounted to more than € 300 m. In February, the EU threatened to cut the ever-increasing AMISOM budget by 20%, but the crisis was resolved in September.

A '5th Ministerial Meeting of the Joint Coordination Mechanism (JCM) of the Regional Cooperation Initiative for the Elimination of the *Lord's Resistance Army* (RCI-LRA)' on 20 May revealed that the LRA problem was still not solved and that combating it seemed to have become an institution in itself. A communiqué was duly released on further action against the LRA. Nor was any headway made in dealing with the crisis in Burundi in the wake of the massive 2015 violence after President Nkurunziza's controversial presidential term extension. The projected intervention force of 5,000 troops never materialised, due to Burundi's adamant refusal.

During the 26th AU summit in January, the AU's PSC had called for increased international cooperation to eliminate the *Boko Haram* terrorist group in Northern Nigeria. The AU supported the Multinational Joint Task Force (MNJTF), formed by the four Lake Chad Basin countries against Boko Haram, and on 29 October handed over a package of material support to the Task Force. In October, the EU announced support for the MNJTF through the AU's African Peace Facility to the tune of $ 50 m.

The AU sent *election observer missions* to a number of African countries: for the 18 February presidential elections in Uganda, the 20 March presidential elections (first round) in the Republic of Congo, the 10 April presidential elections in Chad, the 11 August general elections in Zambia, the 2 October presidential elections in Cabo Verde, and the 7 December presidential and parliamentary elections in Ghana. In no case did the missions see cause to reject the voting procedures or the results, which, in the cases of Congo and Uganda were certainly highly contested. Worst was the report of the AU observer mission to Djibouti's presidential elections on 8 April, which said that the election was "free and credible", but also marred by breaches of the country's electoral laws – a remarkable contradiction masking the deeply flawed electoral process.

As a follow-up to the *Paris COP-21*, 47 of the 54 African member states signed this climate change policy agreement, with two also ratifying it, on 22 April in New York. Despite funding limitations and challenges, several initiatives were taken up in the framework of the agreement, as in the Sixth Conference on Climate Change and Development in Africa (CCDA VI), held on 18–20 October in Addis Ababa. Some countries (such as Senegal) also started planting part of the 'Great Green Wall', a project adopted by AU countries on the sidelines of the COP21 to create a belt of vegetation on the edge of the desert, from West Africa up to the Indian Ocean.

The year witnessed a renaissance of the *APRM*. The 75th meeting of the APR Panel of Eminent Persons was held at the AU headquarters in Addis Ababa on 25–26 January. The work plan presented for the year featured reviews of Chad, Senegal, Sudan and Côte d'Ivoire. A roadmap for the integration of the APRM into the AU was discussed. A Special Summit of heads of state and government took place on 29 January in Addis Ababa with ten presidents and prime ministers in attendance. Kenya's President Uhuru Kenyatta, as chairperson of the APR Forum, bemoaned the concomitant slowdown in the review process and the revitalisation of the APRM. Others in support of such a revival included presidents Zuma of South Africa, Kagame of Rwanda, Ouattara of Côte d'Ivoire and Nyusi of Mozambique. Most speakers linked the APRM agenda with the AU Agenda 2063 and the SDGs. The South African academic Edward Maloka was appointed as the new chief executive officer of the APRM Secretariat. Administrative and financial issues related to the "revitalization of the APRM", which became a guiding slogan for the year, were discussed at the 76th meeting of the APR Panel of Eminent Persons on 26–27 February in Johannesburg (South Africa). The panel's 77th meeting was held in Johannesburg on 20–21 May. It considered review reports on Chad and Senegal and endorsed entering into technical cooperation with the Mo Ibrahim Foundation and the African Capacity Building Foundation as strategic partners.

After the first *second generation APRM country review* was initiated earlier in the year by Kenya, Uganda announced in July its willingness to follow suit. Both states stressed that this underlined their commitment to good governance. The 25th Summit of heads of state and government participating in the APR Forum celebrated on 26 August in Nairobi (Kenya) the successful revival of the APRM, which for the first time since its founding in 2003 adopted a five-year strategic plan. The Forum decided that APRM member states should pay contribution arrears within three years and that annual contributions should double from $ 100,000 to $ 200,000 with effect from 2017. On 17 October, five country review reports for Mali, Mozambique, Sierra Leone, Tanzania and Zambia were tabled before the Pan-African Parliament's third ordinary session held in Sharm El Sheikh (Egypt). It was also announced that Namibia had joined the APRM as the latest member state. After being dormant for several years, the APRM seemed to have entered a new stage in its life.

Democracy and Elections

For an eleventh consecutive year, the North American NGO Freedom House reported a worldwide decline in democracy. As in previous years, SSA was less affected by this decline than North Africa and the Middle East, but this should not distract from the fact that a large number of African countries were experiencing entrenched autocratic rule. Freedom House identified Ethiopia, Mozambique, South Sudan and Zambia as suffering with *eroding democratic institutions*. In all four countries, security forces abused civilian populations with indiscriminate and disproportionate violence. In *Ethiopia*, the state cracked down on the Oromo and the Amhara communities. Harassment of the political opposition took place under the cover of Ethiopia's flawed Anti-Terrorism Proclamation. In *Mozambique*, state violence caused thousands of citizens to flee to Malawi. In *South Sudan*, the peace deal collapsed, which led to renewed fighting between factions loyal to President Kiir and First Vice President Machar. The UNSC authorised a new Regional Protection Force with a stronger mandate to secure the capital but, at the end of the year, the force had still not been deployed. *Zambia* suffered from a very restrictive political environment in the run-up to the elections. After the narrow re-election of President Edgar Lungu, the opposition refused to recognise the election result, which resulted in violence between government and opposition supporters. Among the 11 countries Freedom House labelled as *"the worst of the worst"*, six were located in SSA: Eritrea, South Sudan, Somalia, Sudan, Equatorial Guinea and the CAR. According to the Fund for Peace's 2017 'State Fragility Index', several of these countries were among the ten most fragile countries worldwide: South Sudan, Somalia, the CAR, Sudan, the DRC and Chad. Even in *South Africa*, one of the continent's more stable democracies, Freedom House noted worrying trends and signs of dysfunction. President Jacob Zuma was under mounting political pressure following his involvement in several corruption scandals, and the government's decision to withdraw from the ICC tarnished the the country's international image. Student protests, which had started in 2015, continued to affect university campuses as students demonstrated against tuition fee increases and a lack of racial transformation on campuses.

Presidential elections were held in 17 countries: Benin, Cabo Verde, the CAR (second round of presidential elections held in 2015), Chad, Comoros, Djibouti, Equatorial Guinea, Gabon, Gambia, Ghana, Niger, the Republic of Congo, São Tomé and Principe, Uganda and Zambia. *Parliamentary elections* took place in Cabo Verde, the CAR, the DRC, Ghana, Côte d'Ivoire, Seychelles, Uganda and Zambia. The conduct of these electoral contests often mirrored the nature of the political regime. A few elections are worth mentioning in greater detail as they attracted regional and international attention.

In *Benin* and *Ghana*, elections resulted in yet another peaceful handover of power from government to opposition. The case of Ghana was especially remarkable as the opposition defeated an incumbent, still a rare occurrence in SSA. Democratic norms had become stabilised in both countries. In *São Tomé and Principe*, the opposition defeated Manuel Pinto da Costa, who had served as president in 1975–91 and 2011–16. In *Cabo Verde*, Jorge Fonseca was re-elected in a free and fair contest. *The Gambia* saw the unexpected ousting of long-term autocratic incumbent Yahya Jammeh. To the surprise of many, he initially conceded defeat, only to later rescind that concession. At the end of the year, Jammeh and ECOWAS were locked in a political standoff with ECOWAS threatening to remove Jammeh by military force. The example of the Gambia demonstrated vividly that democratic breakthroughs were still possible in a region of the world that often seems dominated by long-term autocrats. In *Niger* and *Zambia*, elections indicated that the democratic consolidation process was in trouble. In both countries, the government displayed autocratic reflexes. In Niger, the opposition responded by boycotting the run-off. In Zambia, the electoral outcome produced a severe constitutional crisis. In both countries, the recent elections led to the erosion of democratic institutions.

Although many African presidents now respected *term limits*, this was not yet the norm everywhere. President Denis Sassou Nguesso, who had ruled the Republic of Congo for 32 years, secured his re-election through constitutional changes. The same was true for Chad's Idriss Déby and Equatorial Guinea's Teodoro Nguema. In all three countries, incumbents resorted to election rigging, which also affected the outcome in Djibouti and Uganda. In the Comoros, the opposition claimed that the results had been tampered with. In the DRC, elections were scheduled but did not take place. President Kabila, who was scheduled to leave power after the end of his second term, argued that a technical delay in preparing the elections meant that they could not go ahead.

Across the continent, rulers frequently shut down the *Internet* and other media sources in the run-up to elections. According to Reporters Without Borders, *press freedom* was generally under threat. Restrictions ranged from subtle forms of censorship to imprisonment for journalists who criticised their governments. In the last few years, press freedom had come under attack even in those countries that had historically respected press freedom. According to Reporters Without Borders' 'World Press Freedom Index', Namibia, South Africa, Burkina Faso, Mauritania, Mauritius, Madagascar and Senegal were the countries that respected press freedom most. For the first time, Eritrea was ranked worst in the world for press freedom, a position previously held by North Korea. According to Freedom House, the main drivers behind the restrictions on press freedom were political unrest, election-related crackdowns and increasingly repressive leaders. There was no shortage of examples of leaders undermining the ability of the media to report independently. In South Sudan, security forces arrested journalists who reported rights abuses. In the DRC, the murder of Marcel Kalala, who worked for a state-owned television channel, shocked the country in November. In Burundi and Zimbabwe, state repression caused journalists to impose self-censorship.

Unconstitutional Rule, Coups and Armed Conflict

Following the quite dramatic coup attempt in September 2015, the government of *Burkina Faso* announced on 8 October the early detection of a second, less well-prepared coup attempt with potentially only 30 participants. This was reportedly another attempt to bring back the authoritarian leader Blaise Compaoré, though it was questionable that there was a mastermind behind the apparently superficial preparations. With the holding of presidential and legislative elections in the first months of the year, constitutional rule formally returned to the *CAR*.

The constitutionality of regime rule in several countries made headlines. *Burundi*'s political crisis continued, with the opposition not accepting President Nkurunziza's third term in office. However, the regime managed to stabilise its hold on power and Nkurunziza announced on 30 December that he would run for a fourth term if the constitution was changed – a clear sign that this was his new main political goal. Presidential elections in *Congo* (Brazzaville) were overshadowed by renewed violence after Sassou Nguesso managed to change the constitution to allow him to stand for election again. The number of reported casualties in clashes between security forces and militia groups in the Pool area varied wildly from several dozen to a less credible several thousand. Arguably, the most dangerous crisis unfolded in neighbouring *DRC*, where President Kabila, whose mandate ran out towards the end of the year, was not constitutionally allowed to run for a third term. Anti-regime demonstrations met with outright repression and more than 50 protesters were killed by security forces in September alone. A shaky compromise between major political parties to hold elections in 2017 was found on 31 December, but confrontation was brewing in several provinces of this large country. *Gambia* entered a short period of unconstitutional rule after the autocratic Jammeh reversed his initial acceptance of electoral defeat in December.

Demonstrators in the two Anglophone provinces of *Cameroon* not only protested against a recent hardening of government positions in the realm of education policy and interpretation of the law (in favour of the French language), but quickly brought onto the agenda discussions about the legality of the 1972 abolition of federalism. The options being called for ranged from a return to federalism to autonomy or even secession, but met with an uncompromising government response. Three demonstrators were reportedly killed and more than 50 arrested in the protests.

Ethiopia experienced a particularly difficult year, with an extension of the anti-government protests that had started in November 2015. One epicentre of the clashes was in Oromia. On 10–11 January, security forces stormed dormitories at Jimma University and arrested and manhandled many students. In August, the protest reached northern Amhara and more than 100 people were gunned down by security forces. During the *Irreecha* festival on 2 October, the annual Oromo cultural event in Bishoftu (in Oromia, but only 40 km from the capital Addis Ababa), tensions escalated again; government troops used teargas grenades and live ammunition, causing a panic and stampede with 52 people killed, according to official reports. Overall more than 500 people had been killed in further acts of repression since late 2015. The authorities declared a state of emergency and arrested thousands of protestors and individual opposition leaders. Some of them engaged in a hunger strike in July. By 21 December, about 10,000 of the 12,500 detained had been released, but the rest were set to be charged in court with destabilising the country.

The domestic crisis also meant that Ethiopia's security forces were less capable of fighting the al-Shabaab Islamist militia in neighbouring *Somalia*. The continent's largest AU-sponsored peacekeeping operation AMISOM (with over 20,000 personnel), operating in its tenth year, had to cope with a resounding military defeat when a Kenyan company was completely wiped out in the battle of El-Adde (about 150 Kenyan soldiers died at the army base, including all their officers). In the first quarter of the year, some spectacular military actions targeted al-Shabaab. On 8 March, a US drone strike in southern Somalia reportedly killed 150 fighters, and Kenya claimed to have killed 34 fighters on 20 March. However, towards the end of the year, al-Shabaab apparently regained control over some territory after a partial Ethiopian withdrawal. Al-Shabaab managed to carry out targeted attacks on civilians and civilian infrastructure, as well as high-profile attacks on AMISOM facilities throughout the year. In addition, the anti-al-Shabaab coalition had to admit having killed civilians on several occasions. The total number of casualties in all fighting was rising to over 2,000.

International *peacekeeping operations* were prominent in many theatres of conflict, but many missions saw a reduction of personnel. This was the case with the French Sangaris mission in CAR, which ceased operations after the elections. However, the second half of the year saw an upsurge in violent confrontations and about 400 people lost their lives. The MINUSCA mission, with personnel maintained at over 10,000, found itself in difficult situations varying from locality to locality – as a buffer force, as an ally of the government or even of specific armed movements, and sometimes accused of sexual harassment and other abuses. The mission clearly lost credibility, even within the government. Various factions of the original Séléka rebels and other politico-military movements confronted each other or the considerably weaker state security forces, who resented not being systematically armed by international partners. Even harsher criticism was voiced against the slightly extended UNMISS mission in South Sudan (over 12,000 personnel) for failing to protect civilians, one of its essential mandates, in massive military confrontations between forces loyal to President Salva Kiir and those loyal to his rival Riek Machar. This applied particularly to the widespread violence in the capital Juba in July, when the peacekeepers barely managed to defend themselves against well-equipped armies. Even the UN peacekeepers' compound was caught in crossfire. On 16 November, UN Secretary-General Ban Ki-moon warned of a real risk of mass atrocities in the country; about 1,200 people were killed during the year.

The *DRC*'s North Kivu, Tanganyika and Kasai provinces saw major escalations of violence, though constellations were hardly similar. Inter-ethnic clashes were held responsible for the displacement of some 30,000 people in the Kalemie area (Tanganyika province), but the other outbreaks of violence involved organised militias and official security forces. The largest (and most expensive) UN peacekeeping operation on the continent (MONUSCO, with nearly 17,000 troops) concentrated on the Kivu provinces. Despite its massive engagement, the Uppsala Conflict Data Programme still recorded the deaths of 860 people in various forms of violent conflict.

While some of the older UN peacekeeping missions, in Liberia and Côte d'Ivoire, saw major reductions of personnel to figures slightly above 1,000, this was not the case with the MINUSMA mission in *Mali* – which remained at about the same strength as MINUSCA (i.e. above 10,000). MINUSMA was arguably the most dangerous mission, as 39 peacekeepers died in rebel attacks during the year (while the number of civilian casualties fell to less than 200). In one incident on 11 May, a MINUSMA convoy was attacked near Sévaré in the Mopti region and five peacekeepers were killed. The 2015 peace agreement had clearly not solved all the issues of concern.

A smaller UN mission (retaining its approximately 4,400 troops) operated in Abyei, a disputed territory between Sudan and South Sudan, while the very much larger hybrid UN/AU mission, with over 19,000 personnel, continued in *Darfur* (Sudan). On 29 June, the government of Sudan deplored the renewal of the mandate at this high level of troop numbers, claiming that there was evidence that the situation in Darfur justified the mission's drawdown.

Boko Haram, operating from Nigeria, but also solidly embedded in Niger and Cameroon, faced the MNJTF from all four Lake Chad basin countries, which was also capable of following groups of fighters across national frontiers. Chad sent some 2,000 troops to Niger to help fight the insurgency, and the Cameroonian army sometimes operated on Nigerian soil. While the number of casualties fell dramatically in Nigeria, Niger, Cameroon and Chad (to about 3,800, 490, 270 and 0 respectively), there was no reason to declare the insurgency over.

The worldwide trend towards a reduction in *pirate activity* continued and could be very clearly observed with regard to Somali pirates. Only two incidents were recorded by the International Maritime Bureau on the Horn of Africa (plus two in Kenya). The picture was completely different in the Gulf of Guinea, where piracy was on the rise (46 events recorded); 34 crew members were taken hostage and three vessels were hijacked. Most notably, incidents off the coast of Nigeria increased significantly to 36 during the year (making Nigeria the second country worldwide, after Indonesia, for numbers of pirate attacks). Nigerian pirates used modern weaponry and considerable violence and the Nigerian navy sometimes freed crew members in dramatic battles with pirates. There were also six significant incidents at Pointe Noire port in Congo, where robbers repeatedly tried to enter vessels at the outer anchorage in an effort to steal cargo or crew members' personal belongings.

Epidemics and Disasters

Urban *yellow fever* outbreaks at the end of 2015 in Angola spread to neighbouring DRC and from there to Kenya. Another separate outbreak was reported from Uganda. Massive reactive vaccination campaigns in all countries effectively contained the spread within months. According to a WHO report of 28 October, yellow fever was considered endemic in 34 African countries or particular regions. *Cholera* was reported in a total of 17 countries, with the highest numbers recorded in the DRC, Ethiopia, Tanzania and Kenya, amounting to 75% of all registered cases. Other emergencies included polio in Nigeria, encephalitis in Angola and Rift Valley fever in Niger.

Most affected by *humanitarian crises* were close to 15 m people across four Nigerian states (Adamawa, Borno, Gombe and Yobe), with more than 2.2 m people internally displaced. Malaria, chest infections and water-borne diarrhoea were lead causes of morbidity in the camps. The outbreak of new violence in August also turned large numbers of civilians in South Sudan into highly vulnerable internally displaced people and refugees.

In marked contrast to these challenges, which were related to a large extent to destitution, *lifestyle diseases* emerged as a new phenomenon, with diabetes, cancer and heart and respiratory diseases expected to be among the leading killers by 2030. Cases of these non-communicable diseases had more than doubled within a few years. The main contributing factors were identified as unhealthy diets, smoking, alcohol and physical inactivity, which contributed to high blood pressure, obesity, high levels of blood sugar and cholesterol.

The effects of *climate change* continued to impact on the living conditions of many people. Weather-related hazards had increased in frequency and intensity over recent years. A World Bank blog that introduced a new Africa Disaster Risk Management Strategic Framework 2016–20 estimated in November that by 2030 up to 118 m extremely poor people would be exposed to drought, floods and extreme heat. According to a Natural Hazards Vulnerability Index released in March by the risk analysts Verisk Maplecroft, Africa was the continent most vulnerable to natural disasters. Nine of the ten countries ranked as most vulnerable were in SSA (South Sudan, Burundi, Eritrea, Chad, Niger, Sudan, Mali and the DRC). A case in point was the continuing shrinking of *Lake Chad* and the desertification of the surrounding areas, which affected the security of millions of people dependent upon farming or fishing. Insecurity was also considered a factor contributing to younger people's support for Boko Haram as an alternative to deteriorating living conditions and lack of prospects.

Floods and drought related to one of the strongest ever recorded *El Niño effects* affected millions of people in Eastern and Southern Africa, with Ethiopia, Malawi, Namibia, South Africa, Zambia and Zimbabwe among the worst affected. The worst drought for decades hit the eastern highlands of Ethiopia – only to be followed by extreme rainfall. Flash floods destroyed crops and exacerbated already prevailing food insecurity. The 2015/16 harvest season in most countries in Southern Africa was markedly below average and affected food security for more than 100 m people in the region. Increased rainfall recorded in the Sahel region was considered a beneficial side effect of climate change.

An *earthquake* that measured 5.7 on the Richter scale was recorded near the Tanzanian city of Bukoba on 10 September. At least 13 people were killed and over 200 injured in north-west Tanzania and tremors reached as far as Rwanda, Uganda and Kenya.

PART 2

African-European Relations

Christine Hackenesch and Niels Keijzer

In many respects, 2016 defied imagination – or at least expectations – in the evolving Africa-EU relations. While in Africa key steps were taken towards Morocco's accession to the AU, fundamental choices in the opposite direction were faced by the EU following the United Kingdom's referendum in which a narrow majority voted to leave the EU. The year marked an important step forward in EU-Africa economic and trade cooperation through the provisional application of the EPA with SADC and the ratification by a number of middle-income countries of their bilateral interim EPAs. The same UK referendum, however, was a key factor in Tanzania's reluctance to ratify the EAC's EPA with the EU, although concerns over the implications for its industrialisation strategy played a more important part. The same motivation informed Nigeria's blocking of the West African EPA.

Agreement was reached on holding the next Africa-EU Summit in November 2017 in Côte d'Ivoire. High-level statements on both sides acknowledged that Africa's overwhelmingly young population represented a key window of opportunity but also a potential liability for the sustainability of growth while job creation ambitions remained unrealised. The EU therefore proposed 'youth' as the overarching topic for the 2017 summit. The progress made on the trade front, with the EU being highly open to increasing trade in goods with Africa, contrasted with its strong reluctance to facilitate human mobility from Africa to Europe. There was progress in operationalising the EU's Emergency Trust Fund for Africa, but fundamental flaws also emerged in the theory of how to address 'root causes' of migration and the diverging interests of the two continents on this topic.

At the national level, however, EU-Africa relations showed continuity rather than change. For example, the EU was not particularly critical towards Ethiopia and its government's response to civil unrest, but instead signed a migration compact and a 'strategic engagement' framework. The trend was also demonstrated in the EU's limited response to the general election in Uganda, which resulted in a victory for the incumbent president, who had been in power since 1986. This contrasted with elections in the Gambia, which brought the defeat of the small nation's ruler. It was not so much the result that was surprising, but rather the EU's swift and strong support for the newly elected president.

Events at the national level revealed a tension in the EU's approach to shaping its relations with Africa. These were well-captured in the EU's new Global Strategy for Foreign and Security Policy that was adopted in June and replaced the post-9/11 EU Security Strategy adopted in 2003. The EU Global Strategy acknowledged that a 'quantum leap' in European investment in Africa would serve both continents. It

 | DOI 10.1163/9789004355910_003

asserted that the EU should be more flexible and responsive to new developments. Yet EU external action continued to be guided by EU treaties that require the Union to project the values that inspired the start of the European project. One concrete example of the EU facing a trade-off between its values and its interests was the question of how to reconcile its commitment to promoting human rights with initial efforts made during the year to promote 'Turkey deals' with North African states to manage human mobility. This tension was put to the test by the threat of a mass African withdrawal from the ICC, which ultimately remained limited to concrete steps taken by South Africa and Burundi, raising questions regarding the EU's engagement with the continent going forward.

New Developments in European Foreign and Development Policy

In June, immediately after the referendum in the UK, High Representative and Vice President Federica Mogherini published the new *EU Global Strategy for Foreign and Security Policy*. In so doing, she sent out a positive signal that, despite the political crisis, the EU and its member states intended to cooperate more closely on foreign and security policy. Throughout the preparation of the strategy, Mogherini consulted closely with member states and representatives from civil society and the world of research.

The strategy placed a strong focus principally on the EU's relations with neighbouring countries, but also on the EU's relations with the 'neighbours of neighbours', including SSA countries. It included many references to Africa, and the continent and its various regions featured 31 times in the text, compared with 19 references to Asia and four to Latin America. In places, it referred to Africa as a threat to Europe's stability and growth, as when referring to North Africa being 'plagued' by terrorism and violence. The strategy gave priority to promoting both security and resilience. In an implicit yet somewhat ironic reference to the EU's institutional fragmentation, with separate policy frameworks and one EU Directorate-General dealing with North Africa and another with SSA, the strategy observed "growing interconnections" between the two parts of the continent.

Perhaps the most noteworthy part of the strategy was its statement that Europe would "invest in African peace and development as an investment in our own security and prosperity". In addition to calling for effective implementation of existing frameworks for cooperation, the strategy called for a 'quantum leap' in European investment in Africa. To provide an enabling environment for such investments, the EU further expressed the priority aim to make "stronger links between our trade, development and security policies in Africa, and blend development efforts with work on migration, health, education, energy and climate, science and technology, notably to improve food security".

Setting priorities did not provide all the answers, however, including the extent to which the EU desired to differ in its approach from other external partners to the AU. It did not address head-on how resilience would bring security, but instead simply noted an interrelation between the two terms. Nevertheless, the document did present a clear direction, since it defined resilient states as states that "are resilient when societies feel they are becoming better off and have hope in the future". The strategy put a much stronger emphasis on European investment than on European support for good governance and democracy.

On 22 November, the European Commission published a proposal for revising the *European Consensus on Development*, a tripartite political statement adopted in 2005 by the European Council, the European Parliament and the European Commission that set out a shared vision for EU development policy. The Consensus of 2005 had played a key role in informing the general direction of EU development, guiding the elaboration of the EU's financial instruments for development cooperation and developing the policies of those member states that had joined the EU after 2004. The new Commission proposal differed in that its overall aim was to outline a common vision as to how the EU and its member states would promote sustainable development through development policy, as defined by the UN 2030 Agenda for Sustainable Development adopted in September 2015. The proposal came relatively late in the term of the current Commissioner and it followed many operational development policy initiatives, some of which had fundamental implications for EU development policy and operations (such as the EU Trust Fund for Africa). The new Consensus would, however, probably be an important reference document in guiding the next generation of financial instruments for implementing EU development policy for the period 2021–27, including for Africa. Frequent references in the proposal to conditionality and migration 'root causes' reflected the overall ambition as stated in the EU Global Strategy for Foreign and Security policy.

Migration

The EU and its member states, with the parliament watching from the sidelines, confronted the ambition to operationalise the '*Emergency Trust Fund* for Stability and Addressing Root Causes of Irregular Migration and Displaced Persons in Africa' launched in November 2015 during the Valletta Summit. No significant progress was made in terms of the original ambition of the member states to 'match' the funds contributed by the European Commission, which mainly drew from the reserves of the EDF. While documentation material continued to stress that the Trust Fund would allow for 'fast delivery' and 'quick results', policy proposals published by the European Commission and the European External Action Service continued to acknowledge the existence of 'root causes' for migration and forced displacement that the Fund could address. The Global Strategy notably referred to the Trust Fund separately from the instrument of development: through "development, trust funds, preventive diplomacy and mediation we will work with countries of origin to address and prevent the root causes of displacement, manage migration, and fight trans-border crime".

The way in which the Trust Fund functioned and prepared its interventions marked a strong rhetorical break from the 'mainstream' of the EU's development policy as captured in overarching documents, such as the Cotonou Partnership Agreement, the 2000 Development Policy Statement and the 2005 European Consensus on Development. Indeed, the everyday life of the Trust Fund's management showed little emphasis on ownership, partnership or alignment; it allocated funds based on levels of migration rather than needs; it was designed, managed and implemented by Europeans; and it was closely linked to EU interests and used conditionality to promote those interests. There was widespread agreement that these characteristics would form part of future EU development policy.

It became clear that the Trust Fund might only be the beginning, as was seen with the follow-up of a non-paper by Italy distributed in April that called for the creation of a so-called 'Migration Compact'. As central to its proposal, the Italian government argued that "existing initiatives and instruments in the field of external action should be directed (in a coherent way with the internal ones) to developing an active strategy, focusing first and foremost on African countries of origin and transit". In this context, it proposed to create a new EU fund to finance sustainable investments in the region and facilitate European investment, with a strong intermediary role for both the Commission and the EIB.

The Italian government's four-pager proved remarkably effective in informing the European Commission's proposal for migration compacts with Africa that was issued in June. In addition, member states generally appreciated the efforts made to implement the EU's deal with Turkey (even though it later turned out that the main factor driving the reduction of refugee flows was the closing of the so-called Balkan route as negotiated by the Austrian foreign minister). Reflecting EU member states' calls, the Commission's June Communication called for applying both positive and negative conditionality – for the latter singling out development and trade policy as instruments of choice. The migration compacts aimed at improving migration management as well as setting financial incentives for the re-integration of refugees and migrants in their home countries, once their asylum request in Europe had been declined. The EU set aside € 500 m to be channelled via the EU Emergency Trust Fund to those countries that had signed a migration compact, of which Mali was the first. During the year, partnerships with Ethiopia, Niger, Nigeria and Senegal were established. To respond to strong pressure from EU member states, the Commission presented the second progress report on 14 December. In parallel to the initiative, the EU stepped up its travel diplomacy – high level visits by Mogherini as well as several EU Commissioners to Africa increased considerably during the year.

European External Investment Plan

In his State of the Union address on 14 September, the European Commission President Jean-Claude Juncker presented a proposal for a '*European External Investment Plan*' (EEIP) to create incentives for European companies to strengthen their investment in Africa. This plan was originally conceived as the external sibling to Europe's own investment plan (colloquially referred to as the 'Juncker Plan'). It targeted countries in Africa and the EU's neighbourhood and headlined the ambition to deepen partnership, promote a new model for participation by the private sector and further the Sustainable Development Goals. Among the sub-objectives of the investment plan, addressing the 'root causes of migration' also featured, thus reinforcing the EU's assumption that investment provided a means to reduce migration. The Commission planned to mobilise € 3.35 bn (mostly from the reserves of the EDF and from the EU budget), which was then expected to leverage a total investment of up to € 44 bn. If EU member states matched the Commission's funds, up to € 88 bn could be mobilised. The EEIP would consist of three pillars: (1) an Investment Fund for Sustainable Development composed of the existing Investment Platforms for the Neighbourhood and Africa and a new guarantee fund; (2) technical assistance to support local actors and European companies to identify projects that could be supported through the EEIP; (3) cooperation programmes and political dialogue to improve the business environment in African countries. With the exception of the guarantee fund, the EEIP initiative was mostly a repackaging of existing initiatives. The investment platforms for Africa and the neighbourhood were already operating, and technical assistance and political dialogue to improve the business environment was already taking place under the existing instruments. The guarantee fund, however, was a new initiative – the EU could not previously give guarantees to European companies investing abroad; this was mainly a responsibility of member states' institutions (e.g. the Euler-Hermes guarantees in the case of Germany). Some African diplomats, particularly from Southern Africa, voiced concerns that – like the Emergency Trust Fund and migration compacts – the EEIP initiative might again be mainly targeted at those countries in Northern Africa, the Horn of Africa and the Sahel region from which most migrants and refugees were coming. Others cautioned that the EIB would not be well placed to operate in fragile and post-conflict countries as its projects had so far mainly targeted middle-income countries.

Peace and Security

The EU also outlined proposals for reforming its *Instrument for Stability and Peace* (IFSP) and its support for security sector reform. The European Commission together with High Representative Mogherini prepared a legislative proposal to extend the IFSP to allow for supporting the military and they issued a new communication on how the EU intended to support security sector reform. This move was criticised by civil society actors and members of the European Parliament, cautioning that the EU might thereby further enhance security forces in authoritarian regimes.

The EU supported peace and security in Africa through, among other things, missions and operations as part of the EU's Common Foreign and Security Policy. There were *eight missions and operations* deployed in Africa – three in the Sahel region, three in the Horn of Africa, one in Central Africa and another in Libya. Most of them were military training missions (EUTM) or civilian capacity building missions (EUCAP). There was one EUCAP in the Sahel region and one in Niger, and one EUTM in Mali.

On 12 December, the EU decided to extend the mandate of its Common Security and Defence Policy missions in *Somalia*, EUCAP Somalia and EUTM Somalia, until 31 December 2018. EUCAP Somalia aimed at supporting the country in strengthening its maritime security capacity to enforce international maritime law more effectively. It was launched in 2012. The EUTM contributed to building capacities of the Somali National Army. In addition to these two missions, the EU NAVFOR Operation Atlanta, the EU's military operation in the fight against piracy off the coast of Somalia, was extended on 28 November to the end of 2018.

The EU established an EUTM in the *CAR* (EUTM RCA) that was launched on 18 July (with an expiry date in 2020). Its mandate included support for country's authorities in preparing and implementing security sector reform, building capacities and strengthening democratic accountability of the armed forces. This mission, which succeeded the EU military advisory mission (EUMAM RCA), would concentrate on the Bangui area.

On 6 December, Mogherini attended the International Forum for Peace and Security in Africa in Dakar (Senegal). She stressed the importance of crisis prevention and highlighted the importance of economic growth and development in this regard.

Economic Partnership Agreements

2016 was supposed to be yet another year in which the long and contentious episode of the EPAs was to come to a final close. Following a deadline set unilaterally by the EU to complete negotiations by October 2014, a long period of 'legal scrubbing' and translation began that had to be finalised through the subsequent ratification of the EPAs and their coming into force in the course of 2016. This was done through an official ceremony with SADC in the summer, but, for a range of reasons, this endpoint was not reached for West Africa and EAC. Several West African states, including Nigeria as its regional powerhouse, had signalled reservations about signing, while both Uganda and Tanzania indicated in July that the UK's possible withdrawal from the EU meant they were not inclined to sign at that point. Kenya and Rwanda subsequently signed the EPA individually, and Uganda expressed a commitment to append its signature, which the European Commission considered a sufficient basis to continue providing unilateral trade preferences under the EU's market access regulation. A historical irony was that Nigeria and the East African states had previously negotiated trade agreements with the European Economic Community during the 1960s, but neither ultimately materialised, each for its own reasons.

Given the situation in West Africa, the middle-income countries Ghana and Côte d'Ivoire ratified the interim 'bilateral' EPAs they had concluded with the EU in 2007 as the ratification of the regional EPA proved to be unrealistic. The same was done by Cameroon, given that negotiations between the EU and the Central African region had failed to reach any point of conclusion.

What thus remained in terms of EU-Africa trade relations was a mere *patchwork of free trade agreements* (bilateral as well as regional), while a substantial number of African states would now continue to trade with EU under the terms set by its General System of Preferences, including its favourable 'Everything But Arms' scheme for the Least-Developed Countries. This situation was far removed from the shared objective of increased regional integration as expressed in the Cotonou Partnership Agreement, and did not augur well for the implementation of various ambitious trade and investment initiatives, such as the aforementioned EEIP or the AU-led Continental Free Trade Area.

Eastern Africa / Horn of Africa

The EU's relations with *Ethiopia* were particularly tense and controversial during the year. Recent events in Ethiopia confirmed the view that the focus by authoritarian regimes on strong institutions and public goods provision while reducing political spaces would not be stable in the medium to long term. The upsurge in demonstrations against the government that had started at the end of 2014 and accelerated in 2016 indicated public dissent and strong dissatisfaction with government policies. The government's violent response to the demonstrations illustrated the extent to which the regime was shaken by the protests. According to human rights organisations, several hundred people had been killed since the outbreak of the protests. On 10 October, the government declared a state of emergency. In spite of these events, the EU made no public statement criticising the Ethiopian government's response to the crisis during the year. Instead, the EU signed a partnership 'towards an EU-Ethiopia strategic engagement' in the framework of the EU's migration compacts, which provided rhetorical support and external legitimacy for the government. Ethiopia also benefitted from extra aid funds through the Emergency Trust Fund for Africa, even though it was already the EU's largest aid recipient in Africa. In response to strong criticism from civil society activists, the EU pointed out that the extra money would not be channelled through the central government, but instead disbursed through NGOs and aid agencies.

The EU's relations with *Rwanda* were also tense during the year. The EU and some of its member states had criticised the Rwandan government's decision to change the constitution to allow President Kagame to run for a third term. Relations with the EU reached an all-time low in October. During a visit to Rwanda, a delegation of the European Parliament also went to see Victoire Ingabire, a politician from the opposition who had been sentenced to 15 years in prison in 2010 for ethnic-based 'divisionism'. After the delegation's return to Europe, the European Parliament published a resolution on Rwanda, criticising the Rwandan government's position towards Ingabire. The Rwandan parliament, in turn, published a critical response and asked for a travel ban on EU parliamentarians until they apologised.

The crisis in neighbouring *Burundi* escalated during the year and the EU decided on 29 September to renew its sanctions against Burundi until 31 October 2017. The EU's measures consisted of a travel ban and asset freeze against four individuals who were deemed to be particularly responsible for acts of violence and human rights violations, though President Nkurunziza was not targeted. Moreover, the EU did not cut its development aid or trade preferences for Burundi. One reason for the relatively mild sanctions was that the EU supported regional mediation efforts led by Tanzania's former president, Benjamin Mkapa, and did not wish its sanctions to isolate Burundi.

Central Africa

The EU together with the government of the *CAR* and in cooperation with the World Bank and the UN organised a Brussels Conference on the CAR on 17 November. The conference was an opportunity for the CAR government to present its strategy for how to further promote peace, security and stabilisation and support socio-economic development. During the previous three years, the EU had provided more than € 500 m to the CAR in the form of humanitarian assistance or through the so-called Bêkou Trust Fund established in 2014. Although the Bêkou Fund had been somewhat overshadowed by the much larger Emergency Trust Fund for Africa, it in fact performed better in terms of attracting member state financial contributions relative to the level of Commission investment.

The EU followed the political situation in the *DRC* closely during the year. The second term and constitutional mandate of President Kabila came to an end on 19 December, with no date or clear process in place for the next presidential elections. Political tensions in the DRC were thus rising throughout the year. The EU issued two council conclusions, on 23 May and on 17 October, urging the Congolese authorities to respect fundamental freedoms and political rights and the constitutional provisions on the two-term limit. On 23 May, the EU called on the DRC government and the Independent National Electoral Commission (CENI) to create conditions for organising free and peaceful presidential and legislative elections. The EU expressed deep concern over the extreme violence in Kinshasa on 19–20 September, during which about 50 people died and many were injured. On 12 December, the EU Foreign Affairs Council issued sanctions – travel restrictions and an asset freeze – against seven individuals who were responsible for the chain of command related to these acts of violence. On 18 December, the EU called for a continuation of mediation efforts by the Catholic Bishops' Conference to overcome the political deadlock. In response to the security forces' shooting of several protesters demonstrating against Kabila's continuation in power in mid-December, French Foreign Minister Jean-Marc Ayrault urged the EU on 21 December to reconsider the level of its relations with the DRC if the security forces did not cease their violence against peaceful protesters.

In a rather unusual move, the EU made a statement on 19 February that it would not send an election observation mission to the *Republic of Congo*'s presidential elections. The EU raised concern that its recommendations on reforming electoral governance and observing fundamental freedoms, as communicated during a political dialogue meeting on 20 November 2015 and during the election observation mission for the 2002 elections, among other occasions, had not been taken into account by the government. The EU criticised the reforms introduced by a new electoral law as insufficient and likely to increase legal uncertainty. Without explicitly mentioning the issues, the EU thereby hinted at two key changes in the law: the new law lifted both the 70-year age limit and the limit of two presidential terms in order to allow President Denis Sassou-Nguesso to stay in power. The EU pressured the government to respect the fundamental freedoms of opposition candidates and opposition parties during the pre-campaign period as well as the electoral campaign itself. The EU concluded that "the current circumstances preclude the presence of an EU election observation mission during the vote of 20 March". After the elections, opposition supporters took to the streets in the capital Brazzaville. The government violently repressed the protest and about 17 people died. The EU condemned the disproportionate reaction of the security forces on

4 April and urged all actors to refrain from using violence and resolve the disagreement peacefully.

West Africa

The political situation in the *Gambia* figured relatively prominently on the EU's agenda during the year. Ahead of the presidential elections on 1 December, the political climate in the Gambia was very tense. In April, Mogherini's spokesperson highlighted EU concerns about the fate of a leading opposition activist, Solo Sandeng, and other opposition politicians who had been taken into custody. After Sandeng's death in prison, opposition supporters took to the streets. The EU criticised the disproportionate response made by the Gambian security forces against peaceful protesters. Only the AU monitored the elections; the EU and ECOWAS were not present on election day. Against most predictions, the former businessman Adama Barrow won the elections, defeating the incumbent, Yahya Jammeh, who had been in power for 22 years. The EU was among the first to congratulate the new president-elect on 3 December. On 9 December, Jammeh announced that he was no longer accepting the results and called for a new election, triggering a constitutional and political crisis. In a statement on 12 December, Mogherini and Development Commissioner Neven Mimica strongly urged President Jammeh to respect the will of the Gambian people as expressed by their vote and to stand by his earlier acceptance of the result. They highlighted that the EU supported the peaceful and constitutional transfer of power. The EU emphasised its support for the efforts of ECOWAS, the AU and the UN to guarantee a peaceful transition in the Gambia.

The EU participated in an international donor conference in support of *Burkina Faso*'s National Economic and Social Development Plan in Paris on 7 December. After the peaceful change of government and strengthening of democratic rule, the EU and other donors committed to increasing support for the country. During the conference, Development Commissioner Mimica announced that the EU would provide up to € 800 m to support the plan. An important share of the funds would be channelled through direct budgetary aid in the form of a 'good governance and development contract'.

Election Observation

2016 was again a busy year on the electoral front, with 17 African states organising national elections. Each year, the High Representative identifies a number of countries where *EU Electoral Observation Missions* (EOMs) could be deployed, in consultation with the Council of Ministers and the European Parliament. Feasibility missions are subsequently carried out to determine whether an observation mission would be advisable, feasible and useful, and to set conditions for the host government to ensure tha an EOM could operate fully and credibly. This year, four elections, in Uganda, Gabon, Zambia and Ghana, were covered by EOMs.

First up were the elections in *Uganda*, which demonstrated a continuing trend of voter and opposition intimidation during the campaign, while the government also pressured telecommunication companies to suspend access to social media platforms during the general elections. Delays in delivering voting materials to opposition strongholds, notably the capital city Kampala, the teargassing and sealing off of the leading opposition offices, and the announcement of the results before all the votes had been counted led to a situation in which – as one media commentary suggested – Museveni had won more votes than love. With the news that Museveni had gained 60.7% of the votes being announced early, the streets of Kampala were virtually empty when the final results were announced two days after the elections. The EOM's report noted a 'vibrant' campaign period and observed that the election day had generally remained calm and peaceful. However, it also observed the curbing of constitutionally provided freedoms of assembly, association and expression under a controversial public order act, and failure to introduce promised electoral reforms, and noted that the electoral commission had failed to introduce robust procedures so that some 'discretionary decisions' took place during the process. In line with its long list of observations, it put forward 11 recommendations that the Ugandan government could use to organise better elections in future.

Presidential elections in *Gabon* on 27 August were similarly tense. The incumbent, President Ali Bongo, was reported to have won the elections by a tiny margin of 6,000 votes. When the final results were published on 31 August, Gabonese citizens disputed the outcome and violent demonstrations broke out across the country. Several people died and about 1,000 people were imprisoned. Publishing the election result, the Gabonese Constitutional Court confirmed Ali Bongo's rule and suggested only minor modifications to the official results. The EU criticised major shortcomings in the electoral process and urged the strengthening of the independence of the justiciary and the Constitutional Court, which were perceived to be siding with the incumbent president. The EU called on the authorities to improve the transparency of the electoral administration and the counting of the votes as well as to guarantee independent observers to monitor all key stages of the election process. The EU noted 'anomalies', in particular in Bongo's stronghold in the Haut-Ogooue province, where, voter turnout and voter support were close to 100%. On 12 December, the EOM presented its final report in Libreville. The report argued that the pre-election process had not seen major shortcomings, but pointed out that the incumbent's campaign had a substantial financial advantage over those of the other candidates and that the transparency of election campaign finance needed to be addressed. The report particularly criticised the role of the Constitutional Court and its opacity in dealing with appeals by citizens and other candidates. All in all, the EOM report was not as critical as the opposition had hoped, but the EU was also aiming to put pressure on Bongo to ensure that the arliamentary elections – scheduled for December 2016 but then postponed to July 2017 – would better respect democratic principles.

The EU viewed the general elections in *Zambia* as highly competitive, free and fair and prepared in a largely professional manner. Zambia had an ambitious planning schedule, with a referendum, as well as presidential, parliamentary local elections all held on 11 August. President Lungu of the Patriotic Front party was re-elected. The opposition leader Hakainde Hichilema challenged the result. The EOM report made a number of minor recommendations to improve the electoral process and proceedings during election day: it suggested reviewing the electoral legal framework and redrafting some unclear and ambiguous provisions, urged the publication of individual polling station results shortly after their closing, and suggested improvements for the rules and procedures for complaints, among other things.

International attention to parliamentary and presidential elections in *Ghana* in December was high. The pre-election period was marked by strong tensions and observers cautioned that violence might break out after the elections. The former foreign minister Nana Akufo Addo of the opposition New Patriotic Party won the elections, this being the first time in the history of Ghana that a sitting president had not won a second term. To the relief of Ghanaians and international observers, the defeated John Dramani Mahama of the National Democratic Congress accepted the result and the situation remained peaceful. The EOM's end of mission presentation highlighted that the elections represented another milestone in the consolidation of democracy in Ghana. The head of the EOM, Tamas Meszerics, argued that the atmosphere of mistrust and tension during the election campaign could have been avoided and should be addressed for future elections. The EOM report highlighted that the increasing monetarisation of the campaign and the lack of transparency regarding campaign financing should be remedied.

EU Member States' Relations with African Countries

Among the EU's member states, *Germany*'s interest in cooperation with Africa increased most visibly throughout the year. German Chancellor Angela Merkel visited three African countries and the AU in October, her first visit to SSA since 2011. In contrast to her last trip, which was devoted to promoting German business interests, this visit was mainly shaped by the refugee and migration crisis and by efforts to fight terrorist insurgencies. This was demonstrated, for instance, by the selection of her travel destinations: Mali, Niger and Ethiopia. Merkel highlighted that the way Germany and Europe engaged with the African continent was a "strategically important question … If we want to pursue German interests, we have to say that also welfare in Africa is in Germany's interest." In addition, German Finance Minister Wolfgang Schäuble announced that cooperation with Africa would take a prominent role during the German G20-Presidency. He proposed to prepare a 'Compact with Africa' to improve the business environment in a select number of African countries to increase FDI and foster growth and job creation. The compact was prepared by the World Bank, the IMF and the AfDB and was to be supported by other finance institutions and G20 countries. In parallel, Germany's Minister for Economic Cooperation and Development Gerd Müller announced in August that his ministry had prepared a so-called 'Marshall Plan with Africa' to support long-term sustainable development on the continent.

In contrast to Germany, *France* did not engage in issuing new policy proposals with regard to the African continent, striving instead to deliver on its existing commitment, particularly its strong military engagement in Central Africa, which outmatched that of any other EU member state. French President François Hollande visited the CAR on 13 May to prepare for the withdrawal of French troops and to launch investigations into accusations that French soldiers had been involved in the sexual abuse of children during their mission. A few days before the annual 14 July celebrations, Hollande reiterated that France would withdraw her 'Sangaris' mission in CAR, while he also requested additional EU funds to help shoulder its African operations. French Foreign Minister Jean-Marc Ayrault paid a visit to Guinea and Senegal on 10–12 November to discuss bilateral relations and regional cooperation. He also visited Kenya and Tanzania in early August to promote economic relations and review French investments in both countries.

The referendum in which a small majority of *UK* citizens voted to leave the EU also presented key implications for its future engagement in EU-Africa relations. On the morning after the Referendum, Member of the European Parliament Nigel Farage – one of the central figures behind the 'leave' campaign – commented that the exit from the EU offered the UK an opportunity to deepen its ties with the Commonwealth. The coming years would be key to determining whether the UK's reprioritisation of the Commonwealth would have implications for the EU's relations with Africa as well as for relations within Africa itself. One example concerned the implementation of the AU's Agenda 2063, which foresaw further investments in intra-African trade by means of a continental free trade area, with the UK having previously supported a tripartite free trade area that would entail creating a 'Cape to Cairo free trade zone' covering three anglophone regional economic communities.

The Future of EU-ACP Relations

The expiry date of the Cotonou Agreement governing the EU's relations with the ACP (2020) drew closer. On the European side, there was no agreement and rather extreme positions among member states were taken as to how relations with the ACP should look in the future. As for the EU institutions, the European Parliament adopted a position calling for both continuity and change, while the Commission's neutrality in this debate was questioned in view of its leadership's call for a 'post-Cotonou agreement'. The European Commission and European External Action Service published a joint proposal in November proposing building blocks for the EU's negotiation mandate, which would be further discussed by EU member states, the European Parliament and all relevant stakeholders with the aim of adopting a negotiation mandate during the autumn of 2017. Their proposal envisaged the continuation of an 'umbrella agreement' between the EU and the ACP, complemented by regional 'pillars' outlining specific objectives and priorities.

On the ACP side, preparations started early but were moving at a very slow pace, with observers expecting the ACP to opt once again for reacting to the EU's negotiating mandate as opposed to setting out a pro-active position of its own. The clear preference given to Africa in recent EU policy decisions such as the EU Africa Trust Fund, Migration Compacts and the EEIP had affected solidarity among ACP states. In this context, African states did not make public statements on their future alliance with their Caribbean and Pacific states or their partnership with the EU, while the AU also refrained from making statements on the matter.

PART 3

West Africa

Sebastian Elischer

The nature of the political regimes differed substantially across the sub-region. Only a few countries qualified as democratic regimes, most were electoral authoritarian, and a few could be considered authoritarian. Newly elected governments took office in several countries. Others experienced constitutional reform or prepared for upcoming elections. 2016 was a political watershed for the Gambia where long-term autocrat Yahya Jammeh lost the elections. He initially announced his intention to accept the outcome but subsequently refused to stand down. His refusal to honour the electoral outcome provoked a major confrontation with ECOWAS and, at the end of the year, ECOWAS was preparing to oust Jammeh militarily. Most countries showed solid economic growth rates, but little of that progress was trickling down to ordinary citizens. Corruption and inefficiencies continued to plague the region. While in previous years jihadi terrorism affected mainly Nigeria and the francophone Sahel, the terrorist threat was now affecting the political discourse across West Africa.

Regime Dynamics and Human Rights

The nature of West Africa's political regimes and the level of willingness of states to respect human rights differed significantly across the sub-region. In a few countries, democratic rule was the norm. In most of West Africa, citizens were able to exercise some democratic rights, but meaningful democratisation remained an elusive goal. A third group remained in the firm hands of autocratic rulers; democratic rules and human rights existed only on paper.

Benin, Ghana, Senegal and *Cabo Verde* remained the *democratic showcases* of the region. In all four countries, democratic processes were in place and all four complied with basic human rights standards. Benin, Ghana and Cabo Verde held *peaceful presidential elections* and in Ghana and Cabo Verde legislative elections also took place. Benin saw the election of Patrice Talon, a shrewd businessman and political newcomer. In the past, Talon had accused President Thomas Boni Yayi of attempting to orchestrate his murder, but the transition from Yayi to Talon nevertheless proceeded smoothly. Talon emphasised two priorities: the reform of Benin's institutional framework and the fight against public debt. While in Benin the incumbent stood down because he had reached the end of his term-limit, in Ghana President John Dramani Mahama was *voted out of office* by a surprisingly large margin. Voting a sitting African president out of office is still rare and indicates the ebbing away

 | DOI 10.1163/9789004355910_004

of the powers of incumbency. Unfortunately, the run-up to the Ghanaian elections was accompanied by hefty criticism of the Electoral Commission and *violence*. The former was a new phenomenon, but the latter did not come as a surprise, given the large number of violent incidents in the run-up to the election of the presidential candidates in 2015. Despite the *highly polarised political environment*, all parties accepted the outcome of the elections. In Cabo Verde, the opposition won the legislative elections in March for the first time since 2000; the incumbent, President Jorge Fonseca, was re-elected. The turnout was remarkably low (35.5%). The upcoming parliamentary and presidential elections dominated the political scene in Senegal. The revision of the electoral rolls for the 2017 parliamentary elections sparked numerous controversies. A referendum in March on about 15 *constitutional amendments* polarised the political environment further. Almost two-thirds of the electorate endorsed the constitutional amendments that had been put forward by President Macky Sall and his government. Given the growing jihadi threat in the Sahel region, the Senegalese security services boosted security at hotels and prominent places in the capital. The security services also arrested a number of imams as a precautionary measure. Lengthy pre-trial detention and harsh prison conditions remained a major concern.

In *Niger, Mali* and *Nigeria*, citizens were able to exercise some democratic rights. In all three, the *fight against jihadi terrorism* had detrimental consequences for human lives and all three were governed by rulers with *autocratic reflexes*. In Niger, President Mahamadou Issoufou was re-elected in February. The elections damaged the image of Niger as an oasis of political tranquillity. Opposition protestors were imprisoned in highly dubious circumstances. The government also intimidated journalists, which many had thought was a thing of the past. Issoufou's main opponent, former prime minister Hama Amadou, was forced to campaign from his prison cell, where he was awaiting trial for his alleged involvement in an international baby smuggling ring. The accusations against him were never verified. Despite the dismal treatment that Amadou received at the hands of the Nigerien prison authorities, Issoufou was unable to achieve a first-round victory. Niger's war with *Boko Haram* continued unabated and the Diffa region alone received over 300,000 IDPs. The local economy and education system were particularly hard hit. Attacks by jihadi fighters from the area close to the border with Mali were a reminder of the country's *vulnerability* to security threats from the Saharan region. Mali saw a steady increase in political violence, with mounting insecurity affecting populations in the country's central and northern regions. While Mali's domestic security crisis could not be blamed entirely on jihadi terrorism, most attacks were launched by transnational and domestic jihadi groups. The implementation of the 2015 peace accord was uneven and slow and many of its provisions were delayed or simply did not materialise. The political opposition was able to capitalise on the failure of the Keita administration to establish a modicum of stability. Despite the presence of over 13,000 UN troops, Mali's future cohesion as a nation state seemed uncertain. In Nigeria, recently elected President Muhammadu Buhari and his administration got off to a bad start. *Violence* and *organised crime* on an unprecedented scale shattered large sections of the country and the precarious security situation had grave effects on human rights. There was ample evidence that the security forces and local militias killed numerous innocent citizens. Around one year after surprisingly peaceful elections, Nigeria was once more on the brink of political and economic chaos.

Côte d'Ivoire, Burkina Faso and *the Gambia* underwent wide ranging domestic transitions. For Côte d'Ivoire, 2016 was a year filled with important political reforms. In October, the Ivorian people ratified a *new constitution* in a national referendum. Over 93% of voters approved the constitutional draft, with a turnout of slightly over 42%. Following the 2015 presidential elections, the country went to the polls to elect a new parliament in December. The presidential elections had been peaceful, but the relationship between the opposition and the government remained tense, with local analysts and opposition leaders accusing the government of applying 'victor's justice', although President Alassane Ouattara pardoned 3,000 prisoners. Throughout the year, violent clashes occurred in various parts of the country. In Burkina Faso, Roch Kaboré took over the presidency. The government faced a strong opposition. In January, a *terrorist attack* in Ouagadougou left 30 dead and more than 70 wounded. In June, security forces arrested ten people, three of whom were suspected of being responsible for the attack. These domestic attacks and attacks in a number of neighbouring countries gave rise to the perception that Burkina Faso's domestic security situation was deteriorating. The parliamentary opposition challenged the new administration's governance record. It accused the government of manipulating the judiciary and pointed to cases where members of the previous regime, who had been accused of embezzling public funds, had been released without explanation. In May, *municipal elections* took place. The government emerged victorious and took most of the seats. Post-electoral violence was a powerful reminder of how fragile the political consensus continued to be. For the Gambia, 2016 was a watershed moment. Against all the odds, the opposition candidate in the presidential elections, Adama Barrow, caused one of the most surprising *electoral upsets* in the continent's history. In the spring, street protests against electoral reform shook the capital. The heavy-handed response of the government persuaded the opposition to unify, which resulted in the defeat of President Yahya Jammeh. His derogatory comments about the Mandinkas, the Gambia's largest ethnic group, only worsened his position. Diaspora activists sent financial support to the opposition on unprecedented scale and, as a final factor, vote counting was centralised and made electoral manipulation more difficult to achieve. On 2 December, Jammeh conceded defeat, but he reversed his decision on 9 December, provoking furious protest from *ECOWAS* and several Western nations. By the end of the year, the political destiny of the Gambia was still uncertain.

Guinea-Bissau, Guinea, Liberia and *Sierra Leone* suffered from weak state institutions and the long-term implications of the Ebola crisis. In one year, Guinea-Bissau saw the appointment of two prime ministers and the *paralysis of parliamentary life*. AI criticised the government's treatment of prisoners but praised the overall improvement in the human rights situation. There was ample evidence of the mistreatment of *women* in social, political and economic life. The situation in Guinea was more stable. After the re-election of President Alpha Condé in 2015, the year began with the inauguration of the new government. In August, about half a million people followed the call of the opposition parties to demonstrate in Conakry against corruption and economic mismanagement. After long negotiations, the government and opposition agreed in October on a roadmap for local elections, which were scheduled to take place in early 2017 and would be the first local elections since 2005. Guinea's National Human Rights Commission had several of its commissioners dismissed due to lack of financial transparency. In Liberia, the national news was dominated by speculation about *an electoral alliance* for the 2017 elections, masterminded by the convicted war criminal *Charles Taylor*. The Sirleaf government engaged in politically motivated anti-corruption campaigns, which were designed to damage the opposition. *Corruption* and *poor governance* continued to weaken Liberia's economic track record and remained major obstacles in the fight against human rights' abuses. The government of Sierra Leone announced severe austerity measures and also recorded a dramatic increase of its population, according to a new census.

Mauritania and *Togo* remained under the tight control of *autocratic leaders*. Members of the Mauritanian government tried to initiate constitutional changes that would allow President Mohamed Ould Abdel Aziz to remain in power beyond his second term. Aziz declared that he did not intend to seek a third mandate. Attempts to initiate a national dialogue between the government and the main opposition parties failed once again. Following the opposition boycott of the most recent parliamentary elections in 2013, the country suffered from a general lack of accountability and transparency. A blogger who had been accused of apostasy in 2014 remained in custody. In Togo, the opposition remained divided and weak and attempts to implement electoral and other political reforms failed.

Socioeconomic Developments

West Africa continued to be one of the continent's most *vibrant* economic subregions. As in previous years, most countries displayed *encouraging* annual economic growth rates. With the exception of Ghana and Cabo Verde, however, all countries remained at the bottom of the HDI. In almost all countries, *public debt* was on the rise and *corruption* remained a major obstacle to economic growth. Significant *security risks* deterred potential foreign investors.

Cabo Verde enjoyed an increase in tourist arrivals. Its annual GDP growth was estimated at between 3.5% and 4.5%. For the first time in the country's history, the administration announced a halt to recruitment for the *public administration*. The government continued its efforts to foster flight connections with the wider world. *Ghana* continued to suffer from its electricity crisis, growing costs of fuel and a number of new taxes. Its GDP growth rate remained between 3% and 4% and its *debt burden* rose to 70% of GDP. Cabo Verde experienced solid economic growth (estimated at between 3.5% and 4.5%).

The three *economic powerhouses* in the region, *Nigeria*, *Côte d'Ivoire* and *Senegal*, showed solid annual growth rates. Nigeria kept its position as the continent's largest *telecommunications market*. President Buhari's first annual budget included a *staggering deficit* of 30%. The youth unemployment rate was estimated at 60%. During the course of the year, the national currency came under pressure. The naira's massive fall, coupled with declining revenue from oil and gas exports, caused serious concern among the business community. Côte d'Ivoire's impressive estimated annual growth rate of 9% resulted in greater investment spending in education, employment and health. The country supplied 45% of the world's cocoa beans. Nevertheless, *unemployment* remained high and left many families struggling with malnutrition. Senegal achieved low inflation and an increase in the size of its budget. The government prioritised spending on infrastructure. *Bureaucratic blockages* and *corruption* slowed down economic progress in all three countries.

In line with previous years, economic growth remained solid in the Sahel – *Niger*, *Mali*, *Mauritania* and *Burkina Faso*. In Niger, depressed commodity prices led to a fall in the annual estimated GDP growth rate to 3.8%. Rains were deficient and erratic, leading to *flooding* in a number of areas. Trade with Nigeria suffered from the war with *Boko Haram*. The increase in defence spending made the regular payment of salaries in the public sector increasingly difficult. The Malian economy grew by an estimated 5.4%, although the cotton harvest fell 15% short of production goals. Like Niger, Mali invested heavily in its security forces as political violence in the centre and north exacerbated security problems. Annual economic growth stalled in Mauritania (1.5%) as its agricultural and mining capacity expanded only slightly and world market prices for iron ore fell. The EU finally ratified its four-year fishing agreement with Mauritania. In Burkina Faso, GDP grew by 5.5%. The recently elected government drafted a new development plan for 2016–20, which aimed to achieve annual growth rates of 7.7%. In May, the capital faced a severe *drought*, which led to water rationing. Subsequent to the drought, flooding became a significant issue. All the Sahel countries suffered from *malnutrition*.

Guinea, *Liberia* and *Sierra Leone* were still recovering from the *Ebola* outbreak. Guinea's economy recorded an estimated growth of 5.2%, which was surprisingly high. This was due to maintained levels of mineral exports and restrictive fiscal policies. The year also saw the consolidation of the mining sector. Liberia, by contrast, showed no signs of recovery and the economic situation remained dismal, with annual GDP shrinking to 0.5%. The bleak economic outlook was partly the result of a general decline in commodity prices. Around 87% of Liberia's annual budget was spent on public sector wages. Sierra Leone displayed a positive growth rate of 4.3% (coming back from a negative growth rate of -21.1% in 2015). However, according to an IMF report, the country would not return to pre-Ebola GDP per capita levels until 2021. UNICEF directed attention to the high levels of child mortality in SSA and singled out Sierra Leone as a country with a particularly high rate.

Benin, the Gambia, Togo and *Guinea-Bissau* represented the smaller economies in the region. Benin's economic performance recovered from a relative low in 2015. Its economic growth rate climbed from 2.1% to an estimated 4%, although the cotton harvest dropped significantly due to bad weather. Benin remained an important transit country for drugs and weapons. Newly elected President Talon announced his intention to seek closer cooperation with Nigeria to end illegal trade. The Gambia experienced an economically turbulent year due to *external shocks* and the absence of tourism. The annual growth rate fell to 2.4% while inflation rose to 6%. The government struggled to come to terms with a budget. In Togo, the exodus from rural to urban areas continued. *Youth unemployment* reached worrisome dimensions, as did public spending. In Guinea-Bissau, economic conditions improved. Economic growth was estimated to rise to 5.6%, up from 5% in 2015. Security officials were known to be involved in narco-trafficking.

Regional Cooperation and Foreign Affairs

The four regional organisations, *ECOWAS*, the *CEN-SAD*, the *MRU* and the *Liptako-Gourma Authority*, differed significantly in terms of their activity and output. In April, the ECA, the AfDB and the AU Commission launched the Africa Regional Integration Index Report in Addis Ababa (Ethiopia). The report measured the *level of regional integration* in a systematic and transparent manner. On a scale of 0 to 1, ECOWAS came third with a score of 0.509, behind SADC, which scored 0.531, and the EAC, which came first with a score of 0.540. In ECOWAS, Côte d'Ivoire, Togo and Senegal were the best performing countries in achieving regional integration.

Unsurprisingly, *ECOWAS* was the most active and significant regional actor in the sub-region. Over the year, many ECOWAS leadership positions changed hands.

In February, the newly elected *ECOWAS parliament* was sworn in and elected Senegalese-born Moustapha Cisse-Lo as its new speaker. His candidature was unopposed and enjoyed the support of the Anglophone and Francophone members. In May, the ECOWAS parliament called for more legislative powers and the acceleration and widening of regional integration. In April, the *ECOWAS Commission* got a new president, vice president and seven commissioners. Marcel Alain de Souza of Benin was appointed as the new president. He had previously held positions as the internal controller at BCEAO's head office in Benin and director of administration at the BCEAO headquarters. After BCEAO, he had served his country as head of the Department of Economic and Financial Affairs in the Office of the President of the Republic of Benin and as special advisor to the president on monetary and banking affairs.

In June, the 49th *ECOWAS heads of state* summit opened in Dakar (Senegal). Liberian President Ellen Johnson Sirleaf was elected as the new chairperson of the organisation, taking over from Senegal's President Macky Sall. In December, the 50th Ordinary Session of the *ECOWAS heads of state* summit in Abuja (Nigeria) focused on the evolving electoral crisis in the Gambia. Following the refusal of President Jammeh to leave power, ECOWAS issued a strong statement saying it would do everything it could to uphold the result of the Gambian election. ECOWAS further stated that its troops – under the military leadership of Senegal – would oust the Gambian incumbent if he refused to step down by the end of his term in January 2017. In the history of ECOWAS, this was the clearest and most decisive public commitment to honour the electoral outcome in any of its member states. In his New Year message, Jammeh accused ECOWAS of declaring war against the Gambia and her people. He said the Gambia would not be intimidated and reaffirmed his government's determination to defend the country from any external aggression or threat. Although various ECOWAS bodies organised a plethora of seminars and workshops on regional integration through the year, many West African states lacked the will to comply with the rules driving regional integration. The most outspoken critic of this was the director of trade at the ECOWAS Commission, Dr Gbenga Obideyi, who publicly denounced the *inertia* of many national governments in that regard. In July, the secretary-general of ECCAS, Ambassador Ahmad Allam-Mi, and the new resident of the ECOWAS Commission, Marcel de Souza, publicly stated their intention to foster cooperation between the two regional organisations.

CEN-SAD was shown to have the lowest level of regional integration in the AU's report. CEN-SAD defence ministers met in Sharm el-Sheikh (Egypt) in March. With delegations from more than 27 Arab and African states and numerous regional and international organisations, the conference took place under tight security. Large numbers of special forces from both the armed forces and the police were deployed. Interestingly, for the first time in many years, *Egypt* portrayed itself as security guarantor for SSA. The delegates agreed to restructure the organisation's bodies, strengthen the economic, military and security capacities of its member states and bolster cooperation in the face of the challenges and threats posed by transboundary changes in the region. In previous years, CEN-SAD had been largely dormant.

The *MRU* also returned to the world stage after being paralysed by the Ebola crisis. In April, the MRU announced its intention to establish a *legislative body*. In June, the heads of state met in Conakry (Guinea). The meeting did not arrive at any binding decision and did not make any commitment to deeper levels of integration. In October, the *health ministers* of all MRU member states met for the first time in three years and, in December, MRU officials announced the delayed launch of a programme designed to ensure safe drinking water and improved sanitation and hygiene services for border communities. The MRU signed a memorandum of understanding with ECOWAS on border security.

Across the West African sub-region, there was a growing awareness of *jihadi terrorism* and the need to increase border security. A number of countries remained very active in forming bilateral and regional alliances against jihadi groups, including Nigeria, Mali, Niger, Cameroon, Burkina Faso, Benin, Senegal, Mauritania and Togo. The most prominent cooperation scheme in the field of security was the *G5*, which included five Sahel countries: Mauritania, Mali, Burkina Faso, Niger and Chad. Mali remained the prime concern of the sub-region and the international community and more than 13,000 UN military personnel remained deployed there with the *UN-led Multidimensional Integrated Stabilization Mission in Mali* (MINUSMA). Nigeria and, increasingly, Niger remained prominent targets of jihadi attacks. With the exception of the Gambia, all West African countries tried to foster good relations with Western donors and with China.

Benin

Alexander Stroh

The major event of the year was the presidential elections, won by Patrice Talon. The new president portrayed his government and politics as a complete break with the policies of the outgoing administration. After years of ambiguous foreign relations, particularly with donor countries, the new president attracted new donor interest and was able to rely on the anticipated confidence of the donor community. The new administration diversified Benin's portfolio of international partners but its rhetoric still had to translate into action. Economic and social vulnerability remained high, although Benin did not experience any major economic shocks.

Domestic Politics

The election of a new head of state and the first steps of the newly elected Talon government dominated the political agenda. Benin's sixth democratic *presidential elections* had been heralded as a watershed following the heated political debates in recent years under President Boni Yayi's controversial leadership. Yayi

 | DOI 10.1163/9789004355910_005

was constitutionally excluded from standing in the elections as he had reached the end of his second term in office. Although he had been suspected of trying to force through a constitutional amendment that would have allowed him to run for a third term, Yayi respected the two-term limit. He supported the candidacy of his prime minister, Lionel Zinsou.

Zinsou had only returned from Paris in mid-2015 and was a complete newcomer to the domestic political scene. With Yayi's support, he became the presidential candidate of the ruling party 'Forces Cauris pour un Bénin Émergeant' (FCBE). Zinsou also secured the support of Yayi's political ally, Léhady Soglo, of 'Renaissance du Bénin' (RB). Nicéphore Soglo, Léhady's father and former head of state (1991–6) and still the RB's honorary president, publicly deplored his son's decision and condemned the alliance as "high treason", implying neo-colonial sympathies related to Zinsou's deep personal ties with France. In January, the 'Parti pour le Renouveau Démocratique' (PRD) surprisingly joined the 'Republican Alliance' of the FCBE and RB backing Zinsou. PRD founder and leader Adrien Houngbédji had been a fierce opponent of Yayi in recent years and so his election as parliamentary president a few months earlier was widely understood as a major success for the opposition.

On 29 January, the Constitutional Court handed over a list of 36 registered presidential candidates who met all the legal criteria approved by the 'Commission Électorale Nationale Autonome' (CENA). Three of the less promising candidates withdrew their candidacies immediately after they were admitted. Besides Zinsou, the list of the most hopeful presidential aspirants included the businessmen Patrice Talon and Sébastien Ajavon, the experienced politician and international economist Abdoulaye Bio Tchané and former prime minister Pascal Koupaki, who had dissociated himself from Yayi after political and personal disagreements. Most of the country's most experienced politicians – including National Assembly President Houngbédji – were excluded by a constitutional age limit for presidential candidates of 70 years. The majority of the other candidates were former members of parliament or ministers, including close allies of Yayi such as his senior ministers Marcel de Souza (who was also his brother-in-law), Kogui N'Douro and Nassirou Bako Arifari. They all refused to support Zinsou.

Media attention focused on Talon and Ajavon, who were political newcomers like Zinsou. Talon had only returned from Paris in December 2015 following a fierce confrontation with President Yayi, who had accused Talon of attempting to orchestrate his murder. Talon had been sought under an international arrest warrant, but Yayi had eventually dropped the charges. Talon was then able to return to Benin and run for president and to freely organise his candidacy and electoral campaign. Ajavon, who had not previously shown an active interest in politics, entered the race unexpectedly. Talon and Ajavon both were among Benin's richest businessmen; they lacked the organisational support of a political party, but could rely on the support of major media outlets in which they had influence as either owners or investors.

On 15 January, ten presidential candidates revealed the creation of a so-called '*Coalition of Rupture*'. Talon, Ajavon, Koupaki, N'Dourou and Robert Gbian, a retired army general whom the domestic media had originally considered a promising challenger, were among the coalition members and Bio Tchané appeared as the group's spokesperson. The party leaders of the opposition alliance 'Union fait la Nation' (UN) also joined the group. The electoral coalition did not specify any electoral strategy but it was widely assumed that the members would support each other if one of them made it to the second round of the election, united in the simple aim of ending FCBE rule. The campaign saw a surge in the use of modern media. All the candidates presented their presidential manifestos in YouTube videos and, for the first time in the country's history, on 17 March, the two leading candidates took part in a debate broadcast by the national television chanel ORTB ('Office de Radiodiffusion et Télévision du Bénin').

The *first round* was originally scheduled for 28 February but had to be postponed to 6 March because the electoral authorities failed, as they had on several previous occasions, to distribute voter cards on time. The winner of the first round was Lionel Zinsou (with 28.4% of the vote), leading by a narrow margin the runner-up, Patrice Talon (24.8%), closely followed in turn by Sébastien Ajavon (23.0%). Abdoulaye Bio Tchané came in fourth (8.8%) and Pascal Koupaki was fifth in the race (5.9%) and the Coalition of Rupture took all of places two to seven. Only two women ran for president and, together, they took less than 10,000 votes in the first round. Under the absolute majority rule, Zinsou and Talon entered the *second round*. The Coalition of Rupture significantly increased its vote share between the two rounds and, on 18 March, spokesperson Bio Tchané announced that 25 candidates now supported Talon. Two days later, *Talon was elected president* with almost twice as many votes as Zinsou. Turnout had even increased from 3 m to 3.1 m, representing roughly two-thirds of registered voters.

The ECOWAS electoral observation mission, which had deployed 136 observers, was generally satisfied with the electoral process, and domestic civil society groups, on the basis of reports from their own 3,350 observers, agreed with the ECOWAS appraisal. In addition, political parties and the Constitutional Court sent observers to almost every polling station and their complaints and reports helped to invalidate 907 votes for Talon and 222 votes for Zinsou in the second round.

The new president officially assumed office on 6 April. The transition of power from Yayi to Talon was smooth, despite the deep legal conflict that had separated the two men in recent years. On 18 March, between the two electoral rounds, Talon even accompanied Yayi to a three-country summit in Abidjan (Côte d'Ivoire), where they met the presidents of Côte d'Ivoire and Togo.

Talon's government was eagerly awaited after the incoming president had promised to put qualification first and break with the practice of primarily appointing political supporters. Although he did appoint many political newcomers and technocrats, his team of ministers suggested that political alliances drove the selection process. Both Pascal Koupaki and Abdoulaye Bio Tchané received senior ministerial posts, the former serving as chief of the presidential administration ('secrétaire général de la Présidence'), the latter entrusted with economic planning and development. The president's legal counsel and major civil society supporter, Joseph Djogbénou, became minster of justice. Experienced politicians who supported Talon without being presidential candidates themselves assumed responsibility for departments such as the Ministry of the Interior and Public Security (Sacca Lafia), the Ministry for Decentralization and Local Government (Barnabé Dassigli), the Ministry of Industry and Commerce (Lazare Séhouèto), and the Department of Defence within the Office of the President (Candide Azannaï). By and large, however, Talon promoted political supporters to posts whose portfolio corresponded to their professional experience. Sébastien Ajavon was not appointed to the government. Instead, Talon appointed three ministers (of agriculture, secondary education and communication) who were considered close to Ajavon, but Ajavon was allegedly unhappy about the small number of posts his allies had received. In total, the president appointed 21 ministers. This was a small cabinet by national standards, but larger than Talon had promised during the campaign.

Government communication changed drastically. The government relaunched its website, using professionally produced video clips explaining its policy projects, and made presidential decrees and governmental decisions available. The national television station, ORTB, featured government activities, often in cooperation with private outlets. Most notably, the government action programme was presented live from Marina Palace in a talk-show-like setting. The president addressed the audience only briefly before handing over to the specialists in his ministerial team, who discussed individual items of the programme with experts. The *government action programme* had three priorities: first, the consolidation of democracy, rule of law and good governance; second, the structural transformation of the economy; and third, the improvement of living conditions. Forty-five *flagship projects* were proposed in nine strategic sectors, including agriculture, physical and digital infrastructure and tourism. The government estimated the total cost of the programme at slightly above CFAfr 9 trn (approximately € 13.6 bn). It said that about 10% of the funding was already available and that the private sector was expected to contribute about 60% of the budget.

In interviews, Talon emphasised two priorities: the reform of the institutional framework and the fight against public dept. As one of his first acts (Decree 2016–272, 3 May), the president established a political and institutional *reform commission,* headed by the minister of justice. Constitutional law professor Joël Aïvo was named rapporteur and many other high-ranking constitutionalists and academics became commissioners. A similar commission had been appointed by former president Yayi to develop constitutional reform proposals years earlier, but their recommendations had been put on hold because the opposition suspected Yayi of aiming to amend the constitutional two-term limit, which Yayi had always denied. In contrast, Talon proposed to introduce a single-term limit. He himself declared that he would definitely leave office after one term. Though the reform commission report skipped the topic for lack of consensus, the public focussed on the president's term limit proposal. The main opposition parties (FCBE, RB and the Communist Party [PCB], among others) spoke out against the single term. Aïvo handed the commission report to the president on 26 June. Recommendations focussed on less spectacular reforms, such as the creation of a central auditing authority and capacity building in the judicial sector, both key demands of the donor community. Two days later, on 28 June, Talon announced that a constitutional referendum would take place before the end of the year, but this did not materialise.

Nevertheless, a number of low-key *reform processes* were launched. On 17 May, the president decreed a standard model for the organisation of ministerial departments. The model included minimum standards to fight corruption and foster efficiency. On 7 July, the government named provincial capitals for six départements. After previous governments had been unable to resolve the conflicts between competing towns and communities, provincial administrations had not been decoupled since the local government reform in 1999, which had split all provinces in two. On 25 July, the minister of justice announced an increase in judicial recruitment in order to reinforce the capacities of the deficient judiciary. This initiative touched upon the controversial debate about the recruitment process. Reform projects included other sensitive issues such as the reorganisation of the police forces (Decree 2016–685, 7 November). The president commissioned a group of experts to assess a strategy integrating the National Police and the Gendarmerie into one single national police service. In line with the French organisational tradition, the Gendarmerie was part of the armed forces whereas the national police force operated under the ministry of the interior.

In July, local media reported that some government decisions ran against Ajavon's economic interests, including public tendering, but it was unclear whether any government action was deliberately targeting him. However, on 29 October, *Ajavon was arrested* for alleged involvement in drug trafficking. On 28 October, port gendarmes at Cotonou, notorious for decades for drug smuggling, confiscated almost 18 kg of cocaine in a container that had been shipped to Ajavon's firm COMON-CAJAF. At a press conference, a Gendarmerie spokesperson estimated the haul to be worth CFAfr 9 bn (nearly € 758 per gram), but according to the latest data from Australian Criminal Intelligence this was a high estimate compared with street prices in Australia. The actual profit to intermediate traffickers targeting the cheaper European market should be much lower and therefore less spectacular, but the still substantial quantity of cocaine found led to police investigations into the container's addressee. Ajavon denied any connection with drug trafficking and accused the security forces of planting drugs in one of his containers with the aim of humiliating him. He was released following a court order on 4 November. In December, the 'Haute Autorité de l'Audiovisuel et de la Communication' (HAAC) temporarily shut down six media outlets, including Soleil FM and Sikka TV, both owned by Ajavon, but was accused of politicised decision-making, reviving a common criticism of the Yayi presidency.

In early November, the government decided to stop construction work on the *new parliament building* in Porto-Novo. An evaluation report commissioned by the new government found a significant gap between expenditure to date and actual progress with the construction. Around 47% of the project costs had been disbursed but only 38% of construction had been completed. The building site on the bank of the Ouémé River, known to be a flood plain, had lain idle for years due to mismanagement and corruption. The Talon administration stated that it would await a thorough investigation before making any further decisions.

Former president of the Republic Emile Derlin-Zinsou passed away on 28 July at the age of 98. His advice was still sought by many politicians though he had long stepped back from official political engagements. He was an uncle of the defeated presidential candidate Lionel Zinsou.

Foreign Affairs

Beyond relations with its donors, Benin did not pursue any noteworthy foreign policy initiatives. As a member of ECOWAS and the West African Economic and Monetary Union (WAEMU) with close financial relations with France, it continued to commit itself to regional integration without actively pushing for it. Despite Benin's general restraint in taking the initiative to participate in international military activity, it contributed a substantial share of its armed forces to *UN peacekeeping missions*. By the end of the year, almost 1,100 troops and other personnel were serving on UN missions, mainly in the DRC and Mali. The total number of contributions fell heavily compared with 2015 due to a withdrawal from Côte d'Ivoire. In March, 150 troops were committed for the regional battle against jihadism and, in particular, Boko Haram. In 2015, a sub-regional pact between Nigeria and all four of its Francophone neighbours had been launched with French endorsement, and the second summit of coalition members took place in Abuja (Nigeria) on 14 May. President Talon represented Benin, the country least affected by Boko Haram and by far the weakest partner in terms of military capacity. The summit dealt with a comprehensive strategy to address the governance, security, development, socio-economic and humanitarian dimensions of the difficult regional situation.

Beyond this multilateral security meeting, political observers and the media in Benin urgently awaited a bilateral meeting between Talon and his Nigerian counterpart Muhammadu Buhari, given *Nigeria*'s outstanding economic significance for Benin. The state visit took place on 2 August. Marina Palace later disclosed that the two presidents talked about regional security and the strengthening of economic relations, particularly with regard to trade and energy issues. They met again on 3 October to discuss similar topics.

On 11 July in Niamey (Niger), Talon discussed with a selection of Francophone neighbours the revival of the '*Entente Council*', a regional organisation established in 1959 by the then Ivorian president Félix Houphouët-Boigny. It brought together Burkina Faso, Côte d'Ivoire, Togo, Niger and Benin. On 30 July, the president was back in Niamey to discuss trilateral economic relations with Niger's President Issoufou and French officials. French President François Hollande received Talon at the Elysée Palace on 26 April, 12 July and 12 December to discuss the two countries' development partnership and security issues, further strengthening bilateral relations.

The new government made conspicuous efforts to diversify Benin's foreign relations. Talon fostered connections with the *Arab world* by visiting the UAE and Saudi Arabia on 20–22 November, prior to the Afro-Arabian Summit in Malabo (Equatorial Guinea) on 22–24 November. In Saudi Arabia, the president met with the king and the president of the Islamic Development Bank. On 16 October, Senior Minister Bio Tchané held talks in Teheran with *Iran*'s Foreign Minister Mohammad Javad Zarif about bilateral cooperation in the political, economic and academic fields, including banking and agriculture. Beginning in Ankara on 5–6 December, Talon toured *Turkey* and Europe for more than one week. Five accords were signed with Turkey concerning military training assistance, security cooperation, education, information and communication technologies, and archive management. On 8–9 December, Talon met with Belgian Prime Minister Charles Michel and top *EU* representatives, including Council President Donald Tusk, Commission President Jean-Claude Juncker, and Development Commissioner Neven Mimica, in Brussels. After a day in Paris, he continued to *Estonia* on 13 December, where he discussed governance issues with top-level state representatives. Two memoranda were signed with Tallinn's eGovernance Academy concerning cyber security and capacity building for civil servants.

Talon also focussed on *China*. On 7–8 September, he led a delegation to China's Second African Investment Forum in Guangzhou and, on 25 December, he granted an exclusive interview to CCTV's English programme. Meanwhile, Benin decided to close down its embassy in *India* thereby signalling that China's rival was not considered a particularly promising cooperation partner. Benin further closed its missions in Abu Dhabi, Havana (Cuba) and Malabo (Equatorial Guinea), but the total number of *embassies closed* was lower than originally announced. A three-day state visit to Rwanda took place on 29–31 August and was followed by the inauguration of a direct flight connection between Kigali and Cotonou served by RwandAir on 2 September.

Socioeconomic Developments

Two economic heavyweights decided the presidential polls. The 'cotton baron' Patrice Talon and the 'king of poultry' Sébastien Ajavon received almost half of all the votes cast during the first round and their alliance in the second guaranteed Talon's victory. The *two millionaires* had also been economic competitors in Benin's import and export sector and did not share the same interests in all aspects. Soon after the election, domestic observers argued that Talon had not kept his promises to Ajavon with regard to access to government and markets. Instead, the new government committed to transparency and the government action programme 'Bénin Révélé', which was presented to the public on 16 December.

Overall *economic performance* recovered from a relative low in 2015. Economic growth almost doubled from 2.1% in 2015 to 4%, according to IMF estimates, despite unfavourable international conditions and a poor *cotton* harvest. The production of the country's most important cash crop dropped from almost 400,000 tonnes in the 2014/2015 season to a five-year low of 260,000 tonnes, due to weather conditions and a shortage of agricultural chemicals. It was the poorest harvest since the state had taken full control of the cotton sector in 2012. Talon's government promised to revive the industry and handed the production management back to the professional private-sector cotton association, the 'Association Interprofessionnelle de Coton' (AIC). Farmers' representatives complained that any monopoly on control over the cotton sector would be dysfunctional, regardless of whether it was in the hands of the state or private actors. Talon had been one of the founders of AIC, which had managed the industry between 2009 and 2012 with mixed results. Estimates for the following harvest season that began in November predicted a quick recovery of production to around 350,000 tonnes.

Despite the generally positive international expectations about the new government's economic reform capacity, James Roberts of the Heritage Foundation, known for its politically conservative positions, was pessimistic about Benin's prospects: "The poor quality of physical and legal infrastructure, exacerbated by the government's inefficiency in delivering public goods, are serious impediments to long-term economic development. The government of Benin needs to redouble its efforts to fight corruption, over-regulation, and other inefficient practices,"

Roberts stated in the Foundation's online outlet 'The Daily Signal' on 20 September. *Corruption, fraud and smuggling* were major challenges to economic growth. Benin was still considered to be an important transit country for drugs and weapons and the border between Benin and Nigeria continued to be a focus for smugglers. After bilateral talks on 2 August, Talon promised to seek cooperation with Nigeria to end the flourishing illegal trade. Only two days later, on 4–5 August, high ranking customs officers from the two countries met in Cotonou to discuss illegal border activity.

On 11 August, the national government announced its intention to follow the Rwandan example and completely *ban plastic bags*. A bill was announced but had not been introduced by year's end. The proposal came only two weeks before Talon's state visit to Rwanda. The World Bank granted a $ 50 m credit line for the new Benin Cross Border Tourism and Competitiveness project (CBTCP), covering the 2016–21 period. The *tourism* sector was the country's second largest source of foreign exchange earnings and third largest employer.

Bilateral donor relations with one of Benin's biggest donors, the Netherlands, normalised after the change of government. On 29 November, the two countries concluded an agreement for the Omidelta project worth CFAfr 37 bn (approximately € 56.4 m), aimed at improving *sewage management*. The Netherlands, as lead-nation in European water projects, had cancelled cooperation with Benin after a corruption scandal in the sector in 2015.

Burkina Fase

Daniel Eizenga

After the inauguration of Roch Marc Christian Kaboré as president in December 2015, he named his prime minister and new government at the beginning of 2016. The new government faced significant challenges throughout the year, including increased insecurity due to terrorism, an emboldened opposition, and promoting justice and national reconciliation. Security in the northern regions deteriorated significantly as jihadist groups exploited the porous borders between Mali, Niger and Burkina Faso, conducting attacks on security forces and civilians. Relations with Côté d'Ivoire grew tense as former president Blaise Compaoré received Ivorian citizenship in exile and Ivorian officials became implicated in the September 2015 coup d'etat. Burkinabè citizens residing in Ouagadougou also suffered a number of public health crises related to droughts, flooding and outbreaks of dengue fever. However, the government successfully obtained donor support for their National Social and Economic Development Plan promising several development projects and initiatives in the future.

 | DOI 10.1163/9789004355910_006

Domestic Politics

The rise of the ruling party, the Movement of the People for Progress (MPP) and its *new government* marked the beginning the year. The freshly inaugurated president, Roch Marc Christian Kaboré, appointed Paul Kaba Thieba to serve as prime minister on 6 January. By selecting Thieba, an economist and technocrat, Kaboré sought to underscore a break with the former regime of Blaise Compaoré and his own commitment to national development, a key policy item during his campaign. Thieba named 29 government ministers, 25 of whom had not served in the previous administration. Many of the *newly appointed ministers*, like Kaboré himself, had previously belonged to the former ruling party, the Congress for Democracy and Progress (CDP) before resigning in 2014.

Several *supporters of Kaboré*'s bid for the presidency received positions in the government. Simon Compaoré, vice president of the MPP and former mayor of Ouagadougou, became minister of interior security. Rosine Coulibaly, one of seven women in the administration and originally rumoured to be in contention for the premiership, was appointed minister of economy, finance and development. Thieba selected René Bagoro as minister of justice, an important position in view of the numerous court cases in progress against former regime leaders, including members of the 'Régiment de Sécurité Présidentielle' (RSP), which had held Bagoro hostage during their September 2015 coup d'etat.

Kaboré's new government immediately confronted several *security issues*. On 15 January, a *terrorist attack* on a popular hotel and café in downtown Ouagadougou left 30 dead and more than 70 wounded. The majority of the victims were foreigners of more than ten different nationalities. Al-Mourabitoun, a jihadist group led by the Algerian Mokhtar Belmokhtar, claimed the unprecedented attack. French and Burkinabè counter terrorism forces responded, killing three of the attackers.

Over the next several months, many were arrested on suspicion of being connected to the attack. In June, security forces *arrested ten people*, three suspected of being responsible for the attack in Ouagadougou and the rest linked to a terrorist attack on a beach resort in Grand Bassam, Côte d'Ivoire, on 13 March. Thirty-nine people previously arrested on suspicion of involvement in the Ouagadougou attack were acquitted for lack of evidence.

In response to *increased terrorist activities*, and under the direction of President Kaboré, Military Chief of Staff General Pingrenoma Zagré ordered the national armed forces to bolster security by deploying increased border patrols in the north of the country. In March, following the attack in Grand Bassam, France also committed to sending a rapid response team from the National Gendarmerie Intervention Group to be stationed in Ouagadougou to combat terrorist attacks in the region.

Throughout the year, terrorist activities and attacks increased in Burkina Faso's northern Sahel region, particularly the province of Soum. Apparently unrelated, but nevertheless on the same day as the attack in Ouagadougou, Ansar Dine terrorists crossed into Burkina Faso from Mali and *kidnapped two Australian humanitarian aid workers*, Kenneth and Jocelyn Elliot, near the town of Djibo, where the couple had run a clinic for nearly four decades. In February, the kidnappers released Jocelyn Elliot in Dosso, Niger. The Australian government worked with regional partners throughout the year in an attempt to secure Dr Kenneth Elliot's release.

In addition to this high profile incursion by terrorist actors, a *number of skirmishes* took place between armed terrorists groups and Burkinabè security forces in the Sahel region. In Soum province alone, more than ten separate terrorist attacks occurred. The most deadly incident resulted in the death of 12 Burkinabè soldiers on 16 December, when about 40 armed men attacked a military post at Nassoumbou, near the border with Mali. Ansarul Islam, a newly established terrorist group led by Burkinabè national Ibrahim Malam Dicko, later claimed responsibility. The *emergence of Ansarul Islam* at the end of the year set an ominous tone of insecurity, despite government efforts to curtail the spread of insecurity from over the border with Mali.

Kaboré and his government also struggled to demonstrate their control over and support from the military. Nearly a week after the terrorist attack in Ouagadougou, former RSP soldiers *attacked an arms depot* in Yimdi, outside the capital, stealing a cache of weapons. Officials immediately arrested 14 soldiers and one civilian linked to the raid, but others escaped to neighbouring Ghana and Côte d'Ivoire. After a *series of negotiations*, Côte d'Ivoire extradited three soldiers wanted in connection with the arms depot attack and the September 2015 coup d'etat.

Later in the year, Minister of Internal Security Simon Compaoré announced that the government had *foiled a coup plot*. The government alleged that around 30 former members of the RSP had planned to attack several targets, including the Presidential Palace, on 8 October. In response, Kaboré made a direct plea to the armed forces to refrain from entering into the political sphere during a speech commemorating the 56th anniversary of the national armed forces on 1 November. Historically, the Burkinabè government had *struggled to maintain effective civilian control over the military* and these events suggested that the Kaboré administration was encountering similar challenges.

The new ruling party also faced an *emboldened political opposition* as the legislative elections held in 2015 had failed to produce an overall majority of National Assembly seats for the MPP. A parliamentary resolution adopted on 27 January appointed Zéphirin Diabré – runner-up in the presidential election and leader of the Union for Progress and Change (UPC), the party with the second-largest number of parliamentary seats – as the official leader of the political opposition. The UPC routinely *criticised the new administration*'s governance. In June, the UPC accused the MPP of manipulating the judiciary, citing the slow progress made on high profile cases and the observed interference with certain judicial procedures. In particular, the UPC pointed to cases where members of the previous regime who were accused of embezzling public funds had been released without explanation.

However, the UPC failed to establish a strong alliance with other potential opposition parties, suggesting that the *opposition remained fractured and weak*. While the UPC joined with some smaller opposition parties, they failed to form a coalition with the CDP – the former ruling party and the third largest party in the National Assembly. By October, the CDP had formed alliances with other opposition parties including: the Alliance for Democracy and Federation – African Democratic Rally, 'Faso Autrement' and the 'Nouvelle Alliance du Faso'. These parties created a formal legislative bloc known as the Coalition for Democracy and National Reconciliation (CODER). The formation of CODER signalled a *shift in Burkinabè politics* from a system dominated by the ruling party to one characterised by three competing political fronts: the ruling party, the classic political opposition, and the former ruling party recast as an opposition coalition.

This new political reality failed to fully materialise before *municipal elections* on 22 May. A total of 156,693 candidates from 72 political parties contested elections for 19,624 seats in 9,299 municipalities. The MPP emerged as the decisive winner, with more than 11,000 seats. The UPC won the second largest number of seats with just over 3,000, followed by the CDP with more than 2,100 seats. The Electoral Commission estimated voter turnout to be 47%. Despite the MPP victories across the country, certain municipalities highlighted tensions in Burkina Faso's political fabric. *Post-electoral violence* left at least one dead and several wounded, and displaced hundreds in the department of Karankasso-Vigué alone in June. Rioters in Gomboro lynched the newly-elected mayor, Moussa Diallo, and burned down the city hall. The violence dissipated after gendarmes began patrols in the affected municipalities, but tensions at the municipal level continued throughout the year. In July, municipal councillors representing CODER and the UPC *boycotted the opening city council session* in Ouahigouya, protesting against the lack of opposition representation in the leadership of the council.

While dealing with the newly emboldened opposition, the new government also sought to *weaken former leaders* of the CDP. In January, the authorities arrested Eddie Komboïgo and Léonce Koné – former president and vice president of the CDP, respectively – on suspicion of involvement in orchestrating the September 2015 coup d'etat. Both were eventually released from prison on a provisional basis, along with several others suspected of being involved in the coup. However, former foreign affairs minister Djibril Bassolé remained imprisoned throughout the year, as did General Gilbert Diendéré, the former leader of the RSP and of the September 2015 coup d'etat.

The authorities also arrested former prime minister Luc-Adolphe Tiao in September, charging him with intentional assault, complicity in intentional assault, murder and conspiracy to murder. State Prosecutor Armand Ouédraogo brought the charges against Tiao, holding him responsible for the deaths of protesters during the popular insurrection of 2014, which had removed former president Blaise Compaoré from power. Many national and international observers believed these arrests demonstrated Kaboré's desire to maintain his stature as a president capable of getting justice for those who suffered under the previous regime. The arrests also helped to assert his control over the military in the wake of the September 2015 coup. This objective remained paramount throughout the year due to the deteriorating security situation in the north.

Foreign Affairs

The *deteriorating security situation* in the northern regions of Burkina Faso bordering both Mali and Niger received significant attention from regional officials. With the support of the French counter terrorism operation in the Sahel, Operation Barkhane, ministers responsible for public safety in Côte d'Ivoire, Mali, Burkina Faso and Senegal convened in Abidjan (Côte d'Ivoire) on 24 March to discuss counterterrorism measures. The ministers agreed to increase collaboration between their respective security services, but this ultimately failed to put an end to the attacks in northern Burkina Faso.

On 18 May, gunmen attacked a police station in Koutoukou, wounding two officers, and gunmen again *attacked police officers* on patrol near the border with Mali on 31 May, leaving three officers dead. These initial attacks resulted in more patrols and an increased security forces presence in the Sahel region of Burkina Faso, but the strain on the limited security personnel available posed a problem for Burkinabè officials. President Kaboré requested that the UN peacekeeping mission in Mali (MINUSMA), to which Burkina Faso was the eleventh-largest contributor of troops, deploy one of the Burkinabè battalions to secure the Burkinabè-Malian border. Mahamat Saleh Annadif, the UN Special Representative and head of MINUSMA, confirmed the redeployment of these troops to the border by November.

However, these measures were not implemented quickly enough and, on 4 September, a group calling itself the Islamic State in the Greater Sahara, a terrorist organisation led by Abu Walid al-Sahraoui, claimed responsibility for an attack that resulted in the death of a customs official and a civilian in Marakoye, Oudalan province of the Sahel region. Then, on 12 October, the *violence again spilled over* the border when gunmen attacked a police station in Intangom, killing three Burkinabè soldiers and two civilians. The *deteriorating situation* in the north captured the attention of US officials and the American ambassador to Burkina Faso, Tulinabo Mushingi, pledged continued American support for Burkina Faso's fight against terrorism in an October meeting with Prime Minister Thieba.

Faced with the growing domestic insecurity, Burkinabè authorities decided to withdraw from the joint AU-UN *peacekeeping mission in Darfur*. Obeidalla

Mohamen Obeidalle, the Sudanese state minister of foreign affairs, announced the decision in August alongside Rita Solange Agneketom Bogore, the Burkinabè deputy minister of state for regional cooperation. Burkinabè Foreign Minister Alpha Barry then notified the UN that the 850 Burkinabè peacekeepers stationed in Darfur would be withdrawn by July 2017 in order to be redeployed toward domestic security concerns.

President Kaboré led a number of *diplomatic delegations*, including a visit to Brussels (Belgium) on 15 June to participate in the 10th anniversary of European Development Days. During the visit, Kaboré met with his Belgian and Luxembourg counterparts and EU delegates to discuss possibilities for development cooperation in Burkina Faso. In October, Foreign Minister Alpha Barry visited Taiwan and met with President Tsai Ing-wen at the Presidential Palace in Taipei. Barry's visit indicated that Burkina Faso would continue its *recognition of Taiwan*, despite the growing influence of China in SSA. Burkina Faso, along with São Tomé and Príncipe, and Swaziland, were the only three SSA states that continued to maintain diplomatic relations with Taiwan.

Foreign relations between Côte d'Ivoire and Burkina Faso reached new lows at the beginning of the year, but improved later. On 8 January, Burkina Faso issued an *international arrest warrant* for the president of the Ivorian National Assembly, Guillaume Soro, for his alleged involvement in planning the September 2015 coup d'état led by the RSP. A recording of a phone conversation captured two voices, allegedly those of Soro and Djibrill Bassolé, the foreign minister under Blaise Compaoré, plotting the coup and served as the basis for the warrant. Officials in Côte d'Ivoire quickly rejected the warrant and called for the dispute to be handled diplomatically.

Subsequently, on 30 January, Kaboré met with Ivorian President Alassane Ouattara at the 26th AU summit in Addis Ababa (Ethiopia) to normalise diplomatic ties between the two countries. Although an immediate solution did not emerge from this meeting, it was assumed that some diplomatic progress had been made. In February, however, the official legal journal of Côte d'Ivoire published a *naturalisation decree* for ousted president Blaise Compaoré and his son, in effect granting them Ivorian citizenship and protecting them from extradition. Compaoré had sought exile in Côte d'Ivoire following the 2014 popular insurrection that had removed him from power and an arrest warrant for him had been issued by a military court in December 2015 for his presumed role in the 1987 assassination of Thomas Sankara.

In April, the military court cited a number of *procedural errors* in the way the authorities had filed the Soro and Compaoré cases. Following this news, Minister of Justice René Bagoro announced the removal of Lieutenant Colonel Norbert Koudougou, the presiding judge in the case and the recall of civilian delegate judge, Sébastien Rapademnaaba, who was also serving on the case, to the civilian courts. In May, the military prosecutor charged with implementing Compaoré's arrest warrant denied that the warrant had been cancelled. On 6 June, the military tribunal dismissed the case against Soro after Interpol refused to assist with his extradition. Burkinabè Government Commissioner Alioune Zanre called on the Ivorian authorities *to continue the investigation* through a procedure known as denunciation, but the affair between Soro and Bassolé remained unresolved at the end of the year and an investigation into Soro's alleged involvement in the 2015 coup d'etat continued.

In a bid to improve relations between Côte d'Ivoire and Burkina Faso, President Kaboré visited Ivorian President Ouattarra in the Ivorian capital Yamoussoukro on 27–29 July. The meeting revolved around a framework for the *fifth treaty of friendship and cooperation* between the two countries, which aimed to strengthen economic ties and promote strong bilateral cooperation in the fight against terrorism. During the meeting, the *governments signed 13 agreements* regarding, amongst other issues, energy and minerals, road and rail infrastructure, scientific research and technology, culture, diplomacy and defence. Several analysts speculated that the signing of these agreements and the restoration of the treaty confirmed a normalisation of diplomatic relations. On 30 September, the Burkinabè authorities dismissed the charges against Blaise Compaoré for his involvement in the Sankara assassination.

Socioeconomic Developments

Several memorial events took place in Ouagadougou during the year. One year after the 15 September 2015 coup d'etat, which claimed the lives of 15 protesters, the government organised a *memorial ceremony* for the victims. The prime minister and the president of the National Assembly, Salifou Diallo, paid their respects at the city cemetery in Gounghin, a popular neighbourhood in the capital. The government also dedicated a new memorial to former president Thomas Sankara. Serge Bambara, a leader of the social movement 'Balai Citoyen', was at the heart of the project and received the support of Minister of Culture, Arts and Tourism Tahirou Barry. The dedication included a Pan-African symposium, a march of more than 4,000 people, debates on the economy, and a concert in honour of Sankara's ideas and role as a revolutionary leader.

Demonstrators also joined together to *demand justice* for Norbert Zongo, an investigative journalist found dead with three others in a burned out vehicle on 13 December 1998. The demonstration took place 12 December, marking the 18th anniversary of his death. In the 1990s, Zongo had edited the periodical 'L'Indépendant', which had published several critical reports exposing poor governance and corruption under the rule of Blaise Compaoré. His case continued to move slowly through the Burkinabè justice system even after three soldiers were charged with his murder in December 2015.

Another challenge faced by the new administration was to establish a coherent development plan. In July, the council of ministers approved the National Social and Economic Development Plan, which outlined the implementation of *many development projects* from 2016 to 2020. The vast majority of expenditure allocated in the plan required aid from international donors. By December, with support from the UN, EU, World Bank and others, the government *exceeded its fundraising goals* for the plan. The International Islamic Trade Finance Corporation pledged rough $ 875 m and the EU reinforced its support, pledging € 800 m toward efforts to ensure democracy and sustainable development. The primary objective of the plan was to transform living conditions by reaching an average growth rate of 7.7% and by creating about 50,000 jobs per year.

In the *mining sector*, the government began applying a modified mining code that the Transitional Government had promulgated at the end of 2015. However, a number of modifications to the revised code proposed by legislators stalled its implementation, causing the government to recall 316 of 731 mining permits at the end of March. The government justified the *extensive recall* by claiming that time was needed to implement the reforms, update the geological map and attract new investors. These actions caught the attention of and worried several mining companies that had been operating in the country under the rule of Blaise Compaoré. On 22 June, President Kaboré met with several representatives of these companies to assuage concerns about the reforms and give reassurance that Burkina Faso remained an attractive country for mining investment. However, a parliamentary commission later found that the country had potentially lost nearly $ 1 bn to *corruption in the mining sector* between 2005 and 2015 and recommended the indictment of the former minister of mines and several advisors to former president Compaoré.

In *the cotton sector*, Burkina Faso's largest cotton exporter, SOFITEX, received a $ 74 m trade loan from the IFC, the Global Agriculture and Food Security Programme's (GAFSP) private sector window, and Société Générale. The three lenders pledged to provide funds against warehoused commodities to improve SOFITEX's liquidity and ability to purchase crops from 160,000 Burkinabè cotton farmers. Burkina Faso was the largest raw cotton producer in SSA, and this deal helped to strengthen the country's overall exports.

Burkina Faso's cotton association, the 'Association Interprofessionnelle du Coton au Burkina', decided to *ban genetically modified* (GM) *seeds* from US seed company Monsanto following failed negotiations with Monsanto representatives. The association claimed that the introduction of GM seeds caused a drop in the overall quality of the cotton, particularly with regard to the length of fibres. Following the decision to ban the seeds, the government also opted to phase out GM cotton, leading Monsanto to temporarily suspend its operations in the country. Cotton sector forecasters remained optimistic about cotton production in the upcoming harvest season, noting that even though non-GM seeds were more vulnerable to climatic events and pests, the high-quality and longer fibres produced by the seeds would help Burkina Faso maintain its share of the market.

Ouagadougou experienced a *number of public health crises*. In May, towards the end of the dry season, the capital faced a severe drought, forcing the government to implement harsh *water rationing* policies. The city was divided into two sectors and each received only 12 hours of water per day due to extremely low levels at the Ziga Dam, Ouagadougou's main source of drinking water. The government then used tanker trucks to distribute water to deprived residents in some parts of Ouagadougou in an attempt to tackle shortages across the city. The emergency distribution exercise was conducted in collaboration with the National Water and Sanitation Office (ONEA), targeting some of the worse affected districts of the capital. During the water shortage, temperatures soared to 44°C (111°F), exacerbating the situation for many city residents.

The rainy season began in June, putting an end to the water shortage, but there were unusually intense rain storms through August. *Flooding* became a significant issue for Ouagadougou, causing housing damage and destroying granaries. In August, one flash flood *killed 12 people* and critically injured 35. The abnormally heavy rains also led officials of the Volta River Authority to release water from the Bagre Dam south of Ouagadougou. The overflow forced residents in Bolgatanga (Ghana) to flee their homes. In 2015, spillage from the Bagre Dam had killed at least eight Ghanaians in Bolgatanga. The flooding also contributed to an outbreak of *dengue fever* and higher than normal incidences of malaria. International health organisations assessed the progress of these mosquito-borne tropical diseases and issued *warnings against travel* to Ouagadougou. By the end of November, the organisations estimated that roughly 2,000 people in Burkina Faso were carrying Dengue and speculated that dozens of deaths had resulted from the disease.

Cabo Verde

Gerhard Seibert

Three elections shaped the political scene. In March, the opposition 'Movimento para a Democracia' (MpD) won the legislative elections for the first time since 2001. In the municipal elections in September, the 'Partido Africano para a Independência de Cabo Verde' (PAICV) lost six of the eight municipalities it had previously controlled. The MpD increased its share of municipalities from 14 to 18. In the presidential elections in October, the incumbent, Jorge Carlos Fonseca (independent backed by the MpD), was re-elected. Despite the ongoing economic crisis in other sectors, tourism continued to grow significantly.

Domestic Politics

On 20 March, the opposition MpD headed by Ulisses Correia e Silva, former mayor of the capital Praia (2008–16), won an absolute majority of 53.6% of the votes in the *legislative elections*, while the PAICV, headed by Janira Hopffer Almada, received 37.5% and the 'União Cabo-verdiana Independente e Democrática' (UCID) 6.8%.

 | DOI 10.1163/9789004355910_007

Accordingly, the MpD took 40 seats (compared with 32 in 2011) in the National Assembly, the PAICV 29 (38) and the UCID 3 (2) seats. The MpD won a majority of votes in all islands. In Fogo, traditionally a PAICV stronghold, the MpD won for the first time in 25 years. The turnout of the 347,622 registered voters was 65.8%. Hopffer Almada blamed the disappointing result on the low turnout and the fact that 15 years in power had worn out her party. During the campaign, Correia e Silva promised to reduce youth unemployment, introduce free compulsory education until class 12, create 45,000 new jobs and establish political, economic and institutional conditions conducive to economic growth.

On 20 April, the newly elected deputies were inaugurated. Jorge Santos (MpD) was elected president of the National Assembly. Two days later, Prime Minister Ulisses Correia e Silva, replacing José Maria Neves (PAICV), and his 11 ministers were sworn in. The *new government* included four independents. Five previous cabinet positions were dissolved or merged with other ministries. In his inaugural address, Correia e Silva announced the following priorities: improving the business climate to attract more foreign investment, strengthening bilateral relations with Portugal, Luxembourg, France, Spain, Angola, Brazil, the United States and China, and implanting regionalisation through decentralisation by attributing more competences to the individual islands and improving public security. The National Assembly approved the government programme on 24 May with 42 votes (MpD and UCID) against 25 PAICV votes.

On 25 April, 23-year old Manuel António Silva Ribeiro, known as Antany, a member of the armed forces, killed eight soldiers and three civilians, including two Spanish nationals. The crime occurred in Monte Tchota in Santiago, the country's telecommunications centre, which houses the military. Two days after the killings, Antany was captured in Praia. The investigation revealed that he had acted out of personal motivations. The government decreed two days of national mourning in memory of the victims. The tragedy provoked the resignation of the chief of staff of the armed forces, General Alberto Fernandes, who was replaced by General Anildo Morais, the coast guard commander. On 9 June, the government announced that it would pay survival pensions to the families of the eight military personnel killed in the massacre. On 9 November, a military court sentenced Antany to the maximum of 35 years in prison.

In the *municipal elections* of 4 September, the opposition PAICV lost six of its eight municipalities, while the MpD won in 18 municipalities, four more than in the previous elections. Independent groups won majorities in the municipalities of Ribeira Brava in São Nicolau and in Sal Island. Prompted by the PAICV's poor results, Hopffer Almada resigned as party leader and agreed that there was a need for a thorough debate within her party. On 16 October, the PAICV's National Council decided to hold early party leader elections on 29 January 2017. At the meeting, the delegates agreed unanimously to support Hopffer Almada's re-election.

Not surprisingly, Fonseca won the *presidential elections* of 2 October with 93,010 votes (74.1%). Two independent candidates, Albertino Graça, dean of the University of Mindelo, and Joaquim Monteiro, a former independence fighter, received 28,256 (22.5%) and 4,278 votes (3.4%), respectively. The elections were marked by a low turnout of only 35.5%. Although former prime minister José Maria Neves had already announced in April that he would not run for the presidency, the PAICV did not put forward any other candidate in the elections.

Foreign Affairs

Cooperation, foreign investment, regional security and the Cabo Verdean diaspora dominated the diplomatic agenda. On 19–20 January, *Portugal*'s Prime Minister António Costa, Foreign Minister Augusto Santos Silva and Secretary of State for Foreign Affairs and Cooperation Teresa Ribeiro paid an official visit to Cabo Verde. Costa discussed with Prime Minister Neves the third Strategic Cooperation Programme (previously the Indicative Cooperation Programme) for the next five years. Costa declared that, besides education, health and public security, energy and maritime economy would also be integrated in the new cooperation programme. On 17–20 May, President Fonseca was in Portugal, where he was received by President Marcelo Ribeiro de Sousa. In addition, Fonseca participated in a university conference on law in lusophone countries and he also visited Cabo Verdean immigrant communities in several Portuguese cities. From 16–20 June, the new prime minister, *Correia e Silva paid his first official visit to Portugal.* Following talks with Correia e Silva, Prime Minister Costa promised that his country would no longer deport Cabo Verdeans sentenced to prison terms for crimes committed in Portugal.

São Tomé's President Manuel Pinto da Costa visited Cabo Verde on 21–24 January. He was received by President Fonseca, Basílio Mosso, president of the National Assembly, and Prime Minister Neves. In his address at a special session of the National Assembly, Pinto da Costa declared the development cooperation between the two island states to be an excellent example of south-south partnership. On 21–24 February, Neves paid a visit to São Tomé, where he held talks with his counterpart Patrice Trovoada, President Pinto da Costa and José da Graça Diogo, president of the National Assembly. Neves announced the establishment of an embassy in São Tomé to further strengthen bilateral relations between the two archipelagos. On 25 February, Neves, accompanied by a large delegation of businesspeople, left São Tomé for a 24-hour visit to neighbouring Equatorial Guinea to examine opportunities for bilateral economic and business cooperation. During his visit there, he was received by President Teodoro Obiang.

On 15 February, Neves participated in a *business forum in Luxembourg*, where the risk capital investments fund Afroverde 1 was presented. The fund, created by the Ministry of Tourism with the support of the grand duchy's authorities, aimed to attract investments of € 100 m for six projects in the tourism and real estate sectors in São Vicente, Santo Antão and São Nicolau.

From 26 April to 5 May, Cabo Verde hosted for the first time the *annual US Africa Command (AFRICOM) military exercise, Epic Guardian.* The exercise, in which 350 troops participated, included training in the international waters off Sal Island, as well as planning and support by the Praia-based 'Centro de Operações e Segurança Marítima' (COSMAR). Epic Guradian 2016 offered the US and local security forces opportunities to strengthen capacities in communication, logistics, intelligence and crisis planning to improve maritime security in the region. During the exercise, Cabo Verde earned about $ 5 m in taxes and services.

On 11 and 12 October, Correia e Silva and Foreign Minister Luís Filipe Tavares headed a delegation to the 5th Ministerial Conference of the Forum for Economic and Commercial Cooperation between *China and the Portuguese Speaking Countries* in Macau. In his address, Correia e Silva declared that his country was capable of becoming an international service centre, given its rapidly growing tourist industry and favourable location for African, European and American markets. The meeting defined China's cooperation policy towards seven Portuguese-speaking countries for the period 2017–19. Following a meeting with Correia e Silva, Chinese Prime Minister Li Keqiang announced the cancellation of Cabo Verdean bilateral debt of $ 1.54 m and promised additional Chinese grants worth $ 15.4 m.

On their return from China, from 14–16 October, Correia e Silva and Tavares paid an official visit to Luxembourg, where the former held talks with his counterpart Xavier Bettel and Minister of Cooperation Romain Schneider. On 17 October, Foreign Minister Tavares and EU Commissioner for International Cooperation and Development Neven Mimica met in Brussels and signed an agreement on *EU-budget support* worth € 50 m to be disbursed as part of the 11th EDF (2014–20). The signing ceremony was attended by Correia e Silva and EU President Jean-Claude Juncker. The EU support package was aimed at poverty reduction and the promotion of sustainable economic growth and was intended simultaneously to improve the country's competiveness and business climate.

President Fonseca represented his country at two *summits of multilateral organisations.* On 17–18 July, he participated in the 27th AU Summit of heads of state and government in Kigali (Ruanda), where the delegates agreed to use 0.2% of national import taxes to finance the AU budget, set at $ 447 m for 2017. On 31 October–1 November, Fonseca attended the 11th biannual conference of heads of state and government of the CPLP in Brasília (Brazil). At the summit, which also marked the 20th anniversary of the CPLP's founding, the delegates discussed, among other things, measures to improve the mobility and circulation of citizens of the nine member countries in the lusophone community.

On 14–15 November, Correia e Silva and the president of the government of the *Spanish Canaries,* Fernando Clavijo Battle, presided over the 5th annual meeting of the governments of the two archipelagos. The two governments agreed to further strengthen cooperation in the areas of tourism, environment, space utilisation planning, scientific knowledge and economic and international relations. With regard to the last, they decided to develop the region of Macaronesia, together with the Azores and Madeira, as an economic block to take advantage of the commercial opportunities of the ECOWAS region and of relations with the USA, including through AGOA.

Socioeconomic Developments

On 3 January, 'Transportes Aéreos de Cabo Verde' (TACV) was readmitted to the International Air Transport Association (IATA) Clearing House payment system. On 6 January, the government approved the acquisition of TACV debts of € 10.9 m by the 'Caixa Económica de Cabo Verde' (CECV) to consolidate the airline's debts. However, the airline's financial problems worsened over the year. On 27 February, a TACV Boeing 737–800 was grounded at Rotterdam Airport because of outstanding debt payments of almost $ 2.5 m related to the leasing contract for TACV's two Boeing aircraft with the Amsterdam-based Irish company AerCap. In early March, TACV chief executive João Perreira Silva announced the reduction of up to 120 of the airline's 510 staff by December. On 3 May, José Luís Sá Nogueira replaced João Pereira Silva as the airline's chief executive. During the parliamentary debate on the national budget on 14 July, Prime Minister Correia e Silva claimed that the previous government had provided TACV with an annual subsidy of CVE (escudo) 3.6 bn (€ 32.6 m), equivalent to 10.5% of fiscal revenue or 2% of the country's GDP. On 12 November, Binter Cabo Verde, a subsidiary of the Spanish airline Binter Canárias that had connected the Canaries with Cabo Verde since 2012, inaugurated the operation of inter-island flights between Praia, São Vicente, Sal and Boa Vista.

On 31 May, Júlio Morais, president of 'Cabo Verde Investimentos', hosted a delegation of the *China-Africa Development (CAD) Fund*, which intended to invest $ 25 m in the archipelago, particularly in the tourism sector, which accounted for about 20% of GDP. Morais declared that it was a great opportunity for local businesspeople to present their projects to Chinese investors, but also admitted that they had to professionalise and adapt their projects to the CAD Fund's profile. The event included a presentation of the Fund for Development Cooperation between China and the Portuguese-speaking Countries, which had been established in June 2013 with a starting capital of $ 1 bn.

On 27 July, the National Assembly approved the *current national budget* set at about CVE 59.6 bn (€ 539.8 m), of which CVE 40.1 bn (€ 363.2 m) was allocated to current expenditure and CVE 19.5 bn (€ 176.6 m) to capital investment. The budget predicted GDP growth of 3.5%–4.5%, an inflation rate of 1.2% and a global budget deficit of 5.2%. The budget included a putting a stop to public sector recruitment for the entire year.

On 8 December, the National Assembly approved the *2017 national budget*, set at CVE 56.4 bn (€ 510.4 m) with the votes of the ruling MpD. The PAICV voted against the proposal, while the UCID abstained. The budget projected economic growth of 5.5%, an inflation rate of 0.7%–1.7%, and a reduction of the budget deficit to 3%. Public debt was expected to fall from 123.7% of GDP in 2016 to 121.5% of GDP. CVE 40.9 bn (€ 370.2 m) (including interest payments) was budgeted for current expenditure and CVE 15.5 bn (€ 140.2 m) for capital investment.

The number of *tourist arrivals* increased by 75,042 (13.2%) compared with 2015 to a total of 644,429. The UK was again the principal country of origin (20.5%), followed by Germany (11.1%), France and Portugal (10.1% each) and Belgium/Netherlands (9.7%). In the same period, 2,215,892 passengers passed through the seven Cabo Verdean airports, 11.5% more than in 2015. The British Thomson Airways, TAP Air Portugal and TUI Airlines Netherlands were the operators that contributed most to the passenger increase. Sal's Amílcar Cabral Airport accounted for the largest percentage (53%) of international flights, while Praia's Nelson Mandela Airport handled most domestic flights (35%).

Côte d'Ivoire

Alfred Babo

2016 was an after-election year filled with important political reforms, including the establishment of a new executive body and a new constitution, which created a national Senate and the position of vice president. Legislative elections also took place. Cooperative relations with partners from around the globe were maintained. Although the macroeconomic performance continued to improve, the government did not address important social issues and challenges.

Domestic Affairs

Following the 2015 presidential election, a new Ivorian government was formed on 12 January by Daniel Kablan Duncan, the re-appointed prime minister. The presence of women increased substantially, with nine female ministers in the cabinet. The re-elected President Alassane Ouattara had promised a *new constitution* and, on 31 May, he appointed a committee of experts to draft a proposal. According to Ouattara, this initiative aimed to eliminate the 'conflicting' articles in the previous constitution of July 2000 and to ensure institutional coherence. After the National

 | DOI 10.1163/9789004355910_008

Assembly had approved the draft on 11 October, the proposed constitution was submitted to a referendum on 30 October. Despite a few protests and some minor attempts by the opposition to boycott it, the referendum took place and resulted in the adoption of the new constitution with 93.4% of voters in favour of the draft on a 42.4% turnout. The promulgation of the new constitution, now Law No. 2016–886 of 8 November, created the *Third Republic*.

Legislative elections were held on 18 December. Voter turnout was 34.1%. The presidential coalition of the 'Rassemblement des Houphouetistes pour la Democratie et la Paix' (RHDP) emerged victorious, taking 167 of the 255 seats, or more than two-thirds of representatives. Significantly, 75 seats were won by the so called 'Independents', who had emerged as a result of internal crises in a number of prominent political parties such as the 'Front Populaire Ivoirien' (FPI), the 'Parti Démocratique de Côte d'Ivoire' (PDCI) and the 'Rassemblement des Républicains' (RDR), as well as the political coalition of the RHDP itself. While the hardliners in the FPI, led by Aboudramane Sangaré, boycotted the elections, Pascal Affi N'Guessan, the president of the moderate FPI, supported FPI candidates who stood in the elections. The PDCI experienced growing internal opposition from its *young militant wing*, called 'Jeunesse du PDCI' (JPDCI). The party's president, Henri Konan Bédié, angered many supporters when he suggested that the projected unified party that will be drawn from the coalition in power should keep the name of the RHDP and young militants expressed their dissatisfaction with what they called the insignificant benefit of cooperation with the presidential party. On 18 February, around 60 young people, mostly members of the JPDCI, opposed the creation of the RHDP party and tried to prevent a related press conference at the PDCI headquarters. Discontent increased when the RHDP announced the nomination of its candidates for the legislative elections. Several PDCI representatives who did not secure nominations, including members of the leadership, expressed frustration, which led to a *revolt* by PDCI militants. Although the party leadership asked the unsuccessful candidates not to run as '*independents*', many incumbent representatives, including Yasmina Ouégnin of Cocody district and Kouadio Konan Bertin of Port-Bouët ignored this instruction. In response, the governing bodies of the party decided to impose disciplinary sanctions on the independent candidates and 48 members of the Political Bureau and the Committee of Elders were suspended from their functions and from the PDCI. The RDR was affected by similar events. After the nomination of its candidates, several prominent leaders, including departmental secretaries, secretaries of sections and even a top-ranking member, opted to run as 'independents'. The legislative elections also split the governing RHDP coalition, as the presidents Gnamien Konan of the 'Union pour la Côte d'Ivoire' (UPCI) and Albert Mabri Toikeusse of 'Union pour la Démocratie et la Paix en Côte d'Ivoire' (UDPCI) were dismissed from the government. The two parties disagreed over the number of candidates they were allowed within the coalition, and competed against other RHDP coalition candidates in some constituencies.

Although President Alassane Ouattara granted *freedom* to 3,000 prisoners and 100 others benefited from provisional release, only a handful of prisoners were actually released. On 25 January, the case of the murder of the former Ivorian head of the state, Robert Guéï, his wife and his bodyguard, went to trial. The accused were Anselme Séka Yapo, the former chief of security of former first lady Simone Gbagbo, and several other military officers. On 18 February, the trial resulted in ten convictions and 13 acquittals. Three of the defendants, Anselme Séka Yapo, General Bruno Dogbo Blé, former commander of the Republican Guard, and a soldier, Séry Daléba, received life sentences. Simone Gbagbo's second trial opened on 21 May in Abidjan. She was charged with crimes against humanity, crimes against prisoners of war and crimes against civilian populations. The trial had been blocked since late November 2015, following the withdrawal of her lawyers in protest against what they considered irregularities in the judicial process. According to HRW, "The justice system in Côte d'Ivoire continues to suffer from political biases. Five years after the 2010–11 crisis, victims are still waiting for justice. Criticisms still accuse the legal authorities of applying victor's justice." The relationship between the government and the opposition remained tense. Alassane Ouattara met Pascal Affi N'Guessan, the leader of the FPI, on 21 and 31 January. They discussed the release of *political prisoners*, the restriction of bank accounts of Gbagbo supporters and the situation of Ivorian refugees.

Côte d'Ivoire also experienced social upheaval. Violent clashes between Lobi and Fulani farmers in the north-eastern town of Bouna occurred on 24–25 March. This community conflict resulted in 33 dead, 52 wounded and 2,640 displaced. Four more people, including two gendarmes, were killed on 16 November, during violence between the population and the police in the village of Niamoin, 70 km from Bouna. Similar *clashes* occurred in other localities, including in Assoufry (Tanda) on 7–8 March, when a conflict between the village youth and 'Forces Républicaines de Côte d'Ivoire' (FRCI) soldiers left four dead and many wounded. In Katiola, in the north, clashes occurred between young people and police on 3 October, and there were similar conflicts in Yamoussoukro, on 16–17 November.

The Ivorian forces were targeted by unidentified armed men in Nero-Village (Tabou), near the Liberian border on 27–28 March, and an attack on a police station in the town of Daloa occurred on 30 October. On 13 March, a jihadist commando killed 16 civilians and three members of the special security forces at a beach resort in Grand-Bassam. Six assailants were also killed. This attack was claimed by al-Qaida in the Islamic Maghreb (AQIM).

Foreign Affairs

Côte d'Ivoire took over the leadership of the sub-regional economic institution (*UEMOA*) and President Ouattara was unanimously elected as its chair on 8 January.

In the West African region, relations with *Burkina Faso* got back to normal as the Ivorian and Burkinabè presidents met on the sidelines of the AU summit in Addis Ababa (Ethiopia) on 29 January. They pledged to strengthen their security collaboration in the face of growing terrorist threats. Côte d'Ivoire maintained excellent cooperation agreements with *Morocco*. On 16 December, the Consortium Vinci Energies Côte d'Ivoire / EGELEC Maroc signed a CFAfr 28 bn agreement for the construction of the infrastructure associated with the thermal power plant at Songon (a northern suburb of Abidjan). Côte d'Ivoire also consolidated its relationship with *Tunisia*. Ivorian Minister of Agriculture Sangafowa Coulibaly met with his Tunisian counterpart, Saad Seddik, on 15 February and discussed ways to strengthen cooperation between the two countries. In addition, Ivorian Prime Minister Duncan welcomed his Tunisian counterpart, Habib Essid, in Abidjan, on 25 April during the Ivorian-Tunisian economic forum.

In Europe, relations with *France* remained good and French investment in the country rose to CFAfr 672 bn, making France the largest foreign investor in Côte d'Ivoire. Ouattara visited French President François Hollande in Paris on 4 February to discuss bilateral relations, with a focus on security cooperation. In order to strengthen support for the fight against terrorism, France increased its military forces in Côte d'Ivoire from 500 to 900 personnel. Côte d'Ivoire was able to develop new relations with *Turkey* as Turkish President Recep Tayyip Erdoğan visited Abidjan for the first time on 28 February. This visit, occurring almost a year after Ouattara's visit to Ankara, was marked by economic and investment projects. The two heads of state signed cooperation agreements on industry and defence. An Ivorian-Turkish economic forum in Abidjan produced cooperation agreements between Turkish and Ivorian enterprises.

The vice president of the United States' Millennium Challenge Corporation (MCC) visited Côte d'Ivoire on 9 February, reflecting the US's commitment to supporting the country's development. The *USA* initiated development programmes for Côte d'Ivoire, including the McGovern-Dole 'Living for Education' programme, worth more than CFAfr 18 bn over the period 2016–20 to support school canteens. In addition, according to its CEO, Sean Long, US Endeavor Energy, one of the subsidiaries of the private equity investor Denham Capital, agreed with the local Starenergie 2073 to invest $ 900 m to construct a thermal power station and a gas terminal in Songon. In addition, a Côte d'Ivoire-USA economic forum was held in Abidjan on 5 December to promote business and investment between the private sectors of the two countries.

The government continued to cooperate closely with the AfDB, the IMF, the World Bank and the EU to agree *loans and grants*. On 17 November the AfDB approved a € 137.8 m. loan for the Ivorian Electricity Transmission and Distribution System Project and, on 16 December, granted a € 769.8 m. loan for the improvement of Abidjan's urban transportation system. The IMF also agreed in October to finance the National Development Plan for the period 2016–20. Around $ 94.1 m were disbursed immediately. The World Bank provided $ 50 m to modernise trade and freight transport facilities between Côte d'Ivoire and Burkina Faso. It also offered locomotion and computer equipment worth CFAfr 1.0 bn on 23 November to enhance an epidemiological surveillance system and a further $ 50 m to finance an urban drinking water supply project in December. The EU, with the agreement of the Ivorian authorities, opened a regional office of the EIB in November in Abidjan-Plateau and granted, on 20 November, € 80 m (CFAfr 50 bn) to support the government's policies on governance and food production.

Socioeconomic Developments

Côte d'Ivoire was recognised and praised for its multi-level *macroeconomic performance*. In January, the Pan-African Institute Imani Center (Ghana) in partnership with Financial Afrik praised Côte d'Ivoire as the country with the best Ministry of Economy and Finance in the OIF. Regarding macroeconomic conditions (economic growth, employment/unemployment rates, inflation, etc.) and other indicators, the Ivorian ministry outperformed the other 13 OIF countries. The Ivorian average *growth rate* was around 9%, a figure deemed impressive by IMF Deputy Managing Director Mitsuhiro Furusawa. In February, Pierre Laporte, director of World Bank operations in the sub-region, stated that the Ivorian debt burden remained acceptable. According to him, Côte d'Ivoire was "a moderate risk country" that had considerably reduced its level of over-indebtedness. It was also the only country on the African continent to see its *risk profile* improve, with a rating of 'C' by Coface, the French credit insurer.

The *budget* was estimated at CFAfr 5,813 bn, with investment, especially in education, employment promotion and the health sector, being a major item of expenditure. Several *infrastructure projects* were completed. For example, a new power plant 'Ciprel 4' was opened by the Ivorian Power Generation Company (CIPREL) in Vridi industrial zone on 17 February. This steam turbine would enable the country to increase its production of electricity. A Public Health Emergency Operations Centre in Abidjan was inaugurated on 15 February. The purpose of the centre, costing a total of CFAfr 233,888,000 in construction and equipment, was to collect information for strategic decision-making, prevention, epidemic detection and response. In Divo, a medical and surgical unit donated by the Raoul Follereau Foundation (worth CFAfr 716 m) for the fight against buruli ulcer and leprosy was opened by the minister of health and public hygiene. President Ouattara opened two major roads: the 87.5 km Comoé-Agnibilekrou road on 3 December, and the 135 km road from

Boundali to Tengréla (on the Malian border) on 8 December. In cooperation with Morocco, on 18 January, the country launched the first phase of its development of the Bay of Cocody, set to cost of CFAfr 100 bn.

In agriculture, *cocoa* output reached about 1.8 m tonnes – more than 45% of the world supply of cocoa beans. At the beginning of the year, the 'Chocolat Ivoire' brand was launched and was expected to feature on all chocolate products made in Côte d'Ivoire. In order to stimulate local production, Abidjan reduced the 'Single Right of Exit' tax on exports of cocoa. Côte d'Ivoire also led African *rubber* production, with an output of 213,000 tonnes, but demand for rubber was low and prices fell. While several projects to build new rubber plants existed, the fall in prices slowed down investment. Côte d'Ivoire also became the world's largest producer of raw cashew nuts with a 25% market share.

In contrast, *cotton* production dropped by 31% to 310,000 tonnes compared with 450,000 tonnes in 2015. The decline in both the number of producers (from 121,305 to 113,532) and production output was apparently due to climatic factors. Low performance also characterised the *cereal production*, which fell from 1,608,000 tonnes in 2015 to 1,431,000 tonnes, according to FAO. To address this decline, an emergency programme was initiated by the Presidency on 19 December. The government-funded project, worth around CFAfr 100 bn, was intended to enable farmers to produce during all seasons. Gross crude *oil* production rose by 100% to 45,196 b/d in one year (June 2015–June 2016) according to government statistics, the increase being explained by the entry into production of three new wells 'Espoir' (CI-26), 'Baobab' (CI-40), and 'Marlin' (CI-27).

While Côte d'Ivoire improved its macroeconomic performance, it continued to experience *major challenges*. The unemployment rate reached 25%. Many families relied on one meal a day. With the rise in the cost of living, social tensions increased and resulted in several strikes by unions and students. Almost 43% of Ivorian youth were excluded from the school system or did not attend school at all. In many urban and rural communities, populations faced frequent water shortages. During July, violent riots broke out in a number of cities, protesting against the rise in the price of electricity and 58% of the rural population were still waiting to be connected to the electricity grid. The presence of fake and illegal drugs became a major public health problem. The socially unsatisfactory environment led to an increase in illegal *emigration*. Of the migrants who arrived on the Italian coast from January to July 2016, 7% or about 6,500 people, were Ivorians. Côte d'Ivoire thus rose from tenth to fourth place on the list of countries that were the source of illegal immigration into Europe.

The Gambia

Alice Bellagamba

1 December 2016 was a watershed moment in the annals of Gambian political history. With an estimated turnout of more than 70% in a presidential election that was by all accounts deemed free and fair, Adama Barrow, an obscure and lesser-known candidate of the opposition caused a major upset, defeating Yahya Jammeh, the incumbent and long-serving president by 43.3% to 39.6 % of the votes cast. People ran into the streets in jubilation. After having initially recognised the elections as fair and just, on 9 December, Jammeh contested the results. Senegal urged ECOWAS, the AU, and the UN to take all necessary measures to protect the electoral decision and the sovereignty of the Gambian people.

Domestic Politics

The year culminated in the unexpected defeat of President Yahya Jammeh in the 1 December *presidential elections*. For a country that had endured 22 years of a

 | DOI 10.1163/9789004355910_009

brutal dictatorship, the result and the initial willingness of the incumbent to concede defeat was by far the biggest news of the year. In the previous elections in November 2011, Jammeh had won 72% of the votes and defeated Ousainou Darboe of the United Democratic Party (UDP) led coalition by a wide margin. That election, which had been boycotted by ECOWAS observers, had also been considered unfair by AU and EU observers and, in the five years that followed, the political climate had worsened significantly. After a failed coup attempt on 30 December 2014, the Jammeh government had continued to stifle dissent and had further restricted the already very limited Gambian democratic space. The Gambia was ranked 145th out of 180 countries in the 2016 Reporters Without Borders' World Press Freedom Index. In addition to ridding the country of the most prominent dissidents, Jammeh had brought religious institutions and a large number of influential business leaders under state control. Religious and business leaders either financed state propaganda (and stirred popular support in Jammeh's favour) or had to live with the wrath of the autocratic regime. Jammeh had also managed to manipulate civil servants with a careful strategy of demotions and arrests, undermining any serious attempt to unseat him. Although the majority of Gambians, both within the country and abroad, had no illusions about the urgent need for a change of governance, it was unclear how such a change could take place. With a beleaguered Independent Electoral Commission (IEC) and drastic electoral law reforms, many Gambians were of the opinion that a violent overthrow of Jammeh was the only viable option. External observers expected Jammeh's party, the Alliance for Patriotic Re-orientation and Construction (APRC), to consolidate its grip on power especially because his long-term opponent, Darboe, had passed the constitutional age limit for presidential candidates. This made an opposition win all the more unlikely.

In the run-up to the elections, the *national mood changed*. Electoral reform protests in April and the heavy-handed response of the government were important landmark events. The 2015 Elections Amendment Act, passed by an APRC-dominated parliament, had substantially increased the cost of running elections. Registering as a presidential candidate now required a deposit of GMD (dalasi) 500,000 ($ 12,000), a ten-fold increase on the previous registration fees. On 14 April, the UDP organised a peaceful protest march in the suburbs of the capital, Banjul, calling for changes to the Elections Amendment Act. Security forces brutally attacked the protestors and arrested Solo Sandeng, the head of the UDP youth wing. Many others were detained and harassed. Sandeng was allegedly tortured to death and hastily buried. The news shocked the country and the UDP leadership organised a second march on 16 April. On that occasion, party leader Darboe was arrested and detained together with other members of the party's executive. On 28 April, a large crowd marched to Darboe's home, chanting, "We need Solo Sandeng dead or alive." A video started to surface on Gambian social media showing hundreds of people protesting against Jammeh. On 9–10 May, security forces arrested almost 50 people leaving the court hearing against Darboe and his followers. With a deteriorating economy, high youth unemployment, and protests against Jammeh among the Gambian diaspora, these events and the reaction of the international community set the stage for Jammeh's defeat and the subsequent political impasse that gripped the country. On 11 May, in the border town of Farafenni, 235 APRC supporters defected to the Gambia Democratic Congress (GDC) led by Mama Kandeh, a former APRC member of parliament, now estranged from the party.

Disaffection for Jammeh increased on 3 June, when, during a rally in Taliding, a heavily populated suburb of Banjul, he made rude remarks about the Gambia's largest ethnic group, the Mandinkas, calling them "enemies" and "foreigners" whom he threatened to wipe out like flies. In a country with a high inter-marriage rate and solidarity networks, the bold threat that Mandinkas would never hold the office of president in the Gambia was enough to antagonise a large segment of society, irrespectively of their religious or tribal affiliation. This alienated him from his traditional base, especially in rural areas, where he had once commanded a large following, including among the Mandinkas.

The death of Sandeng and the incarceration of Darboe and his party activists were met by wide condemnation from ECOWAS, HRW, AI and the UN Secretary-General Ban Ki-moon, whom Jammeh told to "go to hell". The international outcry against the Jammeh regime emboldened Gambians at home and in the diaspora and unleashed unprecedented fury. Protest took the form of a series of large-scale demonstrations calling for sanctions and regime change in Germany, the Netherlands, the UK, the USA and other locations. On 30 October, eight parties (the People's Democratic Organisation for Independence and Socialism [PDOIS], the National Reconciliation Party [NRP], the Gambia Moral Congress [GMC], the National Convention Party [NCP], the People's Progressive Party [PPP] and the Gambia Party for Democracy and Progress [GPDP]) announced their anti-Jammeh coalition. *Adama Barrow*, the UDP treasurer, who had become leader of the UDP after Darboe's arrest, resigned from his position on 7 November to register for the presidential election as the coalition's candidate. A real estate developer, Barrow had worked for the Alhagie Musa & Sons Company in Banjul before emigrating to the UK, where he earned a degree in real estate management. He had returned to the Gambia in 2006 to set up his own real estate company.

Diaspora activists launched a series of crowd-funding campaigns for Barrow and the opposition coalition through social media and online networks such as 'gofundme'. This commitment to providing logistical and financial support helped fire a vigorous political campaign that eclipsed the APRC and triggered the hope that the opposition would win. Barrow repeatedly declared that he would bring the Gambia back into the Commonwealth and the ICC, and safeguard Gambian civil rights.

Unlike previous elections, when *vote counting* was centralised, the ballots were now to be counted at the polling stations, which made it harder to manipulate votes. There were no reported incidents of violence or irregularities when the polls closed at 5 p.m. on 1 December. A block on the national telecommunication gateway, which deprived Gambians of access to the Internet and all forms of international communication, created an atmosphere of uncertainty and anxiety. The only news that reached the outside was sent through the Senegalese-owned GSM mobile networks. Unofficial results initially reported through social networks and online diaspora radio stations showed the coalition outperforming the ruling APRC party in most of its traditional strongholds. Video streams from the IEC confirmed wide disparities between some of the official and unofficial results that were shared on social media. At 5 p.m. on 2 December, Jammeh conceded defeat to Adama Barrow and the coalition party in a televised telephone call. He declared the elections free and fair, and praised the electoral process as the best in the world. On 9 December, however, Jammeh rescinded his concession, citing allegations of electoral irregularities. The wider international community including ECOWAS, the AU, the UN, the EU, the UK and the USA not only condemned this erratic move but vowed to adopt all necessary measures, including military action, to ensure that the political will of the Gambian electorate was respected. President Macky Sall of Senegal was key in ECOWAS attempts to mediate the impasse.

Foreign Affairs

On 6 October, the National Assembly ratified the International Atomic Energy Agency (IAEA) agreement, tabled by Minister for Environment and Climate Change Pa Ousman Jarju. Minister of Agriculture Ismaila Sanyang also presented a motion in the National Assembly on the International Plant Protection Convention (IPPC) adopted by FAO, which was ratified on 4 October.

In a televised address in March, Minister of Foreign Affairs Neneh Macduall Gaye announced the resumption of diplomatic relations between the Gambia and Mainland *China*. The Gambia had recognised Taiwan in 1995, which had led to a breakdown in relations with China. Diplomatic relations with Taiwan, which funded many development projects and scholarships to Gambian students, lasted until 2013, when the Gambian government for reasons of "strategic national interest" had abruptly ended relations.

Relations between *Senegal* and the Gambia were tense throughout the year. The presence of Gambian dissident elements and coup plotters in Senegal and the refusal of Senegal to extradite them to the Gambia continued to strain relations between the two governments. While Senegal maintained a more indifferent and conciliatory posture, rhetoric from the Jammeh administration pursued the same polemical undertones as before. The most recent dispute, a border closure that had started on 16 November 2015 because of an increase in trade tariffs, lasted until President Alpha Conde of Guinea visited the Gambia on 14 May to resolve the border issue. The sudden death of Sheriff Dibba, the leader of the Gambia transport union, who lost his life in mysterious circumstances in state custody on 22 February, temporarily caused the deterioration of the already very tense situation. After Conde's visit, a high-ranking Gambian delegation visited Dakar (Senegal). The delegation included Minister of Foreign Affairs Neneh Macduall Gaye, Minister of Trade Abdou Jobe, Minister of Justice Fatima Signateh, Minister of the Interior Ousman Sonko and Yam Bamba Njie Keita from the Office of the President. During the meeting, Senegal stressed once again the importance of building a bridge to take the TransGambia Highway across the River Gambia, as the ferry system in use was a major obstacle to the movement of goods and people between the two countries and the alternative was a long detour by road. The Gambian delegation insisted that it was essential to design the bridge in such a way as to allow river traffic to continue to pass. The border was opened in July, shortly before the beginning of the holy month of Ramadan. Immediately after Barrow's election, Senegal's President Macky Sall offered his congratulations, and on 10 December he reacted promptly to Jammeh's 9 December rejection of the election result by urging the international community to intervene to support the sovereignty of the Gambian people.

Socioeconomic Developments

Ranked 175th in the 2015 HDI, the Gambia remained one of the poorest 'Least Developed Countries'. About 48% of Gambians were estimated to be living below the *poverty* line. Rural-urban economic and development disparity remained high. Low agricultural output due to climate change and erratic rainfall patterns significantly reduced export revenues and widened the poverty gap, especially in rural areas. The joint effects of poverty, illiteracy and tyranny had exacerbated social and political exclusion and pushed large numbers of youths into illegal *migration* to Europe. An increasing number of young people were leaving the country in the hope that the EU would not turn away minors.

In his *budget* speech in the National Assembly, Finance and Economic Affairs Minister Abdou Kolley forecast that the 2017 fiscal year would be another difficult period as a result of external shocks that affected agriculture and tourism. Agriculture suffered from the short rainy season, while the country's deteriorating reputation affected tourism. Kolley's budget speech disclosed that average real GDP growth had fallen to 2.4%, well below the 5.6% average growth registered over the period 2007–10. Since 2011, the agricultural sector's contribution to annual GDP had consistently declined, while the service sector had seen a small increase from 62%

in 2011 to 64% in 2015. The industrial sector (15% of GDP) remained unchanged. Consumer price *inflation* decelerated to 6.0% in December 2016, compared with 6.9% in 2015. This was attributed to a decline in food price inflation from 8.4% in early 2015 to 4.8% at the beginning of 2016. Non-food inflation increased from 4.8% to 5.2% in the same period. Volatility in global commodity prices and a further depreciation of the dalasi against the four major trading currencies could cause inflation to rise in 2017. The country continued to struggle with a budget overspend, resulting in substantial domestic borrowing, which reached GMD 4 bn, equivalent to approximately 10% of annual nominal GDP.

Ghana

Jennifer C. Boylan

After eight years of a National Democratic Congress (NDC) government, under two different presidents, the December elections were a referendum on the quality of NDC rule. Ghana also experienced the culmination of three long-term calamities: the last year of a three-year electricity crisis, a third year of diminished GDP growth, and the reverberating effects of massive public scandals exposed in the judiciary and other sectors in previous years. To solve its way out of at least the economic disasters, a series of taxes were introduced via a revised income tax law, an energy sector levy on fuel prices, and the removal of subsidies on electricity and water prices. Ghana had signed up to a three-year IMF assistance programme in 2015, which resulted in a rise in the debt-to-GDP ratio to over 70%, a mere five years after Ghana was the fastest growing economy in the world. President John Mahama tried to answer for the economic calamity by seeking out FDI and implementing massive infrastructure and development projects throughout the year. Ultimately, however, New Patriotic Party (NPP) opposition leader Nana Akufo-Addo won the December election by a nearly 10% margin. The NPP also gained a majority in Parliament, ending the NDC's eight-year control over the legislature.

 | DOI 10.1163/9789004355910_010

Domestic Politics

The 7th presidential elections of Ghana's Fourth Republic were held on 7 December, with incumbent President John Mahama (NDC) again facing Nana Akufo-Addo (NPP). Mahama had first risen to power in July 2012 from the vice presidency after then-president Atta Mills (NDC) died in office. Mahama then won the December 2012 presidential election, and the 2016 elections were thus tantamount to an assessment of the NDC's past eight years in government under two presidents. In recent years, Mahama's government had been plagued by massive *public scandals* involving the judiciary and other sectors. Active civil society pressure groups, such as OccupyGhana, Citizen Ghana and the Let My Voice Count (LMVC) alliance, arose and helped to make voters aware more than ever before of allegations of *corruption* and government failings.

Allegations of corruption continued, and the criticisms hurled at the government travelled all the way up to the president. For example, when it was revealed in June that Mahama had received a vehicle estimated to cost $ 60,000 from a Burkinabe contractor who had recently been awarded two government contracts worth over GH¢ (cedi) 100 m, the public reaction was forceful. Similarly, in the context of a particularly tense election year, two NDC supporters and a talk-show host on 'MontieFM', thereafter dubbed the Montie3, threatened Supreme Court judges, including the Chief Justice, with violence and rape in response to the Supreme Court's ruling against the Electoral Commission in some key cases. The three were sentenced to four months in jail, but only spent one month behind bars after Mahama controversially pardoned their offences. Finally, on 20 November, a claim was made by the NPP that Mahama and his brother had attempted to *bribe* NPP Northern Regional Chairman Bugri Naabu to leave the NPP for the NDC. Though such proposals are made before every election, this allegation of corruption against the NDC resonated with the public and the NPP used the story to portray the government as desperate to win a losing campaign.

This running corruption motif went on to impact the *Electoral Commission* (EC), which was already facing a credibility deficit in the aftermath of the 2013 Supreme Court case challenging the results of the 2012 election. In 2015, Charlotte Osei of the National Commission for Civic Education (NCCE) became the EC chairperson after Kwadwo Afari-Gyan's retirement. There was immediate speculation that Osei would be biased towards the ruling party, not least because the NCCE, which now provided crucial voter education services, had once been an agency staffed with NDC party officials under former president J.J. Rawlings.

The organisation of the elections got off on the wrong foot when the EC requested GH¢ 1.3 bn to implement significant reforms for the upcoming elections, but Parliament only approved GH¢ 825 m (about $ 214 m). One particularly underfunded area was generating citizen awareness about important reforms the EC had implemented since the 2012 election, and this did not help the EC overcome the public's low trust in the institution.

Gearing up to the election, several decisions made by the EC were overturned in court cases. The LMVC pressure group and the NPP opposition demanded that the EC conduct a re-registration exercise over claims that the *voter register* was bloated with the names of under-age and deceased citizens, and non-citizens. An independent panel employed by the EC to review the register ultimately concluded that the register was sound and the EC declined to make any register adjustments. The matter was taken to court. On 4 May, the Supreme Court ruled that the EC must clean up the register by *deleting illegal registrations*, including individuals registered with National Health Insurance Scheme (NHIS) cards, since show proof of citizenship was not required to receive the card. As a result, 56,000 NHIS registrations were deleted, and two re-registration periods were held for those deleted from the register. The politicisation of the register impacted public opinion, and a Centre for Democratic Development (CDD) survey in October found that almost one-fourth of Ghanaians doubted the quality of the voter register.

On 11 October, the EC *disqualified 13 presidential candidates* for submitting incomplete or inaccurate party nomination forms. This matter was also taken to the Supreme Court, which again ruled against the EC and allowed all 13 disqualified candidates an opportunity to amend their forms. Four of the 13 candidates were consequently reinstated.

The EC appeared unprepared when it failed to successfully move the *election date*. The EC had first announced in October 2015 that it planned to bring the 2016 elections forward to 7 November from 7 December, citing the short time available after the December date to hold a runoff election should the need arise. This change needed a super-majority approval in Parliament, however, requiring both NDC and NPP support. Crucially, the EC was late sending the request to Parliament and, given the late notice, as well as the recently perceived close relationship between the NDC and the EC, the NPP minority did not support the reform. The parliamentary vote on 21 July failed to pass the request, so the 7 December date stood.

The EC also encountered problems when early voting for members of the media, security and party officials took place on 1 December and thousands of names were found to be missing from the early-vote register. Though this was initially worrisome, the EC corrected the registers and organised a second day of early-voting on 4 December.

Criticism of the EC was harsh and at times bordered on the obscene (as when an NPP MP accused EC Chairperson Osei of giving sexual favours in return for her appointment to the EC). Osei and the EC maintained a calm and by-the-book composure and by October a CDD survey found that 73% of respondents believed the EC would administer a free, peaceful and credible election, up from 63% in July and an improvement on the low EC trust ratings in the 2014 Afrobarometer survey. When the NPP eventually won the presidential election, beating the incumbent NDC government, the EC was further freed from perceptions of bias towards the NDC.

The *campaign* periods for both parties began informally at the beginning of the year, and accelerated in the few months leading up to December. For the NPP, the major challenge was cementing party unity, as well as making consistent connections between the ruling party's corruption and the economic calamity facing Ghana. The NPP actively pursued party unity, but when former NPP chairman Jake Obetsebi-Lamptey died unexpectedly in London on 20 March, the party had a tragic unifying reason to tie up loose ends.

The NDC's primary campaign focus was on the implementation of development and infrastructural projects, which were particularly increased toward the latter half of the year. The NDC widely touted its 'Green Book' list of government-built projects, but the opposition worked to portray late-in-the-game projects, such as the opening ceremony for the Kwame Nkrumah Interchange at Circle and the inauguration of a $ 170 m road project in the Central Region the week before the election, as election-year gimmicks designed to win votes. The NDC manifesto, unveiled by Mahama in a televised presentation on 13 September, included a pledge to stop seeking IMF bailouts (based on predicted GDP growth in 2017), a one computer tablet-per-student policy, and promises to build five new stadiums.

The NPP heavily criticised the NDC manifesto and unveiled its own carefully calculated document on 18 October. By now, the earlier NPP promise of free secondary school tuition had lost its lustre and instead the NPP now made grand, and potentially unfeasible, promises of the creation of one factory in each of Ghana's 216 districts and an annual development fund of $ 1 m for each of the 275 parliamentary constituencies. In what seemed eerily like a counter to Akufo-Addo's factory promise, in late November Mahama began publicising a project to build a polyclinic or hospital in every district.

Since 2008, the presidential candidates for each party had participated in *presidential debates* organised by the Institute of Economic Affairs (IEA). Early in the year, the IEA scheduled two debates, one in Accra on 22 November and a second in Takoradi on 29 November. In addition to the debates, the IEA also adopted a new speaking forum for the candidates. In response, the Functional Executive Committee of the NDC dramatically announced that it was boycotting the IEA debates because they had not been organised in consultation with the NDC and suggested that the IEA was biased towards the opposition. This move, however, allowed Akufo-Addo, who had not performed well in the 2012 presidential debates, the opportunity to boycott both the IEA debates and a 30 November debate organised by the NCCE. The fact that no debate took place between the two dominant parties in the lead-up to the election lessened the democratic quality of the overall competition.

Violence also marked the elections with significantly greater force than in the past. In reaction to the divisive nature of the competition, the inspector general of Ghanaian Police told reporters on 26 May that the police were considering blocking social media on election day because of the potential for the spread of misinformation and/or threats to the peaceful conduct of the election. Though this policy was not implemented, it presaged the sporadic but contained bouts of violence that did occur in the pre- and post-election period. When violence broke out in the Brong Ahafo Region in early November, prompting the EC to suspend a voter transfer exercise and close the EC office in Kukuom, Akufo-Addo made a speech on 11 November accusing NDC government officials of orchestrating the attacks. The NDC vehemently denied these claims. Violence also broke out between NPP and NDC supporters in front of Akufo-Addo's residence in Nima (Accra), prompting his bodyguards to fire *warning shots*. Following this and other clashes, the Accra Metropolitan Security Committee suspended all campaign activities in the metropolis until election day. Both the *UK and US embassies* released statements on 14 November condemning political violence, and on 29 November *UN Secretary-General* Ban Ki-moon called separately on Mahama and Akufo-Addo to promote peace in the upcoming election. Unsurprisingly, the October CDD survey found that 54% of Ghanaians expected Ghana's politicians to use violence in the context of the December election. On 6 November, the EU election observation mission sent 24 *long-term observers* to each of Ghana's ten regions. A further team of 32 short-term observers was deployed across the country on 7 December, with an additional 31 observers added on election day.

On *election day, queues* began to form before dawn, though the 68.6% turnout was significantly lower than in previous years. The NPP had recruited and trained an enormous *network of party agents* to track polling station results, giving them advance knowledge of the election result. Election observers from Ghana's Coalition of Domestic Election Observers (CODEO), the AU, ECOWAS and the EU were deployed across the 29,000 polling stations and generally rated the election as free and fair. The preliminary EU mission statement released on 9 December summarised the election as "a competitive, transparent, largely peaceful process and a well-managed vote … also marked by a level of tension, misuse of incumbency and some collation problems." Building on a long-term relationship between the NPP and Russia, on 20 December, the Russian Ministry of Foreign Affairs praised the election observation missions from the AU and ECOWAS, but noticeably not the EU, by congratulating Akufo-Addo on his electoral victory.

In the end, Nana Akufo-Addo (NPP) summarily beat John Dramani Mahama (NDC), with 53.9% of the votes against 44.4%. This was the first time an incumbent president had been voted out of power, and was the *largest margin of victory* won by a presidential candidate since the 2000 run-off election. In addition, some 24 incumbent NDC MPs lost their seats, thereby giving the NPP a majority in Parliament for the first time since 2009. The most senior NDC MP loss was Foreign Minister Tetteh in the Awutu Senya West constituency. After the election, it was announced that former president *Mahama's lifetime annual salary* would be 40% of his presidential salary, or GH¢ 22,809. This was up from GH¢ 15,972, but the president would also no longer receive a fully-furnished house in Accra as previous presidents had, although he would still receive a chauffeur for life and two vehicles, to be changed every four years.

Foreign Affairs

The year began with a major *security breach* in West Africa, when 28 people were killed and 56 injured in a 16 January attack at a hotel in Burkina Faso, Ghana's northern neighbour. The attack was carried out by Al-Qaida in the Islamic Maghreb (AQIM) and drew immediate condemnation in a statement by Minister of Foreign Affairs Tetteh. Relatedly, on 16 April a leaked memo revealed that intelligence gathered by the National Security Council Secretariat (NSCS) had identified Ghana and Togo as targets of *possible impending attacks*, following deadly attacks in Burkina Faso and Côte d'Ivoire. Though lamenting the leak, President Mahama acknowledged the memo, and Ghana's Immigration Service reportedly *increased border patrols* and co-operation among agencies in response to the threat.

It was announced in Mahama's 6 March Independence Day address that Ghana would offer *30-day visas on arrival* in Ghana to all citizens of AU countries, and this came into effect in July. The move was intended to increase tourism, which accounted for 5.9% of Ghana's GDP, and to boost trade with AU states. Kenyan President Uhuru Kenyatta was in attendance at the Independence Day celebration.

In mid-March, Foreign Minister Tetteh travelled to *Israel* at the invitation of Prime Minister Benjamin Netanyahu. The visit came as Israel was reportedly aiming to build a stronger relationship with African nations. Tetteh and Netanyahu's discussions focused on economic investments and security concerns.

On 17 March, Mahama's visit to Scotland drew criticism from LGBT rights activists, including members of the Scottish Parliament. The reproach was the result of Ghana's law making *homosexuality* punishable by up to three years in prison. During this visit, Mahama also received an honorary degree from the University of Aberdeen.

On a three-day trip on 17–20 May, promoting Ghanaian business opportunities to Japanese investors, Mahama and Tetteh spoke at a Ghana Investment Forum in Tokyo. Mahama spoke of Ghana's stability and political maturity, commenting that it was one of the most convenient places in Africa for *FDI*. Ghana was in talks with *Japan* to sign a Bilateral Investment Treaty (BIT) but no agreement had been reached by year's end. During this trip, Tetteh also announced that Ghana would be switching to a *chip-embedded passport system*, as required by International Civil Aviation Organization regulations.

On 12–14 June, a visit by President Mukherjee of *India* was the first by an Indian head of state to Ghana. The visit was marked by three MoUs with Ghana, the planting of a sapling as a symbol of friendship at Flagstaff House and the unveiling of a *statue of Mahatma Gandhi* at the University of Ghana-Legon campus. However, it was announced in early October that the statue would be removed after a petition by academics and students protested against Gandhi's use of racist language relatively early in his life in South Africa. Though there was initial worry that this petition could cause a rift in Ghana-India relations, Ghanaian and Indian officials apparently discussed the issue and a decision was made to move the statue to an undisclosed location.

On 19 September, Mahama travelled to New York to attend the 71st session of the *UN General Assembly*. He addressed the General Assembly on 21 September, and referenced Michael Jackson's 1991 hit song 'Heal the World' in speaking on the connections between global development, emigration from Africa and rising xenophobia.

Mahama then headed to Paris on 26 September to give a lecture at UNESCO's International Programme for Development of Communication conference on *universal access to information*. During the trip, Mahama also met with French President François Hollande to discuss energy, agro-business and West African security, among other topics.

Amidst election preparations, it was reported on 4 December that a *fake US embassy* in operation in Accra for ten years had been discovered and shut down by Ghanaian and US authorities. Turkish and Ghanaian organised crime rings had run the fake embassy and issued fraudulent US visas and identification documents, including $ 6,000 birth certificates. It was unclear whether, or how many, individuals had entered the US or other countries using these *fraudulent documents*.

In his first official foreign visit after losing the 7 December election, Mahama travelled to the Gambia as part of an *ECOWAS delegation* to attempt to persuade incumbent president Yahya Jammeh not to contest the Gambian election result and to allow president-elect Adama Barrow to take office. Also in the delegation were President Ellen Johnson Sirleaf of Liberia, President Muhammadu Buhari of Nigeria and President Ernest Bai Koroma of Sierra Leone.

On 15 December, an *EPA between Ghana and the EU* came into effect, as a first step towards a pending EPA between the EU and ECOWAS and UEMOA. These EPAS would increase West African exports to the EU by giving Ghana duty-free and quota-free access to EU markets, while Ghana agreed to decrease its tariffs on EU imports.

Socioeconomic Developments

At the beginning of the year, a barrage of economic policies immediately made life more difficult for the average Ghanaian. The economy had certainly struggled in the previous few years, largely because of the dual impact of a global fall in commodity prices and a three-year electricity crisis. The end of the year would see increases in commodity prices, and particularly oil, as well as the positive effects of some electricity projects coming online, but the outlook at the beginning of the year was bleak.

Global commodity prices had dropped for Ghana's *primary exports* (oil, gold, and cocoa) for a variety of reasons. The most deliberate and uncontrollable was OPEC's flooding the market with oil to drive out competition, which brought the price per barrel down from $ 110 in 2014 to about $ 50 in early 2016. Things were looking up towards the end of the year: in October, the World Bank adjusted its predicted price of crude oil in 2017 up to $ 55 per barrel because OPEC was looking to limit oil production after the previous over supply. The price of gold had dropped significantly in 2015 to its lowest price since 2010, and waxed and waned throughout 2016. In 2014–15, the price of cocoa had recovered from drops in 2012–13, but the price dramatically fell again throughout 2016 to its lowest point in ten years.

In January, Ghanaians awoke to a 27% increase in the cost of fuel, a 59.2% increase in the cost of electricity, and an 89% increase in the cost of water. These *utilities and fuel price increases* also caused the already high *inflation* rate to rise from 17.7% to 19.0%, the highest since January 2013, with food inflation at 8.2% and non-food inflation at 25.5%. The IMF and Ghana's central bank projected that inflation would peak at some point in 2016 and fall to about 10% by the end of the year, but the increase in utility and fuel prices made this goal unattainable. By December, the inflation rate had only fallen to 15.4%.

The reason for the fuel price increase, despite the drop in oil prices, was the addition of the Energy Sector Levy passed in Parliament in December 2015, which accounted for over 50% of the fuel prices consumers were paying. Without the new levy, diesel prices would reportedly have fallen by 10%. Meanwhile, subsidies were taken off electricity and water to increase competition in the utility sector, both to stabilise the economy and to satisfy IMF regulations and, on 13 January, the IMF did indeed approve the third disbursement of aid to Ghana, to the tune of $ 114.6 m.

On top of these increases, on 1 January the Income Tax Act 2015, Act 896, came into effect. Its aim was to simplify and *consolidate income tax law*, but it also introduced some new taxes, including a tax on income earned from investments and on gifts received in the carrying out of business. The fact that this coincided with the fuel and utilities price increases brought a surge of negative public reaction. These economic developments were enough to push workers onto the streets, and they marched through the capital and other cities to express their dismay. The Ghana Private Road Transport Union (GPRTU) also increased fares following the increases in fuel prices.

The three-year electricity ('dumsor') crisis, on-going since 2014, had been difficult to overcome because of Ghana's low GDP growth rate (3.3%) and had also contributed to low productivity, which only further weakened the ailing economy. The electricity crisis finally began to subside, but not before Power Minister Kwabena Donkor resigned in January, as he had promised to do if the power outages did not stop. Electricity projects begun in 2015 and 2016 helped to improve the situation. They included the docking of the first Karadeniz powerbarge, a *floating power plant*, at Tema Harbor in 2015 and a second floating power barge in Sekondi Harbour at the end of 2016, with a combined production of 450 MW. Further, the largest functioning *solar farm* in West Africa (89,760 panels), operated by a Chinese company in Ghana's Central Region, began operation in February, producing 20 MW of power annually.

GDP had hovered around 3%-4% in recent years, and the progress in terms of both oil prices and solutions to the electricity crisis came too late for Mahama's election-year campaign. In April 2015, when debt stood at a concerning 43% of GDP, Ghana had been forced to sign up to a *three-year IMF assistance programme* amounting to $ 918 m. In 2016, debt rose to above 70% of GDP – about the same level as when Ghana had applied for the World Bank's HIPC debt relief scheme under the Kufuor administration. By turning to the IMF, Ghana was able to pay off domestic debt, which typically commanded higher interest rates, but, with inflation devaluing the currency, the repayment of external debt would become harder to pay off.

In addition to the IMF assistance programme, Ghana also began to issue *Eurobonds* to raise money. On 8 September, Ghana issued its fifth Eurobond at a yield of 9.25%, raising $ 750 m in the process. Though still high, interest for this bond was 1.5 percentage points lower than the last Eurobond, issued in October 2015. Current economic challenges and the high debt-to-GDP ratio were cited as reasons why investors continue to demand such high interest rates.

Despite spending constraints imposed by IMF regulations, as the election drew closer, the government began to unveil more and more investment projects. On 30 May, Mahama officiated at the re-opening of the *Komenda Sugar Factory* in the Central Region. The project was largely financed by the Export-Import Bank of India (Exim Bank), with an investment of $ 35 m and, in addition to sugar, was to produce value-added by-products such as energy and alcohol.

On 8 June, Accra became the 467th city to host 'Uber', a door-to-door ride-sharing service that customers could order and pay for with an app. The World Bank reported that *mobile phone penetration* in Ghana now exceeded 100%, up from 1% in 2000.

In mid-August, work commenced on a $ 1.2 bn Eco Park to convert Achimota Forest in Accra into an *eco-tourist destination*. British-based Aikan Capital Ltd was the private partner in the five-to-seven-year project, with the first phase to take two years. The Eco Park was expected to create 4,000 jobs during the construction phase, 2,500 jobs during the implementation phase, and 600,000 visitors annually. According to the agreement, Aikan would operate the facility for ten years, with 20% of the revenue generated going to Ghana's Forestry Commission.

In September, a new pilot *Bud Rapid Transport* (BRT) *system* was launched across major routes throughout the Greater Accra region. Over 250 buses were procured, offering amenities such as USB ports for charging phones, centralised air conditioning, free wi-fi, and reportedly charging the same fares as tro tros. In response, tro tro and commercial drivers threatened to strike, and it did appear that the BRT system was intended to replace tro tro transportation on at least some major routes. The population of Greater Accra was expected to double by 2035, raising concern about the already high levels of congestion and accompanying negative effects on worker productivity. Further, a World Bank report found air pollution had been the cause of 17,524 deaths in Ghana in 2013, a 107% increase from 1990, and dirty fuel emissions from cars sitting in traffic were a major contributor. The buses were intended to offer modest relief from congestion.

On 14 September, it appeared increasingly likely that the *Western Railway Line* would be redeveloped through a potential partnership with the Ghana Ports and Harbours Authority (GHAPOHA) and the Ghana Railway Development Authority. The proposed agreement would empower GHAPOHA to develop the rail line for transportation of goods and services through a $ 100 m public-private partnership with Amanda Holdings.

Also in mid-October, the government approved a project that would *develop the coastline* in Accra, from Osu to Abokobi in the Ga East District. Development would take the form of tourist resort centres including hotels, theme parks, shopping malls, casinos and office complexes. On 14 November, the Kwame Nkrumah Interchange at Circle was inaugurated, having cost a total of € 74 m. Finally, as late as 22 November, India's Exim Bank signed a 12-year financing agreement to fund construction of an 84.8 km railway between Tema and the Lake Volta port of Akosombo.

In January, Ghana, along with Nigeria, Benin, Togo and Côte d'Ivoire, agreed to *ban high-sulphur diesel fuel* imports. A 2015 report by a Swiss NGO claimed that Swiss companies had been selling diesel fuel to these countries with sulphur as high as 3,000 parts per million (ppm), despite the EU having had a 10 ppm limit on its own fuel for the past seven years. Now diesel fuel imports would be limited to a maximum 50 ppm of sulphur.

On 4 May, AngloGold Ashanti Ltd filed a law suit against Ghana at the International Centre for Settlement of Investment Disputes, an international *investor arbitration panel* based in the US, regarding the Obuasi gold mine in the Ashanti Region. The South Africa-based company had ceased mining activities at Obuasi in 2014, citing heavy losses. In 2016, informal 'galamsey' miners infiltrated the mine and the case cited Ghana's failure to protect the operation from *illegal miners*. In early October, Ghana's Mineral Commission gave the illegal miners a 10 October deadline to vacate the mine, accompanied with threats that the military would enforce the order. Despite estimates of as many of 18,000 people mining gold in the area, there was also the danger of alienating Ashanti Region voters during an election year, and nothing was done to address the issue.

In mid-October, a May 'Decisions Memorandum' was leaked, detailing that the government had spent $ 6 m on a *consultancy task force* formed in October 2015 that had begun work on reactivating a previously-halted $ 3 bn loan from China agreed in 2011. The leaked document suggested the $ 6 m would come from the Ghana Infrastructure Fund. The loan had not been reactivated by year's end.

Finally, toward the end of the year, Mahama began to use to his advantage the positive economic predictions for 2017, including a projected increase in global oil prices, improvements in electricity coverage and new oil and gas projects coming online, suggesting that the economy was already beginning to improve under his watch. The economic improvements were not felt soon enough, however, which greatly contributed to Mahama's defeat in the presidential election.

Guinea

Anita Schroven

Guinea lived through a year of challenges. Following the free presidential elections in 2015, citizens were becoming weary of waiting for the alleged democracy dividend, which appeared further away than ever. The international community praised President Condé for his international policies and diplomatic skills, thereby raising his and the country's international visibility. The slowdown of the global economy took its toll. World market prices for minerals declined and made investment in the mining sector unattractive. State revenue declined in turn. Economic tensions translated into political and social tensions, with party politics and perceived ethnic favouritism discrediting the public administration. The government reacted by offering citizenship education training sessions for public administrators. With the end of the Ebola outbreak, the political, social and economic effects of the epidemic became visible. While international investment in public health continued, the better part of the population struggled with the high cost of living, lack of job opportunities and economic instability.

 | DOI 10.1163/9789004355910_011

Domestic Politics

2016 began with the inauguration of a *new government* following the presidential elections in October 2015. President Alpha Condé, newly re-elected, named Mamady Youla, till then head of the Guinea Alumina Corporation (GAC), as his new prime minister. In the president's party, the 'Rassemblement du Peuple de Guinée' (RPG), there was opposition to some of Youla's ministerial appointments. The new government had 31 ministerial and secretarial portfolios and among the appointees were 16 officials who had not previously held ministerial positions. Five women were appointed to the cabinet: Malado Kaba to the Ministry of Economics and Finance, Makalé Camara to Foreign Affairs, Kanny Diallo to Planning and International Cooperation, Christine Sagno to Environment, Water and Forests, and Oumou Camara to Public Works. On 4 January, Condé appointed his close ally Abdoulaye Magassouba, an experienced technocrat, as minister of mines. Magassouba and Kaba were both well respected in their fields and their appointments were intended to boost potential *investors' confidence* in the new government.

During the year, Condé made several changes to the composition of the government and the public administration. By presidential decree, he switched the leadership of Conakry harbour from Mamadouba Sankhon to Hawa Keita Touré, who had previously been general secretary of the Ministry of Commerce.

Condé brought the leader of the second-largest *opposition party*, the 'Union des Forces Républicaines' (UFR), Sydia Touré, into the fold of the newly formed RPG–'Arc-en-ciel' coalition government by naming him as his special representative, thus weakening Touré's hold on his own party. Condé also fomented the animosity between Bah Oury and Cellou Dalein Diallo, the rival leaders of the main opposition party, the 'Union des Forces Démocratiques de Guinée' (UFDG). Bah Oury had spent years in self-imposed exile but returned in January at the president's invitation. On 5 February, he was removed from his position as UFDG vice president amidst *clashes* between his supporters and security forces, during which a journalist, El Hadj Mohamed Diallo, was shot and killed. As a consequence, 22 persons from the UFDG security corps were arrested, all of whom were supporters of party leader Cellou Dalein Diallo. On 8 February, journalists and civil society representatives marched to the Ministry of Justice and called for an unprecedented '*day without media*' on 9 February. For the first time in Guinea's history, there were no newspapers or news on private radio stations. One of those arrested, Mamadou Saidou Bah, died in prison on 11 May. Others remained in pre-trial detention.

On 6 February, the EU election observer mission presented their final report on the *2015 presidential elections*, in which they denounced various irregularities, especially in Condé's home region of Kankan.

On 19 February, a four-day *general strike* over rising living costs led by national trade unions was cancelled after successful negotiations with Special Representative Touré. The agreement came after 16 previously arrested trade unionists were released and the government agreed to lower the costs of fuel and basic commodities. However, trade unions warned that they would resume general strikes if the government did not respect the agreements. Strikes continued to take place on a smaller scale throughout April.

In June, Nawa Damey, the governor of Kankan Region, claimed that several instances of popular disregard for government institutions had taken place. He decried this "insubordination to state authority" and indicated that all radio stations "insulting the president" would be closed down. On a separate occasion, *security forces and local populations clashed* in Mali, Labé region. The confrontation was provoked by soldiers torturing and publicly humiliating a truck driver whose vehicle had happened to delay the journey of the Labé military region's Lieutenant Colonel Issa Camara. After the population attacked the Prefecture building, soldiers started burning the local market in retaliation. Lieutenant Colonel Camara was later dismissed. The incident left 17 persons injured and revealed the growing tensions between state authorities and the wider population, as well as the precarious balance of power between the civilian administration and the military. Since 2010 the military had been slowly removed from government bodies, and international and national observers had acknowledged the efforts made to expand civilian control over the military.

On 17 August, about half a million people followed the call of all opposition parties to a *demonstration against corruption and economic mismanagement* in the capital, Conakry. The march started peacefully, but police fired into the crowd as it began to disperse, leaving one man dead. This led to the arrest of a police captain but his trial was still pending at the end of the year.

In August, the Provisional Commission for Reflection on National Reconciliation (CPRN), which had been mandated by a 2011 presidential decree, submitted its report, which included 22 *recommendations to address political and communal violence*. Notable propositions were justice for key perpetrators, reparations for the victims of violence and an independent truth-telling commission. The National Human Rights Commission ('Institution Nationale Indépendante des Droits Humains'; INIDH), founded in 2015, had not earned public trust or recognition and some of its commissioners were dismissed due to lack of financial transparency.

A fund was established to compensate families who had suffered in the pre-electoral violence in 2013, which saw 60 people die at the hands of security forces and many irregularities in the parliamentary vote. Critics voiced concerns about the lack of judicial follow-up as well as the failure to address similar situations in the 2010 and 2015 presidential elections, and the killing of about 130 unarmed demonstrators in 2007.

Given Guinea's troubled relations with its security forces, the news of Aboubacar Sidiki 'Toumba' Diakité's arrest in Dakar at the end of the year came as a surprise to most Guineans. He was charged with the attempted murder of former president Dadis Camara – both men suspected of being key decision makers in the events leading up to the 28 September 2009 massacre, also known as 'Bloody Monday', when security forces attacked an opposition demonstration, leaving 157 dead and 109 women raped. While it was important for Guinea to address its security forces' violent past, the capacity of its judiciary to do so remained in doubt. The ICC offered to take over the prosecutions in question.

The governing and the opposition parties were scheduled to start negotiations in July for the *delayed local elections*, but the UFDG did not attend a meeting set to take place on 15 July. Government officials subsequently circulated rumours that a coup was imminent, which UFDG leader Cellou Dalein Diallo denied. Alpha Condé and Cellou Dalein Diallo met on 1–2 September to discuss how to resolve the economic and electoral crisis and had further discussions at a private meeting, when Condé visited Diallo to express his condolences on the death of the latter's brother, El Hadj Hady Diallo. These meetings were arranged by Tibou Kamara, a personal friend of Diallo, a political ally of Condé and the brother-in-law of former president Jammeh. On 10 October, after long negotiations, Condé's ruling RPG–'Arc-en-ciel' coalition and the UFDG signed a roadmap for the local elections that had been scheduled to take place under an agreement negotiated with the AU, EU and UN, who were to serve as guarantors. Local elections had been delayed since 2005 and postponed since the initial presidential elections in 2010, leaving local councils effectively without a mandate. Until these elections, local government bodies were to be run by a 'special delegation' selected from the party that had won the relevant electoral district in the 2015 presidential elections. The agreement also foresaw new rules for the National Electoral Commission. The election roadmap scheduled the local elections for February 2017, but they were later postponed again with no date fixed.

In July, Sékouba Konaté, the leader of the AU's standing intervention force and former president of the transitional government after the fall of the government of Moussa Dadis Camara (2009–10), was fined $ 5,000 for money trafficking in the USA. His strained relationship with Condé kept Konaté outside the country.

Foreign Affairs

President Condé travelled extensively during the year and increased the country's visibility both on the African continent and beyond, starting with the World Economic Forum in Davos in January.

Guinea continued to send troops to Mali as part of the MINUSMA forces, currently headed by Guinean mission chief Mahamat Saleh Annadif. Seven of its *peace keepers*, including three women, were killed in an attack by Ansar Dine in Kidal in February. Condé ordered a three-day mourning period to honour the dead soldiers. In addition, Guinea had participated in the Islamic Military Coalition, under the auspices of the OIC, since December 2015 to fight terrorism across the Muslim world. Guinea was preparing legislation to ban women from wearing a full face veil.

In March, the International Organisation for Migration published data indicating that Guineans were the third-largest group of people attempting to cross the Mediterranean Sea towards Europe in the first quarter of the year. The number of *Guinean refugees* continued to grow throughout the year and 14,250 Guineans were officially registered as arriving in the EU, three times higher than in 2015.

On 4 March, during a visit by *Turkey*'s President Tayyip Erdoğan, a number of new cooperation agreements covering defence, health and energy supplies were signed. The Guinean delegation hoped to increase annual bilateral trade with Turkey from $ 69 m to $ 500 m.

Rwanda's President Paul Kagame visited Conakry on 9 March and signed several cooperation agreements concerning cooperation on health, environmental issues and transport.

President Condé attended the inauguration of President Mahamadou Issoufou of Niger in early April.

In June, FAO announced that Guinea had become a signatory to the international accord against *illegal fishing*, which had devastated local fishermen's income and caused the destruction of part of the Guinean coast. The accord would ensure information exchange on vessels that were fishing and unloading illegally.

Also in June, the president participated in the ECOWAS mediation mission to *Guinea-Bissau* to push ahead negotiations for the new government and he also headed the ECOWAS mission to Bissau in September.

Again in June, Condé and Minister for Investment and Public-Private Partnership Kerfala Kamara visited *Moscow* to finalise an agreement between the Guinean state and Rusky Alumine (RUSAL) concerning the Dian-Dian mine. The agreement was expected to ensure the re-opening of the aluminum plant in Friguia at the beginning of 2017 and lead to the construction of a new aluminum plant by the end of that year.

After visiting the UN General Assembly in New York at the end of September, Condé travelled to *China* to sign various cooperation deals, including one for the building of the new hydroelectric dam project in Souapiti.

In the wake of the West African *Ebola* outbreak, the World Bank launched a $ 110 m investment to finance the Regional Disease Surveillance Systems Enhancement Program (REDISSE), a project involving co-operation between WHO, the US Centre for Disease Control and Prevention (CDC) and the Bill and Melinda Gates Foundation. The programme provided Guinea with $ 30 m. On 11 November, the new Pasteur Institute was inaugurated in Conakry in the presence of French Foreign

Minister Jean-Marc Ayrault. Located next to Donka National Hospital, the institute would undertake the investigation of infectious diseases and was another manifestation of closer ties developing between Guinea and former colonial power *France*.

Socioeconomic Developments

Both the Ebola outbreak and the global economic slowdown had a serious effect on Guinea's economy. Despite these challenges, the estimated annual *GDP* growth rate stood at 5.2%, a result of mineral exports and restrictive economic and fiscal policies. The public deficit fell to 1.3%, while government revenue was up 19.2%. Government spending in the public health sector increased from 2.5% to 5% of GDP, indirectly leading to an overall increase in 'pro-poor expenditure'.

Guinea ranked 41st on the Mo Ibrahim Index for good governance, a slight improvement compared with previous years.

Early 2016 marked the end of the *Ebola* outbreak. On 17 March, there was an isolated flare-up in the coastal village of Korobara, which was quickly contained. The World Bank estimated regional economic damage caused by the Ebola outbreak at $ 2.2 bn. The international community had mobilised about $ 1.6 bn to fight the outbreak. Guinea recorded 3,351 confirmed Ebola cases, resulting in 2,200 deaths during the course of the outbreak. After the end of the outbreak, international NGOs published financial and operational reports outlining where the Ebola-related funding had gone. The Guinean government did not provide such reports, but the Ministry of Justice prosecuted NGO-related corruption cases related to Ebola funds. In June, the public prosecutor called for prison sentences for two individuals (one from the national Ebola coordination body and one from the Ministry of Health) who were accused of having stolen € 60,000 of WHO funds. As WHO did not provide any documents or testimony, the two cases remained unresolved at the end of the year. Documentation cited the need for more thorough investigations as it was very likely that similar abuses of public funds had occurred elsewhere and on a larger scale.

With an estimated economic *growth rate* of 5.2%, and the stabilisation of *inflation* at around 8.7%, the IMF granted $ 25.6 m in ECF support and further stated that the recapitalisation of the Central Bank would allow Guinea to enact monetary policies, which it had been unable to do in previous years. In March, the current ECF was extended from June to October to help the country's economic recovery. In May, fiscal policies and the monetary exchange rate were reviewed. The government managed to harmonise the official and the informal market exchange rates. On 17 June, the World Bank announced $ 40 m in IDA credit to assist Ebola-hit communities suffering from food shortages and lack of basic health care. In November, a further $ 25.2 m IMF disbursement took place following the release of optimistic macro-economic figures. On 9 November, Minister of Budget Mohamed Lamine Doumbouya announced an austerity *budget* for 2017 with the aim of limiting the debt that the Guinean government had incurred with private banks in recent years.

The current *hydroelectric output* did not suffice to serve the cities in the north and west of Guinea. Plans for a Sambangalou hydroelectric dam on the Gambia River on the border with Senegal were expected to help alleviate power shortages. The Program for Infrastructure Development (PIDA) under NEPAD (in cooperation with the AU, EU and AfDB) released new funds at the beginning of the year, which increased the number of hydroelectric projects to five. *Electricity shortages* remained the major deterrent for foreign investors.

Bureaucratic challenges were another major burden on the economy. In July, the IMF encouraged the government to look beyond the extractive minerals sector and push for public-private partnerships to bolster investment in infrastructure and agriculture to integrate broad-based economic potential. On 11 July, the World Bank and the Guinean government announced the establishment of a 'one stop shop' to facilitate procedures for investors.

Although the *mining sector* had been shrinking overall, it consolidated its activity during the year. In the area of Boke, bauxite was still being produced, and the Société Minière Boké entered into a public-private partnership with the army's 'Agence du Service Civique d'Action pour le Développement' (ASCAD), which in April announced plans to offer vocational training to vulnerable youths in the area. At the beginning of July, Rio Tinto stopped its production of iron ore in the Simandou region, citing the oversupply of iron ore on the world market. The government called on the company to honour its commitment to expand the development of the world's largest iron ore site. Other co-investors, including the Chinese Aluminum Cooperation (ChinAlCo) and the IFC (part of the World Bank) were also called on to meet their commitments. At full capacity, Rio Tinto was projected to make $ 7.5 bn in revenue and to create 45,000 local jobs, which had been the desperately needed by local populations in recent years but had been slow to materialise. In November, Rio Tinto signed off its 46.6% share to one of its largest partners, ChinAlCo, leaving Rio Tinto to hope for revenues as high as $ 1.3 bn. ChinAlCo now held 87.9% of the project, with the rest shared between the Guinean government and the World Bank. In December, the IFC announced that it would finance the expansion and renewal of the machinery of the Guinean Bauxite Company (CBG) in order to strengthen its capacity and enable it to reach Chinese markets. Soon after, US-based Alcoa (part of Halco Mining Inc.) withdrew from the management board of CBG due to an "internal re-organisation", which drew international attention to its own collaborations with Chinese mining companies. CBG was currently operating in Sangaredi with 2,400 employees, and produced annual export of 15.2 m tones of bauxite.

In August, Guinea joined the International Union for Conservation of Nature, which aimed to achieve the *reforestation* of several regions.

On 18 August, a girl's death from *female genital mutilation* (FGM) led to the arrests of three women. In collaboration with international NGOs, the government called for an end to the practice and the Senegal-based NGO Tostan reported on 20 December that communities across Guinea supported this. This public move was designed to raise awareness of the negative consequences of FGM.

Guinea-Bissau

Christoph Kohl

The year was characterised by a protracted government crisis: against constitutional provisions and ignoring parliamentary majorities, President José Mario Vaz 'Jomav' appointed two prime ministers, provoking political turf wars and parliamentary paralysis. Although crucial judicial rulings went in favour of Vaz, court decisions were heavily criticised because they contradicted earlier judgements. The attorney-general was accused of one-sidedly prosecuting political adversaries and human rights activists criticised the politicisation of the justice sector. Despite intensive mediation efforts by the UN and ECOWAS, a solution to the political crisis had not been achieved by the end of the year and deep political divisions continued to prevail. Political uncertainty caused widespread disappointment and frustration among the population.

Domestic Politics

The *political crisis* restrained the government headed by Prime Minister Carlos Correia of the 'Partido Africano para a Independência da Guiné e Cabo Verde'

 | DOI 10.1163/9789004355910_012

(PAIGC). Correia was a compromise candidate among conflicting factions of the PAIGC, the country's largest political party. President Vaz continued to exercise his power by blocking the appointment of government members he objected to. While a majority of PAIGC members of parliament (MPs) and the party's leadership – together with two minor parties – backed Correia, 15 PAIGC MPs refused their support and sided with Vaz (PAIGC) and the second largest party, the 'Partido para a Renovação Social' (PRS). The renegade PAIGC MPs were expelled from the party in January but refused to vacate their seats. They were eventually forced to leave parliament by a court ruling on 27 January. After the budget was approved on 28 January, the PRS and their 15 PAIGC allies insisted the vote was illegal because of the expulsion of the 15. On 8 February, the court overturned its earlier ruling, and the 15 dissident MPs were reinstated. Similarly, the Supreme Court declared unconstitutional the expulsion of the 15 PAIGC dissenters on 5 April. The international community, notably ECOWAS and the UN, were increasingly concerned about the unfolding situation. Former Nigerian president Olusegun Obasanjo went to Bissau in February and May, and a UN mission arrived in March. None of these interventions yielded any meaningful result and the crisis deepened as parliament was paralysed for months.

Vaz dismissed Correia's government on 12 May, justifying his decision by accusing the government of illegal expenditure, of not fully functioning for months, and of not having its programme approved by parliament. He appointed PAIGC renegade *Baciro Djá* as *prime minister* on 27 May. Djá had been expelled from the PAIGC in 2015 but a court invalidated his exclusion on 4 May. His appointment by the president was a rerun of a procedure the Supreme Court had deemed illegal in 2015. Some local analysts declared Djà's appointment 'illegal' and saw it as a 'presidential coup'. Djá suffered a setback when the nominee for interior minister, Botche Candé (PAIGC), announced on 2 June that he would not accept the position. In a heated atmosphere, some members of Correia's cabinet barricaded themselves in the government building until 9 June. Vaz reportedly impeded negotiation attempts by ECOWAS, the AU and the EU, and the Supreme Court surprisingly ruled on 14 July that Djá's appointment was constitutional. Nevertheless, he was unable to gain a parliamentary majority as the PAIGC faction loyal to party leader Domingos Simões Pereira refused their support.

From August to November, *ECOWAS* sought to broker a solution. The UNSC expressed its concern over the ongoing crisis. On 10 September, the ECOWAS mission agreed on a roadmap in Bissau, but the political situation remained tense and unpredictable.

On 14 November, Vaz dissolved the government, in line with an agreement for a consensus government to be established, brokered by ECOWAS and Guinea's President Condé in Conakry on 14 October. Although the Conakry Agreement provided for a consensual nomination of a *new prime minister*, Vaz declared his intention of appointing one before any mutual consent had been reached and he nominated *Úmaro Sissico Embaló* (PAIGC) on 18 November. However, the PAIGC faction loyal to Pereira, together with two minority parties, refused on 28 November to cooperate with Embaló, regarding him as Vaz's candidate. His nomination was seen as a violation of the Conakry Agreement and of the constitutional right of the PAIGC, as the biggest group in parliament, to propose a candidate. This left Embaló without a parliamentary majority. His cabinet, consisting mainly of former Djá government members of both the PRS and the PAIGC, was sworn in on 13 December. This undermined ECOWAS' intention to announce a new prime minister on 17 December. The PRS demanded Condé's resignation as ECOWAS mediator on 21 December.

Corruption remained a challenge: in TI's 2015 Corruption Perception Index, the country ranked 158th (out of 167). The treasurer of the Ministry of the Interior was arrested in March and charged with misusing funds earmarked for the intelligence services. However, Guinea-Bissau moved up four places in the Mo Ibrahim Index of African Governance, and was now ranked 44th (out of 54).

In February, AI reported improvements in the area of *human rights*, but criticised the treatment of prisoners and the idleness of the authorities. Discrimination against women was widespread, as women's activists Luísa Pereira and Helena Said lamented in March. A US State Department report in April verified their statements and denounced narco-trafficking and violence against women and children as major human rights abuses. The State Department repeated its assessment in June and criticised forced child labour in Qur'an schools, as well as child trafficking. Reporters Without Borders ranked Guinea-Bissau 79th in the 2016 World Press Freedom Index, two places higher than in 2015. On 28 April, the 'Liga Guineense dos Direitos Humanos' (LGDH) pointed to several cases of deaths that had resulted directly from a strike in the health sector. The well-known blog 'Ditadura de Consenso' by journalist and Vaz critic António Aly Silva was hacked in May by pro-Vaz blogger Denílson Ferreira, author of 'Doka Internacional',. In June, Silva received threats by telephone. On 25 May, politicians and Vaz ally Attorney-General António Sedja Mam were accused by the LGDH of being responsible for increasing offences against democratic principles and Guinea-Bissau was ranked 35th in the World Bank's Worldwide Governance Indicators in June. The National Social Media Council criticised the director general of the public radio station, 'RDN', in July for having dismissed the heads of information and editorial policy after they refused to censure a press conference by PAIGC leader Pereira. Also in July, the LGDH criticised the authorities for arresting a PAIGC MP, who had already been sentenced, disregarding his parliamentary immunity. On 18 September, 27 illegal immigrants from Guinea on their way to Spain were rescued from the sea by the authorities and then detained. The LGDH denounced in October the miserable conditions in the country's prisons, pointing to overcrowding and the lack of a high security facility, in the light of a jailbreak by 20 dangerous criminals. In November, the case of an adolescent girl who was beaten by 16 women after she refused to marry was the subject of wide public debate. Human rights activist Fodé Mané denounced impunity and the increase in corruption and political violence since August 2015. In November, the government prohibited several demonstrations, which the LGDH interpreted as a severe restriction of freedom of assembly.

In the *security sector*, the national police commissioner José António Marques was dismissed on 18 January, after he allowed the 15 dissident MPs to enter parliament. In March, Vaz criticised the politicisation of the justice sector. On 28 January, five men were sentenced for a violent assault on the former transport and communications minister, Orlando Mendes Veigas, in 2013. The home of Secretary of State for Transport and Communication João Bernardo Vieira (PAIGC) was burgled on 31 January; his guards were injured and € 3 m was stolen. The navy chief of staff, Sanhá Clusse, died of natural causes on 25 April. In July, several lawyers criticised the nomination of high-ranking military officials, including Carlos Alfredo Mandungal, who was nominated as new navy chief of staff. Prime Minister Djá had made the nominations, although this was normally done by the president. The Global Peace Index released in June revealed that Guinea-Bissau was the most violent lusophone country.

Vaz ally *Attorney-General Mam* initiated a series of corruption investigations of officials who were part of the PAIGC faction that was critical of Vaz. In January, Finance Minister Geraldo Martins, Health Minister Valentina Mendes and the head of the 'Serviço Nacional de Fiscalização de Actividades de Pesca' (FISCAP), Pedro Gomes, found themselves being questioned for alleged corruption. On 12 May and 16 June, Mam prohibited nine members of the dismissed government from leaving the country, including Correia himself. On 18 May, Mam ordered the freezing of all state accounts with commercial banks. On 27 July, Martins was questioned by Mam about loans to commercial banks. Mam ordered the arrest of a Pereira ally, former secretary of state Vieira, for corruption and disrespecting the justice system on 17 August. Vieira was freed by a court one week later.

Political heavyweight and women's rights activist, former speaker of parliament and liberation fighter, Carmen Pereira (PAIGC), died on 4 June aged 79.

Foreign Affairs

On 26 February the *UNSC* extended the mandate of the UN Integrated Peacebuilding Office in Guinea-Bissau (UNIOGBIS) for a further year. On 28 April, Guinea-Bissau and the UN concluded a new partnership agreement worth $ 400 m. In May, Mali's

Modibo Touré was appointed new Special Representative of the UN Secretary-General and Head of UNIOGBIS, replacing Miguel Trovoada of São Tomé e Príncipe who completed his term of office on 30 April.

On 17 February, *ECOWAS* announced the withdrawal of its peace mission in Guinea-Bissau (ECOMIB). Deployed since May 2012, ECOMIB's mandate came to an end in June, but the head of the ECOWAS Commission, Marcel de Souza, declared in August that the pull-out would take place within a year.

In September, the military took part in manoeuvres in Cape Verde by the *CPLP*. In October, the government participated in a summit in Brasília (Brazil) to discuss the free movement of people across CPLP member territories.

On 2 December, reports said that, after discussions among the G7 Friends of the Gulf of Guinea Group, Guinea-Bissau would reinforce maritime security as part of zone G, which also incorporated Senegal and Gambia.

The *Islamist* Cheikh Ould Saleck, who had escaped from prison in Mauritania on 31 December 2015, was captured at the Bissau-Guinean border with Guinea on 20 January and sent back to Nouakchott. On 14 March, investigators said that four men linked to Saleck were in detention in Bissau, two of them having been extradited from Guinea a week before.

Tensions arose between Guinea-Bissau and *Senegal* after a Bissau-Guinean MP, Leopoldo da Silva, was beaten and detained for hours by Senegalese border police officers on 23 November. He had defended a Bissau-Guinean student who had faced a demand for CFAfr 2,000 (about € 3.00) at the border post – an illicit practice commonly applied to ECOWAS citizens.

Vaz increased the number of *state visits* abroad, including to Chad, Congo-Brazzaville, Cuba, Gambia, Guinea, Portugal, and Senegal. His visit to Sudan's President Omar al-Bashir in August provoked negative reactions among the public amid accusations that he was disregarding Sudan's human rights violations. Prime Minister Correia visited Portugal and Senegal, Djá visited Equatorial Guinea, and Embaló visited Liberia.

Accusations already familiar from previous years that officials of the Ministry of Foreign Affairs were selling *diplomatic passports* to foreigners resurfaced in September.

Socioeconomic Developments

Economic prospects improved. The economy had grown by 5% in 2015, and revenues amounted to a record $ 138 m. Even so, the Index of Economic Freedom published by the Heritage Foundation in February ranked Guinea-Bissau 145th (out of 178 countries). An IMF mission visiting Bissau to conduct reviews under the ECF in

March–April spoke of a real GDP growth rate of 4.8% in 2015. The mission predicted an identical growth rate for 2016, and inflation of 2.6% – in comparison with 1.5% in 2015 and a predicted 3% in 2017. The IMF asked parliament to approve the 2016 budget and to improve the private business environment. The World Bank predicted a growth rate of 5.7% for 2016 and 6% for 2017 in June, but in October lowered its forecast for 2016 to 5%. In June, the IMF suspended its budget support due to bailouts of over $ 58 m to local banks. Payments had been ensured by the Pereira government in 2015 to guarantee liquidity but they were rescinded by the Djá government in June. Donors also cancelled budget support worth $ 25 m. To close gaps in the state budget (3.1% of GDP), the government raised $ 18.4 m with the full placement on 14 July of an issue of treasury bonds, to mature in three years at an interest rate of 5.5%. Following an IMF mission in September–October, the government committed itself to submit the 2016 and 2017 budgets to parliament, to implement fiscal efforts and spending controls, and improve administration to close the fiscal gap. Upon approval, accessible funds of $ 7.1 m would become available.

Dependence on *external funds and loans* continued. The AfDB gave $ 29 m to improve governance and electricity supply. The Palace of Justice building, funded and constructed by China, was inaugurated on 27 January and housed various courts and the attorney-general's offices. Funded mainly by the EU, a memorial to commemorate the transatlantic slave-trade was inaugurated in the notorious former Portuguese slave hub of Cacheu in July. In September, China provided $ 12.3 m for housing schemes, scholarships and infrastructure and granted a further $ 16.5 m in November for the construction of a motorway between Bissau and Safim.

Guinea-Bissau continued to attract *foreign investment*. A Spanish consortium announced the construction of low-cost houses and several infrastructure and resource exploration projects. A Senegalese branch of Woodside Energy acquired 65% of an oil exploration block, after signing a production sharing agreement with the British Impact Oil & Gas Ltd (20%) in February. The remaining 15% of shares were retained by a Senegalese-Bissau-Guinean joint company. A Chinese company planned to construct a fish processing plant, according to media report in September. In October, it became known that a Chinese enterprise would contract to build a biomass plant.

The *HIV/AIDS* prevalence in the 15–49 age group remained very high at 5.3%. Three *Zika* virus infections were counted on the Bijágos archipelago in July, causing panic among the population. Malaria affected 160,000 Bissau-Guineans, leaving 680 dead in 2015, according to a WHO report in December.

In July, the media claimed that security officials were involved in *narco-trafficking*. A Portuguese drug mule was arrested by the police at Bissau's airport in June. Former navy chief of staff, José Américo 'Bubo' Na Tchuto, captured by the US Drug Enforcement Administration in April 2013, was convicted in the US for drug-trafficking on 4 October. He was released early, however, and returned to Guinea-Bissau on 22 October and asked the president for permission to resume his military career.

In *communications development*, according to Secretary of State Vieira in February, Guinea-Bissau now had access to a submarine telecommunication cable In April, a Chinese company signed an agreement with the government to construct a new airport, two fishing ports, several residential buildings and power transmission lines. In August, Air Portugal (TAP) announced its intention to resume flights to Bissau, which had been suspended in 2013. Floods hit the capital in August and public electricity blackouts occurred in Bissau in May and December.

Strikes and delayed payments of wages continued to characterise social conflict. In March, nurses complained that they had not received their salaries for 11 months. Employees in the health and education sectors went on strike in March. In July, teachers called on the government to pay their last six months' salaries. Employees of the private telecommunications provider Orange went on strike in August, demanding a salary increase and an end to the salary inequalities between domestic and expatriate staff. Due to service limitations during the strike, Orange was ordered by the regulation authority to pay a penalty of more than $ 1 m. 'RDN' employees went on strike in September. Teachers went on strike again in September and October.

Liberia

Lansana Gberie

Preparations for the presidential and legislative elections scheduled for October 2017 – including the emergence of a multiplicity of political parties, the controversial formation of one coalition that included the party of former president and convicted war criminal Charles Taylor, and preparations for voter registration – dominated public discussions. Corruption scandals rocked the government. Several government ministers, the speaker of the House of Representatives, and the chair of the governing Unity Party (UP) were indicted. The government took over full security responsibilities from the UN Mission in Liberia (UNMIL), including border and maritime patrols, ordinance disposal and VIP protection. President Sirleaf became the first woman to be elected chair of ECOWAS. The UNSC authorised the reduction of the UNMIL mission. The economy stagnated. The country's total revenue for the national budget amounted to only $ 550 m for 2016/2017, a reduction of 11% compared with 2015/16. This was due in large part to the global decline in commodity prices. The IMF estimated a negative growth rate of 1.2% for 2016. Inflation stood at 12.5% by year's end, compared with 7.7% in 2015.

 | DOI 10.1163/9789004355910_013

Domestic Politics

Though presidential and legislative elections were scheduled for October 2017, they already dominated the political discourse. A number of *new political parties* were launched, bringing the total number of registered parties to 23. The new parties included the *Movement for Democracy and Reconstruction* (MDR), whose leader, *Prince Yormie Johnson*, metamorphosed from a feared warlord to a senior senator. In setting up the MDR, Johnson abandoned the National Union of Democratic Progress (NUDR), which he had founded earlier, and on whose platform he had won 11.6% of the national vote in the 2011 presidential elections, in which he came third. The proliferation of new political parties in a country with about 2 m voters led many to speculate about future party mergers or coalitions. However, only one coalition registered to contest the October 2017 elections. This was the *Coalition for Democratic Change* (CDC), an alliance bringing together the Congress for Democratic Change, Liberia Peoples Democratic Party, and the National Patriotic Party. The National Elections Commission (NEC) registered the CDC on 29 December. There were widespread allegations that former president (and convicted war criminal) Charles Taylor had masterminded the alliance, which the CDC hardly denied.

The NEC published the schedule for the 2017 elections on 17 June. It determined that the launch of civic education activities would start in January 2017, that voter registration would take place in February, that the official campaigning period would start on 8 August 2017 and that the elections would take place on 11 October 2017.

A number of *corruption scandals* competed for public attention and commentators speculated that the scandals would damage the prospects of the ruling UP, which in July selected Vice President Joseph Nyumah Boakai as its presidential candidate. On 23 February, Miatta Beyslow, a former minister of commerce and industry, and Nelson Williams, the former managing director of the Liberia Petroleum Refining Company, were indicted by the Liberia Anti-Corruption Commission (LACC) on charges of criminal conspiracy and violations of the public procurement and concessions procedures that had caused the government to lose of more than $ 13 m between 2013 and 2015. The charges against Beyslow were dropped on 20 July but 12 former and current government officials were still facing criminal prosecutions at year's end.

Shortly before the charges against Beyslow were dropped, on 11 May the UK-based campaign group, Global Witness, published a report entitled 'The Deceivers'. The report detailed allegations of *bribery* and other corruption against high-ranking officials, including Senator Varney Sherman, the then chair of the UP, and Alex Tyler, the speaker of the House of Representatives. Global Witness documented that the officials had received tens of thousands of dollars in bribes from Sable Mining Africa Ltd, a publicly listed British company, to facilitate access to valuable mining concessions. In the past, the Sirleaf administration had faced accusations by many Liberians and foreign observers that it ignored corruption allegations against powerful politicians. However, given that the 2017 elections were around the corner and that Vice President Boakai was likely to be a prominent contender in these elections, President Ellen Johnson Sirleaf acted with uncharacteristic urgency. A day after the report was published, on 12 May, she authorised a *special presidential task force* to examine the charges and also formally requested British Prime Minister David Cameron's help in the investigations. Less than two weeks later, on 25 May, upon the recommendation of the special presidential task force, the police arrested Sherman and Tyler. Tyler appeared in court that day under police escort, and, like Sherman, was charged with "economic sabotage, criminal conspiracy, criminal solicitation, criminal facilitation, and bribery". Both men were released on bail but not before they had implicated several other officials in their testimonies. Legislators loyal to Tyler criticised the president for what they described as a misuse of authority. Others critical of Tyler called for his dismissal as speaker. This polarised the House of Representatives. Ultimately, 49 lawmakers (or two-thirds of members of the House of Representatives) signed a resolution calling for the removal of Tyler as speaker and, on 4 October, Emmanuel Nuquay, Representative for Margibi County, was elected to replace him. Within the UP, Sherman's humiliation created great divisions. Many of his supporters vowed to work against Sirleaf throughout her tenure and after.

Though some criticised Sirleaf for her involvement in ordering the special presidential task force to investigate Tyler and Sherman, the disappointing performance of the LACC, which would normally have been assigned such a task, suggested that without her direct involvement nothing might have been done to hold the culprits accountable. The *judiciary's poor record* of successfully prosecuting and convicting powerful individuals or corrupt state officials was illustrated in November, for example, by a Monrovia court's dismissal of a case involving the misappropriation of $ 5.7 m from the sale of petroleum products donated by the Japanese government. In fact, many local analysts feared that the ousting of Tyler as speaker would probably be the only price he would pay for the corruption offences. Upon Tyler's release on an insurance bond of $ 150,000, state prosecutors filed a motion on 27 May in a Monrovia criminal court requesting the court to reject the bond and re-arrest him. The motion was dismissed. Meanwhile, Sherman was released on $ 1.5 m bail on 26 May. The next day a similar request by the state prosecutors on his behalf was also rejected. By year's end, the case was still languishing in court. Several other high ranking state officials were facing trial for the allegations contained in the Global Witness report. They included Eugene Shannon, former minister of lands, mines and energy, who was the main facilitator of the mining concessions deal with Sable. Like Tyler and Sherman, Shannon was also allegedly bribed by the British mining company. Richard Tolbert, the former chairman of the National Investment

Commission, faced similar charges. No verdict was reached in any of these cases or any other case connected with the Global Witness allegations. By the end of the year, Tyler had set up a new political party, the Liberia Peoples Democratic Party, which joined the CDC alliance.

In a report published in August, the UN Secretary General singled out corruption and poor governance as the key remaining *threats to Liberia's stability*. His report also highlighted "suspicion over certain deaths and ritual killings and divisions along religious lines", and noted that "perceptions of discrimination, exclusion and marginalisation along ethnic or religious lines, underpinned by land disputes and historic resentments, continued to pose risks for tensions turning into violent confrontations", all part of the lingering threats to peace and stability in the country. The UN report cited several incidents during the year that raised serious concerns among the international community. They included an incident on 1 April in which about 700 *aggrieved workers* employed by the Cocopa rubber plantation in Nimba County staged a protest to demand several months of salary arrears; and another on 5 April in which workers at the Sime Darby palm plantation in Bomi County demonstrated in protest over the disappearance of a young woman suspected of being the victim of ritual killing. The woman was later found alive. On 9 May, approximately 150 inhabitants of illegally built structures on the University of Liberia's Fendell campus protested against their eviction by the Ministry of Public Works. The protestors temporarily blocked the Monrovia-Kakata highway. *Rape* was a concern throughout the year. The government documented nearly 500 cases. In many rape cases, suspects walked free without a trial. Only seven of 202 cases that resulted in indictments for rape and sexual violence were fully prosecuted. Despite criticisms by human rights advocates, suspects held in *pre-trial detention* constituted over 60% of the prison population nationwide.

The perception of the judiciary as dysfunctional or corrupt meant that public cynicism and distrust of it, as well as of most other government institutions, was widespread and corrosive. On 31 January, the body of *Harry Greaves*, a well-known politician and former managing director of the Liberia Petroleum Refining Company, who had fallen out with President Sirleaf, was found on a Monrovia beach. Going by local newspaper accounts and commentary, many Liberians suspected government involvement in his death. This was largely because, before his death, Greaves had threatened to expose corruption at the National Oil Company of Liberia (NOCAL) when it was chaired by Robert Sirleaf, the president's eldest son. Despite several investigations and the reports of two United States pathologists confirming that Greaves had died of asphyxiation by drowning, many commentators still insinuated that state agents had murdered him. The government requested help from the United States' Diplomatic Security Service, which on 28 July submitted a report concurring with the findings of Liberia National Police (LNP) investigators that it was a case of accidental drowning. Minister of Justice Benedict Sannoh, accused by local media of "mishandling" the Greaves investigation, had already resigned on 11 April and Sirleaf appointed Frederic Cherue, a senator representing River Gee County, to replace him. The affair illustrated the widespread *lack of trust in the Sirleaf government*. In March, a group of political and civil society agitators issued a statement threatening mass demonstrations in Monrovia, which were only called off after the protesters met with UN officials.

The UN and the government accelerated their joint efforts to hand over all *security responsibilities* to the national authorities. In line with UNSC resolution 2190 (2014), this took place on 30 June. At this point, the LNP had 5,142 officers, including 973 women. The overwhelming majority (3,858 officers, including 748 women) were deployed in the capital, Monrovia, and its immediate vicinity; only 1,284 were deployed to the hinterland. The Armed Forces of Liberia, comprising 2,236 personnel (of whom 91 were women), assumed full responsibility for all security operations from UNMIL on 30 April, but UNMIL also had a very minimal presence outside the capital; Liberian soldiers required special per diems before deploying to the hinterland

At least four incidents with implications for *press freedom* were reported. On 7 May, three men severely beat up a radio journalist, Wremongar Joe, for refusing to destroy a video recording of a brawl between a member of the House of Representatives and some spectators during a football match. Then on 7 July, the Liberia Telecommunications Authority ordered the closure of 'Voice FM', a radio station known for its blistering attacks on President Sirleaf. The ostensible reason was that the station, which had been broadcasting for two years, was not properly registered and was therefore using an unauthorised frequency. The station was owned by Henry Costa, a supporter of Sirleaf's key political opponent, Benoni Urey, the political leader and standard-bearer of the All Liberian Party. The station remained closed. On 15 September, the police arrested and detained Festus Poquie, a reporter for the 'New Democrat' newspaper, for republishing an article from London's 'Daily Mail' quoting a political opponent who had described President Teodoro Obiang Nguema of Equatorial Guinea as a cannibal. Poquie was released without charge after the intervention of the Press Union of Liberia and a human rights lawyer. On 7 October, Philipbert Browne, the publisher of the 'Hot Pepper' newspaper, was arrested at his office and jailed in Monrovia Central Prison on charges of libel relating to a story he had published accusing Prince Moye, a UP member of the House of Representatives, or rape. He denied the allegation and filed a libel suit against Browne and the paper's editor, Jah Johnson. The Press Union of Liberia in a statement expressed its shock that the court "would still be treating civil cases as criminal". Browne was released on bail three days later.

However, the *media environment* remained vibrant, with 95 radio stations, 50 newspapers and ten television stations, most of them independent. *Internet* penetration rate, at 5.9%, was below the regional average.

Foreign Affairs

Liberia forged closer ties with its neighbours and regional organisations. A stable security situation in *Côte d'Ivoire* allowed for the voluntary return of 18,729 Ivorian refugees who had camped in the volatile south-eastern part of Liberia. Awareness of the fragility of the region and its vulnerability to sudden upheavals was heightened after a *terrorist attack* on 15 January in the capital of *Burkina Faso*, in which 30 people were killed. A similar attack, on 13 March by three gunmen at a beach resort in Grand-Bassam (Côte d'Ivoire), killed 19 people and injured 33. Responsibility for both attacks was claimed by *Al-Qaida in the Islamic Maghreb* (*AQIM*).

On 6 May, Liberia organised a special *ECOWAS* session on the threat of *terrorism* in West Africa, which brought together security experts and representatives from ECOWAS member states to devise strategies for greater collaboration and information sharing to prevent or combat terrorism in the region. On 16 June, President Sirleaf signed an executive order approving the legal framework for the establishment of a national early warning and response mechanism coordination centre. The following day, 17 June, Sirleaf met with the president of the ECOWAS Commission, Marcel de Souza, to discuss cooperation between Liberia and ECOWAS on security and development issues. The meeting followed Sirleaf's election as chair of ECOWAS on 4 June. That same month, the militaries of Liberia and Côte d'Ivoire had their first joint border security meeting.

As part of this regional outreach strategy, Liberia hosted a two-day session of the *MRU* on 30 November and 1 December. The meeting focused on identifying security challenges in the region. Addressing the *UN General Assembly* on 22 September, President Sirleaf expressed optimism about Liberia's regional initiatives, emphasising that "collaborations at the levels of the AU, ECOWAS and the UN aimed at helping to consolidate peace and security" in Liberia and Africa. "As Chair of ECOWAS," she said, "I can confirm that we are unwaveringly committed to continue, with renewed vigour, efforts for the realization of integration, through infrastructure development, trade and investment, natural resource management, food security, and peace and security."

Sirleaf's international image as something of a superstar was burnished in June when 'Forbes' magazine named her at number 83 on its list of the world's most powerful women. In the United States and Europe, her name was repeatedly mentioned in influential circles as a potential candidate for the position of UN Secretary-General.

On 9 November, Sirleaf stated in an interview that she was "extremely saddened" by the electoral defeat of her friend Hillary Clinton and voiced concern about the prospect of the US undoing some of its favourable trade deals with Africa under incoming President Trump. Many in Liberia feared that this widely reported interview might damage relations with the *United States*, Liberia's most important bilateral partner. In the interview, she expressed concern "as to whether president-elect Trump will have an African agenda, will be able to build bridges with Africa."

Socioeconomic Developments

Liberia's economy showed no signs of recovery from the effects of the Ebola Virus Disease (EVD) and the *decline* in *commodity prices*. There was a slight uptick in the price of *iron ore and rubber* in the last quarter of the year, but this did not trigger any noticeable increase in the production of either commodities, which had seen a reduction during the EVD crisis. Government revenue shrank, and early in the year income projections were reduced to $ 622.7 m (a drop of $ 70 m). The national *budget* for 2016/17 was approved and signed into law on 3 October. It pegged the country's total revenue at $ 556 million, an 11% fall from the 2015/16 budget.

In April, to mitigate the effects of the fall in the prices of cocoa and rubber, the government launched the Liberia Agricultural Transformation Agenda (LATA) to support diversification in the *agricultural sector* as well as to create the foundations for industrial development. The project, supported by the AfDB, began with the official launch of e-registration for all farmers in order to enable equitable distribution of fertilizers and seeds, as well as other support, throughout the country. By year's end, some 450,000 farmers had been registered; it was the first time Liberia had undertaken to create this sort of record.

The macroeconomic situation, however, remained dismal, with real *GDP* shrinking to 0.5%. The IMF estimated Liberia's economic growth by year's end at minus 1.2%. The government's *public sector expenditure* rose significantly, with $ 20 m dedicated to preparations for elections slated for 2017 and $ 10 m for Liberian security agencies to properly takeover security responsibilities from UNMIL. *Inflation* rose to 12.5%. The government attributed this to the *depreciation of the Liberian dollar* against the US $ following the printing and circulation of millions of new Liberian dollar banknotes in October. Both currencies remained legal tender. In compliance with IMF requirements, the government began in October to pay 25% of the wage bill in Liberian dollars in order to enable the Central Bank of Liberia (CBL) to restore its *foreign currency reserves*. Moreover, the CBL issued a regulation mandating that 25% of all inward remittances, via money transfer, be paid in Liberian dollars. This created uncertainty and confusion about the direction of the economy and may have discouraged some investors.

Liberia's large *expenditure* on goods and services (87% of the overall national budget), including *salaries of government officials* and particularly legislators, made matters worse. With a population of just over 4 m, it spent 16.4% of its national budget on sustaining democratic institutions, in particular the Legislature, which received $ 54,027,021 during the year. In contrast, Sierra Leone (with a population of 7 m) spent 0.7% of its national budget on its democratic institutions. Legislators earn about seven times more than their Sierra Leonean counterparts and about four times more than their Ghanaian counterparts; the speaker of the House of Representatives earned $ 444,945 in 2016, more than his counterpart in the United States ($ 223,500). Nevertheless, on 16 February, the Legislature rejected a recommendation by three of its members to reduce lawmakers' salaries by 25%.

Mali

Bruce Whitehouse

Mali experienced a steady increase in political violence, perpetrated primarily by armed jihadi groups and resulting in hundreds of deaths. Mounting insecurity beleaguered populations in the country's central and northern regions, while government and international security forces deployed in these regions were themselves frequent targets of attacks. Little progress was made in implementing the terms of a peace agreement signed in 2015 between northern rebels and the government of President Ibrahim Boubacar Keita, and political opposition to Keita's regime appeared to gain momentum. The rule of law remained tenuous throughout the centre and north, where neither the government nor international forces had effective control over significant areas. Although the national economy continued to grow and commodity exports and agricultural output rose, food insecurity remained a pressing issue for millions of Malians throughout the year.

Domestic Politics

2016 was characterised by a *deteriorating security climate*: an estimated 385 attacks by armed groups were carried out on Malian territory, roughly twice as many as in

 | DOI 10.1163/9789004355910_014

2015, with civilians bearing the brunt of this violence. Most attacks were launched by *jihadi groups* operating in the region, particularly al-Qaida in the Islamic Maghreb (AQIM), Al-Mourabitoune (an offshoot of AQIM), Ansar Eddine and the Macina Liberation Front (MLF). With the increasingly sophisticated use of roadside bombs, car and truck bombs, mortar and rocket salvos, ambushes and raids, fighters affiliated with these organisations extended their reach throughout the central regions of Segou and Mopti, as well as the northern regions of Timbuktu, Gao and Kidal, where such groups had been operating for several years. This violence resulted in at least 332 fatalities, 207 of them civilians. Malian security forces and other agents of the state were also common targets. On 19 July, jihadi fighters assaulted and briefly occupied a Malian army post in the town of Nampala, leaving 17 Malian soldiers dead; this attack was claimed by the MLF. Weeks later, Ansar Eddine fighters took over the town of Boni, burning public buildings and holding a local elected official hostage. These events led President Keita to fire his defence minister, Tieman Hubert Coulibaly, in September and prompted the Malian army to conduct a major security sweep in the Mopti region. On 6 December, unidentified gunmen attacked a prison in the north-central town of Niono, and freed more than 90 inmates. Human rights groups accused both jihadis and government forces of carrying out abuses, including summary executions, torture and arbitrary detention of civilians, mainly in Segou and Mopti. Isolated outbreaks of communal violence were also reported in these regions, and banditry remained widespread further north. In the far northern Kidal region, along the border with Algeria, the Malian state remained entirely absent after the expulsion of its officials and troops from that region by separatists in May 2014. Even in areas nominally under government control elsewhere in the north and centre, half of administrators and other civil servants were absent from their posts due to pervasive insecurity. The Malian government's state of emergency, in effect since 2012, was extended into 2017.

Jihadis also launched numerous *attacks against international forces* operating in Mali. An estimated 75 attacks against patrols and bases of the UN Multidimensional Integrated Stabilisation Mission in Mali (MINUSMA) left 29 peacekeepers dead and another 90 wounded, and MINUSMA maintained its status as the world's deadliest peacekeeping mission. On 21 March, four gunmen assaulted the headquarters of the European Union Training Mission (EUTM) in Bamako but were repelled by private security guards; one attacker was shot dead at the gate and the others escaped, while no one was hurt inside the EUTM compound. AQIM claimed responsibility. In April, Malian security forces arrested an alleged member of Al-Mourabitoune in connection with the deadly November 2015 attack on Bamako's Radisson Blu hotel. Elsewhere, jihadi groups abducted two foreign civilians on Malian soil: in January, AQIM kidnapped a Swiss missionary in Timbuktu and, in December, gunmen kidnapped a French aid worker in Gao, an act the Malian government attributed to Al-Mourabitoune. Neither woman was freed by year's end. In April, Ansar Eddine abducted three employees of the International Committee of the Red Cross near Kidal before releasing them five days later.

Despite international pressure, *implementation of the peace accord* signed in 2015 between Malian authorities and northern rebel leaders (mainly belonging to the Tuareg ethnic group) was uneven and slow. In line with this accord, the government set up a commission to revise the national constitution and appointed governors for two new northern administrative regions in an effort to decentralise state power, but it postponed a planned referendum on constitutional changes. Meanwhile, the establishment of interim authorities for northern regions was a contentious issue. These administrations, intended to integrate former rebel leaders into civilian government in certain northern localities and regions, were controversial with many Malians. On 21 July, during one protest against the new interim authorities in Gao, government forces shot three demonstrators dead and wounded 35. Protestors faulted the peace plan for only rewarding those who had taken up arms against the government. Widespread opposition delayed broader application of the peace accord, while mistrust persisted between the government and supporters of the main consortium of northern Tuareg rebel groups called the 'Coordination des Mouvements de l'Azawad' (CMA). The government and its allied militias boycotted a forum on national reconciliation organised in Kidal in March. From late July to mid-September, sporadic fighting between the CMA and pro-government militias in and around Kidal killed and wounded dozens, further delaying the establishment of interim administrations in the north. The long-awaited disarmament, demobilisation and reinsertion process for civilian combatants also remained stalled, since neither the CMA nor pro-government militia groups provided lists of their personnel to be demobilised. Planned joint patrols between the CMA, pro-government militias and Malian security forces were stymied by disputes over who could participate in them. Overall, progress toward peace was limited and symbolic, such as the July inclusion of CMA representative Nina Walett Intalou in President Keita's new cabinet as minister for artisans and tourism.

The *political opposition in Bamako gained strength* over Keita's perceived failure to address rampant insecurity and corruption. On 21 May, a demonstration against poor governance attracted thousands of people, and police shot one protestor dead on 17 August during a rally urging the release of a detained radio host who had been critical of Keita. Despite such challenges, on 20 November, the government managed to organise long-delayed *local elections* in 647 of Mali's 703 communes. No vote was held in the remaining communes because of either insecurity or the opposition of CMA leaders, who viewed the communal elections as illegitimate under the peace accord. Voter turnout was 43% nationally and reached 60% in Gao.

High-level *legal proceedings* began late in the year pertaining to an imprisoned army officer and the previous head of state he had ousted. Amadou Sanogo, leader of the military coup d'état that drove President Amadou Toumani Touré from office in March 2012, was put on trial in November along with 16 co-defendants, after more than three years in detention. Sanogo and his associates stood accused of killing 21 fellow soldiers who had opposed their junta's rule. In December, however, their trial was suspended until an unspecified date. That same month, Mali's parliament voted to drop charges of treason against former president Touré, whom the Malian government had accused of facilitating the 2012 rebel takeover of northern Mali. While all legal obstacles to his return to Mali were thereby eliminated, Touré continued to live in exile in neighbouring Senegal and gave no indication of any intention to come back to Mali.

Foreign Affairs

Diplomacy was high on the Malian government's agenda for 2016. President Keita maintained an active travel schedule, making 27 trips abroad to 19 different countries, including five trips to France (three for medical purposes and two for private visits).

As in every year since 2012, Mali remained a source of concern to the international community due to rising levels of political violence and insecurity. The *UN* operated MINUSMA, with more than 13,000 personnel deployed to the country. In June, the UNSC approved a resolution to add 2,500 additional troops to the MINUSMA contingent to help it implement the peace accord and protect civilian populations. This expansion came in recognition of the challenges peacekeepers faced in Mali, especially asymmetrical attacks by jihadi groups. No new troops had arrived by the end of the year, however. The Malian government was embarrassed in January, when its voting rights in the UN General Assembly were suspended over non-payment of dues. Its vote was restored in February after the government paid off its arrears and fired its UN ambassador.

France also continued to operate its own military mission, Operation Barkhane, in Mali and four other Sahelian countries. Troops deployed as part of Barkhane conducted operations both jointly with Malian security forces and unilaterally throughout northern Mali in search of jihadi leaders. Three French soldiers were killed and six wounded, all by roadside bombs, during the year. Barkhane's actions generated public opposition within some Malian communities. In April, protestors besieged the airport in Kidal to denounce the French military, and specifically the arrests of three local men whom French forces accused of planting landmines on behalf of Ansar Eddine. The protestors looted and occupied airport buildings, and guards shot two people dead. During the 11-day occupation, both military and relief flights were prevented from landing in Kidal.

The *EU* maintained its EUTM in Mali for a third two-year mandate beginning in May. Under this latest mandate, the EUTM began focusing on developing the internal training capacity of the Malian military rather than on training particular units as it had previously. The EU also increased the budget of its EUCAP Sahel Mali mission, tasked with training Mali's National Police, Gendarmerie and National Guard, from € 14 m to € 19 m. The EU also made efforts to curb emigration from Mali through a € 29 m programme to strengthen Malian border security and combat human trafficking, and through a € 41 m regional programme to build up national police forces in the Sahel. Controversy arose in December over an agreement reportedly signed between the EU and the Malian government to facilitate the repatriation of Malian migrants who failed to win asylum in EU countries. Mali's foreign minister denied having reached any agreement on migrant repatriation, and said negotiations with the EU were continuing on the subject. Malian authorities subsequently sent back to France two deportees who had arrived in the country with EU-issued travel documents, saying it could not verify that the deportees were Malian nationals.

The *USA* continued a gradual increase in support for Malian security forces with a new initiative sponsored by the US State Department to help train and equip Malian gendarmes to respond to terrorist incidents. In September, the US ambassador to Mali called on the Malian government to cut its ties to a northern militia group known as the 'Groupe Autodefense Touareg Imghad et Alliés', leading some government supporters to accuse the USA of meddling in Mali's internal affairs.

Germany stepped up its involvement with Mali. In October, Chancellor Angela Merkel became the first German head of state to visit the country. The German government discussed migration, bilateral aid and increasing its support for peacekeeping operations. A € 115 m bilateral development assistance package was announced for 2016–17, and the German army committed to contributing an attack helicopter unit to MINUSMA to take the place of a departing contingent from *The Netherlands*. A delegation led by *Russia*'s Deputy Foreign Minister Mikhaïl Bogdanov also visited Mali in October and pledged an unspecified package of military equipment to help the Malian government combat terrorism.

Mali's relations within West Africa were dominated by the spread of terrorist activity to neighbouring countries. In January, an attack claimed by Al-Mourabitoune on a hotel in Ouagadougou (*Burkina Faso*) left 30 people dead; in March, gunmen killed 19 at a beach resort in Grand Bassam (*Côte d'Ivoire*) in an attack for which AQIM and Al-Mourabitoune claimed joint responsibility. Following the latter incident, a number of persons suspected of helping orchestrate the attack were arrested in Mali by both Malian and French security forces. Some Malian citizens were also arrested in Côte d'Ivoire and *Senegal* in connection with the killings at Grand Bassam. In October, attackers in *Niger* killed at least 22 government soldiers in Tazalit, at a camp for Malian refugees near the border with Mali. The Nigerien government suggested that the assailants had crossed into Niger from Mali. Increased activity by jihadi fighters in Mali's border zones with Niger and Burkina Faso necessitated closer security cooperation among these governments.

Mali also strengthened ties with a number of states in the Middle East. President Keita travelled to *Turkey* and the UAE. In July, Foreign Minister Mohammad Javad Zarif of *Iran* visited Bamako where he met with Prime Minister Modibo Keita and expressed Iran's support for Mali in its efforts to combat terrorist and trafficking networks.

In August, the first defendant charged with war crimes committed during Mali's conflict entered a guilty plea at the ICC in The Hague (Netherlands). Ahmad al-Faqi al-Mahdi, an alleged member of Ansar Eddine, admitted ordering the destruction of ten historic mausoleums and monuments in Timbuktu during that city's 2012 occupation by Islamist militants. In September, the court sentenced him to nine years in prison.

Socioeconomic Developments

Mali's *economy* expanded by 5.4% according to estimates by the IMF, which continued to disburse loans to the Malian government under an ECF arrangement approved in December 2013. The government's budget forecast for 2017 was CFAfr 2.1 trn (approximately € 3.2 bn), a 10% increase over 2016, with heavy emphasis on investment and security spending. Inflation was low, declining to 0.5% by December.

In the *mining sector*, gold production rose slightly to 50.9 tonnes, 92% of which was generated by industrial mining operations. Small-scale informal mining operations produced the remainder and employed up to one million people in Mali. The government estimated the country's unexploited gold reserves at 800 tonnes, sufficient for Malian mines to maintain current levels of production and allow Mali to be Africa's third-largest gold producer for the next 15 years. Newly opened mines in Fekola and Yanfolila were expected to boost the sector's production further in 2017. In October, the government ordered the temporary closure of the Bamako office of Randgold, one of the largest multinational companies operating in Mali, over alleged non-payment of taxes. Randgold denied having left taxes unpaid, and was allowed to reopen its offices after two weeks while negotiations with the government continued.

In *agriculture*, some 550,000 tonnes of raw cotton were harvested, 15% short of production goals, after late rains delayed the 2015–16 cotton harvest. State efforts to raise producer prices and subsidise fertiliser generated hopes for a more successful cotton harvest in 2016–17. Similar policies were enacted to benefit rice production. Grain harvests were bountiful at some 9 m tonnes, 11% higher than the already successful harvests of 2015 and 35% above the average for the previous five years.

Despite favourable farming output, Mali's population remained vulnerable to *malnutrition*: 25% of Malians were afflicted by food insecurity, according to WFP, and 11.5% of children suffered from acute malnutrition with the highest rates in Gao and Timbuktu. Political violence in the centre and north contributed to this problem and exacerbated the country's outflow of *refugees*: 130,000 Malians remained in refugee camps outside Mali's borders, and growing threats of violence spurred the flow of thousands of new refugees from Mali into Mauritania in October.

Mauritania

Helena Olsson and Claes Olsson

The lack of sustainable and inclusive growth was a major challenge. Nearly a quarter of the population suffered from food insecurity, despite a slightly improved economy. Through its role in the fight against crime and illegal immigration, Mauritania remained one of the EU's privileged diplomatic interlocutors in the field of security and development in the Sahel. Frequent arrests and detentions of human rights activists cast a shadow over the government's claims to being commited to improving the country's human rights record. The president's proposal to abolish the Senate met with strong resistance from the opposition.

Domestic Politics

Two *cabinet reshuffles* took place at the beginning of the year, on 9 February and 27 March. This restructuring was expected to strengthen President Mohamed Ould Abdel Aziz's already strong position. The Ministry of Economics was merged with the Ministry of Finance. Finance Minister Mukhtar Ould Diay had frequently disagreed with the minister of economics, the former chief of Banque Centrale de Mauritanie, Sid' Raïs, and the latter was dropped from the cabinet after the

 | DOI 10.1163/9789004355910_015

ministries were merged. Isselkou Ould Ahmed Izid Bih, a trusted ally of President Aziz, became foreign minister, and Aziz's personal doctor, Boubacar Kane, took over the health portfolio. Mohamed Abdallahi Ould Oudaa, a former chief executive of the state mining group, 'Société Nationale Industrielle et Minière de Mauritanie' (SNIM) took on the water and sanitation portfolio.

In early April, Minister of Justice Brahim Ould Daddah proposed a *revision of the constitution* in order to allow President Aziz to run for a third (and unconstitutional) five-year term. Several ministers supported the initiative. A change to the constitution required a two-thirds majority in both houses of parliament and the government had a two-thirds majority in the National Assembly, but not in the Senate. On 3 May, Aziz suggested that the Senate be abolished and replaced by regional councils ('conseils régionaux'). The opposition claimed that decentralisation would boost regionalism and 'tribalism', and strengthen the control of the ruling party over the legislature. Parliament was dominated by the ruling 'Union pour la République' (UPR; the president's party) while the moderate Muslim party, 'Tawassoul', constituted the main parliamentary opposition. *The main opposition* parties had boycotted the last parliamentary elections in 2013 and so the most influential opposition leaders are not represented in parliament. In late October, the largest opposition coalition 'Forum National pour la Démocratie et l'Unité' (FNDU) mobilised thousands of people in Nouakchott against the president's proposal to abolish the Senate. On 29 November, the FNDU called for a boycott of the *referendum* scheduled for early 2017. On 20 October, Aziz declared that he did not intend to seek a third term and confirmed that he would withdraw a proposal removing the age limit of 75 years for presidential candidates. However, these statements did not usher in more harmonious relations between the government and the FNDU. On 16 September, the government declared that the *national dialogue* (initially launched in late 2015) would start in October, but the FNDU remained reluctant to engage in dialogue with the government and, in the end, the long-awaited talks did not take place.

On 2 February, UN *human rights* expert Juan E. Méndez called on the authorities "to put into practice the existing laws and safeguards for the protection from torture and ill-treatment". The UN special rapporteur on extreme poverty and human rights, Philip Alston, visited Mauritania from 2 to 11 May, to evaluate the country's poverty eradication efforts. On 20 April, human rights organisations urged the government to repeal the death sentence against Mohamed Mkhaïtir and release him with immediate effect. In 2014, Mkhaïtir had used his blog to criticise those who used religion in order to marginalise "certain groups in Mauritanian society". He had been accused of *apostasy* by the Appeal Court in Nouakchott and had been sentenced to death by the Criminal Court in Nouadhibou in December 2014. This was the first time since independence in 1960 that a death sentence had been imposed for apostasy. The appeal court in Nouadhibou confirmed the death sentence on 21 April, but the case was referred to the Supreme Court. On 13 November, the 'Forum des Oulémas et Imams pour la Défense du Prophète', called for the sentence to be upheld. The Supreme Court's decision, scheduled for 20 December, was postponed.

On 14 March, Mauritania ratified the 2014 ILO Protocol to the Forced Labour Convention, against forced labour in all its forms – one of the first African states to do so. However, *slavery* continued to be practised. Anti-slavery activists were frequently harassed, arrested and jailed. Biram Ould Dah Ould Abeid, leader of 'Initiative pour la Résurgence du Mouvement Abolitionniste' (IRA), was freed from jail on 17 May on the orders of the Supreme Court. Two months later, on 19 July, six IRA activists were arrested. On 5 September, 13 anti-slavery activists and IRA members were sentenced to between three and 15 years in prison, although some of the sentences were later reduced. According to the Walk Free Foundation's slavery index released in 2016, about 1% of the population (around 43,000 people) were living in modern slavery and Mauritania continued to have the world's seventh-highest incidence of slavery. On 2 June, 20 civil society organisations protested against a proposed new law that would compromise the right to freedom of association. The protesting organisations believed that this law would continue to limit civil society organisations (which were already restricted) and their possibilities to act.

Terrorism remained a potential threat because of the country's vulnerable geographic position and long and porous borders, and the presence of several terrorist organisations, among them al-Qaida in the Islamic Maghreb (AQIM) and Ansar Dine, which were both operating in neighbouring territories. Nevertheless, no significant terror activities took place in Mauritania during the year. Mohamed Saleck Ould Cheikh, who had been sentenced to death in April 2011 for attempting to commit a terrorist offence and being a member of AQIM, escaped from Nouakchott's central prison on 31 December but was deported back from Guinea to Mauritania on 20 January 2017. In a speech to the nation on 6 June, President Aziz again called on the clerics "to invest more in promoting the values of tolerance and solidarity" in order to tackle extremism.

The government strove to improve Mauritania's reputation for combating *corruption*. The National Commission against Corruption ('Comité National de Lutte contre la Corruption'; CNLC) continued their work but, in the absence of an effective parliamentary opposition, prospects for scrutinising government actions were limited. Journalists trying to investigate corruption and other politically sensitive issues risked prosecution. On 15 July, Cheikh Baye, from the 'Meyadine News' website, who had accused a government official of lying, was sentenced to three years for "using violence against a public official". Even so, Mauritania had the highest press freedom ranking among Arab countries, and was ranked 48th out of 180 countries worldwide by Reporters Without Borders, and classified as 'partly free' by Freedom House. Efforts to strengthen the business environment continued and the World Bank business environment index ranked Mauritania 160th out of 190 countries.

Foreign Policy

Regional security dominated Mauritania's relationships with neighbouring states. Together with Burkina Faso, Chad, Niger and Mali, Mauritania continued to participate in the *G5 du Sahel*, a regional security and development organisation. On 17 June, Foreign Minister Ould Ahmed Izid Bih participated in the G5 Sahel/EU high level meeting in Brussels (Belgium). The meeting was aimed at creating closer ties between the EU and the G5 Sahel in order to combat terrorism, irregular migration and illicit trafficking. Cooperation between the G5 Sahel and EU was expected to be significantly enhanced by the approval of several additional projects, funded by the EU Emergency Trust Fund.

On 3–5 March, UN Secretary-General Ban Ki-moon made an official visit to Mauritania to discuss cooperation between Mauritania and the *UN*, and Mauritanian support for UN peacekeeping missions. At the end of the year, 1,030 Mauritanians were engaged in UN peacekeeping missions.

The strengthening of ties with Arab countries was important for enhancing trade and aid. Mauritania remained attractive to Saudi Arabian investors and encouraged expanding bilateral trade and investment between the two countries. The 2016 *Arab League Summit* was held in Nouakchott on 25–27 June. The event had originally been scheduled to take place in Morocco, but Morocco announced in February that it would withdraw as the host nation. In accordance with the alphabetical order of member countries, Mauritania hosted the summit for the first time since it had joined the organisation in 1973. Although Egypt and Saudi Arabia – the two political heavyweights of the Arab world – did not participate, the meeting was regarded as a success and was expected to reduce the growing domestic criticism of President Aziz's authoritarian leadership.

Diplomatic relations between *Morocco* and Mauritania remained tense. Morocco's decision on 14 August to send security forces to the Guerguerat area on the border between Mauritania and the disputed area of Western Sahara, and the speech by the Moroccan politician Hamid Chabat, secretary-general of the Istiqlal party, in which he called Mauritania "une terre marocaine", exacerbated this tension. Official diplomatic sources claimed that relations between the two countries remained 'excellent'. On 20 December, the 18th session of the Algeria-Mauritania High Joint Commission resulted in 14 cooperation agreements in the fields of justice, vocational training, health, trade and economic sectors of common interest. Algerian Prime Minister Abdelmalek Sellal also disclosed a plan to open a frontier post with Mauritania to facilitate the movement of people and goods and strengthen trade between the two countries.

Relations with the *United States* involved a wide range of issues, including counterterrorism, food security, trade promotion and efforts to strengthen human rights and the rule of law. International observers predicted stronger ties with the US under Donald Trump. In contrast to the outgoing Obama administration, the president-elect was expected to be less likely to focus on human rights abuses and instead value the country's contribution in the war against international Islamic terrorism in the region. Although Mauritania's human rights record was under constant scrutiny by Western donors and domestic human rights groups, the government enhanced relations with China. On 6 May, the Foreign Ministry issued a statement declaring that China's territorial claims in the South China Sea were consistent with the UN Convention on the Law of the Sea.

The Holy See (*Vatican*) announced on 9 December that an apostolic nunciature would be established in Mauritania, while Mauritania would set up an embassy to the Holy See. Around 5,000 Catholics from foreign countries were estimated to be living in Mauritania.

Socioeconomic Developments

China was Mauritania's largest single export destination, receiving more than 40% of total exports. As a consequence, Mauritania's external sector was heavily dependant on Chinese economic development. On 11 May, the IMF concluded its Article IV consultation with Mauritania, recommending policies to support "external stability through greater exchange rate flexibility, supported by foreign exchange market reform and a renewed structural reform effort to support private sector development and job creation". Circulation of money outside the official channels constituted a serious constraint to the effectiveness of monetary policy.

The AfDB issued its *Country Strategy Paper* for Mauritania. The report emphasised electricity supply and agricultural modernisation. The paper did not reveal details about financial assistance but estimated that the strategy would contribute to growth, poverty reduction and a lessening of the country's reliance on the extractive sector. Microfinance being considered to play an important role for small and less wealthy enterprises, a new microfinance bank was opened by the Arab Gulf Program for Development (AGFUND) in Nouakchott early in March. On 9 December, the AfDB approved loans of € 31.3 m and € 9.4 m to Mauritania and Senegal, respectively, to replace ferry services, which had a limited capacity, with a 1,500 m.-long bridge at Rosso, over the Senegal River. The project was co-financed by the Mauritanian and Senegalese governments, the EIB and the EU, to a total of € 87.6 m. The project would contribute to regional integration and boost commercial activity in the region.

Real GDP growth was estimated at 1.5 %. Both agricultural output and mining capacity expanded slightly. The fall in world market prices for *iron ore* at the beginning of the year had negative effects on the country's export income. This changed at the end of the year, when prices rose again from $ 59 per tonne in October to $ 79.4 in December. On 9 February, SNIM announced that Guelb II had started to produce concentrated iron ore and was expected to add 4 m tonnes to the existing annual output of around 11 m tonnes. This also created 1,000 new jobs. It was estimated that the project would cost $ 924 m to complete, and would be funded by AfDB, the 'Agence Française de Développement', the EIB and commercial banks such as 'Société Générale' and BNP Paribas.

On 16 March, Sterling Energy, a company based in the UK, announced that it had completed its withdrawal from Block C-3, located in Mauritanian offshore waters. The decision had been made at the beginning of the year after careful analysis of seismic data. Nevertheless, Sterling continued exploration of another offshore block, Block C-10. On 19 April, Kinross, a Canadian mining company, announced it would invest $ 300 m to expand capacity in Tasiast gold mine, from 8,000 to 12,000 tonnes/day. The investment also highlighted that foreign mining investors remain confident in Mauritania.

The UN High Commissioner for Refugees, WFP and UNICEF urged donors on 11 February to "mobilize the necessary resources to maintain the vital assistance to 50,000 *Malian refugees* in Mberra camp in south-eastern Mauritania". On 14 March, WFP and UNICEF warned that "funding shortfalls threaten their ability to provide essential assistance to some of the most vulnerable families in Mauritania". WFP estimated that 450,000 Mauritanians were in urgent need of assistance. On 17 February, the government announced that import taxes on rice would be raised in order to promote local rice producers. Mauritania's rice production – mostly in the Trarza and Gorgol regions, where the government's decision was appreciated – covered about 75% of national demand.

On 10 May, the EU ratified its four-year *fishing agreement* with Mauritania (provisionally signed in 2015). The bilateral agreement, which allowed more than 100 EU vessels into Mauritanian waters in return for funding for local fishing communities, was unique because it covered a wide range of fish stocks. Nevertheless, critics claimed there was little evidence that EU funding was "helping Mauritanian fishing communities". The critics referred to the fact that, although Mauritania had received more than € 1 bn in return for EU fishing rights over the previous 25 years, there was "little to show how the money has been benefitting local fishing communities or improved the country's fishing sector".

Investments in *renewable energy* were essential in order to extend electricity access in rural areas and counter the risk of environmental degradation. Masdar, a state-run alternative energy company based in the UAE, installed eight new solar energy plants in rural areas. Altogether these would supply a total of 16.6 MW of electricity, sufficient to power about 39,000 homes. The country remained highly vulnerable to extreme weather events and was the fourth most vulnerable country worldwide to drought, according to the Climate Change Vulnerability Index.

Niger

Klaas van Walraven

President Mahamadou Issoufou and his ruling 'Parti Nigérien pour la Démocratie et le Socialisme' (PNDS) consolidated their grip on power, though not without pushing to absurd levels the unorthodox measures by which they hoped to strengthen their position. Opposition leader Hama Amadou of the 'Mouvement Démocratique Nigérien' (Moden-Lumana), who had been arrested in 2015 for alleged involvement in a baby-trafficking scandal, remained in detention. He was allowed to contest the 2016 presidential elections from his cell. Issoufou emerged victorious, though not without an unexpected run-off. The parliamentary polls allowed the PNDS to boost its position in the National Assembly. Although the elections took place in an atmosphere of calm, they were marred by authoritarian interventions, including the arrest of several members of the opposition. The 'Mouvement National pour la Société de Développement' (MNSD) of Seini Oumarou had to cede its leadership of the opposition to Amadou's Moden, which ended ahead of the MNSD in the Assembly. In August, the MNSD joined the presidential majority, which did not bode well for the possibility of political alternation in the future. National security was tested by frequent attacks by Boko Haram fighters in the south-east and raids by insurgents based in Mali. While the humanitarian situation in the south-east

 | DOI 10.1163/9789004355910_016

worsened, the army managed to strike back and engage in counter-insurgency operations together with forces from Chad, Nigeria and Cameroon. Overall, the country held its own, despite being sandwiched between security challenges that caused some serious losses. Rains were deficient, leading to a cereal deficit that would mean earlier shortfalls in 2017. Economic performance was affected by depressed oil and uranium prices.

Domestic Politics

Presidential elections were scheduled for 21 February, together with legislative polls, and a presidential run-off would take place, if necessary, on 20 March. All the tycoons on Niger's political scene entered the fray, joined by various lesser presidential hopefuls. These last included Mahamane Ousmane, who was strong in the eastern city of Zinder but was handicapped by a new party vehicle, and Ibrahim Yacouba, an adviser to President Issoufou, who had been expelled from the PNDS the previous year over an internal dispute. Seini Oumarou and Hama Amadou continued to be the president's main rivals. Oumarou, leading Niger's second party and with his fief in western Tillabéri, hoped to profit from the incarceration of Amadou, who was also from the west (Issoufou being from the central Tahoua region). However, while Amadou's detention was expected to hinder his visibility to voters, his party exploited it by playing the martyrdom card.

Faced with this splintered field, the opposition parties decided to rally behind a single candidate if elections went to a run-off. The effect of this deal, referred to as the 'Coalition pour l'alternance 2016' (Copa 2016), was to allow Issoufou a lead in the first round. The ruling party hoped to transform its incumbency into a 'knock-out' (by taking more than 50% of the votes in the first round), making a second round unnecessary. Issoufou's *campaign arguments* made much of the limited gains in agriculture and infrastructural development. Critics pointed out, not without reason, that the development programme had suffered from increases in defence spending and that the government had used threats to national security as an excuse to harass civil society activists and the opposition.

These accusations centred round *Hama Amadou's treatment.* While the facts of his involvement in the baby-trafficking affair remained unclear, the handling of the case had electoral consequences if not political connotations. Detained in Filingué, 180 km north of the capital Niamey, Amadou had been refused bail in December 2015. This decision was confirmed on appeal on 11 January. A few days earlier, the Constitutional Court had validated his presidential candidature. On 9 February, however, it declared itself incompetent to decide on Amadou's provisional release. This led to a situation in which a principal opposition leader was allowed to contest presidential elections while being kept in detention, barred access to the media and hindered from receiving visitors. Issoufou's administration hid behind the judiciary's independence. The governor of Filingué prison, however, was allegedly transferred after allowing Amadou an opposition visit on 25 January that sealed the Copa alliance.

The run-up to the elections was marred by the government's *authoritarian interventions*, thinly veiled by references to national security. By March, several of Moden's staff were behind bars on charges that varied from creating a disturbance at Niamey airport at the time of Amadou's home-coming in November 2015 to involvement in a ten-year-old corruption case and collusion in the alleged coup attempt in December 2015. Interior Minister Hassoumi Massaoudou (PNDS secretary-general and an Issoufou hardliner), together with Mohamed Bazoum, minister of state at the presidency and campaign manager, accused the opposition of complicity in the putsch. One presidential contender was briefly detained for casting doubt on the reality of the coup. Seven Moden leaders were convicted in July (for the airport disturbance) and released upon completion of their sentence in September. In early February, a Moden-loyal griot who predicted the president's electoral defeat was taken into custody for defamation (griots are used in 'séances de tam tam', political events accompanied by dance and song). Although a court in Niamey freed her on 15 February for lack of evidence, indicating the judiciary's relative independence, this could not conceal the government's reliance on unorthodox tactics. A Moden rally held in Dosso on 2 February was followed by clashes between Amadou supporters and police in Niamey the following day.

Electoral procedures were scrutinised, leading to the removal from the register of 25,000 duplicate names and the elimination of hundreds of 'ghost' polling stations. The exercise was approved by OIF observers. However, on 17 February the Council of State decided to allow 'voting by witness' for those without identity documents (i.e. by allowing a witness to vouch for them – a common occurrence in a poor country like Niger, and such voting had been allowed before). Opposition forces cried foul, arguing that this would open the sluice gates to fraud.

With a reported turnout of 66.8% (rather high by Nigérien standards), the biggest surprise was Issoufou's failure to achieve a knock-out. His support stood at 48.4%, falling short of 50% by 167,000 votes, although he took 12% more than in the 2011 polls and came in ahead of other candidates in six out of eight regions. The interior minister expressed disappointment and admitted that Amadou's detention had helped the Moden leader. The results showed *Amadou's resilience*. He received 17.8% of the votes, taking the lead in the regions of Niamey and Tillabéri. This meant that he had beaten Seini Oumarou, formerly Niger's number 2, who took 12.1%. The leader of the MNSD, which had fractured under government pressure in 2015, lost 11% compared with 2011, most of these votes going to Issoufou, who made inroads in MNSD strongholds in the Maradi and Diffa regions. Of the weaker candidates,

Mahamane Ousmane took 6.3%, indicating the final eclipse of the influence of the former National Assembly chair. Surprisingly, Ibrahim Yacouba, who had broken with the PNDS, took 4.4% of the votes. In the legislative elections, the PNDS won 75 of the 171 seats in an Assembly expanded from 113 seats in 2011. With the smaller parties in the presidential coalition, it secured 112 seats. Moden-Lumana became the second party with 25.

Opposition leaders renewed their call for Amadou's release at Niamey's appeals court, but a verdict was not expected before 28 March, eight days after the run-off. As it was clear that Copa 2016 could never attract more than 40% of the votes, *divisions in the alliance* quickly manifested themselves. The PNDS curried favour with the 'petits candidats'. Ibrahim Yacouba was seen as the key to an Issoufou victory and was won over to the presidential side. On 8 March, Copa called for a boycott of the second round, but as Amadou himself decided to maintain his candidature this was to be partially ignored by voters. In the midst of this confusion, Amadou was hospitalised on 11 and 14–15 March, suffering from exhaustion and eye problems. Prime Minister Brigi Rafini dispatched a medical team, but on 16 March – four days before the run-off – the political tycoon was brought by helicopter to Niamey and flown to France for treatment.

The Electoral Commission reported a turnout of 59.8% in the *run-off*. While the EU and OIF noted the drop in participation, the opposition claimed the figure was closer to 10%-11%. If this was too low, the turnout reported by the Commission seemed high (its website listed turnouts in nomadic regions close to or surpassing 100%). In the run-off, Amadou took 7.5% of the votes, which in the circumstances was an achievement. Issoufou's 92.5% was judged by opposition voices to be of 'Stalinist' proportions. The damage to the political system was illustrated when Copa rejected the result, flatly denying that Issoufou had been re-elected. It rebuffed an invitation to form a government of national unity. To make matters worse, the Supreme Court ruled three days after the polls that civil proceedings on the parentage of the children in the trafficking scandal should be pursued before a criminal prosecution. Consequently, on 29 March, Niamey's appeals court granted bail to Amadou, who stayed in Paris, still under formal suspicion. The procedural logic of the courts allowed opposition politicians to claim that the case had been politically motivated.

The PNDS boosted its majority in the *new cabinet*. Brigi Rafini, not part of Issoufou's inner circle but important, as a northern Tuareg, for the government's stability, was retained as prime minister. Bazoum's appointment as minister of state with a super-portfolio including interior affairs, security and religious issues confirmed his importance (as did Hassoumi Massaoudou's move to defence, a key ministry). Yacouba Ibrahim, the new rising star, became foreign minister as a reward for his support in the run-off.

More than 50 opposition politicians boycotted the Assembly's inaugural session on 24 March, when Ousseini Tinni, PNDS MP for Dosso, was elected parliamentary chair. This meant that both the presidency and the *National Assembly* were now under the control of the same party (the parliamentary chair had traditionally gone to the candidate who came third in the presidential elections). Inevitably, the reality of their defeat forced opposition forces to come back to the fold, returning to the National Assembly and rejoining the Electoral Commission, whose neutrality had become – for the first time in its history – a bone of contention. This put further pressure on Copa 2016 – a coalition of convenience – and notably on the MNSD, which had suffered irreparably through the government's tactics. On 13–14 August, it decided to join the presidential majority. This left Moden out in the cold, especially as Amadou continued in exile. On 31 August, Moden and ten minor groups decided to form a new coalition, the 'Front pour la Restauration de la Démocratie et la Défense de la République', whose strongholds were Niamey and Zinder. A meeting between Oumarou and Issoufou shortly after the MNSD's decision to join the majority was followed on 19 October by a *cabinet reshuffle*. Oumarou was appointed high representative at the presidency and MNSD lieutenants took minor ministries. In the enlarged cabinet, Hassoumi Massaoudou moved from defence to finance, whose minister was ill.

Details emerged over the alleged coup attempt at the end of 2015. Sixteen civilians were kept in detention, as well as 20 military personnel from an elite anti-terrorist unit. The unit was disbanded and its commanding officer detained, as was his deputy who had fled to Togo. The plan for a helicopter-led bombardment of the presidential palace leaked out as putschists sought counsel from marabouts and contacted members of the presidential guard. Although investigators would have spoken to Amadou about the attempt, the involvement of civilian politicians remained hazy.

The *war with Boko Haram* continued unabated. By July, there were more than 300,000 IDPs in the Diffa region. The regional economy had come to a halt, with markets closed and the trade in fish and peppers (key local products) suspended. From November 2015, 100 schools – a Boko Haram target – were moved to safer locations. On 17 March, an army commander became the victim of a suicide attack in Diffa. Around the same time, five suicide bombers, including a young girl, attacked an army detachment further east in Bosso, on the borders of Lake Chad. An army commander was killed and four Boko Haram fighters died, while the girl, who failed to detonate her explosive vest, was shot. Bosso, an exposed locality, was again a target on 19 May, when at least six civilians were killed (four burned alive). The army lost 26 men in a sustained attack on Bosso on 3–5 June. Numerous soldiers were wounded and 55 Boko Haram fighters were reported killed. The insurgents, who included what locals called 'enfants du marabout' (child soldiers, apparently drugged), managed to occupy the town for several days. The population fled (all

6,000, plus 20,000 IDPs). Some 50,000 people made their way west, swelling overstretched facilities elsewhere. Confronted by heavy artillery, army troops withdrew before Niger's two Sukhoi jet fighters and helicopters stationed in Diffa intervened.

The government speeded up a *counter-insurgency operation* planned together with Chadian forces. As part of the four-nation 'Force Multinationale Mixte' (FMM), which included Nigerian and Cameroonian troops, 3,000 Nigériens and 4,000 Chadians swept into Nigeria. On 25–28 July, they liberated Damasak, though not without heavy fighting. The Nigerian border town, on the banks of the Komadougou-Yobé River, had been in the hands of insurgents on and off for a year. Niger's long-term military objective (i.e. pushing Boko Haram towards the islands in Lake Chad and the Nigerian city of Maiduguri, where they could be trapped by FMM troops) still seemed a long way off, however. On 30 July, dozens of inhabitants of the village of Gaduraa were murdered by insurgents. Many had their throats slit. On 2 September, the village of Toumour was targeted – five people died and two were injured. The insurgents fought the village self-defence group, which was armed with bows and arrows. On 12 September, 30 insurgents and five army soldiers were killed in fighting near Toumour. In mid-September, Chadian and Nigérien forces reportedly killed 38 fighters in operations near Toumour and Gueskérou (the latter had been attacked on the night of 14 September, with huts burnt and food supplies looted).

By 30 September, the civilian body count since 6 February 2015 had risen to 177. Nevertheless, Boko Haram appeared to have been dealt a blow, as its attacks grew fewer. On 27 December, the authorities reported the *voluntary surrender of insurgents* – for the first time ever. Around 50 young adults from Diffa (including women) were brought to a centre where they would follow a deradicalisation programme. Many of them hailed from Diffa and had been lured by insurgents with promises of up to $ 500 a month (a fortune by local standards). They would benefit from an amnesty and programmes destined to achieve their socioeconomic reintegration.

Attacks from Mali were a reminder of the country's vulnerability to security threats from the Saharan region. On 17 March, three gendarmes were killed near the Burkinabè frontier by men said to belong to al-Qaeda-in-the-Islamic-Maghreb (AQIM). On 28 April, one gendarme was killed and two wounded in an attack in the Azaouagh region near the border with Mali. The attackers were said to belong to the 'Mouvement pour l'Unicité et le Jihad en Afrique de l'Ouest' (MUJAO) or another Islamist group, Ansar Dine. Later, on 11 September, unidentified men killed two civilians in a UN-run refugee camp in the north-west. Much worse was an attack by 30–40 heavily armed assailants on a camp in the Azaouagh on 6 October. Twenty-two men charged with the camp's protection died. In response, Niger, together with UN and French forces, launched an operation in Mali's Ménaka region. On 14 October, an American missionary in Abalak (between Tahoua and Agadez) was kidnapped, possibly by men belonging to MUJAO. Two guards were murdered. Three days later the army repulsed an attack on the high-security prison of Koutoukalé, 50 km north-west of Niamey, which housed jihadists from Mali and the Boko Haram zone. MUJAO was said to be responsible. On 8 November, five soldiers were killed and three wounded in an attack on the border town of Bani Bangou. Two of the assailants, who arrived with vehicles and motorbikes, were killed. Several local people were arrested on suspicion of complicity.

A *Tubu leader* in the south-east issued a video message in September, announcing the establishment of a rebel 'Mouvement pour la Justice et la Réhabilitation du Niger'. Adam Tcheke Koudigan presented himself as the successor of a Tubu rebel leader in the 1990s, who died in a hospital in Dubai in July, and called for a greater portion of revenues from the oil wealth in his region to be used to benefit marginalised Tubu nomads. In unrelated violence, 18 people died in *clashes between peasants and pastoralists* in the Madaoua region on 1 November. The victims were predominantly women, children and the elderly (seven were burnt alive). The violence was triggered when a herd of cattle devastated a millet field. Hundreds of whipped-up Hausa youths armed with machetes went on the rampage in a Peul village. Local police were overwhelmed.

Foreign Affairs

Western governments remained silent over the deterioration of the political climate, as Niger was seen as a solid partner in the struggle against terrorism. *France* invited Issoufou to the Elysée on 14 June. Afterwards, he dined with Foreign Minister Ayrault. Accompanied by his foreign and defence ministers, he also met French Defence Minister Le Drian, as well as the mayor of Paris, the president of the French National Assembly and representatives of the French employers association Medef. The visit highlighted Niger's privileged ties with France.

Germany boosted its profile with a visit by Foreign Minister Steinmeier, together with his French counterpart, on 3 May. International terrorism had much to do with this, in addition to the problem of illegal migration (the northern city of Agadez being West Africa's main migrant processing point on the route across the Sahara). Chancellor Merkel visited Niger on 10 October and promised $ 27 m in aid, to be targeted at development in Agadez and the procurement of defence equipment. The *US* announced on 30 September the establishment of a base for surveillance drones in Agadez.

Relations with African countries were also dominated by the terrorist threat. After the coming to power of Muhammadu Buhari in *Nigeria* in 2015, relations with Niger's southern neighbour had improved substantially. Nigérien troops could more easily move into Nigeria in pursuit of Boko Haram, while military cooperation also improved. The 8,700-strong FMM force still struggled with a shortage of funds, however. In response to the attacks from *Mali*, the government pleaded for a more offensive mandate for MINUSMA, the UN peacekeeping force stationed there, to which Niger was contributing 1,700 men. At a meeting of the G5 Sahel (Burkina Faso, Mali, Mauritania, Niger and Chad) on 4 March, defence ministers announced the establishment of a rapid intervention and counter-terrorism force to be deployed in areas threatened by AQIM. Technical assistance would be provided by Spain and France, which promised $ 47 m in counter-terror training. *Algeria* decided to improve surveillance of its southern borders, including with Niger, for which 20,000 military personnel would be moved south. Finally, *Libya* remained a source of concern to the government, which spoke of the 'Somalisation' of the country, pleading for renewed international intervention.

Socioeconomic Developments

Rains were deficient and erratic, leading to flooding in the Tahoua and Agadez regions. A dozen people drowned and thousands lost homes and cattle. The *cereal crop* was disappointing. WFP announced that it needed $ 21.4 m to tide over vulnerable groups. On 26 May, the World Bank approved $ 111 m in funds to help improve the agricultural sector. The project, geared at distribution and the use of drought-resistant seeds, would assist half a million people. A local company, 'Société de Transformation Alimentaire', was successful in consolidating production of high-nutrition emergency foods based on local resources.

Due to depressed commodity prices, the *growth rate* fell to an estimated 3.8%, extending the trend set in 2015. However, the IMF (which tends to give higher estimates) readjusted real GDP in 2015 upward to 3.6%. The IMF also raised estimates of growth for 2016 from 4.5% to 5.2%, counting on rebounding prices for natural resources and greater activity in the agricultural sector (but this did not yet include figures on the 2016 cereal crop). Trade with Nigeria suffered from the war with Boko Haram. The *budget* totalled $ 3 bn, slightly lower than 2015. However, the rise in defence spending, while causing imbalances in expenditure, did nothing to diminish the deficit and made the payment of salaries in the public sector increasingly problematic.

In late April, workers at the oil refinery in Zinder went on a three-day strike, disrupting *oil production*, in protest about their pay and working conditions. The refinery suffered from a dispute with the 'Société Nigérienne des Produits Pétroliers' (SONIDEP), the state petroleum company. By October 2015, SONIDEP had failed to pay for Soraz-produced fuel worth up to $ 18.8 m. In June, Soraz was given the go-ahead to export surplus oil on its own account (7,000 b/d being reserved for the domestic market). This would allow it to repay loans made by its Chinese creditors.

Low oil prices, however, continued to cause difficulties. Strike action also took place on 3–5 May at the Cominak *uranium* mine in northern Arlit, where workers protested against the incomplete payment of bonuses. The French nuclear company Areva, plagued by low uranium prices and technical difficulties, stated that payment was subject to a review of 2015 results. While Areva was trying to sell its licence for the development of the huge uranium mine of Imouraren, a Canadian company was awarded a production licence for a site at Madaouela. The government also issued four other licences, one to the Canadian firm and three to African firms, reflecting expectations that the price for yellow cake would slowly recover.

The development of *infrastructure* faced various problems. The state electricity company had to reduce output after its fuel imports from Nigeria fell by two-thirds in April. All regions but one were hit. However, on 9 December, the AfDB approved € 65 m of funding for rural electrification schemes that would extend access to power to 46,000 households (with access for a further 60,000 households planned). The AfDB also gave a loan for improving Internet access; Internet coverage would increase from 15% to 30% of the population. The government confirmed the merger of the state-owned fixed-line and mobile phone companies into a new enterprise called Niger Telecom. In 2015, 36.5% of the population had a mobile phone subscription (and less than 1% a fixed-line). Construction on the Benin-Niger railway BENI Rail stalled. While the 140 km section between Niamey and Dosso was complete, a dispute with a Beninese and French company that claimed to have been granted an earlier contract, forced the French conglomerate Bolloré to halt the planned connection with Parakou and Cotonou on the West African coast. (A similar dispute erupted with a company that had signed a contract with the military government in 2011 for the production of passports.)

In the first half of June, 34 *migrants* who were trying to cross the Sahara via Algeria died of thirst near Assamakka. They had been abandoned by their trafficker and the victims included 20 children. This was not the first incident of its kind. In 2015 alone some 120,000 people had crossed Niger's northern region en route to Europe. On 7 June, the EU announced funding of up to € 60 bn to encourage private investment in West African countries, including Niger. Figures for 2015 showed that Niger was at the bottom of the HDI.

Between January and March, an outbreak of *meningitis* resulted in 61 deaths; 30% of infections were in children. (The 2015 vaccination campaign, in response to a virulent outbreak, had not yet been completed.)

On 19–25 September, university teachers and students went on strike to protest about non-payment of salaries and grant arrears. While the *education* minister blamed this on defence spending, the anti-corruption agency announced that it had found more than 2,500 ghost teachers on the government pay-roll, which had led to substantial losses in funds.

Nigeria

Heinrich Bergstresser

Nigeria faced substantial economic and security challenges throughout the year. Plummeting oil and gas prices coupled with the emergence of new and violent militia groups in the Niger Delta caused the worst recession for 30 years. Increasing violence, and organised crime on an unprecedented scale in central Nigeria and the eastern Middle Belt, compounded the already precarious situation and raised serious questions about the ability of President Muhammadu Buhari's government to handle the multifaceted crises in the financial and economic sectors, as well as the security situation in at least three of the six geo-political zones, namely the North-Central, North-East and South-South. Despite the military's progress in the fight against Boko Haram in the North-East, it was obvious that the security forces were overstretched and thus would have been unable to deal with other security challengers elsewhere.

Domestic Politics

President Buhari and his government got off to a bad start, particularly in the South-South, home of the oil and gas producing Niger Delta and the Ijaw, Itsekiri, Ibibio,

 | DOI 10.1163/9789004355910_017

Isoko, Urhobo and Yoruba. Early in the year, it became clear that the *2009 amnesty programme* had come to a standstill. Several new ethnic-based militia groups such as the Niger Delta Avengers (NDA), Red Scorpions, Niger Delta Greenland Justice Mandate (NDGJM), Egbesu Red Water Lions and Joint Niger Delta Liberation Force, appeared out of nowhere. Following an interlude of relative peace, the region experienced weeks of constant attacks and bombings of oil and gas installations. The affected companies included Chevron, Agip, Shell, Nigerian National Petroleum Corporation (NNPC) and the Nigerian Petroleum Development Company (NPDC). Gun battles involving the police and military forces once again turned the Niger Delta into a veritable battleground. The NDA militia, made up of ethnic Ijaw, was at the forefront of violence, challenging the state and the oil companies with piracy and guerrilla warfare. The public was reminded of the long-lasting civil strife associated with the Movement of the Emancipation of the Niger Delta (MEND), and with the thousands of victims in the early years of the Fourth Republic from 1999. Most attacks, however, took place in Delta and Bayelsa states, causing heavy losses and the deaths of dozens of soldiers, policemen, militia men and innocent civilians. Companies were frequently forced to suspend crude output and withhold gas supply to thermal power stations inside and outside the country. This significantly reduced Nigeria's export capacity and led to export receipt losses of around $ 7 bn.

To the consternation of the federal and the affected state governments, some *militia groups* invaded the creeks along the eastern state borders of Lagos, Ondo and Ogun states. On 5 February, for example, they ambushed and killed half a dozen naval personnel in the Wawa area of Arepo in Ogun state. This was seen as a reprisal against security agents who had previously raided the area as part of 'Operation Awatse' and had arrested a number of pipeline vandals. Nine operatives of the Department of State Service (DSS), also known as SSS, were killed in the same area on 13 September. This incident was probably connected with the killing of four DSS staff in nearby Ishawo area in Ikorodu local government in Lagos state. On 26 July, other militants engaged security forces in Igando in Lagos state. Soon afterwards, on 28 July, a joint task force, comprising navy, army, air force, police, state security service and the civil defence corps, launched an aerial bombardment on enclaves, camps and hideouts of pipeline oil thieves in Lagos and Ogun creeks that lasted for several days. Earlier, in June, the air force had redeployed additional combat and surveillance aircraft and helicopter gunships to the South-South, intending to carry out similar campaigns in the central Niger Delta region.

On 6 June, Vice President Yemi Osinbajo held an emergency meeting in Abuja with all the service chiefs, governors of the region and ministers of defence and petroleum in attendance. As a result, the federal government initiated a somewhat reluctant dialogue with militia groups and stakeholders, including some of the old political Ijaw elites such as octogenarian Edwin Clarke and septuagenarian Alfred Diete-Spiff, the first military governor of Rivers state (as the present Bayelsa and

Rivers states had been known), who together represented the Pan-Niger Delta Forum (PANDEF). On 1 November, in a move aimed at helping to restore peace, leaders of the forum presented a 16-point plan to President Buhari, but the ethnic Urhobo-dominated NDGJM-militias carried out a damaging attack on the important Trans-Forcados pipeline in Delta state on 5 November, signalling that any peace deal was unlikely. In the following weeks, military operations, such as 'Pulo Shield', later renamed 'Delta Safe', 'Tsare Teku', Crocodile Smile', 'Crocodile Tears' and 'Python Dance', led to the killing and arrest of dozens of alleged militia commanders, but the campaigns did not prevent further attacks. Worse still, as part of the 2009 amnesty programme, the government was forced to resume cash payments to repentant militiamen, which had been stopped in February. Unabated killings, kidnappings and bomb attacks forced the government to admit that it would be unable to restore security for the foreseeable future, as it soon became apparent that even the *local elites had lost any respect and authority in their own spheres of influence.*

In the neighbouring ethnic Igbo-heartland, *advocacy groups in favour of an independent Biafra*, such as Indigenous People of Biafra (IPOB), Movement of the Actualization of the Sovereign State of Biafra (MASSOB), the Biafra Independence Movement (BIM) and the Biafra Zionist Movement, regained momentum. Tension grew throughout the year and led to numerous fatalities. On 19 January, in Aba, the hub of Abia state, soldiers opened fire on members of IPOB protesting against the continued detention of their leader, Nnamdi Kanu. Some half a dozen of his followers were killed. In May, further incidents in Anambra, Enugu, Imo and Ebonyi states provoked a chain of violence which culminated on 29–31 May in a bloodbath in Onitsha, in Anambra state. According to MASSOB and IPOB, some 60 members and sympathisers were shot by military forces. AI confirmed these numbers on 23 November, but the army rejected AI's preliminary report, and reported a lower number of deaths. Notwithstanding these events, Osita Okechukwu, the ethnic Igbo director general of the 'Voice of Nigeria', argued at a meeting of the Igbo socio-cultural organisation Ohaneze Ndigbo on 28 September, that the actualisation of Biafra was not feasible.

In several states of North-Central and North-East, particularly Zamfara, Adamawa, Niger, Benue and Taraba, the security situation went from bad to worse. A swathe of destruction affected the northern parts of the southern and eastern states of Cross River, Delta and Enugu. Against the backdrop of an *accelerated militarisation of the region*, cattle rustling – traditionally part of Fulani herdsmen's culture of bravery and prowess – transformed into well organised banditry. In addition, disputes over grazing rights and fertile land led to deadly skirmishes in which hundreds of peasants, herdsmen, soldiers, policemen and uninvolved citizens lost their lives. Zamfara experienced at least two major attacks. On 6 February, gunmen raided Kwanar Dutse community in Maru local government area, gunning down some 50 villagers, razing most of their houses and taking away their livestock.

On 7 November, Bindin village in the same local government suffered another tragedy, when gunmen on motorcycles killed about 50 miners and several gold merchants at a nearby gold mine. In a state-wide broadcast on 21 November, Governor Abdulaziz Yari, trying to address the security challenges by setting up a crisis management committee, disclosed that 155 people had been killed and more than 50 persons kidnapped in the past month.

On 24 January, at least 30 people, including members of a police team were killed by suspected Fulani herdsmen. The group had tried to stop the ongoing raids in the Girei local government (Adamawa state). The attackers were on a revenge mission following earlier clashes with local farmers. In another incident, Kodomun village in Demsa local government of Adamawa state was attacked twice within three days (on 30 July–1 August); dozens of people were killed and many more injured.

Agatu local government in Benue state, *for years a focal point of hostilities* between herdsmen and farmers, was again counting the cost when, at the end of February, incessant attacks on local people by Fulani herdsmen led to the deaths of more than 100 people. Other sources put the number at around 300, with some 7,000 people said to have been displaced and to be surviving in squatter camps. The dispute was not made any simpler by the fact that the hostilities were closely connected with the killing of scores of cattle.

Only after a raid on a community in Enugu state on 25 April, when heavily armed herdsmen killed scores of people, did President Buhari eventually break his silence and order the police and the military to take all necessary action to stop the carnage. The issue of *nationwide grazing reserve centres* re-emerged and, by August and September, the federal government had concluded arrangements to rehabilitate the more than 400 centres and stock routes, mandating 10 state governments to monitor the project. The military launched 'Operation Accord' to tackle the clashes between herdsmen in their own way. On 8 November, the government inaugurated a 16-member technical committee, chaired by Professor Oshita O. Oshita, director general of the Institute for Peace and Conflict Resolution (IPCR), to look into the recurring clashes. Despite these initiatives, deadly incidents in politically volatile southern Kaduna state occurred throughout the year. Endorsed by the president, the state government banned all processions and unlawful assemblies throughout the state on 21 December, imposing a 24-hour curfew in Jema'a, Kaura and Zango Kataf local governments which, except in Kaura, was reduced to a dusk-to-dawn curfew a few days later. Nevertheless, on 26 December, herdsmen were thought to have made an assault on locals, killing at least half a dozen people.

Meanwhile, the precarious security situation in the crisis-ridden North-East gradually improved thanks to an ongoing and better coordinated military campaign by the *Multinational Joint Task Force* (MNJTF). Operations such as 'Lafiya Dole' and 'Gama Aiki' led to the arrest of dozens of Boko Haram commanders, including Mohammed Usman, better known as Khalid al-Barnawi, the rescue of well over a thousand hostages, among them the wife and daughter of the Shehu of Bama, and the death or surrender of several hundred insurgents.

Al-Barnawi was apprehended on 1 April in Kogi state. As a founder of the Islamist splinter group Ansarul (Ansarul Muslimina Fi Biladis Sudan – 'protectors of Muslims in Black Africa'), he had allegedly overseen the bombing of the UN office in Abuja in August 2011. Accordingly, *Boko Haram insurgents lost control of almost all the territory* in Adamawa, Borno and Yobe states, although they retained parts of the notorious Sambisa Forest in Borno state, just 60 km southeast of the state capital Maiduguri. The number of military rank-and-file who fell victim to the terrorists was still markedly high, and did not spare middle-ranking and commanding officers such as Lieutenant Colonels Abu Ali (4 November) and B.U. Umar (15 November). On 16–17 October, the military suffered a humiliating defeat when troops on the northernmost edge of Borno state were forced by the insurgents' superior firepower to abandon their base. They were eventually cornered, and, trying to escape over the Yobe River, most of the soldiers drowned, along with their commanding officer Lieutenant Colonel K. Yusuf. As a result, the military was reluctant to start a major offensive in the forest there, which was full of booby traps, and limited themselves to frequent bombings of Boko Haram camps by jet fighters and drones.

Against this backdrop, *suicide bombings* went on unabated, mostly carried out by young girls. The security forces were unable to prevent all such assaults but managed to foil quite a number. As in previous years, Borno state was the main target of suicide bombings and deadly assaults. On 30 January, more than 60 inhabitants of Dalori village on the outskirts of Maiduguri lost their lives and at least 130 were seriously wounded after a raid by Islamist insurgents. On 28 July, Boko Haram ambushed a UNICEF team returning to the state capital from an IDP camp in Bama. As a result, UNICEF suspended its mission in the area. On 12 October, a bomb blast near Muna Garage, a car park, killed four female passengers and their driver. On 29 October, two suicide bombings, at the entrance to Bakassi IDP camp and the NNPC Mega Filling station in Maiduguri, left several people dead. On 18 November, in a rather rare case, a foiled suicide attack in the city centre led to the arrest of an unhurt female survivor.

On 13 October, 21 of the more than *200 missing Chibok school* girls were released, following a deal brokered by the Swiss government and the International Committee of the Red Cross. Credible sources stated that more than 110 captives were either dead, married off or radicalised and unwilling to leave their kidnappers. Earlier in the year, on 27 January, two female suicide bombers had targeted Chibok market in the local government of the same name and killed more than a dozen citizens.

On 9 December, a twin blast in Madagali in Adamawa state left more than 50 people dead and over 100 injured, reminding the public that the Islamist insurgency was far from over and contradicting the constant claims by the government and military leadership that the crisis in the North-East was ending. On 21 December,

Major General Lucky Irabor, commander of operation 'Lafiya Dole', disclosed that the army had rescued 1,880 women and children in Sambisa Forest and arrested about 500 Boko Haram members, while more than a dozen had surrendered. On 24 December, President Buhari claimed in his Christmas message that the last Boko Haram stronghold, 'Camp Zero', had been seized in a sneak attack two days previously, and that the Islamist insurgency had finally been crushed. At the end of the year more than 1,000 civilians, among them some high-ranking Boko Haram suspects, were arrested in operation 'Rescue Final'.

Throughout the year, *crime was widespread*. Kidnappings, bank raids and murders remained frequent, in spite of the fact that dozens of notorious gangs were apprehended. Clement Abanara and his gang, for example, who were accused of four bank robberies in Lagos state, were arrested in mid-January. On 24 March, Toweki Joseph and his gang were engaged by special police forces while attempting to rob banks and some bureau de change operators at Seme, a border town between Nigeria and Benin Republic. The leaders and most of the gang, mainly ethnic Ijaws, were shot. They had terrorised states in the South-West and South-South for some time and were said to have robbed banks in Lagos and Ondo states, killing several people during their operations. In mid-December, the Lagos state police commissioner disclosed that over the past 12 months, 246 cases of murder and 486 of armed robbery had been recorded in the state.

On 26 March, army colonel Ismaila Inusa was robbed and killed in Kaduna by a four-man gang and his car sold for some NGN (naira) 800,000. Later in June, the same gang and its leader, Emeka Okeke, were apprehended. On 29 May, Thomas Adekoye, a 60-year old surgeon working with the Lagos University Teaching Hospital, was abducted and killed in Ijebu-Itele in Ogun state by suspected sympathisers of a 'native doctor'. On 8 June, the registrar of the Medical Laboratory Science Council, Mrs Olufunke Omotuyi, suffered the same fate in Abuja. She was due for retirement the following month. Shortly before, on 20 May, Denen Igbana, a senior assistant on security to Benue state Governor Samuel Ortom, was gunned down at his residence in Tionsha, close to the state capital Makurdi. The then governor of Ondo state, Olusegun Mimiko, experienced a similar incident when his chief security officer Idowu Oyewole was killed by armed robbers on 20 October, and four days later, in the run-up to the *gubernatorial election* in the state, Afolabi Olaposi, a leadership figure of the All Progressives Congress (APC) in Ondo state, was shot dead after a party meeting in Owo. This was the second APC chieftain to be assassinated, after Franklin Obi, who, together with his wife and son, had been killed by gunmen on 6 March in Omoku in Ogba-Egbema-Ndoni local government in Rivers state. Benue state suffered another blow on 2 October, when armed men attacked a police station in Igumale in Ado local government, killing all four officers on duty. In Sokoto, a Lebanese citizen, Moin Amsuri, a mathematics teacher at the well-known Nagarta College, was the victim of a holdup murder on 28 July.

More *captives were killed* than in previous years. On 5 January, the king of Ubulu-Uku kingdom in Aniocha south local government, Akaeze Edward Ofulue III, was abducted and allegedly killed by Fulani herdsmen. Samuel Okies and Inegite Inibia – the former a nephew and the latter the foster-father of former president Goodluck Jonathan – were taken hostage on 17 February. The nephew was found dead a few days later, but Inegite regained his freedom after more than a month in captivity.

In contrast, hostages such as a traditional Yoruba ruler Oba Gariola Oseni, who was kidnapped on 16 July in Lagos state, and Mrs Margaret Emefiele, wife of the governor of the Central Bank, taken on 20 September in Edo state, were released unharmed on 7 August and 30 September, respectively. In the Lagos case, four men were arrested and put on trial. On 11 November, the king gave evidence and acknowledged that his family had eventually paid a ransom of NGN 15.1 m, although the criminals had initially demanded NGN 500 m. No verdict had been reported by year's end.

On 11 April, *pirates* abducted a Turkish cargo ship. The six crew members were set free after two weeks. Last but not least, the Sierra Leonean deputy high commissioner and high ranking military officer, Nelson Williams, was kidnapped at gunpoint along the Abuja-Kaduna Expressway on his way to Kano on 1 July. The kidnappers demanded a ransom of $ 40 m for his safe return. He was rescued on 5 July. Whether a ransom was paid remained unclear.

This itemisation of criminal incidents in no way completes the list of terror attacks, organised crime, kidnappings, killings and arrests.

Against this backdrop, *jail breaks* occurred in several states: on 24 June in Abuja, on 30 July in Kogi state and on 9 August in Enugu state. On 18 August, a jail break in Ebonyi state failed; several inmates and members of staff were killed. These incidents revealed the dismal prison conditions and the huge challenge of handling thousands of inmates in overcrowded prison cells. They further revealed that prison staff were frequently complicit in many cases. In the aftermath of these events, Comptroller General Ahmed Ja'afaru, appointed to this position on 24 May, dismissed several senior and junior staff.

President Buhari used his executive powers to appoint more chairmen and board members of the numerous *state agencies and federal parastatals*; these short-term lucrative positions served first and foremost to redistribute huge financial resources to the political elite. The appointment of Muhammad Abdallah to the National Drug Enforcement Agency (NDLEA) on 18 January, and that of Ms Adejoke Orelope-Adefulire as senior special assistant in charge of the office for Sustainable Development Goals (SDGS) on 7 March, are examples of such posts. On 18 April, Sule Kazaure became director general of the National Youth Service Corps (NYSC) and, on 24 May, Mohammed Babandele became the comptroller general of the immigration service. New chief executives were appointed to six state media agencies, among them the News Agency of Nigeria (NAN). A change of leadership at the federal budget office took place in June, when Ben Akabueze replaced Tijani Mohammed Abdullahi.

On 21 June, Ibrahim Kpotum Idris was promoted to acting *inspector general of police* after the retirement of Solomon Arase. In early July, against the backdrop of the crisis in the Niger Delta, the president removed Ibe Kachikwu as NNPC's group managing director, appointed Maikanti Kacalla Baru in his place, and dissolved and reconstituted the board. Kachikwu retained his posts as minister of state for petroleum and as the board's chairman. Victor Ndoma-Egba became chairman of the Niger Delta Development Commission (NDDC). The extension of Yemi Kale's tenure as statistician general of the Federation and as chief executive officer of the National Bureau of Statistics (NBC) for another five-year term, which took place in late October, was considered a rare case and an exception to the rule.

Soon afterwards, on 7 November, Sidi Dauda Bage and Paul Adamu Galinje were elevated to the *Supreme Court*, which brought the number of Supreme Court justices to 17 currently on the bench. On 10 November, against common practice, President Buhari swore in the most senior judge, Walter Onnoghen, as acting chief justice after the tenure of his predecessor Mahmud Mohammed had ended the previous day.

In November and December, President Buhari signed 17 bills into law including the 'Prevention of Crime Amendment Act 2016'.

The military redeployed their upper echelons at quite frequent intervals, an indication that *all was not well in the military*, particularly with respect to the ongoing insurgency in the Northeast. On 5 January, Major General Yusha'u Mahmood Abubakar handed over the command of operation 'Lafiya Dole' to Major General Hassan Umaru. Major General Lamidi Adeosun, general officer commanding (GOC) 7 Division, garrisoned in Maiduguri, was deployed to the MNJTF in N'Djamena (Chad) and replaced by Brigadier Victor Okwudili Ezeugwu. On 17 March, Hassan Umaru had to hand over his command to his deputy, Major General Lucky Irabor, and was assigned to the post of chief of training and operations, following the death of his predecessor Abubakar in a road accident not long before. On 14 July, Brigadier General Ali Nani emerged as the new GOC 8 Task Force Division.

Major General Kasimu Abdulkarim was appointed the new GOC 2 Division in Ibadan but later redeployed to take over as GOC of the newly created 6 Division in Port Harcourt. Brigadier C.M. Abraham became acting GOC 2 Division. On 19 November, Brigadier Ebenezer Oyefolu assumed office as GOC 81 Division in Lagos. Operation 'Delta Safe' in the *volatile Niger Delta* also saw a change of leadership when, on 17 November, Rear Admiral Apochi Suleiman replaced Joseph Okojie, making Suleiman the first naval officer in charge of military operations in the region. On 9 December, the army council approved the promotion of 21 brigadiers, 93 colonels and 113 lieutenant colonels to the next higher rank.

Earlier in the year, on 27 February, chief of army staff Lieutenant General Tukur Yusuf Buratai inaugurated a motorbike battalion in Damboa in Borno state to strengthen its counter-insurgency capability, and the army released a further list of 100 suspected members of Boko Haram wanted by the Nigerian state.

The compulsory retirement of dozens of high-raking military officers and several *courts martial* confirmed the incidence of widespread corruption and misconduct, which triggered a major shake-up of the top brass and investigations by the Economic and Financial Crimes Commission (EFCC) against former top military personnel such as retired Air Chief Marshal Alex S. Badeh. Between April and August, dozens of high-ranking officers were sacked for professional misconduct during the general elections in 2015 and the Ekiti gubernatorial election in 2014. In addition, others were sacked and investigated for gun running or for the illegal sale of military equipment. The most striking issue, however, was the alleged involvement of officers in the $ 2.1 bn arms procurement scandal, in which Sambo Dasuki, former security adviser to then president Jonathan, took centre stage.

In early May, two major generals, Ibrahim Sani and Patrick Falola, faced court martial behind closed doors for misconduct and dereliction of assigned duties. While Falola, former commandant of the Military Hospital in Lagos, was demoted to brigadier in September, the fate of Sani, the former chief of the Army Transformation and Innovation Centre, remained unclear. On 10 August, four officers and 16 soldiers were arraigned for having committed various offences within operation 'Lafiya Dole'. In early September, a brigadier was court martialled in a *secret trial* in Maiduguri on charges of selling arms to Boko Haram.

In contrast, on 1 March, the army council commuted the sentence of Brigadier Enitan Ransome-Kuti, who had been disciplined in 2015 for neglecting his military duties. He was demoted to the rank of colonel and the council also quashed his six-month prison term. However, the case highlighted that *procedures within the military* – the retiring or sacking of personnel regardless of their rank – were driven by dubious motives. Other senior officers, such as Major General Ijioma Ijioma and Lieutenant Colonel Mohammed Abdulfatai sought redress at the Industrial Court. The army council was notably absent and cases were still pending at year's end.

In the aftermath of the appointment of Ibrahim Kpotum Idris as the new inspector general, the *police forces underwent major changes*. No sooner had he taken office than he replaced the spokesperson Ms Olabisi Kolawole with Don Awunah. On 1 July, 21 assistant inspectors were compulsorily retired. In addition, within a period of less than four months, seven new deputy inspectors general and two dozen assistant inspectors general were appointed. Promotions and retirements notwithstanding, the police force also had to face adversity: on 23 November, a spokesman revealed that within the past three months 128 policemen had lost their lives in the line of duty, a figure which indicated a significant number of fatalities over the course of the year.

In Edo and Ondo states, statutory *gubernatorial elections* took place on 28 September and 26 November, respectively. The APC candidates, Godwin Obaseki and Rotimi Akeredolu, won the elections. Obaseki was finally installed as duly elected, while Akeredolu was to be inaugurated in February 2017. Earlier in the year, on 9 January, the *Independent National Electoral Commission* (INEC) concluded the ballot in Bayelsa state, which had been partially cancelled in some parts of the state in December 2015. The People's Democratic Party (PDP) incumbent, Seriake Dickson, already had a clear lead and eventually won decisively.

The *INEC* faced 680 legal challenges following the 2015 elections, although only 80 cases were dealt with by the courts. The outcomes of these trials affected federal and state constituencies, meaning that all the disputed governors-elect were eventually confirmed by the Supreme Court. Nevertheless, in Rivers state elections had to be postponed twice due to widespread violence, orchestrated unrest and killings across the state. On 10 December, the elections took place but they were marred by violence, despite the presence of thousands of policemen. The PDP defended its stronghold, but the APC took one senatorial district.

The *precarious security situation* in most parts of the country, often with an *ethnic and sectarian undercurrent*, had grave effects on human rights. On 31 May, Methodus Emmanuel, a trader, was killed in Rafi local government in Niger state by a mob accusing him of blasphemy. Three individuals, including Security and Civil Defence Corps personnel also fell victim to the mob. The issue of blasphemy triggered similar incidents in Kano's Kofar Wambai market on 2 June, where one Bridget Agbahime, an ethnic Igbo trader and wife of a pastor, was decapitated; in Talata Mafara local government in Zamfara state, on 22 August, a student and seven other people were burnt to death. Interestingly, the five suspected perpetrators of the Kano incident were discharged by a magistrate's court on 3 November.

In the aftermath of the killing by armed forces in Zaria in December 2015 of more than 300 members of the Muslim Brethren – also known as the Islamic Movement in Nigeria (IMN), who admire the Iranian revolution and consider themselves as 'Shiites' – the seriously injured leader of the sect, Ibrahim Zakzaky, was still in police custody at the end of the year. Zakzaky's residence was demolished by bulldozers. The official investigation into the killings was deliberately delayed and the Kaduna judicial commission of inquiry, which was boycotted by the IMN, eventually released its report on 31 July. On 6 October, the Kaduna state government declared the IMN to be an unlawful organisation and, in the days that followed, several members of the sect were attacked and killed in the states of Kaduna, Katsina and Sokoto and their properties and vehicles burnt or vandalised. These orchestrated acts were carried out by youth groups. Nevertheless, on 2 December, a federal court ordered the release of Zakzaky within 45 days.

In May, AI accused the military of being responsible for the deaths of babies, children and adults in detention centres, including the notorious Giwa barracks in Maiduguri. In another report, published in September, AI accused the police force, particularly the Special Anti-Robbery Squad (SARS) of *torture and accepting bribes in exchange for freedom*. The inspector general rejected the report as biased and inappropriate and maintained that the police had not been given a fair hearing.

In the so-called 'Apo killings case', the National Human Rights Commission (NHRC) had held the government responsible for the *extra-judicial killings* of eight squatters in September 2013. In June, the ECOWAS court imposed a heavy fine of $ 3.3 m on Nigeria. The Incorporated Trustees of Fiscal and Civil Right Enlightenment Foundation had taken the Nigerian government, the army and the state security service to the ECOWAS court on behalf of the deceased. Earlier, on 19 April, a federal high court in Abuja had rebuffed the federal government's intention of conducting the trial of former national security adviser Sambo Dasuki in secret.

Nevertheless, on 26 February, the Supreme Court once again upheld the legality of the *death sentence* when it confirmed the verdict on Chukwuemeka Ezeugo, popularly known as Reverend King, who had first been arraigned in 2006. Furthermore, Lagos state was in the process of amending the criminal code to allow the death penalty for kidnappers. If the amendment was passed, it would bring Lagos into line with Edo and Ondo states.

On 20 August, Ms Abiola Akiyode Afolabi was elected as chairperson of the *Transition Monitoring Group*, a coalition of around 400 civil society organisations.

Although the president and his government had vowed to take drastic measures against *corruption*, first results were at best mixed and the campaign was making no progress. The arrest of seven high ranking judges on 7 and 8 October on allegations of corruption was seen as a serious blow to the judiciary's reputation. It was reported that a silent power struggle between Justice Minister Abubakar Malami and some courts over the cautious handling of corruption cases might have triggered the arrests. In the end, the judges were released after a few days and were later suspended until further notice. One of the accused judges, Adeniyi Ademola, who was handling two delicate litigation cases concerning Sambo Dasuki and Nnamdi Kanu, was awaiting prosecution. On 21 December, 11 federal high court judges were redeployed, including Okon Abang and Mohammed Liman, who were among those suspended.

On 3 November, the Corrupt Practices and Other Related Offences Commission (ICPC) filed a nine-count charge against Gambo Saleh, the outgoing chief registrar of the Supreme Court, and two other members of staff for diverting NGN 2.2 bn. Shortly before, Saleh had been confirmed by the National Judicial Council to take over as the Council's secretary in mid-2017.

Much earlier, on 2 May, Vice President Yemi Osinbajo acknowledged that about $ 15 bn, provided to support the counter insurgency in the Northeast, had been diverted through *fraudulent arms contracts and theft*. Furthermore, the publication in 'Premium Times' on 5 May of a list of more than 100 prominent Nigerians named in the database known as the 'Panama Papers' had no apparent impact on the investigations.

Apart from taking legal action, the EFCC tried to recover funds by targeting high-ranking former politicians and administrative officers such as Senator Iyiola Omisore, Musiliu Obanikoro and the former comptroller general of the customs service, Abdullahi Dikko, and was successful in recovering more than NGN 1 bn from the former customs boss.

Foreign Affairs

The *relationship with the USA continued to improve*. On 9 February, at a meeting in Washington DC on the regional impact of Boko Haram, Assistant Secretary of State for Africa Linda Thomas-Greenfield announced the resumption of training programmes for Nigerian soldiers, experts on cybercrime and the police, which had been aborted under Buhari's predecessor, former president Jonathan. Soon afterwards, the president returned to Washington to take part in the Fourth Nuclear Security Summit on 31 March. On 20 September, he addressed the 71st session of the UN General Assembly in New York, and held talks with President Obama.

On 30 March, US Secretary of State John Kerry hosted a meeting of the *bi-national commission* and, on 22–23 August, Kerry was in Nigeria on a two-day official visit, where he was received by Nigeria's president in Abuja. One important item on the agenda was talks with the Sultan of Sokoto, the spiritual head of Nigeria's Sunni Muslim community, and with governors from the crisis-ridden North in the Sultan's hometown Sokoto. However, the meeting did not go down well with the Christian Association of Nigeria (CAN), which was denied a meeting with Kerry and accused the US of bias. Later in the year, on 18–20 October, those governors from the North attended a three-day symposium organised by the US Institute of Peace in Washington. In addition, Shaarik Zafar, the State Department special representative to Muslim communities, visited Nigeria on 17–19 October as part of his maiden visit to SSA.

Earlier, Samantha Power, the US representative to the UN, had led a delegation of US military, intelligence officers, business people and the diplomatic corps to Adamawa state capital Yola, the seat of the American University of Nigeria (AUN), underlining their joint determination to defeat the Islamist insurgents and rebuild a *devastated Northeast*.

In June, it was reported that, despite improved relations, the issue of *repatriating looted funds* stashed in US banks by the former military dictator Sani Abacha had been delayed. The matter remained unresolved. According to the US embassy, this was due to the cumbersome legal process and the complexity of the investigation.

On 30 August and 2 September, Facebook founder Mark Zuckerberg, on his first trip to SSA, paid a visit to the Yaba, the technological hub of Nigeria in Lagos, and to Abuja where he was received by President Buhari.

As in previous years, *Nigeria's relationship with Britain was shaped by various legal issues*. The extradition of Ms Franca Asemota, arrested in Nigeria in 2015, was delayed until 27 January. On 4 August, she was finally sentenced to 22 years' imprisonment by the Isleworth Crown Court in London for trafficking Nigerian girls to work as prostitutes across Europe.

Over the course of the year, there *was a further twist in the saga of James Ibori*, who was serving a 13-year prison sentence for money laundering and fraud. When the former Delta state governor was about to be released after serving more than half of his sentence, a British police officer was removed from the UK anti-corruption unit in May, after it emerged that he might have been paid for providing information in the case. More was to come when, in late November, the UK's Independent Police Complaints Commission (IPCC) launched a fresh investigation into alleged corrupt practices of further London Metropolitan Police officers in connection with the Ibori case. On 21 December, Ibori was eventually released, despite attempts by the British home secretary to keep him in prison, pending the ruling on a prolonged asset forfeiture case brought against him by the British government. The request was dismissed outright by a high court judge.

On 4 February, President Buhari attended an international conference on Syria in London. The previous day, he had addressed a special session of the European Parliament and held talks with the chairmen of the European Parliament and the European Commission. This was followed by another trip to London, where he participated in an anti-corruption summit on 12 May, and where, in early June, he underwent medical treatment. The result of the summit was a memorandum of understanding, signed on 30 August in Abuja, which was supposed to provide a mechanism by which *looted funds could be repatriated to Nigeria*, including an amount of £ 300 m kept in the Channel Islands, in Jersey. A similar agreement was reached concerning the return of illegal immigrants and visitors who had overstayed their visas. Earlier, on 13 April, the UK's Minister for International Development Nick Hurd arrived on his first trip to Nigeria.

Although advanced in years, Buhari kept a busy travel schedule, which took him in January to the UAE, where he attended the summit on future energy and signed agreements on returning stolen funds and on the extradition of convicted Nigerians. At the end of the month, he was on a three-day state visit to Kenya, from where he proceeded to the 26th AU summit in Addis Ababa (Ethiopia). In February, he participated in a business forum in Egypt, made the lesser Hajj in Mecca, and attended an OPEC meeting in Qatar. On 14–15 March, the president held talks in Malabo with the president of Equatorial Guinea on maritime security and returned on 23 November for the 4th Africa-Arab summit in the same city. In mid-October, he spent three days on a state visit to Germany, where he met Chancellor Angela Merkel and the then president, Joachim Gauck, whom he had received in Nigeria in February. Gauck had announced that the EU had pledged $ 50 m to support the fight against Islamist insurgents and the resettlement of IDPs. Against this backdrop, the sixth Nigeria-EU ministerial dialogue took place in Brussels (Belgium) on 16 March, focusing on strategic cooperation and migration issues.

On 14 November, Buhari went to the Moroccan city of Marrakesh for the summit on climate change (COP 22), and on 5–6 December, he travelled to Dakar (Senegal) for the International Forum on Peace and Security in Africa. A week later, on 13 December, the efforts of Buhari and his counterparts from Liberia, Ghana and Sierra Leone to persuade their host Yahya Jammeh to concede defeat in the recently concluded Gambian presidential election came to nothing. At the 50th ECOWAS Assembly in Abuja on 17 December, the Nigerian president was mandated to lead an *ECOWAS mediation team to The Gambia.*

The 27th AU summit in Rwanda in July was one of the few occasions in which Buhari was represented by Vice President Yemi Osinbajo.

When IMF Managing Director Christine Lagarde paid an official visit to Nigeria and neighbouring Cameroon on 4–9 January, Abuja was her first port of call. On 8–9 March, Buhari welcomed South Africa's President Jacob Zuma for a two-day state visit. He hosted the 2nd regional security summit on 14 May, which was attended, inter alia, by France's President François Hollande and the presidents of Benin, Cameroon, Chad and Niger. On 2 December, King Mohammed VI of Morocco arrived in Nigeria for a three-day official visit.

Political and economic relations with China were strengthened. Buhari visited Beijing on 10–12 April, with a large delegation of businessmen and ministers, aiming to attract several billion dollars in investment for infrastructure projects such as the coastal railway line, energy, gas and oil pipelines and the downstream sector. As a follow-up, Minister of State for Petroleum Ibe Kachikwu organised the first Nigeria-focused road show in Bejing at the end of June.

On 18 November, a Nigerian, Chijioke Obioha, was hanged in Singapore for *drug trafficking*. Earlier, at the end of July, three Nigerians, along with other foreigners and locals, were executed in Indonesia for similar offences, and more were awaiting execution. In Cambodia, on 6 December, a court dismissed an appeal by another Nigerian, Chineme Nwoko, by upholding a 27-year prison sentence for drug trafficking.

India retained its position as the major importer of Nigerian crude oil, receiving a total of 63 m barrels. In addition, towards the end of the year, Kachikwu negotiated a $ 15 bn oil-for-cash deal aimed at easing Nigeria's depleted reserves of foreign currency and India announced an increased demand for crude.

The *relationship with the UN remained friendly*. Soon after the election of the new Secretary General António Guterres in December, Ms Amina Mohammed, formerly Nigeria's minister for environment, was appointed as his deputy. Earlier, on 26 April, Abiodun Bashua emerged to lead the special investigation into an attack on the UN Mission in Malakal in South Sudan (UNMISS). Against the backdrop of increasing criticism of the ICC and the intention of some African countries to withdraw from the Rome Statute, the Nigerian government pledged its support on 3 November to improve the ICC's mandate.

Last but not least, on 2 June, Mohammed Sanusi Barkindo was appointed secretary general of *OPEC*. He assumed office on 1 August, becoming the second Nigerian to hold that post.

Socioeconomic Developments

Oil and gas prices remained low but gradually rose to above the $ 50 per barrel mark by the end of the year. Despite the modest recovery, renewed civil strife and frequent bomb attacks on pipelines by militia groups seriously affected production levels, which fell to 1.4 m b/d in May, far below the usual target of 2.3 m b/d. However, during the last quarter of the year, production rose, at least temporarily, almost to its normal level.

Foreign reserves decreased to $ 26 bn in December, although the excess crude account gradually recovered and reached $ 2.5 bn by the end of the year. The national currency was also under pressure at a time when the exchange rate had sharply depreciated to close to 500 NGN : $ 1 on the parallel market. The Central Bank eventually applied a currency rate of NGN 305 : $ 1 after it had, in May, rather reluctantly, and only after Buhari's apparent change of heart, allowed the naira to fall to that mark from the previous rate of some NGN 200 : $ 1. Despite the efforts of the Central Bank, the naira's massive fall, coupled with declining revenues from oil and gas exports, gave cause for serious concern both in business circles and among the wider public over the government's ability to handle financial and economic affairs. The government blamed the problem on numerous bureau de change operators who had broken the rules and had traded foreign currency far beyond their mandate. Accordingly, in November, state security staff clamped down on them, arresting about a dozen. Several offices were closed, and markets were raided in various parts of the country in search of illegal foreign currency hawkers.

As in previous years, the signing of the *2016 federal budget*, totalling NGN 6.1 trn ($ 30.8 bn) based on a benchmark of $ 38 per barrel of crude oil, a production of some 2.2 m b/d and an exchange rate of NGN 197 : $ 1 was delayed and only signed into law by the president on 6 May. The budget had already been passed by the National Assembly on 23 March but the president withheld his assent due to controversial projects either added or removed by the lawmakers.

Somewhat surprisingly, the government accepted a *budget deficit* of around 30%, to be financed by internal and external borrowing, the removal of kerosene and fuel subsidies and the imposition of new stamp duties. On 1 November, the government's proposal to borrow $ 30 bn over a three-year period was rejected by the

Senate. Against this backdrop, the AfDB approved a $ 600 m loan the following day, as the first tranche of a $ 1 bn budget support package.

Earlier, on 7 June, the World Bank approved an IDA credit of $ 500 m in support of a 'national social safety nets project', which laid the foundation for the establishment of the country's first system of this kind. Nigeria would contribute $ 1.3 bn.

The *high unemployment rate* particularly among young people, which the Central Bank and the National Bureau of Statistics estimated at almost 60%, prompted several social intervention projects worth billions of naira, among which were the Youths Entrepreneurship Support (YES), the N-Power and the Conditional Cash Transfer (CCT) programme. Inflation soared and soon reached the 18% mark, while the growth rate fell to almost zero, and, on 17 October, the finance minister announced the launch of a development bank early in 2017 aimed at providing small and medium-sized enterprises with easier access to capital.

On 14 December, the government presented its *2017 budget proposal* of NGN 7.3 trn ($ 24 bn), based on a benchmark of $ 42.5 per barrel of crude oil and an assumed production of 2.2 m b/d, while the exchange rate was pegged at NGN 305 : $ 1.

The *enduring power problems* took their toll. Despite billions of dollars having been spent during the previous decade and several restructuring and deregulation reforms, the total power generated by Nigeria's power stations for transmission and distribution was nowhere near the envisaged 6,000 MW. In April, for example, production was 3,700 MW, due to the crisis in the Niger Delta and the disarray within the power sector as a whole. The situation was no better by year's end. Interestingly, according to the Sahara Group, a leading privately owned power, gas and energy conglomerate, businesses and households spent an estimated $ 22 bn on fuel for their generators. Big companies such as the Dangote Group and other plants across the country, however, had built their own power plants and were generating more than 15,000 MW, for the exclusive use of their own companies.

Nigeria kept its position as Africa's largest and most *lucrative telecommunications market*. Almost half of the population had regular access to the Internet. The South African MTN Group saga, which had begun the previous year, was concluded on 10 June. Initially, the Nigerian Communication Commission (NCC) had imposed a fine of $ 5.2 bn – at that time equivalent to NGN 1.04 trn – on Africa's leading provider for failing to deactivate more than 5 m unregistered SIM cards. The fine was eventually reduced to NGN 330 bn, which included a 'goodwill' payment of NGN 50 bn made in February. Accordingly, on 26 December, MTN paid the balance of NGN 30 bn for the current year, leaving the unpaid balance to be paid in tranches until May 2019.

Despite these problems, on 29 June, MTN, the sole bidder, won a 10-year licence to get access to a frequency spectrum, which made *4G LTE* services possible at a fee of about NGN 19 bn.

In addition, on 8 November, Nigeria reached a deal worth $ 5 bn with five international oil companies to cover outstanding financial obligations for joint oil and gas exploration and production. Over the years, Nigeria's state-owned company NNPC had refused to pay its dues and had amassed debts that it was now obliged to pay. Inter alia, this issue highlighted the fact that Nigeria's oil and gas exploration and production costs were comparatively high.

On 29 June, Captain Elechi Amadi (rtd), author of works such as 'Sunset in Biafra' and 'The Concubine', passed away at the age of 82. Later in the year, on 14 September, 93-year-old Ibrahim Dasuki, the 18th Sultan of Sokoto. He had been deposed by the then military dictator Sani Abacha in 1996.

Senegal

Mamadou Bodian

Although the 20 March constitutional referendum dominated domestic politics, it was the legislative elections scheduled for 2017 that was affecting the posturing of Senegal's political players by the end of the year. Other important events included the presidential pardon granted to Karim Wade and the revision of the electoral rolls for the next parliamentary elections. President Macky Sall regained the confidence of key partners and donors. Despite Senegal's being one of the most competitive countries in West Africa, economic performance was poor. Unemployment remained high, especially among the youth.

Domestic Politics

The political atmosphere grew very tense as the country approached the 20 March *referendum* on 15 constitutional amendments. The proposal was submitted by President Macky Sall and his ruling 'Benno Bokk Yaakaar' (BBY) coalition. Sall, elected in 2012, unilaterally announced a reduction of the presidential term from seven to five years, saying he wanted to set an example for other African countries.

 | DOI 10.1163/9789004355910_018

However, in February, he sought the advice of the Constitutional Council – the highest body for the interpretation of the constitution – which ruled that Sall had taken an oath to serve for seven years and so could not shorten his current term. While the presidential majority, comprising the ruling 'Alliance Pour la Republique' (APR) and its allies such as the former ruling 'Parti Socialiste' (PS) and the 'Alliance des Forces de Progrès' (AFP), campaigned for a 'Yes' vote, a majority of the opposition forces – including Abdoulaye Wade's 'Parti Democratique Sénégalais' (PDS) and 'Rewmi', led by former prime minister Idrissa Seck, together with civil society groups such as 'Y'en a Marre' ('We're Fed Up') – joined forces in a loose political platform called the 'Front du non' ('No Front'). They argued that Sall was not bound to follow the Constitutional Council's ruling because it was an advisory rather than a mandatory decision.

On 20 March, 63% of voters in the referendum approved the proposed changes, although turnout was only 38%. Sall's 2012 electoral promise to reduce the presidential term from seven to five years would only take effect from the next presidential election in 2019. Although the opposition criticised this measure, the 15 major provisions in the amendments were widely seen as progressive. They included an age limit of 75 for presidential candidates, the eligibility of independent candidates to stand in all elections, and constitutional recognition of the status of 'leader of the opposition' for the leader of the largest opposition party. The promotion of local governance and development through the creation of a 'Haut Conseil des Collectivités Territoriales' (High Council of Territorial Communities – HCCT) was also part of the proposed changes.

Following the victory of the 'Yes' campaign, political pressures threatened to impede the implementation of the proposed reforms. President Sall, who was seeking to build support around his reform programme, realised the urgent need to negotiate a post-referendum agreement on issues of national interest. On 28 May, he invited the country's opposition, members of the National Assembly, civil society organisations and religious leaders to participate in a *National Dialogue* at the Presidential Palace. The forum discussed political reforms, oil and gas management, security, and peace in Casamance. Discussions also touched on the health and education sectors, both of which faced repeated strikes. Some political parties, including 'Rewmi', and 'Bokk Giss Giss' led by Pape Diop (former president of the National Assembly and the Senate) refused to take part in the dialogue. Others responded positively and welcomed Sall's willingness to resolve major challenges through dialogue. They included the 'Parti Democratique Sénégalais' (PDS), the leading opposition party, which participated in the forum despite the ongoing imprisonment of many of its senior members, including Karim Wade, the son of Senegal's former president Abdoulaye Wade. The National Dialogue gave the opposition an opportunity to criticise some of the government policies that they considered inimical to democracy and the rule of law. Participating members of the PDS called on Sall to release Karim Wade, who had been in detention since April 2013 and had been sentenced in March 2015 to six years' imprisonment on charges of corruption and illegally accumulating a fortune during his father's 12-year rule.

Karim Wade's arrest and prosecution by the 'Cour pour la Répression de l'Enrichissement Illicite' (CREI), a special anti-corruption court, had been one of the high-profile cases in the crackdown on corruption waged by Sall and his release on 24 June after receiving a *presidential pardon* drew mixed reactions. On the one hand, his supporters claimed victory, arguing that his imprisonment had been politically motivated. However, the fact that Karim Wade was appointed by the PDS to be its presidential candidate in 2019 and yet left Senegal for Qatar immediately after his release put the party in an uncomfortable political situation and it remained unclear whether Karim Wade was eligible to run for the presidency. On the other hand, anti-corruption activists such as Mouhamadou Mbodj, the coordinator of the Forum Civil (the Senegalese chapter of TI), raised concerns about Sall's commitment to fighting corruption. Having initially been accused of accumulating a fortune worth more than $ 1.3 bn, Karim Wade had been fined only around $ 230 m as part of his sentence.

Some *institutional changes* and *electoral reforms* took place. Perhaps the most important was the creation of the HCCT under the revised constitution. The operation and authority of the HCCT were defined by the Organic Law adopted on 28 June. On 14 July, another Organic Law set the number of members of the HCCT at 150 'Hauts conseillers' (High Councillors), 70 of whom were to be appointed by the president of the Republic from civil society, socio-professional organisations, religious leaders and citizens, with the remaining 80 to be elected by the 27,000 departmental and municipal councillors by simple majority vote on a departmental list. Each department was allocated at least one but no more than three seats. The election took place on 4 September, though some parties such as 'Rewmi', the 'Grand Parti' led by Malick Gakou, and many others decided not to take part in what they considered to be a budgetary institution devoted to the resettlement of a political clientele. Despite these criticisms, the members of HCCT were inaugurated on 31 October to serve for a five-year term. This new consultative assembly was designed to support the territorial development process and as an instrument for implementing the third phase of the decentralisation policy launched by the government on 19 March 2013. It had 11 technical commissions and was presided over by the secretary general of the 'Parti Socialiste' (PS), Ousmane Tanor Dieng, also a member of the BBY coalition.

The *revision of the electoral rolls* for the 2017 parliamentary elections sparked numerous controversies, though all political actors agreed that such a revision might help to solve the recurring problem of the large number of citizens who had not taken part in elections for a very long time. The main controversy concerned how such individuals should be excluded from the electoral list. In the view of the ruling party, this could only be done through a physical audit of voters. On 11 August, the National Assembly adopted a draft law on the partial revision of the electoral rolls, despite concerns expressed by the opposition during the various working sessions with Minister of the Interior and Public Security Abdoulaye Daouda Diallo. In their effort to ensure that the electoral process would be transparent and protected from fraud, the authorities decided to couple the revision of the electoral rolls with the introduction of biometric identity cards, which ECOWAS had established in March. The primary aim of the cards was to make it possible for residents of the region to travel freely between member countries. However, in Senegal, the new identity card would also serve as a voter identity card for the 2017 legislative elections. Although the Ministry of Interior set up hundreds of permanent and mobile registration centres throughout Senegal and abroad, applications for the new card remained slow at the end of the year.

The instability of the Sahel region increased the fear of *terrorist activities*, given that some Senegalese nationals were suspected of having close ties with Boko Haram and the Libyan branch of the so-called Islamic State. Following terrorist attacks in Mali, Burkina Faso and Côte d'Ivoire in 2015, the authorities worried that Senegal could be a potential target. Early in the year, the intelligence and security forces arrested some imams and radical preachers across the country and security was tightened around leading hotels and other places in the capital, Dakar. The state authorities initially decided to cancel Senegal's annual *Saint-Louis Jazz Festival* scheduled for 4 May, but they eventually reversed this decision and the governor of Saint-Louis, Alioune Aidara Niang, took extra security measures. On 1 June, a court in Kolda (in southern Senegal) sentenced Islamic preacher Ibrahima Seye, arrested on 9 October 2015, to one year in prison for glorifying terrorism and religious intolerance. On 11 October, prosecutors appealed against the sentence on the ground that it was too light and it was increased to a minimum of 30 months in prison.

Lengthy pre-trial detention and harsh prison conditions, including overcrowding, were the most significant human rights concerns. On 17 March, Paul Prince Johnson, a Swedish detainee, died in prison in Diourbel region. The government's post-mortem examination attributed his death to natural causes but AI reported that he had died as a result of inhumane treatment by correctional officers. On 20 September, hundreds of prisoners in Rebeuss, Dakar's oldest and largest prison facility, engaged in a two-week hunger strike to protest against detention without trial for lengthy periods and poor prison conditions. This hunger strike culminated into a prison riot, during which at least one prisoner died and many others were wounded. Following these incidents, Minister of Justice Sidiki Kaba announced that the state authorities would construct additional prison facilities and hire more prison staff.

Reporters Without Borders' World Press Freedom Index ranked Senegal 65th, up from 71st place in 2015. Although independent journalists regularly criticised the government without facing reprisals, censorship and content restriction did occur. On 20 March, the day of the referendum, the authorities attempted to shut down the daily newspaper, 'Wal Fadjri', for allegedly violating the electoral code by announcing election results while the polls were still open.

In the southern Casamance region, between the Gambia and Guinea-Bissau, *deforestation* associated with illegal timber trafficking raised concerns. On 27 May, Senegalese environmental activist and former minister of ecology, El Ali Haidar, disclosed at a press conference in Dakar aerial footage taken during a research trip that showed rosewood logs being collected in Senegal and dropped in neighbouring Gambia, where depots were operating about half a mile from the border. Much of the wood was said to be sold to China. The Senegalese authorities announced new measures to fight timber trafficking. A de facto ceasefire between Senegalese security forces and armed separatists had been in place for many years and France lifted travel warnings concerning Casamance in October. This was likely to boost the tourism industry.

Foreign Affairs

On 4 June, Senegal hosted the 49th Ordinary Session of the ECOWAS Authority of Heads of State and Government. During the summit, Liberian President Ellen Sirleaf Johnson was elected chairman of ECOWAS, taking over from President Sall who had held the position for a year. The summit also deliberated on important issues including the EPA between ECOWAS and the EU, and a report by the Mediation and Security Council.

Taking part in *peacekeeping operations* continued to be a major component of Senegal's foreign policy and defence strategy. In July, Senegal deployed 175 troops in the UN Multidimensional Integrated Stabilization Mission in Mali (MINUSMA), established by the UNSC on 25 April 2013 to support political reconstruction processes in Mali. The mission of this fourth contingent would last for 12 months and would support Malian authorities in the areas of security, stability and the protection of civilians.

Senegal's *relationship with the Gambia* had been dysfunctional over recent years as President Yahya Jammeh had used the Casamance crisis and border closures as leverage when engaging with Senegalese authorities. The border crossing point from the Gambia to Senegal had been at the centre of a long diplomatic row between the two countries, given that a ferry was the only means of crossing the River Gambia to reach Senegal's southern region of Casamance. In mid-February, the Senegalese transport union decided to boycott the Trans-Gambia Highway and divert traffic to eastern Senegal following a decision by the Gambian authorities to increase tariffs on Senegalese trucks crossing into the Gambia from CFAfr 4,000 (approximately \$ 7) to CFAfr 400,000 (\$ 700) per truck. On 15 May, talks between Gambian and Senegalese authorities opened in Dakar to end the 'blockade', which had resulted in significant losses of revenue for both countries. On 25 May, Senegalese road transport unionists ended the boycott after the Gambian authorities decided to scrap the disputed tariff. Beside the boycott and blockade, officials from both countries discussed the possibility of constructing a bridge across the River Gambia to replace the ferry. The AfDB was expected to provide the necessary funding for its construction. The relationship between Senegal and the Gambia took a new turn following the December post-election crisis in the Gambia. President Sall was a key ECOWAS negotiator for a return to constitutional order after long-serving president, Yahya Jammeh, decided to cancel the election results and order a rerun of the 1 December presidential polls, after earlier conceding defeat. Although Sall did not dismiss military intervention to unseat Jammeh, he considered this a last resort. At the end of the year, ECOWAS leaders were still seeking a diplomatic solution to unblock the political stalemate, with Jammeh refusing to concede defeat and hand over power to Adama Barrow, the winner of the presidential elections, and Barrow taking refuge in Senegal.

Senegal remained one of *France*'s main partners in Africa. On 2 March, Foreign Minister Mankeur Ndiaye met in Paris with France's Minister of Defence Jean-Yves Le Drian and Secretary of State for Development and Francophonie André Vallini. On 28–30 March, Vallini met with Senegalese authorities in Dakar. Several topics were discussed, including the development of Senegal, economic cooperation and intelligence sharing to strengthen cooperation on security matters. On 22 September, during a 24-hour visit to Senegal, French Prime Minister Manuel Valls responded to former president Nicolas Sarkozy's controversial comments on France's Gaulish heritage, arguing that the country was stronger because of its diversity. On 18 December, President Sall arrived in Paris on a four-day state visit, the first since Abdou Diouf's in 1992. He met with the French president, the prime minister, the presidents of the Senate and the National Assembly, the mayor of Paris and international business leaders. Sall also travelled to Strasbourg to visit Alstom, the train manufacturer that had just won the Regional Express Train (TER) contract – a project on which work began on 14 December. The French energy group Engie, in partnership with Thales, would design and produce the railway system, which would connect Dakar with its new airport, Blaise-Diagne International Airport (IABD) in Diass (south-east of the capital). The TER project was estimated to cost CFAfr 140 bn, nearly \$ 234 m.

Intelligence and military cooperation became a centrepiece of Senegal's foreign policy, and state officials increased security efforts to counter potential terrorist threats. On 8 February, Senegal hosted for the third time the annual US-led counter-extremism 'Flintlock' exercises for West African forces. This joint exercise was aimed at increasing military cooperation across and security in West Africa, while promoting information sharing and developing interoperability among participating nations. The exercises took place at multiple locations, including at the Senegalese military training base in Thies (70 km from Dakar). Additional training locations included Podor, Bakel, Saint Louis and sites in Mauritania. On 2 May, Senegal and the USA signed a defence cooperation agreement to upgrade an agreement in existence since 2001. The new agreement reflected the many security interests shared by the two countries, including joint military training exercises and the ability to respond to humanitarian and security crises. Senegal's Minister of Foreign Affairs Mankeur Ndiaye argued that the agreement was designed to facilitate the continued presence of the US military in Senegal. On 5–6 December, President Sall convened the *Third Dakar International Forum on Peace and Security in Africa* on the theme: 'Africa and Its Security Challenges: Perspectives for Effective Solutions'. With support from the AU, this two-day forum was attended by African leaders and representatives of regional and international organisations and provided an opportunity to discuss security-related challenges on the continent.

After years of appeals from victims, the former ruler of Chad, *Hissène Habré*, was sentenced on 30 May to life imprisonment for crimes against humanity, war crimes and torture by the Extraordinary African Chambers, an AU-backed special criminal court in Senegal. The trial commenced after a nearly 25-year campaign to bring to justice the former Chadian dictator, who had lived in Dakar since fleeing Chad in 1990. This was the first trial in Africa that relied on the principle of international law and universal jurisdiction, allowing a court to hear a case concerning gross human rights violations committed abroad by foreign actors against foreign victims.

The *relationship with Israel* was marked by diplomatic tension. On 23 December, Senegal, which had become a member of the UNSC for 2015–17, defended its vote in favour of the UNSC resolution condemning Israeli settlements in Palestinian territory as a flagrant violation of international law. Israel decided to recall its ambassador to Dakar and to suspend its aid programme to Senegal, but denied reports of a permanent break in relations.

President Sall and Minister of Foreign Affairs Mankeur Ndiaye took regular trips around Africa and the world. Sall attended the 16th Summit of the OIF on 24–25 November in the Madagascan capital, Antananarivo. On 14 October, he left for Lomé (Togo) to attend an AU Summit on Maritime Safety and Security. On 3–6 August, Ndiaye made a three-day official visit to Japan, a strategic partner of Senegal in the implementation of numerous development projects, particularly in the field of hydraulics. On 10 March, Sall went to Saudi Arabia to attend the closing of the joint military exercise 'North Thunder'. Senegal also welcomed to Dakar many heads of state and diplomats. These included Italian Prime Minister Matteo Renzi on 2 February, Canada's Minister for International Development and La

Francophonie Marie-Claude Bibeau on 31 August, King Mohammed VI of Morocco on 6 November, and President Denis Sassou-Nguesso of the Republic of Congo on 1 December.

Socioeconomic Developments

With a GDP of $ 15.2 bn, Senegal performed poorly on *human development* indicators. Senegal's HDI score for 2015 was 0.466, compared with the global average of 0.883, making it 170th out of 188 countries. *Inflation* remained low, but reached 1% at the end of the year in contrast with a moderate trend of 0.1% in 2015, according to the National Agency for Statistics and Demography (ANSD). Public debt rose to 57.2% of GDP from 56.7% in 2015.

The government *budget* increased from CFAfr 2,869 bn in 2015 to CFAfr 3,022 bn. With recurrent expenditure capped and a rise in tax revenue (surpassing 20% of GDP), the fiscal deficit fell from 4.8% of GDP in 2015 to 4.2%. The subsequent improvement of the government's fiscal position provided room for public investment. In the budget, the government focused on 19 projects under the 'Plan Sénégal Emergent' (PSE), including the Thies-Touba Highway, to foster the structural transformation of the economy. Work at the AIBD had stopped at the end of 2015 but, on 5 February, the Senegalese authorities signed a contract with the Turkish companies Summa and Limak, which would take over from the Saudi Binladin Group (SBG) for the completion of the work. Railway infrastructure was being upgraded and, on 14 December, President Sall officially launched the project to build the TER to connect Dakar with the AIBD. The goal was to help to reorganise and rebalance urban environment in Dakar, to achieve the GDP growth level defined in the PSE.

Bureaucratic blockages and a *challenging business climate* slowed down the implementation of economic planning. Senegal ranked 153rd out of 189 countries in the World Bank's Ease of Doing Business report, compared with the average ranking for SSA of 142nd. Public sector corruption remained an issue despite efforts to combat it. In January 2014, the National Assembly had passed a law requiring state and elected officials and managers of public funds of more than CFAfr 1 bn ($ 1.7 m) to disclose their assets to the 'Office National de Lutte Contre la Corruption' (National Anti-Corruption Commission – OFNAC), but the government had often not enforced the law effectively. On 25 May, OFNAC published it first annual report, which singled out some of the president's allies as among the most corrupt. On 25 July, two months after the report was published, Sall dismissed the OFNAC president, Nafy Ngom Keita and replaced her with Seynabou Ndiaye Diakhaté.

Despite the vulnerability of the overall regulatory environment, the 2015–16 World Economic Forum ranked Senegal as one of the most competitive countries in West Africa (110th out of 148 countries worldwide). Senegal was receiving technical support from the IMF for 2015–17 under a Policy Support Instrument (PSI) to back the implementation of the PSE. The IMF's second review mission in March concluded that the PSI implementation continued to be satisfactory.

Although the *electricity* supply suffered from structural difficulties, new power plants were about to be connected to the electricity grid. On 3 November, President Sall inaugurated a solar energy station at Malicounda (western Senegal) built under a concession contract between the Senegalese national electricity company (SENELEC) and the Italian company Solaria Group, which invested CFAfr 22 bn (approximately $ 35 m). The plant was projected to supply 9,000 households with an annual production estimated at 36 GWH.

Poverty remained high, affecting 47% of the population and *unemployment* continued to be a major concern. According to the national employment survey, unemployment was estimated at 16.6% for Senegalese over 16 years of age in the fourth quarter of the year. Although inequality remained moderate, geographic disparities were very noticeable, with almost two out of every three residents considered poor in rural areas in contrast with one in four in Dakar. On the social front, major *strikes and demonstrations* took place throughout the year. From the beginning of the year to April, university professors' unions, particularly the 'Syndicat Autonome de l'Enseignement Supérieur' (SAES), organised periodic demonstrations to push the government to respect commitments made following the signature of a memorandum of understanding in March 2015. These commitments included the upgrading of university budgets, the reform of academic qualifications, medical care for teachers, and university professors's right to housing. On 20 December, health unions (including Sames, Syntras, Sudtm and Cnts/Santé), which had previously come together under a united front called '2SAU', held a public demonstration in Dakar after several rounds of unsuccessful negotiations with government officials. They urged the government's 'Agence de la Couverture Maladie Universelle' (Universal Health Coverage Agency – CMU) to pay medical bills and demanded that doctors' salaries and allowances be brought into line with those of other senior public sector workers. On 28 April, security forces arrested four members of the 'Non aux APE' coalition, including coalition leader Guy Marius Sagna. They were protesting against the signing of an EPA between the EU and 16 West African states, ECOWAS and the West African Economic and Monetary Union (WAEMU). On 6 June, they were released without charge.

Sierra Leone

Krijn Peters

With President Koroma halfway through his second and final five-year term, the country slowly started to prepare for the next presidential elections. A population census, critical for voter registration, published its findings in April and provoked protests by the main opposition party. The census itself and also the elections had been postponed several times due to the Ebola Virus Disease crisis of 2014–15. Sierra Leone declared itself Ebola free – for the second time – in March. The health crisis resulted in about 4,000 Sierra Leonean deaths and had a major impact on the economy. This, combined with a fall in world prices for iron ore, led to a major contraction of the economy. Nevertheless, growth rates were positive for the first time since 2014.

Domestic Politics

On 13 March, halfway through his second term, President Ernest Bai Koroma of the ruling All People's Congress (APC) party announced a major *cabinet reshuffle* that brought in 13 new ministers and deputy ministers. Sylvia Okayinka Blyden became

 | DOI 10.1163/9789004355910_019

the new minster for social welfare, gender and children affairs, replacing Alhaji Moijueh Kai-Kai, who had recently been sacked along with his male deputy minister. The new minister of works, housing and infrastructure, responsible for one of the largest budgets, was Ibrahim Kemoh Sesay. Sesay had been minister of transport and aviation in 2008 when he was sacked following an investigation into the arrival of a plane with 700 kg of cocaine on board, for which his brother was arrested. Mohamed Bangura, the former leader of the United Democratic Party, became the new minister of information. He replaced Alpha Kanu, who kept a government position as special presidential advisor, a strategy Koroma had often followed in the past to deal with dismissed ministers. Alfred Paolo Conteh was appointed as the new minister of internal affairs. Conteh, a retired army major, had previously been the coordinator of the National Ebola Response Centre, which had been criticised by Auditor General Lara Taylor-Pearce for the way it handled significant sums of aid money. Other appointments included Momodu Kargbo as the new minster for finance and economic development, Nanette Thomas as minister of political and public affairs and Ahmed Khanou as the new sports minister, replacing the disgraced Paul Kamara, who had told the Sierra Leone Football Association to pay nearly SLL (leone) 125 m to be allowed to use the National Stadium for the national team's African Cup of Nations (AFCON) 2017 qualifiers and a friendly match against Malawi. Maya Kaikai became the new minister for local government and rural development and Sidi Yahya Tunis, the former communications director at the Ministry of Health and Sanitation, was appointed as minister of tourism. Tunis had been responsible for communicating health information to Sierra Leoneans during the Ebola crisis, and was rewarded with a ministerial post for his handling of the situation. Bai Mamoud Bangura, a fierce Koroma loyalist and presidential youth aide, became minister of youth affairs. Elizabeth Mans became the new minister for fisheries and marine resources. The changes resulted in Koroma's cabinet having four female ministers. Brigadier General John Milton became the chief of defence staff, with Captain Abdul Rahman Kamar (rtd) named as deputy defence minister. Dr Kaifala Marah, the sitting minister of finance and economic development praised for his many policy reforms during his tenure, became the governor of the Bank of Sierra Leone. He was seen as a possible future presidential candidate.

Provisional results of the *population census*, conducted in December 2015, were released in April, a prerequisite for the 2018 presidential elections, and showed that the population had increased by more than 40% between 2004 and 2015, from 5.0 m to 7.1 m. The $ 10.5 m survey had become political dynamite and it did not take long for the opposition party, the Sierra Leone People's Party, to point out that the population increase had taken place in areas that had traditionally voted for the incumbent party. It further accused APC loyalists of taking key positions in administering the census, which had been postponed twice because of the Ebola crisis. Nevertheless, Gabriel Rugalema, the UN resident coordinator for the census, applauded it, and the quick release of provisional results. The official figures, published in December, showed that at the start of 2016 Sierra Leone's population stood at 7,092,113.

In response to the severe austerity measures announced by the government in October and November, Alie Kabba, the opposition leader and presidential hopeful, said, "The recent abrupt elimination of fuel subsidies by the All People's Congress government and its cascading killer effects, poses very serious threat to the livelihood or ordinary citizens and dangerously toys with the very stability of the state." The cut in oil subsidies was part of a package of measures to reduce the government deficit.

On 16 March, former Civil Defence Forces leader Moinina Fofana was denied bail after breaching the terms of his early release. He was arrested on 10 March for three breaches, which could lead to a new trial and imprisonment. He had been convicted in 2008 by the Special Court for Sierra Leone, and ordered to serve a 15-year prison term but in 2015 he had been granted early release from his imprisonment in Rwanda, where he was serving his sentence, and it had been agreed that he could complete his term on parole.

On 8 June, a spokesperson for the *Special Court for Sierra Leone*, which had completed its activities when it sentenced former Liberian warlord-turned-president Charles Taylor to prison in 2013, announced that another war criminal, Alex Tamba Brima, sentenced in 2008 and serving a 50-year prison sentence in Rwanda, had died at the age of 44. Brima had been one of the leaders of the Armed Forces Revolutionary Council, which overthrew the democratically elected government of Tejan-Kabbah in 1997 and subsequently ruled the country together with the main rebel movement, the Revolutionary United Front of Sierra Leone, during the decade-long civil war. According to the Special Court statement, Brima died at King Faisal Hospital in Kigali (Rwanda) as a result of a serious illness.

Foreign Affairs

On 4 June, during the 49th Ordinary Summit of the ECOWAS Authority of Heads of State and Government, it was agreed that President Koroma, together with the heads of state of Guinea and Senegal, would meet with the key stakeholders in the on-going Guinea-Bissauan political crisis to look for a peaceful solution. On 10 September, both presidents visited Guinea-Bissau as part of the mediation mission.

On 30 June, Sierra Leone's deputy high commissioner to Nigeria, Alfred Nelson-Williams, was *taken hostage* while travelling from Abuja to Kaduna by road. He was released five days later, on 5 July. According to presidential spokesman Abdulai

Baraytay and Deputy Information Minister Cornelius Deveaux, the release was the result of quiet diplomacy. No Sierra Leonean diplomat had been kidnapped for over half a century.

On 6 July, the AU announced that it wanted to pull its AMISOM troops out of Somalia by the end of 2020. Sierra Leone was contributing hundreds of troops to the AMISOM mission.

In November, the Sierra Leonean Armed Forces conducted a *joint military exercise* with the British Army in the Guma Valley, close to the capital Freetown. The jungle warfare training was the first such joint training exercise and was the result of closer military ties between the two countries, initiated under the British dominated International Military and Advisory Training Team (IMATT) Sierra Leone mission, later followed up by International Security Advisory Team (ISAT) Sierra Leone.

Socioeconomic Developments

On 7 September, at a forum in Guangz-hou (China), the World Bank and the Chinese National Energy Administration signed a contract for investment in an *ethanol and biomass project* in Sierra Leone. About 10,000 ha of sugar cane were already under cultivation for ethanol/biofuel production by Addax/Sunbird, a different company, close to Makeni.

Following a visit by an IMF mission between 14 and 27 September, the IMF stated that economic reforms implemented over the previous three years had resulted in economic growth, despite the set-backs caused by the 2014–15 Ebola crisis and a significant drop in world iron ore prices, a major source of export revenue. The 2013 growth rate of 20.7% had dropped to 4.6% in 2014 and had become negative growth of -21.1% in 2015, but *economic growth returned to the positive*, starting from the last quarter of 2015, mainly on the back of new investments in the fisheries, agriculture and mining sectors, and stood at around 4.3%. The post-Ebola Recovery Strategy launched by the Koroma government in 2015 seemed to have started to pay off, focusing on the eradication of the Ebola Virus Disease (EVD); restoring health services; access to water and sanitation; education and protection of the most vulnerable; and economic sectorial response and prudent macroeconomic policies. Many of these points reflected the objectives outlined in the Agenda for Prosperity that had been launched by the government before the Ebola outbreak. Nevertheless, in July the IMF released figures indicating that per capital GDP levels would not return to 2013 levels till 2021.

On 30 March, the IMF concluded its fifth review under the ECF and the 2016 Article IV consultation. It recommended an increase in domestic revenue by removing tax exemptions put in place to lure multi-national corporations to invest in Sierra Leone. The IMF further recommended a broadening of the tax base and the removal of fuel subsidies. In October, the government announced that it would freeze all government projects and, in November, the government announced the end of fuel subsidies, which led to a stark increase in fuel costs. Fuel oil went up from 56 cents to 90 cents per gallon; gasoline and diesel from 67 cents to $ 1.7 per gallon. Furthermore, the government announced that it would implement stricter tax collection mechanisms and cut ministry budgets by scrapping overseas travel and overtime pay.

On 14 July, the World Bank Group approved a joint project with the IDA and the Multilateral Investment Guarantee Agency, to increase *electricity generation* for the capital Freetown. A 57 MW heavy fuel oil thermal power plant would be constructed under the Western Area Power Generation Project to end the recurrent electricity blackouts on the Freetown peninsular. The project was to be financed through a mixture of loans and guarantees worth around $ 200 m. Further improvement in the electricity grid was to take place under the on-going World Bank supported Energy Access Project and the Energy Sector Utility Reform Project.

On 14 January, WHO declared *Sierra Leone Ebola free* following a 42-day period with no new outbreaks. But just hours after the announcement was made in Geneva, a new Ebola case was reported: a 22-year-old woman died close to the Guinea border, resulting in the authorities quarantining 109 people, nearly 30 of them considered high risk cases. On 11 February, four people who had been in close contact with the country's last known EVD patient were released from quarantine. On 17 March, Sierra Leone declared itself Ebola-free for a second time, but vigilance remained in place as on the same day neighbouring Guinea reported two new cases. International support for both further socioeconomic recovery and better monitoring systems was still required. A stronger health and effective disease surveillance system was to be funded with $ 30 m of IDA finance, supported by the Bill and Melinda Gates Foundation and technical support by WHO. Neighbouring Guinea, equally affected by Ebola, and Senegal were also receiving funding under the Regional Disease Surveillance Systems Enhancement Programme. The West African Health Organisation received financial support of nearly $ 25 m to help improve information sharing, collaboration and strengthening the disease surveillance infrastructure in the region, including Sierra Leone. Further support was made available to the country by the World Bank through a $ 10 m IDA credit and a $ 5.5 m grant from the Ebola Recovery and Reconstruction Trust Fund. The project was announced on 30 June. On 9 June, China, through its economic attaché, declared its support for a tropical disease research and prevention centre. In December, the Canadian government announced that it had achieved a major breakthrough in the development of an effective Ebola vaccine. Merck & Co gained the licence to produce the vaccine, which would seek regulatory approval in 2017. The vaccine would provide protection against the Zaire strain, but not against to the Sudan strain of the virus.

On 1 August, UNICEF directed attention to the *high child mortality* in SSA. The UN singled out Sierra Leone, along with Chad, the CAR and South Sudan, as countries with very high child mortality and very high maternity death rates. The data published by the UN in October showed an under-five mortality rate of 161 deaths per 1,000 live births.

According to a report entitled 'Western Africa's Missing Fish' published in June by the UK-based Overseas Development Institute, Sierra Leone was missing out on $ 29 m annually due to *illegal fishing* mainly by South Korean trawlers. According to the report, 44% of all the fish caught illegally were destined for the European market. Moreover, the report accused the Sierra Leone government to sell off fishing rights to other countries, thereby depriving its own citizens of benefiting from the full potential of its territorial waters.

On 24 May, President Koroma launched the Bandajuma-Gendema *highway project*. Financed by the EU, the 103 km highway would link Sierra Leone with Liberia. The following day, Koroma also officially initiated the construction of nearly 33 km of highway between Moyamba town and Moyamba Junction.

On 31 May, the government announced that it would *cancel 57 permits for mining and exploration*. Director of Mines Peter Bangura said, "Companies have either failed to renew their licences or have not undertaken any mining or exploration activity since their licences were issued, despite repeated warning." Argosy Minerals Company, an Australian firm, was particularly affected by the decision.

In March, the World Bank, DFID and the government signed an agreement worth $ 40 m to support the Smallholder Commercialisation and Agribusiness Development Project. The project, worth $ 55 m, would run for five years and would help 50,000 smallholders to access markets, increase agricultural productivity and develop linkages between agribusinesses and farmers. Under the conditions of the project, 40% of the participants would be female and young farmers.

On 3 April, Airtel Sierra Leone commissioned a new data centre in Freetown, worth $ 10 m. Managing Director Dapo Olasope said that this should improve communication for consumers and that it could support 2,000 sites and serve around 10 m customers.

A *new international airport*, planned at Mamamah, Koya Chiefdom, was designed to improve access to the capital and the hinterland. The contract for its construction had been awarded to the Chinese Railway International Consortium in December 2012, but it had run into financial difficulties since then. In February, Koroma announced that he had secured another significant loan from China. The IMF and the World Bank were outspoken opponents of the airport, given Sierra Leone's debt burden. The government had never released the results of a feasibility study carried out by Ernst & Young.

On 3 October, the Mo Ibrahim Foundation published its 2016 Ibrahim Index of African Governance. Out of 54 countries, Sierra Leone was ranked 30th, with a score of 49.4 (out of 100) and with the ten-year trend seeing a slow but steady increase of 3.8 points.

On 16 August, *local protests* resulted in the death of one protester in Kabala in the far north of the country. Young people took to the streets to protest against the relocation of a job training centre. Demonstrators claimed it was a peaceful protest, while the police, who fired the fatal bullet, suggested that protestors had set fire to houses.

On 18 August, a teenage girl undergoing female circumcision (female genital mutilation – *FGM*) died. The girl's aunt and two other women were arrested. About 90% of Sierra Leonean females undergo FGM despite the fact that Sierra Leone ratified the 2003 AU 'Maputo' protocol banning it in 2015.

Togo

Dirk Kohnert

President Faure Gnassingbé acted throughout the year from a position of strength, given the divided and weakened opposition. Overdue political and institutional reforms and local elections were postponed indefinitely. The human rights situation improved slightly, but the regime continued to be describable as 'authoritarian'. In view of the growing jihadi risk in the sub-region, the international donor community rewarded Togo's apparent political stability as an anchor of security in West Africa with a substantial increase in development aid. With promising growth prospects, low inflation and an absence of major external shocks, the government was able to improve the macroeconomic situation.

Domestic Politics

President Faure Gnassingbé focused on foreign affairs and economic development as his overwhelming victory in the 2015 presidential elections consolidated his power base. The opposition coalition CAP 2015 ('Combat pour l'Alternance Politique en 2015'), which had been formed in 2015, remained intact, its main components

 | DOI 10.1163/9789004355910_020

being the 'Alliance Nationale pour le Changement' (ANC), the biggest opposition party, and three smaller parties, the 'Parti Démocratique Panafricain' (PDP), the 'Convergence Patriotique Panafricaine' (CPP), and the 'Parti pour la Démocratie et le Renouveau' (PDR). The opposition tried to mobilise the population to support the political and institutional reforms required for free and fair elections – key demands of the opposition. Local elections had been postponed for 30 years, following the last local elections on 5 July 1987, when the country was still under the late dictator Eyadéma Gnassingbé. During the political upheavals of the 1990s, local elections were not government priorities. In 2001, the government had provisionally installed special delegations intended to be in place until the next local polls. On 26 October, the Council of Ministers nominated new members of the special delegations in the prefectures of Anié and Bas-Mono. The opposition condemned this as a unilateral, partisan and unconstitutional measure. On 11 March, the cabinet had published a road-map for local elections, and in early December, Minister for Territorial Administration Payadowa Boukpessi announced that they would probably take place in July 2018. The opposition accused the government of playing for time in order to tailor the new electoral districts to its advantage. The upgrading of the former sub-prefectures of Mô, Agoè-Nyivé, Oti-Sud and Kpendjal-Ouest (replacing Naki-Est) to prefectures on 27 May was evidence of this view.

Apart from local elections, the demands of the opposition included a limit on presidential terms in office, a reform of the electoral system, a review of the rules applied to impunity for state representatives and the reform of the security services. All these issues should have been tackled by the High Commissariat for Reconciliation ('Haut-Commissariat à la Réconciliation et au Renforcement de l'Unité Nationale'; HCRRUN), which the government had created in 2015 to implement the 68 recommendations of the national Truth and Reconciliation Commission ('Commission Vérité, Justice et Réconciliation'; CVJR), assisted by a civil society platform ('Plateforme Citoyenne Justice et Vérité'; PCJV). However, in retrospect the creation of these institutions served to delay the reforms. In July, the government delayed the implementation of these reforms once again when it referred several outstanding issues to national discussion groups established by the government.

In this political stalemate, the Catholic Church intervened once more and expressed its support for political reforms in a pastoral letter on the occasion of the 56th anniversary of independence. The government was not pleased. Mgr Barrigah-Bénissan, the president of the CVJR, used the occasion of his participation in a national workshop of the HCRRUN in Lomé on 11–15 July to underline the consensus found during the workshop, which supported the limitation of the presidential mandate to two five-year terms and uninominal elections in two rounds for both the presidential and legislative elections. The workshop made three additional recommendations: first, the suppression of the Senate, i.e. the second chamber of legislation which had remained non-operational to date; second, the organisation of local elections following the Ghanaian model, i.e. without party political candidates; third, a more equitable delimitation of electoral districts.

On 28 June, the ANC and a smaller opposition party, the 'Alliance pour la Démocratie et le Développement Intégral', introduced a bill in parliament to amend nine articles of the constitution. The bill envisaged a partial return to the 1992 constitution (adapted to the needs of the ruling Eyadéma regime in a 'constitutional coup' of 2002), including a return to the presidential term limit, but this time dating from the beginning of the president's current term, and a return to a two-round majority system for presidential elections. Additional demands included granting the power to appoint members of the Constitutional Court to parliament instead of to the head of state, who had misused the prerogative in the past in order to install his followers.

The government remained firmly in control of the president. All so-called 'postes de souveraineté' (security, justice, economy, foreign affairs) were held by the ruling party. The Defence Ministry remained (as it had since 2008) in the hands of the president, apparently as precaution against coup attempts. In August, a cabinet reshuffle reduced the representation of women from four in 2015 or 17% (already a cutback from 26% in 2013) to 13%, i.e. three women, in the Ministries of Commerce, Literacy and Postal Services.

The government grew increasingly concerned that terrorist violence would spill over into Togo's territory, given the numerous terrorist incidents in neighbouring countries. The jihadist attack in Ouagadougou (Burkina Faso) on 15 January, the deadly assault on the tourist resort of Grand Bassam (Côte d'Ivoire) on 13 March, following on from the jihadist siege on the Radisson Blu Hotel in Bamako (Mali) in November 2015, all left their mark on the political discourse. The government had deployed more than 1,000 peacekeepers within the framework of the UN peacekeeping mission in Mali (MINUSMA). Five of them were killed in an ambush in central Mali on 29 May. Another peacekeeper from Togo and two Malian civilians were killed in November in an attack on a military convoy.

The growing jihadist threat prompted both the Christian churches and the Muslim Union of Togo ('Union Musulmane du Togo'; UMT) to condemn unanimously any form of terrorism. In February, the president of the UMT, Alhaji Inoussa Bouraïma, and his entourage had already organised a week-long awareness raising campaign in the Muslim communities of all prefectures of the country against the growing terrorist threat from Islamist groups like Boko Haram. Bouraïma repeated his warnings during the opening of Ramadan festivities in the Kégué stadium in Lomé on 7 July.

The human rights situation improved slightly. In 2015, the national human rights commission ('Commission Nationale des Droits de l'Homme'; CNDH) had complained of lack of resources and of the government's unwillingness to cooperate. On

March 11, parliament passed a bill to improve its organisational capacity. However, the local human rights organisation 'Collectif des Associations Contre l'Impunité au Togo' questioned the independence of the CNDH, criticising the influence of the executive within it. On 4 May, five new members of the independent watchdog, the High Authority for Audio-visual and Communication (HAAC), were elected by the National Assembly to supplement four other new members, who had been handpicked by the head of state. One of the latter, Pitang Tchala, a former minister of communications under the late General Eyadéma, became HAAC president. In late July, the opposition accused him of corruption, alleging that he had distributed money from the Presidency to silence more than a dozen journalists.

Following the first Universal Periodic Review (UPR) at the UN Human Rights Council (HRC, in Geneva) in 2011, Togo submitted its second national report on 17 August in order to prove its commitment to consolidating democracy and strengthening the rule of law and to show how it had implemented the 122 recommendations it had accepted in 2011. On 4 November, the UN HRC working group on the UPR adopted its report, which proposed 136 additional recommendations for the improvement of human rights and the rule of law in Togo. Child labour, particularly in the agriculture sector but also in quarries and sand mines, and human trafficking, especially of children, remained serious issues. The worst forms of child labour, including in forced domestic work, were also a result of human trafficking, according to the US Department of Labor 2015 findings published on 30 September. Also, followers of Sufi leaders, known as talibés, were forced to beg for money. AI stated in its November universal periodic review, titled 'A long way to go', that the human rights situation was stagnating. AI called again for the protection of the rights to freedom of association, peaceful assembly and expression in Togo, complaining that security forces had killed and injured many people during peaceful demonstrations, and arrested journalist and human rights defenders during the five-year survey period. It called on the international community to be more vigilant with regard to the human rights situation in Togo.

Both government and opposition made increasing use of Twitter and Facebook to reach their followers. Internet access also improved (7.3% of the population in 2016, against 2.4% in 2008). A major reason behind the growth of Internet access was the fast-growing mobile phone penetration (about 70% in 2014; a 93% growth rate since 2009). Freedom House's overall 'Freedom in the World Rating' improved from the overall status of 'not free' in previous years to 'partly free', mainly due to the peaceful conduct of the 2013 and 2015 elections. Freedom House's 'Freedom of the Press' for raised Togo two places, to 60th out of 100 countries moving it from the 'Not Free' category to 'Partly Free' as a result of improvements in the media environment during the 2015 election period. Opposition candidates had had equal access to the state media and enjoyed a better relationship with the regulatory body and journalists had had greater access to campaign rallies and other events.

The Economist Intelligence Unit's (EIU) Democracy Index 2015 for Togo remained largely unchanged, ranking Togo 130th out of 167 countries with an overall low score of 3.41 out of 10. Accordingly, Togo was still classed as an 'authoritarian regime'.

In view of the apparent unwillingness of the regime to effect any meaningful political change, the population became increasingly disillusioned and alienated by their political leaders. In the 'World Database on Happiness' (an index of subjective wellbeing), the Togolese were among the lowest of the 149 countries surveyed, which was confirmed by the UN World Happiness Report, which ranked Togo as one of the lowest country worldwide (155th out of 157, over the period 2013–15). Nevertheless, some improvements were undeniable. According to the Ibrahim Index of African Governance, Togo was among the top five countries for the greatest improvement in overall governance over the previous decade.

Foreign Affairs

In February, a mid-term-evaluation of NEPAD's APRM, aimed at enhancing good governance, was completed. It included stakeholder analyses of six West-African states (Togo, Ghana, Benin, Mali, Niger, Burkina Faso). The evaluation directed by the national APRM commission in Lomé was still in progress at the end of the year, including regional seminars for capacity building of civil society organisations (CSOs). In June, the first session of the UN Economic and Social Council to evaluate Togo's first Sustainable Development Goals (SDGs) progress report took place. Togo was the first of 22 pilot countries that had committed themselves to participate in this exercise. The report found that the most pressing issues to be solved up to 2030 were youth unemployment, coastal erosion and energy supply. A detailed plan to implement the 17 SDG goals was to be included in the National Development Plan (2018–22), to replace the 'Stratégie de Croissance Accélérée et de Promotion de l'Emploi' (2013–17). The report identified CSOs and the Togolese diaspora, including its remittances, as major actors beside the state for achieving the SDGs.

Togo continued to rank among the most corrupt African states (ranked 107th out of 168 countries, according to TI's Corruption Perception Index), and was also the major culprit in illicit financial transfers worldwide with illicit transfers from Togo representing the equivalent of 76.3% of GDP (2008–13) according to a World Bank study published in September. The most recent example was the Indian corporation WACEM (West African Cement) listed in the Panama Papers. WACEM is heavily involved in Togo's cement industry and has its headquarters in Tabligbo, 80 km north-east of Lomé. In addition, the opposition and media accused Prime Minister Komi Selom Klassou, who, together with other high ranking Togolese officials, was recorded in the Panama Papers as a shareholder in WACEM, of involvement in fraud.

In late October, an extraordinary AU joint summit on Maritime Security and Development in Africa of Heads of State and the AU Commission met in Lomé and adopted a charter on maritime security and safety. The charter was to be incorporated into the 2050 Africa's Integrated Maritime Strategy (adopted in 2012) and aimed at combating piracy, illegal fishing and oil bunkering, as well as trafficking in drugs, arms and human beings in the Gulf of Guinea.

Togo remained permanently reliant on foreign aid. In early January, Germany's Minister for Economic Development and Cooperation Gerd Müller visited Lomé with a business delegation, announcing a new dawn in Togolese-German relations. Berlin considered Togo an anchor of stability in the sub-region that deserved to be rewarded accordingly with an increase in aid of 50% over the commitments made in 2014. On 20 January, Gnassingbé initialled three financial conventions with the Islamic Development Bank (IDB) in Jeddah (Saudi Arabia). The IDB committed itself to a financial package of $ 194 m to boost infrastructure, education and energy projects. On 23 February in New York, Helen Clark of UNDP and Gnassingbé signed an urgency programme for community development. It would be co-financed by UNDP and amount to $ 258 m over three years (2016–18). On 27 April, the president inaugurated the Chinese Dayang motorcycle assembly plant in Notse, 96 km north of Lomé, which would produce over 3,000 bikes a year. In early May, Gnassingbé announced that Togo had joined the African Export-Import Bank (Afreximbank). The deal was expected to attract up to $ 1 bn to support trade activities and infrastructure development in Togo. From 20 July to 10 August, Togo issued its first sukuk-bonds (€ 228.7 m for 10 years, with 6.5% interest), an Islamic mode of financing, provided by a branch of the IDB. Togo was the third state within the UEOMA, beside Senegal and Côte d'Ivoire, to engage in this form of finance.

From 29 May to 2 June, Gnassingbé, escorted by high-ranking diplomatic and economic delegations, made an official state visit to China, which was followed by a visit to Germany on 8–13 June. By the end of the year, the EU, France and Germany had signed commitments totalling € 715 m (2014–20). Europe remained by far the largest provider of development assistance, followed by China. In early June, Beijing had committed itself to the equivalent of € 114 m in project aid, including co-financing the second phase of construction of Lomé-Tokoin airport, which was to be a regional transport hub, similar to the Lomé deep-water port that had been expanded in recent years with Chinese aid. In addition, both Germany and China pledged substantial support for the long-stalled joint Benin-Togo hydroelectric Adjarala Dam Project on the lower Mono River. However, Gnassingbé declared the project suspended on 28 December because of the heavy additional indebtedness that the implementation of the project would have entailed. Beijing pledged itself to cancel parts of Togo's debt and to apply more favourable concessional loans in future. In return, Lomé publicly supported Beijing in its dispute with the

International Court of Justice in The Hague (Netherlands) concerning its territorial claims in the South China Sea. In August, Gnassingbé made an official visit to Israel, his second in less than four years, consolidating the long-standing cooperation between Togo and Israel in security expertise. In return, Lomé offered Israel support at the UN and in the International Atomic Energy Agency vis à vis international criticism of its settlements on the West Bank and its refusal to open its undeclared nuclear facilities to UN inspectors. Shortly after the end of August, Gnassingbé was among the 35 African heads of state attending the grand sixth Tokyo International Conference on African Development (TICAD VI) in Nairobi (Kenya), with 10,000 delegates from the economic community, including 80 major Japanese companies, the first ever Japanese-African summit on African soil. French Prime Minister Manuel Valls again affirmed that Togo had moved in the right direction under President Gnassingbé when he visited Lomé on 28 October, the first visit of a French prime minister to Togo since 1989.

Socioeconomic Developments

Growth perspectives remained favourable with an average GDP growth rate of 5.5% (2015–18; GNI per capita: 1,228 PPP US$). Inflation remained low at about 2%. Multidimensional poverty continued to be high, affecting 55.1% (figures for 2015) of the population although it had decreased slightly since 2011 (59%). The exodus from rural to urban areas continued, with about 40% of the population living in towns, an increase of 160% between 1990 and 2014. Growing youth unemployment reached worrying dimensions. The government had tried to counteract this trend with limited success since 2011 with programmes for unemployed school leavers. The National Agency of Volunteers in Togo ('Agence Nationale de Volontariat au Togo'), which had replaced the 'Programme de Promotion du Volontariat au Togo' in June 2014, had attracted 2,334 volunteers, of whom 1,092 had found employment up to 2016. Overall, 8,906 volunteers (32% women) had participated since 2011 in one of the programmes, of whom 44% had found employment. Inadequate health conditions, notably for the rural poor, were also recognised by the government as major problem. Only 54% of the population had access to clean drinking water and 34% to sanitary facilities. In August, the government signed a Memorandum of Understanding with Ghana to construct a water pipeline from Sogakope on the Volta River to Lomé, in order to provide 4 m people with clean drinking water.

The budget for 2017 was adopted by parliament on 27 December, set at CFAfr 1,227.4 bn, an increase in public spending of 21.6% compared with the budget for 2016. The social sector accounted for 46.8% of expenditure but nothing was apparently provided for the overdue local elections. The ANC voted against the budget.

The EIU expected the deficit to decrease from an estimated 5.8% of GDP in 2016 to 5.5% in 2018.

Environmental degradation continued, with one of the highest deforestation rates in the world. The Environmental Performance Index (Yale University 2016) placed Togo at the bottom of global ranking (161th of 180 countries; score 46.1). Environmental laws and programmes had been adopted long ago but they were inadequate and the government was slow in its implementation. Deforestation rates remained high at an annual rate of 1.4% of the forest. In December, Togo and four neighbouring countries (Nigeria, Ghana, Benin and Côte d'Ivoire) agreed to ban imports of dirty fuels from Europe, which had been revealed by the Swiss campaign group, Public Eye, in September. They had discovered that retailers were exploiting weak regulatory standards in West Africa, dating from the colonial era, in order to dump diesel with toxin levels illegal in Europe and ranked by WHO among the top global health risks, associated with heart disease, lung cancer and respiratory problems. The new stricter standards limited sulphur in fuels from the current 3,000 parts per million to 50 (still above the EU limit of 10 ppm).

Economic freedom, as measured by the Heritage Foundation's Economic Freedom Index 2016, had improved substantially over the last four years (score: 53.6 – up 5.3 since 2012), making Togo's economy the 135th freest of 178 countries worldwide, and 29th of 46 countries in SSA. Thus, Togo moved for the first time out of the 'repressed' category, due to improvements in six of ten economic freedoms, notably investment, trade and business. Nevertheless, the overall Economic Freedom Status still remained 'mostly unfree'. Among the key constraints to promoting shared prosperity, the World Bank listed entry barriers, policies and regulations that distorted private economic activity, and high and distortionary taxation, as well as poor governance.

PART 4

Central Africa

Andreas Mehler

For both political and economic reasons, 2016 was a crisis-ridden year in the sub-region. Elections were held in six of its eight countries but, with the exception of those held in the CAR, they could hardly be interpreted as supporting democratic development. Deadly clashes related to the still bloody aftermath of the civil war in the CAR and Boko Haram insurgencies in the Lake Chad area, as well as domestic political struggles in Gabon and Congo and the constant recurrence of localised confrontations between rebel groups and the government in the DRC, perpetuated what might be seen as a sad routine, though a continuing drama for those directly affected. Oil economies in the sub-region did not manage to cope with the continually low world market oil prices. Both exports and imports, as well as government income and expenditure, decreased in the majority of countries. As new debts were acquired, the economic outlook for the coming two years was rather grim.

Democracy and Elections

With seriously flawed and manipulated elections in Chad, Congo, Equatorial Guinea and Gabon, plus the refusal of the DRC's President Kabila to step down at the end of his mandate, Central Africa again showed little sign of progress towards democracy. With the notable exceptions of São Tomé and Príncipe's routinely open elections and the shaky beginnings of a second democratic era in the CAR (after 1993–2001), prospects for democracy were bleak.

In the *CAR*, the period of transition to constitutional rule formally ended with the inauguration of the newly elected president, Faustin-Archange Touadéra, on 1 April. Results of the legislative elections were only announced later, however, so one core political institution was not yet in place. Both national elections were clearly competitive. In the presidential race, Touadéra's main competitor, Anicet-Georges Dologuélé, had a slight edge in the first round, but this was reversed in the second round, after a complex game of alliances. Another positive achievement was a reasonable 59% turnout on 14 February, given that the elections had to be conducted in the context of on-going localised violent conflicts. Just as in 1993 and 1998/99, international actors and their military presence made it possible for acceptable elections to be held, even though the necessary infrastructure was not guaranteed. This gave rise to doubts that the next elections would suffer from the same shortcomings as all elections between those dates. Another concern shared by both citizens and international partners was that the elections would be

 | DOI 10.1163/9789004355910_021

meaningless without peace. Even a few months after Touadéra's victory at the polls, his government looked ill-equipped to make progress in this regard.

Presidential elections in *Gabon* on 27 August promised to be a very tight contest between the incumbent Ali Bongo Ondimba and the former foreign minister and chairman of the AU Commission, Jean Ping. Ping was able to count on considerable support within Gabon's elite and also from abroad. Only after the election results were corrected did Bongo emerge with 50.7% of the votes, slightly more than Ping's official 47.2%, which led to an immediate challenge.

The *Chadian* presidential elections, held on 10 April in an atmosphere of distrust and fear, produced an expected victory for the incumbent, Idriss Déby Itno (with nearly 60% of the votes), which enabled him to start his fifth term in office. His main challenger, Saleh Kebzabo, despite representing a vast alliance of political parties, was credited with only 12.8% of the votes.

Rather similar results in *Congo*'s scandalous election farce on 20 March (60.2% of the votes going to the incumbent, Denis Sassou-Nguesso, while his main opponents, Guy Brice Parfait Kolélas and Jean-Marie Michel Mokoko, officially received 15.0% and 13.7%, respectively), confirmed a regional trend towards electoral manipulation, comprehensively discrediting elections as means to achieve a change of government.

Quite logically, domestic reactions in Gabon and Congo were wide-scale protests and post-electoral violence, which led to casualties in both countries. The still more *repressive nature of regimes* in Chad and Equatorial Guinea (where the incumbent, Obiang Nguema, was credited with 93.5% of the votes in the presidential elections of 24 April), prohibited such outcries in these countries. However, discontent in Chad was brewing beneath the surface, with civil society and youth groups daring to voice dissent.

The direction taken by the *DRC*, the sub-region's largest country by territory and population, was arguably key for political development in the entire sub-region. Throughout the year, intense debates on the political fate of the DRC's President Kabila did not arrive at a consensus. On the very last day of the year, an agreement between the main parties was signed, setting elections to be held at the end of 2017. Allowing Kabila to remain in office until then was balanced by (1) not allowing preparations for a constitutional referendum that could potentially change core elements of the fundamental law and (2) prohibiting him from running for another term. Enormous technical and financial challenges raised doubts as to whether this plan was realistic and whether Kabila might use this uncertainty to undermine the agreement with the ultimate aim of remaining in office, copying the strategies followed by most of his peers in the sub-region. This was indeed what Cameroonians could expect: Paul Biya would probably run again in the 2018 elections, since the ruling party's 2016 congress was postponed indefinitely and the party's politburo simply extended Biya's mandate as party president by five years, thereby automatically making him the party's candidate in the next race.

Even in São Tomé and Príncipe, the sub-region's only democracy (by most standards), presidential elections held on 17 July were not exempt from suspicion, as the Electoral Commission first announced a slight absolute majority for Evaristo Carvalho and then reduced the figures, necessitating a second round on 7 August. Carvalho then won unopposed after his main rival rejected the official results of the first round.

Instability, War and Peace

Massive escalations in electoral violence were related to manipulated election processes, as noted above, but they were by no means the only sources of serious confrontations.

In the *DRC*, according to the UN High Commissioner for Human Rights, at least 53 protesters were killed by security forces in September, a few months before the official end of Kabila's term in office, when there were no visible signs that he would step down. Bongo's election victory announcement in *Gabon* on 31 August triggered revolts in the two main cities. The National Assembly building in the capital Libreville was set on fire. Attacks on opposition headquarters resulted in two deaths and 19 supporters being wounded. During mounting tensions, as many as 100 people were reported to have been killed, making these confrontations the most serious in Gabon's history, including the aftermaths of the presidential elections in 1994 and 2009, which had also been marked by widespread violent protests against alleged manipulation. Casualty figures for post-electoral violence in *Congo* were difficult to confirm. After targeted attacks on government buildings in Brazzaville, allegedly by former 'Ninja' militiamen, of whom 12 were officially said to have been killed, the government started operations in the traditional hot-bed of contestation in the Pool area, where further assaults by the militia were reported. Local civil society groups estimated that several thousand citizens died, while international sources reported only several dozens.

Anglophone activists in the two English-speaking provinces of *Cameroon* called for separation, or at least more autonomy and recognition of group rights, in the most recent confrontation with the government. Secessionist sentiments had already appeared in the early 1980s and had escalated in the first half of the 1990s, but they were now fuelled by new trends towards centralisation, mostly within the legal system. When English-speaking lawyers went on strike in mid-October, teachers and students in the two provincial capitals of Bamenda and Buea quickly followed suit. Government repression led to the arrest of dozens of activists and the death of three protesters. Although the potential for further escalation mounted steadily, the government did not show any willingness to negotiate or to seek compromise.

After a period of relative calm in the *CAR* around the time of the elections, the second half of the year was marked by more frequent incidents involving violent confrontations. In different constellations and alliances over the territory, four different Séléka factions and four other politico-military movements competed for control not only with weak state security forces and considerably stronger peacekeepers, but also with the so-called Anti-balaka groups which were loosely linked to former president Bozizé (now in exile). The capital Bangui in particular, and the central area of the country, saw many deadly encounters, but the north-west and the south-east were not exempt from violence either. The UN peacekeeping mission met with only mixed success and was therefore strongly criticised by many domestic players, including some from within the government.

Apart from strictly political sources of conflict, other factors clearly played a role in the escalation of violence in rural areas, particularly in border regions. Some of the active rebel movements claimed *religious motivation*. Among those, *Boko Haram*, originally based in Nigeria, received the greatest share of media attention. There were no civilian casualties in Chad and the intensity of terrorist attacks decreased overall in Cameroon, although roughly 100 people were killed in suicide attacks, concentrated in the first quarter of the year. In addition, the Cameroonian army crossed the border into Nigeria as part of the Multinational Joint Task Force on several occasions, maintaining the strength of the involvement of all neighbouring countries in combating Boko Haram. Similarly, Chad sent some 2,000 troops to Niger to help fighting the insurgency. Obviously, the governments in both Yaoundé and N'Djaména feared a spread of the insurgency and the destabilisation of their societies along religious fault lines. The Lord's Resistance Army (*LRA*), apparently only active in the CAR and the DRC, and originally inspired by a Christian sectarian ideology, received less attention from governments and media than in previous years, although their level of activity increased. About 18 civilians were killed and 750 abducted in 106 incidents in the CAR, a steep rise compared with 2015.

The DRC's provinces were not spared from many apparently unrelated violent incidents. The government blamed the Ugandan-based *Allied Democratic Forces*, sometimes presented as a radical Islamist movement, for the massacre of more than 36 people in Beni in *North Kivu* in August, but it appeared that both local militias and government soldiers were also involved in the violence. The attack had been preceded by two other deadly attacks by the same group. The 'Forces Démocratiques de Libération du Rwanda' (*FDLR*) rebels were involved in the killing of 14 people in the same region. The movement's chances of unseating Kagame in Rwanda had clearly become bleak over time and so the FDLR pursued its nonpolitical, material interests almost exclusively in the DRC. An organisational split within the FDLR led to the creation of yet another rebel group in the eastern DRC, the 'Conseil National pour le Renouveau et la Démocratie–Ubwiyunge', and to a substantial weakening of the FDLR. *Kasai* province saw the rise of a new militia headed by a local chief, Kamuina Nsapu, who led attacks against police stations, in one of which he was killed, together with 18 militiamen and 11 policemen. However, his death did not put an end to the movement and, by the end of the year, an estimated 400 people had been killed in attacks and acts of retaliation. The Kalemie area in *Tanganyika* province was the scene of inter-ethnic violence that caused the temporary displacement of some 30,000 people between July and October. South Kivu province was the scene of violence less often than in previous years.

As a result of past and on-going violent conflicts, Central Africa struggled to cope with high numbers of refugees and IDPs, the DRC and the CAR dealing with the highest numbers. The DRC had at year's end a "total number of concern" of over 2.4 m people of whom 1,960,198 were IDPs and 451,280 refugees from neighbouring countries. UNHCR statistics indicated that the CAR alone was the source of 463,759 refugees in the region, making it the seventh-largest country of origin worldwide. The most important host countries for these refugees were: Cameroon (254,633), the DRC (101,866), Chad (64,673) and Congo (30,509). The number of CAR refugees in Congo and the DRC declined fractionally over the year as 34,351 returned to their country of origin. The number of IDPs in the CAR was volatile but declined from over 447,487 to 411,785 at year's end, although each outburst of violence, particularly in the centre of the country, produced new waves of displacement, so there was no reason to be optimistic that the numbers would sustainably decrease in the foreseeable future. Post-electoral violence in conjunction with the resurgence of the Ninja militia, plus government retaliation, led to the forced displacement of some 17,000 people in Congo.

Human Rights and Transitional Justice

Intense violent conflicts were the context of the most horrendous crimes. As a consequence, some of the hottest issues of debate of former years, such as female genital mutilation or discrimination against lesbian, gay and transgender people, were hardly in the focus of human rights defenders, although they were certainly not resolved. The formerly forgotten crisis in the CAR became one of the most pressing issues for human rights organisations. HRW published an entire compendium of its reports and press releases on the country during 2016 (and early 2017), dealing with diverse issues such as executions by rebel forces, abuse by peacekeepers and impunity. On 21 April, a total of 16 human rights organisations signed an appeal to President Touadéra to cooperate fully with the ICC, urging him to take the lead in establishing a Special Court in the country. No concrete steps to prepare for the

Special Court emerged, although the UN peacekeeping mission in the CAR made a list of persons suspected of serious crimes in readiness for its establishment.

A substantial part of *ICC* activity focused again on the Central African sub-region. In the case against the former DRC vice president, Jean-Pierre Bemba, for crimes against humanity perpetrated by his militia in the CAR in 2002, the ICC found him guilty of rape, murder and pillage. In a related trial, on 19 October the ICC found Bemba and his defence team also guilty of bribing witnesses to lie in his favour. Faced with the prospect of further escalations, the ICC prosecutor issued a stern warning to DRC leaders in September, arguing that the aforementioned events would be monitored in detail. Two rebel leaders convicted by the ICC, Germain Katanga and Thomas Lubanga, had returned to the DRC in December 2015 to serve the remainder of their sentences in Kinshasa. After finishing his sentence in January, Katanga remained in detention to face additional charges of war crimes before national courts. Investigations of crimes under international law committed from 2012 onwards in the CAR were conducted by two separate ICC teams working on crimes committed by ex-Séléka and by Anti-balaka forces. Surprisingly, on 21 September, the government of Gabon referred the conflict unfolding between opposing political parties after the presidential elections to ICC Prosecutor Fatou Bensouda. She announced the opening of a preliminary examination on 29 September, and Ping openly supported the procedure; his lawyers presented documentation of alleged crimes against humanity at the ICC in December.

The court case at the Special African Chambers in Dakar (Senegal) against former Chadian dictator *Hissène Habré* was concluded on 30 May. Habré was sentenced to life imprisonment for crimes against humanity, war crimes and torture committed in Chad between 1982 and 1990. On 29 July, the court awarded various levels of compensation to victims of rape and sexual violence and victims of arbitrary detention and torture, as well as prisoners of war and survivors. Habré's conviction was an event without precedent and was generally welcomed by human rights activists. However, given the length of time between the crimes and the judgement, one wondered whether it had any deterrent effect in the fight against a culture of impunity.

Severe human rights violations were perpetrated in the *Boko Haram rebellion* and *government responses* in Cameroon, Chad (and Nigeria). Several organs of Cameroon's security forces were suspected to torturing dozens of men, women and children accused of supporting Boko Haram, some of whom disappeared.

In addition, *contested election processes* were the background of further severe human right violations, for example, in the DRC, where over 100 opposition supporters were arbitrarily arrested and held partly incommunicado for several months. The regime also used the justice system to intimidate and jail opposition leaders for various offences. Similarly, the Chadian regime severely curtailed civil liberties before the elections in April. Among many other incidents, on 6 February, 17 peaceful protesters were arrested and beaten in N'Djaména and tear gas was thrown into their cell. In separate instances, two protesting students were shot dead by security forces and two human rights defenders were threatened with death and left the country. A total of 64 soldiers who had refused to vote for Déby in the presidential elections were arrested and 'disappeared'; only 49 of them were later released. Gabon, long considered a mild autocracy, became a considerably less relaxed place, when security forces used excessive force to disperse demonstrators on several occasions, reportedly leading to 20–50 deaths. On 31 August, an attack by Republican Guards and police on the headquarters of presidential candidate Jean Ping resulted in two deaths, according to the opposition. Protest actions in Congo were frequently banned. Security forces arrested several opposition leaders, including presidential candidate Jean-Marie Michel Mokoko, who was charged with endangering national security. Another candidate, André Okombi Salissa, escaped house arrest. According to an opposition platform, 121 political prisoners were held in detention in Brazzaville's main prison. Opposition leader Paulin Makaya was sentenced to two years in prison in July, after being detained in December 2015 when protesting against the disputed Constitutional Referendum; he was declared a prisoner of conscience by AI. Congo witnessed what was arguably the steepest decline in human rights record within the region, though Equatorial Guinea was still considered the worst country in this regard. Almost expectedly, the presidential elections there were an opportunity for the regime in Malabo to display its readiness to use arbitrary force. Between February and May, more than 250 opposition supporters were temporarily arrested and meetings were crushed.

Shutting down media outlets close to the opposition or interrupting social media services for several months were methods used in many countries including the DRC, Congo, Chad and Gabon. In Cameroon, Ahmed Abba, a correspondent of 'Radio France Internationale' was tortured. The authorities suspected him of hiding information on Boko Haram activities.

Socioeconomic Developments

With an overall growth rate of 0.8% (compared with 2.5% in 2015), the results of Central Africa's economic progress were disappointing. The overall inflation rate was above the 3 % threshold fixed by CEMAC. This reflected the rather unfavourable state of the world market. For the six countries of the CEMAC zone combined, some 70% of the value of exports was based on oil products. The contribution of oil income to GDP differed between countries, but was as high as 85% in Equatorial Guinea, 50% in Congo and 45% in Gabon (2015 figures). With low prices on the world market, four countries – Equatorial Guinea, Chad, Congo and Gabon – were particularly hard hit and consequently had to abandon grandiose infrastructure projects.

The IMF's World Economic Outlook (published in April 2017) drew exactly this picture. Only the CAR (and Cameroon according to AfDB figures) saw a modestly satisfactory *GDP growth* rate of 3.8% according to IMF estimates. However, these were still far from attaining pre-war standards of productivity, with on-going violence in the countryside, including the rather fertile and higher populated areas in the north-west. According to the same source, GDP, imports and exports as well as government revenues all declined in Chad, Congo, Gabon and Equatorial Guinea. Cameroon, the DRC and São Tomé and Príncipe had a somewhat mixed, but certainly not good record. The AfDB's African Economic Outlook provided slightly different figures based on domestic authorities as well as the AfDB's own estimates, but stated quite dramatic losses in GDP per capita for Congo (-5.0%), Chad (-6.7%) and particularly Equatorial Guinea (-11.1%). Economic activity slowed down in most of the sub-region. In April, the BEAC decided to lower the obligatory reserves for commercial banks by 50%, with the aim of liberating some CFAfr 500–600 bn in order to boost the sub-regional economy.

The Index of Economic Freedom (Heritage Foundation) noted relative improvements for the sub-region, starting from a very low level. Five (up from three) countries were now in the 'mostly unfree' category (the DRC – with much better ratings, Gabon, São Tomé and Príncipe, Cameroon and the CAR) and three (down from five) in the worst category of 'repressed' economies (Chad, Equatorial Guinea and Congo, ranked between 162nd and 177th of 180 countries). The World Bank's 'Doing Business' report showed fewer fluctuations, but no single country in the sub-region was well rated; São Tomé and Príncipe ranked best (162nd) followed by Gabon and Cameroon, Congo and Equatorial Guinea. Chad, the DRC and the CAR were among the countries at the very bottom of the ranking (at 180th, 184th and 185th of 190, respectively).

Such indicators could not show the growing significance of shadow economies. Widespread violence, as in the Lake Chad area, eastern CAR and eastern DRC provided opportunities for military entrepreneurs to capture land, control over mines and other resources.

Sub-regional Organisations

CEMAC did not hold an ordinary summit during the year, but instead two extraordinary summits. On 30 July in Malabo (Equatorial Guinea), Abbas Mahamat Tolli, a nephew of Chad's President Déby, was designated the new governor of the BEAC (to take up the post in January 2017), attesting to Déby's extraordinary diplomatic clout (after he secured the position of AU chairman for former foreign minister Moussa Farki). More importantly, the summit on 23 December in Yaoundé (Cameroon) was dedicated to dealing with the financial situation of the entire zone in the presence of IMF Director General Christine Lagarde and France's Minister of Economic Cooperation and Finance Michel Sapin. All the region's heads of state attended to discuss the dire socio-economic situation. A resolution listing 21 measures was adopted to prevent bankruptcy, to some extent linked to the constant deficit in the balance of payments. CEMAC member states continued to export raw materials (particularly oil), but had to import most of the manufactured goods they needed. In light of this, CEMAC decided to enter into deeper discussions with the IMF, although at that stage only two members (Chad and the CAR) had on-going programmes with the IMF. Despite growing discussion in the media about the usefulness of the common currency and the obvious inclination of some external partners to 'adjust' exchange rates, Central African leaders refused to devalue the CFA franc and made it clear that this option would not even be discussed at the summit. Instead, some of the old IMF recommendations of the 1980s were on the agenda again, such as encouraging higher tax revenues and reducing budgetary deficits. The overall solidarity in the zone was tested by Cameroon's signing of a separate EPA agreement with the EU in early August in order to harmonise trade relations between them with WTO rules. However, it appeared completely unrealistic that there would be a sub-regional EPA for Central Africa.

Relatively little activity was recorded for *CEEAC*. However, Rwanda (founding member in 1983), which had left the organisation in 2007, officially rejoined in August. On 30 November, Gabon's President Ali Bongo hosted a summit in the presence of his peers from Rwanda, the CAR and Chad. Although the delegations were specifically invited to discuss the fight against Boko Haram and the situation in Burundi, the CAR and the DRC, the Gabonese opposition also called for the political crisis in the host country to be dealt with.

Angola was clearly pushing the agenda of the ICGLR, which held a summit in Luanda, on 14 June to discuss security and military issues, including a military needs assessment in the CAR plus the security and humanitarian situation in the DRC. Luanda had earlier hosted a Regional Inter-Ministerial Committee (RIMC) on 11 February focusing, inter alia, on a regional initiative on natural resources. Together with the UN, SADC and the AU, the organisation co-hosted an important international summit on the DRC's most recent political crisis on 26 October, again in Luanda.

The *Gulf of Guinea Commission* held an extraordinary summit on 5 September in Malabo. On the agenda was an analysis of the organisation's revitalisation strategy, the related action plan (2015–18) and budget (2016–17). According to an Equatorial Guinean official source, Ghana's application to join the organisation (dating back to 2013) should have been analysed during the summit, but no decisions were reported

(Nigeria being the only West African member state, though the organisation is officially open to all other states on the Gulf of Guinea).

Though no *CBLT* activities at the highest level were reported, it served as a framework for most security cooperation in the Lake Chad area. A Regional Parliamentary Committee met in N'Djaména (Chad) on 3–5 October.

Cameroon

Fanny Pigeaud

The next presidential election, scheduled for 2018, was one of the main preoccupations of the majority of political players, who sought to discern the intentions of 83-year-old President Paul Biya, who had been in power since 1982. The atmosphere appeared increasingly tense within the presidential party, with some of its cadres advocating a change and others supporting the status quo incarnated by Biya. The latter faced two serious crises: a railway disaster involving the French corporate group Bolloré, and large-scale protest movement in the country's two English-speaking regions, which was still ongoing at the end of the year. The armed group Boko Haram continued to pose a substantial threat to security in the north, with implications for the agricultural sector and livestock farming. As a result of the drop in oil prices and the increase in military expenditure, the country's economic situation remained fragile, thus compelling the authorities to turn to the IMF, under pressure from France.

 | DOI 10.1163/9789004355910_022

Domestic Politics

During much of the year, the political elite were on the lookout for any information about President Biya's plans regarding the *presidential election* scheduled for 2018. Cameroonians wondered whether the head of state would remain in office until the end of his mandate, whether he would again present himself as a candidate in 2018, whether he would call an early election, or whether he would change the constitution to create the office of a vice president, who would then become his potential successor. As the months passed, a renewal of his candidacy appeared increasingly likely. Though Biya, always a man of few words, did not personally comment on the subject, some of his close collaborators – including Martin Belinga Eboutou, director of the Civil Cabinet of the Presidency – spoke for him: they launched public appeals calling for him to run again. The decisions taken within the presidential party, the 'Rassemblement Démocratique du Peuple Camerounais' (RDPC) were also a good indicator of Biya's intentions. The party was to organise its five-yearly congress in September, in compliance with the stipulations of its internal statutes to reappoint members of its executive bodies and choose its president, who would subsequently become its candidate for the next presidential election. Though repeatedly announced, the congress never convened: it was replaced in November by a simple meeting of the RDPC political bureau, which decided to adjourn the congress until an unspecified date, and most importantly to extend the duration of Biya's mandate as party president, which effectively made him RDPC candidate for the 2018 presidential election. This decision ensured that the dissensions within the RDPC would not be overly publicised and avoided any public dispute of Biya's mandate as president. In fact, the RDPC appeared increasingly divided over this issue: several of its cadres expressed their desire for change, while others opted for the status quo, fearing a fratricidal war and the loss of their privileges if Biya were to step down. The president's advanced age naturally played an increasingly important role in the reasoning of both groups: all political players were aware that, even if the head of state did not give the impression of wanting to hand over the reins, his years as president were becoming increasingly numbered. In October, a memorandum addressed to Biya and signed by leading members of the Mfoundi Division of the RPDC (equivalent to the political capital Yaoundé), indicated the frame of mind that prevailed among a number of cadres in his party: "Your power is becoming tribal and even familial" and the "Mfoundi and the peoples of the Great Centre and the East are the poor relations of your 35-year reign" were some of the formulations in this open letter, which also accused Biya of being "silent and dismissive". Even though other leaders of the Mfoundi expressed their disapproval following the publication of this text and gave him their support, the sense of unease remained strong.

An isolated incident, widely publicised on social media, came to illustrate the *end-of-reign mood* that prevailed within the presidential party and the country as a whole: on 20 May, the national day, one of the vehicles in Biya's cavalcade broke down in Yaoundé, on May 20 Boulevard, where the annual army parade was to take place under the eyes of the authorities and tight security. Soldiers of the presidential guard had to push the car in full view of an astounded public.

In late October, the authorities and Biya were subjected to strong criticism following the most serious *railway disaster* the country had ever experienced. Having been absent from Cameroon for a month, the president waited two days before deciding to return to Yaoundé – he was in Switzerland at the time. Though he decreed a national day of mourning, he did not visit the site of the tragedy, which occurred on 21 October in the town of Eséka, some 120 km from Yaoundé: a train belonging to Camrail (Cameroon Railways), more than 77% controlled by the French corporate group Bolloré, jumped the tracks. Travelling from Yaoundé to Douala, the country's economic capital, and carrying over 1,500 passengers, its journey ended brutally midway between the two cities. Several of its carriages broke loose and crashed into a ravine, killing at least 79 persons and injuring hundreds. A few hours earlier, the highway connecting Yaoundé and Douala had been literally cut in two following the rupture of a metal duct, which had been in bad state for a long time without any response from the relevant ministry. The network of secondary roads being barely developed, many travellers had opted for the train. In his traditional end-of-year speech on 31 December, the president promised that the in-depth inquiry that he had commissioned to investigate the disaster would uncover the truth. "I will take appropriate action, I have pledged myself to this," he added. However, many citizens doubted that those responsible for the disaster would ever stand trial, although there were numerous indications that the Bolloré group – which was omnipresent in several sectors of the Cameroonian economy and maintained direct ties to the presidential office – had committed several errors. Very soon after the accident, the media published documents and testimonies indicating the possibility that the train had been overloaded and that the majority of its carriages and its locomotive had a history of serious brake problems.

In the latter part of the year, the country also experienced a deep political crisis, the gravest since 2008, between the central power and the country's two *Anglophone regions*, the Southwest and the Northwest, home to 20% of the population. It all began as a simple corporatist mobilisation: English-speaking lawyers went on strike in mid-October, protesting against the lack of an English version of the basic legal texts of the Organisation for the Harmonisation of Business Law in Africa (OHADA) and the increasingly frequent application of the French-language civil code. (The two Anglophone regions that had made up former Southern Cameroon, administered by the British until the reunification of Cameroon in 1961, apply British common law, whereas the eight other regions, in which French is spoken, follow French civil law.) Day after day, the movement grew, in the absence of an adequate response on the part of the government. Students and teachers from the Southwest and the Northwest joined the strike, accusing the authorities of showing little consideration for their educational system. (The two Anglophone regions have also retained the British school system, evaluation methods and certifications, whereas the French-speaking regions adhere to the school system inherited from France.) From 21 November, classes were suspended at schools, colleges and universities in the Anglophone regions. Demonstrations also took place in a number of cities, notably in the most important ones: Buea and Bamenda. Little by little, the demands multiplied, some denouncing the marginalisation of the Anglophone regions in the sharing of power and resources, others calling for a return to federalism or even for the independence of Anglophone Cameroon. The Cameroonian flag was burned by demonstrators, while that of the Southern Cameroons National Council (SCNC), which had been demanding the independence of the Anglophone regions since 1995, was hoisted in front of the regional hospital in Bamenda.

Not unusually, the security forces reacted violently to the *demonstrations*, which led to serious clashes. According to the Social Democratic Front (SDF), the strongest opposition party, three persons died, although the government reported only one death. Several dozen persons, mostly young people, were arrested. There were various attempts at negotiation, notably by Prime Minister Philemon Yang, himself an Anglophone. In December, the head of government set up, among other things, a committee charged with investigating and proposing solutions to the concerns of the Anglophone lawyers. Deeming the government's propositions unsatisfactory, the protesters gradually organised themselves, creating the Cameroon Anglophone Civil Society Consortium (CACSC), an association of lawyers, teachers and members of civil society. While attempting to negotiate, the authorities also declared that they were categorically opposed to any revision of the state's institutional structure. In his end-of-year speech, President Biya insisted that "Cameroon is one and indivisible, and will remain so," accusing "a group of extremist, manipulated, and instrumentalised demonstrators" of trying to manipulate the masses. By late December, this conflict had not yet been resolved. The intelligence services suspected the members of the CACSC of having foreign supporters and of wanting to destabilise the state.

With regard to national security, the armed group *Boko Haram* remained a serious problem throughout the year in the Far North region, even though the actions attributed to it decreased in intensity and were essentially limited to suicide attacks. In January, no less than nine such attacks caused the death of more than 60 civilians. In February, 33 persons were killed and more than 100 injured in the wake of bomb explosions set off by two women during a funeral in Nguetchewe, a town located some 60 km from Maroua, and by two other women at a much used market in Meme, a village near Mora. In August and on Christmas Day, another five persons were killed and at least 34 injured by two more suicide attacks at markets in Mora. Boko Haram, officially operating from Nigeria and relying on a network of local collaborators, was said to have been responsible for the death of 1,500 persons since 2014. Within the framework of the Multinational Joint Task Force (MNJTF), the Cameroonian army crossed the border into Nigeria on a number of occasions. On 19 December, it conducted a raid on Nigerian territory in order to attack Boko Haram in one of its strongholds, some 20 km from the Cameroonian town of Achigachia. Roughly 8,500 soldiers were deployed in the region.

The *security forces* were again accused of *human rights violations*. According to AI, dozens of men, women and children accused of supporting Boko Haram were tortured by soldiers of the 'Brigade d'Intervention Rapide' (BIR), one of the army's elite units, on a military base situated near Maroua, as well as by government agents at the headquarters of the 'Direction Générale de la Recherche Extérieure' (DGRE), an intelligence service, in Yaoundé. Some of the detained persons died under torture, while others were reported missing. The International Organization for Migration (IOM) estimated that the number of persons displaced because of Boko Haram in the Far North had increased from 81,693 to 157,657 between April 2015 and July 2016.

Foreign Affairs

In keeping with his usual practice, President Biya attended very few African and international conferences. He did, however, travel to *Nigeria* on two occasions for official visits (on 2 and 15 May). In January, he welcomed the IMF director Christine Lagarde and he received Samantha Power, the US ambassador to the UN, on 19 April. The government continued to intensify its relations with *China*, Cameroon's most important economic partner. In July, Yaoundé and Beijing signed an agreement providing for the abolition of visa requirements for the holders of diplomatic or official passports from both countries.

Cameroon hosted several *international events*. In May, at Biya's request, the government organised an international conference on the theme 'Investing in Cameroon, Land of Attractiveness', with the aim of persuading investors to take an interest in the country. Several hundred participants attended this event, which was organised by Havas, a subsidiary of the Bolloré group. Manuel Barroso, former president of the European Commission, Donald Kaberuka, former president of the AfDB, and Pascal Lamy, former director-general of the WTO, were among the guests. In late November, Cameroon also hosted the 10th Africa Women's Cup of Nations, in which the national team, the Indomitable Lionesses, were defeated by the Super Falcons of Nigeria in the final. On 23 December, Yaoundé was host to an extraordinary CEMAC summit.

Earlier in the year, Cameroonian leaders, along with ordinary citizens, closely followed the presidential election in *Gabon* on 27 August and the post-electoral crisis that ensued. The majority of the Cameroonian media sided with the incumbent president Ali Bongo, and against his competitor Jean Ping. They believed that this crisis did not so much pitch Bongo against Ping but Bongo against France. In their opinion, Paris sought to remove Ali Bongo from power because a number of measures implemented by his government ran counter to the interests of several French companies. Anti-French slogans resurfaced in the Cameroonian media. According to a source close to the security forces, Biya had sent several hundred soldiers of the BIR to assist Bongo.

The crisis situations in the neighbouring *CAR* and in northern Nigeria continued to have humanitarian consequences for Cameroon: according to human rights organisations, the country was accommodating at least 276,000 CAR *refugees* in camps or host families in the south-western border region, often in difficult conditions. In addition, roughly 59,000 persons fleeing from Nigeria were housed in the Minawao camp, administered by the UN, in the Far North region. Some 27,000 other refugees from Nigeria were also living outside this camp.

Socioeconomics Developments

The *budget* for 2016, which was designed to balance expenditure and revenue, was fixed at CFAfr 4,234.7 bn (€ 6.45 bn), an increase of CFAfr 488.1 bn (more than 13%) compared with 2015. At the end of the year, budgetary resources were estimated at CFAfr 4,218.4 bn, which included CFAfr 356 bn from oil revenues, CFAfr 1,590 bn in taxes and duties, CFAfr 695.9 bn in customs revenue, CFAfr 152 bn in non-fiscal revenue, and CFAfr 1,248.2 bn in loans and gifts. At the beginning of the year, the government banked on an economic growth of 6%, which ultimately turned out to be 5.6% – a drop of 0.2% compared with 2015. This shrinkage was mainly due to the slowdown in oil production (+3% in 2016, compared with +37% in 2015), or roughly 33 m barrels, and by the weakness in global crude oil prices and other raw materials. A portion of expenditure went into the execution of the construction projects for the Africa Cup of Nations, which took place at the end of year, and for the one the country would host in 2019. Part of the budget was, of course, used to finance the war effort against Boko Haram. According to a report published by the IMF in April, the budgetary impact of the increase in security costs amounted to somewhere between 1% and 2% of GDP between 2014 and 2015, in other words CFAfr 189 bn to CFAfr 378 bn (€ 287 m to € 575 m). The budget for 2016 was also marked by the implementation in August of the EPA with the EU – the monthly losses from this agreement having been evaluated at CFAfr 100 m by the Cameroonian authorities.

In late August, the finance minister stated that Cameroon's public debt amounted to CFAfr 4,754 bn, or 27.3% of GDP.

With regard to borrowing, the state of Cameroon floated a *compulsory bond* of CFAfr 150 bn (€ 230 m) in late September, with an interest yield of 5.5%. The funds raised by this bond were to help finance the relaunch of the 'Société d'Expansion et de Modernisation de la Riziculture de Yagoua' (SEMRY) and the 'Société de Développement du Coton' (SODECOTON), a subsidiary of the French GEOCOTON, the expansion of the deep water port of Kribi, the motorway connecting Yaoundé and the international airport of Nsimalen, the enlargement of the Lom Pangar and Memve'ele dams, and a project to supply the capital and its surroundings with drinking water. This was the fourth compulsory bond issued by Cameroon since 2010. The first transaction, which had raised CFAfr 200 bn, had been fully reimbursed in December 2015, according to Finance Minister Alamine Ousmane Mey. In December, the World Bank granted a loan of $ 325 m to allow for the modernisation of the electricity network and to assist in the launching of the newly founded 'Société Nationale de Transport d'Électricité' (SONATREL), tasked, among other things, with the operation, maintenance and development of the public electricity distribution network and its interconnections with other networks. Roughly 74% of Cameroonians were living in areas directly connected to the electricity grid.

In the *agricultural sector* (which contributed approximately 22% of GDP), there was improvement in a number of sectors: cocoa exports increased by 38%, cotton by 31%, and bananas by 7%. The start of production on new plantations and the phytosanitary treatment of old groves explained the increase in cocoa production. However, the situation remained very difficult in the Far North due to Boko Haram raids: according to the Ministry of Agriculture, at least 4,500 ha of land were abandoned, and an investigation conducted by the Ministry of Livestock and Fisheries estimated that Boko Haram fighters had, over recent years, stolen or killed nearly 30,000 head of cattle and nearly 20,000 small ruminants in this region, and that their attacks had led to the closure of some 20 cattle markets, and thus of most the region's selling points. The exactions of Boko Haram also led to a significant decrease in fishing activities in the area of Lake Chad. In May, losses were estimated at nearly CFAfr 55 bn (€ 83.8 m) in the livestock sector and CFAfr 8.5 bn (nearly € 13 m) in the fishing sector. At least 135 cattle farmers were killed. Estimates revealed that the economy of the area most affected by the raids of Boko Haram contributed no more than 5% of GDP, as compared with 7.3% before the appearance of the armed group. Income losses on the national level were said to amount to roughly € 686 m per year, or € 2 bn, since 2014.

Elsewhere in the country, *poultry farming* also suffered significant losses due to an outbreak of avian flu. The epidemic was first detected in May in Yaoundé, before spreading to several other regions, including the West, where 80% of the country's poultry production was concentrated. Tens of thousands of birds had to be slaughtered and the sale of poultry was banned for several weeks. The 'Interprofession Avicole du Cameroun' (IPAVIC) producers' association, which had expected a production of 50 m broiler chickens for the year, had to revise this figure downwards to 30 m. Members of civil society and cattle farmers protested on several occasions against the measures taken by the government, deeming them to be disproportionate and inappropriate. Some even suspected ill-intentioned economic players, in complicity with certain administrative authorities, of attempting to weaken the national poultry sector to benefit poultry importers.

With regard to large enterprises, a plan for the restructuring of the national airline Cameroon Airlines Corporation (Camair-Co) was adopted. It provided for the clearing of Camair-Co's CFAfr 35 bn debt, the purchase of nine additional aircraft, and the opening of new national and international air routes. A new management team was also appointed in August.

The level of *corruption* remained high. 'Opération Epervier', launched in 2006 by President Biya to combat corruption, did not appear to make any progress. One of its most famous victims, Jean Marie Atangana Mebara, was again condemned by a Special Criminal Court on 23 June: he was sentenced to 25 years' imprisonment for the embezzlement in 2003 of nearly CFAfr 3 bn (€ 4.4 m) earmarked for the purchase of a presidential airplane. Atangana Mebara had already received two sentences of 20 years and 15 years in prison for other misappropriations of funds. His supporters continued to denounce the judicial system as being instrumentalised for political purposes. For part of the year, one scandal in particular was widely commented on by the media: a case of misappropriated funds within the 'Banque Internationale du Cameroun pour l'Épargne et le Crédit' (BICEC), a subsidiary of the French group 'Banque Populaire-Caisse d'Épargne' (BPCE) and Cameroon's most important banking network. Senior Cameroonian managers of the bank were imprisoned on charges of embezzling tens of millions of euros over a period of more than ten years. This affair raised many questions among both experts and Cameroonian citizens: many asked themselves how these misappropriations could have gone on for so many years without being detected by successive directors and those responsible for internal audits within the BICEC, all of them French. The National Anti-Corruption Commission (CONAC) celebrated the tenth anniversary of its founding. CONAC announced that it had recovered nearly CFAfr 6 bn (€ 9 m) since its inception and had received 3,268 accusations of corruption in 2015, compared with only 168 in 2008. CONAC also published two reports in the course of the year. The first showed, in particular, that the compensation fund for the victims of the 'Nsam fire disaster' (when an oil depot located in Yaoundé had exploded in 1998, officially causing the death of 250 persons) had been the target of embezzlements amounting to more than CFAfr 14 bn (€ 21 m). The same report also revealed that several ministries, including those of justice, defence, foreign relations, communication, the supreme state audit, and the delegate general for national security had not implemented the National Anti-Corruption Strategy, despite its having been approved by the government and the country's technical and financial partners in February 2011. The second CONAC report showed that the state had lost more than CFAfr 171 bn (€ 260 m) through corruption in 2015. The detected infractions included the failure of the cell phone providers (Orange Cameroun, MTN Cameroon and Camtel) to pay their taxes and duties.

A number of changes were made to the justice system: in June, parliament adopted a *new penal code*, the preceding one having not been revised since 1967. Certain paragraphs in this legislation, which was enacted by Biya on 12 July, were nevertheless heavily criticised by civil rights organisations and opposition groups: the latter were shocked by the fact that adultery, vagrancy and begging were now punishable by imprisonment. Civil rights organisations also deplored the fact that tenants who failed to pay their rent for more than two months could now be sentenced to as much as three years in prison, even though approximately one-third of the country's households were in rented accommodation and nearly half of Cameroonians lived below the poverty threshold. In addition, homosexuality was still a punishable offence and the death penalty was retained. The new code also introduced a system of community work and restorative justice that was meant to reduce the number of short prison sentences. Initially, the text submitted to the vote of the deputies included a provision conferring immunity on sitting cabinet ministers, but protests were so strong that this section of the code had to be removed.

Central African Republic

Andreas Mehler

The transition phase after the overthrow of President François Bozizé in 2013 ended with presidential and legislative elections, but the new institutions barely had an influence on (in)security, and close to none in the eastern half of the country. Large parts of the territory were under the control of rebel movements, though infighting along ethnic (and no longer religious) lines clearly increased. UN peacekeepers were only partially successful in keeping the various armed groups at bay and became increasingly unpopular. The upsurge in violence clearly impinged on economic recovery.

Domestic Politics

A majority of both citizens and international partners were impatiently awaiting the end of the transitional period as the *transitional bodies*, including interim President Catherine Samba-Panza and her government, had lost most of their legitimacy over the preceding years. However, the first round of legislative elections on

 | DOI 10.1163/9789004355910_023

30 January – held in parallel to the first round of the presidential elections – was marred by imperfections, mostly on the level of electoral administration, and had to be annulled early in the year. The results of the *presidential competition* were surprising to many observers. Neither the sons of former heads of states (Désiré Kolingba 12.0%, Jean-Serge Bokassa 6.1%, Sylvain Patassé-Ngakoutou 2.8%) nor the candidate of the oldest political party 'Mouvement pour la Libération du Peuple Centrafricain' (MLPC), Martin Ziguélé (11.4%), achieved the support they had hoped for, but two former prime ministers, Anicet-Georges Dologuélé and Archange-Faustin Touadéra, came top of the list with 23.7% and 19.1% of the votes respectively. Two other candidates (out of 30) had respectable results: the independent Charles-Armel Doubane (3.6%) and Jean-Michel Mandaba of the 'Parti pour la Gouvernance Démocratique' (PGD; 3.1%). Past experience of high governmental responsibility was the only common factor shared by both the candidates who proceeded to the second round. Dologuélé had formed a party in 2013, the 'Union pour le Renouveau Centrafricain' (URCA), while Touadéra presented himself as an independent. When positioning themselves for the second round, to take place on 14 February, Touadéra played on his image as a modest technocrat, while poster images of Dologuélé bursting with self-confidence were omnipresent in the capital, Bangui. Dologuélé clearly had the support of many businessmen, as well as the official endorsement of former president Bozizé, and he also secured the backing of Kolingba, while Touadéra, most significantly, was able to enlist the support of the MLPC. In the end, Touadéra won the second round with a wide margin of 67.3% to 32.7%, according to provisional results announced on 20 February. Dologuélé at first tried to list irregularities in order to contest this outcome, but the gap between the votes was such that he accepted the result "for the sake of peace" and the Constitutional Court quickly endorsed the official result as given by the Electoral Commission on 1 March. Turnout fell only slightly from 62.5% in round 1 to 59.0% in round 2. Touadéra's inauguration on 30 March preceded the official end of the transition period by one day.

The re-run of the first round of *legislative elections* in parallel to the second round of the presidential elections produced clear victories in only 46 out of the 140 single-member constituencies. This meant that the contours of the post-transitional setup became clear only with the holding of the further postponed second round on 31 March, with results announced on 9 April. Touadéra's direct support in the National Assembly appeared limited in a highly fragmented parliament: his opponent Dologuélé could at least draw on his 13 URCA followers, while the 'Union Nationale pour la Démocratie et le Progrès', another new party, won the same number of seats. The parties that were arguably the best established fared moderately well, but experienced a geographically-based shrinking of their support: Kolingba's 'Rassemblement Démocratique Centrafricain' (RDC) was able to win ten seats (four of them in Basse Kotto prefecture), followed by Ziguélé's MLPC with nine seats (five of them in Ouham-Pendé). Bozizé's loosely organised 'Kwa na Kwa' party scored well, with seven seats. Twelve more parties received between one and four seats, while 56 independent candidates were elected, among them Anti-balaka leader Alfred Yekatom, who was under UN sanctions. Results in nine more constituencies were invalidated and partial re-elections had to be organised there. Only 11 women were elected.

Touadéra appointed Simplice Sarandji, his campaign manager and a professor at the University of Bangui, as prime minister on 6 April and Sarandji formed a *government* of 23 ministers on 12 April. With Bokassa as minister of public security and territorial administration, Doubane at Foreign Affairs and Joseph Yakete at the Defence Ministry, three presidential candidates who had supported Touadéra in the second round received meaningful recognition. Two close allies of Touadéra, Félix Moloua and Charles Lemasset, received the Economy and Communications portfolios, respectively, and some further official allies were represented by less well-known individuals, but Dologuélé's URCA also entered government. In contrast to all transitional governments (2013–16), not a single representative of an armed group was included. While the limited size of the government was meant to be a clear sign of modesty, Touadéra extended the size of the president's immediate circle of collaborators, including with some political heavyweights. General Antoine Gambi, chief of staff under Patassé, implicated in the coup against him and later sacked by Bozizé, was made the personal chief of staff at the Presidency. Equally controversial was the nomination of the versatile former minister Fidèle Gouandjika as special adviser. On 6 May, members of parliament elected Karim Meckassoua as Speaker with a simple majority (with Dologuélé and Ziguélé coming second and third). This was interpreted as a sign of reconciliation with the Muslim minority, which had at least partly backed the Séléka rebellion (though not Meckassoua, who had held several ministerial positions in the past).

With the main political institutions in place, Touadéra initiated a first round of consultations with representatives of armed movements on the *demobilisation, disarmament and reintegration* (DDR) process. All the major ex-Séléka factions – 'Front Populaire pour la Renaissance de la Centrafrique' (FPRC), 'Mouvement Patriotique pour la Centrafrique' (MPC) and 'Union pour la Paix en Centrafrique' (UPC) – resented their exclusion from government. They had demanded ministerial positions as a condition for their disarmament and now felt marginalised, while Touadéra stressed that DDR should come first. Presidential advisor Jean Willybiro-Sako was made a special coordinator for this dossier. On 24 August, Touadéra appointed members to an advisory and monitoring committee for the national DDR programme, including two members from the executive branch, one from the National Assembly, one from civil society, three from religious platforms, 28 from political-military groups, and five representatives of the international community.

The president himself met with armed groups during visits to Bouar, Kaga-Bandoro and Bria; in addition, Willybiro-Sako met with 'Rassemblement Patriotique pour le Renouveau de la Centrafrique' (RPRC) and Anti-balaka representatives in Bambari. Most interlocutors expressed their interest in DDR, though expectations varied and were partly unrealistic. Nevertheless, on 3 November, the aforementioned committee unanimously adopted the national strategy on the matter in advance of the 17 November Brussels Donors Conference, at which resources in support of the plan were to be mobilised. Without transparency on budget allocations and entitlements in a full DDR programme, the UN Multidimensional Integrated Stabilization Mission in the CAR (MINUSCA) conducted so-called pre-DDR operations (in Bambari, Bangui, Birao, Bossangoa, Bouar, Bria, Kaga-Bandoro and Ndélé), reaching around 4,000 beneficiaries, who received food assistance and had to participate in short-term labour-intensive activities. Related to the slow process of DDR was the belated start of *security sector reform*. The Ministry of Defence had registered 7,478 members of the CAR armed forces, of whom 3,533 had been verified by MINUSCA as of mid-September. A joint task force of UNDP, MINUSCA, national police and gendarmerie undertook an identification exercise among the internal security forces, which resulted in the registration of 1,874 gendarmes and 1,154 police. In the same period, Touadéra created a presidential security unit, composed of some 175 personnel from the armed forces, police and gendarmerie. Their mission was the protection of residences of high-level government officials in Bangui.

After many postponements, a *reunification meeting of ex-Séléka factions* was held on 18–19 October in Bria, initiated by Nourredine Adam (FPRC). MINUSCA was overburdened with the arrival of between 1,000 and 1,500 armed men and was unable to maintain the status of Bria as a weapons-free zone, but no major incidents were reported. Neither the MPC leadership under Mahamat Al Khatim nor the UPC faction under Ali Darassa arrived for the meeting (according to them because Adam was on the UN sanctions list) and only the FPRC and RPRC signed a joint declaration. Even between those two factions, divisions remained quite obvious, the former being dominated by Runga, the latter by Goula, at loggerheads over the control of the sparsely populated north-east. However, the Bria declaration contained some significant formulations by condemning the continued persecution of minorities by Anti-balaka, allegedly armed by the government, and by calling for a partition of the country, with the north-east under rebel control. The meeting established a so-called High Supreme Council, with Nourredine Adam as president and Zacharia Damane as vice-president, and a National Council on Defence and Security with Abdoulaye Hissène as president. Significantly, the former leader and president of the FPRC, Michel Djotodia, did not take part and was not assigned any role. Observers had doubts as to whether Séléka could be reunified and regain the full strength it had in 2013.

Without tangible progress in DDR, the *security situation* remained volatile and worsened dramatically in the second half of the year. Conflict and security constellations varied from one region to the next, but few areas were constantly at full peace (arguably only the south-west). One hotspot was the capital, where the killing of a Muslim youth by a Christian youth led to inter-communal violence. When security forces detained 26 Muslim traders for days (18–24 June), it led to retaliatory action by the FPRC, who detained six police officers in the PK-5 neighbourhood of Bangui. MINUSCA peacekeepers tried in vain to free them by force on 20 June, killing at least six people. They were released only on 24 June – the same day a non-uniformed MINUSCA peacekeeper was killed. In a reconciliatory move, Touadéra hosted a Ramadan-related dinner on 27 June; he also attended the celebration of the Eid al-Adha holiday in PK-5. But symbolic behaviour was obviously of only limited use. On 12 August, most of the men of an FPRC contingent stationed in PK-5, including Abdoulaye Hissène and Haroun Gaye (the latter under UN sanctions), tried to flee Bangui and were immediately tracked by Anti-balaka, reportedly with the tacit support of civilian politicians. In PK-12, Sibut and Kemio, still close to the capital, clashes occurred. While national security forces had to withdraw due to a shortage of ammunition, MINUSCA's (late) intervention turned into a dramatic show-down with 11 FPRC members it had captured, some severely wounded, while others hiding in the bush later became victims of a man-hunt by Anti-balaka elements; still others were able to reach Séléka-controlled areas. This event not only affected MINUSCA's reputation but also impacted on the balance of power in the PK-5 area in Bangui, where infighting between Muslim self-help groups resulted in the death of two of their leaders. In October, the assassination of a high-ranking army officer and former guard of interim president Samba-Panza triggered a new round of inter-communal violence. The Anti-balaka movement was partly invigorated by the return on 3 August of Jean-Francis Bozizé, son of the former president and former defence minister, despite being wanted on an international arrest warrant for, inter alia, torture and embezzlement. Arrested by MINUSCA and handed over to the government, he was quickly set free again under hypothetical judicial surveillance. Bozizé Jr was clearly trying to reorganise the militant support base of the Bozizé family, potentially preparing for his father's return. While Bozizé Sr had openly supported Dologuélé, it was obvious that Touadéra had been more popular in this camp and this latent sympathy also made some government members quite relaxed about pursuing wanted Anti-balaka leaders, helping to freeze their assets and condemning their violent actions. In the same vein, calls for an end to the weapons embargo so that national security forces could be equipped became increasingly popular, and were supported, for example, by Defence Minister Bokassa. A former member of the Transitional National Council, Gervais Lakosso, organised protest actions against MINUSCA for their alleged passivity in the face of continued violence. On 24 October, a MINUSCA intervention against protesters resulted in four dead and 13 injured, including five peacekeepers.

The *north-west* was definitely not under government control. As a new factor, the MPC moved to the Paoua area in Ouham-Pendé prefecture and formed an alliance with former enemies of the 'Révolution et Justice' militia, which resulted from late January onwards in the occupation or burning of villages close by. An attack attributed to 'ex-Séléka' created panic in Ngaoundaye on 16 June. Further sporadic clashes occurred between, on the one hand, Anti-balaka and the 'Front Démocratique pour le Peuple Centrafricain' (FDPC) and, on the other, Fulani pastoralists and those movements claiming to protect them, such as the 2015-founded 'Retour, Réclamation et Réhabilitation' (3R), the FPRC and the MPC. A rare positive development came in July, when the FDPC released two different groups of hostages and expressed readiness to be disarmed. From April onwards, confrontations between Anti-balaka and Fulani and between 3R and non-Fulani civilians around Bocaranga and Koui increased, with casualties rising, and HRW documented the killing of at least 50 civilians at the end of November. HRW held 3R under 'general' Sidiki Abbas responsible for the displacement of at least 17,000 people (14,000 around Bocaranga, 3,000 on the border with Cameroon).

The *centre* of the country (Ouaka and Nana-Grébizi préfectures) looked even more tense, and in particular Bambari, where a dissident Arab faction of the UPC under Abdoulaye Faya clashed with those loyal to UPC leader Ali Darassa, who repeatedly stated that his mission was to defend Fulani interests. In clashes on 4 July, at least 14 UPC combatants were killed. Thirty-seven dissidents sought shelter in the MINUSCA camp for seven weeks. A first convoy evacuating them to Kaga-Bandoro was stopped in Grimari by Anti-balaka fighters, potentially manipulated by the local district officer (sous-préfet), and had to return to Bambari. Eventually, most UPC defectors were transferred by aircraft to Kaga-Bandoro on 2 September with a view to their early demobilisation. Darassa now consolidated his control over the area, and also over the diamond mining site of Nzako further east in Mbomou prefecture. The UPC was responsible for a number of escalations in October, including the killing of two village chiefs. Shortly afterwards, on 27 October, UPC combatants killed 11 people in the village of Berima and then, on 29 October, six gendarmes sent to investigate the crime. In response, Anti-balaka groups erected road-blocks in a Bambari neighbourhood under their control. However, the Anti-balaka movement was split on the national level between a faction under a degree of control by Maxime Mokom and a faction claiming to be loyal to Edouard Ngaïssona, with the latter faction dominant in Ouaka prefecture. Rather surprisingly, the FPRC and Anti-balaka formed an alliance against the UPC. The UPC ran illegal detention centres and exercised other state-like functions in Ouaka; it also organised forced marriages and used child-soldiers. By the end of the year, new atrocities had been attributed to the UPC, including the execution of over 60 civilians and captured fighters in November and December in or close to Bakala, which also led to new internal displacement. As if this were not enough, a new militia formed on 4 August. The 'Mouvement de Résistance pour la Défense de la Patrie' had some overlaps with the Anti-balaka and issued an ultimatum to MINUSCA to arrest Darassa by 4 October. After that date, the MRDP claimed the shooting at a MINUSCA convoy on 12 October, injuring five peacekeepers (two assailants and one civilian were killed), and it threatened more action, particularly to bring about the departure of the Mauritanian contingent of MINUSCA from Bambari. Kaga-Bandoro was also the scene of serious fighting and looting, in one instance leaving at least 37 civilians and 12 ex-Séléka fighters dead and more than 50 people injured in an attack on an IDP centre. Approximately 6,500 IDPs sought refuge around MINUSCA facilities; both the MPC and the FRSP denied involvement, though fighters were identified as 'ex-Séléka'.

In the *east*, Bria became a further hot spot by the end of November, when about 85 civilians were killed, 76 wounded and nearly 11,000 displaced due to a confrontation between the FPRC and the UPC. Finally, the *south-east* saw an extension of Lord's Resistance Army (LRA) activities. According to the LRA Crisis Tracker, over the year 750 civilians were abducted (and 18 killed) in 106 incidents in the CAR, a steep rise compared with 2015. It was mostly towns in Mboumou, Haut-Mboumou and Haute-Kotto prefectures that experienced LRA attacks.

In light of an obviously weak government and the impression of on-going impunity, it seemed essential that the law to establish a Special Criminal Court signed in 2015 should be implemented. Human rights NGOs estimated that such a Special Court would cost $ 40 m for the first five years. Of that amount, only $ 5 m were raised. Earlier, an initial budget of $ 7 m for starting the Court's operations was drawn up. MINUSCA began to develop a list of persons suspected of serious crimes.

Foreign Affairs

The CAR remained a constant item on the UNSC agenda. On 27 January, by resolution 2262, the UNSC prolonged the comprehensive sanctions regime, including a full arms embargo and targeted sanctions including travel bans and asset freezing, plus an extension of the mandate of the panel of experts, all until the end of January 2017. Furthermore, by resolution 2331, the UNSC decided on 26 July to extend the mandate of *MINUSCA* until 15 November 2017. MINUSCA operated close to the mandated limit of 10,750 military personnel, including 480 military observers and staff officers and 2,080 police personnel. However, the mission faced several critical situations in which it had to deploy force, and faced harsh criticism from various political actors for either not being impartial or being inactive. Past allegations of sexual harassment also kept peacekeepers on the radar of human rights organisations. Responding to reports of atrocities carried out in the country of origin, UN headquarters announced that Burundi's police units (280) within MINUSCA would not be replaced at the end of their assignment in September.

Other external actors faced similar problems. On 7 June, *Uganda* People's Defence Force (UPDF) troops serving under the AU-mandated Regional Task Force (RTF) met violent demonstrators in Zémio after the controversial arrest of a civilian over a stolen UPDF weapon. One Ugandan soldier was reportedly stabbed in the event; in retaliation a civilian was killed by a UPDF soldier. On 25 August, an LRA commando killed a UPDF soldier and wounded two in an attack 60 km north-east of Zémio. On 20 May, the government of Uganda announced that it would withdraw from the RTF mission by the end of the year; but it did not do so.

Touadéra's inauguration ceremony on 30 March was attended by just two heads of state, Denis Sassou Nguesso (Congo) in his capacity as international mediator in the CAR crisis and Equatorial Guinea's Obiang Nguema, but also by two French ministers, Foreign Minister Jean-Marc Ayrault and Defence Minister Jean-Yves le Drian. The official *end of the transition period* had several consequences. With the restoration of a constitutional order, the CAR was readmitted as a full member of the AU on 7 April (after having been suspended in March 2013). It also meant that the mediation role of CEEAC (and Sassou Nguesso) was terminated. Le Drian announced the *termination of the French Sangaris mission*, arguably the most effective unit among all international peacekeepers. Touadéra met French President François Hollande in Paris before and after his inauguration, on 20 March and 20 April, and in Bangui on 13 May, and tried in vain to get guarantees for an extension. Visiting Bangui again on 31 October, le Drian declared the end of the Sangaris mission with its now 900 soldiers, but promised that France would stay engaged via contributions to MINUSCA and the EU Military Training Mission in the CAR (EUTM RCA), with about 350 soldiers. The EUTM RCA, with a nominal strength of 170 personnel and a budget of € 12.4 m in the current year, had a mandate to support the armed forces with strategic advice, education for officers and non-commissioned officers, and operational training. The EU Council adopted the programme on 16 July, with its first mandate expiring in September 2018. Touadéra had a busy schedule with overseas trips, including to Rome on 18 April (visiting FAO headquarters, the Pope, and Italy's President Sergio Matarella), and New York on 8–10 June to attend the UNSC and meet with Ban Ki-moon.

In terms of *relations in Africa*, Toudéra clearly privileged neighbouring countries. Starting with short-term trips immediately after his election, Touadéra visited Chad, Cameroon and the Sudan at least twice, and also Congo, the DRC and Equatorial Guinea. Foreign fighters in various rebel groups originated mostly from *Chad* and *Sudan*, but both governments looked ready to cooperate with the new CAR government. Chadian authorities complained about incursions by armed groups from the

CAR. Quite obviously, however, rebel leader Nourredine Adam was able to travel freely to southern Chad, despite a UN travel ban. New concerns that remnants of the 'Mouvement pour la Libération du Congo' (MLC) were again able to operate from Bangui were voiced after a former commander, Freddy Libeba Baongoli, was seen in the capital and later vowed in a video message to oust Kabila by force. In the ICC case against MLC leader Jean-Pierre Bemba, the verdict was finally declared on 21 March. He was found guilty of crimes against humanity, confirming that he had had effective authority and control over the forces that committed such crimes in Bangui in 2002. On 21 June, Bemba was sentenced to 18 years' imprisonment; he appealed against this verdict.

At the end of the year, *Cameroon* was hosting most of the CAR's refugees (around 260,000), around 7,000 of whom had arrived during the year. Most were concentrated in the sparsely populated eastern region, where refugees from the CAR now represented around one-fifth of the overall population. Illegal smuggling activities – diamonds for weapons – threatened to destabilise the area, with Cameroonian officials probably involved in illegal activities. FDPC rebels operated on both sides of the border. The two other main nations hosting refugees from the CAR were the DRC (103,000) and Chad (71,000). A return intentions survey carried out in December on behalf of UNHCR revealed that 73% of CAR refugees did not intend to go home, citing security concerns.

On 5 December, the *UN Panel of Experts* issued its final report, with many details on the continuation of the war economy. The experts also analysed the growing unpopularity of MINUSCA not only among the population, but also in government circles. Infractions of the sanctions regime were frequent, by both individuals and national authorities, and also by African governments (particularly South Africa, Kenya and Chad) inviting or allowing individuals under sanctions to enter their territory. During the year, Joseph Kony (LRA), believed to be on CAR territory, and his two sons Ali and Salim were put on the UN sanctions list.

Socioeconomic Development

On 20 July, the IMF's Executive Board approved a three-year SDR 83.6 m (about \$115.8 m) arrangement under the *ECF*. \$ 17.4 m of this was earmarked for immediate disbursement to restore macroeconomic stability. This decision was based on the recently concluded Article IV consultations. In the final report, IMF staff presented details of a still sombre picture. This included public debt, which had increased markedly from 23.5% of GDP (2012) to 48.5% (2015), as a result of both the significant fall in GDP and a rise in domestic payment arrears. *Payment arrears* were also accumulated towards a number of bilateral creditors (including recently China, India and the Saudi Development Fund). Capacities to address manifest management problems were critically low. The most relevant ministries (Finance and Budget, Planning, and International Cooperation) and the Institute of Statistics and Prices were understaffed, poorly equipped and working under difficult conditions, '"including a lack of sufficient energy to power computers and office equipment". IMF staff identified three risks to its joint programme with the authorities: absence of political agreement with armed groups, limited experience of the new government, and delayed provision of financial assistance from the international community. The last, according to the IMF, would jeopardise critical reforms, including in the security sector. In fact, the deteriorating security situation was given as major explanation for the revision towards the end of the year of initially optimistic projections. *GDP growth*, initially projected at 5.2%, was estimated at 4.5% in December, while inflation went up from 4.0%to 5.1% – lower than the African average, but also significantly higher than the convergence rate of 3% set by CEMAC.

The weakness of private operators was equally evident, particularly the *financial sector*, the smallest in CEMAC. The IMF termed it "largely underdeveloped" and saw it playing a limited role in supporting the economy. Only about 1% of the population held a bank account and 0.5% had access to credit.

The National Assembly passed a *revised budget* (of CFAfr 259.2 bn in expenses with a CFA 49.2 bn deficit) on 2 October to account for increased spending. According to the new budget, domestic revenue should be kept at 8% of GDP (estimated at $ 1.7 bn), while primary spending would be slightly reduced to 11.3% of GDP. Despite critical discussions, the law was passed by a large majority.

The critical *donor meeting* on 17 November in Brussels came at a moment of waning confidence in the new authorities. However, donor commitments reached a total of € 2.1 bn, about one quarter more than the government had expected. The European Commission pledged € 409 m, while EU member states made additional pledges amounting to € 298 m (for 2017–21). Touadéra admitted having noted some reservations about the government's ability to implement the recovery plan, but committed himself to ensuring that all funds were properly accounted for.

The partial lifting of a *diamond sales embargo* within the Kimberley Process, allowing the export of diamonds produced in the western part of the country, originally only from Berberati, was extended in September to include Boda, Carnot and Nola as 'compliant zones'. The export of rough diamonds from those areas resumed, while export from the eastern production zones (under rebel control) remained banned. However, it was obvious that a major part of the diamonds produced was smuggled out of the country. One indication was that a suspiciously strong and growing number of probably fake Kimberley Process certificates from Cameroon had been issued in previous years, exceeding the total official annual production of Cameroon and most probably stemming from the CAR.

The *humanitarian situation* remained problematic. In a press release on 28 November, the UN Office for the Coordination of Humanitarian Affairs (OCHA) stated that nearly half of the population were still in need of humanitarian assistance. A cholera outbreak in central CAR in summer killed at least 16 people (66 cases were confirmed). By 31 December, only slightly fewer than in 2015, some 460,000 refugees, plus 410,000 IDPs were waiting for improved conditions to return to their home regions.

Chad

Ketil Fred Hansen

The re-election of President Déby Itno on 10 April and the 'austerity measures' introduced by the government on 31 August resulted in massive protests. However, the gang rape of a 16-year-old schoolgirl by young 'untouchables' in Ndjamena on 8 February sparked off even heavier social protests throughout the country. On 30 May, former president Hissène Habré was sentenced to life in prison for crimes against humanity, torture and war crimes in Dakar (Senegal), thus ending more than 20 years' civil struggle to get him sentenced. Strong police and military surveillance proved effective in stopping attacks by Boko Haram on Chadian territory and no deaths resulted from terror attacks during the year. Déby strengthened his international reputation as an unreserved anti-terror ally.

Domestic Politics

Presidential elections, run with biometric voter cards, took place on 10 April. Of the 6.3 m registered voters, some 46,000 were diaspora Chadians. An all-time high 76% of registered voters participated. The 13 challengers to the incumbent were far from

 | DOI 10.1163/9789004355910_024

posing a real threat to him. Déby Itno, representing the 'Mouvement Patriotique du Salut' (MPS), received 59.9% of the votes, granting him a fifth term in office. The strongest opposition came from *Saleh Kebzabo*, representing the 'Union Nationale pour le Développement et le Renouveau' (UNDR), who received only 12.8% of the votes, despite the fact that, in mid-March, a joint force of 13 other political parties called 'Front de l'Opposition pour la République, le Changement et l'Egalité' (FORCE) declared that they were supporting him. In third place came Mbaiherem Laoukein Kourayo, representing the 'Convention Tchadienne pour la Paix et le Développement' (CTPD) took 10.6% of the votes. The opposition described the elections as an "electoral hold-up", while the Independent National Electoral Commission (CENI) proclaimed the elections "free and fair". In Léré, the hometown of Saleh Kebzabo, the population protested massively against the re-election of Déby on 5 May and police brutality led to one death and many injuries. The total cost of the elections, including training of personal and all materials, was estimated by the CENI at CFAfr 47.5 bn (some € 72 m).

Two major *government reshuffles* took place after Albert Pahimi Padacke replaced Kalzeube Payimi Deubet as prime minister on 13 February. On 16 February, Déby replaced 12 of the 26 ministers appointed only six weeks earlier (on 26 December 2015). The second reshuffle, on 14 August, following the re-inauguration of Déby as president on 8 August, installed 22 new ministers. Only six ministers from the February government remained. Numerous minor government changes occurred during the year, most spectacularly the removal of an older brother of the president, Daoussa Déby Itno, as minister of post and telecommunications on 5 May. Throughout the year, Déby issued decrees nominating new governors, prefects and sub-prefects and other public officials, a common way for him to keep the bureaucracy under firm personal control.

On 26 July in N'Djamena, 31 major political opposition parties founded the 'Front de l'Opposition Nouvelle pour l'Alternance et le Changement' (FONAC) under the leadership of Saleh Kebzabo, the 69-year-old head of the UNDR and former minister under Déby. Younger civil society leaders in Chad criticised FONAC for only including the same old, politically powerful men. On 27 December, FONAC changed its leadership and nominated Mahamat Ahmat Alhabo from the 'Parti pour les Libertés et le Développement' (PLD) as its new coordinator, but neither his age (63) nor his former connections with the Déby regime (he was Chad's ambassador to France in 2000) answered this criticism. On 17 November, FONAC held a public meeting at the Abena Stadium in N'Djamena, despite the government banning it "for security reasons". Police intervened with tear gas and dispersed the meeting, arresting some 30 participants, including the head of the political party 'Rassemblement Patriotique du Renouveau' (RPR), Mahama Bechir Barh, and the young activist Mahamat Kally. Twelve of them were held in custody until early December.

Rarely had the regime faced such strong mobilisation by civil society groups. The *social movements* 'Collectif Tchadien Contre la Vie Chère' (CTCVC), led by Nely Versinis Dingamnayal, and the 'Trop C'est Trop!', headed by Céline Narmadj, had been the leading social movements against Déby's regime for some time. Now, a great number of new, and seemingly overlapping, social movements were established, all calling for the departure of President Déby and the restoration of democracy by non-violent means. Many of them were mere umbrella groups of already established civil organisations, while others were brand new creations. The most important included 'Iyina' ('We are tired' in local Arabic), established on 11 January and headed by former student leader *Kaina Palmer Nadjo*, 'Ca suffit', established on 22 February and led by the well-known human rights activist Mahamat Nour Ibedou, the diaspora based 'Projet pour une Alternance Crédible au Tchad' (PACT), established on 23 July in Paris and led by Abdelkerim Yacoub Koundougoue, and finally 'Ça Doit Changer', an umbrella organisation of 15 pupils' and young people's movements, established on 11 November.

On 29 December 2015, well known public figures together with political opposition parties and various civil society organisations, many of them members of FONAC, created the 'Mouvement d'Eveil Citoyen' (MECI), which was said to be closely related to the regime-critical web site www.TchadConvergence.com and an apparently *new politico-military movement* established by former general Mahamat Nouri. Yet another new politico-military movement, called 'Front pour l'Alternance et la Concorde au Tchad' (FACT), was created in April in Tanoua in Northern Chad, led by Mahamat Mahdi-Ali, with some 800–1,500 well-equipped troops. However, Nouri and Mahdi-Ali were not on good enough terms to unite their movements. There was even a skirmish between the two, resulting in some 20 deaths just after FACT was established.

The civil movements used a variety of strategies to challenge Déby and his regime including protests, public meetings, general strikes ('villes mortes'/dead cities) and whistle-campaigns. Among the most important demonstrations were the 15 February rally in N'Djamena and one on 22 February in Faya Largeau protesting at the gang rape of a 16-year-old schoolgirl, nicknamed *Zouhoura*, on 8 February in N'Djamena. Demonstrators asked for "Justice for Zouhoura" and posters proclaiming "Je suis Zouhoura" were frequent both in the streets and on Facebook. Police brutality during the demonstrations led to two deaths. The rapists were all sons of high-ranking regime officials. Zouhoura's uncle, Mahamat Yesko Brahim, with whom she had lived, was a candidate for president in the upcoming elections. After heavy national protests and significant international attention the police jailed the young rapists. On 30 June, the criminal court in Ndjamena condemned the six young 'untouchables' to ten years' forced labour, but at least two of them had been freed or managed to escape by the end of the year.

On 24 February, *'villes mortes'* were organised by various social movements and largely followed by the population both in N'Djamena and the provinces, as a protest against Déby standing for a fifth time in the presidential elections. Schools and markets were closed and traffic was virtually non-existent. Another protest for the same reasons, on 11 March, called for people to blow whistles for 15 minutes in the morning and 15 minutes in the evening, but was less successful. However, when Ibedou and Younous Mahadjir representing 'Ça Suffit', Nadjo Kaina from 'Iyina' and Narmadji from 'Trop C'est trop!' were arrested on 21 and 22 March for planning a civil protest against the upcoming presidential elections, huge protests followed on 30 and 31 March. The four civil society leaders were held in custody until 14 April, when they were all handed down four-month suspended prison sentences for public troublemaking and subversive acts.

Press freedom was limited and journalists worked in an environment of fear and suspicion, although freedom of the media was reportedly improving: Chad jumped seven places up on the Reports without Borders' World Press Freedom Index and numerous independent newspapers were published and distributed in N'Djamena. Among the most influential were the weeklies 'La Voix', 'Abba Garde', 'Haut Parleur' and 'N'Djamena Hebdo'. Among the independent radio stations, 'Radio Liberté' was by far the most influential. The regime *blocked Internet and SMS messaging* on election day. Access to Facebook was restricted to users with a foreign login VPN. On 24 June, Madjissembaye Ngardinon, a journalist employed by 'Abba Garde', was arrested while covering a conflict over land tenure, where the police were involved, and was detained for several days. On 22 July, journalists at the state-owned radio and television broadcasting office went on strike for better salaries and working conditions. On 30 August, the director of 'Haut Parleur', Stéphane Ouaya, was arrested for "fraud and blackmailing" only to be released on 22 September after being tried and acquitted. On 14 November, the local police closed down the community station 'Radio Barkadjé', situated in Kélo town some 400 km south of N'Djamena. The regime accused its director, Edmond Kandi Weidigué, of sedition and kept him in custody for over a week without charge.

Civil liberties were more generally under attack. Out of the more than 40 members of the security and defence forces who went missing immediately after the presidential elections, presumably for not voting for Déby, 23 had not re-appeared by the end of the year. The regime frequently arrested organisers of and participants in demonstrations and held them for some hours or days in custody before releasing them. Former prime minister Dinamou Daram was arrested on 6 October for encouraging citizens not to pay taxes and fines, arguing that the money would only be used for corruption by the regime. The regime released him on 10. December.

However, Déby used also cooption of enemies as a strategy to strengthen his grip on power. Mohamed Ibni Oumar Saleh, son of the opposition leader kidnapped by Déby's security forces on 3 February 2008 and never seen since, returned from exile in France to become the CEO of the state-owned CotonTchad on 1 October. In August, Déby reportedly married a young woman from his home region Amdjaress in order to build relations with the Borgat clan from the Ennedi region. There was lively speculation that he may have done this to strengthen relations with Ali Ordjo Hemchi, head of the 'Mouvement d'Action pour le Changement au Tchad' (MACT), a rebel movement that had recently been silent.

On 30 May, the Extraordinary African Chambers in Dakar sentenced former president *Hissène Habré* to life in prison, finding him responsible for some 40,000 deaths during his presidency (1982–90). More than a decade's work by national and international human rights groups made this case a world first in sentencing a former president for crimes against humanity and torture. He was also ordered to pay victims reparations of CFAfr 10–20 m (€ 15–30,000) Habré rejected the authority of the court but still appealed against the verdict.

On 12 December, parliament replaced the 1964 *criminal code*. Important changes included the abolition of the death penalty (except for acts of terror), a rise in the minimum age for marriage from 16 to 18 years and the inclusion of a penalty for homosexuality.

Foreign Affairs

President *Idriss Déby Itno enjoyed a high standing* among his peers in Africa. He continued as chair of the regional G5 Sahel group and the AU elected him as its chairman for a year on 30 January. On his inauguration as president, on 8 August, 14 African heads of state were present in N'Djamena. In addition, Déby received numerous African presidents in his Rose Palace in N'Djamena throughout the year.

Déby tried to make Chad less dependent of the US and France by fostering relations with regimes in the Middle East and Asia. He *travelled widely* to African countries, the Middle East and Europe, making a total of 37 official visits, more than any other African president. Sudan's President Omar el-Bashir received Déby in Khartoum numerous times and, in February, he travelled to Riyadh (Saudi Arabia), where up to 5,000 of Chadian troops, together with troops from 19 other nations, participated in 'Northern Thunder', the most important Islamic anti-terror military training exercise the world had ever seen. On 30 May, Déby discussed military and financial issues with the crown prince of *Saudi Arabia* in N'Djamena. Déby's relations with King Salman's regime in Saudi Arabia strengthened considerably, as did Chad's relations with *Qatar*. On 3 September, Déby was in China on an official visit discussing business, military cooperation and development assistance with president Xi Jinping.

On 11–13 October, Déby visited Berlin at the invitation of *Germany*'s Chancellor Angela Merkel, who promised close to $ 10 m in humanitarian assistance and military aid to fight terror. Chad also kept strong military links with the US and France. Both securing crude oil deliveries and combating terrorism, including Boko Haram, made the *US* interested in solid collaboration with Déby's regime. The US-led Trans-Saharan Counterterrorism Partnership offered advice, training, intelligence and equipment to Chad's military forces. As one small example, on 8 December, the US delivered the first 20 of 60 promised light armoured combat vehicles to the Chadian Joint Force to help fight Boko Haram.

France also regarded Déby's regime as key for maintaining stability in a troubled region, and supported Chad with intelligence and military training. The French *Operation Barkhane*, consisting of some 3,500 well-equipped French troops including some 200 armoured vehicles, 20 helicopters and three drones, was led from N'Djamena. French troops were present in the capital and also in Abeché and Faya. French Defence Minister Jean-Yves Le Drian made four official visits to Chad (in April, August, November and December). The new French Prime Minister Bernard Cazeneuve chose Chad as the destination for his first trip abroad, on 29 December. This all indicated the importance of Chad for French military engagements in Africa. In early June, Chad sent some 2,000 troops to Niger to help fight Boko Haram. Former Chadian minister of foreign affairs Mahamat Saleh Annadif had taken over the leadership of the MINUSMA operations in Mali on 15 January and, by the end of the year, 1,550 Chadian troops were participating in MINUSMA. On 27 August, four Chadian soldiers died in action in Mali. While official relations between Chad and France were cordial, both French civil society and the Chadian diaspora in France continued to criticise the regime in N'Djamena. In response, Chad's embassy in Paris made wide use of its power to refuse entry visas to French critics.

Chad received huge amounts of *development and humanitarian aid* from the EU and various bilateral donors and UNDP and WFP, as well as other multilateral organisations, had offices in Chad. However, both long-term development aid and short-term humanitarian assistance were underfinanced when compared with the needs. WFP stated that Chad had one of the highest levels of hunger in the world, while UNDP estimated 97% of the population were at risk of contracting malaria. On 11 March, UNDP and the Swiss based Global Fund announced funding of € 59 m to fight AIDS, tuberculosis and malaria, but the majority of aid to Chad was either security related or earmarked to fight terrorism or to support refugees and IDPs. As an example, on 1 August, the EU commissioner for International Cooperation and Development signed a € 50 m support package for the Multi-National Joint Task Force based in N'Djamena, to fight Boko Haram.

Chad hosted a considerable number of *refugees and IDPs*. The most important camps were in eastern and south-eastern parts of the country, accommodating some 300,000 refugees from Darfur some 70,000 from the CAR. On 15 September, the UN's Office for the Coordination of Humanitarian Affairs provided $ 10 m from the UN Central Emergency Response Fund to meet their most pressing needs.

Afraid of being attacked by Boko Haram or other violent groups, some 130,000 refugees and IDPs in the Lake Chad region also required humanitarian assistance. A declared state of emergency continued in the Lake Chad region throughout the year, although Boko Haram 'only' killed three and wounded some 60 in Chad during the year.

Socioeconomic Developments

On 31 August, the government introduced 16 measures to reduce a significant budget deficit. While the regime primarily stressed the low price of oil and the high cost of fighting Boko Haram to explain the difficult financial situation, the opposition added high levels of corruption within the bureaucracy and the political elites, high intelligence and police costs and bad governance as further causes. Salaries for numerous public sector employees had not been paid for months and the state had accumulated unpaid bills for some € 500 m issued by the private sector by the end of August. What the government called "urgent reform measures" were described by the opposition as '*austerity measures*', a term also used by the international media and most of the population.

One austerity measure, the reduction of allowances, came into force on 26 October (Decree 683/2016). Allowances for ministers and high-level personal at the Presidency were reduced to CFAfr 30,000 (€ 45) per day, while other public officers would receive only CFAfr 10,000 (€ 15) per day to cover board and lodging on official domestic duty. This caused four weeks of strike by both judges and doctors in N'Djamena.

Another austerity measure was to cancel scholarships for university students. Up to 2016, university students had received CFAfr 360,000 (€ 550) per year in scholarships. Described by the student union as "academic genocide", the ending of scholarships resulted in massive student protests and the university in N'Djamena did not reopen after the summer vacation. Public sector employees and members of the three major workers associations went on strike for weeks in protest at the non-payment of their salaries. On 28 September, students took to the streets of N'Djamena en masse to protest against the austerity measures.

The national Office for Tourism signed a three-year sponsorship contract with the French football club Metz on 27 August, creating debates in both Chad and France; while the debate in Chad focused the use of public money in the times of crisis and budget deficits, the debate in France focused on accepting sponsorship from dictatorial regimes. While the sum offered to FC Metz was confidential, estimates turn around € 2–4 m a year.

On 5 October, the Court of First Instance in N'Djamena ordered the Doba oil consortium led by *ExxonMobil* to pay $ 819 m in unpaid royalties and in addition, $ 74 bn (close to five times Chad's GDP) in penalties for the non-payment. ExxonMobil appealed on the spot. Negotiations between ExxonMobil and the Chadian authorities started outside the courtroom from mid-November, but the case had not been resolved by the end of the year.

During the last weekend of November, a quarrel between boys playing football in N'Gueli on the outskirts of N'Djamena ended with two Zaghawa players killing a young player of Kreda ethnicity. The affair sparked off a fight between the two ethnic groups that resulted in five deaths and 18 people wounded. The 'Convention Tchadienne pour la Défense des Droits de l'Homme' stated that the escalation of the quarrel was due to Déby's marginalisation of the Kreda (a sub-group within the larger Gouran/Toubou umbrella group known for being active in various military rebel movements) to the advantage of the Zaghawa and the incident was interpreted by most commentators as a proxy-political fight. The minister of interior paid off the Kreda community to keep them calm.

Despite falling oil prices, crude oil was still by far the most valuable export product represented 93% of export value, or $ 1.9 bn. The US purchased 61% of the exported oil while India was the second most important buyer. Cotton, the second most important export product, represented 1.6% of total export value. The USA, India and China overtook France as the most important destinations for Chadian exports, but France remained top of the list of providers of foreign imports (18%), closely followed by China (16%) and Cameroon (14%).

In the midst of the huge financial state deficit and serious austerity measures imposed on the population, the biggest and smartest mall in Chad, the Modern Market, opened in N'Djamena on last weekend in February. It included a 2,600 m² supermarket filled with international food brands. The Chadian elites seemed to manage the economic crisis well.

Rain arrived earlier than usual in most of the country resulting in a 16 % *better harvest* than in 2015. Likewise, grazing for animals was eased by favourable rains, which led to lower prices for meat. In all regions with the exception of the Lake Tchad area, the nutrition situation also improved compared with 2015.

Congo

Brett L. Carter

On 20 March, citizens in the Republic of Congo were called to the polls to elect a new president. Few participated, for no one believed the election would be free and fair. President Denis Sassou Nguesso's government announced his 'victory' in the early hours of 24 March, when it calculated that most citizens in Brazzaville and Pointe-Noire would be asleep. The election was Sassou Nguesso's third since reclaiming power following the 1997 civil war, and the new constitution, passed in October 2015, left him poised to serve at least another three terms. The election elicited widespread protests across the country, which culminated in citizens setting fire to a government building in Brazzaville on 4 April. In retaliation, the government arrested scores of civil society activists and launched a military campaign against the Pool region, outside Brazzaville, which continued through the year. As Western governments condemned the electoral process and subsequent government violence, Sassou Nguesso intensified his diplomatic offensive in Beijing. As global oil prices remained low, the government confronted a financial crisis, with GDP growth falling to 1.7% and external debt rising to 77% of GDP.

 | DOI 10.1163/9789004355910_025

Domestic Politics

The year began with substantial tension, as citizens looked to the 20 March *presidential elections*. Sassou Nguesso announced his candidacy on 25 January, to no one's surprise. Indeed, the October 2015 constitutional referendum had been widely viewed as Sassou Nguesso's attempt to remove term limits, enabling him to retain power with a veneer of legitimacy.

The electoral campaign featured nine *candidates*: Sassou Nguesso, three candidates who comprised the 'moderate opposition' and were financed by the regime, and five candidates who comprised the 'radical opposition'. The five 'radical opposition' candidates claimed membership in the 'Initiative pour la Démocratie au Congo-Front Républicain pour le Respect de l'Ordre Constitutionnel' (IDC-FROCAD), an umbrella alliance that had organised the referendum boycott in October 2015. Of IDC-FROCAD's five declared candidates, three – Guy Brice Parfait Kolélas, Claudine Munari and André Okombi Salissa – had served as Sassou Nguesso ministers for a total of 29 years since 1997 and all three resigned from IDC-FROCAD in protest against Sassou Nguesso's bid for a third term. The two other 'radical opposition' candidates were General Jean-Marie Michel Mokoko and Pascal Tsaty Mabiala, who had served as secretary general of the 'Union Panafricaine pour la Démocratie Sociale' (UPADS) since 2006. Political heir to Pascal Lissouba, the only democratically elected president in Congo's history, Tsaty Mabiala drew substantial support from the southern regions of Niari, Bouenza and Lékoumou. Kolélas, eldest son of a respected former mayor of Brazzaville, drew support from Pool, surrounding Brazzaville. Claudine Munari's popular support was limited mostly to Bouenza.

Although these three candidates' constituencies were relatively circumscribed geographically, two opposition candidates managed to straddle the political divide between northern and southern Congo, and so constituted a profound threat to Sassou Nguesso. General Mokoko, a native of Plateaux, in northern Congo, was Sassou Nguesso's most threatening opponent. Military chief of staff during the National Conference of 1991, Mokoko ordered his troops to guarantee the Conference's sovereignty despite Sassou Nguesso's orders to disband it and for this he was regarded as an icon, a pivotal figure in Congo's democratic transition in the early 1990s. Mokoko's candidacy attracted the support of frustrated northerners and southerners, who regarded him as a champion of democracy. Okombi Salissa, Sassou Nguesso's other chief opponent, was similarly able to bridge the political cleavage between north and south. Also a native of Plateaux, Okombi Salissa drew considerable support from Bouenza, where he had assembled a substantial political machine.

Citizens had few expectations that the 20 March election would be free or fair. The electoral commission was filled with long-time Sassou Nguesso allies, Mokoko was repeatedly threatened with incarceration during the campaign, the EU refused to send monitors, and the government denied entry to AI. To forestall popular protests, *the government suspended Internet access and mobile communications* on 20–22 March. When citizens surrounded polling stations to prevent fraud, the government dispersed them with tear gas. The government even outlawed the use of motor vehicles on election day.

Knowing that Sassou Nguesso's victory announcement would arouse popular anger, the government chose to release *election results* slowly, in stages. The first leak occurred at roughly 2200 hours local time on 21 March, when 'Jeune Afrique', a Paris-based weekly edited by a Sassou Nguesso ally, reported that Sassou Nguesso led initial tallies with 62% of votes cast. The second release occurred at roughly 1800 hours local time on 22 March, when the national election commission announced that Sassou Nguesso had received 67% of votes cast, with only ballots from Pointe-Noire remaining. Sassou Nguesso ultimately claimed 60% of the vote, with a turnout of 69%. In reality, polling stations around Brazzaville were empty until late afternoon, when the regime began bussing in its supporters – many of whom had been paid – to create an illusion of participation.

Of Brazzaville's nearly 2 m residents, only about 200 celebrated Sassou Nguesso's re-election on the streets. The opposition immediately denounced the results as blatantly fraudulent, as did Western embassies. Fearful of an Arab Spring-style revolution, Sassou Nguesso responded by ordering the Republican Guard to encircle the opposition's headquarters and instructing riot police to patrol Brazzaville. Fearful of violence, the population largely stayed at home. Schools and markets remained closed for several days.

On 4 April, a group of young men, in a final attempt to trigger a popular uprising against the government, set fire to the government's administrative headquarters in Makélékélé, one of Brazzaville's nine 'arrondissements' and an opposition stronghold. In retaliation, on 5 April the government launched a *military campaign* against the Pool region. It dispatched ground troops, armoured tanks and attack helicopters. The government justified the military operation by blaming the Makélékélé fire on the Ntsiloulou militia, which was active in Pool between 1998 and 2003, but had effectively disbanded in 2006. Since then, its leader, Frédéric Bintsamou, widely known as Pastor Ntoumi, had lived quietly on a ranch in Tsoumouna, Pool, some 45 miles from Brazzaville. The government's military operations in Pool continued till the end of the year. Since the government denied humanitarian organisations access to Pool, the number of fatalities was unclear. Civil society groups estimated that 15,000 citizens died and perhaps 100,000 were displaced, often seeking refuge in the forests. Munari described the operation as 'genocide'. Pastor Ntoumi was still at large at year's end. Given his proximity to Brazzaville, many citizens regarded the government's inability to capture him as evidence that its military campaign was designed primarily to threaten government opponents into submission.

As the military continued its assault on the Pool region, *the government arrested and tortured dozens of citizens* in Brazzaville and Pointe-Noire. To attract attention to the unfolding humanitarian crisis, IDC-FROCAD attempted another protest in Brazzaville, on 15 April, one day before Sassou Nguesso's scheduled inauguration. In response, the government placed the leaders of IDC-FROCAD under house arrest: Munari, Okombi Salissa, Mokoko, Kolélas, and Charles Zacharie Bowao, Sassou Nguesso's defence minister from 2007 to 2012, and now a particularly strident opponent. The 15 April protest was cancelled, and Sassou Nguesso was inaugurated on 16 April.

On 23 April, Sassou Nguesso appointed as *prime minister* Clément Mouamba, a native of Bouenza, one-time UPADS vice-president, and Lissouba's finance minister in 1992–3. The appointment was viewed as a very modest attempt to mollify southerners. Sassou Nguesso's ongoing campaign of *systematic human rights abuses* ensured that Mouamba's appointment had no such effect. On 15 June, the government arrested Mokoko, who, like all other members of IDC-FROCAD save Kolélas, refused to recognise Sassou Nguesso's electoral victory. Mokoko was charged with 'breaching internal state security'. He was still in prison at year's end, in conditions that many opposition leaders described as inhumane. A similar arrest warrant was issued for Okombi Salissa, who then went into hiding, where he still remained at the end of the year. The government instead arrested his younger brother, who died in police custody on 21 December from injuries sustained under torture. On 10 August, the government arrested Colonel Aimé Portella, brother of the Archbishop of Pointe-Noire; the arrest was widely interpreted as a warning signal to the Catholic Church, which had long been a fierce, if quiet, critic of the regime.

Foreign Affairs

The March presidential election, as well as its aftermath, dominated Sassou Nguesso's foreign policy. Western governments were unanimous in their condemnation. The EU refused to send monitors and the USA announced it was "profoundly disappointed" with the electoral process.

Sassou Nguesso's foreign policy was also animated by the ongoing 'biens mal acquis' (*ill-gotten gains*) corruption investigation. On 2 February, he announced that he had filed a lawsuit in the French courts against 'X' – thought to be TI – a month before. Although the lawsuit was sealed so its details were unclear. Sassou Nguesso's lawyer claimed that 'X' had "attempted to defraud the court". In consequence, Sassou Nguesso claimed, the lawsuit sought the dismissal of all 'biens mal acquis' proceedings against the Sassou Nguesso family, the Bongo family of Gabon and the Obiang family of Equatorial Guinea. In September the Paris 'Tribunal de Grande Instance' announced that Teodorín Obiang, Equatorial Guinea's vice president and son of its president, would begin in January 2017. If Obiang's trial ended with a conviction, most French legal observers expected the Sassou Nguesso family to be targeted next.

Sassou Nguesso faced other legal challenges in foreign courts. Philippe Chironi, along with Lucien Ebata, co-founded Orion Oil, widely regarded as a front company for Sassou Nguesso's money laundering apparatus. A French national, Chironi was also administrator of Forbes Afrique Media Holding, which Ebata had founded with Sassou Nguesso capital. Both companies were registered in Switzerland, and throughout 2016 the Swiss authorities investigated Chironi for laundering Congolese oil revenue to the benefit of Sassou Nguesso. His trial was scheduled for January 2017 in San Marino. Two other European associates, José Veiga and José Mauricio Caldeira, were arrested in February and July, respectively, and both were charged with money laundering by the Portuguese authorities in a case dubbed the 'Route de l'Atlantique' scandal. Veiga and Caldeira were senior figures in Asperbras, a Brazilian firm that had received several major infrastructure contracts from the Sassou Nguesso government in recent years. In December, the Federal Court of *Canada* ruled that Sassou Nguesso's nephew, Wilfrid Nguesso, was *persona non grata*, and so would be refused entry. By virtue of his membership in the Sassou Nguesso family, the Court ruled, Wilfrid belonged to a 'criminal organization'.

With Western governments condemning the March election and European courts pursuing corruption allegations, Sassou Nguesso continued to pursue closer diplomatic relations with *China*. Chinese President Xi Jinping hosted Sassou Nguesso for a state visit in Beijing on 4–8 July. The trip marked Sassou Nguesso's first outside Africa after the March election and his second to China in three years. Sassou Nguesso and Xi announced that the Chinese government would play a central role in building the Pointe-Noire Special Economic Zone, the centrepiece of Sassou Nguesso's plans for a post-oil economy. Construction was scheduled to begin in early 2017. Sassou Nguesso also reiterated his commitment "to work closely with China in international affairs", especially in the South China Sea. Accordingly, China emerged as Congo's leading trade partner, receiving 42.1% of its total exports and generating 20.3% of its total imports.

Sassou Nguesso sought to capitalise on Donald Trump's surprise election as president of the *United States* in November. Buoyed by Trump's apparent willingness to engage with foreign dictators, Sassou Nguesso hired disgraced Republican lobbyist Jack Abramoff, who arranged a meeting between Trump and Sassou Nguesso on December 27 at a charity dinner in Miami, Florida. Sassou Nguesso departed Brazzaville on 26 December, accompanied by the Congolese foreign minister and a coterie of aides. Sassou Nguesso publicised the meeting widely. Communications Minister Thierry Moungalla announced it on Twitter, along with a memo signed by Firmin Ayessa, Sassou Nguesso's long-time aide. The meeting was also announced on Sassou Nguesso's official website, in his propaganda newspaper 'Les Dépêches de Brazzaville' and on Télé-Congo, the state-run television station, which even broadcast a photograph of Trump and Sassou Nguesso embracing. It was clearly a fake, for the meeting was ultimately cancelled after the international press learned of it and Trump's spokesperson even denied that a meeting had ever been scheduled. Sassou Nguesso returned to Brazzaville on 31 December, and was excoriated in the African press after the Trump administration's denials.

Socioeconomic Developments

Congo's GDP, adjusted for purchasing power parity, was estimated to have reached $ 30.27 bn by year's end, up from $ 29.75 bn in 2015, at an estimated growth rate of 1.7%. This represented a sustained decline. In 2010, Congo's growth rate had reached nearly 9%; in 2014, it was 6.8%; in 2015, it fell to 2.3%. The decline was driven by two related factors. First, with the oil sector continuing to account for roughly 80% of government revenue and 65% of GDP, the Congolese economy was sharply affected by persistently low global crude prices. In turn, the government's fiscal position slid into crisis. Government reserves at the central bank fell by 75%, as compared with 49% in 2015, and by year's end were sufficient for only two months of imports. Public debt rose to nearly 80% of GDP, breaching the CEMAC convergence criterion limit of 70%. As crisis loomed, the government was forced to revise its fiscal policy. To do so, it cut public expenditure drastically, especially its construction budget, which, since 2010, had contributed a substantial share to non-oil GDP. By implementing pro-cyclical policies to control its fiscal deficit, the government exacerbated the economic contraction.

The government hoped for some relief in the short term from the Moho Nord oil field, scheduled to come online in early 2017 and produce as much as 100,000 b/d. Congo averaged roughly 250,000 b/d over the year, with Moho Nord, expected to reach 300,000 b/d by 2018. External creditors were sceptical. The Sassou Nguesso government missed a debt service payment on 30 June, and then failed to pay during the ensuing 30-day grace period. By mid-August, all major credit ratings agencies had cut the government's bond rating sharply. By the end of the year, Standard & Poor's had downgraded Congo to B-, from B at end 2015, and Moody's had downgraded Congo to B3, from Ba3 at end 2015. Moody's B3 rating left Congo government bonds a full six notches below investment grade. In August, the government's 2029 dollar bond, issued in 2007 and on which $ 478 m was outstanding, traded at just 67 cents on the dollar. With several substantial debt service payments due in the short term, ratings agencies were giving the Congolese economy a 'negative' outlook by year's end.

Democratic Republic of the Congo

Claudia Simons

The question of whether presidential elections would take place before President Joseph Kabila's mandate expired dominated public debate. 'Dialogue' became the buzzword of the year, with the government and opposition engaging, backing away, boycotting and re-engaging in a series of talks, first under the lead of the government, then under AU mediation and finally under the auspices of the Catholic Church. Various agreements were reached but were never signed by all the parties involved, and always left so many open questions that no solution to the political crisis was found by the end of the year. The political gamble was accompanied by mass protests in the capital, Kinshasa, and other big cities throughout the year, with peaks in September and December. In the shadow of the international headlines focussing on the political crisis and anti-third-term protests, armed violence intensified in both North Kivu und Kasai provinces. The security institutions engaged in gross human rights violations. Amid the political crisis, the economy suffered severely. After years of high growth rates and a relatively stable exchange rate, GDP slumped and the Congolese franc had to be devaluated.

 | DOI 10.1163/9789004355910_026

Domestic Politics

Throughout the year, Congolese citizens wondered whether presidential elections would take place before Kabila's mandate expired on 19 December and whether the president would seek a *third term in office*. The government and the 'Commission Electorale Nationale Indépendante' (CENI) constantly argued that the financial and logistical resources for holding elections were lacking, while the opposition considered this a strategy to delay elections in order for Kabila to stay in power beyond his second and constitutionally prescribed last term. Within this political conflict, 'dialogue' became the buzzword of the year, with a plethora of actors calling for inclusive talks and various, partly overlapping, attempts at dialogue being pursued, rejected, boycotted and re-started.

Kabila himself had already 'ordered' a *national dialogue* by ordinance in November 2015, but important opposition parties decried this effort as manipulation by the government, and so the talks did not take off. Most significantly, an opposition grouping formed in 2015, the G7, refused to enter into dialogue with the government and instead pursued a strategy of election campaigning, putting forward their designated presidential candidate, Moise Katumbi, a former governor of Katanga. UN Special Envoy for the Great Lakes Region Said Djinnit had already in 2015 investigated possibilities of internationally supported dialogue, but handed over the dossier to the AU in January. The latter officially nominated Edem Kodjo, the former Togolese prime minister and former secretary-general of the OAU, as facilitator on 7 April. Just prior to that, on 30 March, the UNSC stressed in its resolution 2277 (SCR2277) the need for an inclusive dialogue between political parties. By late summer, it was still unclear what type of dialogue was to be pursued – an internationally facilitated dialogue under the auspices of the government, thus more or less in line with Kabila's ordinance of 28 November 2015, or a dialogue between political parties as required under SCR2277.

This question also split the *opposition*. The historically important opposition party 'Union pour la Démocratie et le Progrès Social' (UDPS) had initially withdrawn from talks with the government. However, when Kodjo announced the establishment of a preparatory committee for the National Dialogue in April, the UDPS claimed that it should have the right to choose the 30 opposition representatives who were expected to have a part in this committee. After many delays, lists of nominees for membership of the committee were handed in by opposition parties and civil society but, when Kodjo announced the members of the committee on 24 May, they were immediately contested by parts of the opposition and civil society.

Meanwhile, the *Constitutional Court* ruled on 11 May that Kabila could remain president if elections did not take place within the limits of the constitutionally prescribed delay (i.e. in November, as originally scheduled). The ruling became known as the 'glissement' (sliding) ruling, as it was seen by most observers to be a means to delay elections. The court cited Art. 70 of the constitution, which allows the sitting president to remain in office until a new president is installed. The opposition criticised the ruling and argued that, in case of an election delay, an interim president should be installed after the expiration of Kabila's term on 19 December.

Overt government *repression* of the opposition undermined the prospects for serious talks. On 19 April, police attacked the Lubumbashi headquarters of the 'Union Nationale des Fédéralistes du Congo' (UNAFEC) opposition party, part of the G7 opposition platform, which was to host a speech by former governor of Katanga, Moise Katumbi. This sparked protests by opposition followers, to which police responded with tear gas and the arrest of at least 11 people. Only a few days later, on 24 April, the police fired tear gas at a rally of peaceful demonstrators, when Katumbi himself was walking with the crowd. On 4 May, Katumbi made public his candidacy for the presidency. The same day, Justice Minister Alexis Thambwe Mwamba announced an investigation into allegations that Katumbi had recruited foreign mercenaries, including US citizens. Katumbi was summoned to a court hearing in Lubumbashi on 9 May, where he appeared accompanied by several opposition politicians. Several court hearings took place in the following days amidst protests by thousands of followers and clashes between Katumbi associates and police in Lubumbashi. On 13 May, Katumbi was admitted to hospital to be treated for the effects of tear gas during these clashes. Five days later, the court issued an arrest warrant against him but on 19 May the prosecutor agreed to a request by his defence team that he be allowed to seek medical treatment abroad. Katumbi immediately left for South Africa and remained in exile there from where he travelled to various countries and pursued his political ambitions. According to HRW, at least 27 of Katumbi's associates had been arrested between 22 April and 7 May. On 22 June Katumbi was sentenced in absentia in another court case to three years in jail and a $ 6 m fine for selling a house that allegedly did not belong to him.

During a meeting in Brussels (Belgium) on 9–10 June, a number of opposition politicians, including Katumbi and Etienne Tshisekedi, agreed on a joint statement, rejecting dialogue under the auspices of Kabila and calling for dialogue in the form proposed by SCR2277. The opposition statement demanded that the dialogue be mediated by Kodjo and include representatives of the AU, UN, EU and OIF, as well as the USA. However, even after this meeting, the parties could not be brought to the table. Meanwhile, a pro-dialogue group had been formed by other opposition politicians, demanding an end to the blockage of the talks.

It was not till 1 September that the government, a part of the opposition and the facilitator officially started the 'National Dialogue'. Although part of the opposition (including the UDPS) had initially asked for Kodjo to act as facilitator, they rejected him when the dialogue started, arguing that he was biased towards the government. Further points of disagreement were the situation of political prisoners, the fate of Katumbi and Kabila's unwillingness to state clearly that he would not run for a third term. Thus, the dialogue had to be suspended for the first time only two days after its opening. Several suspensions followed over the weeks and the talks, originally scheduled to last for 15 days, dragged on for more than six weeks. On 26 September, Kodjo presented his first proposal for an agreement, but questions around the role of the president, the length of the transition period and the date of presidential elections remained in dispute. On 30 July, the voter registration process started, despite the fact that no one knew whether elections would actually take place. The announcement by the CENI on 1 October that elections could not be held before the end of 2018 clarified this issue, but unsettled the process. On 4 October, opposition heavyweights within the 'Rassemblement des Forces Politiques et Sociales pour le Changement' (hereafter: the 'Rassemblement') – yet another opposition platform that had united in order to stop Kabila from staying in power – under the leadership of Etienne Tshisekedi and Moise Katumbi drafted their demands for an agreement. They accepted the possibility of a delay to elections but Kodjo was to hand over the mediation to another facilitator, political prisoners were to be freed, the CENI was to be dissolved and Kabila was to leave power on 19 December.

The CENI called on the Consitutional Court on 17 September to permit a delay to the presidential elections. The Court repeatedly postponed its decision, apparently waiting for the political dialogue to come to a conclusion. On 19–20 September, one month before the expiry of Kabila's mandate, opposition parties, civil society organisations and youth movements took to the streets, calling for Kabila to leave power. The protests resulted in extreme violence. On 19 September, a mass opposition rally in Kinshasa clashed with police. According to the opposition, at least 50 people died; according to the government a police officer was burnt to death. Overnight on 19–20 September, the headquarters of the UDPS, 'Forces Novatrices pour l'Union et la Solidarité' (FONUS) and the 'Mouvement Lumumbiste Progressiste' (MLP) were set on fire, killing at least four people. Government and opposition accused each other of sparking the violence. In line with human rights NGOs, the UN High Commissioner for Human Rights during a speech in Geneva on 27 September denounced heavy violence by the police, army and presidential guard and referred to at least 53 deaths. On 12 October, the government issued a white paper on these events, stating that only 32 people had died, including three policemen. According to Vice Prime Minister Evariste Boshab, only the demonstrators had been armed and caused the bloodshed, while the police had been carrying only non-lethal weapons.

Hundreds of summary proceedings against alleged demonstrators, organisers and financers of the September unrest were held in Kinshasa. Arrest warrants were signed for at least nine leading politicians, including Tshisekedi's son Félix, the aspiring new leader of the UDPS.

Given the brutal suppression of the protests, the ongoing talks stalled and Tshisekedi and Katumbi decided to withdraw completely. The 'Rassemblement' thereupon became known as the radical opposition rather than those opposition parties that resumed the talks with the government after the protests. During a meeting on 4 October, Tshisekedi and Katumbi decided on their conditions for a dialogue, including a new facilitator and the dissolution of the CENI, but most importantly a clear commitment by Kabila that he would leave power on 19 December. On the same day, during a visit to Dar Es Salaam (Tanzania), Kabila suggested for the first time publicly that elections might not take place in 2016.

The *talks between the government and the moderate opposition parties* came to a conclusion on 17 October, with the signing of an agreement that set presidential elections for April 2018 (at the latest) and proposed that Kabila remain president after the expiration of his mandate. A prime minister from the opposition was to lead a transitional government until the elections. The same day, the Constitutional Court finally agreed that the elections be delayed, as the CENI had asked, arguing that the CENI did not have the capacity to organise elections within the constitutionally foreseen timeframe. The 'Rassemblement' did not sign the agreement, but Kodjo made it clear that the agreement was to remain open to new signatories.

Parallel to the signing of the agreement, on 17 October, a former senior banker at the 'Banque Gabonaise et Française Internationale' (BGFI), Jean-Jacques Lumumba, said in a Bloomberg News interview that, in May, the CENI had paid an excessive fee of $ 2.4 m to the DRC Unit of BGFI for an overdraft facility of $ 25 m, despite the fact that the CENI had already had at least $ 54 m at its disposal. This news not only challenged Kabila's (and the Constitutional Court's) argument that the CENI lacked the funds necessary to run elections, but also added to the opposition's suspicion that the CENI was in fact influenced by the president, given the BGFI's close links to Kabila's family. A close ally of Kabila was directing the BGFI DRC unit and Kabila's sister held around 40% of the shares of the unit. Lumumba left the DRC in June. On 1 November, Belgian Foreign Minister Didier Reynders called for an investigation into possible embezzlement.

Given the failure to come to an inclusive agreement involving all relevant political parties, the *Catholic Bishops' Conference* ('Conférence Episcopale Nationale du Congo' CENCO) began shuttle diplomacy between the signatories and non-signatories to the 17 October agreement. CENCO had been active in the dialogue before but had temporarily suspended participation in response to police violence against protesters in September. Meanwhile, the transitional government, as foreseen in the 17 October agreement, was finally installed on 22 December, with Samy Badibanga as prime minister. Badibanga had been a close ally of Etienne Tshisekedi before the 2011 presidential and parliamentary elections, but after the results of those elections had been announced and Kabila was proclaimed the winner, Tshisekedi had called on his party members to boycott parliament. Badibanga, however, had taken his seat and became president of the UDPS parliamentary group, thereby falling in Thisekedi's bad books. By appointing Badibanga as prime minister, Kabila also bypassed another very important figure within the moderate opposition, Vital Kamerhe of the 'Union pour la Nation Congolaise' (UNC).

During the days before Kabila's mandate expired on 19 December, Kinshasa was plunged into a *state of exception*. In anticipation of massive violence and a prolonged security crisis, the UK and US embassies withdrew their non-essential staff and issued travel warnings. Wealthy Congolese left the city and ordinary people stormed the markets to stockpile fuel and food. From 19 December onwards, many shops in Kinshasa remained closed for about three days. The UN Organization Stabilization Mission in the DRC (MONUSCO) redeployed some of its troops from the eastern provinces to the capital.

At first, opposition parties did not organise demonstrations for 19–20 December but said they would leave the people to express their anger themselves, but after Kabila (unsurprisingly) did not step down at midnight, opposition leaders called for demonstrations, accusing the president of carrying out a coup d'état. In the clashes that followed between police, military and demonstrators, at least 20 people lost their lives and 50 more were wounded in Kinshasa and Lubumbashi. The estimated total number of arrests during the days around 19–20 December varied from 220 to 600.

Among those arrested were 26 activists from the nation-wide civil movement 'La Lucha', who were detained in Goma and Mbuji-Maji. In fact, youth movements such as 'Filimbi' and 'Lucha' became increasingly popular in the political crisis and consequently were increasingly targeted by state repression. 'Lucha', which began as a single-issue movement campaigning for better access to drinking water in Goma in 2013, became internationally famous for its activism against a third term for Kabila on social media and on the street. A month before the end of Kabila's mandate, 'Lucha' and other youth platforms launched the 'bye bye Kabila' campaign. 'Lucha' activists were repeatedly arrested, detained, prevented from gathering or forcibly disappeared.

It was only on 31 December and as a result of heavy pressure by the bishops that an agreement between the signatories and non-signatories to the 17 October agreement was finally signed. It stated that elections should be held in 2017 and that Kabila would remain in office until then but was not allowed to run for another term. Until the end of March 2017, yet another transitional government was to be formed under the leadership of the opposition and was to be tasked with organising the transition process. However, the deal was not personally signed by either Kabila or Tshisekedi. This raised suspicions that the parties involved would not live up to their promises. Most importantly, doubts were still strong as to whether Kabila would eventually leave power as set out in the agreement and Kabila himself made no clear statement about a potential third term, not even during his state of the nation speech on 15 November.

International headlines focussed mainly on violent clashes around the questions of Kabila's third term in the major cities. However, armed violence in the eastern and northern provinces went on and/or flared up throughout the year.

The violence in *North Kivu's Beni territory*, which had started in 2014 and increased in 2015, continued through the year, reaching a new peak on 13 August, with the massacre of between 36 and 51 people (depending on the sources). Following the killings, people in Beni took to the streets, accused the government of inaction and vented their anger by throwing stones at police stations. Only three days before the massacre, Kabila had visited Beni and promised to bring security to the region. Information Minister Lambert Mende declared three days of nation-wide mourning starting on 15 August. Prior to these events, on 21 March, the Congo Research Group had published a report of investigations into the violence in Beni over the previous 18 months. The report drew two main conclusions. First, the Ugandan militia, Allied Democratic Force (ADF), which DRC authorities accused of being the sole author of the violence, was much more rooted in local society than the government believed. The latter portrayed the group as an Islamist force foreign to the DRC. Second, it was not the ADF alone that was carrying out the killings but local militias, as well as soldiers, were also involved in the violence. The report called for an official investigation into the events. The government denounced the report and said it was falsely accusing the 'Forces Armées de la République Démocratique du Congo' (FARDC) as an institution, although the report had only referred to individuals within the FARDC. On 7 January, at least 14 people of the Nande ethnic group were killed in Lubero territory in North Kivu, presumably by 'Forces Démocratiques de Libération du Rwanda' (FDLR) rebels. The same territory saw a massacre of at least 29 Hutu civilians presumably by a Nande militia on 30 November. The FDLR was seriously destabilised over the year, not only by operations by the FARDC, MONUSCO and local militias, but also by internal divisions, which led to a formal split of the group on 31 May. More than 50 officers under the command of former FDLR vice president Laurent Ndagijimana defected and created a new rebel group, the 'Conseil National pour le Renouveau et la Démocratie –Ubwiyunge' (CNRD). As of October, the FDLR had lost many positions and remained almost exclusively in Rutshuru territory in North Kivu province.

The former *Kasai* provinces, the stronghold of opposition leader Etienne Tshisekedi, became a new hot spot for armed violence. In July and August, small attacks by the militia of a local chief, Kamuina Nsapu, targeted police stations in Tshimbulu territory in Kasai-Central. On 8 August, nine people died and, on 12 August, nine militiamen, including Nsapu himself, as well as 11 policemen, were killed in clashes. On 22–23 September, fighting between the same local militia and the army cost the lives of at least 28 people in Kananga. The fighting continued, although little covered in the media, and by the end of the year, experts estimated that at least 400 people had been killed. On 4 October, UN Deputy Special Representative for the DRC David Gressly promised to investigate the situation and increase the number of MONUSCO troops in the area. On 3 October, the civil society organisations of Beni urged the ICC to open a case on the violence. The ICC responded that it was willing to do so if crimes fell within its competences, but that it had to work with the DRC authorities for reasons of complementarity.

Several smaller incidents took place in different parts of the country throughout the year. In *South Kivu*, people took to the streets and engaged in popular justice on 17–18 September to vent their anger about the continuing insecurity and the inability of the police and justice system to respond to it. Offices of the police, the prosecutor and the secret service were attacked and burnt in the localities of Kavumu and Misisi. In Kavumu, a presumed thief was wrested away from the police and burnt alive. In Misisi, two people died and five more were wounded during the confrontations. Earlier, the army and local authorities warned the population of infiltration into Uvira, South Kivu, by Burundian rebels, some of whom had been based in the area for a long time, while others surfaced with the ongoing crisis in Burundi. The government presumed links between these rebels and the M23, a Rwandan-backed rebel group that had made the headlines in 2012, but this was rejected by the M23. A conflict between different ethnic groups in the Kalemie region of *Katanga* province caused the temporary displacement of at least 30,000 people between July and October.

Foreign Affairs

Several *international organisations* were engaged in efforts to end the violence around elections and foster the political dialogue. Two UNSC resolutions directly urged the government to ensure inclusive dialogue and to hold elections on time. SCR2277 of 30 March, renewing the MONUSCO mandate (see below), stressed the need for an inclusive dialogue and served as reference for opposition parties (see above). SCR2293 of 23 June extended the UN arms embargo, asset freeze and travel ban on the DRC until 1 July 2017, calling on the government to ensure the holding of elections in November 2016. On 24 September, the AU, UN, EU and OIF issued a joint appeal for calm, calling for dialogue and the rapid calling of elections. On 13 October, a ministerial visit by SADC to Kinshasa, including the foreign ministers of Angola and Tanzania plus Mozambique's defence minister, discussed the political crisis and promoted dialogue. On 26 October, an international summit to find a solution to the crisis, jointly organised by ICGLR, the UN, SADC and the AU took place in Angola's capital, Luanda. One outcome of the summit was support for the 17 October agreement between the DRC government and one part of the opposition, which allowed Kabila to stay in power after the expiry of his mandate. The UDPS immediately criticised the conclusion.

The government also came under increasing pressure by bilateral partners. On 23 June, Washington imposed sanctions against Kinshasa's police commissioner, Célestin Kanyama. On 16 September, the *US government* threatened to impose additional sanctions on individuals perpetrating violence during protests against Kabila's efforts to stay in power. Only two days later, on 18 September, US Special Envoy Tom Perriello was verbally attacked and physically blocked by a member of Kabila's political party in an area of Kinshasa's Ndjili Airport, which was secured by Congolese authorities. Following the unrest and brutal repression of protests in Kinshasa on 19–20 September, the US Treasury Department imposed more sanctions on 28 September, targeting army general Amisi Kumba and former national police inspector John Numbi. Amisi, alias 'Tango Fort', had come under repeated criticism by the UN Group of Experts, who had accused him of illegal mineral trade and trading arms to militia groups in 2012, among other things. He had subsequently been suspended but was rehabilitated two years later and nominated commander of the first military zone (Kinshasa). Numbi had been cited in news reports over recent years in connection with the murder of human rights activist Floribert Chebeya in 2010. The US Treasury Department accused Amisi of violently repressing protests in Kinshasa on 19–20 September and Numbi of threatening opposition candidates during elections of governors in March. Freezing Numbi's and Amisi's assets remained largely symbolic, however, as experts did not believe they had assets in the US. Defence Minister Crispin Atama criticised the sanctions on 28 September and said the US was biased towards the opposition – and in fact already arming the opposition in Katanga, alluding to the Katumbi case.

Belgium's Foreign Minister Didier Reynder announced on 5 October a reduction of the maximum period for visas for Congolese citizens to six months. The measure was said to apply to Congolese with diplomatic passports, who had previously been granted one-year visas. Reynder justified the measure by reference to the uncertainty following the period after the expiry of Kabila's mandate. According to Reynder, bilateral relations could not continue as usual. He called the measure a sign to the government as well as to the opposition that elections should be held in 2017. After the violence of 19–20 December, the Belgian government said it would re-examine its relations with the government of the DRC.

On 3 October, *French Foreign Minister* Jean-Marc Ayrault called on Kabila to respect the constitution and to not run for re-election. In line with other EU partners, Ayrault announced that France would re-examine relations with the DRC after December 19 and called on the EU to follow suit.

Relations with the *Vatican* were tense, given the clear stance of the CENCO that the president should respect the constitution. On 26 September, Kabila travelled to Rome, where he was received by the pope. No statement was made after the 20-minute meeting; a Vatican communiqué merely stated that the talks had covered the tense political situation and the recent violence. On the day Kabila's mandate expired, the pope received the president and vice president of CENCO and in a public statement urged all parties to refrain from violence. Earlier, in May, after ten years of insistence by the Holy See, the government had signed a framework agreement with the Vatican on the protection of the Catholic Church's property in the DRC.

Several renowned international human rights researchers and journalists were banned. On 7 April, the government expelled Jason Stearns, one of the world's leading analysts of the DRC conflicts and director of the Congo Research Group (CRG), part of the Center for International Cooperation (CIC) at New York University. The official reason for the expulsion was migration irregularities, but the CIC assumed the decision to be in response to a report published by CRG on the security situation in Beni on 21 March (see above). The report was denounced and misrepresented by the DRC authorities after its publication. Immigration officers revoked HRW senior researcher Ida Sawyer's work permit on 3 July, although it had been renewed for three years as recently as May. Sawyer had to submit a new work permit request to renew her original permit, due to expire on 9 August. The request was denied on 8 August and Sawyer was asked to leave the country within 48 hours.

On 30 March, the *UNSC* by SCR2277 renewed the MONUSCO mandate up to 31 March 2017, including its most effective Intervention Brigade. The UNSC decided to maintain its current force levels, despite a 5 January report by Ban Ki-moon to the UN in which he had recommended cutting troop numbers by 1,700. Experts had thereupon raised concerns over a troop reduction. Kabila had been urging the UN to cut their troops for years and the UN had had already decided in 2015 to reduce the number of troops by 2,000.

The *ICC* cases dealing with Congolese citizens made progress. On 21 March, former presidential candidate in the 2006 elections and head of the rebel movement 'Mouvement de Libération du Congo' (MLC), Jean-Pierre Bemba, was found guilty of war crimes and crimes against humanity, more precisely murder, rape and pillage, perpetrated in the CAR between 2002 and 2003. On 21 June, the Court sentenced him to 18 years in prison, eight of which Bemba had already served during his trial. Bemba's defence team appealed on 28 September. On 21 October, the ICC approved symbolic collective reparations for victims of Thomas Lubanga, who had been convicted and sentenced in 2012 for recruiting child soldiers. After an appeal, the verdict had been confirmed in 2014 and, on 3 March 2015, the Court had decided for the first time in its history that the victims would be collectively compensated. It called on the Trust Fund for Victims to identify beneficiaries and decide on appropriate measures. It took over one-and-a-half years for the Trust Fund to present its plan to collectively indemnify the victims through the service-based 'Village Saving and Loan Association' reparations model, a tool to economically empower and improve the livelihoods of victims in five localities.

When the civil war in neighbouring *South Sudan* reached a new peak in July, around 750 South Sudanese civilians, as well as fighters loyal to the former South Sudanese vice president Riek Machar, crossed over into the DRC. After the DRC government asked MONUSCO to take care of the refugees, MONUSCO started in August to evacuate the South Sudanese, many of whom had already died of hunger and disease, disarm the soldiers and then relocate the refugees to various UN bases across the eastern DRC. On 18 August, the UN also confirmed the presence of Riek Machar himself on DRC territory, stating they had handed him over to the DRC authorities – a claim that was denied by the government's spokesperson Lambert Mende. On 24 August, the Khartoum government confirmed that Machar was in Sudan for medical treatment. It was never made public how Machar had left the DRC, but the matter caused diplomatic problems with the Juba government, which accused Kinshasa of helping their enemies. In Goma, where many of the refugees were held, local people demonstrated for the deportation of the South Sudanese soldiers on 2 October, saying they feared that instability would arise from the presence of ever more foreign militias on DRC territory. On 3 October, the DRC government gave MONUSCO one week to remove the refugees from the DRC, stating that they did not want people on their territory who were planning armed actions against their home country. In response, MONUSCO refused responsibility, stating that the government had previously asked MONUSCO to take charge of the refugees and that it was the responsibility of the DRC authorities to find a long-term solution. No third country demonstrated any willingness to accept the refugees, and no solution had been found by the end of the year.

Socioeconomic Developments

After years of high GDP growth rates, *the economy plunged* over the course of the year, with projected growth rates of 4.3%, compared with 6.9% in 2010 and an average 7.7% between 2010 and 2015. Falling international copper and oil prices, which had already led to a first deficit in late 2015, continued to force the government to use their currency reserves. By September, foreign exchange reserves had shrunk by a third since the beginning of the year and reached below $ 1 bn for the first time in three years – enough to cover only 4.4 weeks of imports.

The *fiscal deficit* affected the exchange rate of the Congolese franc to the US dollar, which dropped after five years of relative stability, leading to a perceptible increases in prices for food and other commodities. By February, the franc had already fallen in value by 2.4% and as of June it was down by 4% on the official market and 7% in unofficial trading.

In February, in order to ease the situation, the *Central Bank* 'Banque Centrale du Congo' (BCC) bought francs and increased the percentage of deposits banks were required to keep in the BCC. However, the BCC's space for manoeuvre was limited by the low amount of foreign currency reserves. On 26 January, the Council of Ministers decided on 28 measures to restructure the economy, especially focussing on the fight against fiscal and customs fraud, telecommunications and transport. On 16 May, the government decided to reduce their budget by 22% in order to reduce deficits and prevent further devaluation of the franc. This meant, however, that public sector salaries fell by 30% between June and December and soldiers saw their food allowances cut. School children and their parents also suffered from the drop in state spending, with school fees in Ituri increasing by over 200% for the 2016–17 school year. The opposition platform 'Rassemblement' therefore called for school boycotts in September. On 9 November, students at the 'Institut Supérieur des Techniques Appliquées' (ISTA) demonstrated against rises in fees caused by the devaluation of the franc, setting two cars on fire and clashing with police; at least five students were seriously injured.

On 19 October, the 'Fédération des Entreprises du Congo' (FEC) met with Minister of Economic Affairs Modeste Bahati. As a result, the government approved on 20 October reductions in taxes and customs duties as well as a relaxation of economic border controls for three months in order to facilitate the import of essential commodities. According to Bahati, the government also decided to provide importers with foreign exchange in order to facilitate the import of rice, sugar, oil, fish and other basic needs.

The dire economic situation combined with competition from neighbouring countries caused the closure of a range of significant enterprises. The cement plant at Lukala, close to the Angolan border, shut down at the end of May and, on 1 December, Bralima, one of the leading breweries in the country, closed their Boma factory in Kongo-Central province. Several other factories encountered severe difficulties over the year, leaving hundreds of workers unemployed.

A number of *corruption cases* made headlines. On 29 September, the leading US hedge fund, Och-Ziff Capital Management LP, reached a three-year deferred prosecution agreement with the US Justice Ministry under the Foreign Corrupt Practices Act for corruption in several African countries, including the DRC. Och-Ziff agreed to pay $ 412 m in criminal and civil penalties. As part of the agreement, Och-Ziff issued a public admission of guilt, acknowledging that it had channelled $ 100 m to two Congolese officials via a DRC partner between 2005 and 2015. Although the document did not give any real names, renowned analyst Jason Stearns convincingly deduced that the partner was Israeli businessman Dan Gertler and the officials were Kabila and his former advisor Katumba Mwanke, who died in 2012. Government spokesperson Lambert Mende accused Moise Katumbi of being one of the Congolese officials referred. This accusation came amid fierce political tensions between Kabila and Katumbi, who was putting himself forward as a presidential candidate.

Gertler's involvement in the DRC also came under scrutiny by the UK Serious Fraud Office (SFO) in December for possible violation of British bribery and fraud laws. The SFO led an investigation into Gertler and four former Eurasian Natural Resouces Corporation (ENRC) executives within the framework of a three-year probe into ENRC's acquisition of five cobalt and copper mines in the DRC between 2010 and 2012 – a time when the company was listed in London.

On 16 September, the managing director of Alphamin Bisie Mining (ABM), Richard Robinson, was detained and questioned by a mining sector fraud investigation task team in Kinshasa. ABM, the DRC subsidiary of the Mauritius-based Alphamin Resources Corporation, was involved in a contested tin mining project in Bisie. According to ABM, Robinson was interrogated with regard to the export of mineral samples and subsequently released into custody of the US embassy in Kinshasa. Robinson had previously worked for USAID and had developed a certification programme for conflict-free minerals.

A controversy around the 'Banque Internationale pour l'Afrique au Congo' (BIAC) revealed the instability of the *banking system*. BIAC had long been in trouble and since June 2015 had been under supervision by the BCC. In early February, Prime Minister Ponyo Matata told BCC governor Deogratias Mutombo Mwana Nyembo to suspend a credit line that the BCC had given to BIAC to alleviate short-term liquidity problems. As a consequence, thousands of account holders tried to withdraw their money from BIAC and other banks. After an alleged emergency meeting between Kabila, the finance minister and Nyembo, the latter announced that the government would implement measures to bring BIAC back on track, including an increased credit line by the BCC. On 7 April, Matata confirmed the restructuring and refinancing of BIAC. On 1 June, BIAC was put under provisional administration by the BCC and on 6 June Nyembo filed complaints against seven BIAC senior staff for mismanagement. On 5 August, the BCC announced that a number of banks were ready to buy BIAC but gave no further details. According to the World Bank, the list included one of the most important Kenyan banks, Commercial Bank of Africa.

On 25 July, the World Bank suspended its support for the *Inga III hydroelectric project*. According to the Bank, the strategic orientation that the government had given to Inga III differed from that agreed on in 2014, when the Bank had approved $ 73 m to finance the preparation for Inga III. In May, the Inga III project director said construction could start by June 2017 without studies on environmental and social impact, as foreseen in the World Bank grant. Three consortiums – from China, South Korea and Spain – were said to be interested in developing the hydroelectric dam.

In May, the US company Freeport-McMoRan Copper & Gold announced the sale to China Molybdenum Inc. of its 70% shares in the Bermuda-based TF-Holdings, which in turn held 80% of shares in the massive Tenke Fungurume copper mine in the DRC. On 19 October, the DRC's state-owned mining company 'La Générale des Carrières et des Mines' (Gécamines), which owned the remaining 20% of Tenke shares, filed a complaint against TF-Holdings before an arbitration court in Paris, claiming that Freeport could not sell its shares without the agreement of Gécamines. On 15 November, Freeport's partner, the Canadian Lundin Mining Corporation, also announced the sale of its 30% of shares in TF-Holdings to an affiliate of Chinese private-equity firm BHR Partners. The arbitration was to continue until 27 January 2017.

Equatorial Guinea

Joseph N. Mangarella

The presidential elections, mired in allegations of fraud and abuse, resulted in the extension of Teodoro Obiang Nguema Mbasogo's decades-long rule. Following his re-election, President Obiang named his profligate first son, Teodoro Nguema Obiang Mangue (Teodorín), as first vice president. The predictable decision irked many within the dominant 'Partido Democrático de Guinea Ecuatorial' (PDGE) and the ruling Essangui clan of Mongomo, as Equatorial Guinea would need a responsible and internationally tolerated leader to combat falling oil production, a severe economic crisis and watchful human rights advocates.

Domestic Politics

The upcoming *presidential elections* presented unique concerns for the regime, mostly with regard to the succession of President Obiang, who turned 74 on 5 June. Perhaps as a result, Obiang unexpectedly decreed in mid-March that the election date would be brought forward by several months to 24 April, with campaigning to begin on 8 April. This unconstitutional decision left enfeebled opposition parties

 | DOI 10.1163/9789004355910_027

only a few weeks to prepare and roughly two weeks to campaign, despite reports that the PDGE had already been campaigning. In response to the regime's tactics, a grouping of opposition parties known as the 'Frente de Oposiçión Democrático' (FOD) announced its boycott of the elections. Parties forming the FOD included the 'Convergencia para la Democracia Social' (CPDS), which held the only two non-PDGE seats in parliament, along with the 'Unión Popular' (UP), 'Fuerza Democrática Republicana' (FDR) and the 'Movimiento para la Autodeterminación de la Isla de Bioko' (MAIB). Nine other (nominal) opposition parties lent their support to Obiang's campaign. In the end, Obiang faced six strawman challengers, and on 3 May the Constitutional Court confirmed provisional results, declaring that *Obiang had won a seven-year mandate* with a landslide 93.5% of 301,799 voting electors (a 92.7% turnout).

Perhaps more stunning than Obiang's historically low margin of victory (he had won the three previous elections with more than 95% of the votes) was the degree of *state-sponsored intimidation, media repression and violence* in the months surrounding the election. On 16 January, several leaders of the CPDS were arrested in mainland Bata on dubious charges, while on 12 February family members of the exiled secretary general of the France-based 'Coalición de la Oposición para la Restauración de un Estado Democrático' (CORED) were unlawfully imprisoned. While running the gauntlet of personal attacks by state-owned TV Asonga, the secretary-general of 'Ciudadanos por la Innovación' (CI), Gabriel Nsé Obiang Obono, was banned from entering the presidential race. On 22 April, police in Bata violently attacked and besieged CI's headquarters and demanded that Obono turn himself in, after which at least 23 CI members were sent to the infamous Black Beach Prison. Throughout the year, hundreds more CI supporters would be arrested and released without charge, despite the party's legalisation following the national political dialogue in 2014. On 15 April, the campaign coordinator of the opposition 'Unión de Centro Derecha' (UCD) was likewise detained and reportedly beaten. Such incidents noticeably decreased following the election, with the tragic exception of the beating on 29 November of Joaquin Elo Ayeto, a member of the CPDS's Executive Commission.

In addition to opposition parties, the regime continued its decades-long practice of *targeting civil society and free media* so as to block possible avenues of dissent. On 31 January, the governor of the Littoral Province banned a youth forum organised by the NGO 'Centro de Estudios e Iniciativas para el Desarrollo' (CEID), while the first deputy prime minister for political affairs suspended further activities on 16 March and accused CEID of inciting violence. A cultural theatre group working with UNICEF on HIV awareness was similarly suspended on 20 July for carrying out 'seditious' activities. Early in the year, Obiang banned the broadcasting of the trial of former Ivorian president Laurent Gbagbo before the ICC, while websites deemed critical of the regime remained blocked throughout the year. Finally, a group of

12 foreign journalists from 'Africa24', seeking to cover the elections, were detained at Malabo's airport for several hours on 14 April and had their interviews cancelled. Such abuses led the Committee to Protect Journalists to rank Equatorial Guinea 5th among the ten most censored countries in the world.

Pursuant to Obiang's electoral success, the government was dissolved and reconstituted in June to include an unprecedented 35 ministers and 22 deputy ministers for a population of roughly 800,000, further bloating bureaucracy and expanding political patronage. Key positions in national security were retained by the president's family members, including Minister of National Security Nicolas Obama Nchama, Minister of Presidential Security Antonio Mba Nguema (formerly minister of defence), and Minister of Defence Vicente Eya Olomo (promoted from deputy minister of defence). Most important – and most unsurprising – was the *promotion of Teodorín to first vice president*, first in line to succeed his father. He was the favourite first son of President Obiang and First Lady Constancia Nsue Mangue. Teodorín's financial excesses abroad, relative inexperience and unpredictable nature alienated many in the ruling clan and signalled an incipient power struggle. On 20 July, 'West Africa Newsletter' reported that Antonio Mba Nguema questioned *Teodorín's fitness for office*, while top generals refused him control of the country's weapons systems. Furthermore, events later in the year suggested a growing competition between Teodorín and Gabriel Obiang Lima, the president's second son, who was reappointed as minister of mines to control oil resources.

Foreign Affairs

While the EU echoed the US State Department on 3 May in publicly denouncing April's fraudulent presidential elections, *France continued its years-long pursuit of Teodorín for ill-gotten gains*. After French authorities had seized properties in 2012 and Teodorín's subsequent plea of diplomatic immunity had failed in the French courts, his lawyers had sought arbitration. In early June, however, French prosecutors requested that Teodorín be formally charged with money-laundering and embezzlement, among other offences. On 7 September, 'Agence France Press' learned that *Teodorín would face trial in January 2017*, prompting state-controlled media to decry French 'neo-colonialism'. Finally, on 7 December, the International Court of Justice refused to grant the Equatoguinean regime's appeal based on the Vienna Convention's provisions on diplomatic immunity, conceding nevertheless that the property in question had to be protected by the French authorities.

Alleged public mismanagement resulted in even more seizures within Europe. After lobbying by French authorities, their Swiss counterparts began a preliminary investigation into Teodorín's presumed ill-gotten holdings in mid-October. This led the *Swiss authorities* to seize not only 11 luxury cars on 3 November, but also a

76-metre yacht in the Netherlands five weeks later, claiming in both instances that they were taking possession of public property. Finally, on 1 October, the French telecommunications company Orange seized a Boeing 777 belonging to Ceiba Intercontinental to cover public debts owed to the company, valued at several million euros. Unsurprisingly, the government responded that Ceiba was a private airline and appealed to the French Court of Cassation while tentatively agreeing to service the debt. As a result of the seizure, Obiang was unable to fly to Paris on 10 October to award the UNESCO Equatorial Guinea International Prize for Research in Life Sciences, and was forced to call on the king of Morocco for travel assistance.

Obiang thus continued his pursuit of less investigative allies and business partners who were tolerant of his regime, both within and outside Africa. Jean-Marie Le Pen, former leader of France's National Front party, attended the president's inauguration on 20 May and was reportedly given a helicopter tour of the country's gas installations, while Miao Wei, special envoy of Chinese President Xi, was also in attendance. Many elements of the ruling PDGE, including Teodorín, favoured '*turning East*' to procure investments. The president followed suit with a tour of Arab countries in October, which included discussions in Abu Dhabi on prospects for investment in Equatorial Guinea.

Within Africa, partnerships were strengthened and sustained on the basis of political and economic security. On 25 January, Obiang met with Zimbabwean President Mugabe, a long-time friend, to discuss points of interest for the 27th AU Summit in Kigali in mid-July. On both occasions, Obiang denounced 'negative' journalism, pushed for UNSC reform in his capacity as a member of the 'C-10' group, and advocated pan-African integration and cooperation. The rhetoric had already appeared to bear fruit during the presidential elections, when both CEEAC election observers and the AU's Electoral Observation Mission – headed by Obiang's business partner and former president of Benin, Boni Yayi – praised the election's transparency and high turnout. Furthermore, on 15 September, the *Liberian journalist* Festus Poquie was arrested by the Liberian National Police for re-publishing a UK 'Daily Mail' article critical of the regime in Malabo. The regime expanded its *regional strategy* not only by continuing its track record of hosting elaborately staged summits at public expense (as in November's African-Arab Summit), but also by fielding a candidate for the AU Commission chairmanship, Agapito Mba Mokuy, a long-time advisor to Obiang. Between 13 April and 12 July, Mokuy personally pressed his case in Cameroon, Algeria, Kenya, Burundi and Angola.

Regarding cooperation for economic gain, on 18 February Equatorial Guinea and *São Tomé* discussed plans for a Joint Maritime Development Zone, while on 15 March Obiang and *Nigeria*'s President Buhari signed a Joint Maritime Security Agreement to combat piracy. Cooperation in other sectors was also discussed with Angolan counterparts on 21 May and 9 June. No agreement during the year, however, promised more long-term benefits than that reached on 15 November: after decades of disputes and eight years of UN mediation, Equatorial Guinea and *Gabon* agreed to submit their conflicting claims on the oil-endowed Mbanie islets of Corisco and Cocotier to arbitration at the International Court of Justice. Facing steep economic decline, Obiang had been pressured to find a solution so as to exploit at least some of the islets' reserves.

Socioeconomic Developments

The country faced one of its worst economic downturns since the discovery of significant oil reserves in 1995. Since hydrocarbons continued to comprise approximately 70% of the $ 12.2 bn GDP (2015), chronically *falling production and low oil prices* (around $ 43 per barrel) translated to a contraction of GDP by roughly 10%, announced on the occasion of the IMF's Article IV Consultation concluded in September. The country also faced an IMF-projected -11.8% current account deficit and, thanks to the government's dependence on hydrocarbons for approximately 90% of its revenue, another public spending *deficit* of around -3%. Deficits and IMF input were probably behind parliament's rare decision to bolster tax collection in late summer. However, facing widespread dissatisfaction and growing poverty, the regime pinned its real hopes on quick exploitation of new and old hydrocarbons discoveries, while calls from the IMF and others for economic diversification went largely unheeded.

While *oil production* had peaked at 360,000 b/d in 2005, it was projected to be less than 250,000 b/d in 2016. Now that the country had among the lowest proven oil reserves of SSA's major producers, many firms (including Hess, ExxonMobil and PanAtlantic) either cut their exploration budgets or threatened departure, and neither the Joint Maritime Development Zone signed with São Tomé nor the pending arbitration over the Mbanie islets (with 1.1 bn barrels of proven reserves) would yield benefits anytime soon. The Ministry of Oil, led by Lima, therefore announced on 6 June a *licensing round for 37 unoperated blocks*, 32 of which were offshore (a major selling point). Although authorities were happy to answer the noncommittal inquiries of OMV, Total, Chevron and Kosmos, the government was forced to extend EGRonda's deadline from November to April 2017. Aside from an MoU with Marathon (concluded in February) to supply the liquid natural gas (LNG) train at Punta Europa, *gas ventures* were also stalled when Ophir, the operator of the anticipated Fortuna Floating LNG train, was forced to delay its investment decision because of failure to find partners. Production of 2.6 Tcf of gas reserves would therefore not begin until 2020.

Minor efforts were made to diversify not only the petroleum-dependent state but also its key international partnerships. Following a shakeup at the Oil Ministry, a ministerial contingent opposed to Lima and supported by Teodorín favoured *courting Asian and Chinese firms*, as was revealed when Deputy Oil Minister Ndong attempted in November to award blocks to China's Shaanxi Yanchang and Egypt's Vegas Oil and Gas. Likewise, a $ 2 bn Chinese loan from 2015 made it possible for Equatoguinean authorities to award a contract to a Chinese consortium led by state-owned East China Engineering Science and Technology for the operation of a new petrochemicals complex. The complex would produce fertilizer and help boost the agricultural sector, among the many goals set out in the *National Development Plan Horizon 2020*. Other goals, such as improving the country's business climate and statistical data collection, were less successful. Weaknesses in the former case were on stark display when oil executives from Baker Hughes and ExxonMobil were detained in late October (reportedy at the behest of Teodorín), necessitating the intervention of Western-friendly Lima; both companies were terminating local operations and laying off workers. Along with bad results in the Doing Business Report, the World Bank's Logistic Performance Index ranked Equatorial Guinea among the three worst in Africa, at 156th out of 160 states.

Although the country had one of the highest GDPs per capita in Africa, roughly half of Equatoguineans suffered from *chronic poverty*, as falling public spending and the economic crisis contributed to prevailing social ailments. On 22 March, a study produced for World Water Day revealed that the country was among the five worst in the world in terms of households with access to clean water, while in September UNICEF revealed that 42% of primary school-aged children were not in school, the 7th worst status globally. To make matters worse, the education minister decreed on 18 July that pregnant schoolgirls would be barred from school attendance, so as to discourage 'crime' and 'bad habits'.

Gabon

Douglas Yates

Presidential elections were the main political event of the year. President Ali Bongo, in power since his father Omar Bongo's death in 2009, was sure to win. But his victory was contested, provoked deadly riots and strained relations with France and the USA.

Domestic Politics

On 18 January, opposition parties endorsed *Jean Ping*, former chairman of the AU, as their unique flagbearer to oppose President Ali Bongo in the upcoming presidential elections, officially naming him as the sole candidate of the 'Front de l'Opposition Pour l'Alternance' (FOPA). On 29 February, as expected by all, Bongo announced that he would stand for re-election. That very day, a court in the French city of Nantes dismissed a case filed by his half-sister Pascaline (one of 54 heirs to his father's vast fortune) alleging that Ali's birth certificate was a forgery. Despite this long-standing controversy about his eligibility (because he was said not to be Gabonese by birth but a Nigerian orphan of the Biafran War adopted by the former

 | DOI 10.1163/9789004355910_028

president), on 12 July, the Electoral Commission ('Commission Électorale Nationale Autonome et Permanente'; CENAP), composed mostly of members of the ruling 'Parti Démocratique Gabonais' (PDG), ignored this opposition rumour as calumny, and accepted *Bongo's candidacy* by a simple majority vote.

On 6 June, CENAP set the election date for 27 August, giving any other candidates until 12 July to file their paperwork with the Commission. The official list of *14 candidates* was published on 15 July. In addition to Bongo and Ping, it included an assortment of defectors from the ruling party, such as Raymond Ndong Sima and Casimir Oye Mba (former prime ministers), Guy Ndama Nzouba (former National Assembly president) and Léon-Paul Ngoulakia (former intelligence officer), alongside more traditional opposition candidates who had already run in previous presidential elections, such as Fang politician Paul Mba Abessole of the 'Rassemblement pour le Gabon' (RPG) and Punu leader Pierre-Claver Maganga Moussavou of the 'Parti Social-Démocrate' (PSD), as well as protégés of the late opposition leader Pierre Mamboundou, including Bruno Ben Moubamba (now president of the 'Union du Peuple Gabonais' [UPG]) and Augustin Moussavou King of the 'Parti Socialiste Gabonais' (PSG), and finally a number of unknown minor political figures such as Roland Desiré Minko (who campaigned on redrafting the cooperation accords with France), Dieudonné Minlama Mintogo (an associate of the 2009 challenger, the late André Mba Obame), Abel Mbombe Nzondou (a civil servant close to Ali Bongo's uncle Jéan Boniface Assélé), and Gerard Ella Nguema (a splinter candidate of the dissolved opposition party 'Union Nationale').

By 27 August, Minko, Nzouba Ndama, Ngoulakia and Oye Mba had all withdrawn and come out in support of a *unified opposition under Jean Ping*. A single-round ballot, with 2,500 polling stations, opened for some 650,000 Gabonese voters, out of a population of around 1.8 m. It appears that Bongo had counted on the sheer number of his opponents being his surest guarantee of re-election, so the incumbent pulled no punches, using the nationalist card to undermine his principal rival. The government-run daily newspaper 'L'Union' called the half-Chinese Jean Ping "slanty eyed" ("bridé"), said his campaign was cheap Chinatown junk ("chinetoque") and accused him of selling out his country to Beijing. For his part, Ping lambasted Bongo and Gabon's ruling clique as "Ali Baba and the 40 thieves". Observers were concerned that there would be post-election violence, as there had been after the 2009 presidential elections. French expatriates living in the country were told by their embassy to remain indoors for their own protection.

By 31 August, CENAP announced that Bongo had defeated Ping by 49.8% to 48.2% of the votes, with an unbelievably high turnout rate of over 99% reported in the Haut-Ogooué, where 95.5% were reported as having voted for Bongo. Thanks to this incredibly high turnout (the national rate was only 59.8%), Bongo managed to garner just enough extra ballots to claim victory, winning by the slimmest margin of 5,594 votes, out of a total registered electorate of 627,805. After his *victory announcement* on 31 August, violence broke out in the major cities. In Libreville, the National Assembly building was set on fire, and Jean Ping, who immediately contested the results, saw his headquarters sacked by the forces of law and order, starting with helicopter attacks, then followed by an assault by National Guard 'red berets' that resulted in 19 of his supporters being wounded and two of them being killed. Tensions increased in the weeks after the vote. The opposition said that as many as 100 people had been killed and 1,200 detained by the authorities. By 2 September, at least five people were confirmed to have been killed in the capital and 1,000 more arrested. A curfew continued to be vigorously enforced.

On the night of 4 September, the *Constitutional Court* upheld Bongo's victory and put an end to any legal challenges available to the opposition. Ping's supporters accused Bongo of vote-rigging and EU observers complained that they had not had full access to all districts in Haut-Ogooué province. But the Court only said that it was impossible to recount individual ballots because they had already been destroyed, and furthermore, to add insult to injury, disqualified Ping from putting himself forward in any elections for the next 10 years because, the justices said, he had incited his supporters to violence. It also rejected opposition arguments, concluding that the voter fraud they claimed was marginal and had not changed the fundamental outcome of the election. Although lowering Bongo's disputed score in the Haut-Ogoouéto to 83.2% and the turnout there to 98%, it *increased his total vote to 50.7%*, thereby giving him an electoral majority. Meanwhile Ping's score was reduced to 47.2%. The Court's president (chief justice) Marie Madeleine Mborantsuo, was a former mistress of Ali's father and mother of the budget minister, his half-brother, Fabrice Bongo. This was the second time that the Mborantsuo Court had validated fraudulent Bongo elections, seriously undermining its credibility as an impartial institution.

Bongo was sworn in for another term as president on 27 September, and the next day he appointed *Emmanuel Issoze-Ngondet* as his *new prime minister*, replacing three-time premier Daniel Ona Ondo. Issoze-Ngondet, a diplomat who had previously served as foreign minister, is a member of the *Bakota* ethnic group from the Ogooué-Ivindo province in the deep rainforest interior of the country. His appointment therefore represented a dramatic break with a longstanding ethno-political tradition dating back to the days of the late Omar Bongo that the prime minister would be from the Fang, the largest ethnic group, from the Gabon Estuary. In the new Issoze-Ngondet government, Paul Biyoghe Mba, a former prime minister, was named development minister, Régis Immongault was retained in office as minister of the economy, and Etienne Ndoubou was kept on as oil minister. Despite Bongo's earlier promises to form a more inclusive government, representatives of the opposition were largely absent, with the notable exception of third-place runner-up, Bruno Ben Moubamba, being appointed as deputy prime minister. No one associated with Jean Ping was included in the new government.

One of the biggest changes to the new presidency was the removal of *Maixent Accrombessi* from the centre of power, and his replacement with Martin Boguikouma, a member of Bongo's ethnic Téké, who named his cousin, Vincent de Paul Katoua Soumanga, as the head of the secret services. *Tékés* had been complaining about presidential advisers such as Benin-born Accrombessi and others whom they mockingly called his 'foreign legion'. Soon after the presidential elections, Accrombessi had left the country for Morocco to undergo surgery, and was even rumoured to be dead, until it was announced on 7 September that he was recovering in London. Accrombessi's removal from his post in the presidential palace on 5 October resulted in the rise in influence of Defence Minister Massard Kabinda Makaga, another Téké, who became the principal gatekeeper to the president.

Foreign Affairs

Relations with *France* worsened as the French government under socialist President François Hollande appeared to favour opposition candidate Jean Ping rather than the incumbent Ali Bongo for president. In the immediate aftermath of Bongo's declared electoral victory, on 6 September, France's Prime Minister Manuel Valls caused a diplomatic incident when he called for a recount of the votes in Haut-Ogooué province. This resulted in an angry reply by Bongo over 'Radio France Internationale' (RFI) that it was against the law for him to call for a recount before the Constitutional Council had made its decision on the matter. Valls said that, given the narrow margin of victory and the astonishingly high results in the province, "wisdom demands a recount", but insisted that his principal concern was for the 15,000 French men and women who lived and worked in Gabon.

The French socialist government's preference for Ping appeared to be confirmed when the latter was invited to the Elysée Palace to meet with Thomas Mélonio, presidential advisor on African affairs, and Laurent Pic, chief of staff to Foreign Minister Jean-Marc Ayrault. Ping had been in France since 9 October seeking French politicians who would support his claim to be the legitimate president of Gabon, including meetings with Senator Jean-Marie Bockel, a former foreign minister reportedly removed from that office under pressure from the Bongo clan, Jean-Christophe Lagarde, centrist head of the 'Union des Démocrates et Indépendants' (UDI) party, and Jean-Luc Mélenchon, the far-left presidential candidate in the 2017 elections. Ping also met with the former minister of economy, also a candidate for the presidency, Arnaud Montebourg, as well as Claude Bartolone, president of the National Assembly. But the French government did nothing concrete to help him.

Regionally there was some good news about the dispute over the *Mbanie, Cocotiers and Congas islands*. On 16 November, the governments of Gabon and Equatorial Guinea met in Marrakesh (Morocco), under the guidance of UN Secretary General

Ban Ki-moon, on the margins of the 22nd session of the Paris climate change conference, to sign a historic agreement to resolve their border dispute, which had been poisoning relations for nearly four decades. This ceremony marked the conclusion of a UN mediation process that had started in 2008, when Gabon and Equatorial Guinea had agreed on a compromise aimed at submitting the dispute to the UN's International Court of Justice in The Hague (Netherlands). The bone of contention between these two neighbours was that the largely uninhabited islands were located in waters of the Gulf of Guinea reputed to be rich in oil.

The *United States'* mission in Libreville had demanded the release of several opposition leaders who had been arrested during post-election violence, including Léon-Paul Ngoulakia, a cousin of Ali Bongo and former intelligence boss, who had crossed over to the opposition to run against the president. Ngoulakia spent five days in prison for possession of opposition tracts questioning Ali's birth certificate and supporting Ping's candidacy before finally being released on 28 September. The defamation lawsuit brought by Ali Bongo against French investigative reporter Pierre Péan for his book *Nouvelles affaires africaines* (2014) which started the wave of accusations about Bongo's illegitimacy, was dismissed by a Paris tribunal for lack of evidence. The same is not true for the 'ill gotten goods' affair, for which he will go on trial in Paris in 2017.

Relations with the USA had been strained in recent years by the ongoing investigation into the Bongo family's 'ill-gotten gains' by the US Department of Justice, but the election of Donald Trump as US president on 8 November changed that dynamic, effectively also bringing an end to Ping's hopes of American support for his cause. After an unsuccessful European tour seeking support for his challenge to Bongo, Ping arrived in the USA on 9 November to meet with advisors of the defeated Democratic candidate Hillary Clinton, whom he had met when he was AU chairman and she was secretary of state. But after her defeat in the American presidential elections, Ping appeared to have lost his last hope for American sanctions to be imposed against President Bongo, who on 10 November deftly tweeted his congratulations to the president-elect for his victory. Trump was staunchly pro-oil, and his Secretary of State Rex Tillerson was a former CEO of ExxonMobil. It was reasonable to expect that, given the importance of oil to American strategy in the Gulf of Guinea region, the White House would appreciate the pro-American, pro-oil political positions of Bongo, who was more than willing to provide support for the Trump administration in both Africa and international organisations.

Relations with *China* also improved significantly. On 7 December, Chinese President Xi Jingping and his wife Pen Liyuan posed for photos with Ali Bongo and his wife Sylvie Bongo in Beijing, before a meeting where the two heads of state announced their agreement to pursue a comprehensive cooperative partnership. Bongo had been invited by Xi to make an official state visit, his first since he was re-elected in August, and, following a red-carpet welcoming ceremony at the Great

Hall of the People in downtown Beijing, Xi stressed that the visit showed Bongo's determination to further the China-Gabon friendship. Xi proclaimed that he supported accelerating Gabon's industrialisation process and was ready to push forward relevant cooperative projects, adding that Chinese investment in Gabon's infrastructure construction was encouraged by his government. Xi also announced that China wanted to enhance cooperation in agriculture, tourism, finance and telecommunications. On security, Xi said that China was willing to help Gabon in strengthening the country's law enforcement capacity and in maintaining stability.

Socioeconomic Developments

Low world oil prices continued to trouble the economy, which was still highly dependent on petroleum, accounting for more than 80% of exports, two-thirds of state revenue and 43% of GDP. On 30 June, Gabon officially *re-joined OPEC* after having left it more than two decades before. Omar Bongo had withdrawn from OPEC in 1994 because his government had been unable to pay in its annual membership dues. His son hoped that benefits gained from closer international coordination, as well as technical and other assistance, would outweigh the costs in the long run. Gabon's renewed membership of OPEC followed discussions between Abdalla Salem El Badri, OPEC's secretary-general, and Etienne Dieudonné Ngoubou, Gabon's oil minister. President Bongo wanted to coordinate his production with other oil producers to push for higher oil prices and had asked the organisation for readmission at the December 2015 OPEC meeting; he had requested that membership dues be reduced, but this was refused.

The *Gabon Oil Company* (GOC) signed an oil production contract for Mboumba field, which was set to raise its production to around 1,500 b/d, out of a total national production of 220,000 b/d. GOC had been created in 2011 to own and manage government stakes in oil fields, as well as their revenues, but it had previously mainly focused its activities on selling refined products and crude oil produced by international companies (of which three firms alone, Shell Gabon, Total and Perenco, controlled three-quarters). In 2012, GOC had signed its first exploration and production contract for the marginal field of Remboué, which was given up by Addax Pétroleum. GOC now held an 80% stake and the state 20%.

The Texan independent oil company Vaalco refocused its attention on Gabon with the acquisition of supplementary interests in the Etame Marin oil block. The company's new chief executive officer, Cary Bounds, formerly head of Noble Energy in Equatorial Guinea, had initiated a company retreat from Angola, imposing a reduction of expenses, which allowed Vaalco to generate a profit of $ 2.9 m, an improvement when compared with $ 31 m in losses in 2015. The new oil code gave the state a 20% share in all Gabonese affiliates of foreign oil companies. This, plus the 15% reserved for GOC, meant that Libreville could control up to 35% of new permits.

The decline on the international steel markets resulted in operators in the *manganese* sector closing several mines early in the year. The 'Compagnie Minière de l'Ogooue' (Comilog) suspended production at Moanda, while the Chinese 'Compagnie Industrielle et Commerciale des Mines de Huazhou' (CICMHZ) decided to cease production at Ndjole. Consequently, total national production of manganese fell by 22.6%, representing a loss of some 700,000 tons compared with the same period in 2015. There was better news in the agricultural sector, with Singapore-based Olam increasing *palm oil* and rubber outputs, and in fishing, with Mauritius-based Tropical Holdings, which increased sardine processing at its factory. Average GDP growth reached 5.4%.

São Tomé and Príncipe

Gerhard Seibert

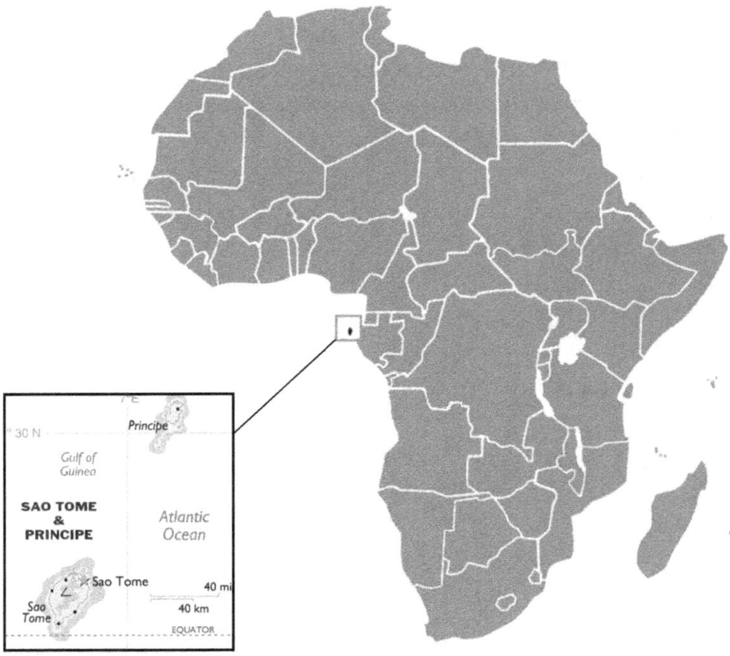

Presidential elections and the diplomatic turn to Beijing were the most important political events of the year. In August, Evaristo Carvalho, the 'Acção Democrática Independente' (ADI) candidate, widely considered a close ally of Prime Minister Patrice Trovoada, was elected president. His election provided Trovoada's ADI with virtually absolute power, since the party now controlled the presidency, government, parliament and São Tomé's district councils. In late December, the government cut off bilateral ties with Taiwan that had been established in 1997 and reinstated full diplomatic relations with the People's Republic of China.

Domestic Politics

A scandal and the annual audit report dominated the political news in the first half of the year. On 9 February, *Justice Minister Roberto Raposo was dismissed* following controversial declarations on the judiciary at a hearing of the permanent

 | DOI 10.1163/9789004355910_029

parliamentary commission of legal affairs on 28 January. During the hearing, Raposo, a former public prosecutor (2006–13), stated that the professional competences of the country's judges were very poor, while the courts were neither independent nor autonomous. Raposo, who had no idea that his affirmations had been recorded, admitted that his statements could damage the government's relations with the judiciary.

On 27 May, José António Monte Cristo, head of the Audit Office ('Tribunal de Contas'), submitted the institution's annual report for 2015. The 40-page document denounced various *violations of established norms in the public administration*, such as deficient organisation and fraud in the recruitment, selection and promotion processes for civil servants. In addition, people were employed or promoted without having the requisite professional qualifications. The report included the audit of the general state account ('Conta Geral do Estado') for 2011. The auditors detected alterations of the approved national budget without the consent of parliament. In addition, extra-budgetary operations had not been duly registered, while accounts of expenditure on personnel and operational expenditure were missing. Only nine entities had duly submitted their annual accounts for 2015 to the Audit Office, as required by law, while 19 public institutions failed to do so.

In the *presidential elections* on 17 July, the ADI candidate, 74-year old Evaristo Carvalho, won with 34,522 votes (49.8%). The two independent candidates from the 'Movimento de Libertação de São Tomé e Príncipe/Partido Social Democrata' (MLSTP/PSD), the incumbent 78-year old Manuel Pinto da Costa and 58-year old Maria das Neves, a former prime minister, received 17,188 (24.8%) and 16,828 votes (24.3%), respectively. Unlike Pinto da Costa, Neves enjoyed her party's official support. The turnout was 64.3%, 4.1% less than in 2011, when the principal contenders had been the same. Due to miscounting at several polling stations, the National Electoral Commission (CNE) initially declared Carvalho to be the new president with an absolute majority of 50.1% of the votes; the error was corrected a few days later. This led Pinto da Costa and Neves to appeal jointly to the Constitutional Court to declare the elections null and void, but in vain. Consequently, Pinto da Costa refused to participate in the second round in protest against the alleged anomalies. It was the first time in the country's 25-year democratic history that a defeated candidate had refused to recognise the election results due to irregularities. On 7 August, Carvalho, who accused Pinto da Costa of refusing to participate in the run-off to avoid electoral defeat, won the ballot unopposed with 41,820 votes (82%), although the turnout was only 46.1%. Despite his boycott, on 3 September, Pinto da Costa participated in Carvalho's inauguration ceremony

On 14 October, Prime Minister Trovoada *reshuffled his cabinet* and restructured several ministries. Simultaneously, he reduced the number of ministries from 13 to 11 to contain public expenditure and increase government efficiency. Ilza dos Santos

Amado Vaz, hitherto head of Customs, was appointed to head the newly formed Ministry of Justice, Public Administration and Human Rights. The public administration department was cut from Américo Ramos' Finance Ministry, which now incorporated the Trade and Blue Economy portfolios. The Ministry of Economy and International Co-operation was entirely dissolved. Manuel Salvador dos Ramos, was replaced as minister of foreign affairs and communities by Urbino Botelho, a senior diplomat. Carlos Olímpio Stock was dismissed as minister of defence and maritime affairs and Minister of Internal Administration Arlindo Ramos took on the defence portfolio. The economist Emílio Fernandes Lima, hitherto director of the oil sector's Records and Public Information Office (GRIP), replaced Carlos Gomes as minister of employment and social affairs. The communications portfolio was transferred from Minister of the Presidency of the Council of Ministers Afonso Varela to Minister of Education, Culture and Science Olinto Daio.

Foreign Affairs

The re-establishment of full diplomatic relations with the *People's Republic of China* was certainly the most significant foreign policy decision for years. On 20 December, Prime Minister Trovoada unexpectedly recognised Beijing's one-China principle and cut diplomatic relations with Taiwan, which had been established by his father, President Miguel Trovoada (1991–2001), in 1997 in exchange for annual development assistance of $ 15 m. Trovoada had reportedly broken with Taipei after the latter had rejected his exorbitant financial demands for bilateral aid, allegedly a sum of $ 210 m. He officially declared that São Tomé could no longer discriminate against the world's second largest economy. Taipei declared that the São Tomé government had ignored 20 years of friendly diplomatic relations and had played the two sides of the Taiwan Strait against each other with financial demands, holding out for the highest bidder. In turn, Beijing immediately showed its appreciation of São Tomé's recognition of the one-China principle and on 26 December re-established full diplomatic relations with São Tomé.

As usual, *Portugal* was another important bilateral partner. On 7 September, Portugal's Secretary of State for Foreign Affairs and Cooperation Teresa Ribeiro and Minister of Economy and International Cooperation Agostinho Fernandes were in São Tomé to sign a new five-year Strategic Cooperation Programme ('Programa Estratégico de Cooperação') worth € 57.5 m covering the period 2016–20, including € 11.5 m in loans. The programme succeeded the four-year Indicative Cooperation Programme ('Programa Indicativo de Cooperação') of € 43.5 m (2012–15). The priority areas of the new programme were identical with those of the previous one and included education, institutional capacity building, professional training, culture, health and social services, which accounted for two-thirds of the funds, as well as justice and security, energy and environment, which represented the remaining third. Ribeiro announced that, under the new agreement, the projects would be evaluated more rigorously and more regularly to guarantee that they met the objectives.

The EU and the CPLP played a prominent role on the multilateral level. On 10 March, Helmut Kulitz, the non-resident EU ambassador and the then Foreign Minister Salvador dos Ramos signed in São Tomé a € 500,000 grant agreement to improve the efficiency of *EU budget support*. This funding was intended to create the conditions for a successful implantation of the 11th EDF, worth € 28 m for the period 2014–20, which focused primarily on the areas of water, sanitation and agriculture. In November, an EU mission met with three government ministers to evaluate the implementation of EU-financed projects. The delegation head criticised delays in the implementation of finance reform and of the water and sanitation plan and asked for greater efforts in project implementation.

During the 11th biannual summit of heads of states and governments of the nine-member *CPLP*, held from 31 October to 1 November in Brasília (Brazil), the former governor of São Tomé's Central Bank, Maria do Carmo Trovoada Silveira, was approved as new executive secretary for a two-year term, while Brazil assumed the CPLP presidency for the same period. At the meeting, São Tomé was represented by President Carvalho.

Bilateral relations with *Cabo Verde* were further strengthened. On 20–24 January, President Manuel Pinto da Costa paid an official visit to Cabo Verde, where he held talks with President Jorge Carlos Fonseca, visited São Vicente and Santo Antão and met with the local Sãotomean immigrant community in Praia. On 21–24 February, Cabo Verde's Prime Minister José Maria Neves paid a visit to São Tomé, where he was received by his counterpart Patrice Trovoada, Pinto da Costa, and the president of the National Assembly, José da Graça Diogo. He also held meetings with the local Cabo Verdean communities in both islands.

São Tomé's controversial capture of oil tankers in 2013 had an unpleasant aftermath. On 5 September, the Permanent Court of Arbitration at The Hague ruled that it had jurisdiction over arbitration proceedings instituted by *Malta* against São Tomé on 22 October 2013. The dispute referred to actions taken by São Tomé against the Maltese-registered Turkish vessel Düzgit Integrity, following its unauthorised entry into the archipelago's territorial waters. Malta argued that the punitive measures imposed had violated the UN Convention on the Law of the Sea and claimed compensation payments totalling $ 12.9 m from São Tomé. The Court found São Tomé's initial measures compatible with international legislation, but considered the imposed penalties to be disproportionate. On 26 September, the two parties had to inform the Court on how they intended to proceed with the dispute in the second phase when the Court would rule on the legitimacy of Malta's damage claims.

Socioeconomic Developments

On 8 January, the National Assembly approved the current *National Budget* of $ 170 m with the 33 votes of the ruling ADI, while the three opposition parties abstained. The budget envisaged economic growth of 5% and a further reduction in the inflation rate to 3.5%. As far as expenditure was concerned, the priority sectors were infrastructure and environment (20.3%), health (14.1%), education (12%), agriculture (6.6%) and security and defence (4.2%). The budget also included an increase in minimum salaries in the public sector from STD (dobra) 975,000 ($ 43) to STD 1.1 m ($ 49) per month. On 19 December, during the parliamentary debate on budget implementation Prime Minister Trovoada admitted that only 45% of the expected 90% of the budget had actually been implemented, since several aid providers had not fulfilled their commitments.

As in previous years, developments in the oil sector had been largely restricted to *changes in block ownership*. On 19 February, the National Oil Agency (ANP) and Equator Exploration signed a 28-year production sharing contract (PSC) for Block 12 in the country's Exclusive Economic Zone (EEZ). Under the agreement, Equator paid a signature bonus of $ 2.5 m for 87.5% of the block, while the ANP held a 12.5% working interest. Under a second agreement, Equator farmed out 65% of Block 5 to the US company Kosmos Energy, which became the operator, while the former kept 20% of the interests and the ANP 15%. In March, Equator farmed out 65% of its interest in Block 12 to Kosmos, retaining a 22.5% stake. On 7 November, the Portuguese Galp Energia acquired from Kosmos 20% stakes in each of EEZ Blocks 5, 11 and 12. The deal increased Galp's involvement in the EEZ from one to four blocks. On 5 December, ANP rescinded the PSC for Block 2 signed in October 2013 with the Hong Kong registered company Sinoangol STP due to the latter's systematic and continuous breaches of the PSC conditions. The decision did not affect the 30% stake of the Angolan Sonangol in the block, acquired from Sinoangol in 2014.

In August, the Joint Development Authority (JDA) in Abuja (Nigeria) transferred the operatorship of Joint Development Zone (JDZ) Block 1 from Equator Hydrocarbons (56%) to PAPIS Energy Solutions (35%), since the former had failed to complete the agreed minimum work programme. In September, the *block ownership was restructured* and new investors were included. The restructuring was also necessary due to the exit of 9%-shareholder Dangote Energy Equity Resources (DEER) from the acreage in July 2015. Under the arrangement, PAPIS and Equator Hydrocarbons kept 31.8% and 10% of the stakes, respectively, while the Nakadu Group acquired 41% of the interests. The remaining 17.2% were transferred to JDZ International Investment Ltd (JDZIIL), the business branch of the JDA, established in 2011 to generate income through investments for the JDA.

On 1 August, the Central Bank (BCSTP) decreed the liquidation of the ailing *Banco Equador* after all attempts to recapitalise or sell the bank had failed. By the end of

2015, Banco Equador had accumulated a loss of STD 236.9 bn ($ 10.7 m). The bank, which had a stock capital of $ 7 m was owned by the Angolan investors Mombaka–Sociedade de Empreendimentos (69.0%), Grupo António Mosquito (21.0%) and local private investors, including the Catholic Church (10.0%). BCSTP governor Maria do Carmo Trovoada Silveira declared that the account holders could only receive part of their deposits, while the remainder would depend on the uncertain recovery of the bank's non-performing loans during its liquidation process.

In mid-November, Buster Bawer, general director of HBD ('Here Be Dragons'), the company owned by the South African IT millionaire Mark Shuttleworth, by far the largest investor in Príncipe, announced the *dismissal of 150 employees* to reduce costs. Bawer announced that he was cutting by half HBD's scheduled investments of $ 11 m for 2017. In addition, the company decided to focus on its core business of eco-tourism and withdraw from agriculture in the Roça Sundy (1,000 ha) and Roça Paciência (100 ha) estates and terminate its engagement in social projects. The socioeconomic impact of HBD's disinvestment in Príncipe (7,300 inhabitants) was significant, since the impoverished island lacked alternative job opportunities.

On 23 November, 'Supermercado Continental', the country's *first shopping mall*, financed by a private Chinese company with $ 5 m, was inaugurated. The five-storey building could accommodate almost 100 shops. Chen Xiao Xian, the Chinese investor's administrator, announced that the project would initially provide 70 jobs for local employees, which could increase to 200 if more shops opened. The mall was the largest Chinese investment in São Tomé since Beijing cut bilateral diplomatic ties with the archipelago in 1997, when the former established relations with Taiwan.

PART 5

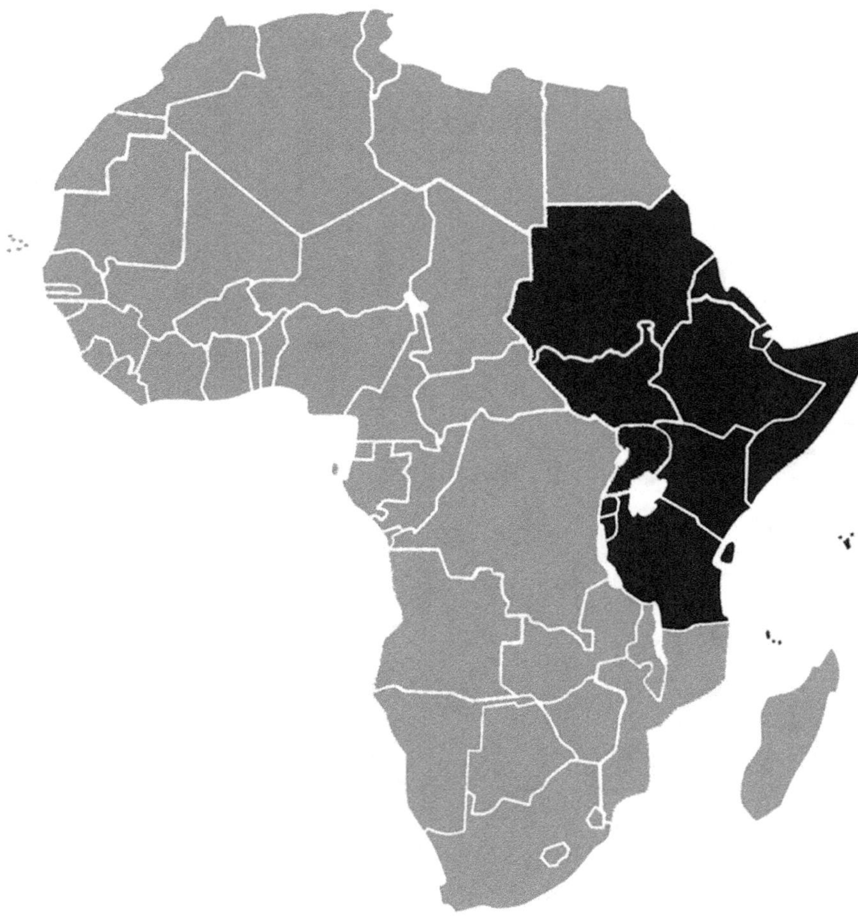

Eastern Africa

Jon Abbink

The Eastern African region experienced political volatility and unresolved governance issues, but achieved relatively good economic growth, with an increase of about 5% in GDP (the highest of the African regions), driven mostly by ongoing infrastructure investments, remittances and FDI. Class and regional inequalities continued to increase. Large-scale investment in energy and in transport facilities was ongoing, and FDI remained significant, despite the political problems and instability that marked certain regions (Darfur, Somalia, parts of Ethiopia, South Sudan, Burundi) and the frequent 'militarisation' of development projects, which kept expropriated or dispossessed local populations at a distance. South Sudan was the worst affected by security problems, due to the dramatic impact of the civil war and political stagnation, which also led to disenchantment among the donor community. Investor interest in the country declined, and the profitability of the oil sector suffered from lower world market prices. The conflict, started by elite groups in 2014, was not resolved but reached an uneasy truce.

Overall, however, Eastern Africa was seen by international capital as a future investment area with good longer-term prospects for growth and market development. The 'new partners', China, India, Turkey and others, continued to make their presence felt and also enlarged their political influence, although some of the countries in the sub-region were slow in developing effective legislation to regulate these investment efforts.

Political developments showed no marked turn toward more public accountability or democratic decision-making. All regimes continued in power, and opposition forces were weakly organised or had no significant impact. Three countries held some kind of elections: Uganda (presidential), Somalia (parliamentary) and Comoros (presidential, and for governors). In all countries, the Executive was dominant over the Legislative and Judicial branches. Several other countries besides South Sudan remained mired in civil conflict, such as Somalia, Sudan and Burundi, while Ethiopia saw mass demonstrations in rural areas and towns, and violent repression.

Humanitarian conditions in several countries remained stark, as in eastern Ethiopia, northern Kenya (drought and livestock death), and in Darfur (Sudan), Somalia and South Sudan, aggravated by drought, violent clashes and food insecurity produced by conflict and the effects of climate change. Populations of IDPs and refugees in Eastern Africa remained in the hundreds of thousands, as did out-migration to other regions, such as the Middle East and Europe.

 | DOI 10.1163/9789004355910_030

Continued high population growth contributed to the effect of conflict dynamics on resources, settlement patterns and urban infrastructures across the sub-region.

Social and religious oppositions continued to play a role in several countries, causing civic tensions and conflict. In Kenya and Somalia, militant radical Islamist groups – al-Shabaab and its subsidiaries – continued to be active and perpetrated numerous terrorist attacks, and Kenya's military in particular, plagued by division and corruption, were not entirely up to the task.

Structures of ethnic and religious tolerance were strained, often driven by elite predation and divide-and-rule policies, conflict over resources (as between Pokot and Turkana in northern Kenya, or in Uganda's new oil areas) or communal rivalry (as in Tanzania). In South Sudan, the conflict that had started on the elite level went down to 'ethnic' community relations and created much societal and economic damage.

The sub-region continued to receive a significant level of ODA funding for developmental and climate change mitigation efforts, estimated on average to be 8–10% of national budgets, and in some countries much more. The six EAC countries received a total of around $ 12 bn. More investments and financial transfers to the region were made for security and peace-keeping, for 'greening' policies and sustainability initiatives. However, the growth of ODA budgets stagnated, in line with a global trend to gradually phase it out and move over to business agreements and trade deals ('trade, not aid').

Political Developments

After a momentous election year for seven countries in 2015, it was back to business as usual. Three elections were held this year, in Comoros (presidential, and for the governors of the three main islands), Uganda (presidential), and Somalia. In dubious electoral exercises, the incumbents in the first two were returned to power. Somalia also started its electoral process, with a federal parliament elected in November via a complex clan delegation system (no universal suffrage), but the presidential elections were delayed to 2017.

Authoritarian rule continued in most countries, despite electoral processes, with close surveillance and waves of repression, except in Tanzania, Seychelles and Somaliland. In Eritrea, no political openings occurred, and young people continued to escape the country in droves for political, economic and social reasons. Rwanda saw continued stifling of political life and civil rights. In Ethiopia, violent repression occurred in the wake of massive popular protests against land expropriation, non-negotiated land settlement schemes and foreign investments, as well as associated political repression. Over a thousand people were estimated to have been killed in the suppression of protests, and scores more were wounded or arrested. The

Ethiopian prime minister announced "deep reform", but by the end of the year it was not clear what was meant by this, and little of it was visible; a number of (vice) ministers were replaced, but no systemic change occurred, and the ruling party did not intend to relinquish power in any way. South Sudan and Sudan remained mired in persistent civil unrest and instability. Across the sub-region, mostly youthful demonstrators demanded more social economic and political rights ('Africa uprising').

Afrobarometer survey data revealed that a clear majority of people expressed a high level of mistrust in national legislatures and executive powers. Political uncertainties in general prevailed. In several countries, worries continued about the proper institutionalisation of power or of democratic structures. For example, Uganda's structures of governance remained strongly dependent on President Yoweri Museveni's person. He neglected to build durable structures that would outlive him, resulting in his decision to groom his son for the succession. But this clearly carried a high risk of instability and decline. The serious clashes in November-December between the security forces and the Rwenzururu Kingdom (in western Uganda), with many people killed, may forebode deep trouble. Uganda was, however, more effective in preventing Islamist violent militancy and radicalisation.

In some areas in the sub-region, there appeared to be in a downward spiral of lawlessness and organised violence for purposes of resource appropriation. This not only emerged in the wake of the South Sudanese civil war and in Darfur, but was also visible in *northern Kenya*, where violence was instrumentalised in the increasingly uncontrolled spaces of, for example, Laikipia, Samburu and Isiolo, and led to pastoralists invading conservancies, private land and the territories of neighbouring groups. Game animals were killed, fences destroyed, livestock sent in to graze on farms and ranches, lodges burnt, thousands of people displaced and several killed. This violence appeared to be the result not only of shortages, drought and climate factors impacting on 'desperate pastoralists', but also of planned action coordinated by elite groups (including MPs from the pastoralist counties), with the help of networks, skilful mobile phone use, M-Pesa cash transactions and social media incitement. State security forces and legal institutions were largely ineffective.

Serious violence also continued in various other countries, such as *Burundi*, which was marked by continued political crisis in the aftermath of the controversial presidential 'elections' of 2015. President Pierre Nkurunziza and his dominant CNDD-FDD party moved to re-establish hegemony, repress all protests and reassert control over state institutions. There was little role for opposition parties, which were not able to present a common front and neither was there serious armed insurgent activity. Efforts toward a political dialogue were made both inside the country and through the mediation of the EAC. Burundi's human rights performance, most notably as a result of the activities of the Imbonerakure CNDD-FDD youth wing, was appalling.

In *Rwanda* the ruling RPF under President Paul Kagame continued to dominate all levels of socio-political life. A year ahead of the 2017 presidential elections, the regime faced limited political opposition, kept in check by repression and arrests. Kagame would stand for a third seven-year term, which was unconstitutional and upset donor countries, but again they did not impose sanctions. Kagame's candidature made his earlier criticism of his Burundian counterpart Nkurunziza's unconstitutional term extension in 2015 seem decidedly hypocritical. Kagame also reshuffled his cabinet and made important changes in the staffing of the security sector.

Uganda's presidential elections, as expected, reinstated Yoweri Museveni and his party also won a majority in the parliamentary elections. His opponents, notably Dr K. Besigye, received more than one-third of the votes, and the process was highly contested. The campaign was characterised by frequent intimidation and arrests of opposition members. Internal political discontent and challenges were on the rise during the year. Overall stability was maintained, but not without rather ruthless enforcement of 'law and order'. Uganda also maintained its persecution of LGBT people.

Tanzania, on the other hand, saw a fresh start with President John Magufuli, in his first full year in office. He took an unorthodox approach, pursuing a strategy of discipline, rigorous cost-saving and anti-corruption measures to reform state institutions. He pushed for higher revenue generation and exercised power by many single-handed directives, by-passing formal procedures (including in the dismissal of top functionaries). Magufuli also took control of the long-ruling CCM party and introduced sweeping changes to its structures so as to consolidate his position. His energetic and anti-corruption stance made him popular among large sections of the general public. There was some curtailing of public activities of opposition parties, and several of their leaders were repeatedly interrogated by police. In semi-autonomous *Zanzibar*, new elections (a re-run vote to improve on the fraudulent process of 2015) were boycotted by the opposition, which led to one-party domination (by the CCM) in the local parliament.

Kenya's public debates were already marked by the preparations for the 2017 elections and their management, eventual political coalitions, etc. Opposition leaders pushed for electoral reforms and new commissioners for the Independent Electoral and Boundaries Commission and mooted a National Super Alliance. The ruling Jubilee Alliance sought to establish a new Jubilee Party. The country also continued to be preoccupied with ingrained corruption, which threatened the political process and the social order. It was a source of popular frustration and anger, in the context of serious inequality, high costs of living and political manipulations. Relations between the government and prominent civil society organisations and the media were also increasingly strained by it.

As noted, *Ethiopia* saw an unprecedented level of civic protest against land expropriations and undemocratic 'developmental' policies, and the stifling of freedoms. There were ethnic overtones, but issues of socio-economic inequality and political abuse were the main causes of the months-long protests, which were not fully extinguished by the end of the year, even though a 'state of emergency' was declared countrywide in October, with the instalment of a new ruling body, the 'Command Post', with extrajudicial authority to 'restore public order' and suppress activism. The overall situation was one of political stalemate, disarray and distrust. No political or other reforms were visible by the end of the year, though a cabinet reshuffle was carried out to at least symbolically address the clamour for reform. Hardly any change was evident in actual policy. Ethiopia's scores fell on the various indexes of 'good governance', business freedoms, media and Internet freedoms.

Eritrea, the most closed country of the sub-region, allowed little assessment of its internal situation, except that the first and only president since independence in 1991, Isaias Afewerki, continued ruling through his single party, the PFDJ, and his coterie. This year marked 25 years of de facto independence from Ethiopia – a 'silver jubilee'. The autocratic political system, still lacking an implemented constitution, continued and the militarised command economy persisted. The open-ended national service for all Eritreans of working age remained in place. The regime offered no reforms or socio-economic improvements, which led to a continuous stream of out-migrants fleeing the country.

In *Comoros*, the electoral process that had started in 2015 (for local councils) was finalised with presidential elections that yielded a win for Colonel Azali Assoumani, who had been at the helm ten years before. The comeback of this soldier-politician, former coup leader and architect of Comoros' existing rotating presidency, or 'présidence tournante', system was remarkable in view of his having only secured 15% of the vote in the first round, but it reflected the fractured political system of this small island nation.

The *Seychelles* saw a new president, Danny Faure, taking over the mandate of long-serving President James Michel and a new political party in control of the legislature. The political process produced ongoing improvements to previously tense relations and authoritarian tendencies.

Somalia remained in many respects the most problematic nation, divided and not making fundamental progress in political order or the alleviation of humanitarian and security conditions. The terror of the Islamist al-Shabaab movement continued, disrupting stabilisation efforts and economic progress. The promise of recovery that had opened up with the 'Somali Compact' of September 2013 receded somewhat. The SFG and the various self-declared regional political units continued to show that they were not competent to govern or to set serious agendas for public policy. Centrifugal tendencies among (sub-)clan groups and self-serving elites prevented major breakthroughs in defeating al-Shabaab and expanding institutional capacity and the federal government's territorial grip. The elections for a new president were prepared but delayed to 2017 because of logistical, political and security problems.

Djibouti saw Ismail Omar Guelleh, inaugurated as president for a fourth term, after a seriously flawed 'election' (in which he won 87.8% of the vote) that capitalised on the opposition coalition's inability to present a united front. In a remarkable statement, the AU said that the Djibouti election breached electoral laws but was "free" and "credible". The president moved to prepare his son-in-law to succeed him, appointing him as minister of health. There was unrest in the country, as the Afar-inhabited north around the town of Obock continued to witness violent clashes between government forces and a militant wing of the 'Front pour la Restoration de l'Unité et de la Démocratie' (FRUD).

In *Sudan*, President Omar al-Bashir kept himself and the hegemonic National Congress Party at the top of the regime after the 2015 'elections'. The regime was not effectively challenged by other political movements; 75% of the parliament was made up of al-Bashir's supporters, and the emergence of other political and civic movements was in fact suppressed. However, two calls for civil disobedience at the end of the year revived discontent with the incumbent Islamist government, in power since 1989. Despite the government's protestations to the contrary, violent conflict, abuse and humanitarian emergency were ongoing in parts of Darfur and South Kordofan (Nuba mountains).

South Sudan did not achieve a lasting peace after the destructive civil war of the past two years, despite mediation efforts by the AU and IGAD. Major problems persisted, not only on the elite level but now also on the ground, between ethnic groups. Efforts to form a transitional government under the terms of the August 2015 peace agreement did not bear fruit. Riek Machar, former vice president turned rebel leader, returned to Juba in April, accompanied by a protection force, to be sworn in, again, as first vice president of the so-called Transitional Government of National Unity (TGoNU), but in July government forces attacked and drove Machar and his forces out of Juba. This seemed to be the end of Machar's role in South Sudan; he was replaced by Taban Deng Gai, former mining minister and member of Machar's party, in a reshuffled TGoNU.

Eastern African countries' scores on the 'political' indexes regarding civil rights, political and media freedoms, etc., were mixed, and overall not so positive, continuing the picture of previous years. Opposition forces and youth movements did not have access to open and secure political spaces. The dissatisfaction was more often than not coupled with socio-economic grievances.

In their global indexes, organisations such as Freedom House, the Committee to Protect Journalists, Reporters Without Borders and HRW ranked most Eastern African countries in the lower half of their tables, indicating serious problems with freedom and tolerance of critical public debate, and often precarious safety for reporters and independent media. Countries such as Sudan, Ethiopia, Djibouti,

Rwanda, South Sudan and Eritrea were doing particularly badly. Internet availability and access grew across the region, with some countries (such as Seychelles) investing in it heavily, but strict control if not repression of Internet freedom also continued in many countries.

On the 176 countries on TI's *Corruption Perception Index*, the sub-region countries remained in the lower ranges, with Somalia again at the bottom (176th), followed by South Sudan (175th), Sudan (170th), and at some distance by Eritrea (164th), Comoros (153rd), Uganda (151st) and Kenya (145th). Best was Seychelles, placed 55th.

While the sub-region made slow but steady economic progress, the picture of economic growth and dynamics was not matched by one of improvements towards freer politics, democratic culture or societal stability or security; as the Economist Intelligence Unit's Democracy Index expressed it: "Elections are routine but democracy is being scaled back." Being involved in (opposition) politics remained quite a risky business.

Transnational Relations and Conflict Configurations

The most important regional conflicts were those in South Sudan, a particularly vicious confrontation, which led to ongoing human misery, severe economic setbacks and unresolved governance issues; the conflict between the Somali federal government and the Islamist terror movement *al-Shabaab* (no rapprochement whatsoever); massive demonstrations with many fatalities in the ensuing violence in Ethiopia; and ongoing internal unrest and harsh repression in Burundi. Djibouti saw armed clashes with an Afar opposition front, the 'FRUD armé'.

The AU met on 30 January for the 28th ordinary session of its Assembly, which launched the theme of 'harnessing the demographic dividend through investments in the youth', a first tentative discussion on the population (growth) issue.

Regional bodies such as the EAC and IGAD tried to enhance their influence in the economic sphere as well as via mediation in political or regional conflicts, such as in South Sudan and Burundi.

The Ethiopian-Eritrean conflict simmered on in its usual low-key mode, with no progress in sight and no reset of political or economic relations between the two. In March, Ethiopian Prime Minister Hailemariam Desalegn issued a threat to take military action against Eritrea in response to alleged acts of 'provocation' and 'destabilisation' (but did not specify). On 12–13 June, there was a flare-up near the border town of Tsorona, leading to clashes between the two militaries and casualties. It was probably sparked off by Eritrean troops chasing Eritrean deserters on Ethiopian soil.

The underlying tensions between Egypt, Sudan and Ethiopia on the Nile issue – focused on the giant Blue Nile or 'Renaissance' dam under construction in Ethiopia – continued and were not resolved, despite the shared 'Declaration of Principles' signed by all three in 2015.

The *Burundi* conflict led to aid sanctions being imposed by some donor partners, including the EU. Diplomatic tensions arose between Burundi, neighbouring Rwanda and Belgium, the country's main bilateral aid donor. There was also international criticism of serious human rights abuse (especially by the youth wing of the ruling Imbonerakure CNDD-FDD). Burundi also withdrew from the Rome Statute on the ICC.

In *Rwanda*, Kagame's decision to run for an unconstitutional third term did not result in loss of support or decreased foreign disbursements from key donors. But bilateral relations with both Burundi and France were strained, while those with Tanzania and the DRC improved.

Uganda felt repercussions from developments in neighbouring countries: South Sudan's state failure caused Uganda to emerge as one of the world's leading host countries for refugees. Its role as an active member of international and African organisations and as an effective regional power was significant, despite its internal troubles.

Kenya remained vulnerable to terror attacks from al-Shabaab and its affiliates among Kenyan Muslims. In November, Kenya announced the immediate withdrawal of its troops from *UNMISS* in Sudan, when the UN secretary-general fired its Kenyan commander, Lieutenant General Johnson Mogoa Kimani Ondieki after a UN investigation found that his lack of leadership had led to a failure to protect civilians in Juba in July, which resulted in the loss of many lives.

Ethiopia kept its prominent position in the Horn region, via IGAD, in the AU and as a participant in AMISOM in Somalia. Despite major internal turmoil and much foreign criticism, it maintained its links with major donor/investor countries and concluded a new 'cooperation deal' with the EU regarding migration schemes and stemming outmigration. There was no further news on the border issue or bilateral normalisation with Eritrea, except for the military skirmish in June.

Eritrea's government was accused by the UN Commission of Inquiry on Human Rights in Eritrea of probably having committed 'crimes against humanity'. The UN Human Rights Council called on UN bodies and the AU to hold perpetrators of human rights violations to account. The EU made little progress towards the implementation of development projects under the 11th EDF. Eritrea's engagement in the Saudi-led anti-Houthi campaign in Yemen continued, and the UAE built a military base at the port of Assab. Eritrea's relations with its neighbour Djibouti did not improve.

Djibouti entered into a military agreement with Ethiopia, which was intended to keep trans-border rebels within bounds. The Chinese-constructed

Djiboutian-Ethiopian Railway connecting the port of Djibouti with Addis Ababa was inaugurated in October, and early in the year China also started the construction of its first naval base in Africa.

Sudan experienced increased tension in its relations with Egypt, was pragmatic towards Ethiopia (in view of expected benefits from the Blue Nile Dam), and confrontational towards South Sudan. Khartoum ended its relations with Iran and closed Shiite schools in Sudan, reinforcing its collaboration with Saudi Arabia and the Gulf regimes, notably in the war in Yemen (in return for substantial financial compensation). The lifting of US sanctions was still under negotiation, while Omar al-Bashir continued to face charges from the ICC for war crimes and genocide, although he continued freely to visit other African countries.

South Sudan was mired in its own problems of violence and communal enmity, but these had a negative influence on the wider region, producing streams of refugees and inhibiting developmental activities and regional cooperation. Mediation efforts to bring the civil war to a good end did not meet with real success.

Tanzania's relations with Western aid donors were somewhat strained over the Zanzibar election issue and dissatisfaction with a lack of basic economic reform measures, but relations with key neighbours and EAC partners improved.

Somalia engaged the continued attention of the international community, which aimed at creating stability, financing the AMISOM forces, and supporting the capacity of governance structures and the federal government's grip on security. Somalia's relations with Kenya (a contributor to AMISOM) were ambivalent and not always positive. For example, the government resented Kenya's decision eventually to close the huge Dadaab refugee camp. Behind the scenes of the parliamentary elections, Qatar tried to get a foothold in Somali politics by sponsoring certain candidates.

The two island states of *Seychelles* and *Comoros* were spared the political turmoil and crisis seen in much of the sub-region, with relatively uneventful foreign policy issues and no major diplomatic problems with either donor countries or trade partners. Seychelles kept up good relations with its neighbours Mauritius, Madagascar, Comoros and Reunion, and worked on its profile as a recognised 'small island developing state'. It held the last of its Somali pirate trials.

Peace-keeping activities with the participation of Eastern African forces continued, and the sub-region's conflict zones hosted the most important of such missions: the AU-UN Hybrid Operation in Darfur (UNAMID) in Sudan, with 19,747 personnel, AMISOM in Somalia, with around 22,000 troops, UNMISS in South Sudan, and the force in the disputed Abyei region of Sudan. This UN Interim Security Force in the Abyei region (UNISFA, 5,300 personnel), with troops from Ethiopia, Rwanda and Tanzania, stayed put during the year, with its UN mandate extended in July, but a solution to the Abyei dispute itself was not brought nearer. No other meeting of the Abyei Joint Oversight Committee took place, reflecting that the Khartoum regime was again playing for time. The UNSC condemned Sudan for its violation of the 2011

Sudan-South Sudan agreement on this region. No more was heard of an Eastern African Standby Force for Burundi, projected to operate there under the AU. In the UN MONUSCO peace-keeping force, operating in the very challenging conflict environment of the DRC, only Tanzania contributed personnel. None of these heavily externally funded operations achieved breakthroughs during the year in bringing contestants to the negotiating table or in establishing conditions for peace.

Socioeconomic Developments

Eastern African *economic growth* averaged about 5.3%, higher than the African average, with Ethiopia, Rwanda and Tanzania being the only countries in Africa to achieve a GDP growth rate above 6%. The World Bank's chief economist for Africa credited this to "stronger macroeconomic policy frameworks, better business regulatory environment, a more diverse structure of exports, and more effective institutions". The exception was Burundi with -1.5% GDP growth, a consequence of the domestic conflict.

The *informal economy* in the sub-region continued to account for some 55% of all economic activity, and growth in general did not lead to more equitable distribution or overall social justice. A general *migration* continued to urban areas from rural areas, which had less access to facilities such as energy, electricity, land and other resources or amenities.

The *HDI indexes* for most East African countries remained largely the same; but measured on the 'multi-dimensional poverty index' (MDPI) – a more realistic measure on overall developmental and rights achievement – the region stagnated, with misery for a large part of the population continuing, but also with slowly expanding middle-class groups emerging and entering into consumerist lifestyles. The problem was the bifurcation of social structures and the exclusion of poor, uneducated and unemployed people, notably in the countryside, among them many youths.

Overall *population growth* remained very high and so did pressure on scarce resources and the natural environment, despite the fact that in Kenya and Ethiopia, for instance, work was put into developing a 'greener' economy'. Environmental issues challenged the economic trajectories, as there was more decline in soil quality, less available land, and damage to biodiversity, ecological balance and wildlife. Long-term sustainability in all these areas, not to mention employment problems, presented major and neglected challenges for the future.

Government spending on agriculture (rural infrastructure, supportive research and technology, and enabling regulatory frameworks) continued to lag behind, reflecting the refusal of most countries' elites to invest heavily in their own smallholder farmers and or do market development. Large-scale land leases to foreign and private companies were popular, but without guaranteed growth figures, and in many places producing disappointing results. Nevertheless, agriculture accounted for one-third of GDP and two-thirds of overall employment. Aims of 'inclusive growth' and fair and equitable distribution across regions and classes were not yet achieved, if they were on national governments' agendas at all. External borrowing remained an important source of funding, but it created risks and vulnerabilities. In most countries in the region, public debt as part of GDP increased, due to more spending on infrastructure investment.

Investments in infrastructure, roads and new energy projects continued, but no solutions were offered to constructively integrate existing (and often food-secure) local economies – such as smallholder agriculture, river bank cultivation, agro-pastoralism or hunter-gathering – in the plans. The rights to land and customary use of commons and pasture areas, or water resources for local peoples, which had been established for ages in these newly opened 'frontier areas', as in Tanzania, Kenya or Ethiopia, were not adequately guaranteed, if at all, leading to gross abuse. One positive point was the recognition in Kenya of a 'Community Land Act' in August, which nominally provided for the "recognition, protection and registration of community land rights". Whether this would be respected in practice was unclear, but in countries like Rwanda, Ethiopia or Eritrea no such recognition was in sight at all.

Most state budgets showed increases funded by both a rise in domestic revenue (taxes, tariffs) and ODA flows. Another steady source of income flowing more directly to citizens and local businesses was the huge remittances received from overseas migrant communities in richer countries in the West and the Gulf region.

State current account deficits of 8%–12% continued to be registered across the region, but domestic tax revenues increased. Only the Seychelles had a tiny deficit of 0.6%. The most dramatic budgetary problems were seen in South Sudan, with a lack of funding sources and around 50% spent on 'security issues'.

Inflationary pressures were a challenge, but the picture was very diverse: extremely high for South Sudan (41.4%) and Sudan (about 19%), low in Comoros (1%), Seychelles (around 0%) and Djibouti (3%), and with the other countries in the middle ranges, from 6% to 12%.

General features in the sub-region's socio-economic landscape were ongoing urbanisation, fuelled by high population growth and the rural crises, and very stubborn (youth) unemployment figures. Somewhat surprisingly, Kenya topped the list here, with 39.1% out of a job according to UN figures. The figures for other key countries were: Tanzania 24%, Ethiopia 21.6%, Uganda 18.1% and Rwanda 17.1%. Policies to alleviate unemployment, including through EU funding schemes to target migratory pressures as well, did not really bear fruit. Urbanisation led to pressure on resources and facilities in the urban conglomerations.

Developments in the various countries showed some notable disparities. *Seychelles* continued on an economic recovery trajectory, and maintained its high HDI profile. Prudent fiscal and monetary policies, including keeping inflation in check, helped consolidate macroeconomic stability, although vulnerabilities to external shocks were still substantial, as the country continued to rely largely on two sectors (tourism and fisheries). Under the post-2015 Sustainable Development Goals agenda, Seychelles undertook to integrate 'green' and 'blue economy' issues faced by island states, such as climatic vulnerabilities and ocean resources. The other island state, *Comoros*, still faced high unemployment, and shortages of food, water, fuel and power were common.

In *Burundi*, the political crisis and international aid sanctions negatively affected the economy and the purchasing power of citizens, and economic growth did not pick up after the violent crisis produced by President Nkurunziza and the elite surrounding him. The gains achieved in the past decade – not only economic but also social and political – were wiped out.

Djibouti was much sought after for its good location and port, and China, apart from starting to construct its first overseas military base there, pledged to finance a $ 4 bn gas pipeline connecting Ethiopia and Djibouti. In spite of the country's economic progress, widespread unemployment and endemic poverty still prevailed.

Information on *Eritrea*'s economy was scant but its economy faltered and suffered from drought as well as lack of foreign investment and mismanagement. UNICEF stated that almost half of the nation suffered from malnutrition. Its neighbour *Ethiopia* showed continued economic growth in terms of GDP and infrastructure investments, although at a slower pace than in previous years. Industrial projects slowly expanded too, accompanied by FDI. Food insecurity caused by both natural and political-economic factors remained a serious problem and endangered the lives and livelihoods of an estimated 5–6 m people, necessitating substantial food aid. Protests and the damage they caused to domestic and foreign-owned companies, notably large-scale agrarian businesses, led to complaints and criticism, albeit short-lived, from investors and donor countries.

In *Tanzania*, relations with Western aid donors were slightly strained over the Zanzibar election issue and dissatisfaction with a lack of economic reform measures, although relations with key neighbours and EAC partners improved. Indicators of macroeconomic performance and growth continued to be strong, despite uncertainty over the government's future course and prevalent liquidity problems throughout the economy, which somewhat stifled the private sector and led to fears about an economic slowdown.

Uganda's economy did moderately well in a global economic environment that was becoming increasingly complex. Oil production, believed by some to be the key to solving all future problems, had not yet begun. Tanzania and Uganda reached agreement over the construction of an oil pipeline from the Ugandan oilfields to the coast – Uganda preferring not to go via Kenya in view of its coastal instability. Kenya went ahead with its own pipeline from Turkana country to Lamu port.

Kenya achieved a GDP growth rate of around 6%, driven by investments in infrastructure and construction, financial services and communications, as well as by rapid urbanisation. A burgeoning middle-class ensured the growth of shopping malls, supermarkets and wholesale and retail trade markets. Implementation of the Standard Gauge Railway and the (downscaled) LAPSSET projects continued. However, high social inequality, high unemployment (topping all countries in the sub-region), and massive poaching, leading to the decimation of wildlife (with consequences for conservation schemes and tourism), represented major problems.

In *South Sudan* the civil conflict overshadowed everything, including economic development, which ground to a standstill. There was an exodus of South Sudanese refugees to neighbouring countries, the economic crisis was severe, oil production was seriously hampered, food production was interrupted, and famine loomed. Foreign investor interest sharply declined as security issues became paramount, and prospects for any short-term recovery looking grim.

Sudan's economy was still feeling the effects of US sanctions, the decline in oil production, and the El Niño climatic phenomenon. The balance of trade remained negative, and inflation suddenly worsened in October following a government decision to stop subsidising basic commodities. The government benefitted from loans from the UAE and Saudi Arabia, but the national currency remained weak and affected by a strong black market.

Rwanda's economy remained resilient and economic growth slightly declined to 5.9% due to lower growth in agriculture, a contraction in manufacturing and construction, and a slowdown in public investment, but the country continued to outperform its EAC neighbours in the fields of public service delivery. A severe drought challenged the government's response to a food security crisis in the eastern part of the country.

In *Somalia*, developments over the year were marked by serious drought and resulting famine conditions, and insecurity hampering trade and business, despite the remarkable versatility of private sector entrepreneurs. Corruption, predatory practices and an unpredictable legal environment had a strongly negative effect on business and discouraged FDI. Foreign donors and other international players (e.g., Qatar) remained important as sources of (government) funding. Private business slowly expanded in all three regions of Somalia and led to some economic growth, despite the adverse conditions. Overseas remittances remained the largest source of income for the Somali population.

The World Bank's *Ease of Doing Business Index 2016* (ranking 190 countries, with New Zealand on 1) showed that Kenya (92nd), Uganda (115th), and Seychelles (93rd) improved on their 2015 rankings. Rwanda, a front runner in earlier years, remained on the same level (56th). Burundi sank to 157th. Lowest ranked were South Sudan at 186th and Somalia at 190th.

On the 188-country *HDI*, all Eastern African countries except the Seychelles ('high') and Kenya ('medium') remained in the 'low' category (lowest of four). Eritrea and Burundi were among the lowest ranked countries of the sub-region.

Patterns of FDI remained favourable across the region, going into large infrastructure projects, agricultural schemes, etc., but their profitability and durability remained precarious because of volatile conditions, very adverse environmental effects, lack of corporate social responsibility concerns and authoritarian implementation via state authorities. Legal, redistributive and 'inclusionary' aspects were often neglected. This sometimes led to massive protests and deep disenchantment in various places, with Kenya and Ethiopia as the main examples (see above).

The role of information and communications technology (ICT), including the development of start-ups and business applications, in the sub-region continued to grow, giving further buoyancy to economic growth and entrepreneurship, but it was very uneven across the sub-region. Kenya was in the lead in this, but other countries faced a relative lack of expansion, politically motivated blockage or excessive surveillance of the Internet (notably in Rwanda and Ethiopia), and limited roll-out of ICT across the country.

Eastern Africa was regularly visited by foreign dignitaries, and in July a remarkable visit was made by Israeli Prime Minister Benjamin Netanyahu to four East African countries, signalling a slow return of Israel to Africa, based on realist business relations and new mutual interests. Accompanied by 80 Israeli business leaders, he went to Uganda, Ethiopia, Rwanda and Kenya.

Sub-regional Cooperation and Sub-regional Organisations

The *most important sub-regional bodies* in East Africa, apart from the AU as a continent-wide organisation, were still *IGAD* and the *EAC*. The seven-member IGAD, representing the Horn countries with a joint population of around 226 m people, continued its series of activities in overall development, and regional peace and security issues, among them a summit in August held in Addis Ababa (Ethiopia) on the South Sudan conflict. There were ongoing projects on development in the sectors of agriculture, livestock economy and fisheries, regional cooperation and infrastructure, and natural resources and environment. IGAD also published its first ever 'IGAD State of the Region Report', providing a good overview of the lasting challenges this region faced as well as a blueprint for changes to be made.

Regarding the EAC, on 15 April, the *Republic of South Sudan acceded to the Treaty of the EAC* and became a full (sixth) member on 15 August. The GDP for the combined six EAC countries (with around 150 m people, of whom 22% were urban dwellers) reached $ 146 bn, and the bloc maintained economic growth despite problems of insecurity, political volatility and corruption. Members of the EAC signed the

'2016 East Africa Code of Conduct', which aimed at enhancing ethical business practices in the region. The 17th EAC summit was held on 8 September in Dar-es-Salaam (Tanzania), and the chief topics of discussion were the organisation's relations with the EU and the conflict situations in South Sudan and Burundi.

An EAC-led process of *mediation on the Burundi crisis*, including through an "external dialogue process", was diplomatically supported by the AU, the EU and the UN. Former Tanzanian president Benjamin Mkapa was appointed to facilitate this mediation process, although it was led by Uganda's President Museveni, but the EAC facilitation had not achieved any meaningful progress by the end of the year. Although the EAC presidency would normally have been taken up by Burundi, Tanzania remained EAC chair for an extra year. But the Burundian Libérat Mfumukeko – widely perceived as ally of the Nkurunziza government – was appointed as the new EAC secretary-general from April onwards. This would allow important leverage over the EAC-led 'dialogue'.

The *East African Legislative Assembly* (EALA), the parliamentary political body of the EAC founded on 28 November 2001, held several sessions during the year. It passed the Disaster Risk Reduction and Disaster Management Bill, an Anti-Trafficking in Persons Bill and a ban on female genital mutilation, and discussed other pieces of legislation, including the Gender Equality and Development Bill and the EAC Polythene Materials Control Bill. While the actual political impact of EALA legislation on member states' national policies was still limited, the EALA was gradually building up a legal corpus that would not fail to reshape the national legal frameworks of EAC countries. Efforts towards the formation of an East African Customs Union and an East African Federation continued.

The *Eastern Africa Standby Force* (EASF), the regional force composed of military, police and civilians mandated to enhance peace and security in the Eastern Africa region prepared to become fully operational in 2017 (having been established in 2007). A reinvention of the Eastern Africa Standby Brigade (EASBRIG), it was part of the AU's African Peace and Security Architecture. The EASF started recruiting civilian personnel to support the troops for its projected 5,000 force during the year. In part because of its long preparation trajectory, as well as its very small scale, there were doubts as to its significance in view of the massive armed conflicts in the subregion, such as in Sudan, South Sudan, Somalia and even Burundi.

Cooperation agreements between Eastern African countries and the EU and other *donor partners* continued, with the EU (and other Western donors) not only funding many peacekeeping operations (such as AMISOM) but also other partnerships. The signing of an EPA with the EAC, foreseen in June and intended to enhance regional integration and economic development, was delayed after criticisms by Tanzania and other countries, although Kenya and Rwanda signed the deal on 1 September. Numerous other EU-Africa activities were also ongoing, such as the promising Africa-EU Energy Partnership (AEEP), but the most important partner of Eastern Africa was China, which made moves to incorporate the sub-region into its 'New (maritime) Silk Road' initiative and continued investing heavily via parastatal companies and providing cheap credit, trade and infrastructural deals. China was also the most visible builder, developing around 42% of all projects in Eastern Africa. Its capital investments during the year increased by an estimated 500% over 2015 figures. Investment in mining was one of its priorities.

Work on the $ 25 bn Lamu Port-South Sudan-Ethiopia Transport (LAPSSET) Corridor infrastructure project, to link Kenya with Ethiopia, Uganda and South Sudan, continued, as did the *Northern Corridor Integration Projects* (NICP), on which the 13th summit was held in Kampala on 22–23 April, to discuss progress on this trans-border infrastructure initiative for integrating the countries in the sub-region, facilitating transport and travel and enhancing global economic connections.

The central theme of the COMESA heads of state and government summit in Antananarivo (Madagascar) in October was 'Inclusive and Sustainable Industrialisation'. The final communiqué struck a positive note, calling for the prioritisation of technology and innovation, SMEs and private sector initiatives. An emphasis on the themes of greening economies, value addition, diversification and capacity building in the public and private sectors was also in line with the new global rhetoric on development policies.

Activities of various of the above regional summits and initiatives seemed to partly overlap with or duplicate those of other regional bodies, such as the ICGLR, concerned since 2000 with security, peace and development issues, the IOC and the IORA (all with Eastern African country membership), but that did not hinder them from convening. The ICGLR held its 6th summit in Luanda (Angola) on 14 June and discussed the vague theme of 'Accelerating the effective implementation of the Pact and its Protocols for a more democratic and stable Great Lakes Region' (referring to the earlier Pact on Security, Stability and Development in the Great Lakes Region).

The *Nile Basin Initiative* (NBI), devoted to one of the thorniest issues in the sub-region – how to use and share the Nile waters so crucial to Egypt's existence – took no major new initiatives during the year. The underlying tension between Egypt and Ethiopia (and Sudan caught between them) about the Blue Nile and the huge Ethiopian dam being built on it, remained unresolved. The NBI also focused on projects for the conservation and protection of wetlands shared by member states and having high ecological value. In this context, the German government, via the 'Gesellschaft für Internationale Zusammenarbeit' (GIZ), funded a $ 6.7 m five-year wetland protection project.

Burundi

Stef Vandeginste

The year was marked by a continued political crisis in the aftermath of the 2015 elections. The dominant party, the CNDD-FDD, underwent restructuring in order to restore its internal coherence and, at the same, consolidate its control over state institutions. Opposition parties remained divided. Despite declarations by some armed movements, there was no significant military insurgent activity. A political dialogue took place both inside the country and under the mediation of the EAC. Aid sanctions were imposed by a number of traditional development partners, including the EU. This gave rise to considerable diplomatic tension between Burundi, neighbouring Rwanda and Belgium, the country's main bilateral aid donor. Burundi's human rights performance, most notably as a result of the activities of the Imbonerakure CNDD-FDD youth wing, was strongly criticised at the international level. Burundi withdrew from the Rome Statute on the ICC. At the socio-economic level, the crisis and the aid sanctions negatively affected citizens' purchasing power.

 | DOI 10.1163/9789004355910_031

Domestic Politics

After its victory at the 2015 general elections, the dominant party *'Conseil National pour la Défense de la Démocratie – Forces de Défense de la Démocratie'* (*CNDD-FDD*) *enhanced its control over state institutions*. At the same time, it tried to address the consequences of the internal rift that had divided the party into two wings, one in favour of President Pierre Nkurunziza's third term in office, the other (known as 'les frondeurs') opposing his continued rule over the party and the country. At the top level of the party, an important reform was decided at the party congress in August. Membership of the 'Conseil des Sages' – the party's main decision-making organ, which in the run-up to the 2015 elections had initially opposed Nkurunziza's term renewal – was reduced to five (from nine), under the chairmanship of Nkurunziza himself. The four other members were longstanding leaders from the early days of the movement's armed struggle, three of them (all Hutu) actively engaged in the military activities of the rebellion and therefore benefitting from the significant historical legitimacy of 'liberating' the country. The new secretary-general was Evariste Ndayishimiye, until then a general in the Burundian army and chief advisor to Nkurunziza. Unlike other party generals, Ndayishimiye's reputation was not tainted by large-scale corruption or command responsibility for human rights violations. Following his election as new party leader, Ndayishimiye tried to shift priority towards economic development, attempting to show that the political crisis had come to an end and that it was time to return to 'business as usual'. Ndayishimiye replaced Pascal Nyabenda, who remained speaker in the National Assembly. He was replaced as chief advisor to Nkurunziza by another former 'maquisard', Gabriel Nizigama. With three more Hutu former rebel leaders in charge of the Army (Prime Niyongabo), the Intelligence Service (Etienne Ntakarutimana) and the Ministry of Public Security (Alain-Guillaume Bunyoni), the military (and, according the many observers, hardline) wing of the CNDD-FDD consolidated its control over the state institutions.

A major concern for the CNDD-FDD leadership was the *internal unity of the party*. Suspected dissidents, or so-called 'undisclosed frondeurs', who remained in Burundi (and in positions in the administration, the judiciary and the security forces) were perceived as potential enemies in case of an attack by an armed rebel movement. Many officials at various levels of Burundi's state institutions, including the ombudsperson, were replaced by presumably more loyal party members. There was also a continuing fear of ongoing contacts between internal dissidents and the 'Parti des Patriotes pour le Développement – Girijambo' (PPD Girijambo), a political movement in exile that united several high ranking CNDD-FDD dissidents under the leadership of Leonidas Hatungimana, former presidential spokesperson of Nkurunziza and brother-in-law of Ndayishimiye. The political action of PPD

Girijambo and other Burundians residing in Belgium was also one of the reasons behind Burundi's strained relations with its main bilateral donor (see below).

At the party congress in August, as well as on various other occasions, Nkurunziza repeatedly and publicly legitimised the continuation of his rule by referring to the 'will of God' and to his 'divine predestination' to lead the country. The *use of religion for political purposes* also showed on other occasions. By the end of the year, five years after she was ordained as a pastor of the Pentecostal 'Eglise du Rocher' (Church on the Rock), of which she was also the general treasurer, first lady Denise Bucumi had established around 50 churches in all of Burundi's provinces. These churches combined religious with humanitarian and political activities. Several high ranking dignitaries and civil servants (most of whom were raised as Catholics) joined the Church on the Rock. Together with national consultations organised by the 'Commission Nationale pour le Dialogue Inter-Burundais' (National Commission for Inter-Burundian Dialogue, CNDI; see below), this paved the way for Nkurunziza's announcement, during a public radio show on the last day of the year, that he might run for an additional fourth term if that was the wish of the Burundian people. In his official New Year's address, he announced the launch of a process to amend the constitution, although he did not specify which provisions were to be amended.

The *opposition parties* – some of which were legally registered while others operated mainly from abroad – remained strongly divided, including internally. The 'Conseil National pour le Respect de l'Accord d'Arusha et l'Etat de Droit' (CNARED), which had been established in July 2015 as an ad hoc coalition bringing together third term opponents from various political backgrounds, continued to suffer from internal rifts and leadership struggles. The formerly single party, the 'Union pour le Progrès National' (UPRONA), generally perceived to be the political entity representing the demographic Tutsi minority, as well as the opposition party 'Forces Nationales de Libération' (FNL), were internally divided into pro-government and a 'real' opposition wings, the latter lacking legal registration. In August, Abel Gashatsi replaced Concilie Nibigira as UPRONA party chair. Within the FNL, rooted in the former rebel movement PALIPEHUTU-FNL and therefore associated with the liberation struggle of the demographic Hutu majority, the division gave rise to a paradoxical situation: while historical FNL leader Agathon Rwasa was vice president of the National Assembly and also appointed three coalition government ministers, he was not a member of the officially registered FNL party, which continued to be led by Jacques Bigirimana, the so-called Burundian opposition leader but in reality an important ally of the CNDD-FDD. This continued undermining of the FNL – potentially benefitting from considerable electoral support – was clearly part of the CNDD-FDD's preparation for the 2020 general elections. On a number of occasions, Rwasa was prevented from engaging in political campaigning and his spokesperson frequently denounced harassment of FNL members by the Imbonerakure, the CNDD-FDD youth wing. The opposition party 'Union pour la Paix et le Développment' (UPD), which was close to former CNDD-FDD leader Hussein Radjabu (who was living in exile in Rwanda and Uganda following his escape from Bujumbura central prison in early 2015), was in turn divided into two wings, one in favour of joining CNARED, the other opposing it. While the government welcomed a dialogue with certain opposition parties, it refused to recognise or talk with CNARED and 34 other political and civil society leaders accused of participating in the military coup attempt of May 2015, against whom an arrest warrant was internationally circulated. Among them were Alexis Sinduhije of the 'Mouvement pour la Solidarité et le Développement' (MSD) and CNARED chair Jean Minani.

In response to the internationally requested inclusive dialogue as a means of settling the political conflict in a non-violent way, two parallel processes took place. One political dialogue was held under the auspices of the EAC, with former Tanzanian president Benjamin Mkapa as facilitator (see below under Foreign Affairs). An *internal political dialogue* continued to be led by the CNDI, a body widely perceived as operating under the strict control of the CNDD-FDD. Hearings were organised in all provinces and in all of them participants voiced remarkably similar concerns and made highly political, sometimes legally complex, recommendations. In August, the CNDI published its interim findings: Burundians wanted their president to be able to serve more than two terms; they no longer wanted former heads of state to be senators for life; and they wanted certain (unspecified) 'errors' contained in the Arusha Peace and Reconciliation Agreement of August 2000 –the country's roadmap to peace and essentially based on ethnic power-sharing – to be corrected; and they wanted a reform of the laws governing political parties, civil society organisations and religious groups. At a meeting in October, CNDD-FDD and some 25 other pro-government parties expressed their support for the CNDI interim findings and called upon the government to launch a constitutional amendment process.

According to the government, *peace and security* were fully restored throughout the country. At a parliamentary hearing in February, Defence Minister Emmanuel Ntahomvukiye acknowledged that three rebel movements (RED TABARA, FOREBU and FNL Nzabampema) had declared war on Burundi, but he insisted that, apart from some terrorist attacks against civilians, they did not constitute a serious security threat. Indeed, none of these three (nor any of the other self-declared liberation movements) carried out any significant military insurgency activity. However, in December, some Burundian military were reportedly killed during an attack on the FNL Nzabampema rebel movement on neighbouring DRC territory. Assassinations of and attacks against high ranking officials symbolised the continued insecurity. In March, Lieutenant Colonel Darius Ikurakure was killed. In April, General Kararuza and some of his relatives were ambushed and assassinated. In July, former government minister and East African Legislative Assembly member Hafsa Mossi was killed. In November, presidential spokesperson Willy Nyamitwe, generally seen as one of the most influential people in Nkurunziza's inner circle, narrowly escaped an assassination attempt. In December, Minister of the Environment Emmanuel Niyonkuru was assassinated. All of these events happened in Bujumbura and, as usual in Burundi, responsibility for these crimes remained unclear. The number of grenade attacks in Bujumbura markedly declined towards the end of the year. This may well have been the effect of a more efficient intelligence system, including the compulsory use of 'cahiers de ménages', a logbook in which residents and visitors to every house in all neighbourhoods of the capital city had to be recorded.

Many eye-witness accounts and international (human rights and other) reports on Burundi confirmed that the *Imbonerakure* youth wing – sometimes also called 'youth militia' – of the CNDD-FDD was the main source of everyday insecurity for ordinary Burundians suspected of supporting the (armed or unarmed) opposition. The Imbonerakure – or newly recruited sections of them, composed of demobilised former rebels – had reportedly transformed into a parallel law enforcement agency operating throughout the country, sometimes in close collaboration with the local police and administrative authorities, and sometimes actually replacing those formal state institutions. Following the assassination of General Adolphe Nshimirimana in August 2015, it remained unclear who exercised central control over the Imbonerakure, some units reportedly operating fairly autonomously. This may well account for the government's legal reform initiative, in October, to establish a national volunteer corps and a division of army reservists. In its official discourse, both the government and the party insisted that the Imbonerakure was a peaceful civil movement engaged in development activities and in non-violent political mobilisation. According to opposition and civil society voices, however, they were responsible for a systematic campaign of killings, forcible disappearances, arbitrary arrests, rape and torture of suspected opponents and civil society activists. Together with the intelligence service ('Service National de Renseignement', SNR), they were accused of eliminating people on a 'kamwe kamwe' (one by one) basis, thus avoiding large-scale and internationally obvious executions. Throughout the year, there were increased allegations that the initially political repression (targeting Nkurunziza opponents) had become increasingly ethnic (targeting members of the demographic Tutsi minority group). This gave rise to alarming reports by some human rights organisations and media channels warning of the risk of a genocide in Burundi. An ethnic census conducted by order of the Senate at the level of the whole civil service further fuelled these fears. Some Tutsi feared that the data collected through the census might be used to target them if large-scale violence broke out.

Accusations of *human rights violations* were also at the heart of Burundi's strained relations with the UN, in particular the Office of the High Commissioner for Human Rights (see also below). In September, the UN Independent Investigation on

Burundi (UNIIB), composed of two experts from the UN and one from the AU, established pursuant to a UNHRC resolution, submitted its final report to the UNHRC. The experts concluded that gross human rights violations were taking place, some of which might amount to crimes against humanity, and urged that independent international judicial processes be set in motion to bring the perpetrators to justice. In its resolution adopted further to the UNIIB report, the UNHRC established a follow-up commission of inquiry for a period of one year, with the purpose of identifying alleged perpetrators. The government strongly protested against the report and the resolution. The three UNIIB experts were declared persona non grata and the government announced it would not grant access to Burundi to the new commission of inquiry. It also suspended its collaboration with the Burundi office of the UN High Commissioner for Human Rights.

The *Truth and Reconciliation Commission* (TRC) continued to face considerable difficulties, including a lack of material resources and donor support, widely perceived political interference in its activities and the general crisis-driven context of fear and distrust discouraging people from participating in TRC activities. Two TRC members left the country and had not been replaced by the end of the year. A law on the protection of witnesses and victims was promulgated in June, which was an essential precondition for the TRC to proceed to the hearings stage of its inquiries.

Relations between the government and *civil society* groups remained tense. Six NGOs, including Ligue Iteka, Burundi's oldest human rights organisation, established in 1991 and symbolically important for the struggle for democracy, were banned. Four other civil society groups were temporarily suspended. New legislation was adopted to regulate the registration and functioning of local and international NGOs. In April, 'IWACU' journalist Jean Bigirimana disappeared, which gave rise to an international campaign in support of local journalists. In December, prominent trade union leader Tharcisse Gahungu was arrested.

According to the government, by the end of the year more than 100,000 *refugees*, out of 265,000 Burundians who had left the country as a result of the 2015 electoral crisis, had returned. However, according to UNHCR, since the influx began as a result of the crisis that started in April 2015, more than 340,000 Burundians had left the country by the end of December. UNHCR verified no more than 7,275 spontaneous returns. In addition, UNHCR reported that 140,000 were internally displaced.

Foreign Affairs

The year was marked by a strong *deterioration of Burundi's external relations with a number of traditional international partners*. In the eyes of the government, an international 'axis of evil' had tried but failed to bring about regime change through the attempted coup d'état of May 2015. For the government, there was no doubt that some international actors – including its main traditional partners, the EU and Belgium – were maintaining their efforts to remove the Nkurunziza regime. To counter this perceived international conspiracy, the government tried to broaden its international network and to establish new international partnerships.

Throughout the year, international involvement with the crisis in Burundi remained intensive. In addition to the internal dialogue led by the CNDI (see above), an *external dialogue process was facilitated by the EAC*, diplomatically supported by the AU, the EU and the UN. At an EAC heads of state summit in March, former Tanzanian president Benjamin Mkapa was appointed to facilitate the mediation process led by Uganda's President Yoweri Museveni. Tanzania also remained EAC chair for an extra year, though the presidency would normally have been taken up by Burundi. In a major diplomatic victory for the Burundi government, the Burundian Libérat Mfumukeko was appointed as EAC secretary-general from April. He was widely perceived as an important ally of the Nkurunziza government, with important leverage on the EAC-led dialogue. The EAC facilitation had not, however, achieved any meaningful progress by the end of the year. Two rounds of talks were held in May and in July in Arusha (Tanzania), while additional consultations took place in December in Bujumbura. A broad range of issues was tabled for the mediation agenda. Without giving any substantive indications about the possible way out of the crisis and while noting a glaring lack of seriousness and willingness of all stakeholders to engage in dialogue, Mkapa announced that his objective was to reach an agreement by June 2017, calling upon all parties involved to prepare for the 2020 general elections. At a controversial press conference at Bujumbura Airport on 9 December, he stressed that there was no more point in questioning the legitimacy of President Nkurunziza. In response, accusing the facilitator of taking a pro-government stance, CNARED withdrew its recognition of Mkapa as facilitator. This risked further side-lining CNARED, which the government refused to recognise as a valuable interlocutor. CNARED requested an international economic and arms embargo to pressure the government to accept a truly inclusive dialogue. Parallel to the EAC-led initiative, the UN continued its own mediation efforts through the UN secretary-general's special advisor Jamal Benomar. In October, increasingly dissatisfied with Benomar's involvement – as well as skilfully playing international actors against one another while, at the same time, buying time – the government requested his replacement.

Three *international initiatives to send an international military or police presence to Burundi failed to deliver*. In December 2015, the AU Peace and Security Council (PSC) had taken an unprecedented decision authorising the deployment of an African Prevention and Protection Mission in Burundi (MAPROBU) for a period of six months with an initial strength of 5,000 military personnel and police. In the absence of the consent of the Burundi government, the decision was referred for endorsement to the AU summit at the end of January. In the run-up to the summit, some AU member states, including Tanzania, expressed reservations about the MAPROBU decision. In the end, the summit did not endorse the PSC decision, which was celebrated as a great diplomatic victory by the government. The implementation of an earlier AU decision to send 200 human rights and military observers to Burundi, with the consent of the government, was delayed because of failure to reach an agreement on the memorandum of understanding defining the observers' mandate. Two UNSC resolutions on Burundi were adopted, in April and in July. The latter requested the UN secretary-general to establish a UN police officers component (of up to 228 police officers), for an initial period of one year to monitor the security situation in coordination with the AU observer mission. The government organised a mass demonstration in the capital Bujumbura to protest against the UNSC resolution. This was but one in a systematic series of *weekly 'popular' demonstrations* – clearly orchestrated and financed by the government – "against international interference in Burundi's internal affairs". In the absence of the consent of the government, the UNSC police presence was not established.

In March, the *EU adopted 'appropriate measures'* – widely perceived as aid sanctions – under article 96 of the EU-ACP partnership agreement. The EU suspended direct financial support to the Burundi administration, but confirmed its intention to deliver development aid and humanitarian assistance to the population. The EU set out specific measures to be taken by the government that could lead to the resumption of full cooperation. These included an inclusive, internationally mediated political agreement to settle the crisis, the lifting of restrictions on independent media and human rights defenders and investigations into human rights violations. In September, the EU prolonged its *individual sanctions* (travel restrictions and an assets freeze) against four Burundians, three on the government side, one on the opposition side. The USA confirmed and extended its individual sanctions to three additional Burundian military (two on the government side and one former lieutenant colonel who fled the country).

Burundi continued to contribute approximately 5,400 troops – six rotating battalions – to the AU's *AMISOM* (AU Mission in Somalia) operation. Its contribution became the subject of important debate. Civil society and the political opposition campaigned against Burundi's continued participation in AMISOM, arguing that this indirectly financed the government. More importantly, under the 'appropriate measures' adopted under article 96 of the Cotonou Agreement (see above), the EU decided to revise payment modalities of its contribution to AMISOM as far as Burundian peacekeepers were concerned. As a result, from March onwards, payments to Burundian AMISOM peacekeepers were temporarily suspended. At the end of the year, Nkurunziza announced that, if no satisfactory solution was found, Burundi would not hesitate to withdraw its troops from AMISOM by the end of January 2017. Burundi also contributed some 850 troops to the UN operation in the CAR (MINUSCA) and a more limited number of police officers to UN operations in Mali, Haiti, Darfur and Côte d'Ivoire. In December, the UN secretary-general announced the opening of an investigation into allegations of sexual exploitation and abuse by Burundian MINUSCA peacekeepers. Approximately one-third of Burundi's armed forces were serving in peacekeeping missions, which indicated the budgetary importance of its international troop contributions.

In October, Burundi addressed a notification to the UN secretary-general announcing its *withdrawal from the Statute of Rome on the ICC*. Together with South Africa, Burundi was the first country in the history of the ICC to withdraw from the Rome Statute. During the parliamentary hearing, it was stressed that this decision was essential to preserve Burundi's sovereignty. Although the withdrawal would not take effect until one year after its notification, the decision was widely perceived as an effort on behalf of the Nkurunziza government to escape international criminal justice. In April, one year after the start of the crisis, the ICC prosecutor announced the opening of a preliminary examination on Burundi. By the end of the year, the prosecutor had not submitted a request for authorisation of an investigation to the pre-trial chamber. Widely criticised at the broader international level, Burundi's withdrawal also had reputational benefits among AU member states insisting on the need to protect Africa against neo-colonial interference with internal affairs.

In January, the UN Group of Experts on the DRC reported to the UNSC that they had met a number of Burundian armed combatants who claimed that at least 400 *Burundian refugees in Rwanda had received military training*, including by Rwandan instructors. Rwanda denied the allegations, but this report further strained diplomatic relations between the two countries. In March, a CNDD-FDD communiqué accused Rwanda's President Paul Kagame of 'attempts to cause genocide' in Burundi. This was followed, in May, by the publication of a 25-page memorandum on Rwanda's 'acts of aggression' by the bureau in charge of communication at the President's Office. In August, bus transport between the two countries was suspended and, in October, there was a diplomatic row over a border incident in Ngozi province. In his New Year's address for 2017, President Nkurunziza warned both Rwanda and Belgium to change their behaviour or Burundi would end its diplomatic relations with both countries.

Diplomatic relations with Belgium – former tutelage authority and Burundi's main bilateral donor – were at an all-time low. Several CNDD-FDD communiqués and statements by the government spokesperson accused Belgium of leading an international conspiracy against Burundi. Belgium was also accused of being responsible for the ethnic divisions in Burundi and for a number of assassinations of Burundian politicians. Party officials requested that the Belgian historical responsibility for the crisis in Burundi be elucidated by the TRC. In December, Burundi recalled its ambassador from Brussels for consultations. Facing international aid sanctions and their increasingly tangible socio-economic consequences (see below), putting the blame on international partners like Belgium had an important domestic rally-round-the-flag effect.

Socioeconomic Developments

In an effort to counter some of the effects of the aid sanctions, the government imposed *new rules on foreign currency account holders* in commercial banks. From April onwards, all NGOs, intergovernmental organisations and all development programmes benefiting from external funding were required to transfer their foreign currency account from commercial banks to the 'Banque de la République du Burundi' (the central bank). In June, the central bank also announced a new partnership agreement with the Russian Gazprombank. This development was illustrative of a larger series of efforts on behalf of the government to diversify its development partners.

Following the international aid sanctions, Burundi increasingly faced a shortage of foreign currency. This also gave rise to *shortages and price increases of imported goods*. On several occasions, there was a shortage of petrol at petrol stations in the capital city. While the official exchange rate for the Burundian franc remained relatively stable, the gap between official and non-official *exchange rates* increased significantly, indicating a further depreciation of the franc. By the end of the year, the value of the euro and the US dollar on the black market was approximately twice that on the official market. This spread reportedly gave rise to an important upsurge in illicit cross-border foreign currency speculation.

Prices for essential foodstuffs (flower, rice, beans, salt, etc.) also rose significantly, adding to an *increase of overall poverty levels* and pushing larger numbers of people out of the monetary economy and back into subsistence agriculture. A new tax raised the price of sugar. Civil servants' and teachers' salaries continued to be paid, although sometimes delayed, but, according to several civil society watchdogs, the purchasing power of large groups of the population decreased significantly. While *inflation* stood at an estimated 5.4%, the projected inflation rate for 2017 stood at 7% or, according to other sources, over 10%. The government increasingly called upon the population to participate in weekly community works (such as the construction of school buildings or health centres, the maintenance of roads, etc.), as part of a larger campaign of promotion of economic self-reliance.

There was an estimated *negative GDP growth* of 1.5% (after a negative GDP of 3.9% in 2015). Expectations for 2017, with the gradual return of political stability, were more optimistic. The 2017 *budget* adopted in parliament projected a 2.9% increase in revenue (and a 5.2% increase in expenditure). This was based, in part, on new taxes on fuel and mobile telephones and on estimated increases in world market prices for tea and coffee, two important exports.

Tax collection improved compared with the politically highly unstable year 2015 (which had seen a 17% decline compared with 2014). According to the 'Office Burundais des Recettes' (tax revenue office; OBR), taxes collected were 6.9% above expectations and 7.9% above the 2015 figures. In June, former AfDB administrator Leonard Sentore was appointed as new OBR director, replacing Domitien Ndihokubwayo, who was appointed as minister of finance.

On the Global Entrepreneurship Index published in November, Burundi ranked 136th (out of 137 countries). On TI's corruption index, Burundi ranked 150th (out of 167 countries). Burundi's position on the World Bank's Doing Business Index slightly deteriorated (to 159th out of 190 countries, compared with 152nd in 2015), the weakest position among EAC member states. On the Global Competitiveness Index of the World Economic Forum, Burundi was ranked 135th (out of 138 countries). The Forum's Executive Opinion Survey listed political instability, corruption, access to financing and inflation as the most problematic factors.

Comoros

Simon Massey

The year was dominated by presidential and gubernatorial elections. In particular, Colonel Azali Assoumani's return as president after ten years witnessed the comeback of a soldier-politician, former coup leader and architect of Comoros' existing rotating presidency, or 'présidence tournante', system. Under his predecessor, Ikililou Dhoinine, the country's economy had continued to underperform, with GDP falling from a growth rate of 3.5% in 2013 to 1% in 2015. Unemployment remained high and shortages of food, water, fuel and power were common. However, given its history of coups, mutinies and secession, the relative political stability of the country under Dhoinine's leadership marked out his time in office as a qualified success. The conclusion of his mandate also completed the first cycle of the rotating presidency system, the constitutional and electoral arrangement devised to check secessionist pressures in the two less populous islands of Nzwani and Mwali, and to ensure power sharing at a federal level within the Union of Comoros.

 | DOI 10.1163/9789004355910_032

Domestic Politics

All three islands having supplied a president of the Union, the constitution required that the cycle start again with a president from Ngazidja. The first round of the *presidential election*, held on 21 February, was restricted to the electorate of Ngazidja and had a field of 25 candidates.

The voters faced a choice between experienced politicians and personalities from civil society, both representatives of political parties and independents, including Mohamed Daoud, the mayor of Moroni, Hamidou Bourhane, who had been president of the National Assembly until January 2015, former chief of staff, General Mohamed Amiri Salimou, and the prominent Franco-Comorian lawyer Said Larifou, leader of the 'Rassemblement pour l'Initiative de Développement de la Jeunesse Avertie' (RIDJA). However, four other candidates ultimately dominated the vote. Dhoinine's preferred candidate was the sitting vice president for finance and the economy, Mohamed Ali Soilihi, the official candidate of the 'Union pour le Développement des Comores' (UPDC), the largest single party in the National Assembly, with eight out of 24 seats. For Soilihi, the advantages of incumbency were offset by a faltering economy, unpaid public sector salaries and rumours of corruption. Another confidant of Dhoinine, the governor of Ngazidja, Mouigni Soilihi Said Baraka, faced the challenge of appealing to voters from Nzwani and Mwali, where he was little known. Sambi's party, Juwa (meaning 'Sun' in Shikomori), gave its backing to a former foreign minister under Sambi, Fahmi Said Ibrahim, who, though leader of the 'Parti de l'Entente Comorienne' (PEC), stood as an independent. Finally, Azali Assoumani, the former president, sought to play down the coup that had originally brought him to power, rather accentuating his role in devising the electoral system that had underpinned the relative stability of the past 15 years, and his unique experience as the only former president in the electoral field.

The role of the large Comorian *diaspora* was more pronounced than in previous elections. Based mainly in mainland France, the number of Comorians living abroad was estimated at 150,000. Increasingly influential in the electoral process largely as a result of its financial influence – with the diaspora contributing around a quarter of the Union's total GDP – the original intention for the elections was to extend the franchise to expatriates. Ultimately, however, citing 'technical reasons', the 'Commission Électorale Nationale Indépendante' (CENI) blocked this decision, so the role of the diaspora in the election, notably its money and influence, remained significant but was no longer crucial.

The provisional *results of the first round* were announced by the CENI on 24 February. The turnout was 74.4% of a registered electorate of 159,000 and the result was tight, with Soilihi winning 17.6% of the vote, Baraka 15.1% and Assoumani 15%, leaving Ibrahim, with 14.5% of votes cast, excluded from the second round. The peaceful conduct of the election was commended by the AU. Claims from the

Ibrahim camp, and from 18 other candidates, that the vote had been fraudulent did not gain traction and calls for a general strike were ignored.

As the election from then on encompassed the other two islands of the archipelago, the tenor of the campaign became more charged. A fire bomb attack on the Ministry of Foreign Affairs in Moroni just before campaigning began for the second round evidenced a deep-seated frustration amongst the electorate, particularly young voters, with the political class's inability to resolve the high unemployment rate, shortages of food and energy, and chronic inadequacies in infrastructure, as well as inadequate health and education provision. Nzwani saw the most disruption, with violent confrontations between rival supporters erupting after former president Ahmed Abdallah Sambi came out in favour of Assoumani.

The *result of the second round* was very close. The turnout was 69.1% of a registered electorate of 301,000 across the three islands. Assoumani came out the winner with 41% of the vote, followed by Soilihi with 39.9% and Baraka third with 19.2%. The outcome was rejected by Soilihi, who claimed that the vote on Nzwani was seriously flawed with voters prevented from participating and incidences of fraud. These objections were upheld in part by the Constitutional Court and a repeat of the second round of voting was ordered in 13 constituencies on the island. This *partial re-run*, held on 11 May, resulted in Assoumani increasing his majority to 41.6%, with Soilihi dropping to 39.7% and Baraka dropping to 18.9%.

As well as voting in the presidential poll on 10 April, the three islands also voted in the *gubernatorial run-offs*. The results were disastrous for Dhoinine's UPDC. On Ngazidja, the ruling party's Hamada Moussa took 38% against 62% for Hassan Hamadi, who benefitted from splits in the Assoumani camp to get to the run-off, and ultimately received Assoumani's backing. On Mwali, Dhoinine's wife Hadidja Aboubacar received 37% of the vote against 67% for Mohamed Saïd Fazul, a former president of Mwali and fervent opponent of Dhoinine.

The fractious presidential campaign on Nzwani was mirrored in the gubernatorial elections. In the run-off, the UPDC's candidate and sitting governor, Annisi Chamsidine, faced the Juwa party candidate, Abdou Salami Abdou. During the campaign, frequent violent confrontations took place in front of the 'Commission Électorale Insulaire Indépendante' (CEII) offices in the island's capital, Mutsamudu. There was confusion over the outcome, with first Chamsidine and then Salami Abdou being declared the victor. Both candidates alleged incidences of fraud on polling day and the Constitutional Court ordered *re-runs of the gubernatorial vote* in the same constituencies where re-runs in the presidential vote had been ordered. Salami Abdou was ultimately declared the winner, meaning the UPDC failed to win the governorship of any of the three islands.

Neither the presidential nor the gubernatorial campaign was conspicuous for novel approaches to the Union's longstanding economic and social problems. However, it was clear that whichever candidate won, with six political parties and three independents represented in the National Assembly, and with *no single dominant party*, discrete alliances would need to be formed in order to pass each piece of legislation. The increasing fragmentation of Comorian electoral politics left Assoumani, who received just 15% of the first round vote compared with Dhoinine's 28% in 2010, and whose party, the 'Convention pour le Renouveau des Comores' (CRC), had only two seats in the National Assembly, less able to dictate the legislative agenda than his predecessor.

During his first months in office, Assoumani intervened to lower the cost of living by cutting domestic petrol prices, public transport fares and some foodstuffs. He also signalled his intention to reduce government spending by cutting the public sector workforce. This ambition would bring him into conflict with vested interests and the public sector trade unions. Paradoxically, despite his ambition to cut the national wage bill, Assoumani decided to raise the salaries of some ministers.

Foreign Affairs

As the former colonial power, *France* remained Comoros' most important economic, political and cultural partner. Yet despite the closeness of the ties between the two countries – about 300,000 Comorians were living in France and the French treasury guaranteed the Comorian franc – the question of whether the archipelago's fourth island, *Mayotte*, was Comorian or French remained seemingly intractable. From the Comorian perspective, France had reneged on the original rules of the independence referendum and opted to retain control of Mayotte. Since 2011, Mayotte had been a full department of the French republic. Moreover, since 1995, France had severely restricted visas for Comorians, leading to a crisis involving tens of thousands of migrants making the perilous sea crossing every year, many motivated by much higher living standards on Mayotte, but others simply seeking to visit family. Many drowned and others were held in migrant centres before being returned.

In his September speech to the UN General Assembly, Assoumani called for a renewed dialogue with France over the sovereignty of Mayotte. He also raised the issue with President François Hollande in October, when he made his first official visit to France following his election. However, with successive referendums in Mayotte reaffirming an overwhelming commitment to remain part of France, there was no prospect of the island being returned to Comoros. Like previous Comorian heads of state, Assoumani had to tread a delicate path. National honour required Comoros pursue its claim to Mayotte, whilst diplomatic and practical efforts had to be made to cut the level of migrant deaths at sea. However, given the importance of the relationship with France on many levels, Assoumani had also to maintain constructive relations with the former colonial power.

Comoros continued its long-standing *'open-door' policy*, seeking to maintain good relations with Western powers, Middle Eastern states and its regional neighbours. For many years, it had been one of the few countries to be on good terms with both the *United States* and *Iran*. However, in recent years, as the rivalry for hegemony in the Middle East between Iran and *Saudi Arabia* had intensified, so Comoros had come under pressure from Riyadh to break relations with Tehran. In January, the Dhoinine government officially severed diplomatic relations with Iran, citing that country's interference in the internal affairs of some Arab states. This decision followed the injection of $ 40 m in budget support from Saudi Arabia in late 2015 to settle the unpaid salaries of public sector workers and clear the state's debt to the central bank. Breaking diplomatic ties with Iran also had a theological dimension. Comorians being predominantly Sunni Muslims, the links forged with Shia Iran, notably under the Sambi presidency, were viewed with suspicion by many. In October, the minister of the interior restated the prohibition of non-Sunni Muslim rites in public and private places, re-emphasising Comoros' support for Saudi Arabia with regard to Iran.

The decisive shift toward Saudi Arabia and the wider Arab Middle East was also emphasised by the opening in June of a secretariat dedicated to Comorian relations with the Arab world. In May, the then Minister for External Affairs Abdoulkarim Mohamed indicated publicly that Comoros was willing to discuss granting economic citizenship to Kuwait's stateless 'bidun' population.

Apart from the rupture with Iran, the open-door policy remained in place. In particular, cooperation with *China* was courted. In May, in addition to a defence agreement and a port management venture agreed in 2015, it was announced that there were plans for Sino-Comorian collaboration in areas including infrastructure, health, energy and fishing.

Socioeconomic Developments

Economic growth continued to slow to an estimated 0.7%, down from 1% in 2015. This continued decline was caused by delays in infrastructural improvements, the shortfall in *electricity* production and a drop in the production of two key *export crops*, cloves and ylang-ylang, which contracted by 45% and 10% respectively. Mid-year figures indicated that *FDI* had fallen to $ 5 m in 2015 from $ 14 m in 2014 and a high of $ 23 m in 2011.

The IMF released a report at the end of the year commending the new government's commitment to stabilising the fiscal situation. Assoumani met with Comorian banking leaders to urge a simplification of international fund transfers to encourage FDI. At the same meeting, he assured them that the government should be treated like 'any other client' when it came to government lending.

The *inflation* rate for the year was 1%, the result of low international food and oil prices as well as the restraining effect of membership of the franc zone, with the Comorian franc pegged to the euro (CF 492 : € 1) and guaranteed by the French treasury.

Despite recording substantial current account deficits in the three preceding years, mid-year figures from the Banque Centrale des Comores (BCC) indicated that in 2015 the country had, for the first time, registered a *surplus*. The surplus of CF 2.6 bn was the result of a reduction in imports as a consequence of lower oil prices, a drop in equipment imports and a rise in secondary income, notably a 3.4% rise in remittances and the $ 40 m in budgetary aid received from Saudi Arabia.

However, the single largest shift in the current account, amounting to a drop in the services deficit of 90% from the previous year, was result of the CF 7 bn income from the sale by the Dhoinine government of a second *telecoms* operating licence to the Madagascar-based firm Telecom Malagasy (Telma), which brought to an end the monopoly held by Comores Télécom (Comtel), a government-owned company. The introduction of competition in the sector was applauded by the IMF. The high cost of telecom services in Comoros – with broadband at $ 80.2 a month compared with an average for low-income countries of $ 44.9 – had been largely attributed to Comtel's monopoly. Telma complained that Comtel had denied it access in Moroni to the Eastern African Submarine system (EASSy), the fibre-optic cable network that connected countries in the region. It was hoped that the fourth-generation and fibre-optic networks that Telma was promising to deliver would have the potential to increase Internet usage in Comoros, which in 2015 stood at 7.5% compared with 22.5% in Africa overall.

Djibouti

Nicole Hirt

Presidential elections were held on 8 April, and Ismaïl Omar Guelleh was re-elected to serve his fourth term by 87% of the vote. The weak opposition coalition had not been able to agree on a common strategy to counter the political supremacy of Guelleh and his UMP coalition. The president's son-in-law, Djama Elmi Okieh (dubbed 'Djama Speed'), was appointed minister of health and given substantial political power as Guelleh's possible designated successor. The Afar-inhabited north around the town of Obock continued to witness violent clashes between government forces and a militant wing of the 'Front pour la Restoration de l'Unité et de la Démocratie' (FRUD), and Djibouti entered into a military agreement with Ethiopia, which was supposed to keep the rebels within bounds. The Chinese-constructed Djiboutian-Ethiopian Railway connecting the port of Djibouti with Addis Ababa was inaugurated in October, and China, which had started the construction of its first naval base in Africa in Djibouti early in the year, pledged to finance a $ 4 bn gas pipeline connecting Ethiopia and Djibouti. In spite of the country's economic progress, widespread unemployment and endemic poverty prevailed.

 | DOI 10.1163/9789004355910_033

Domestic Politics

President Ismaïl Omar Guelleh (widely dubbed IOG) retained control over all aspects of Djibouti's political and economic life and continued to rule the country after winning the *presidential elections* that took place on 8 April with 87% of the vote. He started his fourth term as president with the support of the governing 'Union pour la Majorité Presidentielle' (UMP) coalition, which was dominated by Guelleh's 'Rassemblement Populaire pour le Progrès' (RPP) and retained personal control over the military, the police and the security forces. Parliament's role in politics was limited in the face of the president's dominance in affairs of state, and the *political opposition coalition* 'Union pour le Salut National' (USN) remained weak and lacked a common strategy. While one faction of the USN had opted for a boycott of the election, two other factions nominated their own candidates to run against Guelleh: Mohamed Daoud Chehem and Omar Elmi Khaireh, who received 7% and 2% of the vote, respectively.

Guelleh did not accept election observers from the EU, and so the AU was the only international body that was present on the ground with *election observers*. Remarkably, they declared the election process 'free and credible', despite the fact that representatives of the opposition complained that many of their supporters had been barred from entering the polling stations.

Shortly after his re-election, Guelleh started to establish his son-in-law, *Djama Elmi Okieh* (often dubbed 'Djama Speed') as his designated successor. He had been married to Guelleh's youngest daughter Haibado since October 2014. Guelleh appointed him as minister of health and gave him permission to appoint ten out of 14 cabinet members. Simultaneously, *Guelleh's wife Kadra Mahamoud Haid* tried to bring her son from her first marriage with Abdallah Mohamed Kamil, an ethnic Afar, into the competition for the succession to the president. Her son *Naguib Abdallah Kamil* held the post of general secretary to the Prime Minister's Office ('Préfecture') under Prime Minister Abdoulkader Kamil Mohamed, an ethnic Afar. He enjoyed the *support* of *the Afar*, who made up about one-third of the population.

In spite of the strong political influence of the female members of Guelleh's family, *women* were politically underrepresented in public offices. Only seven of the 65 members of the National Assembly were female, and Hasna Barkat Daoud, who had served as the only female member of the cabinet, was not re-appointed to her former post as minister for the promotion of women, family welfare and social affairs after the April elections.

The *political climate* remained repressive and opposition politicians and human rights activists were harassed in the run-up to the elections. *Press freedom* remained strictly limited; the government controlled the state-owned radio and television and the newspaper 'La Nation'. No independent media were allowed to work in the country, but the opposition Internet radio station, 'La Voix de Djibouti', broadcast from France. Djibouti was ranked 172th out of 180 countries in Reporters Without Borders' press freedom report. On 8 April, members of a BBC team who had interviewed the foreign minister and a candidate of the political opposition were arrested by security officers, questioned for several hours and subsequently expelled from the country without explanation.

In mid-April, President *Guelleh sued Facebook* Ireland for publishing what he claimed were offensive posts related to his person. He demanded that the Facebook accounts in question should be closed and the identities, names, e-mail addresses, telephone numbers, and postal and IP addresses of those associated with the accounts should be revealed. The proceedings were struck out by the Irish High Court on 20 October.

Harassment of the political opposition and human rights activists continued. On 31 December 2015, human rights activist and co-founder of Djibouti's Human Rights League, Omar Ali Ewado, was arrested after publishing a list of the victims of the violent suppression of a public celebration by government forces in the same month. He was accused of spreading false news and in January was sentenced to three months' forced labour for "public defamation". He was released on 14 February, however, after the Court of Appeal had decided that the reasons for his imprisonment were not valid.

The *trial of Abdourahman Boreh*, an influential businessman and former director of Djibouti's Port Authority, at the London Court of Arbitration ended with his acquittal on 2 March. The Republic of Djibouti had brought charges of fraud, bribery and corruption against him. In June, the court refused permission to appeal against the judgement in favour of Boreh, which brought an end to a trial that had lasted for eight years and cost Djibouti's state treasury about $ 90 m.

Clashes between government troops and FRUD-Combattant (or 'FRUD armé'), the militant wing of the FRUD, continued in the Obock region, inhabited by the Afar minority. In late February, the construction of the Chinese naval base began near Obock, and in March, Guelleh decreed that a fish farm financed by a French investor should be built north of Obock. This was seen as land grab by the local population, and support for the armed wing of FRUD increased. In mid-March, FRUD armé fighters carried out several attacks in the area, and the Djiboutian army reportedly retreated with six wounded soldiers. About half of Djibouti's armed forces were members of the Yonis Moussa clan (within Issa). Civilian members of this clan had been attacked by security forces during a religious festival in a suburb of Djibouti-Ville in December 2015, probably in the context of the president's private vendetta against Abdourahman Boreh, a member of the Yonis Moussa. This might have reduced the troops' loyalty to the president and could have contributed to the low morale of the armed forces.

On 14 October, the Djibouti Court of Appeal ruled that Mohamed Ahmed 'Jebha', a FRUD leader who had been in jail since 2010, should be released because his detention was arbitrary and the court considered him a political prisoner. The authorities had accused him of being an agent paid by Eritrea. Prime Minister Abdoulkader Kamil Mohamed declared that he would refuse to abide by the court's ruling.

Foreign Affairs

Djibouti continued to maintain close relations with all neighbouring countries in the Horn of Africa except Eritrea and maintained its strategic position in the wider regional and international context. The small country played an active role in supporting *international anti-terrorism activities* in the region and hosted a growing variety of *international military facilities.*

There was no progress in the Qatar-mediated peace process between Djibouti and *Eritrea*, based on an agreement from 2010, and neither was progress achieved towards the final demarcation of the contested border, which was monitored by a small contingent of Qatari military observers. During a visit to Qatar on 29 February, President Guelleh stressed that a settlement of the conflict would depend on the release of the remaining Djiboutian prisoners of war (POWs) held by Eritrea. On 18 March, the Eritrean government handed over four Djiboutian POWs, who were flown home on a Qatari plane, accompanied by Qatar's Foreign Minister Mohamed bin Abdul Rahman Al Thani. Eritrea stressed that it had no other POWs in custody and claimed that out of seven POWs originally taken during the armed border clashes between the countries in August 2008, two had escaped, one had died and the remaining four had been released. Pro-government Eritrean websites claimed that the conflict had now been settled peacefully, which was one precondition for the lifting of UN sanctions imposed on Eritrea since 2009. However, Djibouti claimed that Eritrea had released only four out of 19 POWs, and Djibouti's permanent representative to the UN described Eritrea's behaviour as "characterized by denial, procrastination and obfuscation" in a letter to the UN secretary-general dated 31 March.

One reason for Djibouti's refusal to normalise relations with Eritrea, beyond the fact that the government suspected Asmara of supporting the FRUD armé forces that operated close to the Eritrean border, was its strong relationship with Eritrea's arch-foe *Ethiopia*. Djibouti and Ethiopia remained economically interdependent and maintained close and cordial relations, while the process of *economic integration* continued. On 5 October, the Chinese-constructed and financed new *Ethiopian-Djiboutian Railway* line was officially inaugurated. It connected the port of Djibouti with Addis Ababa and was intended to facilitate land transport significantly. The fourteenth high-level Joint Commission meeting with the participation of Djibouti's and Ethiopia's foreign ministers, Mohamoud Ali Yusuf and Tedros

Adhanom, took place on 18–21 July. Both government representatives stressed their countries' close mutual ties. In May, Djibouti and Ethiopia signed a *security agreement* that allowed Ethiopian troops to enter Djiboutian territory without prior consent, to use Djibouti's military facilities and to intervene in internal conflicts. This included the presence of Ethiopian troops around Tadjoura, aimed at containing the uprisings in the Afar-inhabited regions.

Djibouti's government continued to support the AU peacekeeping mission *AMISOM* in *Somalia.* On 28 February, Djibouti hosted the summit of countries contributing troops and police to AMISOM. On 25 October, four peacekeepers from Djibouti were killed in a car bomb attack carried out by *al-Shabaab* militia near Beletweyne. On 20 March, Djibouti officially opened a *diplomatic office* in *Somaliland* and became one of three countries, along with Ethiopia and Turkey, that indirectly recognised Somaliland as an independent territory.

Due to its important geo-strategic location, Djibouti continued to host a variety of international *military bases* that served the purposes of surveilling international maritime routes, controlling piracy and fighting militant Islamist groups. The *USA* maintained a contingent of 4,000 troops and civilian personnel at Camp Lemmonier, which also served as one of the world's largest *drone bases* for targeted assassination attacks on radical Islamists and hosted a counter-terrorism unit. On 21 January, *China* and Djibouti signed an agreement that paved the way for China's first "logistics and fast evacuation base", or in other words the first Chinese naval base on African soil, for an initial ten-years lease period. Construction began immediately and, in early February, a first contingent of 300 Chinese troops arrived at the location near Obock. China planned to station up to 10,000 troops upon completion of construction.

France also maintained a strong military presence in its former colony and had 1,450 troops stationed in Djibouti. The country also hosted a small Japanese military camp with 180 troops, and *Japan* negotiated with the government of Djibouti to lease additional territory to enlarge its base to counter China's presence on the ground. The EU's Djibouti-based anti-piracy operation, Atalanta, also continued, and accordingly Djibouti further developed into an *internationalised military zone.*

In addition, *Saudi Arabia* announced plans to establish its own military base on Djiboutian territory and, in mid-January, Djibouti's foreign minister told the 'Financial Times' that Saudi Arabia and his government were working on a common security agreement. In an attempt to further improve relations with Saudi Arabia, President Guelleh severed diplomatic relations with *Iran* in January and re-established diplomatic ties with the *UAE* in the same month, following Saudi mediation. Guelleh had severed diplomatic ties with the UAE in May 2015 in connection with his cancellation of the port management contract with Dubai-based DP World due to his personal feud with former port manager Boreh. Saudi Arabia and the UAE were interested in strategic relations with Djibouti to improve their standing in their struggle against the Houthi rebels in Yemen.

Socioeconomic Developments

The government continued its strategy of transforming Djibouti into a modern city state and international service centre with the help of *substantial inflows of FDI* for major infrastructural projects. This process was accelerated by the agreement with *China* on its *naval military base* near Obock, since China was ready to engage massively in Djibouti's infrastructural development. One of the major projects envisaged was a *gas pipeline* connecting Ethiopia and Djibouti, worth about $ 4 bn and financed by the Chinese POLY GCL Petroleum Group Holdings. The 700-km pipeline was expected to be finished by 2019 and was to link gas extraction fields in Ethiopia with a liquefaction plant to be constructed in Damerjog in Djibouti and a new export port terminal.

Similar plans to construct a *fuel pipeline* from Djibouti to Awash in Ethiopia to transport fuels from the port of Djibouti to inland Ethiopia also made progress and, in March, South Africa-based infrastructure development group Black Rhino presented a feasibility study. However, the construction did not begin due to funding restraints.

Progress was made towards the government's aim of expanding the *renewable energy* sector and exploiting the country's high potential for geothermal energy. In early October, the first *geothermal drill* was launched at Gaale-le-koma near Lake Assal. However, this project led to rising tensions between ethnic Afar and Issa, because Guelleh's favourite Djama Elmi Okieh had declared the area, which had previously been administered by Afar-dominated Tajoura, as a part of the Issa-dominated Arta district. In January, the Swiss renewable energy firm Green Enesys started the construction of a 30 MW *photovoltaic project* worth $ 390 m in the Grand Bara desert. There were also plans to construct a 60 MW *wind farm*, to be financed by Qatar. However, it was doubtful that Djibouti could achieve its aim to become energy self-sufficient by 2020 due to rapidly rising levels of energy consumption and the government's lack of a comprehensive electrification strategy, combined with the monopoly of the state-owned 'Electricité de Djibouti' (EDD) on power generation and limited private investment opportunities.

Despite the government's formal commitment to its development agenda, *'Djibouti Vision 2035'*, Djibouti's rapid economic growth was mainly related to infrastructure development based on currency influx through the international military bases and FDI. It lacked a strategy to reduce endemic *high levels of poverty* and *unemployment* and low levels of education among the majority of the population.

At the same time, the administration was characterised by a nepotistic network dominated by the president's family clan, along with a lack of transparency and high levels of *corruption*. TI's corruption report ranked the country 99th out of 176 countries.

Macroeconomic performance was reasonable, with an IMF-estimated GDP growth rate of 7% over the coming years. Consumer price *inflation* stood at 3% during the year. The *fiscal deficit* stood at 16% of GDP, and, contrary to previous estimates, it was projected to fall to 6.1% in 2018 due to lower public spending on infrastructure projects and increased income from re-export revenues. *Foreign exchange reserves* stood at $ 349 m. The Djibouti franc (Dfr) remained pegged to the US dollar at a rate of Dfr 177 : $ 1 under a currency board arrangement. The *structural trade deficit* narrowed slightly, and according to Economic Intelligence Unit's 2016 estimates, exports of goods and services amounted to $ 140 m compared with imports worth $ 991 m.

The government's efforts to mobilise revenues continued to be hampered by extensive tax exemptions for FDI projects, and a reform of the tax system as recommended by the IMF had yet to make progress. The general *business environment* remained heavily restricted, and Djibouti was ranked 171st (out of 190 listed countries) in the World Bank's 'Doing Business 2016' assessment.

The *IMF* did not enter into a new ECF agreement with Djibouti and recommended in its July country report that the financial infrastructure should be further developed and access to small credits should be eased. The *unemployment* rate was estimated at 48% and 22% of the population continued to be living in *extreme poverty*. Humanitarian aid was needed by 282,000 people, including the local poor and more than 22,000 refugees, as well as regional migrants trying to reach the Arabian Peninsula through Djibouti. The WFP supported about 67,000 people with food aid and food for work programmes. The Global Hunger Index ranked the country 105th out of 118, and Djibouti's 2015 HDI ranking was 168th out of 188 countries.

The national airline *Air Djibouti*, disbanded seven years before due to technical problems, was relaunched and offered flights to regional destinies such as Ethiopia, Saudi Arabia and Somalia.

Eritrea

Nicole Hirt

Twenty-five years after its de facto independence from Ethiopia, Eritrea celebrated its silver-jubilee but still lacked an implemented constitution. The autocratic political system under the unelected President Isaias Afewerki prevailed, and the militarised command economy persisted. Time-unlimited national service for all Eritreans of working age remained in place and the resulting mass exodus continued. The UN Commission of Inquiry on Human Rights in Eritrea confirmed that it had good reason to believe that crimes against humanity had been committed by the government. In July, the UN Human Rights Council welcomed the Commission's findings and called on UN bodies and the AU to bring to account those who had perpetrated human rights violations. The diaspora remained politically split and respective groups organised pro-and anti-government demonstrations. Eritrea's engagement in the Saudi-led anti-Houthi campaign in Yemen continued, and the UAE built a military base at the port of Assab. The EU made little progress towards the implementation of development projects under the 11th EDF, and UNICEF stated that almost half of the nation was suffering from malnutrition.

 | DOI 10.1163/9789004355910_034

Domestic Politics

A quarter of a century after Eritrea's de facto independence from Ethiopia, the political system remained autocratic and President Isaias Afewerki was unchallenged in his position as the unelected ruler of the country. No progress was made on the process of drafting a new constitution, which had been announced by the president two years earlier. On 22 January, Isaias stated in an interview with local media that he was no longer thinking about a new constitution, but rather about a regulation concerning the "structure of the government".

On 24 May, the *Silver Jubilee Independence Day* was celebrated with carnivals and exhibitions, recalling the country's 30-year independence struggle. In his speech on the occasion, the president stressed that, in the face of ongoing "hostility and other anti-Eritrean agendas", resilience, patriotism, hard work and sacrifice were needed to counter the "enemy challenge", referring to the unsolved border conflict with Ethiopia and the UN sanctions imposed on the country.

The *cabinet was not reshuffled*, and the post of minister of defence remained vacant. General Sebhat Ephrem kept his post as minister of energy and mines, but at the same time *Hagos Ghebrehiwet 'Kisha'*, the head of economic affairs of the ruling People's Front for Democracy and Justice (PFDJ), was referred to as 'head of Eritrean economic affairs and of the National Mining Corporation' by government media. This was a clear indication of the extent of the power of the position he had held since independence, overseeing the revenues not only of the ruling party's but also of the whole country. The cabinet met only once, on 11–12 August, and discussed means to control *corruption*, unbalanced monetary circulation and illegal transactions, which were considered root causes of high consumer goods prices. On 5 October, Eritrea's permanent representative at the UN, *Girma Asmerom*, one of the country's most senior diplomats, died at the age of 66. He had served as ambassador to South Africa, the EU and the AU before taking up his post in New York in 2013.

It seemed that the power balance among the *military leadership* remained unchanged, with Major General Phillipos Weldeyohannes retaining his supremacy over other high-ranking officers. Elderly citizens continued to be forced to carry arms and patrol their neighbourhoods as militias and to participate in regular military training sessions, despite growing passive resistance against these programmes, which often took place during harvest times.

In July, the Afar People's Party, a group of about 400 fighters headed by Alo Aydahis that had been part of the Asmara-based umbrella of Ethiopian opposition groups called 'Ethiopian National Salvation', defected and returned to their homeland. Following the defection of the leadership of the Tigray People's Democratic Movement in 2015 and with the absence of Ginbot 7's leader Dr Berhanu Nega from Asmara, Eritrea's influence on *armed Ethiopian anti-government groups* seemed to have diminished.

The *mass exodus* induced by the time-unlimited national service continued unabated. Up to November, UNHCR Ethiopia counted more than 162,000 Eritrean *refugees*, an increase of more than 30,000 compared with 2015, and stated that more than 81,000 Eritreans had disappeared from the camps and were believed to have either settled in Ethiopian cities or continued on to other destinations. Similar numbers of Eritrean refugees were hosted by Sudan, but exact numbers of new arrivals were not available. During May, the Sudanese authorities deported at least 442 refugees back to Eritrea and, on 6 May, 377 people were arrested near Dongola while trying to reach the border with Libya. Among them were 313 Eritreans, including 13 children. They were accused of illegal entry and deported on 22 May without being granted access to UNHCR, which had reported the deportation of 129 Eritreans a few days earlier. On 23 May, about 900 Eritreans staying in Khartoum were rounded up and arrested. These actions may have been intended to demonstrate Sudan's willingness to comply with European demands to curb the flow of refugees towards Europe in the framework of the multilateral *Khartoum Process*. Nevertheless, *human smuggling and trafficking* continued with the involvement of transnational criminal networks.

The *human rights* situation remained appalling, and civil liberties were non-existent. Reporters Without Borders gave Eritrea the lowest ranking in their Press Freedom Index for the eighth consecutive year, stating that at least 15 journalists remained behind bars. There was no news regarding the fate of the surviving *members of the G15*, a group of prominent PFDJ members who had questioned Isaias's wide-ranging powers and the lack of democracy before being imprisoned in September 2001. None of them had been brought before a court of law or allowed access to lawyers or contact with family members. It was unclear how many of the group had survived the harsh conditions of detention.

Religious freedom was not granted and Jehovah's Witnesses and Pentecostal churches remained prohibited, while the state's involvement in the religious affairs of the permitted religious communities – Orthodox, Catholic and Lutheran Christianity and Sunni Islam – continued. On 6 August, eight months after the death of government-imposed Orthodox Patriarch Abune Dioskoros, the Eritrean Holy Synod published a statement, announcing that Abune Antonios, who had been dismissed as patriarch of the Orthodox Christian community in 2007, had apologised for his earlier mistakes and resumed his duties. However, no third party had been witness to this process, and branches of the Eritrean Orthodox Church in exile as well as human rights groups expressed fear that the elderly patriarch had signed the statement under severe pressure by the government authorities.

Eritrea's *judicial system* remained in a poor state and suffered from constant government interference, lack of qualified legal practitioners and lawyers and a complete lack of checks and balances. It was unclear whether and to what extent the new *civil and penal procedure codes* introduced in 2015 were being implemented, but informal litigation based on customary procedures continued to be the basis of civil jurisdiction and conflict resolution. In March, the US Library of Congress published the new law texts online and noted that there was evidence that the transitional laws that had been put in place after independence (mostly decrees issued by the president in the absence of a functioning legislative body) were still being applied, and that the government had failed to announce a date for the implementation of the new laws. In practice, imprisonment for political reasons as well as arrests for alleged criminal offences continued to take place without any formal legal process.

Corruption remained endemic, and high-ranking PFDJ cadres and military personnel accepted bribes from conscripts for holiday leave permits or national service exemptions and were involved in *smuggling goods* and *trafficking conscripts* over the borders. TI's Corruption Perception Index ranked Eritrea as highly corrupt (164th out of 176 countries). The clandestine resistance movement 'Arbi Harnet' (Freedom Friday) reported that on 22 October a pickup truck carrying seven young adults and three children was ambushed for unknown reasons near Haykota at the Sudanese border on the orders of a senior divisional commander. Shoot-to-kill orders against individuals who tried to cross the border illegally had been in place for more than a decade, but had not been carried out on a regular base in recent years due to the growing involvement of military officers in the trafficking of national service recruits.

In a letter dated 9 May, the *Commission of Inquiry on Human Rights in Eritrea* (COIE), established by the UN Human Rights Council (UNHRC), reiterated that no progress had been made regarding the human rights situation and stated that it had good reason to believe that "*crimes against humanity*, namely, enslavement, imprisonment, enforced disappearance, torture, other inhumane acts, persecution, rape and murder, have been committed in Eritrea since 1991" by officials at the highest levels of the state and the PFDJ, as well as by military commanders. The COIE criticised the continuation of *time-unlimited national service*, which amounted to systematic forced labour under highly abusive conditions. The COIE referred to Minister of Information Yemane Ghebremeskel, who had revoked promises made by the PFDJ's Head of Political Affairs Yemane Gebreab during speeches to international audiences in 2015 that the duration of the service would be reduced to its original period of 18 months. Ghebremeskel stated in February that national service was a necessary measure of self-defence and should continue to be prolonged. On 9 May, a member of a Swiss-German fact-finding mission and representative of the Swiss Secretariat for Migration stated that "Eritrea officially went back on its promise of shortening the required national military service".

On 14 June, Foreign Minister Osman Saleh responded to the report during the 32nd session of the UNHRC and accused the COIE of making extreme and unfounded charges with no solid or legal evidence, claiming the report was politically motivated. However, on 1 July the *UNHRC adopted a resolution* that welcomed the COIE report and condemned in strongest terms the gross human rights violations committed by the government of Eritrea and expressed deep concern about the lack of civil liberties and the detention of journalists, human rights defenders, political actors, religious leaders and practitioners. It called on UN bodies including the UNSC, and also on the AU, to take appropriate action to bring to account perpetrators of human rights violations, including possible crimes against humanity.

The *Eritrean diaspora* remained split between supporters and opponents of the government. Prior to the launch of the COIE report, the government carried out a campaign to collect *counterstatements* by some 45,000 diaspora Eritreans, who signed a pre-written document rejecting the COIE findings. Ironically, the government, which had not granted the COIE access to Eritrea and had protested that the report was based on the testimonies of Eritreans living outside the country, mobilised the diaspora rather than Eritrean residents to participate in the campaign.

On 21 June, government supporters from various European countries gathered in Geneva to hold a rally to denounce the findings of the COIE, while, on 23 June, government opponents from across Europe demonstrated in favour of the COIE's work.

Foreign Affairs

On 10 November, the UNSC voted, with ten votes in favour and five abstentions, to extend for a further year the *targeted sanctions* imposed on Eritrea that had been in place since December 2009 (resolution 1907/2009) and December 2011 (resolution 2023/2011). The UNSC urged the government of Eritrea to provide information concerning the fate of a number of missing Djiboutian prisoners of war who had been held by the Eritrean authorities since 2008. Representatives of the countries that abstained stressed the lack of evidence for Eritrean support for the al-Shabaab militias in Somalia and suggested preparing a roadmap for gradually lifting the sanctions.

Eritrea continued its strategic *military partnership* with *Saudi Arabia* and the *UAE* in the coalition against the Houthi rebels in Yemen. In December, US-based global intelligence company Stratfor reported massive construction activities at the port of Assab, supported by satellite images of the construction site that showed aircraft shelters, a naval dock and housing facilities for military personnel. Prior to the 1998–2000 border war, the port had served as a sea outlet for landlocked Ethiopia but had later fallen into disuse. Eritrea's engagement with the anti-Houthi coalition might be an attempt to secure much-needed resources such as fuel and hard currency. On 15 March, Isaias visited *Qatar* and was received by the Emir Sheikh Tamim bin Hamad Al Thani to discuss regional and international issues. On 11 October, Isaias travelled to Abu Dhabi and met the UAE's Crown Prince Sheikh Mohamed bin Zayed al-Nahyan, the deputy commander of the UAE armed forces.

On 29 November, Isaias was received by *Egypt*'s President Abdel Fattah al-Sisi in Cairo, allegedly to discuss projects related to fishing and agriculture. However, several analysts interpreted the invitation as a signal to Ethiopia, which had tense relations with Cairo due to the construction of the Grand Ethiopian Renaissance Dam on the Blue Nile.

The stalemate between Eritrea and *Ethiopia* continued, and on 12 June there were serious *military clashes* at the border near the town of Tsorona, probably causing *hundreds of casualties*. Each side accused the other of having initiated the skirmishes. Ethiopia's Information Minister Getachew Reda claimed that Eritrea had started the fighting to divert public attention from the COIE's accusations that the government had committed crimes against humanity, while Eritrea's ambassador to Kenya, Beyene Russom, stated that Ethiopia had instigated the violence to exploit the negative publicity caused by the "false" COIE report. The Eritrean opposition website awate.com suggested what might be a more probable explanation, namely that deserting Eritrean army recruits had crossed the border and been followed by Eritrean troops. They were reportedly first repulsed by members of armed Eritrean opposition groups hosted by Ethiopia and later by soldiers of the Ethiopian National Defence Force. The US, the AU and the UN expressed deep concern and called on both parties to use utmost restraint and to refrain from any activities that might aggravate the situation. The outbreak of clashes called to mind the *international community's failure* to pressure both parties to find a lasting solution to their ongoing political and diplomatic crisis and to pressure Ethiopia to abide by the 2002 ruling of the *Eritrea Ethiopia Boundary Commission*, which had awarded the contested border town of Badme and its surroundings to Eritrea.

Relations between Eritrea and *Sudan* remained close and, on 24 February, Foreign Minister Osman Saleh and his permanent escort on foreign missions, presidential adviser Yemane Gebreab, visited Sudan on behalf of Isaias, delivering his message to President Omar al-Bashir.

No high-level meetings took place between Eritrea and *Russia*, but a number of Eritrean students took part in a Russian scholarship programme. *Israel* continued to coerce Eritreans into departing 'voluntarily' to either *Rwanda* or *Uganda* with $ 3,500 and a laissez-passer in their hands, or alternatively face prolonged detention in prison-like conditions at the Holot facility. According to human rights organisations, more than 3,000 Eritrean and Sudanese refugees had left Israel in these circumstances by 2015 and were stranded in Uganda without refugee status.

The number of *Eritrean refugees reaching Europe* via the Mediterranean fell to 20,000 from over 30,000 in 2015, possibly due to the increased danger of arrest and deportation by Sudan and to a lesser extent by Egypt, which caused a shift from Sudan to Ethiopia as the first country of exile, as the latter provided better physical security for the Eritrean refugee population.

European governments continued to court the Eritrean regime in an attempt to limit the refugee influx. On 29 November, the *European Parliament* hosted a conference under the heading 'Eritrea – opportunity for development', which was attended by Eritrea's Minister of Information Yemane Ghebremeskel and Christine Umotoni, UNDP's resident representative in Asmara and a notorious apologist for the Eritrean regime, as well as by ambassadors and representatives of Germany, Sweden, Ireland and the UK. Eritrean and European *human rights activists* had protested against the conference, given the government's role as possible perpetrator of crimes against humanity. The meeting also stood in stark contrast to a declaration by the European Parliament on 8 March, in which it expressed its concern about the deplorable human rights situation and demanded an end to time-unlimited national service. On 8 September, presidential adviser Yemane Gebreab was invited to a panel discussion by *Germany*'s 'Afrika Stiftung' (Africa Foundation). United4Eritrea, a German-based anti-government civil society organisation, was critical that neither members of the political opposition nor human rights activists had been invited to the event. On 23 August, Foreign Minister Osman Saleh visited the *Netherlands* and discussed bilateral relations with his Dutch counterpart Bert Koenders.

Relations between the *USA* and Eritrea remained poor, and no ambassadors were exchanged. Relations with *China* were positive, and a high-level Eritrean government delegation led by the PFDJ's head of financial affairs Hagos Ghebrehiwet 'Kisha' attended the China-Africa Cooperation Forum on 26–30 July in Beijing, according to the Ministry of Information's website shabait.com.

Socioeconomic Developments

Eritrea's command economy remained under the firm grip of the ruling PFDJ and the military leadership, and private small business activities were severely restricted. Following the *currency reform* of 2015, which had forced all Eritreans to exchange the nakfa (ERN) notes in their possession for new ones and to deposit all cash exceeding ERN 20,000 in a bank account, the *withdrawal of cash* was *heavily restricted*. The undeclared *aims of the reform* had been to contain inflation, corruption and the hoarding of bank notes in the absence of investment opportunities, as well as the introduction of cheques as the medium of economic transactions. The permitted limit for cash withdrawals was ERN 5,000 per family per month. If more money was needed, as in the case of weddings, people had to apply to the local administrations (*memhedar*) for permission and were obliged to deliver receipts for their expenses to the authorities. Larger expenses such as for the purchase of cows and sheep were meant to be handled by cheque, but in spite of the government's aim to bring about a change from a cash-based to a cheque-based system, cheques were in short supply. The official exchange rate remained fixed at ERN 1: $ 1, and the diaspora continued to use the *Hawala system* to remit money to their relatives at home. Accordingly, black market rates reportedly dropped from about ERN 44: $ 1 prior to the reform to around ERN 25 : $ 1, still significantly different from the overvalued official exchange rate.

The usual *shortages* of basic consumer goods and fuel continued, as did regular electricity blackouts throughout the country, including in the capital Asmara. This was due to the poor state of Eritrea's only electrical power plant in Hirghigo, near Massawa, after years of inadequate maintenance. Despite a drought that had affected the entire Horn of Africa region, President Isaias denied any possible *food shortages*. In early February, he told state media that the current harvest shortfall would not lead to a lack of supply because the government had accumulated strategic food reserves. In stark contrast, a UNICEF report spoke of an "ongoing nutrition and food insecurity crisis" that had been exacerbated by poor rains throughout 2015. The report indicated a deterioration of the nutrition situation in four of the country's six regions, namely Anseba, Gash-Barka, Maekel/Central Region and Southern Red Sea Region, where malnutrition rates had risen over the past three years. The report indicated that 1.5 m individuals, among them 725,000 children, were affected by severe malnutrition and needed food aid. Given that the Eritrean National Statistics Office had estimated Eritrea's resident *population* at 3.5 m in 2014, this meant that close to half of the population was severely malnourished. The actual number of Eritreans living inside the country was unclear because no population census had ever been carried out, either before or after independence. The World Bank estimated Eritrea's population at about 5 m.

The Warsay-Yikealo Development Campaign, introduced in 2002 as an 'open-ended' *national service programme* remained in place, and accordingly Eritreans aged between 18 and 50–60 years were forced to perform *systematic forced labour* for companies owned by the ruling PFDJ, on cash-crop farms run by the military or in the public administration. Most teachers and health workers were poorly paid conscripts, which led to deteriorating standards due to a lack of motivation and high fluctuation rates, because many of the affected individuals opted to flee the country rather than serving as conscripts for life. In August and September, a *cholera epidemic* in the Gash-Barka region caused numerous deaths, but was concealed by the government until reports by 'Arbi Harnet' activists about the outbreak of the disease were widely shared on social media by diaspora groups.

On 28 January, Eritrea's Minister for National Development Giorgis Teklemichael and the head of an EU delegation to Eritrea, Christian Manahl, signed a *National Indicative Program* (NIP) under the 11th EDF. The *EU* pledged € 200 m over the next five years for the country's *renewable energy sector* and for *governance*. While it seemed reasonable to invest in renewable energy infrastructure in order to overcome the chronic electricity shortages, the EU's aims to improve public financial management, modernise the financial sector, enhance economic planning and put Eritrea on a sound statistical basis, as well as to implement the recommendations of the UN-led Universal Periodic Review on human rights, seemed rather illusive, given that Eritrea's finances had been deliberately concealed since independence and were secretively managed by the PFDJ's head of financial affairs. In addition, Eritrea had an explicit policy of withholding statistical data. It also remained unclear how the EU intended to improve the human rights situation on the ground. The only project that had been announced by the EU Commission under the NIP by the end of the year was the planned installation of a photovoltaic mini-grid solar system costing € 8 m in the Southern Region.

Statistical data were unreliable and erratic. School enrolment rates were estimated at 42% at primary level, while the secondary school enrolment rate was 22% and the tertiary rate just 2%. The literacy rate for 15–24-year-olds was indicated – surprisingly – as being around 90%. The World Bank did not indicate an *inflation* rate due to a lack of data, while the Economic Intelligence Unit estimated inflation at 11.8%. *Economic growth* depended heavily on the copper and zinc exports of the Bisha mine and was estimated at around 4%. The mine, a joint venture between the Canadian Nevsun company and the Eritrean National Mining Company, remained the only operational extraction site in the country. The current account balance was estimated at -4.2% of GDP.

On 4 December, *Qatar Airlines* suspended flights to Asmara after two years. Despite various attempts, Eritrea had failed over the years to establish a national airline, allegedly due to government interference and economic mismanagement. The only international airlines flying to Eritrea were Turkish Airlines and Egypt Air.

Ethiopia

Jon Abbink

All the year's events were overshadowed by persistent demonstrations and protests by, mainly rural, people against political repression and perceived inequalities in land allocation and against dispossession. The lives of hundreds of people were lost in violent repression, and there were also tens of thousands of arrests. Bloodshed and anger dominated the country for months, and demonstrations and pockets of armed resistance persisted even after the declaration of a 'state of emergency' in October and the instalment of a new ruling body, the 'Command Post', which took extrajudicial authority to "restore public order" and suppress activism. The overall situation was one of political stalemate, disarray and distrust.

In international affairs, Ethiopia kept its prominent position in the Horn region, via IGAD, in the AU and as a participant in AMISOM in Somalia. It maintained its links with major donor/investor countries and concluded a new 'cooperation deal' with the EU.

Economic growth – GDP and infrastructure investments – continued, although at a slower pace. Industrial projects slowly expanded, accompanied by FDI. Population growth remained high, as did out-migration, running at close to 100,000. Food

 | DOI 10.1163/9789004355910_035

insecurity due to both natural and political-economic causes remained a serious problem and endangered the lives and livelihoods of an estimated 5–6 m people.

Drought again struck in some areas, necessitating substantial food aid. The militant protests and the damage they caused to domestic- and foreign-owned companies, notably large-scale agrarian businesses, shook investor confidence and led to complaints and criticism, albeit short-lived, from donor countries. Investors' hesitation did not prevent most of them from continuing their economic planning and partnership with government agencies. The political system, however, faced unresolved problems in accommodating people's grievances and addressing issues of lack of accountability and socio-political inequality.

Domestic Affairs

Ethiopia's political system continued to be marked by autocratic rule, with a one-party government and parliament since the last elections in 2015. The Ethiopian Peoples Revolutionary Democratic Front (EPRDF) also retained control of all public offices and the army. No opposition representatives led any public body or administration. The political process and national policies remained top-down dirigiste and strongly controlled. Domestic tensions over lack of accountability, few media freedoms, politico-economic inequality, corruption and the absence of political dialogue perpetuated discontent below the surface. In rural areas, tensions were fuelled by large-scale land deals and land alienation, which victimised locals by side-lining small-holders and agro-pastoralists. New enterprises only absorbed a fraction of these people.

The year saw dramatic civil unrest and repression, with at least 800 (and according to some opposition circles, several thousand) public protesters killed, and more injured. Tens of thousands were arrested, often arbitrarily. Such numbers had never been seen before, and the unrest – due to people clamouring for land rights, justice and government accountability – persisted throughout the year, with many attacks on property. Later in the year, some protesters turned to sporadic armed resistance, but had little organisation and no opportunity to effect systemic changes. The protests were concentrated in the Oromiya and Amhara regions, but there was also unrest in Benishangul-Gumuz, Afar and the Southern regional state, where 'ethnic clashes' and repression occurred. The Somali Region saw a low-key rebellion continue, but without major armed clashes. Core issues underlying the year-long protests were: lack of political freedoms, loss of (access to) land, poor compensation for land loss, and identity issues, which played out against perceptions of a government often seen as arrogant, intimidating and routinely overreaching its powers.

The protests in Oromiya, the largest region, were a continuation of the 2015 rebellion against the (now suspended) Addis Ababa Masterplan, which had aimed to expand the metropolis into Oromiya farmlands. During the year, protests spread to other towns, including Woliso, Chiti, Wonch'i, Ambo, Ajo, Hagere Mariam and Shashemene. Government vehicles were stoned and destroyed on the roads and government offices and enterprises were looted or torched.

A major drama occurred on 2 October in the town of Bishoftu (Debre Zeit) in Oromiya on *Irreecha* day, an annual Oromo cultural festival to mark spring, instituted in the 1990s. An estimated 80–90 people died and hundreds were injured. The proceedings had turned political, and security forces fired teargas and live ammunition into the crowd. Panic followed, and in the stampede many died, being trampled to death or falling into ditches. Messages of condolence were issued by Amhara and other protest leaders, and popular anger, notably in the Oromo areas, rose rapidly. This incident and the shockwaves it sent out were the probable trigger for the government's declaration on 9 October of a *state of emergency* (SoE) across the entire country.

The protests in Amhara Region and elsewhere were caused by feelings of political marginalisation, economic inequality and, more particularly, identity issues, including, for example, the status of the Wolqait region, historically part of Gondar (Amhara). July saw the arrest of Colonel Demeqe Zewdu, a retired military officer and a key member of the Wolqait Identity Committee, which was agitating for the return of this area to the Amhara Region from Tigray (to which it had been annexed in the 1990s). During the arrest, a fight ensued between his armed escort and the police/security forces, and several people were killed. Unrest spread against a background of already long-standing issues of land loss, perceived marginalisation and lack of freedoms. Other Wolqait Identity Committee members and leading young demonstrators, including Ms Nigist Yirga, were later abducted.

In the weekend of 6–7 August, protests took place in several locations in Amhara, and some 100 demonstrators were shot and killed. In the same month, protests also flared up in Oromiya and the South (Shashemene town). Dozens of farms and businesses were attacked and damaged, among them the Esmeralda flower farm near Bahir Dar, the FV SeleQt vegetable farm, the Africa Juice company and the Turkish textile firm Saygin Dima. In addition, more than 60 trucks and cars seen as belonging to the government or to certain state-linked companies were torched and destroyed. The protests hit not only foreign farms perceived to have neglected the rights of (displaced) locals, but also state/party enterprises. On 4 October, an animal farm in Wonji owned by the tycoon Mohammed Al-Amoudi, who was close to the regime, was torched and, the next day, a gas depot in Dire Dawa was damaged. In early December, a 60 ha state sugar plantation constructed by TPLF's metals and engineering company MeTEC in Jawi, Gojjam, was partly burned down (for the second time).

Security units used lethal force to subdue the protests. They usually gave protesters one warning to disperse or turn back and opened fire on the crowds if they did not obey, which led to high numbers of deaths. The units (often special federal forces, not the regional police) also avoided communication with protesters.

The SoE affected not only the regions in turmoil but all other areas too, both rural and urban, although some parts, such as the Southern capital of Hawassa, had not seen any protests at all. The new authority structure under the SoE was the *'Command Post'*, a unit consisting of the prime minister, chief-of-staff, minister of defence, a Tigray People's Liberation Front (TPLF) vice prime minister and one senior TPLF Central Committee ('Politbureau') member. This junta-like committee, as some called it, had supreme authority and behaved like a new 'sovereign'. It could act at will to restore order and suppress unwanted protests, some of which had taken on a violent character. Under the Ethiopian constitution – a product of the ruling party in 1994 – an SoE could be declared under conditions of: external invasion, a natural disaster, an epidemic, or "a breakdown of law and order which endangers the Constitutional order and which cannot be controlled by the regular law enforcement agencies and personnel" (Art. 93). Observers both within and outside Ethiopia doubted the validity of declaring a (nationwide) SoE, because the protests, in so far as they damaged property and constituted public protests against failing governance, could also have been tackled through law enforcement under the Criminal Code. But the government identified the unrest as a *systemic threat*: people wanted to change the political system. In general, the Ethiopian people responded with scepticism, defiance and a sense of humour to the impositions of a regime of exhaustive restrictions, with online parodies on the SoE proclamation appearing.

The emergency regulations led to an increased military presence, mass arrests and even house-to-house search campaigns in all areas of unrest, although protesters developed alternative methods of resistance, such as the 'dead city' campaigns – wholesale strikes that paralysed public life. Even some religious festivals were boycotted. This led the security forces again to try to force people to open their businesses and offices.

Despite the SoE, protests went on in subdued forms in many areas. Some armed resistance took place in isolated parts and border areas of the north and west. The low-key insurgency of Ogaden rebels in Somali Region 5 also continued.

Foreign NGOs and aid workers complained of the restricting impact that the SoE had on their work; they felt they could not report on the real needs of the people (in the face of impending drought) or had to slow down their activities.

As part of its campaign, the government, using the sole Internet and telecoms provider Ethio-Telecom, repeatedly *shut down the Internet and social media* (Facebook, Twitter, WhatsApp, Instagram, etc.). On 7 June, the government had rushed through parliament a 'computer crime law' with very restrictive clauses that provided for even more government control over the Internet, including Facebook posts. Internet shut-downs caused significant damage and delay to the business sector because essential communication was hampered. This became worse under the SoE.

In general, *media freedoms and civil society organisations suffered.* On 27 May, the journalist Muluken Tesfaw (of the weekly *'Ethio-Mihdar'*) was arrested when interviewing people evicted in connection with the Blue Nile dam construction. On 1 October, a critical blogger, Seyoum Teshome, was arrested and other journalists remained in jail. Prime Minister Hailemariam said on 6 December in an interview with the BBC: "We are ready to be criticized by any journalists because we know we are not perfect", but the practice did not match the rhetoric.

At the end of the year, government figures stated that *some 2,400 people were to appear in court, and some 9,800 of those arrested had been released.* The opposition gave much higher numbers of arrests. The prisoners held in camps were subjected to a "re-education, training and disciplining" campaign. They were forced to 'repent' and ask for pardon before being released. Descriptions of life in the camps by former inmates spoke of intimidation, humiliation and abuse. By imposing this form of punishment, the government in effect denied that those arrested had any legitimate grievances and implied that they were just 'criminals'. It was clear that correct mechanisms for accountability and dealing with criticism and grievances were not in place. Opposition parties had no demonstrable connection to the protests. One opposition leader said: "We were unprepared for this and we could not influence events." Most protests were spontaneous and sudden, although they had become contagious, spreading via word of mouth and social media. As they went on, a degree of coordination and local organisation emerged, but trans-regional or 'Oromo-Amhara' alliances did not materialise, due to distance, somewhat different agendas, organisational problems and preventive action by the authorities. In some areas, local authorities and militia joined the protesters and some local self-government units were set up.

Business life suffered many setbacks as a result of the unrest. The situation also led to absurd practices, such as flower producers in the Sebeta, Tulu Bolo and Adama areas transporting their produce in *armed convoys* to the export points. In many areas, agrarian enterprises and state plantations had been provided with armed guards before.

The unrest also caused power vacuums in which *'ethnic' animosities* were whipped up and played out: some minorities were routed, as in Dilla town, for example, where Gurage and northern traders and shopkeepers were attacked by local Gedeo people, and in Gondar, where 'Tigrayan' businesses – or at least TPLF-linked interests – were targeted. In ugly violence on 6–7 October, dozens of people, mostly of Amhara descent, were killed in the town of Arsi Neghele (Oromiya). Superficial Western journalism sometimes appeared to 'ethnicize' the protests, framing them in terms of ethnic oppositions, but this was a misjudgement of the fundamental *social and economic contradictions* of Ethiopia's developmental model, which had led to the marginalisation of people.

On 13 September, more than a dozen people were killed by security forces in Konso, where local people had petitioned and demonstrated for separate district status. Some 4,000 people also fled the area. The Omo Valley saw continued tension due government investment projects such as sugar plantations displacing and cowing local people. There also was continued resistance to (forced) villagisation. In March, shocking photographs of slave-like abuse of local people in the South appeared in social media and on some Ethio-diaspora websites. There were also *clashes between 'rival' ethnic groups*, such as in February in Gambela Region, a very volatile region due to the displacement of many Anywa to make way for commercial, state-supported agricultural enterprises and the influx since 2014 of around 250,000 Nuer refugees fleeing South Sudan's civil war. Anywa and Nuer people clashed, leading to dozens of deaths, even among the regional police force, which split along ethnic lines.

The government's economic policy under the Growth and Transformation Plan II focused on large-scale commercial agricultural development and on 'transforming' the smallholder sector. The land taken from smallholders and agro-pastoralists leased to investors or exploited by state companies reached an estimated surface of more than 2.5 m ha (of the projected 3.5 m). The vast majority of smallholders affected were displaced and poorly compensated, which fed resentment. Only a few found jobs on the new farms, and new farmland elsewhere was not given to them.

International criticism from foreign donors and institutions of the way the authorities handled the protests fell on deaf ears, and the latter predictably rejected any intervention by international and UN observers to investigate the killings. Criticism soon subsided: donor statements again had no bite due to lack of interest, lack of commitment to a rights agenda and an overemphasis by Western and other donors/ trading partners on Ethiopia as a "strategic partner and emerging economy". The government saw its harsh repression to stop the protests at all costs as justified and continued to repeat its refrain against 'illegal protests' by 'anti-peace elements'. No accountability probes into excessively violent army, federal police or militia practices were carried out. In general, there were no political structures or procedures in place to account for abuse or respond to charges, grievances or even alternative views and policies. In interviews with global media (as on 9 March with 'The Guardian'), Prime Minister Hailemariam showed nominal awareness of Ethiopia's problems, such as 'lack of a democratic culture', 'bad governance', corruption and youth unemployment, but his government's policies to deal with those problems were falling short. His remark in the interview that Ethiopia was "an island of stability in a troubled region" rang hollow at the end of a year that was marked by domestic repression and the curtailing of civic freedoms.

On 12 November *Merera Gudina, leader of the legal opposition party, the Oromo Federalist Congress, was arrested*, a politician not known for any violent or insurrectionist agenda. He was detained at Bole Airport on his return from a meeting at the European Parliament, where he had been invited to testify on the unrest in Ethiopia. The government claimed that he had met and 'conspired' with two declared government opponents, Berhanu Nega (of the Ginbot-7 movement) and the 2016 Olympic 10-km silver medallist Feyissa Lilesa, who had made the crossed-arm protest gesture after his race. Merera's arrest and other measures against opposition voices seemed to reveal the government's insecurity and fear of any dissenting opinions. The SoE was thus used to interpret the clauses of the already extremely strict anti-terrorism law of 2009 very stringently and to declare critical voices as criminal, if need be. It appeared to many observers that the government was again revealing that it was aware of its unpopularity but incapable of cultivating dialogue or negotiation.

After the wave of open protests had subsided toward the end of the year, Hailemariam announced a "new approach" and promised to weed out government officials who "had abused the public's trust" by their corrupt and illegal practices. He also said talks would be held with excluded groups that had grievances. On 1 November, the government announced a reshuffle of cabinet ministers: 21 new appointments were made, bringing the total, including both new posts and replacements, to 30. In a televised presentation of the new ministers, the prime minister explicitly mentioned their 'ethnicity', presumably to show that the government was responsive to ethnic inequalities, but this was felt by many to be embarrassing and irrelevant.

Under the SoE, those arrested had limited recourse to the usual rights, such as *habeas corpus* and appeal. While many thousands were detained, put in prison camps and subjected to forced 'rehabilitation', none of the people's concrete grievances were addressed, except rhetorically. The prime minister and government spokespersons repeatedly muttered about "the need to be more attentive to the people", and "to address the problems that were overlooked", but no comprehensive solutions or new policies were forthcoming by the end of the year; it was all about restoring order and the *status quo*.

Internal relations between the four constituent parts of the ruling EPRDF were sometimes tense, and rivalries as well as disagreements on how to handle the protests and address the apparent popular grievances were evident. Some leading members of the Oromo People's Democratic Organisation (OPDO) and the Amhara National Democratic Movement (ANDM) were accused by the leadership of sympathising with the protesters. At the same time, the leadership, notably of the ANDM and the OPDO constituent parts, tried to operate more independently from the EPRDF overall structure.

Although the overall system of governance itself was not reformed, selected (former) high-level party members were charged with crimes and sentenced, including the former head of domestic intelligence (Ethiopian National Intelligence and Security Service or NISS), Woldeselassie Woldemichael, who was convicted on charges of corruption and sentenced to ten years in prison.

After the death of numerous protesters in Oromiya and Amhara in early August, even *the UN High Commissioner for Human Rights called for a probe by international observers*, decrying the impunity, but to no avail. Ethiopia lived up to its reputation as a 'hard-line autocracy', as it was classified by the German think-tank BTI. The US State Department's annual report on human rights also confirmed a string of abuses, bad prison conditions, torture, disappearances and impunity of the security forces.

Inter-religious relations between Christians, Muslims and traditional religionists, despite a general accommodative attitude, were often marked by underlying tensions and rivalry, but no large-scale violent clashes occurred. In the countryside, however, Protestant Evangelicals (many of whom were recent converts) and followers of traditional religions were engaged in frequent conflicts.

Foreign Affairs

Foreign policy was made by the ruling EPRDF without interference from other groups, either domestic or foreign. Ethiopia's regional role in Eastern Africa was recognised and it remained a partner in global efforts to stem Islamist terrorism. At the same time, it was strongly dependent on humanitarian aid and development funds from donor countries and institutions. The government manoeuvred between new donors and partners such as China, India and Turkey and the traditional Western and other donor countries. In March, Ethiopia began its campaign for a non-permanent seat at the UNSC for 2017–18.

On 21 September, the EU, mindful of the growing migration threat and the unrest fuelled by the 'youth bulge', concluded a $ 500 m job-creation scheme deal with the government to be implemented in the coming years.

Ethiopia retained its prominent position in the IGAD, the AU and the AMISOM force in Somalia and maintained its contingents (around 8,100 personnel) to various UN missions (including in Sudan's Darfur and Abyei regions).

Relations with Kenya, Somaliland, Sudan and especially Djibouti were peaceful and fairly close, with mutual agreements, cooperation and high-level visits. South Sudan was problematic because of that country's internal disarray. Ethiopia favoured Salva Kiir to continue as leader and on 28 November refused entry into Ethiopia for rebel leader Riek Machar.

There was no improvement in relations with *Eritrea*. On 12 June, armed clashes, resulting in a "significant number" of casualties, were reported between Eritrean and Ethiopian forces near the border town of Tsorona, with each side predictably blaming the other for starting the incident. Eritrea claimed to have killed over 200 Ethiopian troops. In February, Ethiopia had accused Eritrea of fuelling anti-government protests in Ethiopia. It later also accused Egypt of supporting the protesters – without any evidence.

Prime Minister Hailemariam made various foreign trips. On 7–9 April, he visited Ghana to strengthen bilateral relations. On 14 June, he was in Brussels and signed a joint declaration with the EU, 'Towards an EU-Ethiopia Strategic Engagement', on security matters, migration and economic cooperation. He went to Kenya on 22–24 June for talks on security issues, border management, economic relations (with a business forum) and the on-going Lamu Port-South Sudan-Ethiopia-Transport (LAPSSET) Corridor project. On 28 October, he visited Juba (South Sudan) to press for calm in the border area, for a peace deal, and for improved economic relations. On 20 November, he was in Saudi Arabia, meeting with King Salman and business people.

Ethiopia received visits by a significant number of *foreign dignitaries*. *Brazil's Minister of Foreign Affairs Mauro Vieira* visited Ethiopia on 8 March and met with the prime minister and with AU leaders, and an Ethio-Brazilian business seminar was held. On 7 July, the *Israeli Prime Minister Benjamin Netanyahu* visited with a delegation and discussions were held during an Ethio-Israel business summit on more future cooperation in agriculture, water management, technology and tourism development. Several agreements were signed. *German Chancellor Angela Merkel* came on 11 October for a visit to the AU headquarters in Addis Ababa and for talks with the government. Merkel declined to give a speech to the one-party dominated parliament and in a conversation with Hailemariam advised him to open up political dialogue and reduce the costly repression in the country. On 11 November, *Canada's Foreign Minister Stéphane Dion* visited during an African tour, appealing for proper handling of the political unrest and for opening a dialogue process. A Saudi business delegation headed by the chairman of the Saudi Development Fund paid a visit on 14–16 December for a meeting with the Ethiopian prime minister that focused on 'investment opportunities'.

The Nile question remained a bone of contention. Although in March the 'Declaration of Principles', a tripartite agreement on the Nile waters, was concluded between Sudan, Egypt and Ethiopia, misgivings were not resolved, especially between the latter two countries. Egypt continued to be fearful of expected negative effects of the huge Renaissance Dam on levels and quantity of water reaching the country downstream. Sudan tended to favour Ethiopia, as it would have future benefits from the use of the accumulated water and the electricity generated by the Ethiopian dam. Egypt hinted that if there were no guarantees regarding its share of the Nile waters – its essential lifeline – it would keep all options open. In the wake of this Declaration of Principles, it was agreed that there would be a comprehensive scientific investigation of the dam project and its likely effects on the Nile water flow, but this had not started by the end of the year.

On 21 July, Ethiopia, Djibouti and China announced the launch of a *$ 4 bn natural gas project*, based on future exploitation of the large Ogaden gas reserves.

An unexpected armed incident occurred on 15 April, when a well-organised party of *Murle raiders* from the Pibor area in South Sudan crossed the border into western Ethiopia (Gambela). They raided 20 villages, took hundreds of cattle, kidnapped 108 children and killed 208 local people (from the Nuer). Before the Ethiopian army could retaliate, they withdrew to South Sudan, which was in turmoil because of the civil war. In the subsequent weeks, the Ethiopian army unilaterally crossed the border and retrieved some children and cattle. In the south-west (Bench-Maji Zone), there were repeated violent incursions and cattle raids by South Sudanese Toposa into Ethiopian territory – a long-standing problem.

Socioeconomic Developments

The country's population, economic output and GDP all increased, although investments, exports and imports slowed down, partly due to world market developments, climatic problems and the social unrest, which also hit tourism revenues. However, figures cited on the country's economy were often approximations, and different sources showed remarkable divergences.

The country saw continued drought and related climatic challenges, leading the government, as in previous years, to appeal for aid for around 9 m *people in need of food* at the beginning of the year. Later, this figure fell to 5.6 m. The areas most affected were Somali Region, Afar and Central-East Oromiya (including Arsi). Tens of thousands of livestock were reported to have died and crop production was affected. The government spent some $ 380 m on the problems itself but, despite increased agrarian production, 'productive safety net' programmes and an improved early warning and logistics system, no durable solution to the recurring El Niño-driven challenges was in place. High population growth contributed to the problem. The food relief industry, led by WPF, USAID and the EU, again came to the rescue.

GDP at year's end was around $ 62.5 bn, having shown a real-terms growth rate of about 6.5%, significantly down from previous years. Apart from world market developments, this was partly due to the unrest and mass protests, which led to damage and shook investor confidence. A stiff state-led economic policy restricting the role of the private sector did the rest. Various state ventures did not produce expected profits, either. For example, the huge sugar plantations in the South did not come out of the red, due to massive costs, the declining world sugar price and looming global over-production. Per capita GDP was said to be $ 719.

Agriculture's share in GDP was 36% (still employing about 80% of the population), services represented about 47%, and manufacturing 17%. Industrial production grew at an estimated 9%, so above the GDP growth rate. Agricultural growth was down to 2.9%.

The *state budget* (the Ethiopian budget year runs from July to July) reached $ 10 bn, while expenditure amounted to $ 11.8 bn. The *current account deficit* thus stood at 10.2%-10.5% of GDP. Taxes and other revenues generated some 14.6% of GDP.

The annual *IMF Article IV consultation* was concluded in October, and the IMF warned that debt increase was a risk, exports had underperformed and the current account deficit remained high. It blamed the region's drought for " ... supply shock, necessitating scaled-up food imports". Again, nothing was said on the state-dirigiste economic policies and the lack of political and economic freedoms, despite that fact that they impinged on the performance of the national economy.

On 17 December, the 1,870 MW *Gibe III hydro-electric dam* was officially opened, although it had gone on the grid earlier. In December, it was reported that water levels in the Omo River and of Lake Turkana (in the Ethiopia-Kenya border area) had already dropped by 1.7 m., affecting downstream fisheries, river-bank cultivation sites and other sources of livelihood for local people. Kenya's government, having little interest in the arid northern frontier areas and its populations near Lake Turkana, did not respond.

Work on the huge $ 4.8 bn, 6,000 MW Renaissance Dam on the Blue Nile progressed slowly, but was said to be 70% complete at year's end.

Another infrastructure project, the Chinese-financed 700 km, $ 4 bn *Addis Ababa-Djibouti rail link*, was completed and formally inaugurated on 5 October in Addis Ababa by Prime Minister Hailemariam and President Guelleh of Djibouti. Additional railway lines were planned.

The new $ 300 m Hawassa Industrial Park was officially opened on 13 July.

According to Prime Minister Hailemariam's six-months' report to parliament on 10 March, *export revenues* had reached $ 5.3 bn, but the IMF and other sources referred to a sum of around $ 3 bn, with coffee still as the top crop (27% of exports), followed by oilseeds (17%), vegetables, including *khat* (17%), gold (13%), and flowers, live animals, raw leather products and meat products (about 20%). This represented a decline in exports of around 7% compared with the same period in the previous year.

Low export revenue-generating capacity remained the economy's Achilles heel and had not shown a structural breakthrough in recent years. *Imports* again dwarfed exports to the tune of $ 14.5 bn., although this was $ 1 bn down from the previous year. The large trade deficit thus continued, compensated for by foreign aid flows and remittances from the Ethiopian diaspora. The country struggled with foreign currency scarcity.

Inflation went ahead at an estimated 9% per year, with the birr (ETB) reaching 22 to the dollar. Experts estimated the currency to still be *overvalued* by around 20%–40%. Real estate prices and house rents in Addis Ababa rose very rapidly.

The *public debt* at year's end stood at slightly over $ 36.9 bn, or 54.2% of GDP (up from about 49.6% the previous year, a 12.8% rise). The amount of *external* debt reached $ 23 bn. China was the largest creditor, with about $ 17 bn in outstanding loans, followed by India, Turkey and the World Bank. The rapidly mounting debt (from $ 14 bn in 2011) caused several Ethiopian and international economic experts to express concern about the sustainability of Ethiopia's financing model, all the more since the profitability of various new major projects and enterprises left much to be desired. The IMF, however, stated that, despite increased vulnerability, Ethiopia's "risk of external debt distress remains moderate" (in part because 70% of the debt was owed to 'official creditors', not trade and commercial-based ones). The previous budget (of July 2016) reserved a substantial chunk of around $ 633 m (or ETB 13.9 bn) for debt repayments.

There were estimates of *illegal money transfers* – capital flight – out of the country of some $ 2–$ 2.5 bn – representing a higher share of GDP than in any other SSA country. The organisation Global Financial Integrity suspected that, as in other countries, import-export businesses and some government officials were involved – both regularly conniving with the banks. As the government (ruling party) controlled close to half of the Ethiopian economy, their involvement was more than likely. Export or import trade misinvoicing and 'leakages' in the balance of payments were the predominant tricks.

Remittances by overseas Ethiopians – both declared and undeclared – amounted to $ 3.4 bn, much more than annual export revenues, and again showing the developed world's extra impetus to the country's economy. On 8 June, it was announced by the US Securities and Exchange Commission that Ethiopia's electric utility ETTC had agreed to pay them nearly $ 6.5 m to settle charges that it had violated US securities laws due to failure to *register* bonds sold to US residents of Ethiopian descent.

In the Heritage Foundation's annual *Index of Economic Freedom*, Ethiopia again came out as 'mostly unfree' – a qualification highly familiar to private-sector business people, small entrepreneurs and traders. The ruling party and its large business conglomerates were still seen as dominating the economy, using insider knowledge, patronage and often unfair business practices. The country continued to suffer from *corruption*, buttressed by the stories of ordinary people, office workers and business people. On TI's Corruption Perception Index, Ethiopia was 106th of 176 countries, a slight drop, but still comparatively modest for Africa.

Social and income inequality increased somewhat, with the GINI coefficient reaching 33.6, slightly higher than in 2015, but the data on which this was based were shaky. A small party-linked and business elite continued to increase its wealth rapidly. On Oxfam's Multidimensional Poverty Index (MPI), Ethiopia had an 87.3% 'MPI poor' population, higher than East Africa's average (70%).

Most economic figures confirmed the picture of a skewed, externally dependent economy that lacked sufficient export revenue-generating capacity and was propped up by remittances from the Ethiopian diaspora, donor aid money, and loans, particularly from China. The long-term vulnerability of the economy remained.

Population growth remained at a high 2.7%, and the total population, according to the UN Population Division, reaching 101 m, though other sources put it some 5–6 m lower. The increase for the year was more than 2.2 m people – reflecting a basically unsustainable pace in view of the limited resources and economic prospects. The birth rate in urban areas fell slightly, but the urban population still increased by about 4%, mostly due to rural-urban migration.

Population growth went along with a rapidly *dwindling agrarian/natural resource base*: in many parts, land scarcity became more acute, leading to group conflict, attempted cultivation of marginal areas, loss of vegetation, drying out of the land (due also to excessive planting of eucalyptus trees), and water scarcity. Efforts to reclaim eroded land were successfully undertaken in some parts of the northern highlands, but in other regions erosion continued unabated.

The number of *refugees* in Ethiopia reached about 783,000, 45% of whom were from South Sudan. UNHCR again bore the major responsibility for assisting them, with a budget of $ 280 m (but with a funding gap by October of 62%). An estimated 38,000 Eritrean refugees/migrants crossed the border into Ethiopia (paying an average of $ 2,500 each to smugglers), bringing the total to some 163,000. Most of them stayed in camps, while others moved on to Sudan and the Mediterranean coast, heading for Europe. About 94,000 Ethiopians migrated (fled) to Yemen, remarkable in view of that country's heavy suffering from armed conflict and severe economic decline. The migrants hoped to move on to Saudi Arabia or the Gulf States. The risks were high, but the reason most given was to "… seek the opportunity to have a better life", at whatever cost. In a reverse movement, some 3,400 Yemenis fled to Ethiopia.

Contraband and illegal economic practices were on the increase, among them human trafficking, and smuggling or illegal sales of wildlife products. The latter sector increased significantly, amidst slackening prevention policies. At a meeting of the Horn of Africa Wildlife Enforcement Network on 7–8 December, it was said that cheetahs and animal products such as ivory, rhino horn and antelope skins were most traded, notably to countries in the Arabian Peninsula and Far East. This was a further sign of the precarious state of Ethiopia's ecology and environmental situation.

Kenya

Gabrielle Lynch

Dominant issues in 2016 were electoral management, the formation and consolidation of political coalitions, and spiralling corruption. Although not scheduled until 8 August 2017, the forthcoming polls overshadowed political debate and activities during the year. Opposition leaders pushed for electoral reforms and new commissioners for the Independent Electoral and Boundaries Commission, and mooted a National Super Alliance, and the ruling Jubilee Alliance sought to establish a new Jubilee Party. The forthcoming elections also fuelled corruption, as incumbents and aspirants at all levels – from those running to be members of county assemblies up – sought to fund their campaigns, and devolution continued to provide new opportunities for accumulation. Unprecedented corruption – in the context of high levels of inequality, costs of living and salaries for elected officials – constituted a source of popular frustration and anger, and strained (already tense) relations between the government and prominent civil society organisations and the media. Relations with these key actors were then further undermined by the government's use of a history of ethnic violence within the country, and of an ongoing external threat from al-Shabaab (the radical Islamist group based in neighbouring Somalia), to insist upon the need for unity and cohesion in the interests of stability and development.

 | DOI 10.1163/9789004355910_036

Domestic Politics

The *Jubilee Alliance* and the principal opposition coalition – the *Coalition for Reform and Democracy* (CORD) – maintained a combative relationship. In particular, opposition leaders blamed the government for spiralling corruption and economic hardship, and claimed that it was getting ready to rig the 2017 election; while the Jubilee Alliance criticised the opposition for being overly critical and dismissed it as divisive and desperate. This context ensured that an array of government policies and projects became mired in a war of words, as was exemplified in an exchange between President Uhuru Kenyatta and Hassan Joho, the Orange Democratic Movement (ODM) deputy and governor of Mombasa, in January over the government's decision to sell land titles to squatters at the long-disputed Waitiki farm in Kwale through individual government loans of KSh (shilling) 182,000. According to the government, this decision embodied their commitment to address *historical land injustices*. However, it was rejected by the opposition, and Joho called on people to refuse to pay, arguing that the government should simply clear the loans, as it had done for some coffee farmers in central Kenya.

In this context, and under the leadership of Raila Odinga and Kalonzo Musyoka, CORD insisted on the need for *electoral reforms* and the removal of all *Independent Electoral and Boundaries Commission (IEBC) commissioners*. This campaign drew upon a sense (particularly prevalent in opposition strongholds) that the 2007 and 2013 elections had been stolen, as well as upon revelations of corruption in the Interim Independent Electoral Commission of Kenya (which had been superseded by the IEBC in 2011), and claims that preparations were afoot to manipulate the 2017 polls. The latter included rumours that a National Youth Service (NYS) registration drive was being used to add young Kenyans to the electoral register without their knowledge; that foreigners were being registered along the Somalian and Ugandan borders; and that a by-election for the Kericho County senatorship in March was rigged in favour of the government's preferred candidate.

In their bid to push for reforms, CORD organised a series of *protests* in Nairobi and a number of other cities and smaller towns across the country during April and May, which culminated in violent confrontations between demonstrators and security forces. The clashes included the use of police batons against protestors outside the University of Nairobi's main campus by General Service Unit (GSU) officers and the fatal shooting of two men in Siaya County. In June, a compromise agreement was finally brokered whereby *new commissioners* would be recruited and greater reliance would be placed on *election technology*. However, at year's end, new commissioners had yet to be appointed, and the government and opposition continued to argue about whether an electronic voter identification system should be supported by a manual one.

As debate over the management of, and rules for, the 2017 election persisted, the IEBC continued to update the *voter register* through a continuous registration process and the first of two mass registration drives (the second to follow in the early months of 2017). However, the IEBC fell far short of its (admittedly ambitious) targets, fuelling talk of a more general problem of political apathy. Questions were also raised regarding the high number of *voter transfers* between wards, constituencies and counties, which appeared to be facilitated by candidates at different levels seeking to boost their support in the forthcoming party primaries and/or general election. In turn, reports of relatively high registration rates in several counties along the Somalian and Ugandan borders supported rumours of voter importation.

In April, the intervention of the ICC came to an end after the Office of the Prosecutor (OTP) vacated the case against Deputy President William Ruto and radio presenter Joshua arap Sang. This followed the withdrawal of charges against the former head of the civil service, Francis Muthaura, in March 2013, and President Kenyatta in December 2014. Ruto and Sang had initially been charged for their alleged role as indirect co-perpetrator and contributor, respectively, to the commission of crimes during the post-election violence of 2007/8. However, while the government lauded the collapse of this case as further proof of Kenyatta's and Ruto's innocence, and organised a mass thanksgiving ceremony in Nakuru town, the OTP insisted that charges were only dropped because it was impossible to fully investigate and prosecute the crimes, and continued with its investigations into witness tampering.

With the ICC cases at an end, the Jubilee Alliance focused on the consolidation of Kenyatta's party, The National Alliance (TNA), and Ruto's United Republic Party (URP) into the Jubilee Party (JP), which officially became a single entity in September. This concerted effort at *party-building* included the opening of new offices across the country, a national membership drive and intense campaigns ahead of a series of by-elections – most notably, for the member of parliament for Malindi constituency in Kilifi County and senator of Kericho County in March. These efforts sought to establish a positive momentum ahead of the 2017 election; they also constituted part of a broader political strategy by Ruto and his allies to establish a network across the country that could later be used to support his succession to become the JP *flagbearer in 2022* (when, if the JP won in 2017, Kenyatta would have to step down due to a two-term limit).

The *by-elections* in Malindi and Kericho revealed an ongoing regional and ethnic divide. Malindi, situated in former Coast Province, together with parts of western Kenya, constituted the main stronghold of the ODM, the principal opposition party, headed by Odinga. Ongoing support was evidenced when the ODM retained the Malindi seat with relative ease, while the JP won the senatorship in Kericho in an area dominated by Ruto's Kalenjin community. Moreover, while the credibility of the latter was disputed by the political opposition, it constituted a severe blow to Ruto's two main *Kalenjin rivals* – Isaac Ruto (the governor of Bomet County) and Gideon Moi (the senator for Baringo County, head of the Kenya African National Union [KANU], and son of former president Daniel arap Moi) – who had both campaigned for the defeated KANU candidate, Paul Sang.

As the government sought to institutionalise the JP, opposition leaders began negotiations for a new *mega-alliance*. This included Raila Odinga of the ODM, Kalonzo Musyoka of Wiper, Moses Wetangula of FORD-Kenya, Musalia Mudavadi of the Amani National Coalition (ANC), Gideon Moi of KANU, and Isaac Ruto – who launched the new 'Chama Cha Mashinani' party (CCM) in July. However, while negotiators suggested an array of new positions as a way to include different interests – with mooted posts including a first and second deputy president, a prime minister and two deputy prime ministers – the question of who would be the presidential candidate of the National Super Alliance (NASA) remained unresolved. The coalition also failed to agree on an alliance structure or manifesto. Negotiations were complicated by rumours of a rift between Odinga and Musyoka, and by reports that *Gideon Moi* was undecided about whether to join NASA or the JP – with many speculating that a faction within the JP was trying to position Moi as the party's candidate for 2022. This was fuelled by reports that many within Kenyatta's Kikuyu community blamed Ruto for rampant corruption, still believed that he had been involved in organised attacks against Kikuyu during the post-election violence of 2007/8, and did not want him to succeed Kenyatta in 2022.

Competition for *county assembly seats* and *governorship* positions increased markedly, as many senators announced their intention to run for the latter, and many wards gained the attention of successful businessmen and/or professionals. In the process, a number of border disputes, local resource conflicts, and appointment processes became further politicised, and *inter- and intra-communal tensions* increased. This included areas with a history of tension and violence – such as the Nandi/Nyanza and Kericho/Nyanza borders, and Kwale and Bungoma counties – but also some counties – such as Meru – where new tensions were fostered between communities following the formation of the county as a new political unit.

In many counties, these dynamics were complicated by ongoing discussions about whether *negotiated democracy* agreements reached in 2013 – which had seen elders and leaders in various counties agree to share seats between different ethnic groups and clans – should still hold in 2017, be renegotiated or be abandoned. These debates became particularly heated in parts of northern Kenya – with Garre elders in Mandera County, for example, insisting that all elected officials should stand down so as to allow for the representation of other clans. Increased interest in the county assemblies was in part a reflection of the responsibilities and powers that the new devolved units enjoyed, but was also fuelled by the associated opportunities for accumulation.

According to several commentators in the national press, *corruption* reached unprecedented levels, as the devolution of power to 47 new counties in 2013 continued to bring new opportunities for graft and heightened competition provided strong incentives. However, media attention focused largely on national-level scandals, including the fate of the country's Eurobond billions and NYS funds, and allegations that around $ 300 m had been misappropriated from the *Ministry of Health*. The scale of graft prompted public demonstrations and further displays of force – with anti-corruption protestors in November, for example, beaten up by police and dispersed with tear gas.

While devolution continued to shape politics in new and unexpected ways, the *police reforms* that had also been envisaged as part of the 2010 constitution stalled. In particular, the ongoing vetting of police officers by the National Police Service Commission – which was meant to increase public confidence in this critical institution through public hearings – attracted little attention, while *extra-judicial killings* increased. The latter grabbed the headlines in July when a human rights lawyer, Willie Kimani, his client, Josephat Mwenda, and their taxi driver were killed, allegedly by an Administrative Police officer after they were abducted following a court hearing regarding police harassment. However, while the killing of such a high-profile individual was unusual, violent intimidation and killings were not. Young male residents of informal settlements constituted the vast majority of victims. Yet public condemnation was muted, with many Kenyans welcoming heavy-handed tactics on social media as a way to tackle crime and terrorism.

The number and scale of *terrorist attacks* by al-Shabaab was significantly lower than in any of the previous five years. Nevertheless, a series of relatively small-scale attacks in the north led to loss of life. At the same time, reports of radicalisation and al-Shabaab recruitment in former Coast and North Eastern provinces, the government's failure to address the familiar Muslim narrative of 'historical marginalisation', and Kenya's ongoing involvement in a military operation in Somalia, ensured that the possibility of future attacks remained a real and pressing threat. In this context, steps were taken to develop a national policy on *countering violent extremism* (CVE); the government continued to develop new community policing structures, such as the new 'nyumba kumi' (ten houses) initiative; and the international community supported various local and international organisations to carry out CVE programmes.

The country continued to suffer from other forms of *insecurity*. They included the proliferation of loosely affiliated criminal gangs in Mombasa and Kisumu; the invasion of ranches and conservancies in Laikipia County towards the end of the year by herders from Samburu County; and retaliatory *cattle raids* between neighbouring communities in parts of the southern and northern Rift Valley. However, while the border between Pokot and Turkana counties in the North Rift had been particularly troubled in early 2015, an inter-communal peace drive in mid-2015 held for much of the year.

The government continued to face strained relations with prominent *human rights organisations* as officials sought to quell critical voices and simultaneously encourage self-censorship. With relations between these vocal organisations and the government at a nadir, *religious leaders* gained greater prominence after they helped to negotiate an agreement between the government and opposition over the IEBC and were increasingly seen as potential mediators in any possible election-related conflicts in the year ahead.

Disagreements between the government and commercial *media* proved less visible, as private threats to redirect government advertising and to refuse to pay subscription fees continued to encourage substantial *self-censorship* by individual journalists, editors and media houses. The exception was the Nation Media Group's decision to sack a senior editor, Denis Galava, and a leading cartoonist, popularly known as Gado, in January and March, respectively, which led them to sue the media house on the grounds that they had been fired due to "government pressure".

The *judiciary* continued to provide an important check on government, and issued a number of rulings against the Executive to protect various rights including the right of assembly. The judiciary also continued to provide an important avenue for protest and several government directives – such as a decision to close Dadaab refugee camp in northern Kenya – were challenged through the courts. A number of cases relating to the post-election violence of 2007/8 – including those related to sexual and gender-based violence and police shootings – also continued throughout the year. In June, *Chief Justice* Willy Mutunga stood down and was replaced by Justice David Maraga, who had risen from the High Court in 2003 to the Court of Appeal in 2012. Maraga was chosen over a number of eminent judges, legal practitioners and scholars. As a career judge, he was widely seen as a less contentious choice than his predecessor, who had been a vocal human rights lawyer and activist, but he was also generally perceived to be clean and fair.

Parliament failed to discuss the *Truth Justice and Reconciliation Commission* report, which had been pending since July 2013. However, steps were taken to establish a *Restorative Justice Fund*, which had initially been announced by President Kenyatta in his 2015 state of the nation address, and which sought to compensate victims of select gross human rights violations through a fund to be administered by the attorney general's office.

Foreign Affairs

The year began with the government still engaged in a multi-stranded campaign to mobilise domestic, pan-African and international support against the *ICC*. The aim was to *counter-shame* the Court by depicting the OTP's charges as "baseless" and "biased", and as "detrimental to regional peace and development", with the accusation that the charges targeted "democratically elected leaders" of a regional powerhouse in an area wracked by terrorism. This campaign bore significant fruit, as the 26th AU summit of heads of state and government in January adopted Kenyatta's proposal to develop a road map for the mass withdrawal of African nations from the Rome Statute. In turn, Kenya's position contributed to the rise of anti-ICC feeling across the continent, and thus probably contributed to the announcement in October of South Africa, Burundi and Gambia to withdraw from the Rome Statute, alleging that the Court was "neo-colonial" and "anti-African". However, with the withdrawal of charges in April, the government of Kenya turned its attention to other priorities: regional security, large-scale infrastructure projects and economic agreements.

With Ruto freed of charges at the ICC, relations between the government and two key donors – the *USA* and the *UK* – continued to improve. In the run-up to the 2013 elections, the Jubilee Alliance had accused 'the West' of being behind Kenyatta's and Ruto's troubles at the ICC, leading to increasingly strained relations, particularly with the UK and the US. However, after Jubilee's electoral success, these donors had adopted a more conservative approach that relied on *quiet diplomacy*, as reflected in the behind-the-scenes role that the American ambassador and British high commissioner helped to play in negotiating an agreement between the government and political opposition over the IEBC.

However, this did not prevent the government from scapegoating donors when it served their interests, as occurred, for example, in December, when President Kenyatta referred in his Jamhuri (or Independence) Day speech to the possibility of *foreign interference* in the country's elections. Kenyatta went on to note that money was already coming in "from abroad in the guise of supporting good governance or civic education", but that the "true intention is to influence our electoral choices". His message was clear: "This is our country, and no one should ever try and control our choices for their selfish interests." The impact of Kenyatta's warning was swift, as several donors pulled funds set aside to support *civic and voter education* projects by local civil society organisations.

The decision by the British public to leave the EU through the *Brexit* referendum in May, and the election of the controversial Republican candidate, *Donald Trump*, in the American polls in November, raised questions about what the rise of right-wing populist politics in the West would mean for Kenya. The sense, at least in the short term, was that the country would continue to be valued as a key ally in the 'war on terror' and, more specifically, in the struggle against al-Shabaab in Somalia, but that there would be less interest in domestic politics, and less funding for governance and development projects.

The Kenya Defence Forces (KDF) continued to be involved in Somalia as part of the *AU Mission in Somalia* (AMISOM), which was primarily funded by the EU with additional support from the US. In 2014, *al-Shabaab* had declared that their struggle had turned fully to Kenya in response to the country's invasion of Somalia in 2011 and alleged atrocities by KDF soldiers, and they continued to cite the invasion – together with the "suffering of Muslim communities" in Kenya – as the reason for their efforts to establish cells and conduct attacks on Kenyan soil. However, unlike in recent years, the worst attack by al-Shabaab against Kenyan nationals occurred within Somalia when, on 15 January, militants overran an AMISOM operating base garrisoned by KDF troops at El Adde. The government did not release information on the number of casualties, or on how many soldiers were deployed at El Adde, but al-Shabaab claimed that over 100 soldiers had been killed. The base had been particularly vulnerable due to its poor operational set-up and procedures – its remote location in an area in which al-Shabaab retained considerable freedom of movement and difficult relations with the local population. Poor communications with Ethiopian troops stationed relatively close by also meant that the response team had to come all the way from Kenya.

The government renewed its efforts to *close Dadaab* – a cluster of five refugee camps in Garissa County, home to around a quarter of million Somalian refugees – on the grounds that it was a *source of insecurity* and hotbed for al-Shabaab recruitment and activities. However, following pleas from the UN and international aid agencies, the government announced in November that it would postpone the camp's closure for a further six months on *humanitarian grounds*. Uncertainty surrounding the camp's future was further fuelled by a legal challenge brought before the High Court by the Kenya National Commission on Human Rights and a local civil society organisation, 'Kituo cha Sheria', that the government's directive was discriminatory and contrary to international law. This case was still ongoing at the year's end.

Relations with the UN soured after Secretary-General Ban Ki-moon sacked the Kenyan commander of the *UN Mission in South Sudan* (UNMISS), Lieutenant General Ondieki, in November after a UN special investigation found that a lack of leadership had culminated in a "chaotic and ineffective response" to fighting in Juba in July. In response, the Ministry of Foreign Affairs announced that Kenya would *withdraw its troops* from South Sudan and accused the UN of unfairly attributing "fundamental structural and systemic dysfunctionality" within UNMISS to a single individual.

Politicians from both sides of the divide became involved in the *Ugandan elections* in February: the deputy president joined President Museveni on the campaign trail in eastern Uganda in an effort to mobilise his Kalenjin kinsmen from the local Sebei community to vote for Museveni and ruling National Resistance Movement, while Odinga openly supported the country's main opposition leader, Kizza Besigye, and the Forum for Democratic Change. Museveni's victory in the polls reinforced a close working friendship between the two regimes and with Kagame's Rwanda in what had become known as a 'coalition of the willing'.

However, despite this friendship, Uganda continued to develop its plans to build an oil pipeline from the Ugandan oil town of Hoima to Tanga in Tanzania, rather than through the Kenyan oil town of Lokichar and on to Lamu port on the coast through Kenya's insecure northern belt. This further undermined plans for the *Lamu Port Southern Sudan-Ethiopia Transport Corridor* (LAPSSET), which – when launched by former president Kibaki in 2009 – had included plans for a new road, railway and pipeline across the three countries, as well as a port and oil refinery in Lamu and an international airport in Isiolo.

While LAPSSET continued to be downscaled, significant progress was made on the Mombasa to Nairobi section of the *standard gauge railway* (SGR), with plans to later link the SGR to Kampala in Uganda and Kigali in Rwanda. The Mombasa-Nairobi section, which was 90% funded by a loan from the China Exim Bank and constructed by Chinese companies, provided an important example of the increased presence of *China*. The Chinese government helped to fund and/or construct a number of major infrastructure projects, and Chinese companies continued to be involved in a number of other industries; most notably construction and import/export markets.

In May, Kenya's ongoing efforts to revive the Hoima-Lamu pipeline resulted in a diplomatic incident with its southern neighbour, *Tanzania*, when – during a joint visit by Ugandan and Kenyan officials to analyse the proposed Hoima-Tanga pipeline – Tanzanian authorities *confiscated the passports* of top Kenyan officials, including the Energy Cabinet Secretary Charles Keter, and denied them access to Tanga port. This incident reflected a broader context in which Kenya and Tanzania competed to be the region's transport hub and Tanzania sought to curtail Kenya's dominance within the EAC. Relations were further strained by *Uganda*'s President Magufuli's refusal to sign an EPA between the EAC and EU in July, which was supported by Kenya, and by his failure to attend the Tokyo International Conference on African Development in Nairobi in August. The diplomatic situation was then exacerbated by popular comparisons on social media between Magufuli's 'cleansing operation' and hardline stance on corruption and unnecessary expenditure, and Kenya's spiralling graft and lack of accountability, through the popular hashtag #WhatWouldMagufuliDo. Nevertheless, both countries made a concerted effort to make a show of cordial relations during Magufuli's first *state visit* to Kenya in October, when he was received with great pomp and ceremony, including a grand guard of honour inspection and 21-gun salute. Other state visits during the year were made by the Nigerian President Muhammadu Buhari, South African President Jacob Zuma, Japanese Prime Minister Shinzo Abe, and Indian Prime Minister Narendra Modi.

Kenyatta continued with his record of regular *state visits* abroad as – in addition to attending the AU summit in Ethiopia in January – he made state visits to Sudan, Botswana, Israel, France, Germany and Belgium. He also attended the Northern Corridor Integration Project Summit, President Museveni's inauguration, the 40th Anniversary of the Entebbe hostage crisis, a Diplomats' Forum in Uganda, the World Economic Forum and ordinary AU summit in Rwanda, the EAC summit in Tanzania, an IGAD summit on South Sudan in Ethiopia, an AMISON summit in Djibouti, IGADS's extra-ordinary summit in Somalia, Ghana's Independence Day, an AfDB meeting in Zambia, the ICGLR in Angola, an AU summit in Togo and the UN Climate Change Conference in Morocco.

Socioeconomic Developments

Real *GDP growth* remained buoyant at around 6%. This was driven by investment in infrastructure and construction, financial services and communications, as well as by rapid urbanisation, a burgeoning middle class and the growth of shopping malls and supermarkets, which ensured the relatively rapid growth of the country's wholesale and retail trade markets.

Devolution continued to be associated with visible signs of development across much of the country, as *county-level projects* such as roads and clinics went hand-in-hand with the construction of new hotels and retail outlets in county headquarters. Such physical evidence of a new redistribution of resources through the county governments also helped to ensure that – despite the localisation of corruption, exacerbation of ethnic tensions and new or higher levies at the local level – most Kenyans remained broadly supportive of the devolution of power.

While the economy continued to diversify, *public infrastructure* investment once again proved to be the strongest sector. This reflected the government's development plans, which continued to be articulated through *Vision 2030* – a plan that had been initiated under former president Kibaki and which included a series of ambitious and high-profile infrastructure projects, such as the SGR and a downscaled LAPSSET.

These projects came into direct tension with *conservation* efforts. The worst affected was *Nairobi National Park*, with agreements reached between various ministries and the Kenya Wildlife Service in 2015 that allowed the SGR to cut deep into the Park, and for Nairobi's southern by-pass to hive off another area. Community groups and conservationists also continued to oppose the construction of a new *coal-fired power station* in Lamu. While the government praised the economic benefits, including new jobs, activists raised concerns about the distribution of such benefits, potential harms and the environmental and human health costs.

In April, the governments of Uganda and Kenya confirmed that they would develop separate export pipelines for their *oil resources* from Loima and Lokichar in Turkana County, respectively. Together with a low global oil price, and ongoing disagreements between the government and Turkana politicians about how to share future oil revenues between the national and county governments, this decision cast a shadow over the likely profitability of the country's oilfields. However, the exploitation of oil continued to move forward and, in October, a Joint Development Agreement was concluded between the government and the UK company, Tullow Oil, on structures for the development of the export pipeline. In March, Tullow also announced that it had discovered "an active petroleum system with significant oil generation" in the Kerio Valley. The export of *sand minerals* also increased by almost 9%, while foreign investors prospected for other rare minerals – including gold in western Kenya.

Wildlife poaching continued to be a serious problem, with elephants, rhinos and lions the main targets. In April, the government burned 100 tonnes of ivory – including elephant tusks, ivory sculptures and rhino horn confiscated by the authorities, said to be worth up to $ 105 m – in a ceremony in Nairobi National Park. This action was intended to shock the world into recognising the scale of the problem, and to display Kenya's commitment to tackling it. President Kenyatta also demanded a total ban on the *trade in ivory* to protect the future of wild elephants.

The ongoing fall in animal numbers raised further concerns about the future of Kenya's *tourist industry*, largely reliant on visitors to the country's game parks and coastal beaches. However, following a slump in 2014, the sector continued to pick up as a result of improvements in security, the removal or downscaling of travel advisories imposed in 2014, and an increase in the number of middle- and upper-class domestic tourists. It was also assisted by steps taken by the government, including a decision to waive visa fees for children under 16 and to reduce park fees from $ 90 to $ 60.

Poor rains in late 2015 led to a rise in food prices at the beginning of the year and contributed to an *inflation rate* of almost 8%. Inflation then fell to 5% in the middle of the year before rising to just over 6% in the fourth quarter after the failure of the short rains. Two years of *poor rains*, together with population growth and increased livestock, also raised the spectre of drought, food shortages and livestock deaths, and prompted the need for food relief and cattle purchases in northern Kenya.

Food shortages in the north also brought attention to high levels of *inequality* within the country, which continued to be a source of widespread frustration. More specifically, while absolute poverty levels continued on a trajectory of gradual decline, many complained of inequalities, the *high salaries paid to elected officials* and endemic corruption. At the year's end, these frustrations contributed to a national *strike by doctors* demanding the implementation of a Collective Bargaining Agreement (CBA) that had been signed by the government in June 2013. The CBA covered issues of remuneration (including a proposed 300% pay rise), promotions, training and working conditions. In 2015, the Kenya Medical Practitioners, Pharmacists and Dentist's Union had taken the government to court over the Ministry of Health's failure to enact the CBA and, in October, the Labour Court ordered the CBA's registration. However, the Ministry continued to insist that it lacked the funds to implement the agreement and this refusal – in a context where the Ministry had recently been implicated in a $ 300 m corruption scandal and where the country's lawmakers were the second highest paid in the world – led many to reject the government's stance and to demand *#lipakamatender* or 'pay it like a government tender'. As a result, the doctors went on strike and onto the streets with significant popular support.

The *education sector* also faced serious problems, including a number of *arson attacks* on schools by students in the middle of the year, with over 20 incidents reported in July alone. This was not the first time that this month had witnessed such a spike, with over 20 incidents of secondary school buildings being set alight reported in June and July 2008, and at least eight in July 2013. Many blamed youth delinquency and a lack of discipline in schools. However, a more persuasive explanation was that many students saw violent protest as the only effective way to draw attention to their grievances, with arson as a preferred choice due to its destructive capacity and the relatively limited chances of the perpetrators being caught.

Tighter monitoring and supervision of the year's Kenya Certificate of Secondary Education (KCSE) examinations – which had historically been associated with widespread claims of malpractice including the leaking and sale of exam questions – led to a sharp dip in overall grades awarded. This had serious implications for the *higher education* sector, with the possibility that the country's 33 public universities would absorb almost all of the qualified students, leaving many of the country's 35 private universities in a critical situation.

In May, Kenya's anti-doping organisation for sports was declared non-compliant by the World Anti-Doping Code, which put Team Kenya's participation in the *Olympic Games* in Rio in August at risk. However, the International Olympic Committee (IOC) decided not to ban the team as a whole and left it to the international federations governing each sport to decide whether Kenyans were eligible to compete. In the absence of a clear steer from the IOC, the individual federations decided to allow athletes from Kenya – as well as from Russia where similar allegations were made – to participate. In early August, the World Anti-Doping Agency removed Kenya from the list of non-compliant countries after parliament revised the relevant legislation, which was then signed into law by Kenyatta in June. Allegations of mismanagement and corruption continued to mar the Games, however, including claims that fewer kits were distributed to team members than those provided by the American International, Nike, while some coaches were left out of the Olympic Village and other 'joyriders' were accredited. Nevertheless, Kenya regained its status as having some of the world's best athletes, coming 15th in the medals table overall with 13 medals: six gold, six silver and one bronze. This reversed Team Kenya's poor performance in the 2012 Games, when they had sunk to 28th place (with 11 medals and only two gold) after being ranked 13th in the 2008 Games (with 14 medals including six gold).

Rwanda

Yolande Bouka

The ruling Rwandan Patriotic Front continued to dominate all levels of socio-political life. The regime, led by President Kagame, faced limited political opposition a year ahead of the 2017 presidential elections. Kagame reshuffled his cabinet for the first time in two years and made important staffing decisions in the security sector. Rwanda continued to outperform its EAC neighbours in the fields of public service delivery, but a severe drought challenged the government's response to a food security crisis in the eastern part of the country. Kagame's decision to run for a third term did not result in loss of support or a drop in foreign disbursements from key donors. Bilateral relations with both Burundi and France were strained, while those with Tanzania and the DRC improved. The economy remained resilient and economic growth declined slightly to 5.9% due to lower growth in agriculture, a contraction in manufacturing and construction, and a slowdown in public investment.

Domestic Politics

A year ahead of the *2017 presidential elections*, the ruling Rwandan Patriotic Front (RPF) continued to dominate all levels of socio-political life. The year began with

 | DOI 10.1163/9789004355910_037

President Paul Kagame announcing that he would stand for the 2017 presidential elections. This followed a successful campaign to amend the constitution allowing him to stand for a third term of seven years and potentially two additional five-year terms, drawing the criticism of donors. The USA was among the first to express its disappointment, arguing that the *constitutional amendment* "threatened democratic consolidation" in Rwanda. Kagame responded to critics by stating that his candidacy was a response to the 'popular will of Rwandans' concerned with security, continuity and development. The majority of *opposition parties* in Rwanda were deferential to the ruling party and supported Kagame's candidacy, with the exception of the Green Party. The opposition in exile vehemently opposed the move, but its lack of a foothold in Rwanda limited the impact of its protests. Finally, the state continued to keep a very tight control on the political space, with a poor *human rights* record and restrictions on freedom of speech and political competition, making any real challenge to Kagame's candidacy unlikely. As a result, most observers argued that everything remained the same and Kagame was likely to achieve an easy win in the upcoming presidential elections, as in 2003 and 2010 when he won 95% and 93% of the votes, respectively.

Kagame replaced ruling party members in key positions in his government. Some of these changes reflected the need to adjust personnel and institutions to bring them more into line with the country's development objectives, such as the merger of the Ministry of Trade and Industry with the Ministry for the EAC. However, some *cabinet changes* raised questions about the position of some of Kagame's previously closest allies in government. In August, the outspoken permanent representative to the UN, Ambassador Eugene Gasana, was recalled from New York following a cabinet meeting chaired by Kagame. Gasana was a close confidant of the president and had held the UN post since 2009. There was no government comment on the recall. Minister to the EAC Valentine Rugwabiza was appointed as the new envoy. In July, award winning Minister of Health Dr Agnes Binagwaho was sacked after five years in office. Her dismissal came at a time of growing concern in the health sector, including a rise in cases of malaria and alleged mismanagement of resources.

Important changes also took place in the *security* sector. In February, Major General Richard Rutatina was dismissed as head of military intelligence while Major General Jacques Musemakweli was promoted to army chief of staff. Major General Alex Kagame replaced Musemakweli as commander of the Republican Guard. Kagame's October cabinet reshuffle also included the removal of his close ally and longest-serving minister, Musa Fazil Harerimana as head of the Ministry of Internal Security. His responsibilities were transferred to the Justice portfolio at a time of growing concern about potential radicalism within the Muslim community in Rwanda. In recent years, Kagame had routinely made changes in senior military posts, perhaps indicating a lack of trust on his part. Since the end of the genocide, the military and security services had been key to maintaining the stability of the political elite and the primary tools of state coercion and enforcement of norms and securitisation of development. However, since the early 2000s, growing divisions in the RPF and the higher echelons of the armed forces had led to a number of defections later in the decade, notably some of the founding members of the Rwanda National Congress (RNC), who were former senior members of the RPF. Concerns of infiltration within the security apparatus had resulted in waves of arrests and internal purges in the army. At the end of March, the head of the Presidential Guard, Tom Byabagamba, and Brigadier General Frank Rusagara (rtd) were convicted of inciting rebellion and sentenced to 21 years in jail.

The *death of King Kigeli V*, Jean-Baptiste Ndahindurwa, in October in the USA, where he was living in exile, also sent ripples through the Rwandan community at home and abroad. He had been overthrown during the Hutu Revolution immediately before Rwanda's independence in 1962 and had lived in exile ever since. In the late 1990s, a group of Rwandans had called on him to participate in Rwanda's reconciliation process, but this had not been well received by the RPF-led government. Kagame had supported the return of the king as a private citizen, but cautioned him and his supporters against attempts "to disrupt the political order". King Kigeli chose to remain in exile. His death was followed by a lengthy legal battle about his burial site.

Human rights organisations such as AI and HRW continued to accuse the Rwandan government of closing the political space by harassing and intimidating political opponents. The RPF government often boasted of its widespread support among the population, but opposition parties remained constrained in their activities. The only registered opposition party challenging the RPF during the upcoming presidential election was the Green Party, which also challenged in the Supreme Court the constitutionality of the constitutional amendment on the extension of presidential terms. The party and its supporters were reportedly threatened. The chairperson of the opposition party 'Forces Démocratiques Unifiées' (FDU Inkingi), Victoire Ingabire, remained in prison serving her eight-year sentence for "endangering state security" and "promoting ethnic divisionism". In 2015, Ingabire had launched an appeal before the African Commission on Human and Peoples' Rights (ACHPR), a regional human rights body operating under the aegis of the AU, but to no avail. Her appeal hinged on the claim that the Rwanda government had violated her rights and freedoms under the Universal Declaration of Human Rights. Rwanda had signed the ACHPR Charter in 2013 but announced in March that it would withdraw from the clause that allowed individuals and NGOs to sue governments. The process would take 12 month to come into effect and in June the court declared that Rwanda's withdrawal had no bearing on pending cases.

Given the difficulties in operating freely in Rwanda, political dissidents chose to operate from outside the country. However, over past decades, the *opposition in exile* had been shown to be fractured and weak. In November, Thomas Nahimana, a controversial Catholic priest turned politician, attempted to return to Rwanda after having fled to France in 2005. His aim was to register a political party to participate in the 2017 presidential elections. It was unlikely that Nahimana would have been permitted to participate in the electoral process, given that some of his past public comments had been deemed to constitute 'genocide denial' and 'genocide ideology' by the Rwandan authorities and could result in jail time and permanent disqualification from competing for elected office if he were found guilty. Nahimana's attempt to return to Rwanda was thwarted when Kenyan authorities stopped him from proceeding to Kigali on the orders of Rwanda's Immigration Directorate. This not only frustrated his plans to run for office, but also created division among the opposition in exile. His decision to return to Rwanda for the 2017 election elicited mixed reactions from members of the political opposition platform composed of five leading parties in exile. The opposition abroad was further weakened by a split in the RNC in July, which came on the heels of on-going divisions between two of the group's founding members, Kayumba Nyamwasa and Theogène Rudasingwa. News of the break-up was welcomed within RPF ranks.

Despite Rwanda's unexpected official commitment to implementing most of the recommendations of the UN Universal Periodic Review to improve its human rights record, the RPF government remained heavily criticised for its lack of substantive progress and its continued *repression of the press* and civil society organisations, which limited the space for criticism and oversight of the government. While Rwanda's legal framework guaranteed media independence, the press remained tightly controlled. International organisations and local journalists reported that the regime routinely arrested, intimidated and jailed journalists for criticising the presidency or for reporting security issues and human rights abuses committed by the RPF. In February, for example, the Rwanda National Police detained two journalists who were preparing a report on tax evasion involving the country's main stone quarry. The media law amended in 2013 was supposed to expand the rights of journalists but it also created a regulatory body with powers to set conditions for both local and foreign media outlets to operate in Rwanda. It was reported that, since the May 2015 ouster and subsequent exile of its elected chairperson Fred Muvunyi, the Rwanda Media Commission, a self-regulatory body which sometimes intervened on journalists' behalf, had lost its independence and its ability to protect the freedom of the press.

Similarly, *NGOs* engaging in human rights monitoring were kept closely under the control of the state. Domestic NGOs focusing on human rights were limited due to internal conflict, self-censorship and, at times, government interference. In May, Epimack Kwokwo, a Congolese national and former executive secretary of the League for Human Rights in the Great Lakes Region ('Ligue des Droits de la Personne dans la Région des Grands Lacs'; LDGL), was expelled after the government refused to renew his work visa. When LDGL's registration was renewed, many members alleged that the government had manipulated its electoral board to insert pro-government members into the leadership. HRW also faced continued difficulties operating in the country after its 2015 and 2016 publications of reports on the unlawful detention of vulnerable people at the Gikondo Transit Centre. The government revoked its Memorandum of Understanding (MoU) with HRW and suspended its registration, forcing the head researcher to leave the country and fire the local staff. While the MoU was later signed, the organisation did not resume its operations, given its unregistered status.

Security remained a priority and the government welcomed news of the arrest of a few senior members of the Rwanda rebel group, 'Forces Démocratiques pour la Libération du Rwanda' (*FDLR*): in May, the Congolese authorities arrested the group's chief of staff, General Leopold Mujuambere, and, in October, Habyarimana Mucebo, the FDLR's intelligence chief, was captured in Rutshuru, north-eastern DRC. While Rwanda maintained that the FDLR continued to be a significant threat to its peace and security and alleged that the group had established a presence in Burundi since 2015, most analysts believed that the group's capabilities had weakened and, following recent offensives by both the Congolese and the UN, posed very little threat to Rwandan interests. Moreover, the arrests of key high-raking FDLR personnel might indicate a fragmentation of what was left of it. In January, a suspected Islamic State (IS)-affiliated imam was shot dead by police and a few alleged associates were arrested. Unlike its neighbours in the EAC, Rwanda did not participate in the AU Mission in Somalia (AMISOM), so analysts doubted that Rwanda might be a target, although it could be a potential recruiting ground for attacks elsewhere. In September, Rwanda tightened security after Rwandan military patrolling the Bugarama sector in the south-western district of Rusizi shot and killed two people suspected to be 'infiltrators' from Burundi.

The government continued to seek the extradition of *genocide suspects*. In previous years, a number of countries such as the Netherlands and Canada had readily extradited genocide suspects to Rwanda. In November, Canada deported Henri Jean-Claude Seyoboka, a former government soldier during the genocide, who had sought asylum there in 1996. Seyoboka was accused of failing to mention his military connections when he sought refugee status. In September, Leopold Munyakazi, an alleged key ideologue of the genocide, was extradited from the USA. Other countries declined returning suspects to Rwanda and opted to try them under universal jurisdiction. In July, a French court convicted two former local officials for their crimes during the genocide. Both men were sentenced to life in prison. In November, the Catholic Church in Rwanda issued an official apology for the role its clergy had played during the 1994 genocide.

Foreign Affairs

Relations with *Burundi* continued to be strained. Tensions between the two countries had emerged at the end of April 2015 when Burundi's President Pierre Nkurunziza announced his candidacy for a third term, despite being barred by from doing so by the constitution. Nkurunziza's candidacy led to a crisis marked by protests, political violence, an attempted coup and a mass exodus to neighbouring states. Burundi accused Rwanda of supporting coup plotters and the armed rebellion, while Rwanda accused Burundi of harbouring members of the FDLR. While Rwanda denied its involvement in the rebellion, a UN panel reported in February that Burundian refugees had been recruited at a refugee camp in eastern Rwanda in May and June 2015, and given two months' military training. Furthermore, a US Senate Foreign Relations Committee meeting held in the same month pointed to Rwanda's involvement in Burundi. Rwanda's Foreign Minister Louise Mushikiwabo responded by announcing that the government intended to expel Burundian refugees, citing security concerns. The refugees were never expelled, but tensions continued. In March, Rwanda's former ambassador to Belgium, Jacques Bihozagara, who had been arrested in Burundi at the end of 2015 on suspicion of espionage, died in prison. His death shocked the Rwandan government. Tensions between the two countries also had an economic impact. In August, Burundi, imposed a ban on food exports to Rwanda, citing food security concerns. This in turn resulted in an increase in prices of produce in Kigali, forcing Rwandan consumers to turn to more expensive Ugandan and Tanzanian food items.

There were slight improvements in the relationship between Rwanda and the *DRC*. In August, the DRC's President Joseph Kabila met Kagame in Rubavu to discuss security issues and the FDLR. In a joint communiqué, the two sides noted their intention to work in their mutual interests and agreed to strengthen bilateral cooperation, particularly in the areas of cross-border trade and energy. Rwanda's exports to the DRC represented 75% of its informal cross-border exports. Shortly thereafter, Rwanda re-joined ECCAS, of which the DRC is also a member. Rwanda had first joined in 1981, but had left citing the need to focus on its membership in the EAC and COMESA. The return repositioned the country to benefit economically, politically and diplomatically in the Central African region.

Since the 2015 presidential elections in *Tanzania*, relations with Rwanda had steadily improved. Diplomatic relations had been tense for over a decade, but worsened after Tanzania's former president Jakaya Kikwete had suggested that Rwanda engage in negotiations with the FDLR following years of efforts to eliminate the group. The suggestion angered the Rwandan government and relations did not improve as the Burundi crisis unfolded, when Rwanda and Tanzania took opposing stances on the issue, with Kikwete being seen a key ally of Burundian President Nkurunziza. After President John Magufuli replaced Kikwete, Rwanda and Tanzania renewed diplomatic and economic ties. In February, Kagame hosted Ambassador Tanzania's Foreign Minister Augustine Philip Mahiga at Village Urugwiro in Kigali. During the visit, Mahiga minimised the seriousness of Burundian claims that Rwanda was contributing to the instability in Burundi, marking a shift in Tanzania's position. In April, Magufuli visited Rwanda to join Kagame in the commemoration of the anniversary of the Rwandan genocide and, in May, Kigali hosted the first ever

Tanzania-Rwanda Trade Forum. The strengthening of economic ties helped smooth negotiations on Rwanda's future use of Tanzania's Central Corridor, a large railroad project set to connect Burundi, Rwanda, Uganda and the eastern DRC to Dar es Salaam port.

There was a slight improvement in relations with *South Africa.* Diplomatic relations had been severed in March 2014 after South Africa linked assassination attempts of opposition members on their soil to the Rwandan government and members of Rwanda's diplomatic corps in the country. South Africa then expelled three Rwandan diplomats and Rwanda reciprocated by expelling six South African diplomats. Prior to the incident, South Africa had been one of Rwanda's major trading partners and a common destination for Rwandan students and businesses, and with no functional consular services, trade and travel between the two nations dwindled. While both countries had agreed to resume normal relations in 2015, little progress was made until April when the diplomatic missions resumed operations, although tensions remained.

After a few years of normalisation, relations with *France* took a turn for the worse in October, when France announced that it was reopening an investigation into the shooting down in 1994 of the plane carrying the former Rwandan president Juvénal Habyarimana. A court sought the testimony of former General Kayumba Nyamwasa, living in exile in South Africa, who claimed that Kagame had been involved. Nyamwasa was the alleged target of an assassination attempt planned by the Rwandan government in 2014, which contributed to the lifting of diplomatic relations. Two weeks later, Rwanda accused 22 French officers of helping to plan and execute the Rwandan genocide. The National Commission for the Fight against Genocide accused these individuals of complicity and of having perpetrated acts of genocide. Among those accused by the Rwandan government was General Jacques Lanxade, special chief of staff to French President François Mitterrand from April 1989 to April 1991 and army chief of staff from April 1991 to September 1995. The report alleged that he was aware that the Habyarimana regime was planning a mass killing of Tutsi but continued to provide training and weapons. Unlike in 2006, the Rwandans did not expel the French ambassador, but relations between the two countries remained strained.

Rwanda continued to market itself as a *regional hub*, in which the completion of the new Kigali Convention Centre was instrumental. In May, the country hosted the World Economic Forum for the first time. In July, heads of states and their AU delegations descended on Kigali for the bi-annual AU summit. The summit concluded with a number of initiatives including plans for self-sustainable financing, a long-term mantra of the Rwandan government despite its heavy dependence on foreign assistance. During the summit, heads of state and government tasked Kagame with leading efforts to reform the AU Commission and the AU to make them more efficient.

Socioeconomic Developments

Rwanda's *development and economic performance* remained strong, with a GDP growth of 5.9% and with agriculture, services and industry all recording strong performances. This was less than the 6.5% growth recorded in 2015, partially due to lower growth in agriculture linked to drought, a contraction in manufacturing and construction, a slowdown in public investment, and a tightening of monetary conditions. Throughout the year, the government intensified its public commitment to private sector growth, infrastructure development and urbanisation. Rwanda's long-term development goals defined in a strategy entitled Vision 2020 (launched in 2000) sought to transform the country from a low-income agriculture-based economy to a middle-income country by 2020. In order to achieve these long-term development goals, the government had formulated a medium-term strategy. The second Economic Development and Poverty Reduction Strategy (EDPRS 2, introduced in 2013) had outlined an overarching goal of growth acceleration and poverty reduction through four thematic areas: economic transformation, rural development, productivity and youth employment, and accountable government.

The World Bank's *Doing Business Index* reported that Rwanda had improved its ranking to 56th out of 190 countries from 59th in 2015 (the 2015 published rank was 62nd, but 59th captures revised factors and changes in methodology). The government was aware that the still largely informal *private sector* had to play a bigger role in ensuring economic growth. In October, Rwanda Development Board chief executive Francis Gatare stated that Rwanda aimed "to harness the role of the private sector in accelerating economic growth to make the country even much easier and conducive in conducting business". The *agricultural sector* continued to be the driver behind Rwanda's economic growth, accounting for 35% of GDP and most of the workforce. However, the government also made strides in investing in and promoting the services sector, particularly tourism. *Tourism* earnings reached $ 400 m, up from $ 318 m in 2015, largely due to a 4% boost in visitors in line with the government's target. Rwanda demonstrated its ability to grow its tourism industry, enabled by a stable environment, wildlife attractions and drops in tourism in Kenya as a result of security concerns. Beyond tourism, the government aimed to improve its *manufacturing* industry. To support Rwanda's 'Domestic Market Recapturing Strategy', the government embarked on a 'Made in Rwanda' campaign, launched in February, to encourage consumption of locally produced goods. The government was also successful in attracting foreign investors. In December, Volkswagen announced that Rwanda would be part of its 'Volkswagon South Africa' (VWSA) expansion and opened an assembly plant in Rwanda.

At 6.4% in August, down from 6.9% in July, *inflation* stayed above the government target of 5%. The rising cost of food was partly attributed to Burundi's ban on food exports (see above). Another contributing factor to price increases was

Rwanda's widening current account deficit. The central bank attempted to alleviate the impact by intensifying its foreign exchange market interventions, which stemmed the rate of currency weakening.

A major obstacle to private investment and development of the private sector remained the country's *poor infrastructure* and lack of access to electricity. Only about 25% of the Rwandan population had access to electricity. The government aimed to increase the power grid capacity to 563 MW by 2018 and to cut the cost of electricity, which was much higher than in other EAC countries. In May, the government launched a power plant that used methane gas from Lake Kivu (shared with neighbouring DRC), officials said, adding 26 MW to the grid. This project had the potential to address economic, development and environmental issues as several studies cited by the government had raised the alarm about the risk of environmental disaster if methane build-up in the lake were not addressed. They suggested this project as a way to reduce methane in a controlled manner, via extraction or use in power generation. In November, the Rwanda Utilities Regulatory Authority announced the reduction of the cost of electricity for both financially constrained households and major industries. Other infrastructure improvements included plans announced in September for the building of a new Bugesera International Airport, located 40 km from Kigali, with capacity for 4.5 m passengers a year, compared with the approximately 1.6 m capacity of the current airport.

Rwanda met most MDGs and continued to improve *living standards*, as evidenced by a two-thirds drop in child mortality and the attainment of near-universal primary school enrolment. The government promoted its expanded maternity leave programme to guarantee working mothers full pay for three months. Under the previous scheme, mothers only received a full salary during the first half of their 12-week maternity leave and 20% in second half. In the *health* sector, national HIV/AIDS prevalence remained stable at 3% in 15–49-year-olds. Rwanda also achieved one of the highest national antiretroviral therapy (ART) coverage rates on the continent, reaching 78% of those eligible, based on the new WHO ART guidelines. The Ministry of Health launched a new campaign for communities to take the lead in the distribution of ART. Despite these achievements, several health challenges remained. These include *malnutrition*, with 38% of under-fives still stunted, and a rise in the incidence of malaria. These concerns were compounded by a severe *drought* that left 100,000 families in the Eastern province without sufficient food. While the government blamed climate change for the drought and ensuing famine, analysts cited poor agricultural policies and under-funding, which failed to address recurring food security issues in the region.

Seychelles

Anthoni van Nieuwkerk and Jon Abbink

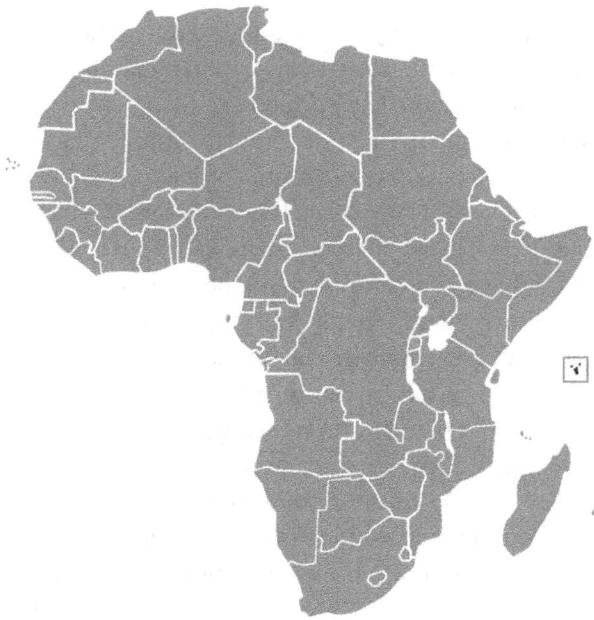

Seychelles saw a new president and political party take control of its legislature, overseeing the ongoing normalisation of a previously tense political setting. It maintained its HDI profile. Under the post-2015 SDG agenda, the country undertook to advance the need to integrate green and blue economy issues faced by island states, such as climatic vulnerabilities and ocean resource use. The economic recovery trajectory was maintained, particularly by keeping inflation in check. Prudent fiscal and monetary policies helped consolidate macroeconomic stability but vulnerabilities to external shocks were still substantial, as the economy continued to rely largely on two sectors: tourism and fisheries.

Domestic Politics

October saw the *swearing-in of President Danny Faure* of the ruling People's Party (Parti Lepep) to complete the five-year term of outgoing President James Michel,

 | DOI 10.1163/9789004355910_038

who resigned on 16 October. Michel's resignation followed the earlier *parliamentary elections* of September, when the opposition coalition 'Linyon Demokratik Seselwa' (LDS) took control of the legislature from the ruling Parti Lepep for the first time in the country's history. Faure had previously been vice president and a former finance minister and had served as a governor of the IMF, the World Bank and the AfDB.

After years of animosity and distrust between the political opposition and Michel and his long-ruling Parti Lepep (or People's Party, the name the Seychelles People's Progressive Front adopted in 1999), *amendments to electoral legislation*, already passed in December 2014, raised hopes of a more open political climate and fairer chances for the opposition in the 2016 elections. After more than two years of discussions in the Electoral Reform Forum, new, more transparent regulations for the functioning and financing of political parties and for a new permanent voter registration system had finally been introduced. The long-criticised media situation had also improved.

These notable changes in the political environment encouraged key *opposition leaders* to announce early in the year that they would participate in the September elections, in contrast to the 2011 election boycott by most opposition parties. Several new political parties entered the political landscape.

The Mo Ibrahim Index of African Governance placed Seychelles fourth out of 54 African nations on a broad range of *governance*-related criteria, up two places from 2015. The report suggested that island nations off the coast of Africa were performing better than most of their continental peers, with Mauritius taking the number one spot and Cabo Verde in third place. Seychelles recorded improvements in most of the four main index categories except for 'Safety and Rule of Law', where it slid to fifth place overall. Some of the sub-categories that showed the most improvement were in 'Rural Accountability and Transparency', 'Transparency of State-Owned Companies' and 'Women in the Judiciary'. The sub-categories that saw the most deterioration were 'Workplace Gender Equality', 'Human Rights Violations' and 'Political Violence'.

In September 2015, the government had approved a spatial framework for the future of Seychelles to 2040, providing policy across a range of topics to guide development, inform lower-tier policy, including land use plans, and inform decision making. The *Seychelles Strategic Plan* comprised an integrated national Strategic Plan, a Framework Plan for the most populous island (Mahé), and a detailed Masterplan for the capital city Victoria. The plan was the first strategic planning document of its kind in Seychelles. Alongside the National Development Strategy and Seychelles Sustainable Development Strategy, the plan would now act as the third pillar for decision-making. Throughout the year, the plan was used to determine planning applications by the Seychelles Planning Authority and was also used by ministries and external bodies to make strategic decisions and guide overall decision-making.

Despite demonstrable progress with democratic governance, several issues remained. Concerns over government *corruption* continued to focus on a lack of transparency in the privatisation and allocation of government-owned land, as well as Seychelles' facilitation of dubious international financial transactions. A 2011 report released by the auditor general had already revealed nearly two decades of dysfunctional government finances, including unprofessional record-keeping, illegal procedures and embezzlement. Seychelles received a score of 55 (where 100 equals 'very clean') in TI's Corruption Perceptions Index.

The government kept much of the nation's *media sector* under control including the daily 'Seychelles Nation' newspaper, the online resource Seychelles News Agency, and the only television station. Several newspapers were in circulation, but most showed partisan ties or were government-run. *Human rights* groups and other NGOs continued to operate. Workers had the right to strike, but only if all other arbitration procedures had been exhausted; foreign workers who went on strike were subject to deportation. Collective bargaining was rare in practice.

The *judiciary* was generally seen as independent. Because of the low number of legal professionals in Seychelles, the country had a good number of expatriate judges serving fixed-term contracts on the Supreme Court. In the legal sphere, Seychelles was one of the rare African countries to decriminalise gay sex (in May).

The Seychelles Court of Appeal tried several *Somali pirates* during the year. In November, it acquitted five suspects for lack of evidence and had them deported to Somalia. A second appeal case on piracy upheld the earlier sentence of eight Somalis to 14 years' imprisonment. This case concluded the nearly 20 Somali piracy cases brought to Seychelles courts since 2011. The country's prisons held 22 convicted Somali pirates serving their jail sentences.

Remaining security threats were in the main restricted to the drugs trade, but the US Office to Monitor and Combat Trafficking in Persons reported that Seychelles was a source country for children subjected to sex *trafficking* and a destination country for foreign men and women subjected to labour and sex trafficking, despite some government efforts to counter this.

Foreign Relations

Throughout the year, the government prioritised *bilateral cooperation with immediate neighbours* – Mauritius, Madagascar, Comoros and Reunion – in the areas of fisheries, tourism and health, as well as in combating drug trafficking and illegal fishing.

To rationalise its regional integration objectives, the country was developing a *regional integration strategy* to guide its policies and implementation under the various African regional economic communities and multilateral agreements. With bilateral and double taxation agreements with 29 countries, and being a services-based economy, Seychelles continued its open trade regime: 94% of imports entered at a zero tariff, with average tariffs of 4.6% on agricultural and 0.3% on non-agricultural products. Nonetheless, according to the Global Competitiveness Report (GCR) 2015–16, Seychelles' standing in terms of openness of the economy slipped to 97th out of 144 countries in 2015–16, compared with 92nd in 2014–15, and 80th in 2013–14, with 'access to finance' remaining the most significant obstacle. A poorly educated workforce and low work ethic were identified by the GCR as additional obstacles to economic performance.

Seychelles, as a *Small Island Developing State* (SIDS, recognised as a group at the UN Conference on Environment and Development of 1992) with limited natural resources but endowed with an exclusive economic zone (EEZ) of 1.3 m km² of ocean, pursued its national interests via a combination of the so-called 'green economy' and the 'oceans economy' or 'blue economy', in which the country was a self-declared pioneer. The concept was based on harnessing *local marine and related land resources* in a responsible, sustainable and connected manner as a mainstay of long-term development. In this context, the FAO director, José Graziano da Silva visited the Seychelles on 2–3 September for talks with then President James Michel. On 12–19 January, Michel was in Abu Dhabi to attend the Second Blue Economy Summit as well as the World Future Energy Summit of the Abu Dhabi Sustainability Week. On 28 September, he spoke at the Clinton Global Initiative Special Session on Sustainable Oceans, on the sidelines of the UN General Assembly's general debate.

High profile visitors to the Seychelles were rare but included UN Secretary-General *Ban Ki-moon*, who on 10–11 May visited the Supreme Court Annex, an infrastructure project constructed by UN Office on Drugs and Crime under its global maritime crime programme (for piracy trials).

Under the post-2015 SDG agenda, the country undertook to advance the need to further integrate green and blue economy issues faced by island states, such as climatic vulnerabilities and ocean resource use, pointing this out as an issue to monitor. With the help of the UN Department of Economic and Social Affairs, the country was one of the first SIDSs to pilot a 'vulnerability-resilience profile' to articulate sustainable development from an island's perspective.

It was expected that President Faure and his new cabinet and senior civil servants would review the country's foreign relations, with the aim of adjusting bilateral and multilateral relations to the benefit of the country's growth and development prospects.

Socioeconomic Developments

Seychelles' medium-term *growth outlook* was moderate, with an estimated GDP growth of 3.1%, projected to rise to 3.7% in 2017. The traditional tourism and fisheries sectors were expected to continue to drive growth in the medium term.

Prudent *fiscal and monetary policies* helped consolidate macroeconomic stability but vulnerabilities to external shocks were still substantial. Seychelles' fiscal policies in recent years resulted in an overall budget surplus of 1.4% of GDP, down from 1.9% in 2015 and 2.2% in 2014. GDP per capita reached $ 14,760, the highest in Africa. The Central Bank of Seychelles (CBS) pursued a tight monetary policy to keep *inflation* in check at -0.8%. The CBS used treasury bills as its main monetary policy instrument.

The strong *tourism* sector continued to buoy Seychelles' economy; visitor numbers rose by 9.8% to reach a record high of over 300,000 (compared with a local population of approximately 97,500). Overall, output was estimated to have increased by 4.4%, a robust pace, albeit moderating from the very rapid average annual expansion of about 6% from 2010 to 2015 (fuelled by construction and tourism-related activities).

High transport costs and the limited potential for economies of scale continued to make it difficult for Seychelles to compete through low prices, and it developed its focus on quality products instead, although the range was very limited: processed fish, refined petroleum, unfilleted frozen fish, cement, and animal meal and pellets.

Domestic demand was also boosted by an approximate 25% increase in the minimum wage, and 40% increase in the universal pension. Despite this, inflation remained subdued, helped by moderate global food and fuel prices. Strong import growth probably caused the *current account deficit* to increase slightly from 17.3% in 2015 to 17.7%, despite the solid growth of exports. The Seychelles rupee depreciated slightly, by 2.7% against the US dollar, while gross official reserves fell to $ 523 m in December, equivalent to about four months' imports.

The *national budget* was $ 605 m, with a 0.3% deficit. More spending was projected for education, health and 'anti-corruption efforts'. In December, Finance Minister Peter Larose announced a new tax on property owned by non-Seychellois citizens for the next budget year. Seychelles' macroeconomic reform programme, supported by an IMF Extended Fund Facility, anchored fiscal policy around running sizable primary surpluses (3% of GDP), and this was achieved, helped by recent strong revenue outturns offsetting the sharp increase in social spending. In its December report, the IMF complimented the government on its macro-economic performance but advised it to work more on reducing poverty and debt.

For the third quarter of the year, the *unemployment* rate was 4.5%, indicative of a tight labour market in line with generally robust recent economic conditions.

Rising labour demand was met by a surge in *expatriate workers*, whose numbers as measured by new and renewed Gainful Occupation Permits rose to 16,792, approximately doubling since 2014 to account for about a quarter of the total workforce, and employed mostly in construction and tourism.

The HDI measuring long-term progress in three basic dimensions of human development (a long and healthy life, access to knowledge, and a decent standard of living) gave the Seychelles a value of 0.782, placing it in the 'high human development' category and 63rd out of 188 countries and territories. Seychelles topped the Index as the highest-ranking African country, closely followed by Mauritius (64th), Algeria (83rd) and Tunisia (94th), all in the 'high human development' category.

Environmental issues were integrated into the national curriculum and across various important sectors, such as tourism, the country's coastal waters being home to giant tortoises and sea turtles, for example. The Seychelles Sustainable Development Strategy 2010–20 aimed at ensuring that the country would meet the needs of present and future generations regarding environmental management and climate change. Though a small island country, Seychelles claimed to be a leader in biodiversity maintenance, although it had a high degree of environmental vulnerability. The government reaffirmed its commitment to becoming a green economy by 2020.

Seychelles continued to face a number of *challenges*. Above all, the country suffered from insufficient economic diversification and vulnerability to external shocks, relying mainly on two sectors, tourism and fisheries (notably the export of canned tuna and prawns). One problem was the continued dependence on the import of food (90%), another the virtual absence of manufacturing. Development of the private sector would be paramount in achieving a more diversified economy. However, Seychelles' private sector required a more enabling environment to fully exploit its potentials and expand into new business areas. It was noteworthy that Seychelles made some progress in improving the *business environment*. The World Bank Doing Business report ranked Seychelles in 95th position, up nine places from 104th in 2014. Its *Internet* service, supplied by three government-regulated Internet service providers, was well-developed, boasting the 'highest speed' in Africa, and 57.9% of the population had access to it.

Several bottlenecks continued to stifle the business environment, however. These included the high cost of electricity and several impediments to establishing a new business, and growth would need to be made greener in order better to protect Seychelles' fragile natural environment from the adverse impacts of climate change.

Somalia

Jon Abbink

Developments in Somalia were marked by three main issues: serious drought and resulting famine conditions (again necessitating large-scale international humanitarian assistance); preparations for the upcoming presidential elections; and ongoing issues of security and governance. The 'promise' of recovery that had appeared on the horizon a couple of years before seemed to dissipate, despite the conclusion of the 'Somali Compact' in September 2013, the gradual retreat of the Islamist al-Shabaab terrorist movement, and the slow reconstitution of the Somali Federal Government (SFG). The SFG and the various self-declared regional political units continued to show they were hardly competent to govern or to set serious agendas for public policy. The country did not achieve major breakthroughs in either defeating al-Shabaab or expanding its institutional capacity and territorial grip on the country because of perennial centrifugal tendencies among (sub-)clan groups and self-serving elites. The elections for a new president, announced in 2015, were prepared, but were eventually delayed to 2017 because of logistical, political and security problems. Foreign donors and other international players (e.g., Qatar) tried to actively influence the process and remained important as sources of funding. Private business slowly expanded in all three regions of Somalia (Puntland,

 | DOI 10.1163/9789004355910_039

Somaliland and South-Central), bringing some economic growth despite the conditions of drought, major insecurity and uncertainty. Overseas remittances remained the largest source of income for the Somali population. The number of IDPS stayed in the range of hundreds of thousands, due to famine conditions, livelihood crises and insecurity.

Domestic Developments

The Somalia Federal Government (SFG) based in Mogadishu continued to rely strongly on security control by forces of the multinational peacekeeping mission, AMISOM, but the Somali National Army (SNA) played a growing role, despite its organisational weaknesses. Among the army's problems were the lack of stable and predictable salary payments, and (sub-)clan divisions. Abuse of the civilian population was also frequently reported, hindering acceptance and the cooperation of the populace with the federal government. The army of the self-declared independent Somaliland Republic was in a better state, reflecting a more stable and unified political entity, despite its continued lack of international recognition and unresolved political tensions. AMISOM, with contingents from Uganda, Burundi, Djibouti, Kenya, and Ethiopia (in total 22,126 troops), entered its tenth year and extended the 'secure territory' in Somalia. But the coordination and policy aims of the five national components were sometimes at odds, and some of its personnel were implicated in abuse and illicit sales of weapons and ammunition. The EU continued to cover most AMISOM funding (at around $ 21 m per month), but during the year there were some scuffles around the funding model (e.g., a cap on troop allowances), especially after the problems in Burundi, and to control rising costs. In October, Ethiopia withdrew 2,000 of its estimated 7,000 AMISOM troops.

Much of the year was dominated by preparations for the *federal elections*, which were not by universal suffrage or proportional or district representation but by clan structure and a delegation system. Puntland and South-Central Somalia were the two large regions where they were to be held, and their leaders met to discuss the scenario. On 3 April, SFG Prime Minister Omar Abdirashid Ali Sharmarke signed a new agreement in Garowe city with the authorities of Puntland on the electoral procedure for the upcoming presidential elections, the constitution of a new Upper House of parliament and on the 'Roadmap 2020'. The signing was witnessed by UN, AU, EU and IGAD representatives. One of the clauses was that the previously followed but contested '4.5 formula' – with most members of parliament to be selected from the four large clan families and the rest from the smaller clans and groups – would no longer be followed after the next elections (for 2020), where a 'one person, one vote' principle would be implemented. The autonomy of Puntland within the federal union was confirmed.

In October, the complicated electoral process began, with three phases: selection of the 54 members of the Upper House (the first ever), the Lower House, and the president (who would nominate the prime minister). Each regional administration (Puntland, Southwest State, Juba and Hiraan-Shabelle) nominated its members of the federal Upper House, reflecting a careful representation on the basis of clans. Some Somalilanders event sent delegates, but without the consent of the Somaliland government. The prescribed constitutional quota of 30% female candidates was not reached in any region, but about 24% of those ultimately chosen in November were women. For the 242-member Lower House (the 'House of the People') the representatives were selected along clan lines by a 14,025-member electoral college chosen by clan elders. The various candidates and coteries jockeyed for position via a series of alternative strategies ranging from discussions and persuasion to lobbying and 'buying' or bribing future voters. This led some observers to speak of the process as not an 'election' but a 'selection', if not an outright 'buying' of candidates. Nevertheless, the process established a new mode of practising federalism in the country, based on new federal units that could each deliver their own representatives: no longer was everything decided in Mogadishu. All this did not lead, however, to a resolution of the tensions and grievances between certain clans, e.g. the Abgaal(-Hawiye) and their long hostility toward the SFG.

The inauguration of the *two chambers of parliament* for a four-year term finally took place on 24 December, in the presence AU and AMISOM representatives and various diplomatic corps members. It was greeted with cautious hope, despite the non-transparent 'vote-buying' and jostling, corruption and intimidation, based (again) on clan-lines, elite interests and money flows. There was international and donor country criticism but also an air of acceptance of the perennially complex and opportunist nature of Somali politics. The third stage in the process, the actual *presidential elections*, was delayed to early 2017.

As to governance, the SFG made a little *progress in institution building*, but again nothing substantial, as internal clan-based and regional rivalries, personal ambitions, and lack of accountability and financial transparency kept causing problems. The SFG and the various 'federal member states' did not make much headway on the constitutional regulation of their powers of authority, as agreed upon in the 2013 'Somali Compact' between the SFG and the international (donor) community. By year's end, the latter as usual pressed for results and 'solutions', instead of allowing for time and experimentation with the new political dispensation.

The radical-Islamist 'Harakat al-Shabaab al-Mujahiddiin' (*al-Shabaab*) remained active as an insurgent movement with no positive agenda and perpetrated a continuous string of 'suicide bomber' and mortar attacks on hotels, state offices, AMISOM and government personnel, army posts and civilians. Under its 'emir' Ahmed Omar (alias Abu Ubaydah), its leader since late 2014, no policy changes were noted. The movement continued to avoid all-out battles, which they knew they would lose.

Through their intimidating and violent tactics, their foreign funding (including from some Somali diaspora circles) and their economic and networking activities, they retained an influence well beyond their numerical strength as an organised military movement. This was apparent in the fact that, in some areas of rural Somalia, notably in the Gedo region, al-Shabaab even had some grudging support. It could play on continuing (sub-)clan rivalries in various areas, such as between the Hawiye and the Marehan-Darod in Gedo and Juba, and between Habr Gidir-Hawiye and Bimaal-Dir in the 'Southwest State' and pose as a mediator. In fact, the countryside remained the sector of Somali society that was most neglected by both federal authorities and donors, making it vulnerable to anyone offering a perceived advantage or income. In the second part of the year, when another (predicted) major drought was nearing, al-Shabaab positioned itself as a service provider to get food relief to needy rural people. In addition, the movement pursued its major economic interests in the illicit trade in charcoal, wildlife products and weapons, and also levied taxes on the rural transport of goods.

Al-Shabaab was involved in a steady stream of *violent actions*, bombings and hit-and-run attacks, with many hundreds of deaths and massive destruction of property. On 15 January, a large-scale assault on an AMISOM base in El Adde, near the Kenyan border, led to the killing of about 200 mostly Kenyan soldiers. On 21 January, there was an attack on Lido Beach in Mogadishu, a popular spot, with restaurants visited by townspeople, and at least 20 civilians were killed. On 28 February, 14 people were killed and many more wounded in a terror attack on a hotel in Mogadishu. On 9 June, several hundred al-Shabaab militants attacked an Ethiopian base near Halgan town with a massive suicide car bomb crashing through the gate and then sustained back-up gunfire. They inflicted a dozen casualties, but failed to capture the base. Over 100 militants were reportedly killed. Also in June, al-Shabaab attacked the base in Lego, in Lower Shabelle region, killing dozens of soldiers and seizing military equipment. In late August, the AMISOM base at Janale, south-east of Mogadishu, was targeted in similar fashion, and dozens of soldiers were killed. On 15 November, al-Shabaab retook the town of Tyeglow in west Bakool region, killing over 20 Somali army troops and injuring dozens more. The capital Mogadishu was also hit regularly, with car bomb attacks claiming dozens of victims, as on 26 November, when 11 people were killed and a score seriously injured.

The USA maintained its presence in the region and carried out a number of strikes aimed at al-Shabaab leaders, such as on 27 May, just after an al-Shabaab attack on a Mogadishu hotel, when a top leader and attack strategist, Abdullahi Haji Da'ud, was killed in an airstrike. On the same day, Somali special forces in Jubaland took out a group of 16 armed militants, including Mohamed Ali 'Dulyadin', held responsible for the 2015 Garissa University massacre in Kenya.

The instability of the SFG led to widely known embarrassments, as when the Somalia National Army (SNA) withdrew from Merca town on 12 July, allegedly because SNA soldiers' salaries remained unpaid. This allowed al-Shabaab to move in again.

The AMISOM forces and the Somali national army had control of most towns and cities and main roads, extending their reach, but were vulnerable to massive hit-and-run attacks on bases and did not succeed in dislodging al-Shabaab groups from the forested areas in the riverine South and near the Kenyan border.

While al-Shabaab's hold on territory in South-central Somalia generally weakened during the year, its presence strengthened in Puntland, where al-Shabaab-linked groups were already active in the 'Afmadow and 'Al Miskaal mountain regions near Bossaso. Puntland's government was considered weak, understaffed and ill-paid, as it received much less financial and army training support from donor countries than the SFG, and its intelligence services were infiltrated by former al-Shabaab members. Puntland also provided a location closer to Yemen and thus could facilitate al-Shabaab financial and arms trafficking links with the al-Qaida groups operating there. These well-funded and well-armed groups were seen as a source of more advanced arms, including ATGMs (anti-tank guided missiles). The existing links between the two movements (arms, propaganda, funds, security training and media productions) were set to expand. Another reason for al-Shabaab to expand in Puntland was probably to prevent the emergence in Somalia of the 'Islamic State' (IS), with which the movement had an ambivalent relationship. Pro-IS fighters were already present in Somalia, however, and one contingent briefly seized the small coastal town of Qandala, east of Bossaso, on 26 October, retreating into the 'Afmadow mountains when a Puntland army force approached. In April, a prominent al-Shabaab convert to IS, Abdulqadir Mumin – before 2010 a radical Islamist preacher in London and Leicester, who had been tolerated by the British authorities – appeared in an IS propaganda video, showing him in a small training camp with supporters, brandishing assault rifles, grenade launchers and machine guns. Al-Shabaab's 'security branch', the 'Amniyat', was reported to have eliminated various 'defectors' to IS, as they wanted to keep the Somali monopoly on radical Islamism for themselves, and also for business reasons. Al-Shabaab also gained some influence elsewhere, in Mudug and Galgaduud, thus making up for their losses. One aim was to regain access to sea ports.

There was *no political rapprochement at all between the SFG and al-Shabaab*, due mainly to the latter's lack of interest.

Other armed groups, such as political and clan militias, also perpetrated violence, in regional power conflicts or clan and business rivalries, which claimed hundreds of victims. Much of the violence occurred on and near the main roads.

Respect for *political and civil rights* remained precarious, and the media and NGOs were often under threat. Journalists were regularly the targets of assassination attempts (and three were killed), mostly by al-Shabaab but some by unknown assailants, and pro-government circles did not escape scot-free. More than a dozen journalists were arrested. Media outlets and newspapers were also regularly closed down, including the Mogadishu-based 'Xog Ogaal' newspaper on 15 October, whose editor was arrested. On 23 June, Puntland police raided the offices of 'Radio Daljir' and silenced its broadcasts, giving as the reason its interview with anti-government rebel Abdisamad Mohamed Galan, a former regional governor.

In Somaliland, media and civil society freedoms also came under more pressure in the wake of a deteriorating democratic atmosphere. On 24 March, for example, the daily 'Codka Shacabka' (Voice of the People) was closed down, and several journalists were arrested during the year.

In the *Somaliland-Puntland* border area, the military standoff on the disputed territories of 'Ayn, East Sanaag and Sool (in Somaliland) continued, with no political resolution in sight.

On the *piracy* front, there were still some incidents (some 15–16) by year's end, but no major hijackings; the new targets were smaller foreign fishing boats. The reduction was due to the international anti-piracy mission patrolling Somali waters, not to a decline in the capacity of (potential) pirates: the 'infrastructure' of piracy operations still existed. Over the year, about 39 crew members from international vessels continued to be held hostage in Somalia, 26 of whom (from the Taiwanese ship FV Naham 3) were finally released on 22 October, after almost five years of captivity.

Foreign Affairs

The international community's diplomatic and humanitarian involvement with Somalia remained substantial, with UN agencies, the AU, donor countries and various aid organisations trying to provide political, military and humanitarian support and to enhance stability in the region.

Relations with neighbouring countries were stable although the *Kenyan presence in Somalia*, as part of the AMISOM forces, repeatedly generated controversy as a result of continued reports of Kenyan troops' harsh practices and involvement in illicit activities. Kenya also announced its decision to close down the huge Dadaab refugee camp in northern Kenya, implying a gradual (forced) return of the Somali refugees there.

Saudi Arabia cosied up to the SFG in order to undercut Iran's influence in the region. It offered an immediate aid package of $ 50 m if Somalia would cut ties with Iran, which the SFG did on 7 January, officially declaring that there was, of course, 'no link' between the two events.

Somalia, as a 'problem child' in Africa, was frequently visited by members of the international donor community concerned with issues of security, political reforms and development, and there were a number of other prominent *foreign visitors*.

On 13 March, the new head of the UN Assistance Mission in Somalia, Michael Keating, came to Mogadishu on 18 January, and visited Somaliland on 13 March to meet the leadership. In May, Turkish President Recep Tayyip Erdoğan paid a visit, aiming to underline Turkey's 'anti-colonial' support, cement a durable alliance and further business connections. He opened Turkey's large new embassy and signed bilateral agreements. On 2 June, UK Foreign Minister Philip Hammond met with the Somali prime minister and president and discussed security issues, UK financial support and the electoral process. The UK was the only European country that maintained an embassy in Mogadishu. On 26 August, a Japan-Somalia foreign ministers' meeting took place in Nairobi (Kenya) between Japanese Minister for Foreign Affairs Fumio Kishida, and Abdisalam Hadlie Omar, his Somali counterpart. On 13 September, Kenya's President Uhuru Kenyatta was in Mogadishu for the 28th extraordinary summit of IGAD.

The leaders of Puntland and the SFG exchanged visits regularly and also visited Ethiopian authorities in Addis Ababa several times, reflecting their close security cooperation.

There was no movement towards any international recognition of the self-declared independent *Somaliland Republic*.

The *SFG President Hassan Sheikh Mohamud made several foreign visits*. He was in Djibouti on 28–29 February but he cut his visit short following the terrorist attack by al Shabaab on a hotel in Mogadishu and also postponed a visit to Sweden, planned for March. He was in Kenya on 6–7 June to tour the Dadaab refugee camp (which the Kenyan authorities intended to close in stages) and for talks with his Kenyan counterpart. In August, he was in Jijiga (Ethiopia) to meet the Ethiopian Somali Region's president and, on 22 August, he travelled to Abu Dhabi (UAE) for talks on economic, security and political cooperation. In June, the president reportedly visited Israel (which does not have diplomatic relations with Somalia) and met in Tel Aviv with Israeli government officials. Not much publicity was given to the visit, which was neither confirmed nor denied by either country, but the president allegedly met with Israeli Prime Minister Benjamin Netanyahu. In April, the president was in Washington, DC, and gave a talk at the US Institute of Peace.

In April, SFG Prime Minister Omar Abdirashid Shermarke visited Moscow for talks on security matters, trade and cooperation.

On 19 May, representatives of 15 member countries on the UNSC paid a one-day visit to Somalia to urge the government to implement the country's 2016 electoral model.

Socioeconomic Developments

The main threats to orderly economic development were *drought and political insecurity*. In the early months of the year, after failing rains in the previous season, livestock herds were in steep decline across all three parts of Somalia, leading to emergency situations and the need for humanitarian aid for several hundred thousand people. Migratory drift towards the towns started and relief agencies appealed for massive aid, projecting that 3.7 m people would be in need by July. Also, in Somaliland, an unprecedented 200,000 people were estimated to be in need of humanitarian aid due to the severe drought, which affected livestock herding and cultivation and led to significant livestock deaths and thousands of people moving to cities and seeking alternative resources.

The three Somali regions had *no unified economic or development policy* and lacked efficient statistical and data-gathering services, but the World Bank estimated that the GDP of SFG-controlled Somalia (i.e., including Puntland) reached about $ 6.2 bn, with GDP per capita at $ 450 and an estimated poverty headcount rate of 51.6 %.

Statistical information on the country was incomplete and rather unreliable, so estimates had to be used again. *Exports* accounted for about 14% of the GDP of the SFG, and the large *trade deficit*, with 60% more imports than exports, was off-set by the usual flow of remittances from Somalis overseas (some $ 1.3 bn) and by international aid funds. This confirmed the country's continued strong dependency – amounting to 'life support' status – on outside resources, and its lack of a strong domestic economic base. Government *tax-generating capacity* did expand to about $ 120 m, but was still mainly based on trade taxes, despite an ambitious new financial plan by the authorities to implement indirect taxation alongside trade taxes. Pressure from donors played a role, but the target to generate about 64% of the national budget from domestic sources seemed unrealistic. Institution-building by the SFG and the Puntland authorities continued at a very slow pace and made no real breakthroughs.

Corruption remained alarmingly high in the entire country, although much less so in Somaliland. It was prevalent in government institutions, the private sector and the aid organisations, who worked with or were dependent on, for instance, 'gate-keepers' around IDP settlements and famine victim communities, who asked for bribes. Again, Somalia topped the list of TI's Corruption Perception Index as the most corrupt country in SSA.

The *SFG budget* was $ 246.3 m, a 24% increase on 2015, with a whopping 85% of the total spending allocated to the administrative and security sectors. Economic and social services sectors accounted for only about 10%. The declared aim was to cover 64% of the budget from domestic revenues (especially new sales taxes and VAT), and the rest from foreign donors.

The *budget of Somaliland* was $ 295 m, an increase of 13% compared with 2015. The security sector and 'the rule of law' were prioritised, with infrastructure (road building and water management) in second place. On 5 September, it was announced that Dubai Ports World (DP-World) had won a 30-year concession to run the port of Berbera in a joint venture with the Somaliland government.

The *humanitarian situation* remained drastic, with an estimated 45% (4.9 m people of the 11 m total population) suffering from drought and food insecurity (in fact, famine conditions) and in need of life-saving and livelihood support. Some 1.5 m people were living as IDPs in camps, mostly near the big towns. Another approximately 920,000 people were refugees in neighbouring countries (Ethiopia, Kenya and Yemen). A flow of Yemeni refugees to Somalia – a total of around 35,000 – continued throughout the year. International organisations such as the International Committee of the Red Cross, Médecins Sans Frontières, the Swedish SIDA, and the WFP continued to provide massive assistance to the refugees, IDPS and other Somalis in need with cash relief, food-for-work programmes, healthcare, water and sanitation services, seeds and seedlings provision, medical aid, livestock disease treatment, etc. Aid per capita in Somalia was estimated at $ 97, but the aid agencies did not solve any structural problems and were said by some local NGOs and activists even to perpetuate the misery.

The *education* situation remained dire, with 1.7 m school-age children (about half) still out of school and the quality of education provided low.

Livelihoods remained very precarious due to conflict, and unsettled economic and property issues, precarious environmental conditions and unresolved disputes over land and resource access, most of them lingering on since the years of civil war.

In general, *social conditions* were unsettled, with high levels of crime, insecurity and *gender-based violence* in an inveterate patriarchal society, with young women, widows and even married women quite vulnerable to abuse.

In the midst of human misery, *environmental issues* were not high on the agenda but the destruction of the country's forest and wood resources steadily continued, as did largely unchecked pollution, water contamination, overgrazing and soil erosion. In March, the SFG established an 'environment wing' within the Prime Minister's Office with support from UNDP, but environmental policy was still in its in infancy.

South Sudan

Daniel Large

The year began with efforts to form a transitional government under the terms of the August 2015 peace agreement. Riek Machar, former vice president turned rebel leader, returned to Juba in April, accompanied by a protection force, to be sworn in as first vice president of South Sudan's so-called Transitional Government of National Unity. This was short-lived. In July, government forces attacked and drove Machar and his forces out of Juba. Machar was replaced by Taban Deng Gai in a reshuffled Transitional Government of National Unity. Conflict spread, with devastating humanitarian consequences and an exodus of South Sudanese refugees to neighbouring countries. By the end of the year, as the conflict entered its fourth year following the eruption of violence in December 2013, the context in South Sudan was much changed from when the peace agreement had been signed in August 2015: the conflict had expanded, the opposition was fragmented, the economic crisis was severe, famine loomed and ethnic hate speech ran at alarming levels. The launch of a National Dialogue in December by President Kiir appeared highly unlikely to address such issues. Instead, the government seemed intent on pursuing a military solution amidst a widening war. While the August 2015 peace agreement continued to be formally in place, in practice it had collapsed.

 | DOI 10.1163/9789004355910_040

Domestic Politics

The year started with efforts to form a *Transitional Government of National Unity* (TGoNU) as prescribed by the August 2015 Agreement on the Resolution of Conflict in South Sudan (ARCISS). While these dominated attention, outside Juba fighting spread in western Equatoria, Bahr el Ghazal and elsewhere, despite a ceasefire. The efforts to form a TGoNU became deadlocked, meaning the original deadline of 22 January was missed. Meanwhile, attempts to promote unity in the Sudan People's Liberation Movement (SPLM) also failed. The government part of the *SPLM* held an Extraordinary National Convention in January at which President Salva Kiir announced the reunification of the party. The main SPLM-in Opposition (SPLM-IO) boycotted the event, but its chief negotiator, Taban Deng Gai, attended the opening and closing sessions.

Amidst mutual blame, and token efforts by the government to redeploy Sudan People's Liberation Army (SPLA) forces outside Juba in line with the terms of the agreement, further steps were taken to form a TGoNU. In February, James Wani Igga, the former vice president, was sworn in by President Kiir to his new position as second vice president, and Riek Machar was reappointed as first vice president despite not being in Juba. Meanwhile, in March, SPLA General Chief of Staff Paul Malong Awan reshuffled the top command of the army and Kiir fired Minister for Foreign Affairs and International Cooperation Barnaba Marial Benjamin, who was replaced by Deng Alor Kuol.

Following advance deployment of about 1,370 *SPLA-IO* troops, and after protracted uncertainty and dispute about the manner of his return, notably regarding security, Machar finally returned to Juba in April and was duly sworn in as first vice president of the TGoNU. The resulting presence of SPLA-IO forces within Juba predictably resulted in tensions between opposition and government forces. The security terms of the ARCISS had, in effect, positioned opposition forces in close proximity to government forces within the capital.

The *newly formed TGoNU* finally held its first cabinet meeting on 6 May. New Minister of Water Resources and Irrigation Mabior Garang de Mabior was forced by Kiir to leave the meeting for being inappropriately dressed. A far more serious and violent *expulsion* – that of Machar and his SPLA-IO forces from Juba – occurred not long afterwards. On 8 July, the eve of the fifth anniversary of South Sudanese independence, *heavy fighting* erupted in Juba between SPLA and SPLA-IO forces. It started when Machar was meeting Kiir inside the Presidential Palace in Juba, and quickly spread. There was a relative lull on 9 July, South Sudan's fifth Independence Day, but fighting resumed as the SPLA used heavy artillery, tanks and helicopter gunships to attack opposition forces in parts of Juba. There was fighting close to UN bases, amidst a clampdown on UN movements and attacks on UN Mission in South Sudan (UNMISS) personnel. Fighting continued until 11 July, when a ceasefire was announced. *Machar fled* under fire through Equatoria and eventually crossed into Garamba Park in the neighbouring DRC.

While the causes and motivations were disputed, key military figures in the SPLA had strongly opposed implementation of the ARCISS and appeared to be attempting a military solution. The Juba fighting had destructive consequences, and not just within Juba. As SPLA-IO fighters fled from the capital, violence rippled out to other parts of South Sudan and the humanitarian situation deteriorated precipitously.

Following the fighting, *Taban Deng Gai*, the former SPLM-IO chief negotiator and governor of Unity State, was appointed first vice president on 26 July, after Machar failed to return to Juba by 23 July. Machar denounced the move as a 'conspiracy' to overthrow him. Soon afterwards, Kiir sacked ministers allied to Machar (the ministers of the interior, petroleum, higher education, labour, water, and lands and housing) and replaced them with ministers linked to the new vice president.

The question of the *legitimacy of Taban Deng's new position* and whether it was consistent with the ARCISS was initially controversial within and outside South Sudan. The SPLM/A-IO Political Bureau stated from Khartoum that South Sudan had slid "into another round of civil war" and "that the people of South Sudan should brace for long-term popular armed resistance led by the SPLM/SPLA(IO)" against the Kiir government. After criticising Taban Deng's appointment as going against the 2015 agreement, the chairman of the Joint Monitoring and Evaluation Commission (JMEC), Festus Mogae, eventually said they supported his appointment; there was no choice.

After July, *opposition forces denounced Kiir* for abrogating the ARCISS by attacking Machar and his forces in Juba. Many declared the agreement 'dead'. A meeting of opposition groups held in Nairobi (Kenya) in August challenged government claims that the ARCISS could be implemented, and declared the overthrow of Kiir's government as its ultimate objective. The SPLM/A-IO Political Bureau called for a reorganisation of its forces in order to "wage a popular armed resistance against the authoritarian and fascist regime of President Salva Kiir in order to bring peace, freedom, democracy and the rule of law in the country".

There was *further fragmentation of opposition forces* amidst fluid, militarised politics and a series of defections to the opposition, and from the opposition to the government. In September, the former minister of agriculture, Lam Akol, formed a *new rebel faction*, the National Democratic Movement, as an umbrella grouping of armed and unarmed opposition groups. The SPLM-Democratic Change Party, the party he had previously founded, elected Onyoti Adigo, previously minority leader in the national legislative assembly, as its new leader.

While the events in Juba around the creation, destruction and re-creation of a TGoNU, and interest in and concern at ARCISS implementation, dominated attention, *conflict proliferated throughout the country*. Many parts of South Sudan experienced hostilities and inter-communal violence. There were attacks on UN-protected

IDP camps, as in February, when Dinka men in SPLA uniforms attacked a base hosting Nuer and Shilluk IDPs in Malakal, killing at least 30 and burning shelters. There were regular accusations that the August 2015 deal had been broken through military action by government and opposition forces, with periodic heavy fighting in parts of greater Upper Nile, including around Malakal. Much of the fighting occurred in Bahr el Ghazal and greater Equatoria. In June, clashes between the SPLA and armed groups around Wau, in western Bahr el Ghazal State, forced thousands of civilians to flee the area. A state of emergency was declared in Wau, and Kiir replaced Governor Elias Waya Nyipuoch, who had criticised SPLA abuses, with Andrea Mayar Achok. Areas of former Central and Western Equatoria also *saw deepening conflict.* This partly involved pre-existing grievances but was further driven by new SPLM/A-IO military movements.

After July, *Machar was militarily and politically weakened.* In late November, a meeting in Khartoum of the SPLM/A-IO saw Henry Odwar, an Equatorian, appointed deputy commander in chief, and Tingo Peter, a Fertit, SPLM/A-IO secretary general. A union between SPLM/A-IO and Equatorian groups was formed, with General Martin Kenyi, an Equatorian, in charge. The government and the SPLA proceeded to *crackdown on local communities* in greater Equatoria on the grounds they were supporting the rebels. Kiir made a public threat to assume personal military command in the field of the fight against Equatorian militias. Such SPLA counterinsurgency operations, including in Yei, predictably only worsened grievances, fuelling a cycle of *more entrenched violence*, civilian casualties and deaths. What made this trend worrying was the more explicitly ethnic edge to much of it. The targeting of civilian transport and the killing of Dinka civilians in Equatoria triggered calls for revenge Dinka attacks on Equatorian civilians.

Even before the July violence, the *creation of 28 states* via unilateral presidential decree in October 2015 *meant further political disruption* amidst a proliferation of political administrative units. In January, the Shilluk unseated their 'reth', or king, Kwongo Dak Padiet, who was perceived as aligned with the government and accused of supporting the creation of the 28 states. The redivision of South Sudan continued to be a divisive political issue throughout the year. This perceived violation of the ARCISS and opposition to the Jieng [Dinka] Council of Elders was one factor behind the resignation of an SPLA deputy chief of general staff, the Bul Nuer leader Lieutenant General Bapiny Mantuil Wichjang, in October.

On 14 December, Kiir launched a process of *'National Dialogue'*, ostensibly aimed "for forgiveness", appointing members to a new National Dialogue Committee. The initiative was predictably condemned as bogus by Machar and other opposition parties.

The more politicised and polarised atmosphere saw a further deterioration in the environment for *human rights* and civil society. South Sudan's Legislative Assembly passed a controversial bill in February, which was duly signed into law by President

Kiir, that gave the government sweeping powers to regulate, shut down, and seize assets of non-governmental and civil society organisations based on declarations or activities deemed political. Civil society actors were also harassed and threatened by agents of the Internal Security Bureau of South Sudan's National Security Service under Akol Koor. Shortly before a visit to Juba by a UNSC delegation in September, the government threatened to shut down or deny registration to a number of civil society organisations.

It was a bad year for South Sudan's *media*. The country ranked 140th out of 180 on the World Press Freedom Index, and fifth in the list of countries where most journalists were killed with impunity, according to the Global Impunity Index compiled by the Committee to Protect Journalists. Armed attacks against, and intimidation of, journalists and newspapers continued amidst an intensified atmosphere of repression. In March, Joseph Afandi, a writer with the Arabic daily 'Al-Tabeer' was found beaten and tortured in a Juba cemetery after being abducted by security forces. In October, another journalist, Malek Bol, was abducted and tortured. In July, the veteran journalist and editor of the 'Juba Monitor', Alfred Taban, was arrested and detained after publishing an op-ed calling for the replacement of the South Sudanese leadership. His newspaper was shut down briefly following his arrest. Another newspaper, 'The Nation Mirror', was shut down indefinitely in September after it ran a front-page story about a report by 'The Sentry', an initiative of George Clooney and John Prendergast's 'Enough' project, detailing corruption by South Sudan's ruling elite. The authorities closed a radio station in November and expelled an American journalist in December.

Beyond traditional media, hate speech and incitement to violence mobilised by *social media* and involving the global diaspora increased. In October, the government disproved rumours of Kiir's death. These had raised fears about conflict between competing power factions over the future of the presidency. In response to these rumours, the government said it could be forced to disconnect social media and other online media that had been circulating 'false information' about the president's health.

Foreign Affairs

South Sudan's relations with *Sudan* continued in a stop-start pattern: signs of promised progress on key areas were frequently called into doubt before further agreements were made. The result was fluid relations reflecting unresolved underlying tensions between the two countries. In February, Sudan's President Omar al-Bashir affirmed that river transport with South Sudan, halted for four years over security concerns, would resume. Both governments signed a number of security arrangements in June, including immediate re-deployment of joint military forces along the Safe Demilitarized Border Zone, a plan to stop supporting and harbouring rebels, and the opening of crossing points. They also agreed to the redeployment of forces in Abyei during a meeting of their Joint Political and Security Mechanism. After denying that there were any Sudanese rebels on its territory, in October South Sudan gave them an ultimatum to leave. In November, Kiir and al-Bashir met during the African-Arab summit in Malabo (Equatorial Guinea), and agreed on open borders between their countries.

Both the government of South Sudan and the SPLM-IO undertook *diplomatic visits abroad* as part of efforts to support and promote their different positions on the ARCISS before and after July. *Riek Machar* travelled frequently before July: he met Uganda's President Yoweri Museveni in January, Egypt's President Abdel Fattah al-Sisi in February in Cairo, and South African President Jacob Zuma and Kenya's President Uhuru Kenyatta in March. After he fled Juba in July, travel became harder as the government of South Sudan sought to apply pressure on him through regional partners.

The new first vice president, *Taban Deng*, fronted efforts to garner support for South Sudan's newly constituted government after July, leading delegations to Khartoum for talks with al-Bashir. He made a number of visits further afield, including to the USA to address the 71st session of the UN General Assembly in New York. As part of an apparent effort to reposition American support for the new TGoNU, US Ambassador to the UN Samantha Power, and US National Security Advisor Susan Rice held talks with Taban Deng in September and October. Meanwhile, Deng Alor met *China*'s Foreign Minister Wang Yi in Beijing in late July and, in a sign of enhanced relations between Juba and Cairo, South Sudan's Minister of Water Resources and Irrigation Sophia Pal Gai met her Egyptian counterpart in November.

South Sudan's relations with *Ethiopia* were complicated. A cross-border raid attributed to Murle tribesmen in April left more than 200 Nuer dead in the Gambela region of western Ethiopia. Ethiopian troops briefly deployed to Boma state in South Sudan to secure the return of abducted children. Relations with Ethiopia became strained after July, when Addis Ababa supported international pressure to deploy additional UNMISS peacekeepers in Juba and there were calls for Ethiopian troops to lead such a Rapid Protection Force. However, relations improved over mutual security concerns. Ethiopia declared Machar would not be welcome and Taban Deng visited Addis Ababa in September for talks with Prime Minister Hailemariam Dessalegn. In October, President Kiir and Hailemariam signed an MoU on trade, borders and military cooperation during a visit to Juba by the Ethiopian Prime Minister. In December, South Sudan asked Ethiopia to shut down all SPLM-IO offices in the country.

Besides other key neighbours, *South Africa* was also involved in South Sudanese affairs. Machar visited there in February and October. The South African government was at pains to call his February trip a 'private visit', but Machar nevertheless met President Zuma. In September, another South Sudanese government delegation visited South Africa, this time led by Taban Deng, who sought to muster support for the post-July 2016 TGoNU and opposition to Machar.

It was a year of high-level *international visits to South Sudan*. UN Secretary-General *Ban Ki-moon* visited Juba in February and his new Special Envoy for Sudan and South Sudan, Nicholas Haysom of South Africa, made his first visit to Juba in September. In the same month, a delegation of the UN Commission on Human Rights in South Sudan, which the UN Human Rights Council had created in March, visited the country and expressed grave concern at ongoing impunity and the slow pace of implementing the ARCISS. A UNSC delegation visited South Sudan on a fact-finding mission on 2–5 September, intended to show its commitment to peace. After visiting South Sudan in November, Adama Dieng, the UN secretary-general's special adviser on the prevention of genocide, expressed strong concerns about the "strong risk of violence escalating along ethnic lines, with the *potential for genocide*". The Ban Ki-moon amplified international concern in November when he warned the UNSC of a "very real risk of mass atrocities" in South Sudan and that UNMISS was not capable of preventing mass killings. Finally, US Secretary of State John Kerry visited Nairobi in August, offering new aid and accepting Taban Deng Gai's appointment as first vice president. In September, US Special Envoy Donald Booth informed the US Congress that Machar should not return to Juba. Afterwards, IGAD and AU statements stopped calling for his return; Machar had gone from being a recognised part of the peace process to an exiled and isolated rebel leader.

UNMISS faced criticism over its failure to protect civilians during the July violence in Juba, which also saw the deaths of two Chinese UN peacekeepers. This fighting exposed the weakness of the mission: government soldiers engaged in murder, rape and torture, including against international personnel, and looted $ 30 m worth of food, fuel, equipment and vehicles from WFP. The UN Secretary General fired the Kenyan commander of UNMISS, Lieutenant General Johnson Mogoa Kimani Ondieki, in early November after a UN investigation found that the failure to protect civilians in Juba in July was due to a lack of leadership. In response, the government of Kenya announced the immediate withdrawal of its troops from UNMISS. The *UK*, however, deployed peacekeepers to the mission and, in November, *Japan* approved deployment of a new Ground Self-Defense Force contingent.

The challenges facing UNMISS, as well as aid agencies, were greater than ever, especially after July, when 'access incidents', including *violence against humanitarian workers*, spiked. There was pervasive looting, road insecurity, ethnic targeting, harassment, threats of detention, and attacks against and expulsions of international staff, including the head of the Norwegian Refugee Council. Anti-UN sentiments were compounded by the UN's role in airlifting Machar and his forces from within the DRC in August, and by UNSC Resolution 2304, adopted in August. This resolution condemned the July fighting, called for a permanent ceasefire, and approved the deployment of an additional 4,000-strong peacekeeping – or Rapid Protection Force – force in Juba, which became a major point of contention with the government. The JMEC returned to South Sudan after temporarily operating from Addis Ababa. In December, the UNSC rejected a draft US resolution imposing an arms embargo and further sanctions. The government welcome the resolution; SPLM-IO expressed outrage. The UNMISS mandate was extended through 2017 and David Shearer, a former New Zealand politician, replaced Ellen Margrethe Loej as its head.

After July, there was concern that the move by opposition forces into the *DRC* and their location in other neighbouring countries could regionalise the conflict. This was compounded by SPLA ground and air attacks on Machar's forces inside the DRC in August. *Kenya* was concerned about the economic impact of South Sudan's conflict and South Sudanese refugees on its territory. In November, Kenyan authorities deported James Gatdet Dak, the spokesman for the SPLM-IO and a registered refugee, from Nairobi to Juba after he spoke favourably of the firing of the Kenyan UNMISS commander, Lieutenant General Johnson Ondieki.

Socioeconomic Developments

Government finances continued to be badly affected by reduced *oil production*, as the sector struggled to deal with the impact of previous and new conflicts. Production from Upper Nile ran at around 120,000 b/d in May (down from around 329,000 b/d in 2011). Efforts to boost output were disrupted by continuing fighting in oil producing areas. China National Petroleum Corporation employees were evacuated after the Juba fighting in July, leaving a skeleton staff to maintain operations. Oil income was further decreased by subdued international oil prices and Juba's fixed oil transit fee agreement with Sudan. Juba sought to lower its oil transit payments to Khartoum, while Khartoum sought political concessions in return. In December, South Sudan's Petroleum Minister Ezekiel Lol Gatkouth and his Sudanese counterpart agreed to extend the 2012 cooperation agreement on oil revenue payments for three years.

Other economic problems included *deficit financing* caused by the devaluation of the South Sudanese pound (SSP) and the printing of money, hyperinflation, growing fuel shortages (due, in part, to the insecurity of supply routes from Uganda), and a resort to subsistence economy amidst the disruption of livelihoods by conflicts. The South Sudan National Bureau of Statistics reported that the consumer price index rose by 682.1% between September 2015 and September 2016. In June, the black market currency exchange rate was 50 SSP : $ 1 compared with the official Central Bank rate of 35 SSP : $ 1; by the end of the year, the value of the pound had dropped by nearly 90%.

South Sudan's *draft budget* for the fiscal year 2016–17 was presented late, in October, by Minister of Finance and Planning Stephen Dhieu Dau, who noted that it was "impossible to overstate the gravity" of South Sudan's economic situation. Estimated to total SSP 22.3 bn, the budget allocated SSP 11.045 bn for the security sector (mostly for salaries, but including SSP 1.983 bn for "operation costs" and SSP 307 m for "new capital expenditures"). It allocated SSP 5 bn for "the implementation and consolidation of Peace", some to be disbursed through security organs or the Presidency. Education (SSP 1.4 bn), health (SSP 588 m) and social and humanitarian affairs (SSP 177 m) received far less, but were to be supplemented by off-budget donor support.

Juba made further efforts – mostly unsuccessful – through its foreign relations to secure *financial support from external actors*, including China. The economic crisis affected the ability of the South Sudanese government to operate abroad, including its ability to pay its diplomatic corps and embassy rents. Despite its economic difficulty and predicament, in March, South Sudan was admitted to the EAC as its sixth member state.

There were further *indications of economic stress*. South Sudan's main non-oil foreign investor, SABMiller, announced that it would close brewing operations at its factory just outside Juba due to a foreign exchange shortage and the difficulties of importing raw materials. There were *strikes* by school teachers. Academic staff at five universities ended strike action in July after receiving assurances from the government that their demands over unpaid salaries would be met. While officially having a Fiscal Stabilisation Action Plan, *debt* as of 30 June ran at SSP 35.137 bn, of which SSP 14.931 bn came from direct borrowing from the Bank of South Sudan and SSP 11.410 bn from advance oil sales. Overall, as the IMF declared in December, South Sudan faced "massive economic challenges".

Food shortages evolved from looming threat to, by the end of the year, warnings of famine. A 'borderline famine' situation was declared in February in parts of Unity state, with insufficient and unreliable evidence hindering a proper determination of famine. In June, *FAO, UNICEF and WFP* warned that almost half of South Sudan's population faced severe food shortages and an 'unprecedented' level of food insecurity. In November, there were warnings of a soaring risk of *starvation and famine* as a result of the impact of conflicts spreading to rural areas and disrupting access to agricultural land. There were chronic food deficits in greater Upper Nile, northern Bahr el Ghazal, and greater Equatoria, where agricultural production was disrupted in areas affected by violence.

An important change was the marked increase in the numbers of South Sudanese *refugees* fleeing the country. The July fighting in Juba catalysed a further exodus of more than 185,000 people. By the end of the year, the UN reported the number of IDPs as 1.83 m, and the number of South Sudanese refugees in neighbouring countries including Ethiopia, Uganda and the DRC as 1.3 m.

Sudan

Jean-Nicolas Bach and Clément Deshayes

President al-Bashir kept himself and the hegemonic National Congress Party at the top of the regime. They were not challenged by other political movements, as 75% of the parliament was made up of al-Bashir's supporters after the 2015 elections, and the emergence of other political and civic movements was suppressed. However, two calls for civil disobedience at the end of the year revived discontent with a government that had led the Islamist regime since 1989. 2016 was also marked by ongoing violent conflict in parts of Darfur and South Kordofan, although the government asserted that these conflicts had ended. At the regional level, relations remained tense with Egypt, pragmatic towards Ethiopia, and confrontational towards South Sudan. Collaboration with Saudi Arabia and the Gulf regimes was strengthened, notably in the war in Yemen. Diplomatic relations with Iran were severed and Shiite schools in Sudan were closed. The lifting of US sanctions was still under negotiation, while al-Bashir continued to face charges of war crimes and genocide at the ICC. The economy continued to be affected by US sanctions, weak oil production and El Niño. The balance of trade remained negative, and inflation suddenly worsened in October following the government decision to end subsidies

 | DOI 10.1163/9789004355910_041

on basic commodities. The government benefitted from loans from the UAE, but the national currency remained weak and affected by a strong black market.

Domestic Politics

The year was politically, socially and militarily quite intense. After the 're-election' of Omar al-Bashir in May 2015 and the very low turn-out in these *elections*, the regime faced significant social contestation, while the civil war was ongoing in Darfur and the Nuba Mountains, and several *rebel groups* were still very active in the Blue Nile Region. The most significant groups were the Sudan Liberation Army Abdel Wahid Nur (SLA/Nur), the Sudan Liberation Army Minni Minnawi (SLA/MM), the Justice and Equality Movement (JEM), and the Sudan People's Liberation Movement North (SPLM–N). All these groups had been allied within the Sudan Revolutionary Front (SRF) since 2010, although this alliance was weakened by leadership disputes in 2015 and 2016.

In September in El Fasher (North Darfur), President al-Bashir announced the 'return of peace' in *Darfur*, in the presence of Chad's President Idriss Déby and the emir of Qatar, although large parts of Darfur were still facing a substantial level of violence and fighting, especially around the Djebel Marra area. Furthermore, the ceasefire talks under the auspices of the AU between the regime on the one hand and the SLA/MM and the JEM on the other, remained in deadlock. The process of segmentation of the Darfurian rebel groups went on and not only led to several splits within the three main rebel groups – SLA/Nur, SLA/MM and JEM – but also made it difficult to face the offensives launched by Sudanese government forces. It appeared that the SLA/MM and the JEM had lost most of the areas they used to control. Smaller groups emerged from the weakening of the rebel groups, and attempted with some success to negotiate a separate peace with the government. AI, for its part, accused the regime of using chemical weapons against civilians in the Djebel Marra area, still under the control of the SLA/Nur. The Sudanese government denied these accusations.

As foreseen in the *Doha Document for Peace in Darfur* of 2011, a *referendum* was finally held in the region in April. It mainly offered a choice between the current situation of division of Darfur into five different states, and the creation of one Darfurian regional state. The first option (supported by the regime) found 98% support, which led to the dissolution of the problematic *Darfurian Regional Authority* (DRA), run by El Tijani Sese since the Doha agreement. Before the vote, many calls from political parties, civil society organisations, rebel groups and local leaders of displaced people to boycott the referendum were followed by large segments of the Darfurian population, so the representativeness of the poll was not credible.

In the meantime, several clashes had occurred between students calling for the boycott and the security forces in Darfur's major cities and in Khartoum. The opposition denounced the result as a "falsification" or a "farce", while the government welcomed the outcome.

Another point of concern in Darfur was that of recurrent *tribal clashes* in various areas. It seemed the intensity of violence had decreased but these incidents remained one of the main factors contributing to insecurity in the area. Numerous confrontations occurred between the Rizeigat, Ma'alya, Salamat, Fellata and Misseryya, among others. Some tribes, including the Salamat and Fellata, negotiated peace through the mediation of the DRA and exchanged compensation for the loss of their kinsman and livestock. Several reconciliation meetings between tribes were held in order to avoid retaliation and the spiralling of violence. In addition, a 'Social Peace Conference' was held in May in Nyala in the presence of the states' governors, Native Administration members and tribal leaders in order to ease tensions.

The situation in the *Nuba Mountains* and the Blue Nile was less complicated, even though the population was facing high levels of violence. The SPLM-N still held on to large parts of the South Kordofan region and was able to repel various attacks from the Sudanese army and militias. The SPLM-N and the JEM from Darfur also gave military support to President Salva Kiir's troops in the South Sudanese civil war.

Social and political discontent increased and protests reached their peak during the last months of the year in various sectors. Conflicts over land and water continued in a significant number of locations and were especially strong in El Gereif in Khartoum around land issues, and in the city of Gedaref and the neighbourhood of Al Fitehab in Omdurman over the shortage of drinking water.

Sudan also witnessed major social conflict, with *strikes and protests* by doctors throughout the country, teachers, especially in Kordofan, and students in several universities (including Khartoum, Gedaref, Kassala, Atbara, El Obeid and El Fasher). Doctors' and teachers' strikes were strong and organised without the involvement of unions or organisations controlled by the governing National Congress Party (NCP). The doctors organised their strike through the creation of an independent body, the Central Committee of Sudanese Doctors. The teachers' strikes included threats to boycott examinations in Khartoum and Kordofan and some areas of Darfur. Their main demands were for the payment of salary arrears, better working conditions and better access to healthcare for the people. *Universities* in the main cities also witnessed important tensions for various other reasons. The Darfurian student associations launched two campaigns, first to oppose the Darfur referendum, and second against tuition fees for Darfurian students. Indeed, the student associations advocated for the exemption of registration fees for Darfurian students, as agreed in the Doha Peace Agreement. Several clashes occurred in various universities and some university administrations responded by withholding the results and diplomas of numerous Darfurian students. An additional conflict took place at Khartoum University after the announcement of a plan to move the university premises from the city centre to a southern suburb. Even though the university denied this plan, large demonstrations took place inside the university, leading the authorities to close down the campus for several months.

The government's systematic *response to these protests* and demonstrations was detention and repression. Numerous union leaders, students and teachers were detained for periods ranging from a few days to several months. This repression was especially violent towards Darfurian students, although many activists from other areas also reported being victims of brutality and torture by the security services during their arrest and detention.

Social contestation culminated in a call for *civil disobedience* launched in November by unknown online activists. This call spread among the population through social media and was supported by several political movements and parties. Social tensions increased after the surprise announcement by the government of a liberalisation of petrol prices and an increase in electricity tariffs at the beginning of November. A few days after the liberalisation of fuel and electricity, the Central Bank of Sudan (CBS) *cut subsidies* on imported medicines, leading to a doubling of prices. November saw immediate demonstrations by university and secondary school students, Facebook protests by women's groups and strikes by pharmacists. For the population, the cut of subsidies echoed the events that led to the uprising of September 2013, when more than 200 demonstrators had died. The call for three days of civil disobedience was joined, not without some hesitation, by most of the political parties and civil society, and attempts were made to organise the struggle. The call was for the population to stay at home during three days of civil disobedience, not to go to work, and to avoid moving in the city to escape repression. The first three days of the campaign were relatively successful, with very low activity in the capital and some of the major cities. However, the second call for civil disobedience in December did not attract massive support by the population, even though the scale of support and preparation by political organisations, rebel groups and NGOs was considerable. The government and the opposition indulged in a war of images, opposing pictures and videos of empty streets and closed shops on the one hand, and scenes of normality on the other. During this period, dozens of activists, citizens and pharmacists were arrested.

In the Economist Intelligence Unit Democracy Index, Sudan was still classified as an *'authoritarian state'* (ranked 151st of 167 countries). Civil liberties and the activities of political parties were forcibly restricted, and opponents and activists were often fiercely repressed.

Opposition parties and allied bodies, such as the Sudan Call and the National Consensus Forces, faced tensions between their members and were weakened by their difficulty in reaching a consensus or establishing a common stance. Tensions developed especially around the necessity or desirability of negotiating with the regime in the framework of the so-called 'National Dialogue'. Part of the opposition was under pressure from the AU and the international community and signed the AU High Implementation Panel (AUHIP) peace roadmap, put in place to oversee the outcomes of the National Dialogue. This led again to tensions with political and civil society organisations opposed to any negotiation with the current government. This new roadmap appeared to have reached a stalemate at the end of the year. A new opposition alliance, the Future Forces of Change (FFC), was created in February and attracted a few small, mainly Islamist, political parties. The FFC included several groups that had seceded from the governing NCP, such as the Reform Now Movement of Ghazi Salah El Din, but was already facing several splits at the end of the year, as it appeared unable to find a common position on the National Dialogue and relations towards the armed movements.

The *National Dialogue process* was completed in October, although most opposition and armed groups had boycotted it, considering it a "theatre" or pure "farce". Supported by the international community, the Dialogue's aim was to work on the future constitution and to prepare for the formation of a government of national unity to be led by a prime minister appointed by the president. The recommendations of the National Dialogue would have to be implemented in 2017, even if the opposition and some participants in the Dialogue questioned the desire of the NCP to implement some specific recommendations, such as freedom of speech, freedom of the press and equality among citizens regardless of ethnic or religious belonging.

In fact, while the National Dialogue was going on, the *freedom of the press* continued to deteriorate. The few independent newspapers (mainly 'Al Jareeda', 'El Ahram el Yom', 'El Tayyar' and 'El Ayam') had editions seized several times during the year. The Sudanese Journalist Network (SJN) reported 58 press freedom violations in the last quarter, including 38 confiscations of newspapers and print runs, and 11 arrests and summons of journalists. SJN reported an increase in violations during the civil disobedience movement. Censorship under the supervision of the National Intelligence and Security Service pursued the aim of weakening the newspapers economically, in addition to judicial and physical pressure. Reporters Without Borders ranked Sudan as 174th out of 180 countries in its Press Freedom Index. Freedom House also defined Sudan as 'not free' with regard to press freedom and freedom of the Internet. They reported a constant increase of arrests and prosecutions over previous years under the IT Crime Act. In response to the escalation of the situation, journalists organised some rallies and limited strikes.

Foreign Affairs

President *al-Bashir continued to face ICC charges* of war crimes and genocide in the eastern Darfur region in the 2000s. However, like his Kenyan counterpart, al-Bashir kept trying to use these charges as a means to reinforce his legitimacy on the internal political scene, publicly accusing the ICC of representing "neo-imperialist justice controlled by the whites". He also continued to urge his African counterparts to officially withdraw from the ICC and, despite the international arrest warrant, he was still hosted in neighbouring countries, including in Uganda in May, in Egypt in February, and in Ethiopia at least twice, in April and November.

At the regional level, relations with *Egypt* remained strained around at least three important issues. First, Sudanese officials regularly accused Cairo of hosting Sudanese opposition groups, not blaming President Abd al-Fattah al-Sisi by name, but rather condemning the Egyptian regime at large and the Egyptian intelligence services in particular. Second, the Grand Ethiopian Renaissance Dam remained a source of regional tension. In spite of Egyptian resistance and veiled threats against Ethiopia, the Ethiopian authorities continued to maintain that the dam (under construction since 2011) would start operation in 2018. The Sudanese regime had traditionally supported Egypt and the colonial treaties (of 1929 and 1959), until a historical redefinition of its geopolitical position in 2012 aligned it to Ethiopia's new hegemonic position in the region. Low-level negotiations were ongoing between the three countries, although no significant progress was achieved. Finally, a third source of tension between Khartoum and Cairo remained over the Halaïb Triangle on Sudan's north-eastern border with Egypt. The area was still administered by Egypt but was claimed by Khartoum as Sudanese territory and Khartoum publicly accusing Egypt of having annexed the Triangle in 1995.

Internal conflicts continued to have regional ramifications. In the southern part of the country, for instance, the situation remained tense on the border with *South Sudan*, especially in the South Kordofan and Blue Nile regions. The UN reported that one of the main rebel movements in Darfur, the JEM, was still operating in South Sudan "as a result of the Government's effective counter-insurgency strategy" in Darfur. Another notable rebel movement from Darfur was operating from Libya – the SLA/MM. The UN also accused these two groups of being engaged in criminal and commercial activities in Libya and South Sudan. In South Sudan, the JEM alongside the SPLM-N (an armed movement from the Nuba Mountains/South Kordofan, active since 2011) benefited from the support of Salva Kiir's governing SPLA/M, conducting joint military actions against SPLM-IO (the armed opposition to Salva Kiir led by Riek Machar) mainly in Unity state around Bentiu, causing mass displacement of local populations. The war in South Sudan and its remaining connections with internal conflicts in Sudan (notably Darfur and South Kordofan) also continued to deeply affect trade relations not only between Sudan and South Sudan, but also between South Sudan and *Uganda*. This partly explained why Khartoum and Uganda's President Yoweri Museveni continued to develop closer ties. Museveni started organising informal meetings with the JEM and the SLA/MM in Kampala from May onwards, to which Sudanese official and AU-UN Mission in Darfur (UNAMID) representatives would be invited.

One of the most notable developments regarding Sudan's role in the broader region was its relations with *Middle Eastern and Gulf regimes*. Dramatic changes took place in Khartoum's foreign policy: the breakdown of relations with *Iran* on the one hand, and the deepening of its relations with the Gulf regimes on the other. One explanatory factor was the conflict that was affecting Yemen in the aftermath of the 2011 popular uprisings and the vacuum created by the fall of the Abdullah Saleh regime. The conflict in Yemen and the new religious alignments it engendered (Sunni vs. Houthis-Zaydis) also affected the countries in the Horn of Africa, including Sudan. Pragmatically blurring former alignments, Sudan fought along with Saudi, Eritrean and Emirates partners in order to avoid the destabilisation of the strategic Red Sea corridor. Khartoum notably contributed by maintaining its troops within the so-called Arab coalition (largely led by Saudi Arabia) against the Houthis with a contingent estimated at more than a 1,000 soldiers. This put an end to relations with Sudan's former partner, Iran. Two major events that emphasised this turn-around were the Iranian military attaché's departure from Khartoum without being replaced, and the government's official announcement of the closure of Iranian-sponsored Shiite schools, claiming that Sudan had enough challenges to cope with in terms of ethnic and tribal issues and did not want to import Sunni-Shiite divisions and related problems into the country.

Saudi Arabia was not the only Gulf regime to strengthen its ties with Sudan during the year. *Qatar* was also very involved diplomatically and also scientifically, sponsoring archeological projects in Sudan and continuing to offer very attractive university scholarships and positions, in order to attract the best students and professors to, for example, the Doha Institute. The *UAE* was also very influential. The Abu Dhabi Fund for Development, for instance, promised to deposit $ 400 m in the CBS to help Sudan face economic and financial challenges. The UAE was also said to have played a significant role in the conduct of negotiations between the USA and Sudan concerning the lifting of sanctions.

Negotiations continued with the *USA* towards the eventual *removal of the sanctions* imposed since 1997. A set of preconditions were proposed by the American administration, among which was a decrease in Khartoum's involvement in South Sudan, a reduction of military offensives in the 'Two Regions' (South Kordofan and Blue Nile) and in Darfur, collaboration in the fight against terrorism, and the improvement of humanitarian access to the field. These negotiations may explain al-Bashir's successive announcements of cessations of hostilities in June for four months in the 'Two Regions', then in October for two more months, and again in December for one additional month. Sudan also effectively collaborated in the 'war on terror', not only in Yemen but also in the fight against the Lord's Resistance Army. On 23 December, Moez el Fezzani was extradited to the USA. He was considered responsible for many international terror incidents, including the attack on the Prado Museum in March 2015. Other terrorists were also allegedly extradited. Sudanese efforts to facilitate access to the field for humanitarian agencies were formalised by a new regulation issued in December. Travel permits were delivered more easily, although only the following months would show the effectiveness of this new policy. No specific requirements were set by the USA regarding human rights improvements. Thus, as Khartoum worked hard to maintain good relations on the international scene, it kept up internal repression and continued to impose the terms of 'dialogue' in domestic policy. Eventually, despite these efforts on the part of the Sudan government, the Obama administration decided not to lift the sanctions in October, announcing their continuation for one more year, and not to remove Sudan from the list of regimes sponsoring terrorism.

Sudan continued to collaborate with the *EU* on the *migration* issue, pursuing the so-called Khartoum Process initiated in November 2014. In June, the EU member states confirmed the 'out-sourcing' of border controls to African regimes beyond the Mediterranean Sea and released a plan aimed at urging migrants to stay in Africa. Some € 8 m would be spent in the coming five years on training border policemen and financing development projects in the relevant African countries. Sudan effectively reinforced the control of its borders with Chad and Libya, using mobile Rapid Support Forces. The EU denied sponsoring any Sudanese security agency, but opposition groups expressed concern about such support from the EU for a non-democratic regime, which they accused of using the former Janjaweed as border guards (within the Rapid Support Forces). But Sudanese nationals remained one of most numerous groups of asylum seekers reaching Europe: they were, for instance, the third largest group of asylum seekers in France, after Syrians and Afghans (with 5,201 applicants).

Sudan was hosting more than 3 m *IDPs* and about 450,000 *refugees*. Among refugees, a recent study by the International Organisation for Migration, based on a limited sample of 308 interviewees, considered that Sudan remained an important transit country for Eritreans, Ethiopian, Nigerians, Somalis and Syrians. Among the refugees, the South Sudanese were still in a precarious position, as only the most recent migrants fleeing the conflict in South Sudan could benefit from refugee status. Thousands of South Sudanese thus remained stateless: no longer Sudanese, but not South Sudanese refugees either.

Arrivals of *Syrian nationals*, mostly fleeing the war in Syria, remained high, following the trend started in 2011, and above all after 2015. Their choice of Sudan could be explained by the closure of the Turkish route following the EU-Turkey Agreement of 18 March. It was also the result of a strong welcoming policy initiated by the Sudanese government and facilitated by direct flights from Damascus (operated by Fly Damas and Cham Wing). In effect, Syrians entering Sudan were not considered refugees by UNHCR but "brothers and sisters" and could move around and access

Sudanese schools and universities without a visa. They were mostly concentrated in the capital Khartoum and were estimated to number 200,000 at the end of the year.

Socioeconomic Developments

High *population growth* continued, with 60% of the population below the age of 25, and with a median age of 19.6. The *literacy* rate remained around 73%, and around 2.7–3 m school-age children did not attend school according to UNESCO and World Bank data. *Economic growth* remained positive (around 3%) and GDP was estimated at $ 94.3 bn ($ 27.5 bn in agriculture, $ 20.7 bn in industry and $ 51.8 bn in services).

On 6 December, the minister of finance reported to the national parliament that the deficit in the 2017 state *budget* would rise to SDG (pound) 19.5 bn ($ 3 bn), up from SDG 13.3 bn (about $ 2 bn) in 2015 and SDG 12 bn ($ 1.8 bn) in 2014. Debt represented almost 63% of GDP. The state budget was SDG 67.5 bn ($ 11.1 bn). The growing budget deficit could be partly attributed to heavy government spending in the military and security sectors, the deficiency of administration, the lack of cash reserves and the weakness of the industrial sector. The US-based Enough Project stated in a report in August that, according to Sudan's 2016 national budget, 76% of government expenditure was channeled to the defence, police and security sectors, while only 8% of projected expenditure was earmarked for agriculture, manufacturing, health and education.

Inflation continued to increase, especially toward the end of the year: it rose from an annual average of 17%–19% to 29.5% in November, even though controlling inflation remained a stated high priority of the Sudanese authorities. This rise was mainly due to the worsening of economic conditions following the government decision in October to stop *subsidies* on basic commodities – petrol, fuel, medicines and electricity – which the government announced it was not able to afford. This resulted in a sudden 30% increase in petrol prices at filling stations and a 50% rise in electricity costs. The government reacted by increasing civil servants' salaries by 20% in November and threatening the population with severe punishment for popular protests – making explicit references to the 2013 movements.

In November, while domestic transport tariffs were soaring, the government also liberalised the official hard currency tariffs for a number of imported goods and services. After the CBS cancelled the the exchange rate of SDG 7.5 to the dollar for the import of medicines, the rate rose to SDG 17.5 to the dollar and medicine prices doubled and in some cases even tripled. At the same time, the Civil Aviation Corporation officially requested airlines flying to Sudan to adopt a rate of SDG 15.9 to the dollar and the prices of airline tickets immediately rose by more than 150%. As the ongoing shortage of hard currency at the CBS continued to push up the black market rate, the government decided on an economic reform programme, which, according to al-Bashir, was needed "to avoid the collapse of the country". The commercial exchange rate that banks and foreign-exchange bureaus were allowed to use was lowered from around SDG 6.7 : $ 1 to SDG 15.8 : $ 1 (more or less the same as the black market rate). The CBS kept its official pegged exchange rate of around SDG 6.2 : $ 1, only available for limited purchases of foreign currency.

Bank operations and international transactions remained complicated due to this conjuncture and the persistence of US sanctions, resulting in high import financing costs, which according to the World Bank might "... result in greater reliance on cash transactions and associated AML/CFT risks".

The World Bank further expressed concern about the continuing widening of *external imbalances* in 2015–16, "due to low commodity export prices, expansionary policies, and insufficient exchange rate adjustment". Sudan's top *export* destination countries were China (about half of exports), the UAE (around 14%), and Saudi Arabia (about 12%). According to new figures from the CBS, total export earnings in the first half of the year were $ 1.5 bn, down from $ 1.8 bn in the same period in 2015. Sudan's two largest sources of export earnings in the first half of the year were *gold and livestock*. The minister of mines announced that 42 mining companies were operating in gold extraction throughout the country. The profits of the Khartoum-based Ariab Mining Company increased by 18%. Some 26 tonnes of gold were extracted, coming mainly in the Northern regions, Kordofan and Darfur, and the minister of mines announced that revenue from gold would amount to around $ 1.2 bn by the end of the year (officially $ 1.0 bn – CBS). *Livestock* export earnings were broadly steady, at $ 417.6 m in the first half of the year (compared with $410.4 m in 2015). The main factor behind the fall in export earnings was the decline in prices for sesame and crude oil. Earnings from *sesame* exports fell from $ 305 m in the first half of 2015 to just $ 164.7 m in January–June 2016, despite a slight increase in export volumes (up from 187,000 tonnes to 197,000 tonnes).

Although Sudan and South Sudan found a basis for discussion in February (to pay a total transit fee $ 15 per barrel), it was still difficult to estimate Sudan's earning from the export of *South Sudan's oil* via the only pipeline through Sudan to the Red Sea. 'The Economist' noted, however, that "in the past the exports have brought in at least $ 50 m a month – and usually nearer to $ 100 m – to Sudan". Concerning Sudan's own production and exportation of oil, the earnings from *crude oil exports* were officially estimated at $ 335.7 m, compared with $ 627.1 m in 2015. The reduction was primarily the result of lower average oil prices, but probably also reflected greater domestic consumption. According to recent figures from the CBS, oil export revenue amounted to only $ 176.4 m during the first half of the year – 40% less than in the first half of 2015, which was already well down on previous years' oil export earnings, according to 'The Economist'.

Saudi Arabia invested in Sudan's large *hydroelectric energy projects*, including dams in Kajbar, Dal, El Shireik, Upper Atbara and Setit. The proposed construction was opposed by residents of towns along the Nile, who feared displacement (as reported on opposition-related 'Radio Dabanga'). The planned Kajbar Dam on the Nile's third cataract would create a reservoir of 110 km^2 and generate 360 MW. According to 'International Rivers', the project would displace more than 10,000 people and submerge an estimated 500 archaeological sites. The Dal Dam on the second cataract would have a capacity of 340–450 MW, and would displace at least 5,000 people.

Tanzania

Kurt Hirschler and Rolf Hofmeier

President Magufuli, in his first full year in office, stringently pursued a hitherto unaccustomed leadership style, stressing discipline, rigorous cost-saving and anti-corruption measures in state institutions, pushing for higher revenue generation and exercising power by continuous single-handed directives (including dismissals of top functionaries), often without regard for formal procedures. This earned him popularity among large sections of the general public, but also raised fears about authoritarian tendencies and a loss of space for dissenting voices (including the media). Public activities of opposition parties were curtailed and some of their leaders were repeatedly interrogated by police. A repeat of the allegedly fraudulent 2015 elections in semi-autonomous Zanzibar was boycotted by the opposition and led to a single-party situation in parliament. Magufuli took control of the dominant long-ruling CCM party and introduced sweeping changes to its structures in an attempt to consolidate his (not entirely undisputed) position. Relations with Western aid donors were slightly strained over the Zanzibar election issue and dissatisfaction with a lack of economic reform measures, while relations with key neighbours and EAC partners improved. Indicators of macroeconomic performance and growth continued to be strong, but uncertainty over the government's future course and

 | DOI 10.1163/9789004355910_042

prevalent liquidity problems throughout the economy somewhat stifled the private sector and led to fears about an economic slowdown.

Domestic Politics

Throughout the year, President John Pombe Magufuli showed that he had no intention to slow down the pace of *implementing his agenda* of 'Hapa Kazi Tu' ('here only work'), the slogan of his 2015 electoral campaign. In his *fight against corruption, inefficiency and embezzlement of public funds*, he and his subordinates sacked or transferred more than 300 civil servants, among them the heads of the Tanzania Revenue Authority, Tanzania Investment Centre and several other institutions. Ministers and other senior leaders followed Magufuli's example of dismissals for alleged non-performance. Misappropriation and theft of public funds, fraud, violation of regulations and other illegal practices were revealed, ultimatums were set and even senior civil servants were fired in numerous state agencies and authorities. Some of those who lost their jobs over accusations of fraud, theft, corruption and the like, found their bank accounts frozen and were brought before the courts.

In the *fight against misappropriation of public funds* and to *reduce government expenditure*, the government also addressed the problem of so-called *ghost workers*, i.e. 'employees' of public sector institutions who did not exist (or had died) but whose names nevertheless appeared on the payrolls. In a nationwide audit between March and September, more than 16,000 ghost workers were detected and removed from the public sector payroll. All civil servants were required to prove their identity and their qualifications.

Various measures were introduced to *reduce government expenditures* and to *increase revenues*. This included a consistently restrictive approach towards foreign travel for state functionaries and government workshops in luxury resorts, as well as salary cuts for senior civil servants. Although welcomed by the general public, the *austerity policy* had some negative consequences for the economy and on the social situation of the poorer segments of the population (such as budget reductions in the Health Ministry leading to medication shortages in government hospitals). Strict controls were introduced to *increase tax discipline* and to *reduce tax evasion.* In addition, *new taxes* were introduced, including on mobile phone transactions, in the already highly-taxed tourism sector, and on transactions on the Dar es Salaam Stock Exchange. There were, however, fears that some of the new taxes would hit small businesses and the general population too hard. Local governments were urged to increase their own revenues, prompting some authorities to introduce several questionable taxes on small businesses. In response to complaints, Magufuli decreed that these local taxes should only be collected from larger businesses.

As promised during the election campaign, *school fees were abolished* up to lower secondary school level. The government also abolished additional charges that had been demanded in primary schools (such as parents' contributions to security, cleaning, construction of classrooms, etc.). This led to a dramatic increase in enrolment, especially in primary schools. Although extra operational funds were provided by government, it became obvious that schools were not prepared to accommodate such large numbers of students. A severe lack of classrooms, furniture, textbooks and teachers was reported. Audits and investigations revealed that fraud, theft, corruption and related vices were rampant in the education system. Nearly 7,500 students attending a special diploma course in education at the University of Dodoma were suspended after an investigation by the Ministry of Education showed that they lacked the required qualifications. Almost 500 students at a private university were suspended by the ministry for similar reasons.

Following established party tradition, the chairman and former president of CCM ('Chama cha Mapinduzi' / Revolutionary Party), Jakaya Kikwete, handed over the *CCM party chairmanship to Magufuli* at an extraordinary CCM congress on 22 July. Rumours that the party would break with this tradition and continue with Kikwete until regular party elections in 2017 indicated that some CCM sections were not happy with Magufuli's fight against corruption, since it posed a threat to their own personal interests, but he was unanimously elected by the nearly 2,400 delegates. In mid-December, the CCM National Executive Committee (NEC) proposed *several wide-ranging changes to the CCM constitution*, which remained to be approved by an extraordinary congress in February 2017. The changes focussed on reducing the membership of key decision-making organs. The NEC was to be reduced from 388 to 158 members and the Central Committee from 34 to 24. Under the new composition, MPs were no longer allowed to be members of both bodies. While the size reduction of the two organs was widely welcomed, the exclusion of MPs was received more negatively as a measure to restrict democracy and participation within the party. There were proposals for several party posts to be abolished and the frequency of party meetings to be reduced.

The government's stern measures found wide *approval from the general public*, as they tackled crucial weaknesses in Tanzania's political and administrative system, such as negligence, theft, embezzlement, corruption, wastefulness – and impunity. Furthermore, they were directed against members of the state apparatus, who were widely perceived as selfish profiteers of Tanzania's economic growth (which had failed to benefit the majority of poor people) and seen as responsible for the poor results of development achievements. A representative opinion poll, conducted in June by the civic-empowerment NGO Twaweza, showed that 96% of Tanzanians approved Magufuli's activities and 70% stated that services of government institutions had improved under his presidency. Although several of his austerity measures had (short-term) negative effects on many people, Magufuli maintained the image of a *man of the small people*, who was targeting the allegedly greedy and corrupt big fish in order to help the poor and provide better services for them.

Many observers, however, expressed some *scepticism* as to whether these measures would in the longer run bring the desired results. The new political style was characterised by surprise visits by the president, ministers or other office holders to government institutions. Whenever they discovered any deficiencies, they either fired the officers responsible or gave them a specified short time to fix the problems. This *authoritarian leadership style* tended to instil a culture of fear rather than one of dedicated work. There was criticism that government employees were punished without correct procedures being followed and in some cases even by violating human or civil rights. There were also questions as to whether the frequent ultimatums and dismissals undermined established mechanisms of the democratic political process and would in the longer run weaken state institutions. Another point of criticism was that the shortcomings that led to the punishment of individual civil servants had often been caused by structural problems such as underfunding.

Having been elected as CCM chairman, Magufuli informed the party congress that he was determined to accomplish the *shift of the seat of government* from Dar es Salaam to *Dodoma* by 2020. Dodoma had officially been declared Tanzania's capital city in 1973, but plans to move the government had never been implemented. Questions immediately arose concerning the high costs and logistical challenges of such a move. An estimated 120,000 government employees and their families would have to be transferred, with virtually no preparations made so far. On 30 September, the office of Prime Minister Kassim Majaliwa moved to the new capital.

There was no development in the stalled *constitution review process*. Although it had been among CCM's pledges in its 2015 election manifesto, Magufuli made clear that it was not among his government's priorities. However, civil society organisations such as the Tanzania Constitutional Forum called on the government to continue the process, which had been controversially aborted in April 2015, and made suggestions on how to restart it.

Magufuli translated his *'here only work' slogan* not only into tackling corruption and wastefulness, but also into actions *against criticism, democracy and activities of the political opposition*. It emerged that he was much less open to criticism and media freedom than his predecessor Jakaya Kikwete had been. He also seemed to have little sense of the role of a political opposition, as he expected it to remain silent and not to interrupt government in its work. Several *opposition politicians were temporarily arrested* during the year, and two *radio stations and one newspaper were banned* for allegedly inciting violence and publishing seditious material.

The government charged several people under the restrictive *Cybercrimes Act* of 2015 and other laws. In June, one man was sentenced to three years in prison or a fine of TSh (shilling) 7 m for allegedly insulting the president on social media and another separately faced the same charge. In September, five people appeared before the court and a university lecturer was also arrested, again on the same charge. On 13 December, Maxence Melo, co-founder of the popular whistle-blowing and discussion site 'Jamii Forums', was arrested under the Cybercrimes Act for refusing police demands for forum members' personal data; subsequently, the police raided the 'Jamii Forum' offices. In mid-December, parliament finally, after years of controversial discussions, endorsed the *Media Services Act*, which called for increased professionalism in the media sector. It required every journalist to seek accreditation from a newly created government-appointed board, which could also revoke the accreditation. Media organisations were strongly critical that the new regulations imposed government control on journalists' work and heavily curtailed press freedom.

In January, Information Minister Nape Nnauye announced that the government would *stop the popular live broadcasting of parliamentary sessions* by the public Tanzania Broadcasting Corporation (TBC) to reduce the allegedly high costs. This brought objections from media and human rights organisations and from opposition parties, who accused the government of censorship – since the live broadcasts were among the rare opportunities the opposition had to publicise its positions to the electorate. A Twaweza opinion poll showed that 79% of citizens rejected the government's decision and 92% regarded the live broadcasts as important. Although the major opposition party, CHADEMA (Party for Democracy and Progress), offered to pay for the service, live broadcasts ended on 19 April. TBC subsequently distributed selected debate highlights to private TV stations.

In June, *CHADEMA* announced that it was to stage *nationwide protests* against the ban of live broadcasts of parliamentary sessions and against Magufuli's leadership style, which they described as dictatorial. After CCM stated that they would counter CHADEMA's protests with their own public rallies, the *police banned all political rallies* for security reasons until further notice. On 23 June, Magufuli banned all political rallies and public demonstrations until the next elections in 2020, arguing that it was now time for work and not for politicking. CHADEMA launched a *campaign against dictatorship* (Ukuta) and called for demonstrations in a '*Day of Defiance*', to take place on 1 September. However, the police reminded CHADEMA of the existing ban and went even further, *banning internal party meetings* on the grounds that they served to create chaos. Several CHADEMA leaders and party members were temporarily arrested for incitement. In an atmosphere of rising tensions, religious leaders, political analysts and human rights activists called for dialogue and CHADEMA finally called off the demonstrations. Magufuli's popularity and his fight against corruption and public sector slackness, which the opposition had always demanded, made it difficult for the opposition to attract much attention. They therefore increasingly concentrated on his controversial leadership style and growing authoritarian trends.

Although still unsolved, the *Zanzibar crisis* faded from the political limelight after the nullified 2015 elections were repeated on 20 March. After the nullification, Seif Sharif Hamad, the secretary general of Zanzibar's main opposition party, the CUF (Civic United Front), had *called for dialogue* to resolve the crisis instead of conducting a re-run. Nine rounds of closed-door meetings between Hamad and high-ranking CCM officials, including Zanzibar's President Ali Mohamed Shein, were held, but without arriving at a solution. After two months of negotiations, Hamad told a press conference on 11 January that the talks had failed to reach a consensus and called upon Magufuli to help finding a solution acceptable to all. Magufuli remained reluctant to intervene, saying the matter rested with the Zanzibar Electoral Commission (ZEC). In early February, he eventually declared that he saw a repeat election as the best solution to the political deadlock and called on the CUF to take part. On 22 January, ZEC Chairman Jecha Salim Jecha announced *20 March* as the date of the *election re-run*, which was to be conducted with the same candidates as in the 2015 polls – even if parties refused to take part in the repeat exercise. The CUF governing council formally decided on 28 February not to participate and most other small and politically insignificant parties followed suit. The *elections* were conducted with a heavy *police and military presence. Shein*, the incumbent president, *received 91.4%* of the votes, while second-placed Hamad Rashid Mohamed (Alliance for Democratic Change) took just 3%. CCM candidates won all the seats in the House of Representatives, the parliament of semi-autonomous Zanzibar. According to the ZEC, voter turnout was 67.9% (341,865 voters), but the CUF challenged the figure, claiming it had counted only 100,726 voters (20%).

Western donors reacted with strong disapproval to this electoral process. On 22 March, the embassies and high commissions of 16 Western donors, including the US and the EU, issued a joint statement regretting the ZEC's decision to hold the re-run without a negotiated and mutually accepted agreement. They also made clear that they expected the Tanzanian government to find a solution to the impasse. In reaction, the US *Millennium Challenge Corporation* (MCC) cancelled a grant worth $ 472 m (designated for rural electrification). The MCC had already twice postponed the approval of the grant due to concerns about corruption and bad governance and said this final cancellation was based on the MCC's dissatisfaction with the government's non-adherence to democratic principles.

Zanzibar's 2010 constitution required the president to form a *Government of National Unity* (GNU) from all parties elected to the House of Representatives and to appoint the first vice president from the strongest opposition party, which had to have secured at least 10% of the votes. These regulations had been introduced before the 2010 elections to allow the CUF a share in the government and to calm the ever-growing tensions between the two rival camps, which had resulted in deep divisions in Zanzibar's society. But with no opposition MPs in parliament, Shein could neither form a GNU nor appoint a first vice president. Instead, he appointed to the House of Representatives three members of small parties that had not boycotted the election re-run and also made them ministers in his new 15-member cabinet.

After five years of relative harmony under the power-sharing arrangement of the GNU, Zanzibar had in practice returned to a *one-party situation and the politics of exclusion*. Despite continuing problems and distrust between the two camps, the GNU had been the precondition for reducing political tensions and reconciling Zanzibari society, which was also split along party lines. By terminating the CUF's participation in the GNU, the CCM had excluded about half of Zanzibar's population from political participation and also put societal peace and cohesion at risk. However, it appeared that Zanzibaris preferred political acquiescence and agony to open protest – probably a consequence of bad experience from the pre-GNU period. After the repeat election, the CCM simply continued with business as usual and showed no inclination to make conciliatory moves towards the CUF.

The *CUF tried to win international support*: Hamad travelled to the US, Canada, the EU and several European countries in July, where he met with representatives from political parties, democratic institutions and the ICC, accusing the CCM of violating democratic principles and human rights. He also presented a six-point plan to resolve the crisis, which included the formation of an interim GNU headed by a Zanzibari personality not affiliated to any party. That interim GNU was to prepare elections within six months, to be held under the supervision of a neutral international body. Hopes that Magufuli could try to reconcile the two parties were dashed during his first visit to the isles after his election. In a speech in Pemba in early September, Magufuli strongly criticised Hamad and the CUF, telling them that the elections were over and they had to wait until the next round in 2020.

The *CUF's exclusion from the formal political process* also had consequences for the party itself. It owed much of its support to Hamad's popularity and he had for years managed to hold different factions together and avoid a radicalisation of party members and supporters who were sceptical about his conciliatory approach towards the CCM. Although some within the CUF (like some within the CCM) found this hard to accept, the establishment of the GNU as a means for the CUF to participate in government had strengthened his position against more radical tendencies. Now that his dialogue-oriented approach had failed, it remained unclear whether the 72-year-old Hamad could maintain his authority. But even the future of the party remained uncertain. A severe *leadership wrangle* posed a first challenge, when its former chairman, Ibrahim Lipumba, reclaimed his previous position in June. He had stepped down in August 2015 in protest against Edward Lowassa's nomination as the opposition coalition's presidential candidate and was due to be replaced at the CUF's national congress. Lipumba's intention to return was strongly rejected, mainly by the Zanzibar wing and Hamad. The eruption of chaos at the congress on 21 August revealed a deep rift between the primarily Zanzibar-based Hamad wing and the Lipumba wing, which got most of its support from the Mainland. Although a large majority seemed to support Hamad's faction, the congress failed to resolve the leadership question and the CUF remained split and weakened until the year's end.

Foreign Affairs

Magufuli paid much *less attention to foreign policy* and diplomacy than his predecessor, focussing energetically on domestic issues. But he placed some new emphasis on *regional cooperation in the EAC*, where Tanzania had been somewhat side-lined in recent years. Mainly to reduce costs and to demonstrate his concentration on urgent domestic reforms, Magufuli skipped several international meetings, where Tanzania was represented by Vice President Samia Suluhu Hassan or ministers. Magufuli made only three foreign visits: to Rwanda (April), Uganda (May) and Kenya (November). During the EAC summit on 2 March in Arusha, *Tanzania's tenure as chair* was extended for another year. Magufuli declared his intention to extend his anti-graft and austerity approach to the EAC, demanding, amongst other measures, reductions in costs for travel and extravagant conferences. Relations with the EAC's neighbours improved noticeably, since Magufuli's administration displayed a much more active approach towards the EAC integration process and focussed more on business cooperation and joint infrastructure projects than on political issues. This was, however, somewhat contradicted by the imposition of stricter rules for Tanzanian work permits for foreigners, including those from EAC countries.

Under Magufuli's presidency, *relations with Kenya* had somewhat cooled, partly due to suspicions about his personal friendship with Kenya's opposition leader Raila Odinga and to complaints about difficulties faced by Kenyans working or running businesses in Tanzania. Ugandan and Rwandan decisions to construct important infrastructure projects (oil pipeline and railway line) across Tanzania and not through Kenya – as earlier agreed – and Tanzania's rejection of the EPA between the EU and the EAC, which Kenya had already signed, further exacerbated the long-existing rivalry. During Magufuli's state visit to Kenya in early November, he and President Uhuru Kenyatta nevertheless reaffirmed their commitment to strengthening ties.

The government displayed only a modest commitment to attempts to resolve the two major current *crises in the East African region*. Tanzania's former president Benjamin Mkapa was appointed as facilitator of the *Inter-Burundi Dialogue* at the EAC summit in March. In several consultative meetings, a roadmap for the dialogue was developed and presented to EAC heads of state on 8 September. The future of this roadmap remained uncertain, however, since Burundi's opposition alliance accused Mkapa of having sided with Burundi's President Pierre Nkurunziza, who had refused the alliance's participation in the talks.

According to UNHCR, Tanzania was hosting more than 235,000 *Burundian refugees* in camps in western Tanzania. After the CCM had played a positive role in 2015 in reconciling warring factions in *South Sudan*, no further Tanzanian activities to mediate in the continuing civil war were reported.

Magufuli's efforts to curb corruption and waste earned Tanzania *worldwide approval*, but relations with *Western donor countries* remained somewhat ambivalent. On the one hand, they welcomed the government's reform efforts, which they had been calling for for years. Tanzania was one of only two African countries invited to the UK's Anti-Corruption Summit in London in May. On the other, they were critical about the evident erosion of democratic governance, including through harassment of opposition parties and restrictions on press freedom, freedom of expression and freedom of assembly. The handling of the Zanzibar election crisis was another major point of criticism. Some Western countries and institutions still continued to provide substantial aid, but were reluctant to provide unspecified budget support. Asian countries, specifically *China* and *India*, remained equally important as investors and providers of credit for Tanzania's economic and infrastructure development.

Socioeconomic Developments

According to most standard indicators, the overall *macroeconomic performance* was again quite satisfactory, in line with the strong continuous growth trend that had persisted since the early 2000s. Tanzania remained in the top group of the fastest-growing and most consistently performing economies in Africa, although it was still characterised by a very low level of material wealth for the vast majority of the population (about one-third were living below the poverty line). In the 2016 *HDI* (data for 2015), Tanzania was again ranked 151st (out of 188 countries) in the 'low human development' category. The average *per capita income* (in nominal terms) was estimated to be around $ 1,000 per year – thus practically attaining the government's declared goal of reaching the status of a 'lower middle-income country'. The per capita income (in PPP terms) was calculated at $ 2,467 in 2015.

Tanzania's economy continued to remain remarkably resilient in a difficult global setting of continued financial uncertainties and weak growth in SSA. This was partly due to the fact that the level of monetisation of the economy and the degree of outward trade openness were still considerably lower than the SSA average, thus shielding the country from negative repercussions. The *GDP growth rate* was estimated at 7.0%, slightly lower than planned (7.2%), but similar to preceding years and consistent with the growth trend over more than a decade. Climatically, it was by and large a fairly regular year, but the normal year-end rains failed in many parts of the country, raising fears of serious food shortages (which were denied by government). The *agricultural sector* again performed poorly, with a growth rate of just above 2%, and the food stock of the National Food Reserve had to be run down to 90,000 tonnes by the year's end, compared with 180,000 in 2015 and 466,000 in 2014. The main *drivers of growth* continued to be the communications, mining and services sectors, while manufacturing industries (after remarkable expansion in recent years) were hampered by difficulties in obtaining credit and a slowdown of demand due to a general shortage of liquidity throughout the economy. For some years, expectations of a faster and more fundamental transformation of the economy had been linked with prospects for substantial natural gas production (based on significant proven reserves), but, with depressed global oil markets, full commercial exploitation (including liquid natural gas [LNG] for export) did not appear realistic before sometime in the 2020s. Tanzania's ranking was just slightly improved at 116th (out of 138 countries) in the World Economic Forum's Global Competitiveness Index, and at 132nd (out of 190 countries) in the World Bank's Doing Business report. In the World Bank's 2015 Country Policy and Institutional Assessment, Tanzania scored 3.6 (out of 6); despite a slight deterioration compared with 2008, it remained well above the SSA average, ranking joint sixth of 38 countries assessed. This appraisal reflected the government's relatively prudent management of the economy.

Headline *inflation* was successfully contained close to the medium-term target of 5%, at an average rate of 5.2% for the year. For a fourth consecutive year, a prudent monetary policy thus met its desired target. Contrary to a substantial depreciation of 24% against the dollar in 2015, the *exchange rate* of the shilling remained unusually stable throughout the year, reaching TSh 2,173 : $ 1 at year's end. This was largely the result of a tight liquidity situation in the domestic banking system and above all of a significantly improved balance of payments situation. For a second year running, the *structural trade deficit* was brought down by a further 33% from $ 5.6 bn (2014) and $ 4.4 bn (2015) to $ 3.0 bn, principally as a result of a much reduced (by 12%) import bill of $ 8,661 bn. This fall was largely due to a sharp decline in the import of capital goods (as a result of reduced large investments) and consumer goods. Export earnings grew by 5.3% to $ 5,689 bn, mainly from minerals and a recovery of traditional agricultural exports (by 12%). Manufactured goods fell in value by 20%. On balance, two-thirds of Tanzania's import needs were covered by its own export earnings – the highest ratio ever achieved. Coupled with a strongly improved surplus (by 83%) in the service sector account (largely from tourism, the main foreign exchange source), this led to the *current-account deficit* being almost halved (from $ 4 bn in 2015 to $ 2 bn), equivalent to an estimated 4.4% of GDP (exceptionally low compared with around 10% in previous years). *Gross foreign exchange reserves* remained practically unchanged; by the end of December they amounted to $ 4.3 bn, sufficient to cover 4.2 months of imports of goods and services. While the *external debt* had been substantially reduced in the early 2000s to a low of $ 4.2 bn in 2006 as a result of debt cancellations under the HIPC initiative, it had recently been increasing again rather fast. External debt reached a new high of $ 17 bn at year's end (compared with $ 16.5 bn in 2015). Almost 80% of the debt was owed by central government and 20% by the private sector; 47% of the debt was owed to multilateral agencies and 11% to bilateral donors, with the remainder composed of commercial debts and export credits. A debt sustainability analysis indicated that the value of the external debt was equivalent to 19.9% of GDP, well below the critical international threshold of 40%, implying that Tanzania's debt was quite sustainable.

IMF missions visited Tanzania in March and October to conduct the fourth and fifth reviews of the country's performance under the current three-year *Policy Support Instrument* (PSI). Macroeconomic performance was judged to have remained strong and the medium-term outlook was seen as favourable. Most assessment criteria under the PSI and all indicative targets were met. The IMF welcomed the authorities' ambitious reform and development agenda, but also pointed to downside risks to economic growth in the short term, stemming from the current tight stance of fiscal and monetary policies, the slow pace of credit growth, the laggard implementation of public investment programmes and private sector uncertainty about the government's new economic strategies. The pace of structural reforms was also seen as in need of acceleration.

On 8 June, Finance Minister Philip Mpango submitted the current government's maiden *budget for fiscal year 2016/17* to parliament. It was premised on a fairly optimistic economic outlook and foresaw *highly ambitious targets*, assuming significant progress in improving public-sector efficiency and revenue generation. Total expenditure was budgeted at TSh 29,540 bn (about $ 13.5 bn), a staggering increase of 31% over the 2015/16 budget figures. An unprecedented 40% of the total budget was earmarked for development expenditure, while previously well over 70% had always been allocated for recurrent expenditure (mainly salaries for about 550,000 civil servants). The revenue forecast was composed of domestic tax and non-tax revenue (51% and 9%, respectively), domestic and external borrowing (25%) and external financing from development partners (12%). There was a cautious estimate that only 1.6% was expected to come in the form of external general budget support (GBS), based on recent experience of donor countries withholding promised GBS as a sign of disapproval of certain government actions. With stricter enforcement of existing tax regulations and a widening of the tax base (for example, by introducing VAT for tourism-related services despite sharp protests from the tourism industry), the tax share of GDP was expected to rise to 13.8% (still low by comparable SSA standards), and a slightly rising fiscal deficit of 4.5% of GDP was foreseen.

The *2015/16 budgetary outcome* was marked by the satisfactory achievement of most domestic revenue targets (except for local government authorities), but by external financial shortfalls and a continuing decline in grants. Recurrent expenditure was somewhat higher than budgeted, while only 87% of budgeted development expenditure was in fact used. The fiscal deficit turned out at around the targeted 3.5% of GDP. In March, Magufuli stopped the ongoing settlement of considerable payment arrears that had accumulated over the years (e.g. to contractors, suppliers, pension funds), totalling about 1.9% of GDP by mid-2016, pending a general review of genuine verified arrears. *Budget execution* during the first half of 2016/17 was slower than expected, largely on account of ongoing external financial shortfalls. Tax revenue was broadly in line with the ambitious targets, due to rigorous collection efforts by the tax authorities. Spending (particularly development expenditure) was, however, considerably lower than budgeted, due both to slow disbursements of aid funds and to delays in spending authorisations stemming from insufficient planning capacities.

The new *2nd Five-Year Plan 2016/17–2020/21* provided the medium-term framework for the government's ambitious goal of transforming Tanzania into a semi-industrialised *middle-income country by 2025*. However, uncertainties about the government's concrete intentions and about Magufuli's often spontaneous directives led to a widely-felt atmosphere of insecurity, particularly with respect to private sector activities. Some critical observers even sensed a partial return to authoritarian state-led economic strategies, reminiscent of Tanzania's socialist past under Julius Nyerere, although the government officially stressed its unequivocal support for private-sector activities. The anti-corruption and revenue-generation drives, coupled with problems in the banking sector (a sharp increase of non-performing loans and a shift of all public-sector accounts from commercial banks to the Bank of Tanzania [BoT] in response to a Magufuli directive), contributed to a widely-felt liquidity squeeze and a slowdown of private-sector activities. In line with advice from the IMF, the BoT eventually began to ease the liquidity situation for the private sector. Magufuli's reformist steps thus proved to be somewhat disruptive in the short run, but were expected to be beneficial in the longer term.

The improvement of Tanzania's physical *infrastructure* as a precondition for faster industrialisation continued to be a major focus of the government's development strategy, but the pace of implementation often remained somewhat uncertain. The long-endured situation of insufficient electricity generation and frequent *power failures* saw a noticeable improvement, with 45% of available generated power already coming from natural gas and with further expansion underway. With more exploration activities, the volume of *proven gas reserves* was updated to 75 trn cubic feet, but no decision for the construction of an LNG plant for gas export was in sight. TANESCO, the heavily loss-making parastatal *power utility*, continued to be a major financial burden on the government; it had accumulated large arrears with its suppliers (mostly private energy producers) and had simultaneously been unable to recover huge arrears from its customers (including government departments, specifically Zanzibar). An 8.5% electricity tariff increase, approved for January 2017, was abruptly stopped by Magufuli for fear of social protests while looking for a more sustainable solution.

In February, Uganda agreed to the construction of a 1,120 km *oil pipeline* from its oil fields (Hoima) across northern Tanzania to the export port of Tanga; this decision overturned earlier plans to build the pipeline across Kenya and was viewed as a victory in the perennial competition between Kenya and Tanzania. China offered a credit of $ 7.6 bn for the construction of a new *standard-gauge railway* to replace the existing dilapidated central railway line, but plans remained to be finalised in 2017. The start of Chinese-financed projects to develop large *coal and iron ore deposits* in south-western Tanzania was further delayed, awaiting the conclusion of protracted discussions over government subsidies. In August, the government *banned the import of coal* to strengthen the local coal industry, but this met with strong protests from local consumers (specifically the cement industry) due to the low quality of local coal. This led to a major conflict over a cement factory in Mtwara, opened in 2015 by Nigerian billionaire Dangote with a $ 500 m investment; it had created 10,000 jobs and supplied a third of the local market. Dangote threatened to close the factory because promises by the previous government had not been met. Only upon Magufuli's intervention was a solution found that allowed the factory to obtain gas at an acceptable price.

In July, the government backed away from the expected ratification of the long disputed EPA between the EAC and the EU, citing newly arising uncertainties over Brexit and fears over its negative consequences for Tanzania's future industrialisation. With diverging positions of Kenya and Rwanda, no common EAC position had been found by year's end. In November, parliament unanimously rejected the EPA and supported the government's stance. The EPA question clearly underpinned the government's latent protectionist and nationalistic economic tendencies, which were also visible in a number of other domains.

Uganda

Volker Weyel

Though not much of a surprise had been expected, the presidential and parliamentary elections, held early in the year, were the major domestic event, together with their aftermath. This partly overshadowed the unfortunate developments in neighbouring countries, which all had their repercussions on Uganda. South Sudan's state failure caused Uganda to emerge as one of the world's leading host countries for refugees. Its international standing mirrored its role as an active member of worldwide and African organisations as well as being an effective regional power. Internal political challenges were on the rise, but overall stability was maintained, though at the price of ruthless enforcement of what the government in power deemed to be law and order. In a global economic environment that was becoming increasingly complex, the economy did moderately well. Oil production, believed by some to be the silver bullet for all problems, did not commence, with various preparatory measures still in the offing.

 | DOI 10.1163/9789004355910_043

Domestic Politics

On the day of the *election for the presidency and Uganda's 10th parliament* on 18 February, the rule of Yoweri Kaguta Museveni, who was sworn in as president on 29 January 1986, had already clocked up 30 years. The results of the polls saw again a *large majority for the incumbent and the ruling National Resistance Movement* (NRM). Ahead of the elections, state actors created an intimidating atmosphere. Opposition politicians were arbitrarily arrested and their rallies obstructed, and journalists were harassed. But for the first time two televised debates between the presidential contenders took place, one in January without and one in February with the participation of the incumbent. On the eve of election day, social media platforms were closed down by the state. Voting was generally peaceful, though marred by a good number of irregularities. Conspicuously, in some urban areas (presumed to be opposition-leaning) voting materials did not arrived till the afternoon; some Kampala polling stations had to re-open the following day. On the evening of 18 February, there was a tense atmosphere outside district counting centres, police using teargas in some cases, and in the capital the presidential candidate of the main opposition force, the Forum for Democratic Change (FDC), was detained when trying to investigate alleged rigging.

Foreign *observers* were present. Former Nigerian president Olusegun Obasanjo, head of the Commonwealth observer group, summarised the main concerns, saying, "Uganda has fallen well short of meeting many of the key democratic benchmarks for the conduct of credible elections." Key points of criticism were "the increased prevalence of money in politics, the misuse of state resources, and the competence, credibility and the ability of the Electoral Commission to manage the process effectively", all already mentioned by the 2011 Commonwealth observers. Obasanjo expressed "profound disappointment that none of the previous recommendations have been substantively addressed". Similarly, the EU mission noted the "orchestrated use of state resources and personnel for campaign purposes" and the absence of any "legal measures to ensure a level playing field in the campaign". It found that "the Electoral Commission (EC) lacked independence and transparency" and noted that the "entire tallying process lacked transparency and checks against electoral malpractice". The AU mission concluded more benevolently that the elections "were largely peaceful, but not without shortcomings".

Apart from Museveni, seven other *candidates* stood for president, the most notable being former prime minister and NRM secretary-general Amama Mbabazi and previous FDC party leader Dr Kizza Besigye Kifefe. The others included a former vice-chancellor of Makerere University, a gospel evangelist, a retired general and one female contender. Mbabazi stood as an independent. FDC candidate Besigye ran against Museveni for the fourth time. According to the results declared by the EC, the incumbent won 60.6% of the vote, compared with 68.4% in 2011, 59.3% in 2006 and 69.4% in 2001. Besigye received 35.6% (2011: 26%, 2006: 37.4%, 2001: 27.7%), and Mbabazi only a humiliating 1.4%. Voter turnout (10.3 m of 15.3 m registered voters) reached 67.6%. The president was inaugurated on 12 May. His new term of office would run to 2021, but the question of possible succession continued to be a popular subject of speculation. The name of his son Muhoozi Kainerugaba, head of the Uganda People's Defence Forces' (UPDF) Special Forces Command (SFC), was usually mentioned; in May he was promoted to major general.

The elections to *parliament* were based on first-past-the-post majority voting in the 290 constituencies and for the 112 district women representatives. Voting for the representatives of special interest groups (ten for the army, five each for youth, persons with disabilities and workers) took place in a separate process. The NRM won a resounding victory, while the FDC took only 36 of the 427 seats in parliament (8.4%). The Democratic Party (DP) had 15 legislators, the Uganda People's Congress (UPC) six. Opposition in parliament faced an NRM camp not only consisting of the 294 declared party members (68.9%) but also including many of the 66 'independents' and the military MPs, who had no formal party affiliation. Speaker Rebecca Kadaga, first elected by the 9th parliament in May 2011, was re-elected on 19 May, as was her deputy and rival Jacob Oulanyah (both NRM). Winifred Kiiza (FDC), district woman representative for Kasese, became 'Leader of Opposition in the House'. One-third of the MPs were women, most of them having been elected to the reserved seats. Only a few female candidates won in the regular constituencies. On 1 July, four new districts became operational, and in those four additional district women representatives were elected on 29 August, all belonging to the NRM, raising the number of MPs to 431. In addition, there were a number of ex-officio MPs without the right to vote, namely ministers (including the prime minister) who had not stood for parliament or had failed to be elected.

Among the *elected MPs* were three descendants of former presidents. Taban Idi Amin (NRM), Idi Amin Dada's grandson, won a constituency in Bunyoro; James ('Jimmy') Akena (UPC), son of Apolo Milton Obote, succeeded in Lango; Henry Okello Oryem (NRM), son of General Tito Okello Lutwa, gained a seat in Acholi. A first was the election of an MP of the Jewish faith (though listed by parliament as 'Budhist'), Rabbi Sizomu Wambede (FDC), who was elected in Bugisu and belonged to the tiny Abayudaya community, which had its origins in the embracing of Judaism by a warrior from Buganda in the 1920s. With regard to religion, the largest group were the Anglicans, followed by Catholics (the reverse of the picture countrywide). Pentecostals followed some way behind, but demonstrating their increased role in recent years, and before Muslims. Regarding training and profession, teachers, social workers and administrators were best represented. In the elections for district chairpersons and councillors that followed (in most cases on 24 February), Besigye ally Erias Lukwago was re-elected lord mayor of Kampala.

Immediately after the elections, Besigye scorned the EC and called the results a fraud, but the FDC, regarding any legal recourse as futile, did not take its objections to court. Mbabazi, however, petitioned the Supreme Court on 1 March to annul the elections, alleging various offences committed by Museveni during the electoral period, including his 'illegal nomination'. On 31 March, the Court, though acknowledging some instances of non-compliance by EC officials and interference by security forces, unanimously dismissed the petition. Besigye declared himself the 'people's president', claiming to have won 52% of the vote, and staged a 'swearing-in' at an undisclosed place, circulated on YouTube the day before Museveni's inauguration. This was followed by a *'defiance' campaign* with demonstrations intended to bring him to power. The strategy was criticised within the FDC and attracted neither lasting nor large-scale support, but it did lead to a number of clashes between his supporters and the police, to Besigye being charged on 11 May with treason and jailed for two months before his release on bail, to further multiple arrests mostly for a few hours only and to court summonses. Besigye was subjected to prolonged de facto house arrest, his home being blocked by police, but he was not prevented from travelling abroad for a couple of weeks. Police action against Besigye's supporters included the caning of people lining the streets to greet him on his way to the FDC headquarters in July. The public outcry led to an internal police investigation against the men involved.

While the 1995 constitution had limited the number of cabinet ministers to 21, a 2005 amendment allowed for "such number of Ministers as may appear to the President to be reasonably necessary for the efficient running of the State". On 17 June, parliament approved an increase in the number of cabinet ministers to 31 and of ministers of state to 49, thus creating 82 top positions (including the president and vice president). The list of appointees had already been announced by the president on 6 June. In the *new government*, Vice President Edward Kiwanuka Ssekandi was reappointed, as was Prime Minister Dr Ruhakana Rugunda. The two deputy prime ministers, Moses Ali and Ali Kirunda Kivejinja, also returned, indicating an attempt to achieve regional and religious balance: the president and prime minister being Anglicans from Ankole and Kigezi in the west, the vice president being a Catholic from Buganda and the two deputy prime ministers being Muslims from West Nile and Busoga, representing the north and the east, respectively. Among the cabinet ministers, the majority were from the west and Buganda, the home regions of the majority of Ugandans.

A number of seasoned politicians were dropped, including controversial characters such as Jim Muhwezi, John Nasasira and Abraham Byandala, whose names had figured in corruption cases. Defence Minister Dr Crispus Kiyonga, sole winner of a constituency for Museveni's Uganda Patriotic Movement in the 1980 flawed elections, lost to an FDC candidate. However, another 'historical' politician, Justice Minister Major-General Kahinda Otafiire, was reappointed, despite having stood unsuccessfully as an independent, and having earlier failed to be nominated in the NRM primaries. Another loser in the NRM primaries, Idah Nantaba, was elected as an independent; after having been an outspoken defender of tenants' rights as state minister for lands, she now was appointed state minister for information and communications technology. The president's wife, Janet Museveni, previously state minister for Karamoja, now headed the weighty Education and Sports Ministry. Betty Amongi, a UPC MP and wife of UPC MP Jimmy Akena, an ally of Museveni, became minister of lands, housing and urban development. The president also enlisted the 2011 Uganda Federal Alliance contender for the presidency, Beti Kamya, and appointed her minister responsible for Kampala City. Also drawn from the opposition ranks, Florence Nakiwala Kiyingi became state minister for youth and children's affairs; a DP member and former office-holder in Buganda kingdom, she had stood unsuccessfully for parliament. Tito Okello's son, Okello Oryem, was reappointed as state minister for international affairs. Christopher Kibanzanga, brother of Rwenzururu king Wesley Mumbere, became state minister for agriculture. For the portfolios of internal affairs and of security, men with a military background were appointed: General Jeje Odongo and Lieutenant-General Henry Tumukunde.

The *political parties* continued to be characterised by internal conflict, particularly the 'old' parties, the DP and UPC. DP party head Norbert Mao was not able to run for a seat in parliament since the EC in 2015 had determined that he was too late submitting his forms. UPC President Olara Otunnu resigned, as announced earlier, and handed over to his deputy, Joseph Bossa, at the end of May. The struggle with Akena's faction continued. A court ruling allowed Akena to continue to use the party offices occupied by his supporters in 2015 until such time as the leadership dispute was settled, but the wealthy Milton Obote Foundation (close to the party and owner of Uganda House, a commercial building in central Kampala and site of the UPC offices) remained on Bossa's side.

New *legislation* was introduced. The Financial Institutions (Amendment) Act, 2016, was passed by parliament on 6 January, and received presidential assent on 19 January; it provided for Islamic banking and for agent and branchless banking. The Anti-Terrorism (Amendment) Act, 2016, was passed on 7 January and assented to on 19 January, to update the definitions of 'terrorism' and 'acts of terrorism'. The Non-Governmental Organisations Act, 2016, signed into law by the president on 30 January, established the National Bureau for Non-Governmental Organisations, tasked "to register, regulate, coordinate and monitor" NGO activities. The Children (Amendment) Bill, 2016, passed by parliament on 2 March, was signed into law on 20 May. It sought to protect children from all forms of violence, including sexual abuse, child sacrifice and child trafficking. Guardianship was restricted to Ugandans; inter-country adoption was seen as a last resort. Signed into law on 19 November, the Income Tax (Amendment) Act, 2016, was applied retroactively from 1 July. The bill had been passed in March; since it included a provision by which MPs exempted themselves from paying tax for emoluments other than their salaries, it was rejected in May by the president. Museveni later returned it twice more, but was overruled by parliament and approved it on 15 November.

For the second time, Uganda underwent the Universal Periodic Review in the field of *human rights* by the UN in Geneva in November. As in 2011, among the issues addressed by Human Rights Council members were infringements of the right of assembly and inappropriate action taken by the security forces. In response to concerns raised about attitudes towards homosexuals, the foreign minister stated that no discrimination based on sexual orientation would be tolerated. In the same month, a provision in the Equal Opportunities Commission Act, 2007, which could be read as allowing the use of sexual orientation as the basis for denying certain persons the right to complain, was scrapped by the Constitutional Court.

The fight against *corruption* remained an uphill task. A prominent case of theft of pension funds concluded with the conviction of three public servants, including one high-ranking bureaucrat, by the anti-corruption division of the High Court in November. A former permanent secretary in the Ministry of Public Service received a seven-year prison term and two others were sentenced to five and ten years in jail. Parliament's Committee on Statutory Authorities and State Enterprises was able to recoup some misused public funds and also recovered from Chinese contractors working on highway improvements a sum of well over $ 20 m that had been intended to compensate people affected by the works. "This money was put on fixed deposit accounts since 2013 for some individuals to profit from," according to Speaker Kadaga.

Some notable threats to *internal security* occurred. In June, Gulu Central Police Station was attacked by people claiming to belong to a 'National Democratic Alliance'. Shortly after, the commander of Entebbe air force garrison, a colonel, was arrested for subversive activities; soldiers and an opposition MP suspected of involvement also went to jail. The Muslim community had suffered from a spate of murders of senior clerics in recent years and the Allied Democratic Forces (ADF), who had formerly fought against the government but had long since been active only in the DRC, were alleged to be involved. The Ugandan authorities described the ADF as having links with Islamists and as a potential threat to the west of the country. Muhammad Kiggundu, a former ADF commander who had renounced rebellion and became integrated into the UPDF, was gunned down on 26 November in Kampala. The trial of 13 defendants charged with involvement in the 11 July 2010 terrorist attacks linked to al-Shabaab (Uganda's '7/11') ended on 26 May with eight of them sentenced to long jail terms.

After clashes in 2012 and 2014, conflict in the *Mountains of the Moon*, the Rwenzori mountain range, resurfaced. After the local elections that followed the presidential and parliamentary polls, fighting spurred by allegations of rigging broke out in a number of places between ethnic groups. At least 45 people lost their lives and 8,000 were displaced. Further escalation occurred at the end of November. Suspicious activities of a Bakonzo militia believed to favour secession (and to have linked up with Congolese Bakonzo to form a 'Yiira Republic') and the reluctance of Rwenzururu king Wesley Mumbere to respond to President Museveni's demands to disarm his 'royal guards' eventually culminated in disaster. Mumbere's residence was attacked by the UPDF and police Field Force and burned down. The king was arrested on 27 November. It was thought that more than 150 people may have died, including at least 14 police. The opposition criticised the use of maximum force by the government and suspected that the motive was to punish the locals, the majority of whom had voted for the FDC.

Makerere University was placed fourth among the top 15 African universities by the 'Times Higher Education World University Rankings', being the only one of the first six that was not situated in South Africa. Even so, it was not spared from problems. Beset with staff and students strikes and conflicts over various types of grievances, it was even temporarily closed at year's end.

The Uganda Cranes, the national *football* team, defeated the Comoros on 4 September, and thus, after 38 years, qualified for the Africa Cup of Nations to be played in 2017. No Ugandan athlete left the Rio Olympics with a medal, but David Emong won the country's first-ever *Paralympic* award on 16 September, a silver medal in the men's 1500 metres event in the T46 category.

The internationally-acclaimed Disney movie *'Queen of Katwe'*, based on the true story of a girl from a poor Kampala neighbourhood turned chess champion, had its Ugandan premiere in October.

On 29 November, the Ma'di bowl lyre music and dance of the Madi people in northernmost Uganda was added by UNESCO to its List of Intangible *Cultural Heritage* in Need of Urgent Safeguarding, Uganda's sixth entry in this international register.

For the first time, 16 February was observed as a public holiday devoted to the memory of Anglican Archbishop Janani *Luwum* who was killed on that day in 1977 on the orders of Idi Amin. Robert *Kitariko*, a former secretary-general of the DP, born in 1933 in Kigezi, died on 18 January. Joshua Wanume *Kibedi*, 1941-born former brother-in-law and foreign affairs minister of Idi Amin and a cousin to Second Deputy Prime Minister Kirunda Kivejinja, died on 13 June in London. Kibedi, a member of one of Busoga's 11 royal clans, had been appointed by President Museveni as chairman of the Uganda Citizenship and Immigration Board in 2012. DP Secretary-General Mathias *Nsubuga*, born in 1956 and hailing from Buganda, died on 18 December.

Foreign Affairs

Uganda excelled as a pioneer in the UN's *2030 Agenda* process, since in New York in July it was among the 22 states delivering voluntary national reviews on their readiness to implement the Sustainable Development Goals (SDGs). The 2015 Paris Agreement, which aimed to enhance the implementation of the UN Framework Convention on *Climate Change*, was ratified on 21 September, the government having committed itself in 2015 to a 22% reduction in carbon emissions by 2030. Other actions were more controversial, notably *Museveni's criticism of the ICC*. Despite having become a state party to the Rome Statute in 2002 and having played host to the ICC Review Conference in 2010, Uganda became a vocal critic of the ICC because of its alleged "preoccupation with Africa". Taking the opportunity of his inauguration, Museveni denigrated the court as "a bunch of useless people". ICC indictee and Sudanese President Omar al-Bashir was one of the guests, Uganda ignoring its obligation under the Rome Statute to arrest him. Withdrawal from the ICC was threatened but not implemented. The trial of Dominic Ongwen, a former senior leader of the Lord's Resistance Army (LRA) apprehended in the CAR in 2015, opened on 6 December in The Hague.

In Entebbe on 4 July, *Israel*'s Prime Minister Benjamin Netanyahu commemorated the rescue of the hostages taken by Palestinian and German terrorists 40 years before and the death of his brother Yonathan in that operation. The same day, Museveni hosted a regional heads of state and government summit meeting with Netanyahu on counter-terrorism. It was attended by the presidents of Kenya, Rwanda, South Sudan and Zambia, Ethiopia's prime minister and Tanzania's foreign minister. The leaders and the Israeli prime minister "agreed to strengthen cooperation on security, fight and defeat terrorism and all crimes that are associated with it, including cyber crime". In October, Netanyahu described "Uganda's support for Israel in international forums" as of "great importance to us, as is your facilitating our return to the African Union as an observer State" and alluded to a "strategic partnership" between the two countries.

Two *mediation* attempts by Museveni on regional issues proved futile. His efforts in favour of an intra-Burundian dialogue, later being pursued by former Tanzanian president Benjamin Mkapa as 'facilitator', lacked tangible results. The informal mediation role in the Darfur conflict that Museveni assumed in May led to his meetings with two rebel groups in Kampala on 19 October and 31 December, apparently without consequences. Former vice president Dr Speciosa Kazibwe was nominated as candidate to chair the AU Commission, but eventually withdrew due to lack of support. On 23 October in Geneva, Speaker Kadaga was elected chairperson of the Inter-Parliamentary Union's African group.

Within the *EAC* (which on 2 March decided to admit South Sudan as its sixth member), on 23 April the 13th Northern Corridor Integration Projects Summit took place in Kampala, with Burundi and Tanzania remaining observers. Yet an important shift in relations with the neighbours took place when the summit "agreed that two crude oil pipelines … will be developed by Kenya and Uganda respectively", one from the Kenyan oilfields to the Kenyan port of Lamu, the other from Hoima to the Tanzanian port of Tanga. Thus earlier plans for a joint Ugandan-Kenyan endeavour were abandoned.

Bilateral relations with *Sudan* continued to improve. On 10 October, together with the presidents of Chad, Egypt and Mauritania, Museveni witnessed the conclusion of Sudan's National Dialogue process in Khartoum (involving numerous political parties and armed movements, though boycotted by the major ones). The presidents of Uganda and the *DRC* met on 4 August in Mweya Safari Lodge and agreed to share intelligence information. The issue of the repatriation of former M-23 fighters cantoned in Bihanga military camp remained unresolved. Gold smuggling from the DRC continued, the ultimate export destination being Dubai.

The greatest challenge unfolded at the northern border. Ever since mid-December 2013, refugees had arrived from *South Sudan*, fleeing the turmoil there. When events there took an even more dramatic turn in July, the increasing inflow became a heavy burden. UNHCR's Bidibidi camp in Yumbe district opened in August and became the fastest growing refugee settlement in the world. Uganda became the African country hosting the highest number of refugees, the figure reaching 940,800 by year's end, ahead of Ethiopia, and taking fifth place of all host countries. The UPDF again evacuated Ugandan citizens but ruled out another military intervention in the country.

In foreign relations, Uganda shifted from its long-standing association with *North Korea* to collaboration with South Korea, since international enforcement of sanctions against North Korea became more serious. South Korea's President Park Geun-hye, on a state visit at the end of May, appreciated Uganda's implementation of UNSC Resolution 2270 of 2 March strengthening the sanctions regime. Uganda terminated its programmes in the field of police with North Korea and military cooperation ceased by the end of the year. Chief of Defence Forces Katumba Wamala visited South Korea in early October, soon to be followed by SFC commander Muhoozi calling on the Army Special Warfare Command there.

Though criticising Museveni's domestic actions as "contraven(ing) the rule of law" and "jeopardiz(ing) Uganda's democratic progress", US Permanent Representative to the UN Samantha Power praised Uganda in the UNSC on 21 March as "a critical contributor to peace and security, especially through its long-time contribution to the African Union force in Somalia". By its Resolution 2297, adopted unanimously on 7 July, the UNSC authorised the AU to further deploy the AU Mission in Somalia (*AMISOM*) up to a maximum level of 22,126 uniformed personnel until 31 May 2017. Uganda, still contributing the biggest contingent with more than 6,000 soldiers, occasionally pondered ending its engagement. The UPDF continued to receive substantial construction and military hardware from the US, including forklifts, trucks, armoured personnel carriers and mine-resistant ambush-protected vehicles to be used for its AMISOM contingent. Uganda was seen by the US as "a partner nation and ally in global missions". At home, the UPDF embarked on setting up a mountain warfare force with French assistance in Kasese district.

'Green Berets' (US Army Special Forces) supported UPDF operations within the AU Regional Task Force (AU-RTF) in the CAR against the scattered remains of the *LRA*, whose head Joseph Kony still dodged his pursuers. Uganda announced the withdrawal of its AU-RTF contingent by September, later postponed to year's end and again stretched until April 2017. In October, US President Barack Obama extended 'Operation Observant Compass' for six months only. The UN continued to see the LRA as a threat to regional security.

Interpol's General Assembly, meeting in November in Indonesia, decided to hold the 2018 global police gathering in Kampala.

Two politicians who rose to international prominence during the year had roots in Uganda. Priti Patel, born in 1972 in London, the daughter of Ugandan-Asian refugees and previously the UK's work and pensions minister, became international development secretary in the new UK cabinet in July. Danny Antoine Rollen Faure, born in 1962 to Seychellois parents in Kilembe, was sworn in as president of Seychelles on 16 October.

Socioeconomic Developments

On 6 June, the *IMF* Executive Board completed the sixth Policy Support Instrument (PSI) review and approved a one-year extension of the programme, a mechanism that concentrated on advice and monitoring. An IMF team visited Kampala again in October, preparing the conclusion of the seventh review under the current PSI. Programme performance under the PSI was seen as "mixed". Uganda's "economy performed reasonably well in a complex environment" was the message summarised in the mission's report of 16 December. In the financial year 2015/16 (i.e., from July 2015 to June 2016), real GDP growth "slowed marginally" to 4.8% from 5% in 2014/15. "Lower than expected nominal growth and election-related spending resulted in missed revenue and deficit targets." Structural reforms went ahead, "albeit with many delays".

In contrast to the 2011 election year, no serious inflationary pressures were experienced. The average headline *inflation* (which included food crops, fuel and electricity) for the calendar year came to 5.5%, slightly above the 5.4% recorded for 2015. The Bank of Uganda (BoU) was able to reduce the central bank rate (i.e., the lending rate to banks) from 17% in October 2015 to 13% in October 2016 and 12% in December. Commercial banks had to come to grips with bad loans; in June the non-performing rate reached 8.3%. The Crane Bank, the third-largest domestic bank, experienced more than 20% of non-performers and became insolvent, prompting the BoU to take it into statutory management in October since it was seen as "systemically important".

Partly due to the strengthening of the US currency, the shilling (UGX) had depreciated by 17.5% against the dollar during the calendar year 2015. In 2016, however, the real effective *exchange rate* depreciation was lower. In September, on a year-on-year basis, the currency even appreciated by 7.8% against the dollar. The level of international reserves remained adequate, equivalent to approximately four months of imports.

Finance Minister Matia Kasaija read the *2016/17 budget* on 8 June; on 3 May it had been approved by the 9th parliament, then still in office. Under the timely heading 'Enhanced Productivity for Job Creation', it provided for expenditure of UGX 26,361 bn, equivalent to $ 7.9 bn. The rise from the 2015/16 appropriation of almost UGX 24 trn to more than UGX 26.3 trn constituted an increase of about 9%, though in dollar terms it appeared less dramatic compared with the $ 7.6 bn in 2015. External financing was projected to be UGX 6.5 trn, 24.8% of the total, mainly made up of concessional and non-concessional loans plus some grants. The *tax* base was to be expanded "by gradually formalizing the large informal sector, improving efficiency in tax collection and compliance". Tax increases hit the usual suspects, with rises in excise duties on diesel and petrol, cigarettes and sweets. The more affluent were targeted by quadrupling registration fees for personalised number plates. The emphasis of the budget allocations was again on infrastructure. Looking back, the budget deficit for 2015/16 was estimated at 6.4% of GDP, largely financed by external borrowing and "to a lesser extent by domestic borrowing equivalent to 1.6% of GDP".

The final results of the *2014 census* were released in March, putting the 2014 population total at 34.6 m, slightly lower than in the provisional results (34.8 m). The average annual population growth rate (2002–14) was 3%. In Uganda's SDG review document, concern was cautiously expressed that all "efforts to leave no one behind could be undermined by the fact that the increasing numbers pose a burden on the available resources thus affecting service delivery levels".

After having cancelled funding for a roadworks project in the west of the country on 21 December 2015, "due to contractual breaches related to workers' issues, social and environmental concerns, poor project performance, and … serious allegations of road workers' sexual relations with minor girls in the community", the *World Bank* on 8 January suspended the disbursement of funds for two other projects, also overseen by the Uganda National Roads Authority (UNRA), "pending a review and strengthening of the capacity of UNRA to adhere to the required environmental and social standards". Later, the World Bank decided to put in place a Global Gender-Based Violence Task Force to provide advice "on best practices for reducing risks to community safety in connection with our development projects". More general dissatisfaction came to the fore when the World Bank decided to withhold any new IDA lending, effective from 22 August, while reviewing the portfolio in consultation with the government. Critical performance issues included "delays in project effectiveness, weaknesses in safeguards monitoring and enforcement, and low disbursement".

At the beginning of July, it became known that the Russian enterprise Rostec had withdrawn from a project to construct an *oil* refinery after disagreement on payment terms. On 30 August, developers Tullow and Total were granted oil production licences.

The Parliamentary Forum on *Social Protection*, launched in early 2014, was reinstated in October. Speaker Kadaga pointed out that there was a tendency in society to neglect old people instead of giving them the special attention they needed, particularly those who lived alone.

Issues concerning *land*, including evictions, were a perennial source of debate and conflict; on 8 December, the president set up a commission of inquiry into matters of acquisition, administration, management and registration of land.

The entrenchment of *corruption* in the country was reflected in TI's 2016 Corruption Perceptions Index, which ranked Uganda 151st of 176 countries (compared with 139th of 168 in 2015), far behind Rwanda and also worse than Tanzania and Kenya, though better than Burundi and South Sudan.

PART 6

Southern Africa

Henning Melber

It was mainly 'business as usual' for the sub-region for the second consecutive year with a limited number of elections, but governance issues in several countries nevertheless provoked protest, unrest and contestation in domestic policies, causing a certain level of policy turmoil. Bumpy roads in Zambia and Lesotho, growing political-economic uncertainty in Angola and Zimbabwe over succession issues to the longest serving heads of state in the region, dos Santos and Mugabe, continued scandals under the Zuma administration in South Africa, major corruption issues in Malawi and the damaging consequences of the disclosure of secret loans in Mozambique, made headlines and had negative consequences for the domestic situation.

The Angolan, Namibian and South African economies were possibly hit hardest for different reasons, including the slump in the oil price (Angola), the effects of drought and previous overspending by government (Namibia) and economic mismanagement and dubious appointments in state administration (South Africa). In particular, the weakening of the Angolan and South African powerhouses in the sub-region affected the overall economic performance of neighbouring countries, as did the general decline in commodity prices on the world market, which had a negative effect on resource-based economies.

In addition, floods and drought hit many rural communities in most countries and water shortages seriously impacted living conditions in urban areas too. The ecological vulnerability of the sub-region to effects of climate change became ever more visible and indicated serious challenges for the future, while concerted efforts by SADC states to promote integration and invest in preventative measures continued to lack the necessary political will to meet the challenges. After several years of high economic growth, hard times had arrived. Despite these setbacks, the sub-region continued to score best in terms of governance compared with other parts of SSA.

Elections, Democracy and Human Rights

Zambia held general elections for the presidency, the National Assembly, local government councils and mayors/council chairpersons on 11 August. Voters chose between nine presidential candidates and 13 political parties. It was a tight race between the two old rivals Edgar Lungu of the Patriotic Front (PF), seeking re-election as head of state, and his main rival, Hakainde Hichilema of the United

 | DOI 10.1163/9789004355910_044

Party for National Development (UPND). After an election campaign that saw several violent incidents Lungu was re-elected by a narrow margin of 50.4% of the votes to 47.6% secured by Hichilema. The PF also emerged as the biggest party with 42% (80 seats), followed closely by the UPND with 41.7% (57 seats). The main loser was the former government party, Movement for Multi-Party Democracy (MMD), which did not put forward a presidential candidate. The number of parliamentary seats it held fell from 55 to three, when it won only 2.7% of the votes. Hichilema rejected the election results as fraudulent but failed both to prevent Lungu's swearing in and to secure a recount. Violent protests in UPND strongholds resulted in the arrest of over 300 people. The municipal elections were also a close race between the two parties, with the PF securing 50 electoral victories and the UPND 48. The head-to-head race and tight outcome did not bode well for the future political climate. A referendum held in parallel to the general elections sought support for a constitutional amendment that would both add to and reduce civil liberties by strengthening socio-economic rights on the one hand while on the other prohibiting same sex relations and abortion. The referendum turnout did not reach the necessary minimum 50% and so failed.

South Africa was the battleground for heavily contested local (municipal) elections. Their results were a blow to the governing African National Congress (ANC), which lost its control over the Johannesburg, Pretoria (Tshwane) and Port Elizabeth (Nelson Mandela Bay) metropolitan cities to opposition parties, despite remaining the strongest party with a total of 54% of votes countrywide. The Democratic Alliance (DA) not only emerged as the strengthened political alternative but was also able to extend its earlier control over Cape Town to a two-thirds majority. The election results also confirmed that the Economic Freedom Fighters (EFF) had managed as a party to establish themselves as a meaningful force able to upset balances of power. The sobering results for the ANC signalled voters' growing frustration with the Zuma administration.

Presidential succession was at the core of domestic politics in *Angola* and *Zimbabwe*. Angola's Josè Eduardo dos Santos of the Movimento Popular de Libertação de Angola (MPLA), in office since 1979, announced that he would retire in 2018. With elections scheduled for 2017, this still left room for speculation as to who might be selected as his replacement and whether he planned to remain in charge of the party, despite continued indications of his health problems. Meanwhile the battle over the succession to Robert Mugabe (in office since 1980) continued among various factions of the Zimbabwe African National Union-Patriotic Front (ZANU-PF). Although the party nominated Mugabe again as its candidate for the next presidential elections in 2018, the 93-year old autocrat's deteriorating health suggested that a potential successor might be required at any time. Internal party rivalries resulted in the expulsion or side-lining of several potential candidates during the year and absorbed much energy, but the divided and weak opposition parties were unable to exploit this focus on intra-party matters.

The tense domestic policy situation in *Lesotho*, with a confrontation between Phakalitha Mosisili – leader of the Democratic Congress (DC) and in charge of a fragile seven-party coalition government – and Tom Thabane of the opposition All Basotho Convention (ABC), continued to paralyse any transition to some kind of stability in the mountain kingdom. The ongoing feuds and power struggles, involving army and police as important if not decisive factors of influence, also negatively impacted on relations with SADC and its efforts to mediate through South Africa's Deputy President Cyril Ramaphosa. Political turmoil continued unabated.

Rumours about a coup d'état marred domestic politics in *Madagascar*, but despite constant pressure caused by political instability the government managed to handle the challenges. In *Mauritius*, even though the country continued to receive high marks in political rankings, the relatively stable political environment was eroded by a constitutionally dubious announcement by Prime Minister Anerood Jugnauth that he was to hand over the role to his son in what was dubbed a monarchy-like succession arrangement. A reform of the electoral act introduced by the government in *Botswana* provoked massive protest by the opposition parties, afraid that it would create opportunities for manipulation by the introduction of electronic voting machines. *Malawi* politics remained marred by massive corruption scandals.

The political opposition parties in *South Africa* articulated growing frustration with government policy amidst increased public protest against President Jacob Zuma's policy of self-aggrandisement, which, despite mounting dissent and criticism, continued to be tolerated by a majority of office-holders within the governing ANC's essential political organs. But opposition within the ANC to the continued backing of the party and state president mounted. Open demands for his resignation coincided with opposition parties' failed efforts to seek his impeachment. Despite lack of public support, the hitherto most controversial and least accepted head of state since the first democratic elections remained in office and survived damning reports by the public protector and a ruling by the Constitutional Court that he had violated the constitution.

On the occasion of the annual SADC summit, HRW published on 30 August a document that expressed concerns over the *deterioration of human rights* in Angola, Mozambique, Swaziland, South Africa and Zimbabwe. The statement lamented the severe curtailing of rights to freedom of expression and association in Angola and the excessive force, arbitrary arrests and intimidation by state organs to prevent peaceful anti-government protests, strikes and other gatherings. In Zimbabwe, "no progress toward justice for human rights violations during past political violence" was observed. Rather, police applied outdated and abusive laws to curb freedom of speech and assembly. Arbitrary detention and unfair trials remained the order of the day in Swaziland under the draconian Suppression of Terrorism Act, which was applied to restrict political activism. Human rights abuses also increased in Mozambique, with a new escalation of conflict between the Frelimo government and Renamo. An erosion of respect for the rule of law was also diagnosed in South Africa, along with growing xenophobic tendencies and concerns over the extreme levels of rape and other forms of violence against women. While the government of Botswana continued to promote a value-based foreign policy in support of human rights and related normative frameworks, its domestic policy with regard to minority rights remained restrictive and at best reluctant.

Media freedom was also a matter under scrutiny and of concern, as governments seemed increasingly to consider further infringement on the independent press. Stronger control of social media was another emerging feature. Print and broadcast media were under threat and limited in their freedom in several countries. In Zambia, several of the print, broadcast and electronic media were restricted in their operations. In Angola, journalists and media were exposed to even stricter limitations and interferences. New media laws increased restrictions on print and social media and a newly created body under MPLA control was tasked with the accreditation of journalists. Media repression also increased in Lesotho, and censorship continued in Swaziland's media, while the state-owned public broadcaster in South Africa was put under stricter administrative control by the governing ANC to ensure loyal and selective reporting. As in previous years, Namibia remained the highest-ranked country on the continent in media freedom and compared favourably even with some established Western democracies.

Police state methods of repression remained a threat to social movements, other civil society actors and members of political oppositions in several countries in the sub-region. In Zimbabwe, the leader of the campaign #ThisFlag was arrested and after his release left the country, seeking temporary refuge in the USA. This and several other spectacular cases of draconian, unlawful prosecution testified to the continued repressive nature of Zimbabwean government politics and a strict clampdown on political opposition. Political activists remained at risk of being abducted and 'disappeared'. The same risks faced activists in Angola, where social protest was met by state terror and extrajudicial killings became widespread, while the military conflict over the Cabinda province continued. In Mozambique, the violent conflict between the governing Frelimo and the Renamo opposition included not only military encounters but also the use of hit squads to eliminate individuals through targeted assassinations.

Despite all the limitations and concerns listed above, the sub-region – as in previous years – ranked in the overall aggregate based on the scores of the 12 countries by far the best on the continent in the *Ibrahim Index of African Governance*. The overall governance score was 58.3 (African average: 50.0). All indicators scored higher than the African average. The sectors performed as follows (compared with the SSA average): Safety and rule of law – 63.3 (52.1), participation and human rights – 59.7 (50.0), sustainable economic opportunity – 50.5 (42.9) and human development – 59.9 (55.0). The *Freedom House Index* on Freedom in the World placed the countries in the following categories (from best scores to worst): Mauritius, Botswana, Namibia, South Africa as 'free', Lesotho, Malawi, Madagascar, Zambia, Mozambique, Zimbabwe as 'partly free' and Angola and Swaziland as 'not free'. The comparison between the rankings of different agencies displayed once again the inconsistencies and deviations in the way countries were classified.

Socioeconomic Developments

According to a SADC report released in July, the sub-region faced severe consequences of the El Niño-related *drought*. Crop failures and poor harvests resulted in an estimated shortfall of 9.3 m tonnes of cereal production. An estimated 643,000 drought-related livestock deaths were reported in Botswana, Swaziland, South Africa, Namibia and Zimbabwe alone. A statement released on 26 July appealed for $ 2.4 bn in relief aid to help 40 m people suffering from hunger. The USA ($ 300 m), the UK ($ 95 m) and the EU ($ 66 m) responded with pledges. At an *Africa Drought Conference* in Windhoek (Namibia) on 15–19 August, it was estimated that 52 m people in the sub-region were food insecure, with numbers rising.

The *macro-economic outlook* of SADC's Regional Vulnerability Assessment and Analysis programme (RVAA) warned of the backdrop of currency depreciations in countries such as Angola, Malawi, Mozambique, South Africa (which by implication included Namibia, with the local currency pegged to the rand) and Zambia. Dependency on food imports from beyond the region meant that currency depreciations presented significant challenges. The majority of countries also relied on commodity exports. With commodity prices generally lower than average, depressed economic growth ensued. The regionally still very high prevalence of HIV/AIDS (see below), with an average of 11.4%, and high malnutrition rates, added considerably to levels of vulnerability and compounded the problems.

The chronic shortage of electric *power supply* was exacerbated during parts of the year by the lack of rain and its negative impact on the generation of hydroelectric power. The regional dependency on power supplies from South Africa remained another vulnerability during times when South Africa faced problems generating sufficient power for its own demands. Most countries remained unable to meet their peak demands and power cuts often occurred as a necessary regulatory intervention. Investments in renewable, particularly solar, energy were discussed as a priority. A regional strategy promoting cleaner energy was designed, and experts endorsed a Regional Renewable Energy and Energy Efficiency Strategy and Action Plan for 2016–30 in October at a validation meeting in Johannesburg (South Africa). The AFDB estimated the overall hydropower potential in SADC countries at about 1,080 terawatt hours per year (TWh/year) but the capacity utilised was just under 31 TWh/year.

While the dimensions and the devastating effects of the scourge of *HIV/AIDS* were decreasing in the region, data released for 2016 by UNAIDS still indicated high prevalence rates with massively negative impacts on living conditions and economic consequences for most of the countries in the sub-region. Swaziland, with an HIV/AIDS prevalence rate of 27.4%, and Lesotho, with 22.9%, continued to have the highest levels in the world, while South Africa with 6.3 m infected people remained the country with the world's biggest HIV epidemic in terms of numbers. In Zimbabwe, which also remained among the most affected countries (ranked fifth in terms of proportion of population), estimates suggested that nearly 1 m children had been orphaned by AIDS.

Individual *economies of SADC countries* performed differently, but in general the trend was a decline due to the unfavourable effects of falling commodity prices on the world market as well as economic mismanagement and abuse of public funds. Angola's economy was suffering from the continuing drop in oil prices. The loss of revenue also affected directly the decline of individual purchasing power that had previously benefitted the Namibian economy through Angolan consumers. Equally negative were the effects on the region of the economic woes in South Africa, since the economic powerhouse's weakness directly impacted on other economies in the neighbourhood. The ongoing devaluation of the South African currency also included the Namibian dollar, directly pegged to the rand. This had dramatic effects on the latter's debt servicing in hard currency, which increased considerably for the amounts borrowed. Rating agencies responded to the economic weaknesses in both countries by downgrading their credit status. Despite such increased pressure on resource-dependent economies, Botswana managed to handle the impasse in a way that allowed it to retain positive credit ratings by influential international agencies.

State capture (meaning control of public assets by a clique in government in collaboration with members of the private sector) became the new watchword for the characterisation of South Africa's economy under the Zuma administration. The release of a report by the public protector offered damning evidence of the abuse of political influence and power for personal gain. This kind of privatisation of public resources had already been a long practised way of handling the Angolan economy under the dos Santos family's 'oiligarchy'. This, combined with the fall in oil-related income, also directly affected the already inadequate government delivery of social and public services, with a further negative impact on living conditions for ordinary people.

The government of *Mozambique* came under pressure with the revelation of secret loans on a grand scale, which had fuelled massive embezzlement and misappropriation of funds. The scandal impacted on foreign support and resulted in the shelving of aid by donors and international financial institutions. This exacerbated the country's socio-economic woes and necessitated a 10% cut in the planned state budget. Other consequences were a drastic increase in inflation, a dramatic devaluation of the local currency and a massive increase in interest rates – all negatively affecting the local economy.

In *Namibia*, the hitherto good economic record was seriously damaged. Triggered by consecutive years of a government policy of overspending to stimulate the economy through public tenders, liquidity problems caused a fiscal crisis. The state budget had to be adjusted downwards and major foreign loans were required to keep government finances operational. These added to a massive increase in the public debt and the highest budget deficit since independence. Delays in payments to local contractors for delivery of work executed through state tenders added to an economic crisis, which, in combination with a water shortage, seriously affected the local construction industry. Retrenchments added to the already high unemployment figures. With economic contraction, the country's hitherto positive international standing was severely damaged.

Economic woes also seriously hampered developments in *South Africa*, where the economy also contracted. The setbacks were partly the result of controversial policy decisions by President Zuma. His collaboration with the Gupta family, dubbed 'state capture' (see above), resulted in many political and public appointments that aimed to fully control the country's economy for the benefit of a small circle of business men and political office-holders.

TI's *Corruption Perception Index* ranked the countries of the sub-region (without listing Swaziland), overall less favourably than the governance indicators suggested, though surprisingly with regard to some countries such as South Africa and Angola, which had improved scores compared with 2015. The overall ranking was as follows (2016 ranking [out of 176 states], score/change from 2015): 35th Botswana (60/-3), 50th Mauritius (54/+1), 53rd Namibia (52/-1), 64th South Africa (45/+1), 83rd Lesotho (39/-5), 87th Zambia (38/-), 120t Malawi (31/-), 142nd Mozambique (27/-4), 145th Madagascar (26/-2), 154th Zimbabwe (22/-1) and 164th Angola (18/+3).

Sub-regional Organisations

All 12 countries of this sub-region were members of *SADC*, which also included the DRC, Seychelles and Tanzania. A Double Troika Summit of heads of state and government of SADC and the Organ on Politics, Defence and Security Cooperation was held on 18 January in Gaborone (Botswana) to discuss the situation in *Lesotho*. It urged the government to comply with the recommendations in the report by the Commission of Inquiry and received a SADC Facilitation Mission report by the South African Deputy President Cyril Ramaphosa, the appointed SADC facilitator. It noted with concern that constitutional, public sector and security sector reforms had not yet been undertaken and tasked the government with submitting a progress report to the summit in August. In July, SADC facilitated a technical workshop in Lesotho on security sector reforms to improve trust among various stakeholders. In November, members of the SADC Oversight Committee supported Lesotho in implementing constitutional and security sector reforms.

The 36th *SADC summit* took place in Swaziland's capital Mbabane on 22–31 August. The theme was 'Resource Mobilisation for Investment in Sustainable Energy Infrastructure for an Inclusive SADC Industrialisation for the Prosperity of the Region'. The ordinary summit of heads of state and government was held on 30–31 August. As the outgoing chairman, Botswana's President Ian Khama expressed concern over the region's deteriorating access to water and energy supply. He identified food insecurity, inherent poverty and the escalation of poaching and illegal wildlife trade as major challenges. As usual, the hosting head of state, Swaziland's King Mswati III, took over as chairperson for the next one-year period. During the meeting, the summit elected South Africa's President Zuma as SADC deputy chairperson. Tanzania's President John Pombe Magufuli, was elected as chairperson of the SADC Organ on Politics, Defence and Security Cooperation. He succeeded Mozambique's President Filipe Jacinto Nyusi. Angola's President Josè Eduardo dos Santos was elected as the Organ's deputy chairperson. With Zuma's fate in doubt and the announcement of dos Santos's retirement, the anticipated future office-holders might no longer be available by the time they were expected to assume their duties.

In his acceptance speech, King Mswati III announced his sponsorship of the establishment of a *SADC University of Innovation and Transformation* to be operational by the next summit with an intake of 300 funded students (20 from each member state). But he also asked his fellow heads of state for support for this "imaginative initiative". SADC Executive Secretary Stergomena Lawrence Tax declared that the five-year investment plan for the implementation of the SADC *Regional Agricultural Policy*, drafted in 2014, had been finalised to ensure long-term food security and the reduction of social and economic vulnerability. She also reported that the roll-out of regional projects by the SADC Regional Infrastructure Development Master Plan was on course. The summit approved the Revised SADC Protocol on *Gender and Development*. It contained new provisions on gender-related challenges, including climate change, child marriage, sexual and reproductive health and reproductive rights. It also addressed gender disparities in media, information and communication. A baseline study on *trafficking in persons* in the region was also presented.

The SADC RVAA programme (see above), operational for a decade, held its regional annual dissemination technical forum on 6–8 June in Pretoria (South Africa). A senior officials meeting of member states followed on 9–10 June. Delegates endorsed the Regional Synthesis Report on the State of *Food and Livelihoods Vulnerability* in the SADC Region, which was released at the 36th summit.

The official communiqué declared that the summit had agreed to support Botswana's Minister of Foreign Affairs and International Cooperation Pelonomi Venson-Moitoi as SADC candidate for the *African Commission* position. Member states expressed concern over the situation in the DRC and encouraged stakeholders in Lesotho to participate in the reform processes. It had also agreed on the operationalisation of the SADC *Regional Development Fund* and appealed to "Member States to urgently ratify the Agreement in order to facilitate mobilization of resources to finance key regional projects and programmes, giving further impetus to preparation of infrastructure and industrialization projects". Given that in the past less than one-tenth of expenditure for SADC projects had been covered by member states, this would be an important step towards less dependency on donor funding and more self-reliance and ownership.

The SADC *Peoples' Summit* took place in Manzini (Swaziland) on 16–19 August under the theme 'A Peoples' driven SADC committed to total liberation for all'. Over a thousand representatives of social movements and other civil society organisations held a People's Tribunal on Transnational Corporations and adopted the Manzini Peoples' Declaration. The strongly worded document diagnosed an "ongoing and deepening multi-crisis as a consequence of neoliberal economic policies" and condemned the escalating "capture and control of peoples' means of production such as land, water, seeds, forests and seas". It accused political and government elites of complicity with transnational corporations and stated: "We see greater levels of poverty and unemployment as a result of the inappropriate development models that are based on extractivism, exploitation of people and violation of Human Rights." The Declaration also observed a "continued deterioration in democracy and good governance", which had marginalised the youth from the regional development process.

The *SADC Tribunal* remained a bone of contention. Ahead of the summit, 16 NGOs from nine of the SADC member states acted in a Coalition for an Effective SADC Tribunal and issued a statement on 17 August. They complained that the revised Tribunal Protocol was not compliant with the SADC Declaration and Treaty and undermined the protection of human rights, since it prevented other than state parties from access to the court. They urged member states not to ratify the revised protocol but to advocate an inclusive Tribunal serving the people of the region.

As chairperson of *SACU*, the oldest customs union in the world, operational for 105 years, South Africa's President Zuma visited Botswana, Namibia and Swaziland between 18 and 21 April for consultations on how best to follow up on earlier decisions taken at the end of 2015 at a high-level meeting held in Windhoek. He added a visit to Lesotho on 9 June. In a subsequent consultative move, the finance ministers of all five SACU member states (Botswana, Lesotho, Namibia, South Africa and Swaziland) attended after an interval of two years a 3rd Ministerial Retreat on

20 June in Johannesburg to discuss how the SACU roadmap adopted in late 2015 should best be taken forward. At the core of the negotiations was the SACU revenue-sharing formula, which in the view of South Africa was unfair, being too beneficial to the other members but not in the interest of South Africa. With an ailing economy, the regional economic engine had run out of steam and was starting to explore cost-cutting measures. This made SACU revenue-sharing a bone of contention, especially since the other SACU members depended on this revenue to a considerable extent for their annual budgets. The revenue-sharing formula had three components: the customs share component, allocated on the basis of each country's share of intra-SACU imports; the excise component, allocated on the basis of each country's share of GDP; and the development component, fixed at 15% of total excise revenue and distributed according to the inverse of each country's GDP per capita. Figures indicated that SACU revenue transfers accounted on average for 30% of Botswana's revenue, 35% of Namibia's, 44% of Lesotho's and 50% of Swaziland's, making their state budgets vulnerable in case of any cuts through redistribution by use of a different formula. The plans to adjust revenue distribution therefore provoked serious concerns and objections from the smaller economies, while the financial crisis in South Africa added to that country's ambitions to seek a compromise in her interest. A SACU heads of state summit, planned to be held during the year, did not materialise.

After many years, the *EPA* negotiations finally produced legal results. On 10 June, the six-member SADC EPA Group (Botswana, Lesotho, Mozambique, Namibia, South Africa and Swaziland) signed an agreement with the EU after lengthy and at times controversial negotiations, with Angola having an option to join the agreement in the future. The other eight SADC members (the DRC, Madagascar, Malawi, Mauritius, Seychelles, Tanzania Zambia and Zimbabwe) were negotiating EPAs as part of other regional groups, namely Central Africa, Eastern and Southern Africa and the Pacific island states, respectively. In 2015 the EU had been the largest trading bloc with the SADC EPA group, trading in goods to the value of almost € 32 bn from the region (mainly minerals and metals as well as agricultural products), while exporting mainly manufactured goods (such as vehicles, machinery, electrical equipment, pharmaceuticals and processed food) of almost the same value to the region. The breakdown of the total trade of almost € 63 bn over the year (including Angola's oil exports) documented the continuing skewed terms of trade as signified by the exchange of mainly unprocessed raw materials from the region for value added commodities from the EU member states. Although celebrated as a success story, it hardly contributed to development-oriented, diversified and sustainable economic growth paths as proclaimed by the EU signatories.

Angola

Jon Schubert

While the family of President dos Santos consolidated its grip on the economy, the head of state indicated he would retire from active politics in 2018; this was confirmed later in the year when the ruling party nominated its candidates for the 2017 elections. Although this heralded the possibility of future political change, domestic politics continued to be dominated by the ruling party. The economic crisis worsened, and the persecution of dissidents continued, putting a damper on Angola's activities on the international stage, which were markedly reduced in comparison to the previous year.

Domestic Politics

In March, President José Eduardo dos Santos announced his *retirement* "from active political life in 2018". As he had repeatedly made similar announcements since at least 2001 without following through, this was met with a healthy dose of scepticism, especially as the date, 2018, was after the next elections, scheduled for 2017.

 | DOI 10.1163/9789004355910_045

To many, this implied that dos Santos would run again as the top candidate of the Popular Movement for the Liberation of Angola ('Movimento Popular de Libertação de Angola'; MPLA) in 2017, and hand over power to his chosen successor after the elections. Dos Santos was reconfirmed as the party's president unopposed at the MPLA congress in August. Two of dos Santos's children, José Filomeno 'Zénú' dos Santos and Welwitschea 'Tchizé' dos Santos Pego, were elected to the party's Central Committee, and Defence Minister João Lourenço was elected party vice president, rather than any of the usual suspects from the party's 'old guard', such as previous party vice president Roberto de Almeida.

This further fed speculation that had already arisen in January that Lourenço might be selected to run as the party's number two after dos Santos in the 2017 elections, rather than current Vice President of the Republic (and number two) Manuel Vicente. In December, however, much to everyone's surprise, the party's Central Committee 'leaked' the MPLA's list of *candidates for the 2017 elections*, which, instead of José Eduardo dos Santos, featured Lourenço as the party's number one, and hence presidential, candidate, followed by Bornito de Sousa, the current minister of territorial administration (who was in this function also responsible for the organisation of the elections) as number two and thus the probable future vice president. This also confirmed Vicente's slow but steady fall from grace, which was compounded by his indictment in Portugal in February for active corruption.

Other noteworthy reshuffles during the year included the appointment of Augusto Archer de Sousa Mangueira as new minister of finance and Manuel da Cruz Neto as new head of the civilian office of the presidency, replacing Edeltrudes da Costa. Da Costa had, in his previous functions, ordered the National Bank to transfer funds abroad to companies held by friends of his; in the wake of his dismissal, President dos Santos also ordered the freezing of any transactions previously ordered by da Costa. This did not impede the governor of the National Bank, José Pedro de Morais, from speaking to the 'Financial Times' in January about how Angola was a leading force in fighting money laundering in Africa; accordingly de Morais was also dismissed in April, and replaced by the hitherto low-profile Valter Filipe. The previous governor of Kuando Kubango, General Francisco Higino Carneiro, was made governor and first party secretary of Luanda, replacing the 'firebrand' Bento Francisco Bento, who was relegated to second vice president of the National Assembly. In Kuando Kubango, Carneiro was replaced by Pedro Mutindi.

At year's end, there was therefore much speculation as to whether Lourenço's likely ascent to power did indeed herald the beginning of some form of political change for Angola. However, he was widely regarded as a safe choice signalling more of the same, as he had proven his loyalty to dos Santos after an earlier fall from grace, as well as having impeccable party and army credentials.

Moreover, as the *dos Santos family* consolidated its stranglehold on key economic assets throughout the year, it became clear that whoever would succeed dos Santos as president of the republic would be economically dependent on the dos Santos family. Dos Santos issued a decree that attributed the upgrading of the Corimba Bay Road in the capital, Luanda, at a cost of $ 567 m, to a consortium led by a company owned by his daughter Isabel. He also put her in charge of the General Metropolitan Master Plan for the restructuring of Luanda, the commission for the readjustment of the oil sector, and the restructuring of the state oil company Sonangol. The last, however, was only the first step in completing *Isabel dos Santos*'s near-total control over Angola's political economy, as in June the president appointed her CEO of Sonangol. All these contracts and nominations violated the law of public probity, and her appointment at the helm of Sonangol in particular even met with some, ultimately futile, opposition from within the MPLA. State media rushed to her defence, saying that the promotion of Angola's most successful entrepreneur to head Sonangol demonstrated the company's strategic importance to the president and that she was the perfect person to turn it around. Isabel dos Santos herself denied any irregularities in her appointment and said she had only been made CEO on the strength of her impeccable track record as a businesswoman. Twelve Angolan lawyers also filed an appeal against this appointment with the Supreme Court. The appeal was at first ignored; the Court then announced in October that it had asked for and received clarifications from the president, Isabel dos Santos and the attorney-general regarding the appointment. The court did not reveal any of the content of these clarifications, and on 29 December confirmed the appointment.

This further confirmed the *politicised nature of the judiciary*, as similar earlier formal complaints against high-ranking office-holders for corruption and abuse of power – the attorney-general, army generals, province governors or the president of the Republic himself – had not been followed up and were dismissed by the public prosecutor's office. The judiciary also demonstrated its subservience to the regime in two sham trials that had both started in 2015: on 28 March, the 'Angola 15+2' activists, who had been arrested in June 2015, were sentenced to prison terms ranging from two to eight years, for "preparing acts of rebellion and association with criminals". Following widespread outcries both at home and abroad, Angola's 'roving ambassador' Luvualu de Carvalho stated that 99% of Angolans did not care about the sentence, and compared the activists to terrorism suspects in the US, reaffirming the jurisdiction of Angola's judicial institutions to carry out the trial.

A little later, the Supreme Court approved a habeas corpus petition by the activists' defence team, and they were provisionally released in June, but subject to travel restrictions. In October, the Court ordered an amnesty for the 17 activists, a move largely viewed as political decision to prevent the activists from arguing their case and most likely proving their innocence before the Supreme Court, given the widespread negative publicity for the regime the case had attracted. On 5 April, the leader of the 'Light of the World' sect, José Julino Kalupeteca, was sentenced to

28 years in prison for killing nine police officers during the Mt Sumi raid in April 2015. In September, there were also reports that security forces had killed 13 families of followers of Kalupeteca in Kwanza-Sul province.

A lone bright spot was the release on 20 May of Cabindan activist Marcos Mavungo, by the Supreme Court, which decided there were no concrete facts proving the crimes of which Mavungo had been accused and for which he had been sentenced. Also, online activism continued, despite government attempts to clamp down on Internet expression. In March, it was also revealed that Angolans had used two mobile Internet services made available for free to customers in 'developing countries' – Facebook Free Basics and Wikimedia Zero – to embed and share large media files such as music and movies behind innocuous image links.

In February, the Movement for the Lunda Tchokwe Protectorate held a demonstration in Cafunfo, Lunda Norte province, to demand greater autonomy for the *Lunda provinces*. In the same month, the Front for the Liberation of the Enclave of Cabinda (FLEC) announced the resumption of its armed struggle for the independence of the oil-rich *Cabinda province* from Angola. Following the 2012 elections, FLEC had signalled in vain to the Angolan government its readiness to start a fresh dialogue about substantial autonomy for the province. However, with no government response, the movement resumed its attacks in February and March. These were downplayed by the authorities, but FLEC claimed to have killed a total of about 40 Angolan soldiers. In May, five men in a speedboat also allegedly boarded a Chevron oil platform off the coast of Cabinda to deliver a warning from FLEC, inciting foreign workers to leave the province. Following the death of FLEC's longtime historical leader Nzita Tiago in his Paris exile in June, FLEC further intensified its military activities, claiming in September to having killed over 50 people during August. In October, however, the movement's spokesman, Jean-Claude Nzita, accused the Angolan Armed Forces of killing several FLEC commanders in the neighbouring Republic of Congo, and appealed for a resumption of dialogue.

Extrajudicial killings were also on the rise in the diamond-rich Lunda provinces, as well as in the shanty towns and suburbs of Luanda. According to the investigative news site 'Maka Angola' in September, the Criminal Investigation Service ('Serviço de Investigação Criminal': SIC) of the National Police was carrying out a crackdown on suspected criminals, and had shot and killed over 100 people since the beginning of the year. Other human rights violations included arbitrary and extrajudicial detention and the denial of access to justice, degrading treatment of prisoners, police violence and the use of torture. Arbitrary *housing demolitions* in the peripheral neighbourhoods of Luanda also intensified again, leading to the forced relocation of residents and individual cases of deaths during the demolitions or the protests against them.

Media freedom was also constantly restricted. In late January, for example, a majority of the few independent weekly newspapers could not be published, allegedly for technical reasons at the printing press. However, Angolan journalists suspected that the press, owned by generals close to the presidency, had refused to print news about the Kalupeteca trial. Another new weekly, 'Relatório 10', launched in October saw its first issue withheld from circulation after someone bought up the entire print run. In January, journalist Mayama Salazar was detained on fabricated charges by the SIC. On various occasions, journalists were intimidated, arrested or impeded from accessing informants and sites.

'*Rádio Ecclesia*', the Catholic Church's independent radio broadcaster, which had for years been applying in vain for a licence to broadcast beyond Luanda, was also beset by problems. In May, its director, Father Quintino Kandanji, very publicly stated that he had refused an EU grant of € 149,631 and that the broadcaster would "not sell out to foreign interests" – a statement very much in line with the government's take on foreign coverage of the trial of the 'Angola 15+2' (see Foreign Affairs, below). The EU delegation stated in response that the amount was simply owed by 'Ecclesia' as a return from a previous grant that had not been used. It later transpired that Kandanji had received a $ 50,000 grant from the Ministry of Social Communication, though he himself denied this. Given that, ever since Kandanji had taken over the direction of 'Ecclesia' in 2011, programmes had been cancelled and reporters had started complaining about a climate of censorship, it came as a relief to many when in September the Vatican suspended Kandanji at the request of the Church's lay members.

A new package of *media laws*, pushed through parliament by the MPLA majority on 18 November, included additional restrictions on print media, social media and the activity of journalists, including the creation of a Regulatory Body for Social Communication (dominated by the MPLA), which would henceforth be responsible for the accreditation of journalists.

Although *opposition parties* voted against these laws, their scope for counterbalancing the MPLA's dominance was still limited. The government postponed local elections – again. In May, a rally by the main opposition party, the National Union for the Total Independence of Angola ('União Nacional para a Independência Total de Angola'; UNITA) in Benguela was attacked by MPLA supporters, leading to the death of three civilians. Similar acts of violence and intimidation were registered across the country throughout the rest of the year. Following the beginning of the electoral registration process for the 2017 general elections, opposition parties also complained, but to little effect, that the new electoral register law 'gutted' the competences of the nominally independent National Electoral Commission by transferring responsibilities to the Ministry of Territorial Administration.

Foreign Affairs

External relations were overshadowed by the economic crisis and the international attention given to the trial of the 'Angola 15+2' activists. With international pressure mounting to set the activists free, Foreign Minister George Chicoty in May accused the *EU* of "manoeuvres to destabilise Angola and its government", a statement that was widely met with ridicule and exasperation amongst Angolans.

In February, the European Commission asked *Portugal* to clarify whether recent acquisitions by Isabel dos Santos in Portugal had violated anti-corruption laws. The indictment of Vice President Vicente further soured relations with the former colonial power, which dropped to third place on the list of Angola's major sources of imports.

That top spot was taken by the *USA*, whose imports to Angola rose by 62% compared with 2015. However, the USA sharply condemned the sentencing of the '15+2' in an April report on "serious human rights violations", which was strongly rejected by the Angolan secretary of state for human rights. Relations with *Israel* were also suspended after Angola voted in favour of a UNSC resolution condemning Israel's settlement policy in the West Bank, a resolution made possible by the abstention of the USA.

Relations with *China*, Angola's main commercial partner over recent years, were also affected by the oil price crisis, with commercial exchanges dropping by 35% in the first half of the year compared with the same period in 2015. In August, the China Development Bank refused to extend further credit to Sonangol, citing "lack of contractual compliance". Nonetheless, China remained a major supplier of imports, and the China-Angola investment forum, held on 7–8 November, was evidence of continued investor appetite. Angola also continued active commercial exchanges with *France* and *Russia*, especially in the area of defence procurement.

Relations with Angola's other main Lusophone partner, *Brazil*, were overshadowed by on-going corruption investigations against former Brazilian president Luis Inácio 'Lula' da Silva and two companies, Petrobras and Odebrecht, both with extensive interests in Angola. This led the Brazilian Development Bank to suspend payments to Angola and Mozambique in October. Cultural exchanges remained important, however, as evidenced by the signing, on 2 March, of an agreement to lay a subsea fibre-optics cable between Angola and Brazil – though this venture was to be financed by the *Japan* Bank for International Cooperation.

Closer to home, Angola was re-elected for a second two-year term to lead the *ICGLR*, the other member states having approved of Angola's management of the crisis in 2014–15. Angola was also elected to head the *SADC parliamentary forum* in November, though a report published in July confirmed that Angola had the lowest "levels of integration" of all the regional body's member states. In terms of its relations with the CPLP, the International Institute for the Portuguese Language revealed in January that Angola had not ratified at any level of government an orthographic agreement on new rules of spelling. Though the Institute underlined that Angola remained "fully committed" to implementing the reform, it had to take into account local realities and would proceed with the implementation "at its own pace".

Relations with the neighbouring *DRC* remained ambivalent; although the two countries signed a commercial agreement for the joint exploration zone in January, Angola's Oil Minister Botelho de Vasconcelos accused the DRC of violating the agreement in late April. Angola also followed the political unrest in the DRC closely, withdrawing its diplomatic staff in September, and reaching a point in October where the army chief of staff, General Nunda, had to deny the involvement of any Angolan troops in the country's internal conflicts.

Socioeconomic Developments

Due to continuously low world oil prices and the subsequent drop in government revenues, the year began with a cut in fuel subsidies, resulting in the third *hike in fuel prices* at the pump in less than a year. This in turn prompted collective taxi operators to raise their fares from 100 to 150 kwanzas (AOA), which the Ministry of Finance accepted, in contrast to their response to earlier attempts to adjust the fares. This prompted widespread, though ultimately ineffective, popular outrage.

In January, the kwanza fell to a record low since 2001, after the National Bank of Angola allowed the *currency to depreciate* in response to falling export earnings. While the official rate dropped from about AOA 135 to AOA 156 to the dollar, street exchange rates rose to AOA 280 : $ 1. In early April, the informal rate peaked at AOA 620, levelling at about AOA 400 to the dollar at year's end, meaning that the kwanza had effectively lost 75% of its value since the onset of the oil price crisis. Accordingly, *imports dropped*, as importers were sitting on stacks of useless and depreciating kwanza and had no, or increasingly difficult and costly, access to hard currency. Given the country's strong import dependency, the prices of food supplies rose steeply. Though the government introduced price controls for basic foodstuffs in March, many suppliers and supermarkets started *rationing food*, which led to an expansion of the black market, with speculative and arbitrarily rising prices. As local salaries, paid in kwanza, also lost value by the day and many companies suspended salary payments altogether, there was a resurgence in *strikes* – for example by teachers in Bengo province, and by dock workers in the port of Lobito, both in September, as well as at Bolloré Africa Logistics Angola, in November.

Despite these worrying developments, the government played down the crisis. In February, Defence Minister Lourenço said the current crisis was "nothing compared to the war". Authorities also talked up the country's economic recovery, especially when in May Angola briefly overtook Nigeria as *Africa's largest oil exporter*, with production of about 1.7 m b/d. However, both the slight rise in crude oil prices and Angola's regaining of the first place amongst Africa's oil-producing nations were largely to do with security issues in Nigeria, which led to lower production levels there, rather than with any structural improvement in the Angolan economy. Moreover, the high levels of debt that Angola had contracted since 2010 and the taking up of new oil-backed loans, together with the renegotiation of repayment deadlines with China since early 2015, meant that three-quarters of these revenues from oil exports were used for debt servicing.

In April, the government submitted a request for a bailout to the *IMF*. Despite the government's evident failure to heed the lessons from the previous shorter price crash in 2008/09, the IMF agreed on 14 June to support the government under the Extended Fund Facility (EFF) scheme with a $ 4.5 bn loan package, which would have required further improvements regarding budget transparency. However, on 30 June, following reports that the government had secured an additional $ 1 bn in syndicated loans from commercial lenders through Goldman Sachs, President dos Santos reportedly personally turned down the IMF's EFF package, saying the country only wanted to pursue talks on the IMF's annual assessments of the Angolan economy. This decision was described as "negligent" by financial analysts, and as "credit negative" by ratings agency Moody's.

All the while the president's son, José Filomeno 'Zénú' dos Santos presided over the country's $ 5 bn *sovereign wealth fund*, nominally created to help buffer the Angolan economy against oil price shocks, but which was busy investing in luxury properties abroad, and paying exorbitant consultancy fees to companies that existed only on paper and had an ownership structure surprisingly similar to Zénú's own investment bank, Quantum Capital. In September, it was also revealed that the fund had lost $ 486 m in its first two years of operation; clarifications were not forthcoming. Moreover, given that in March, Angolan economist Carlos do Rosado stated that the assets of Angolan leaders held in foreign banks totalled $ 28 bn, i.e. more than the country's foreign exchange reserves of $ 24 bn, and that General Kopelipa, the head of the president's security cabinet, made news in August by ordering the production of bottles of Spanish wine with his head on the label, the lack of success in addressing the economic crisis appeared again more like a question of a lack of political will and misplaced priorities rather than capacity.

The death in February of Lúcio Lara, one of the MPLA's first generation leaders was then also met with much sadness, as Angolans said that with Lara an earlier, perhaps 'cleaner' era of the MPLA had finally ceased to exist.

The state oil company *Sonangol*, arguably the government's most important single source of revenue, was also in trouble because of the low oil price. Following the controversial appointment of Isabel dos Santos as CEO in June, she announced ambitious plans to improve the company's performance by reducing wasteful spending and trimming core operations back in line. While some commentators saw the restructuring and the appointment of new board members with proven track records and technical competence as a positive signal, inside commentators spoke of a climate of "mistrust", akin to a hostile takeover, with permissions and competences revoked, and entire floors and office suites declared off limits to existing staff. Angolan investigative journalist Rafael Marques said that Isabel's appointment was equivalent to "putting the fox in charge of the henhouse". Given that most of her seed capital for other business ventures had, in fact, been taken out of Sonangol, she was likely to use the opportunity to cover up any traces of previous financial misdeeds. Indicative of such practices was the announcement in December that Sonangol would source all its Christmas gift hampers from the Candando supermarkets, owned by Isabel dos Santos, while during the year the company also hired a consulting company and a human resources service provider owned by her.

More evidence of Sonangol's mismanagement emerged over the year, without any of the proposed measures having yet had any impact. In July, it was revealed that Sonangol owed $ 13 bn in outstanding debts to Standard Chartered Bank (UK); while the new leadership of the company obtained a reprieve of 45 days to clarify its financial positions, there were reports that manoeuvres were under way to improve the appearance of the company's financial situation. In October, the US oil company Chevron also demanded the payment of $ 300 m from Sonangol for its share of the operating costs in Block 0 in Cabinda, which Sonangol had stopped honouring since June, while in November employees complained that they had to bring their own toilet paper to work. Minor rays of light for the oil sector were the announcement of the discovery of two new commercially viable oil deposits in the Lower Kwanza Basin and the resumption of production at Angola LNG, the liquefied natural gas plant in Soyo.

In addition to her dealings at Sonangol, Isabel dos Santos, through her mobile phone company Unitel, acquired in October a controlling stake in Banco Fomento de Angola; in December, she also announced that her beer bottling plant in Luanda would henceforth produce the Portuguese brand Sagres for the local market, as well as a new local brand, Luandina. This was already the second *new domestic beer brand* in the year, after Refriango launched in March its new Tigra beer, which it started exporting to Portugal in September.

In March, a *steel mill* opened 40 km north of Luanda, with the intention of turning the country's scrap metal – mainly obsolete weapons and discarded material from the civil war – into new steel, with a view to making the country a supplier, rather than an importer of steel by 2020.

Food scarcity was a continuous problem, with UNICEF revealing in May that close to 100,000 children were facing serious and acute malnutrition, especially in the drought-affected southern provinces of Cunene, Huíla and Namibe, where media reported in February that people were eating 'weeds'. MPLA Deputy João Pinto had his own Marie-Antoinette moment when he said in February that everyone had to tighten their belts and that "instead of eating expensive beef steaks, we'll eat tuna steaks". This was somewhat ironic as the Ministry of Commerce had just issued new licences for *tuna fishing* off Angola's southern coast to foreign fishing fleets, a deal from which both the production and the revenues would probably flow abroad. The imposition, in July, of an obligation for *ambulant street vendors* to acquire a commercial licence to carry out their trade legally, allegedly for reasons of public health, was widely seen as further unnecessary administrative and legal hassle for the largely female workforce, who were already struggling to make ends meet in Angola's informal sector. Angolan sociologist Pedro de Castro Maria commented that, given the general difficulties Angolans had in acquiring identity documents, the measure would probably push informal vendors further into informality and illegality, especially as even people with formal salaries in the public sector had often to resort to some form of informal side-line to sustain their families.

Luanda's rubbish crisis also continued, despite the creation of a presidential commission to address the issue and the introduction of refuse taxes in March. Increasingly insalubrious conditions in the capital, combined with drastically reduced health funding, resulted in a dramatic *yellow fever outbreak*, the world's worst since 1986. The high mortality that ensued was largely a result of a combination of low vaccination rates, poor sanitation, weak diagnostic capacities and ineffective and insufficient treatment, as hospitals lacked even basic supplies such as latex gloves and clean water. In March, UNITA activists who wanted to donate blood at the Luanda General Hospital were also turned away by the hospital's management, though it transpired that the hospital was ordered to do so while the MPLA's youth wing, the JMPLA were donating blood. From January till May, the Ministry of Health officially recorded 277 deaths, though the actual number was probably higher. In November, the ministry also admitted it had insufficient supplies of tuberculosis vaccine, and malaria and cholera remained major health issues.

Though dropping slightly from 2015 to an estimated 75.6 per 1,000 births in the first year of life, *infant mortality* remained among the world's highest at 120/1,000 under-fives, and more than 30% of children showed physical signs of malnutrition such as reduced body height.

This overall underfunding of social spending was aggravated by general budget cuts and higher levels of debt servicing, and was certainly not helped by the fact that *defence spending* remained Africa's highest both in absolute and per-capita terms, higher than the defence expenses of South Africa and Nigeria combined.

Botswana

David Sebudubudu

The year was dominated by preparations for celebrations for the 50th anniversary of Botswana's Independence on 30 September. This coincided with the launch of Vision 2036 as Vision 2016 drew to a close. Opposition coalition talks were also in motion. A vocal foreign policy continued, with open disparagement of countries that debased the ideals of democracy and human rights and good governance – much to the chagrin of most of its African peers and resulting in a degree of isolation. Socio-economic barriers and risks continued to pose challenges; the economy remained vulnerable to external oscillations and failed to realise broad-based growth.

Domestic Politics

Whilst the Botswana Democratic Party (BDP) maintained its dominance of the political scene, the year was preoccupied with preparations for celebrations to mark 50 years of Independence. However, there were some *changes in party affiliation*: the previous speaker of the National Assembly and former minister, Margaret Nasha, resigned from the BDP on 24 January and joined the opposition coalition, the

 | DOI 10.1163/9789004355910_046

Umbrella for Democratic Change (UDC), as a member of the Botswana Movement for Democracy (BMD). Her resignation sparked the wrath of her former party, including President Ian Khama, who declared that she was ungrateful to the BDP, and "power hungry", an assertion that Nasha denied. She criticised Khama for failing the country and said he would have no legacy to show for the period of his presidency, and also noted that Khama had curtailed debate within the BDP. These sentiments were echoed by Kenny Kapinga, former Botswana ambassador to Zimbabwe, and deputy commissioner of police, on 7 November at a press conference as he joined the Botswana Congress Party (BCP). Kapinga declared, "He [Ian Khama] has stifled debate over everything, rules by fear and has paralysed institutions all of which play according to nobody but his rules alone."

A *BDP Special Congress* took place in Mogoditshane on 22–23 July, in line with the 36th Mmadinare National Congress decision. The party decided, amongst other things, on timelines for holding party primary elections in both constituencies controlled by the opposition and itself, in October 2017 and October 2018, respectively. The BDP also considered rules for selecting its candidates for the 2019 general elections and welcomed Okavango MP, Bagalatia Arone, who had left the BCP and joined the BDP in June. The BDP's recruitment posture was in motion throughout the year.

The *Botswana National Front* (BNF) held its 17th National Congress in Francistown from 16 July. Duma Boko was unchallenged as party president. Prince Dibeela was voted in as vice president and Moeti Mohwasa was elected secretary-general. Abigail Mogalakwe and Noah Salakae were elected party chairperson and treasurer, respectively. Nelson Ramaotwana was voted secretary for international relations and Elmon Tafa secretary for political education. Justin Hunyepa, Tona Mooketsi and Eithopa Mokeresete were elected publicity and information secretary, national organising secretary and secretary for labour, respectively. Peter Makwati was voted secretary for economic affairs. The BNF celebrated the 50th anniversary of its founding in Mochudi, where the party had been created in 1965.

The *Botswana People's Party* (BPP) held its congress in Tati Siding on 16–17 July. Motlatsi Molapisi was unopposed as party president and Mbaakanyi Lenyatso was voted in as deputy president. Richard Gudu was elected party chairperson, and Botho Seboko and Otlaadisa Otlaadisa were returned as secretary-general, and deputy secretary-general, respectively. Tonkomani Dan was elected party treasurer, and Thabani Peter publicity secretary.

Meanwhile, *BMD factional wrangles* played out in public, with cracks in the party's national executive committee (NEC) being reported – with one faction led by the party president and his vice president, and the other by the chairperson and secretary general. The party's divisions mainly centred on Sydney Pilane's disputed return to the party. His renewed membership was not accepted by Gaborone North constituency, but was subsequently approved by Mochudi West constituency with the support of the secretary-general and party chairperson – without involving the NEC or the party president. As a result of divisions relating to Pilane's membership, some party structures (regions) called for a special party congress. These requests were rebuffed by the NEC in August as those who made them failed to satisfy the party's constitutional requirements for a special congress to deal with problems besetting the party. It was reported that Pilane, a founder member of the BMD who quit in 2012, had ambitions to run for the party presidency in 2017. Furthermore, it was reported in November that the BDP was actively recruiting members, mainly from the BMD, and some of those recruited cited leadership divisions within the BMD.

Opposition cooperation talks, underway since 2015 between political parties affiliated to the UDC (BMD, BNF and BPP) and the BCP, could not be concluded by the end of the year despite a resolution being anticipated in the media. Remarkably, the Botswana Federation of Public Sector Unions (BOFEPUSU), which had publicly affirmed its backing for the UDC in the 2014 elections, called for "fruitful cooperation talks" between the UDC and the BCP. Earlier in the year, the UDC and BCP entered into a Memorandum of Understanding through which they pledged to support each other at by-elections. Four *council by-elections* were held, with the opposition parties (BCP and UDC) and the BDP winning two each. In November, the BCP Women's League held is conference in Letlhakane.

On 30 September, President Khama led the country's vibrant celebrations for the *50th anniversary of Independence*. This coincided with the launch of its Vision 2036 as Vision 2016 drew to a close. Swaziland's King Mswati III and Lesotho's King Letsie were guests at the celebrations. Media reports suggested that Minister of Foreign Affairs and International Cooperation Pelonomi Venson-Moitoi had indicated that eight SADC heads of state were expected to attend. Those who did not make an appearance included Zimbabwean President Robert Mugabe. Media reports cited differences between Khama and Mugabe as the reason. Khama had been one of Mugabe's fiercest critics; he had called on him to step down and accused him of running down the Zimbabwean economy. The government of Zimbabwe rejected these suggestions.

Several *legislative amendments* were approved. In October, Khama restructured ministerial portfolios and established two new ministries following an amendment of the Ministerial Offices (Maximum Number) Act in September, which enlarged the number of ministers from 16 to 18, and assistant ministers from 8 to 10. In line with this restructuring, Khama rationalised his *cabinet*, with Thato Kwerepe, Itumelelng Moipisi, Biggie Butale and Kefentse Mzwinila being appointed as assistant ministers. In October, parliament elected Mephato Reatile and Bogolo Kenewendo as 'specially elected MPs' in accordance with a constitutional amendment that raised the number of specially elected MPS from four to six. A divisive amendment of the *Electoral Act* was also approved, which, amongst other things, introduced electronic voting machines, removed supplementary voter registration and increased fees for parliamentary and council candidates at general elections. These changes were vehemently opposed by the opposition parties. The BNF suggested that it might not participate in the 2019 elections, while the BCP cautioned that the use of electronic voting machines might lead to violence.

Issues of *corruption and maladministration* persisted, despite Botswana being ranked amongst the least corrupt countries in Africa. Allegations of corruption and wrong-doing in a number of parastatal organisations, including the Botswana Railways, the Botswana Investment and Trade Centre, the Botswana Trade Commission and Botswana Tourism Organisation, amongst others, were exposed and widely reported, with some being investigated by the Directorate on Corruption and Economic Crime (DCEC), and others by a parliamentary committee. All this suggested that corruption might be on the rise. In November, BDP MPs Guma Moyo and Thapelo Olopeng (the latter Minister of Youth Empowerment, Sport and Culture Development), successfully challenged a decision to freeze the accounts of their company at the High Court, thus frustrating efforts of the state to keep their accounts frozen. The two business associates were being investigated by the DCEC. Despite widely publicised accusations of corruption against Director General of the Directorate of Intelligence and Security Services Isaac Kgosi, regarded as a close ally of Khama, there was no move towards laying charges. Nevertheless, the Whistle Blowing Act was approved in July, ostensibly to demonstrate government commitment to containing corruption.

Matters relating to the *judiciary* and its independence continued to attract public interest. A tribunal appointed by Khama in 2015 to investigate four suspended High Court judges was yet to commence its work because litigation on the suspension was pending, while doubts concerning the independence of the judiciary continued. In September, the International Commission of Jurists urged Khama to uphold judicial independence. In December, media reports suggested that the Law Society of Botswana had decided to report Chief Justice Maruping Dibotelo to the Judicial Service Commission for "acting selectively" against the four judges. One of the suspended judges, Key Dingake, had emphatically declared his disapproval of "executive minded judges".

The government and *trade unions*, especially those affiliated to BOFEPUSU, continued their discordant relationship. In April, the Industrial Court invalidated a 3% salary rise for public service employees passed by government without reference to the Public Service Bargaining Council (PSBC), which was consistent with a 2015 High Court ruling. Following the withdrawal of the Botswana Public Employees Union (BOPEU) from BOFEPUSU, BOPEU contested the eligibility of BOFEPUSU to be represented on the PSBC. In June, the Court of Appeal allowed both BOFEPUSU and BOPEU to sit on the PSBC after satisfying the agreed threshold. The government continued its efforts to weaken trade unions by ensuring a successful revision of the Trade Disputes Act in September. The amendment expanded the categories of employees considered to be providing essential services, and the government thus succeeded in restricting the number of public service employees who could take part in a strike, much to the disapproval of BOFEPUSU. This suggested that the government, especially under Khama, was not keen to see strong trade unions emerging in the country.

Meanwhile, tense relations with the *media* continued. The government persisted in its 2014 charge of sedition levelled against the editor of the 'Sunday Standard' newspaper, Outsa Mokone, regarding a story that "detailed the president's involvement in a car accident". Interestingly, media reports in November criticised a private radio station, 'Gabz FM', for sacking Reginald Richardson and Keikantse Shumba, and associated their dismissal with a protest registered by the BDP "with the 'Gabz FM' management for airing a voiced-over clip of an alleged meeting between Vice President Mokgweetsi Masisi and some UDC councillors and members", purportedly without offering the party an opportunity to be heard. Richardson was instrumental in the 2014 'Gabz FM' parliamentary and presidential candidates' debates, in which the BDP had not taken part. Subsequently, there were suggestions that the radio station had been 'captured', which 'Gabz FM' rejected.

With respect to issues affecting the *San/Basarwa*, the leader of the First People of the Kalahari (FPK), Roy Sesana, appeared to have mellowed towards the government. Media reports in June that suggested he had been offered a government job (as a community facilitator) without consulting Survival International (SI), a key associate in supporting Basarwa against their ill-treatment by the government, particularly since the government's discontinuation of services in the Central Kalahari Game Reserve (CKGR) in 2002. Critical services had been reinstated in the CKGR, but the FPK continued to campaign for "the restoration of full residency rights to everyone with CKGR roots". It was also reported in June that the government had initiated a dialogue with Basarwa following a meeting between Sesana and Khama. Media reports also suggested that, following this meeting, Khama had established a team led by Minister of Foreign Affairs and International Cooperation Pelonomi Venson-Moitoi. The other members were Minister of Local Government and Rural Development Slumber Tsogwane, and Minister of Environment, Wildlife and Tourism Tshekedi Khama. Venson-Moitoi was quoted in the media as saying that the team had immediately ended the water problem the Basarwa had been facing. Nevertheless, SI continued its CKGR campaign.

The government maintained its hardened attitude towards *minority groups and their rights*. Interestingly, the courts continued to be inclined to protect and uphold those rights. Media reported that America's special envoy for human rights of lesbians, gays, bisexual, transgender and intersex (LGBTI) persons, Randy Berry, visited Botswana in January and was hosted by the American Embassy in Gaborone – which had openly declared its support for *gay rights*. It was reported that Berry "interacted with civil society representatives, government leaders, and members of the media to better understand the legal and social context for LGBTI individuals in Botswana". The government claimed not to be cognisant of the visit, although an assistant minister of local government and rural administration, Botlogile Tshireletso, and former president Festus Mogae were amongst those who attended a US embassy dinner in Berry's honour. Tshireletso had openly declared support for gay rights. It appeared that the government was not yet ready to openly affirm its position on gay rights, a politically sensitive issue in cultural terms. In March, however, the country's highest court, the Court of Appeal, confirmed a 2014 High Court ruling that permitted Lesbians, Gays and Bisexuals of Botswana (LEGABIBO) to register and be accepted as a lobbying group, ending a protracted tussle between LEGABIBO and the government regarding LEGABIBO's recognition and registration. LEGABIBO was consequently registered as an NGO by the Registrar of Societies on 29 April.

The government persisted in enforcing its clandestine *deportations of non-nationals*, whose rationality is considered somewhat doubtful. In February, it was estimated that there had been 2,400 such deportations since Khama assumed the presidency in 2008, which was in line with his intolerant leadership style. Interestingly, the minister of defence, justice and security declared in July that 62 persons had been killed by security agencies since 2008. Deported non-nationals included Stephen Anderson, an American pastor, who was allegedly deported in September for promoting 'hate speech' after declaring on 'Gabz FM' that gays and lesbians should be "stoned to death". Anderson's remarks and visit to Botswana met with disapproval, particularly from LEGABIBO and its members.

Foreign Affairs

On 18 January, Botswana hosted the *SADC Double Troika* Summit of Heads of State and Government, representing Botswana, Mozambique, South Africa, Swaziland, Tanzania and Zimbabwe, to evaluate the political and security environment in the region, with a special focus on Lesotho. Botswana hosted another SADC Double Troika of Heads of State and Government meeting on 28 June. On 21 January and 24 March, consistent with the upfront policy it had adopted in 2008, Botswana deplored terrorist attacks in Burkina Faso and Brussels (Belgium) and called for sustained efforts against terrorism.

Botswana denounced a nuclear test by *North Korea*, and urged that country to respect and uphold the relevant UNSC resolutions, as its actions threatened world peace. It also called for stern action against North Korea. Consequently, on 3 March Botswana applauded the UNSC for embracing further sanctions against North Korea, and on 12 July further stated its discomfort concerning North Korean sustained missile tests, which it considered a "threat to international security". Botswana reiterated its unease at the North Korean nuclear test on 9 September.

Botswana also declared its disquiet at the worsening conflict and security situation and reports of human rights abuses in Burundi, and called for an end to the conflict. On 17 February, it also decried the intensification of the *Syrian conflict*, and called for cooperation amongst concerned parties to bring hostilities to an end. On 8 September, Botswana restated its concern about Syria, particularly alleged crimes against humanity, and further criticised the UNSC for its inability to successfully bring the conflict to an end.

On 17 February, Botswana called on claimants to the South China Sea Islands to follow established international structures in addressing their disagreements, causing a diplomatic tiff with *China*, which affirmed its position regarding the South China Sea. Media reports subsequently suggested that China had closed its embassy in Gaborone for an indefinite period. On 22 February, Botswana declared its unease concerning the conduct of the Ugandan elections and on 12 July decried "renewed hostilities and fighting in Juba" (South Sudan) and called for an end to the conflict. On 8 March, Botswana donated foodstuffs to Lesotho. On 12 December, Botswana denounced Gambian President Jahya Jammeh for flouting democratic ideals after he refused to accept his election defeat by Adama Barrow and annulled the result. On 21 December, Botswana criticised the DRC for failing to conduct elections as expected.

On 22 March, Botswana applauded the *ICC* for convicting Jean-Pierre Bemba of the DRC for crimes against humanity. Botswana remained categorical in its support for the ICC. On 25 October, Botswana criticised South's Africa intention to pull out from the ICC's Rome Statute, and used this opportunity to reaffirm its own commitment to it, sparking a diplomatic row with South Africa. On 24 November, Botswana condemned attacks on ordinary citizens in Syria and Yemen, and also criticised Russia for intending to pull out from the Rome Statute.

On 9 December, Botswana voted in support of the UN General Assembly resolution that called for "an immediate cessation of hostilities in *Syria* and humanitarian aid access throughout the country", and denounced Russia and China for using their "veto power to counter resolutions which are intended to address humanitarian crisis…". Botswana further insisted on a truce in Yemen, where massacres had been reported.

Minister of Foreign Affairs and International Cooperation *Pelonomi Venson-Moitoi* attended the 28th Ordinary Session of the AU Executive Council on 27–28 January, the 26th Ordinary Session of the Assembly of AU Heads of State and Government on 30–31 January in Addis Ababa (Ethiopia), and the 31st session of the UN Human Rights Council from 29 February to 2 March in Geneva (Switzerland). On 23 March, Venson-Moitoi was recommended as the Southern Africa regional candidate for the position of AU Commission chairperson, but she failed to attract sufficient votes at the 27th Ordinary Session of the Assembly of Heads of State and Government in Kigali (Rwanda) on 17–18 June. Botswana's Delegation to the 27th Ordinary Session of the Assembly of Heads of State and Government was led by Vice President Mokgweetsi Masisi. President Khama did not attend, despite Botswana's Venson-Moitoi being a candidate in the critical election of the AU Commission chairperson. Venson-Moitoi also attended the 15th session of the Africa-Nordic Meeting of Foreign Ministers in Oslo (Norway) on 26–27 May.

High profile visits continued, demonstrating that Botswana was maintaining its foreign policy. Senator Jeff Flake led a US Congress delegation to Botswana on 17–19 February and, amongst other things, commended Botswana for its anti-poaching stance. Another US Congress delegation, headed by Senator Lamar Alexander, visited on 1–2 June, while US Assistant Secretary for African Affairs Linda Thomas-Greenfield visited on 29 June. South African President Jacob Zuma visited on 18 April, Kenyan President Uhuru Kenyatta on 27–29 June, and Namibian President Hage Geingob on 11–12 July. There were also visits by Chile's Vice Minister of Foreign Affairs Edgardo Riveros Marin on 2 September, and Singapore's senior minister of state at the Ministry of Defence and Ministry of Foreign Affairs, Mohamed Maliki Bin Osman, on 5–6 September.

President Ian Khama visited Mozambique on 23–25 May, and attended the 36th SADC Summit of Heads of State and Government on 29–31 August in Mbabane (Swaziland), where he handed the revolving position of chairperson to Swaziland. He also attended the inauguration of Zambia's President Edgar Chagwa Lungu on 13 September, celebrations for Lesotho's 50th anniversary of Independence on 4 October, and the 3rd session of the Botswana-South Africa Bi-National Commission (BNC) in South Africa on 11 November.

Socioeconomic Developments

The economy continued to be trapped in *mineral sector* dependency and attendant commodity vacillations, despite government efforts to widen its growth base. On 7 October, the government announced the closure of BCL and Tati Nickel Mines and put them on interim liquidation, citing, amongst other things, a fall in commodity prices (copper and nickel) and an increase in operational costs. The closures resulted in over 5,000 employees losing their jobs.

The economic situation remained stable, despite challenges associated with a commodity driven economy. The *2016/2017 budget* set revenue and expenditure at P (Pula) 48.4 bn and P 54.4 bn, respectively, and a huge preliminary deficit of P 6.1 bn was suggested. Minerals continued to be a leading source of revenue at 35.2%, followed by customs and excise at 24.3%, whilst non-mineral revenue was put at

21.2%. The country maintained relatively healthy foreign reserves although they fell steadily, from P 84.9 bn in December 2015 to P 76.8 bn in December 2016.

However, *social risks* (particularly unemployment, poverty, inequality and HIV/AIDS) persisted in blighting the socio-economic outlook, despite efforts to contain them. In August, the Unemployment Movement of Botswana, held a protest outside parliament, and clashed with police, denouncing a rise in unemployment and calling on government to "address their plight". Unemployment was estimated at 19.8% while poverty was put at 19.3%. The latest estimates (2013) put HIV prevalence at 18.5%, one of the highest in the region. Several programmes were in motion to contain the threat posed by HIV/AIDS. For example, the government reported that about 90% of those infected with HIV were receiving treatment whilst mother to child transmission was reduced to below 2%.

No improvement was recorded with respect to inequality, with the country's Gini coefficient put at 0.645. As a result, *social security programmes* continued to be a priority. In December, the government stated that the temporary labour intensive programme was enlisting 63,688 people monthly, while the supplementary feeding programme reached around 299,096. In addition, support was received by 105,754 old age pensioners, 35,713 destitute persons, 34,264 indigent students, 29,828 orphans, 1,795 World War II Veterans and 1,303 home-based patients. The National Service Programme had 13,474 young persons registered as of June while there were 3,452 interns registered on the National Internship Programme, according to details provided in the State of the Nation Address. These programmes may not be sustainable in the long term owing to the economy's narrow growth base. The economic growth rate was 2.9%, which was less than the 4.2% initially anticipated.

Inflation continued to be stable, and stood at 3.0% in December, in line with the Bank of Botswana's target range of 3%-6%, compared with 3.1% in December 2015. In terms of the World Economic Forum's 2016/2017 *Global Competitiveness Index*, Botswana showed a slight improvement, ranked 64th of the 138 countries evaluated, compared with 71st in the 2015/2016 report. Botswana also retained optimistic credit ratings, with an A2 from Moody's and an A-2 from Standard and Poor's.

Lesotho

Roger Southall

The seven-party coalition put together by Phakalitha Mosisili, leader of the Democratic Congress (DC), following the February 2015 election was always destined to be unstable. Although he was once again prime minister, Mosisili's coalition majority in parliament was wafer thin and, as the government progressed, its internal tensions became increasingly manifest. Ironically, this flowed most notably from divisions between the Lithope and Lirurubele factions within the DC (led by Mosisili and Monyane Moleleke, deputy leader of the DC, respectively). They culminated in Mosisili's removal of Moleke as minister of police and public safety and his transfer to the prime minister's office in November, along with the dismissal of four other ministers, allegedly for colluding with the opposition. It subsequently emerged that Moleleke had forged an agreement with the former prime minister, Tom Thabane, leader of the opposition All Basotho Convention (ABC), to oust the government.

 | DOI 10.1163/9789004355910_047

Domestic Politics

The *report of the SADC Commission*, chaired by Botswana's Judge Mphaphi Phumaphi, into instability in Lesotho was made public in February. Its principal purpose had been to enquire into the killing by soldiers of Brigadier-General Maaparankoe Mahao in June 2015. Mahao had been appointed commander of the Lesotho Defence Force (LDF) by the then prime minister Tom Thabane in place of Tlali Kamoli, only for Kamoli to be re-appointed to his position in May 2015 by Mosisili after the latter had resumed his post as prime minister. The LDF had claimed that Mahao had been killed in a skirmish after he resisted attempts to arrest him for alleged involvement in plotting a mutiny within the army. The Commission, which first met in Lesotho on 20 July 2015 under an initial 60-day mandate (later extended by a further 30 days), had heard testimony from government officials and civil society, as well as from opposition parties, the Lesotho Mounted Police Service and the LDF themselves. During this process, Judge Phumaphi had clashed repeatedly with members of Mosisili's government and senior army officers over what he deemed to be their evasiveness in failing to answer questions about matters they should have known about or their refusal to allow soldiers implicated in Mahao's death to testify. In turn, the government had publicly criticised the judge for hearing testimony from former prime minister Thabane and other opposition politicians (who had fled Lesotho following Mahao's death) in South Africa (claiming that the Commission had been established under Lesotho's domestic law).

It was against this fraught background that the *findings of the Commission* concluded that "on a balance of probabilities", Mahao had not resisted arrest; that the degree of force used to arrest him was not commensurate with the danger he had posed by his possession of a pistol; and that there had been a failure by the LDF to properly preserve evidence of what had occurred. The Commission concluded that Mahao had been murdered, rather than shot and killed. Indeed, it reported that it was extremely doubtful that Mahao had been involved in the alleged mutiny plot, "bearing in mind that before he was shot and killed, there had been threats to his life coming from the LDF". Furthermore, there were divisions within the LDF, and anomalies relating to the charges of mutiny. The report went on to recommend that the 23 soldiers facing mutiny charges should be granted amnesty from criminal prosecution. Indeed, given that soldiers charged with mutiny had been subject to torture, it concluded that "the alleged mutiny might have been a fabrication". The report went on to endorse Mahao's appointment as commander and the removal of Kamoli from the same post by Thabane as legal. In contrast, while the subsequent removal of Mahao by the incoming Mosisili government had also been legal, it had been accomplished in a flawed manner, as had been the re-appointment of Kamoli. The Commission further found that Kamoli's re-appointment had imperilled security, not least because Kamoli had perpetuated divisions within the LDF by vowing to deal with those who had celebrated his removal. The flight of opposition leaders to South Africa and subsequent boycotts of parliament by the opposition parties was a further manifestation of political instability.

The *recommendations of the Commission* included: first, that the government should ensure that criminal investigations into Mahao's death be pursued vigorously; second, that Kamoli should be relieved of his duties as commander of the LDF, and all army officers implicated in cases of murder, attempted murder and treason should be suspended immediately while investigations into their cases were carried out; third, given that some of the country's political and security problems emanated from its constitution, deficiencies and overlaps within the latter should be addressed urgently; and fourth, that implementation of reforms (of the constitution, security sector, public service and information services and media) should be accelerated, as recommended by the SADC Mission to Lesotho, which had been headed by Cyril Ramaphosa during much of 2015.

Unsurprisingly, the Phumaphi Report met with a *hostile reception in Maseru.* The SADC leadership met with Mosisili to discuss the report on 18 January, only to be faced with a refusal to receive it. SADC promptly threatened to suspend Lesotho from the regional organisation, whereupon the government reluctantly accepted the report, formally tabling it in parliament on 8 February. However, the tabled version omitted the names of certain LDF officers who were implicated in human rights violations, including torture and other ill-treatment, and the killing of Brigadier Mahao. In addition, the legitimacy of the report was directly challenged by a court case whereby Lieutenant Colonel Tefo Hshatsi, one of those implicated in the murder of Mahao, sought to nullify its findings on the grounds, first, that the Commission, especially Justice Phumaphi, had been biased against him and had violated his constitutional right to be presumed innocent until proven guilty by a competent court; and second, that the Commission had violated its terms of reference by hearing evidence in South Africa. In response, SADC reiterated that any court decision against the Commission of Inquiry would have no legal effect. The Mosisili government was further alienated by what it regarded as SADC's threat to Lesotho's sovereignty and lack of impartiality, and had sought to delay publication of the report to give time for editing out anything deemed likely to threaten the country's peace and security. In this regard, the government had met a particular opponent in South Africa's President Jacob Zuma, who had stated on 19 January on the South African Broadcasting Corporation's 'Morning Live' programme that SADC would unilaterally release the report and push for the complete suspension of Lesotho from the regional body. Zuma's remarks met with no surprise in Maseru, where it was felt that he had aligned himself with Thabane, who when he was prime minister had appointed as advisers the controversial Indian Gupta family, who were close to Zuma. In turn, Mosisili, on his return to office, had terminated the arrangement with the Guptas, and revoked their diplomatic passports. Mosisili was naturally vocal in his rejection of any suggestion that Lesotho be suspended from SADC, claiming that any such move would be invalid while a case concerning the legitimacy of the Phumaphi Commission was still before a court of law.

Meanwhile, Mosisili was facing other pressures. There was particular opposition to an *Amnesty Bill* that the government was seeking to process through parliament, which would grant amnesty to any members of the army, police, national security services, correctional services and 'other persons' for any offences committed between January 2007 and December 2015. The amnesty would extend to any members of the LDF whom the Phumaphi Commission had recommended should be subject to prosecution. Civil society organisations objected to what they considered the government's attempt to construct a "culture of impunity". More forcefully, US diplomats warned that the passing of the Bill would imperil Lesotho's continuing favourable access to the US market under AGOA, thereby endangering the jobs of the 30,000 workers in Lesotho's textile industry.

Tensions between the government and SADC continued, with the former missing a deadline to file an update on progress in implementing the Phumaphi report. However, on 20 June, Mosisili presented an update in parliament, while stating that SADC's recommendations were not binding. At a further SADC meeting on 28 June, it was resolved that SADC would assist the government to develop a "comprehensive road map" with clear time frames for the implementation of all SADC decisions and recommendations, notably those pertaining to reforms of the security sector and the constitution. It also called upon all opposition leaders in exile to return to Lesotho to participate in the reform process.

The appeal met with no response, opposition leaders having received no guarantees of their safety. Meanwhile, the political situation remained tense and volatile. *Media repression* increased. Journalists working in the broadcast, print and social media faced threats, and some were physically attacked. On 23 June, 'Lesotho Times' reporter Keiso Mohloboli was interrogated at police headquarters and pressured to disclose her sources for an article alleging that Tlali Kamoli would receive an exit package of M (maluti) 50 m (around $ 3.5 m). She was arrested the following day, along with the newspaper's editor, Lloyd Mutungamiri. The newspaper's owner, Basildon Peta, was charged in turn with criminal defamation following publication of a column that had satirised Kamoli. On 9 July, gunmen attacked and injured Mutungamiri in his home driveway. Mohloboli fled the country, fearing for her life.

The SADC meeting on 28 June had given Lesotho until August to start implementing the reforms, but August came and went. Subsequently, Cyril Ramaphosa met with the three exiled opposition leaders (Thabane, Theselle Maseribane of the Basotho National Party, and Keketso Rantsho of the Reformed Congress of Lesotho) in Pretoria (South Africa), where they were joined by opposition leaders from within

Lesotho. Ramaphosa briefed the leaders on SADC's efforts to consolidate peace and stability, highlighting the *appointment of a SADC committee* to oversee the recommended reforms, notably those of the security sector and the constitution. He further indicated that he would soon pay a visit to Lesotho to introduce members of the oversight committee to all relevant stakeholders.

This formed the backdrop to the dramatic events of the next few days. On 8 November, the government announced that it had concluded negotiations with Lieutenant General Kamoli, who would retire as commander of the LDF on 1 December. However, hopes that this would stabilise the *fragile political situation* were immediately dashed by Mosisili's redeployment of Monyane Moleleki, his party's deputy leader, from the key post of minister of police to the prime minister's office (where it was presumably felt he would be under firmer control). The National Executive Committee of the DC, which was controlled by Moleleki's *Lirurubele* faction, responded by ordering Mosisili to pull out of the seven-party coalition, which they accused of corruption, nepotism and undermining relations with development partners. Subsequently, four ministers (and two deputy ministers) who were aligned with Moleleki were dismissed. When another DC minister joined them by resigning a few days later, it was clear that the end of the government was in sight. Moleleke's faction declared that they were ready to form a new government, claiming that they had the support of at least 21 members of the ruling coalition, and that they were ready to go into coalition with Thabane's ABC. In response, the government sought to stand firm, insisting that the prime minister would only leave office if he lost a vote of no confidence, with Deputy Prime Minister Mothetjoa Metsing hinting that opposition MPs who had been in exile for more than a year might be disqualified from participating in such a vote by their lack of attendance at parliamentary sittings. This threat was backed up by reports that police were arresting, or ready to arrest, MPs who were attempting to cross the floor and rumours that the government wanted to clamp down on social media. Deputy Prime Minister Metsing meanwhile claimed there was no crisis in Lesotho, only a thriving democracy.

Foreign Affairs

The *tensions between Lesotho and SADC* were reflective of deeper undercurrents. Lesotho's politicians were acutely aware of their country's lack of effective sovereignty and of the determining influence of outsiders. The budget was hugely dependent upon development assistance; electoral and military affairs were heavily subject to SADC influence; employment was critically reliant upon AGOA and the export of labour to South Africa; and Lesotho depended on imports from South Africa for virtually all consumer and capital goods. In addition, although benefitting financially from the export of water to South Africa via the Highlands Water Project,

Lesotho was becoming increasingly subject to South Africa's strategic security and political concerns. Further anxieties amongst Lesotho's political elite were aroused by the activities of a People's Charter Movement, which called for the incorporation of the country into South Africa.

In August, it was reported that South Africa's Water Affairs Minister Nomvula Monkonyane had insisted on new terms of reference for the R (rand) 26 bn *Polihali dam*, originally scheduled for completion in 2018 but repeatedly delayed (now supposedly due for completion in 2025). Senior departmental officials with the South African ministry, who asked not to be identified, stated that Monkonyane was demanding that the main contractor chosen to design and build the dam should share 20% of the contract with a black empowerment partner. It was further claimed that the minister favoured LTE Consulting, reportedly an African National Congress donor, for that role. LTE was already the subject of a probe by the Special Investigating Unit relating to alleged flawed tendering processes regarding water and sanitation contracts in the South African province of Gauteng. Meanwhile, it was further alleged that Monkanyane had removed South Africa's chief delegate to the Highlands Water Project, Dr Zodwa Dlamini, who had ten years' experience in mega-water projects, to facilitate the inclusion of LTE in the project, replacing him with Bheki Nkosi, who had served as her provincial minister for infrastructure when she had been premier of Gauteng. Ministers in Mosisili's cabinet were said to be colluding with Mokonyane in their eagerness to use the Highlands Water Commission as a source of patronage.

Socioeconomic Developments

Minister of Finance Dr 'Mamphono Khaketla presented her *budget* on 22 February. The total recurrent expenditure estimate of M 11,485.8 m was complemented by proposed capital expenditure of M 5,004.7 m. Partly because of the depreciation in the value of the rand (to which the maluti was tied), public debt had increased to M 867 m. She also noted that Prime Minister Mosisili had urged Basotho and development partners to respond to a need for M 585m in drought relief. Critics on the relevant parliamentary committee complained that the budget lacked creativity and failed to deal with the pressing problems of declining custom revenues from SACU, an increasing public sector wage bill, and a low capacity to spend the capital budget. They doubted that a budget deficit of 10% of GDP was sustainable and called for increased efforts to mobilise domestic revenues whilst cutting back on unnecessary expenditure, notably on travel and transport of government officials. The committee failed to mention that, were the unwieldy seven-party coalition to fall apart, the government would need to look well beyond its proposed budget to fund any consequent election.

Madagascar

Richard R. Marcus

The perpetual fragility of the position of President Hery Martial Rajaonarimampianina was softened by decisive wins. The senatorial elections of 29 December 2015 resulted in a 60% majority for the president's New Forces for Madagascar party. Political uncertainty and policy clashes led to the dismissal of Prime Minister Jean Ravelonarivo, the appointment of Olivier Mahafaly Solonandrasana, and a subsequent cabinet reshuffle, but Rajaonarimampianina showed a greater propensity for political survival than many had predicted. The economy was relatively stagnant due to external shocks, political instability and dangerously weak institutions, but macroeconomic stabilisation paved the way for increased international financial support. The year closed with significant political uncertainty and unimpressive economic growth, but the government exceeded expectations by merely surviving. Former presidents Marc Ravalomanana and Andry Rajoelina, as well as a growing litany of political upstarts, were already jockeying for support from key political and private sector elites in anticipation of the 2018 presidential elections.

 | DOI 10.1163/9789004355910_048

Domestic Politics

It was uncertain whether President Rajaonarimampianina would survive the year politically. There were fairly regular rumours of an imminent *coup d'etat*; the military leadership was uneasy with the status quo; the president and prime minister did not appear to share a common vision for the country; much of the politically powerful private sector had reversed its support for the president; civil society, the key to the peace agreement brokered in 2012, was highly fractured; and the opposition, particularly supporters of former president Marc Ravalomanana, was impatiently creating new strategies. The president abruptly dismissed Prime Minister Jean Ravelonarivo on 8 April, taking much of the cabinet by surprise. No immediate reason was given for the dismissal, but there had been public squabbling over development policy, particularly as it related to the national road system, crime and traffic in the capital. There was also much speculation that Ravelonarivo had ultimately lost the support of key individuals in both the private and public sectors, which were moving towards political networks close to former presidents Marc Ravalomanana, Andry Rajoelina and Zafy Albert, as well as former prime minister Camille Vital, the last three of whom actively sought to block Ravelonarivo's initial appointment. The president appointed Minister of Interior and Decentralization Olivier Mahafaly Solonandrasana as prime minister on 10 April. Mahafaly named a new cabinet, retaining his own cabinet portfolio. Of the 32 members of the cabinet, six were reshuffled to new positions, 13 retained their posts, and 13 new cabinet members were appointed. The new prime minister was immediately beset with expectations that he could address critical legal reforms, create a greater balance of power, and use his cabinet, replete with technocrats, to address core sectoral challenges. By December, none of these problems had abated but it became increasingly clear that money and energies were being focused on the 2018 presidential elections rather than the removal of Mahafaly. This was a sign of client maturity but should not be mistaken for institutional strength. Nearly every major sector including banking, mining, education, health care, water and land lacked measurable accountability and remained in desperate need of both legislative and policy reforms.

When new senators took their seats in January it should have been a sign of normalisation. After all, this was the first time the *senate* had sat since its dissolution with the overthrow of Ravalomanana in March 2009. Unfortunately, the upper house lacked the power of the National Assembly. Part of this was a procedural problem: following the 2010 constitution and the electoral code, 42 of the senate's 63 seats were elected indirectly by approximately 12,500 local level counsellors and the remaining 21 seats were appointed by the president. Since his party, the New Forces for Madagascar ('Hery Vaovao ho an'i Madagasikara'; HVM) had dominated the preceding local elections, no other outcome was imaginable. Yet, because the electorate had no direct link to the process and did not necessarily vote for the same party in local and national elections, the process largely failed to build internal legitimacy and to catapult new political leaders onto the national stage. At the same time, the president hoped that the new senate would strengthen his position. Concern mounted that he would call snap elections and dissolve the National Assembly in an effort to strengthen his legislative position, a move successfully made by Ravalomanana in 2007.

Political energy was mainly spent on the realignment of *opposition forces* and their sources of funding in advance of the 2018 presidential elections. Rajaonarimampianina was expected to run for a second term, but he was viewed as ineffective and highly vulnerable. He had won only 16% of the votes in the first round of the 2013 elections and it was considered unlikely that he could fair better. He continued to show that he was a practical political operative by simultaneously relying upon technocrats and cultivating informal networks to stay in power. But he was not successful either at growing institutional capacity politically or economically or at safeguarding nascent institutions from exploitation by predatory elites. Ravalomanana was active through the year, demonstrating that he would probably be the strongest opposition Rajaonarimampianina would face. He spent much of the year rebuilding both his private sector relationships and his political networks. Once a lay-leader in the Protestant Church of Jesus Christ in Madagascar ('Fiangonan'i Jesoa Kristy eto Madagasikara'; FJKM), Ravalomanana also re-established important links with this politically powerful organisation. Madagascar's semi-presidential system required that a president needed to gain 50% of the votes, which generally forced a run-off election. While there would probably be dozens of candidates in the first round, it was again only Ravalomanana, Rajoelina and Rajaonarimampianina who appeared to gain any footing during the year.

Governance indicators (Mo Ibrahim Index, V-Dem, World Bank and Freedom House) were mildly positive. However, the starting point was low, with Freedom House giving a total freedom rating of 56/100, comparable to Bhutan and Guatemala. Crime in urban areas reached unusually high levels. Progress had been slow and political entrepreneurs had learned to profit on the sidelines, making it very difficult to cultivate change and leading to criticism from international organisations. For instance, Madagascar had applied to join the EITI in 2008 but the application process was suspended in 2011, resuming in 2014 after Rajaonarimampianina was elected. At a December presentation of the 2017 EITI Madagascar work plan, Daniela Randriafeno, executive secretary of EITI in Madagascar, stated that she hoped Madagascar would seek EITI validation in 2017 but expressed concerns with regard to the mining and petroleum industries in such areas as transparency in the collection and distribution of revenues (which required a revision of the mining and petroleum codes), property disclosures, transparency of geo-scientific information and transparency of permits and permit processes.

On 12 December, former president Didier Ratsiraka set four conditions for the *2018 presidential elections.* While the signal that he might run appeared quixotic for the octogenarian, who had led the country from 1975 to 1993 and 1997 to 2002, his points reflected profound concerns expressed by many parts of civil society and the international community: rewrite the 2010 constitution of the 4th Republic, replace the Independent National Electoral Commission (CENI), change the electoral code, and modernise the voting system. These were perennial issues raised to challenge the structure of governance and of the state itself. Most analysts agreed that the constitution was an incoherent text, muddying not just responsibilities between the executive, legislature and judiciary, but the nature of decentralised and regional governing entities. Hery Rakotomanana, CENI's director, had the challenging job of improving CENI's communication and voter awareness strategy, revising and improving the security of the electoral register, and creating a new legal framework for the upcoming elections, while building trust in CENI amongst civil society organisations and the political parties that it was charged with overseeing. Rakotomanana sounded a pessimistic alarm on 15 November, when he said, "It must be recognised that until this day our electoral register is failing … for a population estimated at more than 23 million, we have only 8.6 million voters." The electoral code was designed on the assumption that there would be an annual revision of voter lists but this had not happened. There had been a widespread desire locally and amongst international interlocutors to address shortcomings in the electoral code, most notably the rules for electioneering and campaign finance. Other institutions required under the 2010 constitution that it was hoped would be created during the year included the High Court of Justice, the High Council for National Defence and the High Council for the Defence of Democracy and the Rule of Law, but these hopes were not realised and there was significant criticism that the executive was reluctant to engage in building institutions that might constrain presidential powers.

The *legal process* was frustrated. In its first ordinary session, from 3 May to 1 July, the National Assembly adopted 28 of the proposed 33 laws, bringing renewed accusations that it was there merely to ratify the wishes of the president. The implementation of laws seen as politically inconvenient often took years, with some clauses never implemented at all. For instance, the Mining Investment Law, a source of significant revenue, included guarantees that the environment would be restored and protected, but these were never implemented. As of 14 September, only 106 of 207 legislators and 12 of 63 cabinet ministers had declared their assets, in direct violation of the law. The lack of public information about assets and interests meant that the flow of informal political relationships was protected at the expense of transparency and accountability.

With few of these issues addressed by year's end, the likelihood of reforms had faded. The legislative process remained in disarray, the cabinet was unstable and there were relatively high barriers to communication and functionality. A question of the order of reforms remained. The electoral code had yet to be adopted as a bill by the Executive and prospects faded as the president was preparing for the 2018 elections. On 5 October, the CENI reached an agreement with civil society representatives on many points of the electoral code. However, some of the reforms related to it that were demanded by civil society organisations in December were not in line with the constitution, begging the question of how many of the reforms would be possible in advance of a constitutional revision that would surely not take place before the 2018 elections. Finally, with nine constitutional revisions and four republics since 1960, there was hardly reason to automatically trust that institutions would be constructed with accountability measures and be able to hold sway over the politicians who created them. The Malagasy body politic was poised to enter 2017 with little success but with hopes of muddling through and survival, putting off systemic crises for the future.

Foreign Affairs

The general trend in *ODA* was positive, with an increase of 7%, according to the most recent figures (2015) to a total of $ 677 m. The World Bank was the largest donor, granting $ 253 m, followed by the EU ($ 116 m), the United States ($ 98.7 m), and France ($ 85.9 m). During the political crisis (2009–2013), international donors overwhelmingly discontinued direct work with the government, shifting funding to education, health, humanitarian aid and other areas where direct support was most feasible. In 2016, education and health retained significant funding at 17% and 16% of overall allocations, but were overtaken by programme support, which accounted for 30% of funding. Humanitarian aid levels remained relatively constant but, with increased funding, dropped to 4% of the total. UN organisations were the most significant donors during the political crisis but their support dropped off. The UN Development Assistance Fund (UNDAF), established in 2015, confirmed late in 2016 an increased commitment of $ 523 m for the remainder of the period 2015–19 to cover poverty reduction in vulnerable populations, public institutions and civil society development, and access and use of sustainable social services. A conference of donors held on 1–2 December led to tensions over the president's commitment to governance reforms, but Rajaonarimampianina defended himself, arguing that he was satisfied with the results and was dedicated to fighting corruption, establishing good governance and improving the business environment.

The most important international event was the 16th *IOF Summit* held on 26–27 November. It brought delegates together to enhance the promotion of the French language and cooperative relationships between the 84 member states. Making Antananarivo the venue was at once a statement by the OIF about the importance of Madagascar to the organisation and a political statement by the Madagascar government.

From 10 to 19 October the 19th *COMESA Summit* was held in Antananarivo. The focus was to grow opportunities for Madagascar to find new markets to grow "inclusive and sustainable industrialisation". The relative absence of heads of state – only six attended – was largely viewed as a criticism of Malagasy governance. Although this was an exclusively economics-focused meeting, the fact of COMESA being based in Zambia and predominantly Anglophone, renewed a cautious challenge to Madagascar on how it should navigate sometimes conflictual memberships in COMESA and SADC (whose 36th Annual Summit was attended by Rajaonarimampianina in Swaziland on 31 August). The direction of foreign policy indicated a development approach. On 14 October, COMESA Secretary General Sindiso Ngwenya stated that COMESA was calling for a paradigm shift towards regional integration that recognised and accepted the need for robust institutional and governance structures, signalling a shift in organizational structure and priorities towards regional industrialisation. This effectively supported policies introduced by the Ravalomanana presidency (2002–9) at the expense of narrower bilateral arrangements favoured by other Malagasy politicians and the OIF.

The *United States* continued to increase its presence. On 14 April, US Ambassador Robert Yamate met with the director general of BIANCO ('Bureau Indépendant Anti-Corruption'), the Malagasy government's anti-corruption bureau, to lend his support to the embattled agency. Forty-five new Peace Corps members were sworn in on 3 May. An Emergency Relief Fund to combat drought was increased on 28 October from $ 3.7 m to $ 32.1 m. In November, a joint US-Malagasy delegation unveiled its new US-supported border security database at Ivato International Airport, and, while the US condemned Madagascar for human rights abuses, human trafficking, weakness of courts and crackdowns on journalists and free speech in its 2016 Human Rights Report, it gave positive support to government efforts to address such abuses and electoral processes and was less critical than many others in the international community.

With Rajaonarimampianina and former president Andry Rajoelina holding their orientation towards France and Ravalomanana holding his towards other countries, international alignments proved important to domestic political jockeying. Ravalomanana as the leading opposition figure was notable in his move away from French relations in favour of relations with a broad array of countries, particularly the US, Germany and South Korea.

Socioeconomic Developments

Madagascar remained vulnerable to economic shocks. The country was given a score of 0.512 on the *HDI*, dropping from 154th to 158th of the 186 countries on the list and continuing a long-term trend since 1990 in several key indicator areas. Some 64.3% of the population lived in rural areas according to World Bank data. With an (Atlas) Gross National Income per capita of $ 420, Madagascar had one of the lowest fiscal yields in the world; 87.7% of the population were living on $ 1.25 per day and 95% on under $ 2 per day. The HDI reflected that the richest quintile of the population averaged 9.8 years of schooling compared with 1.7 years for the poorest quintile. The rural poor were far less likely to learn reading, writing, mathematics and other critical skills and had become trapped in a poverty cycle. Similar stagnation was also notable in gender development, with perpetually fewer opportunities for women in adult literacy, which had dropped from over 70% in 2000 to 64.7% in the most recent measure (2015), and in inequality. Life expectancy showed a modest improvement but remained low at 65.5 years. Food prices stabilised after several turbulent years, but in the main the socioeconomic picture was one of slow deterioration.

At $ 9.7 bn in 2015, *GDP* showed a gross expansion of 3.1%, but with a population growth rate of 2.8%, it was noticeably flat. Claims on central government expanded by more than 25% and inflation ticked up from 6.6% to 7.6%. Agriculture continued to contribute a steady 26.5% of total GDP, while industry accounted for 16.9% and services 56.6%. The price for Malagasy vanilla, which accounted for 79% of global supply, continued to soar from an international market rate of $ 11/kg in 2011 to $ 193/kg. While supply shortage fed high profits for international companies, it took its toll on the local work force and sparked syndicated networks of vanilla thieves that defied government control. The World Bank's *Doing Business Index* scored Madagascar at 167 out of 189, slightly worse than the 164 score for 2015. This reflected a perpetually low building quality control score, high electricity costs and, worse, an average of 450 days required to connect to electricity, high costs and heavy bureaucratic procedures for starting a business, low corporate transparency, low shareholder governance, and a comparably high profit tax rate of 38%. All of this was discouraging a sea change in domestic private sector risk-taking and international investment.

Extractive resource industries were an exception to the general private sector stagnation. With a long history of artisanal mining, there were more than 100,000 jobs in the sector but they provided low incomes and accounted for less than 1% of GDP. The growth of two large industrial mining projects, QMM in the south and Ambatovy in the north-east, had led to investments of $ 7.2 bn and $ 930 m in the late 2000s. Industrial mining had grown from representing 1% of GDP in 2012 to 6% and was poised to reach 14% of GDP by 2025. It accounted for 30% of all exports and this was expected to grow to 50% in the coming five years. In February, Madagascar Oil, an American company, led a consortium to win the first environmental permit for *oil exploration*. Tsimiroro Block 3104 had 150,000 barrels in store from its Stream Flood Pilot Facility, but this had seismic implications. September updates showed estimated reserves of nearly 2 bn barrels in Tsimiroro. The company proudly touted that 90% of jobs had been filled locally, that there had been $ 303 m of private capital investment, and that schools and healthcare facilities had been funded at the point of extraction. The state-owned Office of National Mining and Strategic Resources estimated that Madagascar had a total geological reserve of about 1,500 bn barrels of oil. It committed to auctioning off 40 offshore blocs in 2017 and planned to extend VAT holidays to encourage exploration as it had for Tsimiroro. Ambatovy and QMM have led to complementary *infrastructure development* including roads, ports, railways and drinking water treatment.

Industrial mining accounted for over 20,000 local jobs and was expected to grow to over 67,000 by 2025. Other projects – Toliara, Sakoa and WISCO – had already received permits and were poised to begin increasing extraction of coal, ilmenite, zircon and iron ore. This increased activity in mining and oil extraction held high potential as a catalyst for growth. However, mining analysts, civil society organisations, and economists were concerned that the governance challenges, questions about royalty distribution and socioeconomic impacts, legal and institutional frailty and political instability could undermine the positive impact of the sector windfall. As put by TI's country director, Randria Arson, on 16 May, "Licensing without scrutiny has become a problem for the government. These permits pose environmental problems, security and governance issues since some of these were issues to the limit of legality." The challenge going forward would be for a weak government with limited legal capacity to ensure new wealth was leading to extraction-driven economic growth rather than being a natural resource curse.

Malawi

George Dzimbiri and Lewis Dzimbiri

Issues concerning poor socioeconomic and political governance featured prominently during the year. The continued abuse of public funds in public services, which resulted in slowed progress in service delivery, was central to concerns in various quarters of Malawi society. The ruling Democratic Progressive Party (DPP) faced criticisms from various actors over poor governance, misplaced priorities and poor social services, including a shortage of medicines in health facilities and the inability to employ nurses and doctors trained at public expense when there were vacancies in hospitals. Both intra- and inter-party squabbles between key political parties and actors featured prominently. The shortage of maize, on-going inadequate power supplies, rising commodity prices, the continued withholding of budgetary support by donors and unfavourable tobacco and tea prices had a detrimental effect on the economy. The Malawi kwacha (K) continued to depreciate during the second part of the year, resulting in rises in commodity prices and the general cost of living. This prompted strikes for wage increases in both the private and public sectors.

 | DOI 10.1163/9789004355910_049

Domestic Politics

The political arena was characterised by both *intra- and inter-party conflicts*. Intra-party conflicts were noticeable in both the opposition parties and in the ruling DPP. On 1 February, violence erupted within the People's Party (PP) at a political rally held in Mzuzu and at least nine people were injured. The violence started when the acting president of the party, Uladi Mussa, physically attacked the former vice president of the party, Khumbo Kachali, for allegedly bringing divisions within the party and demanding a leadership change in the absence of the founding president, Joyce Banda. On 2 February, the PP fired its provincial governor for the North, Christopher Ngwira, who was alleged to have organised thugs to disrupt a political rally in Mzuzu. PP Publicity Secretary Ken Msonda claimed that Ngwira had proved to be a nuisance and unrepentant following similar acts of thuggery in the past. In a related development, the member of parliament (MP) for Mzimba Hora was also expelled from the party for declaring that the party's former vice president, Khumbo Kachale, should replace party president Joyce Banda, who had been outside the country since losing the May 2014 elections. Further, on 24 August, MP for Zomba Mtonya, Patrick Makina was expelled from the PP on allegations that he had not worked in the interest of the party. Conflicts also rocked the Malawi Congress Party (MCP). On 30 August, the party expelled Felix Jumbe, MP for Salima Central, for gross indiscipline. In September, MCP president Lazarus Chakwera announced the suspension of two of its members, Jessie Kabwila, MCP spokesperson, and Joseph Njobvuyalema, MP for Lilongwe Mapuyu South, who were alleged to have plotted with others to take over the leadership and destroy the party's headquarters. The ruling DPP was also beset by internal squabbles. On 13 September, the party summoned Bon Kalindo, MP for Mulanje South, to a disciplinary hearing for championing semi-naked demonstrators protesting in Lilongwe to push for stronger actions by the government and the public to stop the notorious practice of attacking and killing persons with albinism.

Inter-party conflicts also emerged. On 20 February, opposition PP officials made scathing criticisms of President Peter Mutharika in Lilongwe at Masintha Ground, where the PP held a rally. They alleged that he had failed to manage the country and called for him to resign for failing to resolve the maize crisis that had hit the country, amidst electricity blackouts and water challenges in the cities of Blantyre and Lilongwe and in various districts. In a related development, the leader of the opposition and MCP President Lazarus Chakwera led opposition MPs in attacking Muntharika's state of the nation address on 20 May as lacking in substance and failing to give adequate details of progress made in fighting corruption and other ills such as electricity blackouts and water shortages, as well as other social and economic challenges facing the country.

The government was also at loggerheads with *civil society organisations* (CSOs), including faith groups and human rights organisations, over social services and economic challenges. On 19 February, the Public Affairs Committee called for Mutharika to resign within 30 days for failing to resolve the hunger crisis that was looming large, among other things. On 13 March, bishops of Malawi's Catholic Church issued a pastoral letter in which they strongly criticised the government for socio-political and economic issues facing the country. The Episcopal Conference of Malawi released a statement on 13 March. Headed 'Mercy of God as a Path of Hope', it criticised the government for persistent hunger, the rising cost of living, the overall shrinking of public service delivery, theft of government money and misplaced priorities in policy-making and implementation processes. On 20 June, the Church of Central Africa Presbyterian Nkhoma Synod came out strongly against the government over albino killings and called on the government to protect people with albinisms. On 12 November, Mutharika was bitterly criticised by university students and CSOs in the education sector for his silence on the closure of five institutions of higher learning (Lilongwe University of Agriculture and Natural Resources Natural Resources College, the Polytechnic, a constituent college of the University of Malawi, Malawi University of Science and Technology, Malawi College of Health Sciences and Mzuzu University), which had been shut down for various reasons, such as disputes over rises in fees, demands for salary increases and water problems. On 7 December, members of various Christian denominations took to the streets in a nationwide protest against a proposed Pregnancy Termination Bill and pro-homosexuality campaigns that were being mounted by certain segments of the community. The march was organised by the Episcopal Conference of Malawi and the Evangelical Association of Malawi under the banner: 'Citizens March for Life and Family'. The demonstrators appealed to MPs and the government always to remember that it was their duty to pass laws that were in line with the country's culture, beliefs and values. The religious bodies had asked MPs to reject what they called "killing of unborn life".

On 7 April, Mutharika announced a *cabinet reshuffle*. He fired Allan Chiyembekeza, who was replaced as minister of agriculture, irrigation and water development by George Chaponda, former minister of foreign affairs. The new face in the cabinet was Aggrey Masi, who was appointed deputy minister of defence, replacing Malison Ndau, who was promoted to minister of transport and public works. On 3 May, Mutharika appointed Bright Molande, former director of information in the Ministry of Information, Communications, Technology and Civic Education as his director of communications. He later appointed him as his third press aide since taking over government in 2014. On 1 August, Mutharika replaced army commander Ignancio Maulana with his former deputy Griffin Supuni-Phiri. Like his predecessor Henry Odillo, who was to remain on the government payroll until his retirement in 2019, Maulana was appointed to head the security section of the National Food Reserve Agency until he reached the mandatory retirement age of 60.

Various laws were adopted. On 17 July, MPs unanimously passed the long awaited Copyright Bill to help artists benefit more from their work and protect their products from exploitation. Parliament also debated and passed three land-related Bills on 22 November. During the debate, a number of MPs expressed misgivings before grudgingly voting in favour. The new laws were aimed at empowering Malawians to acquire and own land, unlike in the past when all land had been vested in the president. On 13 December, parliament passed the much-awaited Access to Information Bill after the government had previously made several objections to some of its provisions. Mutharika had declared that he would not assent to the bill if the government's proposed amendments were rejected. Minister of Information and Civic Education Malisoni Ndau described the passing of the bill as a great step.

Foreign Affairs

Malawi continued to receive *international financial support.* The UK government released K 4.8 bn as a humanitarian response to the food crisis that affected people country-wide. Visiting Secretary of State for Scotland David Mundell announced additional funding in a discussion he held with Mutharika at State House in Lilongwe on 16 February. The Japanese government provided over K 5.5 bn in response to humanitarian needs during the same month. The assistance followed Mutharika's call for support to complement his government's resources to assist food insecure households following the 2015 floods and prolonged dry spell, which had hit some parts of the country. On 22 December, the Indian government gave Malawi K 723 m in aid to buy medical equipment for Mzuzu hospital in response to an appeal by Mutharika for humanitarian assistance following the natural disaster that Malawi had experienced early in the year.

Malawi returned to the *IMF programme* that had gone off track. An IMF mission was in the country from March 9 to determine whether to resume the $ 150 m ECF programme that had been declared off course in September 2015, following the government's failure to meet agreed targets after registering a scary K 78 bn in domestic borrowing at the end of the 2014/15 financial year. This had been reduced to K 4.3 bn by the end of December 2015, the first half of the 2015/16 financial year, but the IMF nevertheless declared that the 2015/16 national budget, which amounted to K 929 bn, was unsustainable and advised the government to revise it downwards. Later, the government complied by trimming the budget by K 23.7 bn. On 23 March, the IMF mission chief Oral Williams declared that Malawi had met programme targets for domestic financing and domestic borrowing.

Fraud amounting to K 184 m in embezzled funds was detected at the Malawi Embassy in Ethiopia on 18 April. This led to the suspension of Doreen Kapanga and Fletcher Chowe, Malawi's deputy ambassador and first secretary for administration and finances, respectively. On 17 May, the new Indian Electricals Ltd announced plans to invest about $ 15 m in setting up a manufacturing plant within a period of four months, which was expected to create jobs and help to scale up efforts in the provision of electrical industrial machinery. The World Bank approved a $ 17 m grant (about K 12 bn) for tuberculosis treatment on 31 May, Malawi being one of the four Southern Africa nations to benefit from the World Bank $ 122 m funds.

On 20–23 July, Jill Biden, the wife of the US vice president, visited to engage government and civil society partners on issues related to economic empowerment and educational opportunity for women and girls. In mid-September, Mutharika left for New York to give a speech at the UN General Assembly later that month. His month-long disappearance from the public scene prompted widespread speculation that he was either critically ill or dead. Speaking for the first time after his extended trip to the US upon his arrival at Kamuzu International Airport, Mutharika, who could not use his right hand but used the left to greet dignitaries welcoming him, said he was in "excellent health".

On 21 December, Malawi signed a Memorandum of Understanding with the Tanzanian government on the *Songwe River Basin* Development Programme. The Songwe River defines the boundary between Malawi and Tanzania before it runs into Malawi. The river's instability, flooding and constant change of course as it meanders to Lake Malawi had been a source of concern to authorities in both countries.

Socioeconomic Developments

The *cost of living* continued to rise. Prices of basic foodstuffs in both supermarkets and local markets started rising from January and February, leaving many feeling hopeless. On 7 February, the Malawi Energy Regulatory Authority increased electricity tariffs by 7.5% from K 53.69 to K 57.72 per kilowatt. During the same month, maize prices continued to skyrocket, with private traders selling at K 15,000 per 50 kg bag. According to John Kapito, executive director of the Consumer Association of Malawi, the shortage and high prices of maize on the market had contributed to the high cost of living. He described the situation as "the worst ever recorded scarcity of maize and of higher prices since Malawi embraced the subsidised agricultural farm input in the production of maize". On 17 March, prices of diesel, petrol and paraffin were also increased. The price of petrol went up by 4.4% from K 711.90 to K 743.30 per litre, while diesel was up to K 722.80 from K 671.30 per litre, a 7.7% increase. Paraffin rose to K 580.40 from K 526.30 per litre. On 3 June, Illovo Sugar (Malawi) Limited, the major sugar manufacturer, announced that it was increasing sugar prices by an average of 8%. Retailers were selling it at K 650 per 1 kg packet, while hawkers set the price at K 700 and above. A bale of 20 1 kg packets increased to K 13,054.99 for brown sugar and K 13,106.25 for white. Illovo attributed the price adjustment to fundamental market factors including inflation, the cost of electricity and the depreciation of the kwacha against the dollar. On 1 September, Blantyre Water Board (BWB) quietly raised water tariffs by 23%, effective from 1 July, after government approved the request for the increase. This came after the country's five water boards (Blantyre, Northern Region, Southern Region, Central Region and Lilongwe) had increased the price of water by between 10% and 45% in September 2015.

According to the Center for Social Concern (CSC) report of July, the average national *cost of living* had increased by 0.26% from K 160,660 in June to K 166,086 in July. CSC said that the increases would continue during the time of acute food shortages, especially of the staple grain, maize, since food accounted for about 50.2% in the consumer price index. In its statement, CSC revealed that the cost of living for an average family of six in the cities of Lilongwe and Zomba and the peri-urban area of Mangochi had risen in the month of July from K 182,484, K 157,450 and K 167,109, respectively, to K 187,652, K 162,090 and K 172,609. On the other hand, the report also showed that prices of maize, green vegetables, electricity, house rentals and water were the main factors contributing to the rise in the cost of basic needs in Lilongwe, Zomba and Mangochi.

The year also witnessed *shortages of medicines and blood*, which seriously affected many hospitals. By 3 February, Kamuzu Central Hospital was hit hard as the blood in the hospital's blood bank ran short. This development forced medics at the hospital to start rationing blood and other medical supplies. One glaring example of the critical shortage of blood was the strategy to give just one pint (450 ml) to an adult in need of blood and 300 ml to a child, regardless of how much blood they needed. Essential medicines such as antibiotics and painkillers were scarce in most public hospitals, which had nearly exhausted most of their drug budgets by February. Minister of Health Peter Kumpalume admitted during a mid-year budget review that most district hospitals had no stocks of drugs, as district health officers had used up more than half of their funding for drugs six months before the next budget. Some of the most affected district hospitals were in Ntcheu, which had used 87% of its allocated funding, Dedza (80%), Mulanje (71%), Thyolo (82%) and Karonga (80%).

On 22 February, the government reduced its domestic borrowing by 88% from K 36.2 bn to K 4.3 bn. Political commentators welcomed the development, given that, over previous years, Malawi's domestic debts had been rising significantly, with consequent negative effects on the economy. Similarly, the private sector described the development as 'good news' as it had been complaining of being crowded out of the financial market by the government's insatiable appetite for domestic borrowing. On 26 February, the *kwacha exchange rate* reached the point of equilibrium and started to stabilise. In some authorised dealer banks, the kwacha seemed to have slightly gained against the dollar. However, during November the kwacha depreciated by 8.0% against the dollar as a result of a low inflow of foreign currency. On the other hand, on 26 March, inflation rate fell by 1.3% to 22.1%. The National Statistical Office attributed the drop to a decline in food inflation due to increased supply of cereals. Similarly, during October, Malawi's inflation rate fell to 20.1%, a drop of 1.1%, reflecting declining food inflation (to 25.4% from 27% in September). Similarly, non-food inflation fell by 0.7% to 15.2%. Malawi's inflation rate remained one of the highest in COMESA under the harmonised consumer price index.

On 26 June, the IMF predicted a gloomy future for Malawi, reiterating that the economic situation was still challenging with no signs of hope. The IMF said in its June report that the macroeconomics situation remained difficult. This came less than a week after the IMF's board had approved the disbursement of $ 76.8 m to Malawi under its ECF programme, which was later extended to December following a letter of intent from the Malawi government. According to the IMF, the performances of most economic indicators remained poor. Restoring macroeconomic stability was the most critical short-term priority. On the other hand, the IMF recommended that the fall in inflation would necessitate the implementation of a credible budget in the 2016/17 fiscal year in line with sustainable financing.

Low prices, high leaf rejection rates and frequent market closures affected Malawi's *tobacco* industry. Tobacco continued to face a lot of challenges in all the auction floors and the tobacco market was described as very disappointing to farmers. It was reported that overproduction resulted in buyers failing to absorb all the leaf that was brought to the auction floors. Latest statistics from Tobacco Control Commission (TCC) showed that a total of 159.5 m kg of the green gold had been sold at an average price of $ 1.51 per kg in all auction floors. According to a TCC report, tobacco sales for the month of October alone reached $ 56 m (compared with $ 79.6 m during the same period in 2015) from the auctions, representing a 26% decrease. The 2016 season for tobacco sales was officially closed on 20 December with a total sum of $ 275.85 m. The total sales for tobacco for the previous year amounted to $337.40 m, representing an 18% fall. The tobacco selling season, traditionally ending in November, was extended twice to make room for more sales. This indicated that substantial quantities of tobacco remained to be sold as of November as a result of a high rejection rate and overproduction, and showed that tobacco sales faced huge challenges. In a related development, the price of *tea*, the country's second main foreign exchange earner, dropped by 20% in the second quarter (April to June) to around $ 2.90 (K 2,100) per kg from $ 3.63 (K 2,600) per kg, a development that put pressure on the foreign exchange reserves. In its financial and economic review, the Reserve Bank of Malawi attributed the declining prices to the supply glut in Kenya, Africa's number one tea producer.

International rankings differed. The HDI report for 2015, released on 9 February, ranked Malawi 173rd out of 188 countries and showed that the scores for Malawi continued to be low at 0.445, below the SSA average of 0.518. The report revealed that women were disadvantaged in both paid and unpaid work and ranked Malawi as 'low', with countries whose people were highly dependent. Countries that ranked above Malawi included South Sudan (167th), Solomon Islands (156th) and Swaziland (150th). Similarly, in November, Malawi scored poorly on the Global Entrepreneurships Index, ranking 130th out of 137 countries. In October, Malawi improved by eight places on the World Bank Doing Business Index from 141st to 133rd. The report, released on 26 October, noted that Malawi had made it easier to start a business by eliminating the legal requirement to use a company seal, making it optional for entrepreneurs as well as for getting credit. Along with these developments, the World Bank gave Malawi a score of 76.73 out of 100 from an overall Distance to Frontier score, compared with 54.39 the previous year.

A dry spell affected some parts of Malawi, resulting in some food insecurity. In April, almost 6,000 victims of *floods* in Mzuzu city risked contracting cholera as the government had not yet provided them with sanitation facilities in the five camps where they were seeking shelter. The floods were caused by a week of heavy rains in Mzuzu city, and a total of 1,265 houses also collapsed in the townships of Masasa, Mchengautuba, Chibavi, Salisbury line, Katawa, Zolozolo and Chibanja. Cholera cases in Karonga reached 175 as communities in the district grappled to return to normal life following floods. Eight people were reported to have died of diarrhoea in Karonga district alone. As of 24 May, the Ministry of Health reported 16 new cases of cholera. In November, the government admitted that the number of people requiring *food assistance* had risen from 6.5 m to 6.7 m following a second Malawi Vulnerability Assessment Committee report.

On 31 June, parliament passed the K 1,149 tr 2016/2017 *national budget* after a total of K 8.6 bn had been added by means of a supplementary order paper to the initial K 1.41 tr that the finance minister had wanted the law makers to approve. In reaction, the World Bank described the budget as unsustainable.

There was a decline in the *crime rate*. In October, police in the Southern Region reported that they had reduced crime from 7,272 cases in 2015 to 4,121 representing 43%, while traffic cases had been reduced by 25% compared with 2015. However, *security issues* were a major concern. The number of murders of albinos continued to rise in the first few months of the year. During March alone, a total of 11 albinos were reported killed and 2016 was described as the worst year ever for this crime. An AI report revealed that in 2015, 45 incidents including killings, attempted killings, abductions and attempted abductions, as well as the opening up of graves of people with albinism had been reported.

Labour conflicts and other forms of protest by employees against their employers took place. In February, local staff at the Chinese-owned Golden Peacock hotel went on strike to force management to review their salaries and other conditions of service, which employees viewed as poor. They also accused some members of the hotel management of both physical and verbal abuse and threatened to continue boycotting work until their demands were met. According to the general manager, Jenny Jiang, management had not received any notice of the strike but was surprised when no workers arrived for work. The staff and management were yet to start discussions amid disagreements over what format the talks would take due to the absence of any recognised union or working committee to represent the striking staff. Lecturers at the Polytechnic, a constituent college of the University of Malawi (UNIMA), went on strike on 21 March demanding a 30% pay increase. The UNIMA Council rejected the demand, arguing that introducing the rise in UNIMA's four colleges would inflate the budget by about K 6 bn. This would in turn lead to the suspension of most operations in the University. First Discount House (FDH) Financial Holdings Ltd, a parent Company of FDH Bank and the Malawi Savings Bank, made 250 of its 1,020 employees redundant on 11 April as part of its restructuring process. They included senior managers in the Malawi Savings Bank to reduce duplication of managers. The restructuring process came amidst adverse economic conditions that were affecting the country. In June, Judiciary employees gave the government a seven-day ultimatum to address their concern over lower salaries and poor conditions or face a nationwide strike. Initially, the employees planned a sit-in, but the government intervened and asked them to return to work with assurances that their concerns would be considered.

Mauritius

Tor Sellström

As the Alliance Lepep (People's Alliance) coalition government enjoyed a comfortable parliamentary majority and no elections were scheduled for 2016, the domestic political scene was expected to remain stable. In September, however, Prime Minister Anerood Jugnauth announced his intention to step down and hand over the premiership to his son, Finance Minister Pravind Jugnauth. The constitutionality of the decision was strongly contested. In addition, Deputy Prime Minister Xavier-Luc Duval and his Mauritian Social-Democratic Party left the ruling coalition in December. By year's end, political stability had been replaced by uncertainty. Adding to the short- to medium-term concerns were the consequences of the revised double taxation agreement with India and of the British referendum vote to exit the EU. With regard to Mauritius' claim to the British-held Chagos archipelago, critical reversals were registered when the UK government decided against resettlement of the Chagossian people and announced that the defence agreement with the US was to be extended for a further 20 years. GDP growth was estimated at 3.8% and Mauritius continued to lead African rankings on governance, economic development and social welfare. With no military forces, the country was not involved in any armed conflict.

 | DOI 10.1163/9789004355910_050

Domestic Politics

Following its convincing electoral victory in December 2014, the *Alliance Lepep*, led by Premier Sir Anerood Jugnauth and composed of the Militant Socialist Movement, the Mauritian Social-Democratic Party and the 'Muvman Liberater' (Movement for Liberation), launched an anti-corruption campaign. While the main casualty was the defeated prime minister and leader of the Labour Party, Navin Ramgoolam, a number of high-ranking state officials were dismissed. Opinion polls showed these measures were popular, but irregularities and discord within the ruling coalition started to damage its popularity and effectiveness: its favourable opinion rating of 84% in December 2014, had fallen to 62% in April.

Cabinet changes took place early in the year. On 23 March, Minister of Environment Raj Dayal, a former Police Commissioner, was forced to resign after being accused of taking bribes in connection with a housing project. On 14 March, the outspoken Finance Minister Vishnu Lutchmeenaraidoo left his position to become foreign minister. Initially, the finance portfolio was taken over by Anerood Jugnauth himself. In late May, he appointed his son, Pravind Jugnauth, to this significant position, but only after the latter had been cleared by the Supreme Court of charges of conflict of interest dating back to his first term as finance minister in 2009–11. The reshuffles, in combination with perceived non-transparent changes in the highest echelons of parastatal companies, notably the dismissal on 28 October of the successful CEO of the national carrier Air Mauritius, Megh Pillay, created *frictions within the governing coalition*. They culminated in December, when Deputy Premier Xavier-Luc Duval and three other ministers from the Mauritian Social-Democratic Party opposed a proposed constitutional amendment to create a Prosecution Commission, left the government and joined the political opposition. Duval was replaced as deputy prime minister (and as minister of tourism) by Ivan Collendavelloo, leader of the 'Muvman Liberater'.

What really emboldened the battered opposition of the Labour Party and the Mauritian Militant Movement was the announcement on 12 September by the 86-year old Anerood Jugnauth that he intended to step down and hand over the *premiership* to his son, Finance Minister Pravind Jugnauth. Since independence, politics in Mauritius had been dominated by a few dynastic families and largely characterised by electoral calculations and intrigues, but never had a similar quasi-monarchical succession been declared without prior elections. Dubbed 'the *papa-piti* (father-son) deal', the arrangement was denounced as unconstitutional and strongly rejected by the political opposition, and provoked widespread protests. However, Sir Anerood dismissed the critics and maintained that the transition was in line with the constitution, arguing that Jugnauth Jr was the leader of the ruling Militant Socialist Movement and that the party enjoyed the necessary parliamentary support,.

Finally, the *prosecution of former prime minister* Navin Ramgoolam remained on the domestic agenda throughout the year. Briefly arrested in February and May 2015 and charged, *inter alia*, with bribery and money laundering, the reinstated leader of the Labour Party made several court appearances. In the process, most of the charges were struck off, but the money laundering case was postponed until early 2017.

Foreign Affairs

In the area of foreign policy and international relations, no major shifts took place. With economic rather than political or ideological considerations as its guiding principle, the Alliance Lepep government continued the traditional, consensus-based outreach in which the consolidation of Mauritius as a *trade, transport and communications hub* between Europe, Asia and Africa played a paramount role. As before, the small island nation had to navigate the growing rivalry in the Indian Ocean between the two Asian giants, India and China.

This said, Mauritius had to face *three new significant challenges* to its future international economic and political relations: trade adjustment to the EU in the wake of Brexit and EU reforms; adaptation of the financial services sector to the revised taxation agreement with India; and a way forward on the Chagos question following the extension of the lease agreement between the UK and the US regarding the military base on Diego Garcia.

Traditionally, Mauritius' leading export markets were the UK and France, each representing around 12% of foreign sales. Clothing, textiles and sugar were the main exports to these markets. Against this background, the outcome of the June 2016 British referendum on *Brexit* introduced considerable strategic uncertainty. In his 29 July budget address for 2016/17, Finance Minister Jugnauth underlined the challenges and the need to reposition Mauritius' significant textiles and clothing sector in order to remain competitive in Europe. To this end, he announced that, over a two-year period, the government would underwrite a 40% reduction of freight costs by Air Mauritius, targeting EU markets other than the UK.

Unrelated to Brexit, the marketing in Europe of Mauritian *sugar* was another major concern. Following an overhaul of the EU Common Agricultural Policy regime, European reference prices and production quotas were set to be removed in September 2017. The predictable outcome was a surge in European beet production and a corresponding drop in cane imports. While several African countries would be hard hit, as a high-cost producer with limited access to alternative markets, Mauritius was in a particularly vulnerable position. Over 90% of its sugar production went to the EU, and although the industry's contribution to the national economy had fallen considerably over the previous decade – and the government had launched a number of initiatives to diversify production – it remained critical to employment and export earnings, accounting for almost 10% of foreign sales.

Originally signed in 1983 and a cornerstone in Mauritius' economic diversification and emergence as an international finance centre, the *Double Taxation Avoidance Agreement* with India was amended in May. The significance of the agreement was illustrated by the fact that Mauritius had accounted for around a quarter of all foreign investments into India in 2014/15. Increasingly, however, the Indian authorities had argued that the funds largely represented domestic capital merely routed via Mauritius to avoid Indian taxes. The issue had been raised by India's Prime Minister Narendra Modi during his visit to the island in March 2015. After thorny negotiations, a revised agreement was signed 14 months later, while India was also revising a similar agreement with Singapore, Mauritius 'competitor' in this field. According to the new protocol, the possibilities of so called 'round-tripping' would be closed down by April 2019, with a designated transition period coming into effect in April 2017. Although the short- to medium-term economic consequences were difficult to assess, they were likely to be considerable and news of the revised agreement was not well received by operators within the Mauritian offshore sector. At the same time, the broader Mauritian business community was looking forward to opportunities under a new bilateral *Comprehensive Economic Cooperation and Partnership Agreement* (CECPA) with India, including a Preferential Trade Agreement, which was being negotiated during the year between the authorities in Port Louis and New Delhi.

As before, the Mauritian government actively and firmly raised the twin issues of the Chagossian people's right to return to the *Chagos archipelago* and of Mauritius' territorial sovereignty over the islands, held by the UK as its colony of the British Indian Ocean Territory (BIOT) and, under an agreement with the US, housing a military base on *Diego Garcia*. Noting that the British government had not acted on various international rulings, notably the verdict reached by the Permanent Court of Arbitration in The Hague (Netherlands) in March 2015, Prime Minister Jugnauth had announced to the UN General Assembly in September that Mauritius had submitted a request for "an advisory opinion by the International Court of Justice (ICJ) on the legal consequences of the separation of the Chagos archipelago from Mauritius in 1965". It was, he emphasised, the responsibility of the UN to complete the process of decolonisation. However, before the request had become operational, British Foreign Minister Boris Johnson declared that his government wished to engage in a dialogue with Mauritius "in order to sort out the matter by June 2017".

This was not to be. Citing "security interests", in mid-November, the UK government unilaterally announced that it had "decided against resettlement of the Chagossian people" and that the UK would "continue to welcome the US presence [on Diego Garcia]", adding that "the agreements [with the US would] continue as they stand until 30 December 2036". Prime Minister Jugnauth and the leader of the

Mauritius-based Chagos Refugees Group, Olivier Bancoult, condemned this decision, underlining that it was not only unilateral, but also “taken in utter disregard of international law and the human rights of the Chagossian community”. A week later, Mauritius re-submitted its request for an advisory opinion by the ICJ to the president of the UN General Assembly.

During the year, several delegations from *China* visited Mauritius to discuss plans raised at the Forum on China-Africa Cooperation (FOCAC) summit in Johannesburg (South Africa) in December 2015, notably in the fields of transport and energy. To further consolidate the island's position as an aviation hub, an Africa-Mauritius-Singapore-Asia Air Corridor initiative was launched.

Often called ‘Little India’ on account of its majority Indo-Mauritian population group, bilateral relations with *India* occupied prime place beyond the double taxation agreement and the CECPA partnership. The first instalment of a $ 53 m four-year *concessionary credit* from India was disbursed. Introducing the 2016/17 budget, Finance Minister Pravind Jugnauth clarified that about half of the funds had been set aside for a metro express transport project in and around Port Louis with the balance earmarked, *inter alia*, for social housing for the poorest citizens and for the provision of digital tablets to primary school children in grades 1 and 2. The use of the considerable credit was further discussed when Jugnauth Jr visited India from 12 to 18 September.

In the area of *maritime security*, relations with India were further strengthened and their joint interest in securing the sea lanes of communication and combating the threats of unlicensed fishing, trafficking and piracy in the Indian Ocean, was reflected in India's Defence Minister Manohar Parrikar's official visit to Mauritius on 10–12 December. Under agreements signed in March 2015, he delivered an Indian-built vessel to the Mauritian coast guard and two helicopters to the police force. In addition to adhering to the African position on *UNSC reform*, Mauritius reiterated its backing for India's aspiration to take a permanent seat on the UNSC. As a small oceanic nation, it also supported the establishment of a dedicated seat for the grouping of Small Island Developing States (SIDS).

Historically close relations with *France* continued in a number of fields, not least with regard to international tourism. More than 400,000 French passport holders visited Mauritius during the year, of whom more than a quarter of a million were from metropolitan France and almost 150,000 from the sister island of Reunion. Nevertheless, among outstanding issues remained the French hold over the island of *Tromelin*, claimed by Mauritius. In his address to the UN General Assembly in September, Prime Minister Jugnauth stated that “the decolonisation of Mauritius would not be complete until the issue of Tromelin is resolved”, urging France “to pursue the dialogue with Mauritius for the early resolution of the dispute”.

As regards continental Africa, Mauritius continued its ‘*Africa strategy*’, launched in 2012. Agreements on the establishment and management of Special Economic

Zones were signed with Ghana, Madagascar and Senegal. In addition to promoting Mauritian business ventures under the Mauritius-Africa Fund, the Alliance Lepep government also intensified the marketing in Africa of Mauritius as a tourist destination, "in particular targeting the new rich", as stated by Finance Minister Pravind Jugnauth. In this respect, South Africa maintained its position as an important partner, with more than 100,000 visitors to the island.

Socioeconomic Developments

Mauritius' *macroeconomic performance* improved. GDP growth was estimated at 3.8%, less than hoped for, but higher than expected and described by Finance Minister Jugnauth as "honourable", given the unfavourable international context. The construction sector registered a slight growth of 2% after five consecutive years of contraction, and several key economic sectors grew by more than the national average. This was notably the case with the financial services sector and with information and communications technology, with growth of an estimated 5.7% and 6.5%, respectively.

Above all, *tourism* continued to surge, with no fewer than 1.3 m visitors setting a new record for the third year in a row. The total number of tourist arrivals was 10.8% higher than in 2015. As before, visitors from France accounted for the largest number, amounting to 21%, with those from Reunion (11.5%) and the UK (11%) in second and third place. Despite the improved frequency of flight connections with China, the number of Chinese tourists fell by 12% from 90,000 to 79,000. This shortfall from an important emerging market was compensated by a higher number of Indian visitors, increasing from 72,000 in 2015 to 82,000.

Whereas the year-on-year inflation rate of 1% was low, *unemployment* remained high, standing at 7.6% in the third quarter, slightly higher than the year before. The high rate was largely due to a persistent mismatch between education and the skills required on the labour market. As defined by the World Bank, *absolute poverty* was, however, minimal, affecting a total of only 6,400 families. Describing the pockets of indigence as "an aberration", during the year the Alliance Lepep government launched what it termed a 'Marshall Plan Against Poverty'. Under this scheme, all affected adults would be given a monthly subsistence allowance of MUR (rupees) 2,720, 40% higher than the World Bank threshold of $ 3.1 per day. As Mauritius had been lagging behind for decades with regard to *gender equality*, the government also launched various initiatives in this respect, including the requirement that public companies listed on the stock exchange should have at least one woman on their board of directors. To monitor progress in gender equality, the introduction of a Gender Development Index for Mauritius was announced.

Mauritius' lead in Africa with regard to *governance and socio-economic achievement* was again confirmed by various international classifications. It remained within the UNDP 'high' category for human development and was placed number 1 in Africa. With regard to governance, it again ranked top out of 54 nations on the Ibrahim Index of African Governance, a position it had retained every year since 2000. On TI's global Corruption Perception Index, it was ranked 50th, down five places from 2015, but only bettered in Africa by Botswana and Cape Verde. And on the World Bank's ease of doing business list, Mauritius ranked 49th in the world, but first in Africa.

Mozambique

Joseph Hanlon

The year ended with a New Year ceasefire in the on-going low-key war with the Renamo armed opposition. But more than politics, the year was characterised by dramatic events linking foreign policy with the economy. Revelations that secret loans had totalled more than $ 2 bn was an economic and political bombshell, which also impacted on external relations. The IMF cut its programme and donors cut budget support, leading to a foreign exchange crisis. The metical was devalued by 58% and annual inflation was 20.6%. A parliamentary commission declared the debt to be illegal and unconstitutional.

Domestic Politics

Despite being the main opposition party in parliament, *Renamo* had always maintained an armed militia, and on-and-off military actions had continued since 2013. Renamo head Afonso Dhlakama declared that Renamo had won the 2014 national elections in six of the 11 provinces, and he demanded the right to nominate governors in those six provinces. In fact, Dhlakama won more than 50% of

 | DOI 10.1163/9789004355910_051

the presidential vote in two provinces and the largest vote in five provinces, and Renamo won a majority of seats in provincial assemblies in three provinces. On 15 January, Dhlakama declared that he would seize control in all six provinces in March, and that he was not prepared to negotiate. After Dhlakama's motorcade was shot at twice in September 2014, he had remained in his bush headquarters in the deep forest at the base of the Gorongosa Mountain, communicating with the outside world only by telephone. Renamo maintained permanent bases in four central provinces: Sofala, Manica, Tete and Zambézia. Renamo attacks took place in those four provinces, and later in the year in Inhambane, Nampula and Niassa as well. In March, police attacked the tourmaline mine in Mavonde, Manica, which is next to a Renamo base and is one source of Renamo finance.

Fighting in Tete had driven 4,000 *refugees* into neighbouring Malawi by the beginning of 2016; by March, the number had risen to 10,000, and many refugees blamed government troops who in turn accused them of supporting Renamo. For its part, Renamo sometimes attacked villages, burning houses and any official buildings and stealing medicines from health posts. By April, more than 100 schools were closed due to the fighting. Thirteen decomposing bodies were found under a bridge on the N1 road in Sofala in May. By July half the refugees had returned home, but three refugee centres remained in Manica province, housing 2,000 people fleeing the fighting.

Both sides resorted to *assassinations*. Renamo targeted lower-level government officials and chiefs and community leaders allied to the ruling party, Frelimo. On the other side, higher-level Renamo leaders were shot and the government was accused of having a 'hit squad'. Renamo secretary general Manuel Bissopo was seriously injured and his bodyguard killed in a drive-by shooting in Beira on 20 January. On 9 April, Jose Manuel, a Renamo-nominated member of the National Defence and Security Council, was shot and killed, again in Beira. Manuel Lole, a former Renamo member of the Council of State, an advisory body to President Filipe Nyusi, was killed on 13 July in Chimoio. Perhaps the most serious assassination was that of one of the Renamo negotiators in the peace talks, Jeremias Pondeca, who was gunned down in Maputo on 8 October; he was also a Renamo nominee to the Council of State. During the year, at least nine other Renamo figures were killed, including five members of provincial assemblies and one member of a provincial election secretariat.

The *hostilities escalated* on 11 February when, for the first time since June 2015, Renamo began to attack road traffic. Initial attacks took place on the 100 km section of the N1 main north-south road between the River Save and Muxungué in Sofala province – the same section of road where convoys had been in force in 2013–14 and which had also been attacked in the 1982–92 war. Military convoys were introduced on this section of road on 15 February. Following further attacks, a second convoy was introduced on the N1 further north, between Maringué and Caia, on the south bank of the Zambeze River. Attacks on the N7 road going north from Chimoio to Tete led to a third convoy from June. On 6 June, Renamo fired on a train, carrying coal from Moatize to Beira port; one of the drivers was injured by flying glass; a second attack followed and the line was temporarily closed to coal shipments. When it reopened, Renamo shot at another train on 25 July, and it was temporarily closed again. On 3 and 6 October, Renamo opened fire for the first time on trains on the northern railway line to Nacala port. Sporadic attacks continued through the year. Speaking in parliament on 23 June, Agostinho Vuma, a Frelimo MP and a senior figure in the Confederation of Mozambican Business Associations, said that, since October 2015, there had been 107 Renamo attacks, in which 40 people had died and 79 had been seriously injured.

Nyusi and Dhlakama finally spoke on the telephone on 15 and 16 June, and agreed there could be *talks about talks* between the two sides, but not at presidential level. Nyusi accepted Dhlakama's demand for international mediators, which the government had always opposed. A four-point agenda was agreed, with two items put forward by each side. From Renamo, "governing the six provinces won by Renamo and integrating Renamo military cadres into key positions in the armed forces". From the government, an immediate end to hostilities and the disarmament of Renamo.

Negotiations began on 20 July with government and Renamo teams of six on each side. In addition, Renamo and the government each asked three eminent people or institutions to name mediators. Renamo identified the EU, the Vatican, and South Africa's President Jacob Zuma. The government identified three former presidents and prime ministers: Ketumile Masire (Botswana), Jakaya Kikwete (Tanzania) and Tony Blair (UK). Each of these sent one or more delegates, making a total of 13 mediators (which meant the mediators needed mediation to agree on how they were going to act). The EU named Mário Raffaelli, an Italian politician who was the chief mediator of the 1990–2 Rome peace talks, and who effectively became the chief mediator here too. But the talks did not advance and were suspended on 25 August. There were three more rounds of talks – on 12–30 September, 18–28 October, and 16 November to 15 December – after which the international mediators left Mozambique, giving up on the stalemate. Rafaelli had tabled a paper on 27 September on how Renamo's demands could be incorporated, and also proposed a ceasefire. On 26 December, Dhlakama and Nyusi spoke on the telephone. Dhlakama announced a New Year *cease fire* (later extended until March 2017). This was a unilateral ceasefire by Renamo, but it was announced by Nyusi, who did not publicly reciprocate. But military actions were restricted, and convoys to escort traffic through three sections of road were stopped.

The war had several special characteristics. In Mozambique, the military had always been kept in a state of weakness, in part to prevent a military coup. Under President Armando Guebuza (in office from 2005 to January 2015), the power of the military was further weakened, while the security services ('Serviço de Informações e Segurança do Estado' [SISE], which is under the Presidency) increased in importance. The war against Renamo was largely fought by the riot police (FIR; Forca de Intervencao Rapida, rapid intervention force) under the Interior Ministry. Both sides seemed to try to *limit casualties*: Renamo attacks on villages and government attacks on Renamo bases were announced in advance; villages and bases were left undefended so there were few injuries and only damage to structures. Renamo attacks on road traffic in most cases consisted of a few shots from a distance, often aimed at bus drivers. Renamo used a strategy of low cost but high profile actions intended to frighten people and show it could attack at will. For example, four Renamo gunmen seized the head of the Tica, Sofala, administrative post when he was addressing a public meeting, and they also took the local *regulo* (chief), and killed them both on 2 September. In an attack in Murrupula district, Nampula, a group of 10 men, only two of whom were armed, attacked on 27 August. "They sang happily and said they were Renamo," said one witness. They told people to flee their houses and run into the bush. A witness said they did not want to kill anyone, and just wanted to ransack. The government tended to use targeted assassinations, which forced the Renamo local leadership into hiding. The result on both sides was maximum disruption with minimum casualties.

President Nyusi used his second year in office to slowly take more control by the *replacement of officials* named by former President Guebuza. In March, Nyusi appointed Julio dos Santos Jane as commander of the police, replacing Jorge Khalau, who had been named in 2008 by Guebuza. Khalau had been unable to stop organised crime infiltrating the police. Two highly respected technocrats were replaced as ministers by *political appointments*. Pedro Couto was sacked as Minister of Mineral Resources and Energy on 29 September, and replaced by Leticia da Silva Klemens, who had no experience in government or of minerals. Frelimo Political Commission member Conceita Sortane was named education minister on 26 November, replacing Jorge Ferrão. Couto and Ferrão were seen as two of Nyusi's most important appointments – respected, honest technicians who could bring about change. No reasons were ever given for ministerial changes, but it was rumoured that the gas companies pushed the sacking because Couto was driving too hard a bargain.

Frelimo announced that its next congress would be held in Matola (near Maputo) from 26 September to 1 October 2017, which would test the balance of power between the Guebuza and Nyusi factions in the party.

Targeted attacks continued. Public Prosecutor Marcelino Vilanculo was gunned down and killed on 11 April as he returned to his home in Matola. Vilankulo was investigating the wave of kidnappings of businessmen (mostly of Asian origin) that had hit Mozambican cities since 2011. In particular, he was investigating Danish Satar, nephew of Momade Assife Abdul Satar ('Nini'), one of the men convicted in 2003 for ordering the assassination of the country's top investigative journalist, Carlos Cardoso. Vilanculo was also looking into the assassination in March 2015 of the prominent Franco-Mozambican constitutional lawyer, Gilles Cistac. On 20 and 23 May, two people who had spoken out against the government were the victims. José Jaime Macuane, a commentator on the Sunday night television talk show 'Pontos da Vista' ('Points of View'), was kidnapped, shot and left crippled. João Massango, president of one of the small green parties, who was the organiser of an upcoming demonstration, was severely beaten. There were also nasty and racist campaigns organised by trolls on social media, attacking critics of the government, including 'wanted' posters with pictures of the targeted individuals.

Foreign Policy

Secret foreign borrowing dominated the year. It was revealed that only a small part of an $ 850 m Eurobond for a new state-owned fishing company was destined to be used for fishing boats, with the bulk of it to be paid for patrol boats and other military equipment. In March, the government said it could not make the next repayment and asked for rescheduling, which was accepted by creditors on 29 March. But the 'Wall Street Journal' revealed on 3 April that, hidden in the debt rescheduling documents, was substantially more secret debt.

It soon emerged that five secret *government-guaranteed loans* had been made to three state companies, all set up especially to take the loans and controlled by SISE. The first had been syndicated loans in 2013 to a coastal security company, Proindicus: $ 504 m arranged by Crédit Suisse and $ 118 m arranged by the Russian bank VTB. Next had been two bond issues in mid-2013 to a tuna fishing company, Ematum ('Empresa Moçambicana de Atum'): Crédit Suisse $ 500 m and VTB $ 350 m. President Guebuza, French President François Hollande and shipyard owner Iskandar Safa had been present at a 29 September 2013 ceremony at the Cherbourg shipyard in Normandy. The final syndicated loan was for $ 535 m, arranged in 2014 by VTB, and had been for a new ship repair company MAM (Mozambique Asset Management).

The revelation caused an international explosion. In 2015, the *IMF* had agreed a loan of $ 283 m under its Standby Credit Facility (SCF) and the first instalment of $ 119 m had been released in December 2015. But on 15 April the IMF announced that it had cancelled a mission to Mozambique scheduled for the following week, and would not release the second tranche of the loan. The IMF was particularly offended because it had not been told about such a large borrowing when the SCF loan had been agreed. It became clear that the loans had been arranged in such secrecy that members of the new government that had taken office in January 2015 did not know about it; it was only confirmed to parliament on 8 June by Prime Minister Carlos Agostinho do Rosário. All that Economic and Finance Minister

Adriano Maleiane, already in Washington for the spring meetings of the IMF and the World Bank, could do was promise to provide more information.

By the end of April, all members of the group of 14 (G14) *budget support donors* had suspended their contributions to the government budget, although other project aid continued. Maleiane said that donor budget support stood at $ 467 m per year, corresponding to 12% of the state budget, and on 4 May he announced the first budget cuts. In May, donors made clear that any direct aid to the government budget would only be resumed when Mozambique had a new *IMF programme*. This effectively put the IMF in charge, but on 18 May IMF Managing Director Christine Lagarde told the BBC that, by keeping the loans secret, the Mozambique government was "clearly concealing *corruption*". Thus Lagarde said on the record what donors and lenders had only been willing to say in private: that some money from the secret loans had been used corruptly.

The *G14* sent the government a letter in mid-May saying that the secret loans were "perceived by partners as a serious breach of trust, poor governance and lack of fiscal responsibility". Their immediate demands included a full list of government and government-guaranteed debts, a full list of state-owned companies, a report on "extra budgetary expenditure", and a "forensic audit" of the secret loans. The government offered a joint task force, but this was rejected by the G14. Interviews made clear that donors felt personally offended; government ministers and officials had lied to them about low levels of military spending and borrowing. Mozambique had been seen as a success story, and now donors had to admit they had been wrong.

In mid-year, the government strategy was largely to hope that *alternative funding* would – materialise – that they could get money from China or Russia or as capital gains tax from the gas fields, or that donors would ease up (as they had always done in the past). Ministers kept saying that nothing wrong had been done and that the debt would not affect government spending – even as it was not paying its bills. In June, the IMF finally sent a mission, but only to gather information. When the mission left on 24 June, it issued an unusually strong statement, making clear that it did not accept what had been presented to it by the government, and that any resumption of lending was a long way off. It called for "substantial fiscal and monetary tightening" – in other words, serious austerity. Most significantly, the mission demanded "an international and independent audit".

On 24 July, Nyusi again rejected IMF and donor demands for an international forensic audit of the $ 2 bn secret debt. He said the issue was being considered by two Mozambican sovereign institutions, parliament and the Attorney-General's office ('Procuradoria-Geral da República'; PGR), and that was sufficient. But, faced with devaluation, inflation and donor intransigence, the resistance soon collapsed. On 31 August, Nyusi announced that after nearly 30 years at the IMF and 39 years outside the country, Rogério Zandamela would returned to Mozambique to head the Bank of Mozambique ('Banco de Moçambique'; BdM), and he took up his post within days. On 10 September, Nyusi quietly admitted that he would not oppose an *external forensic audit*; on 15 September, he had a more cordial meeting with IMF head Lagarde in Washington and an external audit was announced, but it would be carried out within the PGR. On 4 November, it was announced that the multinational risk management firm Kroll, one of the best known forensic auditors, had been selected, in agreement with and funded by Sweden and the IMF. Kroll was given only three months to carry out the audit (later extended by one month).

Socioeconomic Developments

The IMF predicted *GDP growth* of 3.4%, compared with 6.6% in 2015. Mozambique had turned to the IMF in 2015 in response to falling commodity prices, a drop in exports and lower investment. The sudden cut in the IMF loan and donor budget support sharply exacerbated the *economic squeeze*. The government delayed payments to its suppliers, which had a knock-on effect within the private sector, as overdue receivables increased and companies had no cash to pay their own bills. There was a shortage of dollars. By June, local businesspeople reported that they were unable to obtain dollars for imports, and some imported items such as rice disappeared from the market. There was little new construction in Maputo; some building projects were slowed or stopped. Many companies reduced staff. Rents, especially in older buildings, fell significantly.

Following the IMF's rejection of the government's response to the debt crisis, the Council of Ministers, in a special session on 7 July, announced that the *state budget* was being cut by 10%, or Mt (meticais) 24 bn ($ 375 m). The main cuts were in spending on new building projects and on fuel and travel, including per diems. The budget did not include any payments on government guaranteed debts, which Economy and Finance Minister Maleiane said had been judged to be "non-essential". The original budget had projected inflation of 5.6%, but Maleiane forecast 16.7% (and it actually rose to 25.5%), which meant that spending cuts were, in practice, much larger. In a statement to the press, Maleiane blamed the economic crisis on the usual collection of drought, flood, war and global economic situation, but did also mention the drop in donor aid – without actually referring to the secret loans. On 23 August, with the year more than half over, Maputo city cut its budget by 37%, partly because aid and other external funding was down by 73%.

Civil servants and many company employees had been accustomed to receiving a *Christmas bonus* equivalent to one month's salary, thus known at the '13th month'. On 27 December, Maleiane announced that the bonus would be halved for most civil servants, while higher-paid staff, from heads of departments up to ministers, would receive no bonus. Maleiane blamed the cut in donor budget support, which in turn was a response to the secret debt.

On 26 July, parliament set up its commission to investigate the *secret loans*. The committee was to have 10 Frelimo, 6 Renamo and 1 'Movimento Democrático de Moçambique' member – in proportion to each party's parliamentary seats. But Renamo voted against and did not take its seats on the ground that such an inquiry could not be credible if it was dominated by Frelimo. The chair was Eneas Comiche, an MP and former finance minister. Highly respected, he had not been allowed by Frelimo to stand again as mayor of Maputo in 2008 because he was too honest. The *Parliamentary Commission* took evidence in secret, its report was secret, and the report was debated by parliament in secret on 9 December, but the report was then released and proved to be a bombshell. Although originally presented to lenders and the public as a loan for tuna fishing, the main purpose of the $ 2 bn borrowing was military, and the proposals had been made by the SISE. "Fishing is not the main activity of Ematum," confirmed António Carlos do Rosário, a senior SISE official and CEO of the three companies. The main purpose had been to create a coastal security system for the Mozambique Channel. The Commission questioned the "high degree of secrecy". Rosário said the contract had been given to Constructions Mécaniques de Normandie–Abu Dhabi MAR (CMN/ADM) as a negotiated contract, without a public tender. CMN/ADM had also negotiated the financing. The money had gone directly to CMM/ADM without passing through the Mozambican treasury; Mozambique had received equipment and services but not the money. A key issue was that, although the loans had been made to three private companies, the companies were owned by the state and the loans contained government guarantees signed by then Finance Minister Manuel Chang and then National Budget Director (and later vice-minister) Isaltina Lucas. The guarantees renounced all sovereign immunity, and claimed that the government complied in all aspects with its obligations to the IMF and the World Bank. This was manifestly false, and the IMF had cut off its loan to Mozambique precisely because it was not informed about the loans.

On 23 May, MAM failed to make the first $ 178 m payment on the MAM loans – but there was no attempt by borrowers to enforce the state guarantee. There was a growing discussion about the government guarantees on the $ 2 bn loans. Prime Minister Carlos Agostinho do Rosário told parliament on 8 June that "the government only assumes that part of the debt that is proven to be applied to things in the public interest". The PGR announced on 14 July that the *secret loans* were in violation of the budget law, and thus were a "criminal offense in the form of abuse of office". The Parliamentary Commission said "it must be understood that the guarantees issued are void", since the constitution required that loans and guarantees be approved by parliament, which had not been done, and the guarantees exceeded the limits set in the 2013 and 2014 budgets.

Some of the *secretly financed boats* paid for by the loans were in the port of Maputo for all to see. At least 20 fishing boats were also sitting in the harbour, unmaintained and literally rusting away. In May, Maleiane told parliament that, even though the boats were built in a French shipyard, they could not be used for tuna to be exported to Europe, and required expensive refitting. “The Ministry of Defence was not consulted,” Defence Minister Atanásio Salvador M’tumuke told the Parliamentary Commission, and the equipment purchased was not suitable. Equipment began arriving in 2016. “Bought, through which money, we do not know; if we have debt, we do not know, but there are the objects. Airplanes are in the air base, the ships are in our naval bases,” he said. Carlos Xavier, director on the National Navy Institute (‘Instituto Nacional da Marinha’), told the Commission that the fishing boats were unsuitable, because “they have restricted range” and the manufacturer specified that they could only operate in waves up to two metres high. “The commission notes that the financial projection was based on unsustainable and hypothetical assumptions,” it said in its report, and there was no way the companies could repay the loan.

The local currency, the metical (Mt), was dramatically devalued during the year, from Mt 45.9 = $ 1 at the start of the year to Mt 71.2 = $ 1 at the end of the year, a 58% *devaluation*. This had a direct effect on the size of the debt, because debt was denominated in dollars but paid in meticais. Combined with the secret $ 2 bn debt, this made Mozambique’s total debt “not sustainable,” the government told creditors on 25 October. Much of Mozambique’s imports of food and other goods came from South Africa so the exchange rate to the South African rand (ZAR) was politically important. Indeed during its decade in power the government of Armando Guebuza had maintained an overvalued exchange rate and tried to keep the rate below Mt 3 = ZAR 1. This kept food and clothing prices low in the capital Maputo and staved off riots like those caused by price rises in 2010. But in 2016, the exchange rate went from Mt 2.9 = ZAR 1 to Mt 5.2 = ZAR 1, an 82% devaluation. The overvalued exchange rate meant that many things that could be produced in Mozambique, from rice to shirts, were imported instead. The end-of-year exchange rates were seen as approximately correct. But years of an overvalued metical meant that there were no local production facilities, and the very high interest rates made it impossible for business people to invest to produce goods inside the country.

Interest rates and reserve requirements for banks were increased dramatically during the year. The base rate, the BdM lending rate to commercial banks (‘taxas de juro das Facilidades Permanentes de Cedência de Liquidez’), was raised from 9.75% to 23.25%, and the interest rate paid on compulsory deposits with the BdM (‘taxas de juro das Facilidades Permanentes de Cedência de Depósitos’) was raised from 3.75% to 16.25%. *Annual inflation* hit a peak of 25.5% in October, and for the year 2016 was 20.6%; the biggest contributors were food, up 30.6%, and clothing, up 30.0%. The World Bank, in its ‘Mozambique Economic Update’ published on 12 December, noted that food accounted for 48% of the Consumer Price Index, but amounted to more than 70% of the expenditure of the poor. Thus, when official inflation exceeded 25%, it was actually 33% for the poor.

Airlines and airports became a major issue. In May, it was reported that Mozambique Airlines ('Linhas Aéreas de Moçambique'; LAM) had trouble sourcing fuel and flights from Maputo to Johannesburg and had to leave with enough fuel for the return trip because they could not refuel in Johannesburg. On 12 September, the chair of LAM, Antonio Pinto de Abreu, said LAM had cancelled its order for three Boeing 737 Next Generation aircraft "because it is unable to pay". LAM admitted to having debts of $ 139 m. On 25 October it was announced that the Brazilian aircraft maker Embraer had admitted it paid a bribe of $ 800,000 to "a high level official" at LAM to secure the sale of two aircraft for $ 65 m. The Brazilian Federal Public Prosecutor's Office named those who received the bribes as José Viegas, chair and CEO of LAM for 24 years (1987–2011), and Mateus Zimba, who had worked for Enron and Sasol. Nacala international airport, the most modern airport in the country and opened with great fanfare by President Guebuza in 2014, remained virtually unused, the only flights being by LAM to and from Maputo. On 1 June, the government announced that it would try to privatise management of the airport in the hope that a private company could attract foreign airlines and charter companies to fly there. The airport, on the site of a former military airport, had been designed and built for $ 216 m by the Brazilian construction giant Odebrecht. In a plea bargain with the US Department of Justice, Odebrecht admitted that between 2011 and 2014, it had made *corrupt payments* amounting to $ 900,000 to win the contract. These included approximately $ 250,000 paid to a high-level government official in exchange for Odebrecht obtaining favourable terms on a government construction project, which the government had not been inclined to agree. Nacala airport was the only Odebrecht construction project in Mozambique at the time. Details released by the US Department of Justice showed that it cost significantly less to bribe Mozambican officials than those in other countries: Odebrecht and Embraer had paid less than 1% of the value of the respective contracts.

The first World Bank economic update on Mozambique, published in May, hammered Mozambique for the unaccountability of *state companies*. They were accused of implementing large public investment projects that were not profitable, while receiving non-concessional credits. State enterprises that were losing money included LAM, telecommunications ('Telecomunicações de Moçambique'; TDM), mobile phones (M-Cel), airports ('Aeroportos de Mocambique'; ADM), electricity ('Electricidade de Moçambique'; EDM) and petrol (Petromoc), the May and December Bank reports noted. Only the railways ('Caminhos de Ferro de Moçambique'; CFM) and the hydrocarbons company ('Empresa Nacional de Hidrocarbonetos'; ENH) were profitable.

Economy and Finance Minister Maleiane said on 5 September that the *state business sector* consisted of 13 public companies, two state companies, and 109 companies in which the state held shares. Twenty companies regarded as "strategic and viable" were analysed with a view to restructuring to make them "capable of competing with other companies on the market". TDM would be merged with M-Cel, and measures were already being taken with the Mozambican Post Office, ADM, LAM, and STEMA (which ran the grain terminal in the port of Matola). Of the 109 companies in which the state held shares, 64 were not viable and would be sold off or liquidated. Many had been abandoned 40 years before, when their original owners fled shortly after independence, and had been kept running by the state.

There was also concern about massively *inflated contracts*. 'Africa Confidential' revealed on 13 May that the cost of the BdM building in Maputo had jumped from $ 90 m to $ 300 m, with kickbacks and 'commissions' accounting for some of the cost inflation. Work started on the Maputo-KaTembe suspension bridge, which will be a dramatic landmark but came with a high price tag – two loans from the Export-Import Bank of China totalling $ 754 m. A more modest but totally adequate bridge could have been built for one-third of the cost.

ProSavana was originally a Brazilian-designed and Japanese-funded project to attract giant Brazilian *agribusiness* to set up huge plantations in the Nacala corridor, but the initial 2009 plan foundered because of a major international campaign to defend the land rights of local peasants, and because visiting Brazilian businesspeople found there were no large tracts of land available. Brazil had dropped out because of its own financial problems, and Japan had moved to redesign it to support small farmers, spending the year trying to write a strategic plan. During the year, civil society split; non-government forums in the ProSavana area decided to work with Japan to try to gain support for peasants, while NGOs in Maputo continued their 'No to ProSavana' campaign, saying Japan was not to be trusted and that a land grab was still planned. CEPAGRI, the Agriculture Promotion Centre ('Centro de Promoção de Agricultura'), was closed by the government on 12 October. It had been created a decade before to promote large-scale agricultural investments, but none of them had succeeded.

HIV/AIDS remained a major problem, with 11.5% of 15–49-year-olds infected; Gaza was the worst province with 25.1% infected. Mozambique had the 8th-highest prevalence rate in the world, the seven worst-affected countries all being in southern Africa. Deputy Health Minister Mouzinho Saide reported that 1.5 m people were infected and there were 107 deaths per day from AIDS.

The daughters of two former presidents were attacked by their partners, dramatically raising the issue of *violence against women*. The daughter of former president Guebuza, Valentina Guebuza, head of family businesses and one of the wealthiest women in Mozambique, was shot and killed by her husband Zófimo Muiuane on 14 December. And the trial began of Rofino Licuco, from 2012 to 2015 the boyfriend of Josina Machel, daughter of first president Samora and Graça Machel. He was charged with beating her so badly on 17 October 2015 that she was blinded in her right eye.

Poverty decreased very slowly, while inequality increased, according to an analysis by the Ministry of Economy and Finance presented on 26 October. It was based on four national family expenditure surveys, carried out every six years. Although the percentage of people living in poverty had fallen in the previous 18 years from 69% to below 50%, the population had been growing faster, so the actual number of those living in poverty rose from 11 m to 12 m between 1997 and 2015.

El Niño brought a second year of drought to much of southern Africa. Mozambique was less affected, with normal rains in the north, but there was a serious drought in the southern provinces of Maputo, Gaza, and Inhambane.

Namibia

Henning Melber

During the second year of his presidency, Hage Geingob's administration continued announcing ambitious plans and statements selling Namibia as a showpiece of African progress and development, but little translated into visible practical reforms to improve the living conditions of the poor. Geingob continued to travel extensively, promoting Namibia abroad as an investment opportunity, while constitutional matters, the proposed enforcement of shared company ownership with the formerly disadvantaged, and new exploitation of resources, which at times clashed with environmental concerns, became contested matters at home. Increased government expenditure in combination with sluggish economic growth created precarious fiscal constraints, which required budgetary cuts and a prudent financial policy. The effects of climate change, not least a severe water shortage and a devastating drought, added to a critical situation, while matters of ethnicity and regional representation emerged as a controversial subject in politics.

 | DOI 10.1163/9789004355910_052

Domestic Policy

Several *judicial matters* entered the headlines. During February, the High Court heard the case of four SWAPO Youth League activists who had been expelled by the party leadership, and ruled on 22 April that this violated party regulations. The expulsion of Elijah Ngurare, Job Amupanda, Dimbulukweni Nauyoma and George Kambala had to be revoked, though the claimants were not entitled to keep their previous positions. SWAPO complied with the ruling, but officials repeatedly demanded that they should terminate their membership. On 8 June, the police banned demonstrations in Windhoek on the grounds that they would clash with a series of international events in the capital. The object of the ban was a demonstration organised by the reinstated party activists for 16 June in protest against the plans for the construction of an expensive *parliament building*, while urgent matters such as urban land development and ownership remained neglected. The march by several hundred mainly younger people was ultimately re-routed.

A legal battle evolved around Namibian *citizenship*. On 23 June, the Supreme Court ruled that the locally born son of a Dutch couple resident in the country with work permits since 2006 was entitled to a birth certificate and citizenship. In defiance of the ruling, Attorney General Sacky Shangala and Minister for Home Affairs Pendukeni Ivula-Ithana asked the cabinet for a constitutional change, which was rejected. They submitted a bill to parliament in mid-July to change the citizenship law, and this was adopted by the National Assembly (NA) within days. In response to strong protests, a hearing was held in the National Council (NC) on 29 July, at which legal experts criticised the initiative as a violation of the rule of law. Ivula-Ithana dismissed this criticism in a public statement on 1 August and the SWAPO party chief whip in the NC instructed MPs to pass the bill to be gazetted just before the ruling of the Supreme Court came into effect. On 2 July, however, the cabinet decided to comply with the Supreme Court's ruling. On 3 August, the NC unanimously rejected the Namibian Citizenship Amendment Bill as unconstitutional and referred it back to the NA. On 12 August, President Geingob declared that the executive should not sidestep decisions made by the judiciary. The Bill was officially withdrawn from the NA on 18 October.

Controversies also erupted over the nomination and appointment of five new *electoral commissioners*. Based on a constitutional amendment and law reform in 2014, eight candidates were selected during July by a parliamentary committee without any wider public consultation. The short-list was submitted to the president, who made a final decision on who should be nominated and submitted to the NA for appointment. *Party funding* totalling N$ 116 m, allocated for the 2015/16 financial year to the eight political parties represented in parliament, remained unaccounted for by all the parties, with the single exception of the Democratic Turnhalle Alliance, in violation of the statutory obligation to present accounts.

Farmland remained a contested matter. On 24 August, a second land reform conference was announced for later in the year to address the unequal distribution of privately owned land. Foreign interests, mainly German and South African, still held 247 farms covering 1.2 m hectares. The conference was postponed, but the land issue remained a matter of concern. Lawmakers indicated their intention to eliminate absentee landlordism, but a land bill was withdrawn from parliament in late November after criticisms of its shortcomings and demands that the land conference should be held first.

Resettlement was controversial too and became a matter of *ethnic animosity*. On 3 December, Deputy Minister of Land Bernardus Swartbooi publicly criticised his minister, Utoni Nujoma, for allocating land in the southern regions to people from the north, while those who had been victims of land grabbing during the German colonial times remained landless. On 6 December, President Geingob demanded a public apology, but Swartbooi refused to comply and was supported by several agencies of the Nama, Damara and Herero. After a heated exchange in State House, Geingob asked Swartbooi on 13 December to resign. While Swartbooi declared that he would not resign but would wait to be dismissed, State House announced on 15 December that Geingob had accepted Swartbooi's "verbal resignation" and replaced him with the deputy minister of poverty eradication and social welfare, Priscilla Boois. Several demonstrations by members of minority ethnic groups protested against the dismissal. On 16 December, marchers to the Land Ministry in Windhoek demanded that land stolen under German and South African colonialism be handed back to the affected groups.

At a press conference on 13 December, Geingob accused *traditional leaders* of playing the tribal card for personal reasons. He associated their role with the Bantustan empires of the Apartheid era, while claiming that Namibia was more united than ever before. Tensions related to agencies based on population groups also erupted over the results of elections to the central committee at the *Women's Council* congress on 10–11 December. After the delayed announcement of the elected members, criticism mounted over the Council's leadership, in which women originating from the former Ovamboland were over-represented. Comments suggested that this did not reflect voting patterns or contribute to all-inclusive nation building.

As a member of the *UN Human Rights Council*, Namibia was one of four African states that abstained on a resolution adopted on 30 June in favour of appointing a monitor to protect and advocate Lesbian, Gay, Bi- and Transsexual rights. It was argued that such rights were not yet internationally codified and guidelines were therefore lacking. However, Namibia voted in favour of a resolution in support of promoting and protecting the space for civil society actors to strengthen universal rights to freedom of expression and association. At home at the end of August, the attorney general insisted in response to a recommendation by the UN that the common law on sodomy would be neither repealed nor amended to allow same-sex marriages.

On 29 August, Minister for Information Tjekero Tweya announced that government planned to regulate and punish the *media* through a regulatory body incorporated in the draft Access to Information Bill. After heated public debates, the minister declared in early September that he was not planning to restrict media freedom. The cabinet decided in November, much to the concern of independent media houses, to give preference to state owned newspapers when advertising.

Foreign Affairs

A number of high-ranking *foreign visitors* included on 19–20 April President Jacob Zuma, who discussed SACU matters with President Geingob. India's President Prenab Mukherjee used a state visit on 15–17 June to explore possibilities for the supply of uranium for peaceful purposes. Prime Minister Modibo Keita of Mali arrived in mid-August on a four-day working visit. He extended an invitation to Geingob to canvass the international community for support for Mali's security efforts aimed at bringing an end to terrorism.

Geingob embarked on a series of *foreign visits* beyond attendance at continental and international summits. His frequent absences from home, as well as the large entourage that accompanied him and the related costs, were a matter of public debate. Among others, he was in Sweden on 26–27 May, on a state visit to Botswana on 11–13 July, and in Lusaka (Zambia) on 29–30 July. From 10 September to 4 October he was on an *extended stay in the USA*. He spoke at the opening sessions of the 71st UN General Assembly and visited several universities. Accompanied by a large delegation that included business people, he promoted investment opportunities on several occasions. An official visit to France (27–29 November) also served the promotion of business relations and was followed by a visit to the UK. Geingob interrupted his visit to Europe to attend together with former presidents Nujoma and Pohamba and others the ceremony commemorating *Fidel Castro* on 30 November in Cuba. In recognition of Cuba's crucial role before and after Independence, three days of national mourning were declared on 2–4 December.

Bilateral *negotiations with Germany* over the recognition of the genocide committed under German colonial rule against mainly the Herero and Nama (1904–8) resulted in several rounds of meetings between the special government envoys, Ruprecht Polenz and Zedekia Ngavirue, amidst mounting criticism from representatives of the descendants of the affected groups for the failure to include them. On 25 November, at a meeting in the German embassy in Windhoek between Polenz and delegates of the Nama and Herero, tensions escalated, when Polenz declared that the genocide was not comparable to the Holocaust. A walk-out by the delegates, who felt racially insulted, caused chaos and several parties and other agencies subsequently demanded the expulsion of the Germany's Ambassador Christian Schlaga.

A UN panel of experts criticised Namibia's close cooperation with *North Korea* as a violation of the sanctions imposed by the UNSC. The government argued that the ties were rooted in North Korea's support for SWAPO's liberation struggle and that no new collaboration had been entered into after the adoption of sanctions. However, ongoing public works, in particular the building of an ammunition factory outside Windhoek, involved North Korean firms and advisors. On 30 June, after a visit to North Korea by Foreign Minister and Deputy Prime Minister Netumbo Nandi-Ndaitwah, the Foreign Ministry announced that contracts with two North Korean companies had been terminated. The statement stressed that "warm diplomatic relations" continued to be maintained. In late August, a North Korean delegation headed by the former foreign minister met SWAPO party officials. According to Pyongyang, it was an official state visit, though it was not disclosed by the Namibian authorities. Local media also reported that the construction works by the North Korean company at the military basis outside Windhoek were continuing.

Jointly with South Africa, Zimbabwe and Japan, Namibia was at loggerheads over the limited legalisation of the *ivory trade* with the majority of members at the International Union for Conservation of Nature World Wildlife Congress, which in mid-September prepared decisions to be presented to the 17th meeting of the Conference of the Parties to the Convention on International Trade in Endangered Species in Johannesburg. A submission by Namibia and Zimbabwe that they be allowed to sell large stocks of ivory on a controlled market was rejected by a majority of member states on 26 September on the grounds that past experience indicated that this would stimulate further poaching.

On 18 and 21 November, the UNHCR discussed allegations of torture and inhumane treatment of vulnerable persons in Namibia brought by the *UN Committee Against Torture*, including the situation in prisons and psychiatric institutions as well as the treatment of refugees and asylum seekers, long and illegal pre-trial detention and the high incidence of rape, often of children. In a related matter, many of those released at the end of 2015 after up to 15 years' imprisonment without conviction following the Caprivi High Treason trial initiated compensation claims. Despite having been at the forefront of campaigning in 2015 for a withdrawal from the *ICC*, Namibia did not join those African countries that terminated their membership.

Socio-economic Developments

Minister of Finance Calle Schlettwein presented the *annual budget* for 2016/17 on 25 February. He indicated that remuneration expenditure and related budget subdivisions were "a cause for concern". Debt had sky rocketed from N$ 35.95 bn in 2014/15 to N$ 59.79 bn in 2015/16 and was projected to rise to N$ 63.73 bn, or 37% of GDP, in

2016/17. This exceeded not only the projected revenue of N$ 57.84 bn but also, and for the first time, the non-interest expenditure for the year of N$ 61.12 bn. Interest payments for debt increased from N$ 3.13 bn in 2015/16 to N$ 4.88 bn, or 8.5% of estimated revenue income, while a return of N$ 2.96 bn to the SACU Common Revenue Pool signalled that this important source of income had declined. While education expenditure, at a total of N$ 16.2 bn (24.5% of total government spending), remained the highest item, investment in the maintenance of law and order totalling N$ 13.01 bn (mainly composed of N$ 6.6 bn for defence and N$ 5.1 bn for safety and security) was higher than for the Ministry of Basic Education, Arts and Culture (N$ 12.79 bn) and Health and Social Services (N$ 7.23 bn or 10.9%). The freeze of a (inflation adjusted) wage bill for the public sector and a moratorium on recruitment were announced. The budget deficit of about N$ 8.1 bn, was projected at 4.3% of GDP. Schlettwein emphasised that the budget "marks a firm commencement of the fiscal consolidation programme that curtails the negative effects of excessive budgetary expansion and fiscal austerity". The emphasis was on a 'pro-growth' and not a 'pro-poor' budget. A shift towards a more progressive tax system was announced, but not yet specified, to contribute "positively to the social objectives of reducing income inequalities".

In his State of the Nation Address on 5 April, Geingob presented his *Harambee Prosperity Plan* (HPP) for 2016 to 2020. It added several concrete goals to the National Development Plan 4 and Vision 2030, which was adopted as the blueprint for Namibia's future under the country's first president Sam Nujoma. The HPP stressed the elimination of 'hunger poverty' and the creation of jobs, among many ambitious priorities and targets. On 13 December, Geingob and his team presented a Harambee review for the year and claimed that most of the targets were on track. Calling himself a dreamer, the president outlined his vision that the country would have 80%–90% of the population in the middle class and eradicate absolute poverty, while ownership of property would continue to be respected. Despite the budgetary constraints, he insisted that the Namibian house remained politically and economically stable.

On 12 August, Geingob signed the *Namibia Investment Promotion Act*, which he had originally initiated as minister for trade and industry (2008–12). The law authorised government to limit foreign involvement in certain sectors of industry and resource extraction (such as uranium) to avoid external control. It aims at the gradual Namibianisation of the economy, starting with the retail sector. A *Business and Intellectual Property Authority Act*, signed at the same time, formalised the establishment of an entity tasked with the registration of businesses and the protection of business and intellectual property.

The planned new legislation to enhance *economic empowerment* for what was termed previously disadvantaged persons (PDP), known as the New Equitable Economic Empowerment Framework (NEEEF), remained controversial. The draft required that PDPs have a minimum 25% ownership in local companies and at least 50% participation in management. The private sector, including business associations, considered the intervention damaging for the investment climate and tantamount to compulsory nationalisation. On various occasions, Geingob made conflicting statements on the NEEEF, but ultimately confirmed the intention to implement it.

The local financial investment company Simonis Storm Securities warned in early August of the dramatic level of *government borrowing*. State debt had skyrocketed by 415% from N$ 12.1 bn in January 2010 to N$ 62.1 bn in June 2016 and government debt stood at 43.3% of total debt compared with 24.7% recorded in January 2010. Finance Minister Schlettwein agreed on 10 August that this was a worrying trend that transgressed the 35% GDP limit set by government. "Unfortunately", he added, "we did not create a lot of jobs." Addressing Finance Ministry staff on 19 August, he reiterated that the state's financial liquidity faced serious restrictions due to the more limited borrowing options. On 12 September, the finance minister instructed that all state tenders be put on hold until a budget review for 2016/17 had been undertaken. The local Construction Industries' Federation reacted with shock and warned in a strongly worded statement that many of the 450 member companies and their workers might face drastic consequences.

On 2 September, the international ratings agency Fitch downgraded the *economic outlook* from stable to negative, mainly because of the increase in government debt from 23.2% of GDP to 38.2% from the end of 2014 to the end of 2015 and the worst deficit in the country's history of 8.3% of GDP in the current budget. Other contributing factors were the decline in SACU revenue, lower company and income tax receipts than expected and the anticipated negative effects of the proposed NEEEF on foreign investment. An *IMF mission* visited on 8–21 September for the Article IV Consultation. It predicted a decline in annual economic growth to 2.5%, but expected some recovery in 2017 with the opening of new mines. Risks identified included the volatile SACU revenue, further falls in commodity prices and possible sovereign debt credit downgrades. During his visit to the USA, Geingob indicated on 19 September that the government planned to raise a total of US $ 5 bn (in South African currency) through state bonds and concessional loans over the next ten years to invest in the diversification and industrialisation of the economy.

On 27 October, Finance Minister Schlettwein presented the *mid-year budget review* to parliament with a diagnosis that the economy "has never before been in such a precarious situation". The GDP was revised downwards by 16.1% or some N$ 30.54 bn, while revenue was expected to fall by 9% or some N$ 6.23 bn compared with the original forecast. He indicated liquidity constraints, not least by high budget deficits and the consequent erosion of market confidence in government bonds and bills. He identified reduced expenditure and containment of public debt as priorities. As a result, a total of N$ 5.5 bn in expenditure cuts were identified. On

2 December, Moody's revised Namibia's *credit risk outlook* from stable to negative, but affirmed the long-term issuer and senior unsecured ratings at Baaa3 in expectation of a robust growth outlook, debt metrics and political stability. On 7 December, the Bank of Namibia confirmed weak *economic growth* at an estimated 2.5%, mainly due to decreased production of diamonds, zinc, cement and blister copper and a decline in the construction, agriculture and transport sectors. The annual inflation rate was projected at 6.7% while international monetary reserves stood on 30 November at N$ 25 bn, estimated as equivalent to about 3.3 months of import cover. Economic growth contracted in the second (-1.5%) and third (-1%) quarters of the year. The *recession* suggested that the annual growth rate of 2.5% might not be achieved.

At a press conference on 8 December, Schlettwein confirmed that *cash flow problems* were affecting payments for goods and services. He offered exceptional tax discounts and an amnesty to enhance tax revenue from those who were in arrears with payments to the tax authority. The dire situation was exacerbated by huge road tenders entered into by the Roads Authority (RA) of the Ministry of Public Works without proper authorisation and tender procedures, amounting to payments in the region of N$ 2 bn in the near future. The RA claimed that the decisions were made on instruction by "the highest offices".

The devastating El-Niño-induced drought resulted in serious *water shortages*, which affected not only rural communities but also Windhoek and other towns. Dam levels had dropped on average to a third of their volumes by mid-year and experts warned that consumption would have to be reduced by 30%–60%. Continued unsustainable consumption levels required drastic restrictions. Several industries (including beverages and the construction sector) were affected. Some companies reduced or stopped production. In December, dam levels necessitated a reduction of water supply to the capital.

A five-day *African Drought Conference* took place in Windhoek on 15–19 August. Agricultural output, which had since 2013 been the main source of direct and indirect income for 70% of the population, was impacted by the worst drought for 80 years, and shrank by 12%. The 2015 maize harvest had been 44% lower than in 2014 and it was estimated that 120,000 tonnes of maize had to be imported. Massive food price increases accompanied the shortfall, adding to *food insecurity*. Some 600,000 people were recipients of drought relief food. The economic impact of the drought was estimated by mid-year at over N$ 4 bn. On 29 June, Geingob declared a drought-related *state of emergency*. A few days earlier, Finance Minister Schlettwein circulated an instruction to all ministries that vacancies in government services could no longer be filled, since money had been re-allocated to drought relief and emergency food programmes. This moratorium affected the planned recruitment of some 15,000 civil servants; 100,700 people were employed by the state against 116,500 posts originally budgeted for.

The massive decline in the price of oil and the effects on the economy in *Angola* negatively impacted on the Namibian economy. The number of Angolans visiting for medical treatment or shopping dropped significantly and affected the retail and services sector. In particular, many shops in the erstwhile boomtown of Oshikango on the border with Angola and home to many larger scale traders (mainly from China but also other countries), significantly reduced or completely closed their businesses, leaving thousands of people unemployed.

A controversial project for *marine phosphate mining* in combination with onshore phosphate processing plants some 120 km south-west of Walvis Bay was granted environmental clearance by government, despite strong objections from environmental groups and the fishing industry, thereby in principle allowing investment in the planned activity. It was estimated that the project, undertaken by Namibia Marine Phosphate (NMP), would yield 1.8 bn tonnes of phosphoric sand with a N$ 5.2 bn capital investment. The main owner is Mawarid Mining LLC, owned by the Omani businessman Al-Barwani, with Havana Investment of Knowledge Katti as a local partner holding 15%. Minister for Environment and Tourism Pohamba Shifeta announced to the NA on 19 October that NMP had received environmental clearance in a letter dated 5 September. By then, the time for any objections had lapsed. Minister of Fisheries and Marine Resources Bernard Esau challenged this procedural flaw, while his colleague responded that the Fisheries Ministry had not used the time to make submissions. The fishery industry reacted with concern that its future might be at stake given the possible environmental damage. Esau tried to revoke the permission through a cabinet decision at the end of October, but faced resistance. A heated parliamentary debate on 28 October, during which the opposition left in protest, showed that the cabinet was divided. The Namibian constitution anchored environmental protection as a priority, and the matter could have ended up in the Supreme Court. On 2 November, Shifeta, in a U-turn, set aside the certificate granted to NMP by the environmental commissioner. The Ministry of Fisheries and interested parties were notified that they were to finalise their responses to the NMP environmental report within three months.

In mid-May, the government established Namib Desert Diamonds (Namdia), as a local agency in *diamond trading* on the basis of a ten-year marketing and sales agreement with the De Beers group for the distribution of up to 15% of total diamond production of Namdeb, in which the government held 50% as a joint venture with De Beers. On 16 November, an investigative report in 'The Namibian' revealed dubious deals by Namdia through grossly undervalued sales to undisclosed clients in Dubai with subsequent re-sales with up to 500% profit margins, instead of sales on the local market. It alleged that Namdia was controlled by a cartel of highest-ranking political and state office holders also linked to top officials in the Presidency.

On 2 August, the deputy health minister confirmed that *AIDS* remained the lead cause of death among adults. Namibians living with HIV were estimated at some

215,000, including 17,000 aged between 10 and 19, with approximately 42,500 people not yet on anti retroviral treatment; 27,000 mothers were enrolled in prevention of mother-to-child transmission.

Poaching continued unabated. By November, 47 rhinos had been poached during the year, and at the end of November a Chinese national was arrested in Johannesburg, on transit from Windhoek to Hong Kong, carrying 18 rhino horns. Namibia was listed as Africa's top destination for *cyber criminals* as a result of a well-developed communications network and banking sector, combined with a legal system inadequate to deal with cyber crime.

South Africa

Sanusha Naidu

It was an intense year in South Africa's domestic and international political and economic landscape. Following on from the fallout of the firing of Finance Minister Nhanhla Nene in December 2015, the Zuma administration faced a divisive political landscape enshrouded in economic uncertainty. The fifth local government elections took place. They were significant indicators of the mood of the electorate, and how voter behaviour was impacted by questions of political legitimacy, loyalty and the effect of a failing economy. Domestic political and economic affairs dominated the year, especially around issues that exposed the vulnerabilities of the ruling party and the Zuma administration.

Domestic Politics

As usual, the ruling *African National Congress* (ANC) began the year with its statement marking the founding of the party on 8 January. Hosted at the Royal Bafokeng Stadium in Rustenburg, the actual celebration rally appeared to attract a near capacity crowd. The ANC saw this as a positive indication of support. Analysts and

 | DOI 10.1163/9789004355910_053

commentators, however, cautioned that filling seats at rallies did not correlate with electoral loyalty or support. The 104th anniversary celebrations were the platform to provide a backdrop for the ANC election manifesto for the local government elections to be held in the second half of the year. The theme of the statement was 'The Year of Advancing People's Power: Local government is in your hands'. It aimed at refeshing the party's footprint and a reconnection with its branch and grassroots constituencies. The statement provided the context for the ANC's priority policy areas and was seen as a lead-up to the State of the Nation address (SONA), which would inform the government's policy agenda over the next 12 months. Facing stronger competition from other parties, the ANC was in danger of losing critical support, especially in the eight metropolitan municipalities, where its weaknesses were exposed.

Given the state of affairs that the party found itself in, President Jacob Zuma, addressing the rally, emphasised several main points as part of the *local government* focus. In addition to the values and calibre of representatives, he recognised the prevalence of economic inequities in society. He argued that this was the result of historical injustices having not being addressed by reversing the economic dispossession and disempowerment of the black South African majority. He noted that a radical economic transformation agenda was needed that would align the moral imperative with economic imperatives. Underpinning Zuma's speech was the theme that racism still remained a prevalent scourge. The statement and Zuma's speech came under scrutiny. Commentators pointed to a lack of clarity on several issues, such as the government's plans to deal with the overhaul of ailing state-owned enterprises, wastage and corruption, the weakening currency and job creation.

On 11 February, Zuma delivered his ninth *SONA* to the joint houses of parliament. In the run-up to the speech, analysts argued that this would be one of his toughest addresses, given the ailing economy and a domestic political landscape marred by corruption, capture of public wealth and manipulation of state resources. The president himself was perceived as compromised, having been implicated in scandals, including 'Nkandla-gate' – the furore over the cost to the public purse of the upgrading of his personal residence – and some opposition parties such as the Congress of the People (COPE) objected to his delivering the address at all on the grounds that he had violated the presidential oath of office.

Other political parties such as the Economic Freedom Fighters (EFF) raised similar objections to Zuma's presence in the parliament, and chanted "Zupta must fall" – a pun on the president's association with the Indian Gupta family and the level of their political influence. While COPE and the EFF staged a *walk out from the National Assembly* (NA), other opposition parties that remained in the chamber seemed uninspired by the address. Mmusi Maimane, the leader of the official opposition party, the Democratic Alliance (DA), felt that the speech did not reflect a coherent road map to show how the ruling party was going to address the economic challenges of poverty, inequality and job creation. Others, such as the Inkatha Freedom Party (IFP), highlighted that by acknowledging that 5% growth rates could not be achieved, the president had inadvertently admitted that "we are in dire straits" economically. Analysts and commentators criticised the president for a missed opportunity to provide clear leadership on tackling corruption. As one analyst commented, "Mr President this should start with you." Overall, the speech was criticised for not providing a clear plan for fighting recession, a possible credit rating downgrade and job losses. However, the antics of the night by the EFF, in particular, and earlier protest marches that ended in violent clashes with the police overshadowed the event.

On 24 February, Finance Minister Pravin Gordhan delivered the *budget speech*. If there were mixed reactions by business to Zuma's SONA, the corporate sector was definitely looking to Gordhan to provide some concrete policy certainties as regards the economic landscape. The speech was delivered in a sensitive political climate and against the backdrop of deep-seated divisions in the ANC. Gordhan was serving a second term as finance minister after the fallout surrounding the dismissal of Nhanhla Nene. He was found to be in a minority in the ANC, fighting against the factions who did not take kindly to his strategy of applying fiscal austerity measures to government expenditure and procurement restrictions to state tenders. The speech was premised on a narrative expressed by the online news agency, 'Daily Maverick', as "South Africa cannot spend what it does not have." The need for tightening government expenditure, raising taxes and increasing social development programmes were key hallmarks. Many saw the minister as trying to rebalance and shift the country's resources towards economic growth, with little room for flexibility. At the heart of the speech was the message that the political and economic governance of South Africa needed to be redefined to address greed and the manipulation of resources. Gordhan cautioned in interviews following the speech that "There are many parts of transacting between government and business, which have gone seriously wrong and, if we don't stop this, we're going to become a kleptocracy … there is far too much corruption. There are too many extractors." Gordhan was praised by sections of the business community, media and some government and opposition actors and his speech was received internationally with cautious optimism. Some local economic actors believed that Gordhan might have managed to buy South Africa some time with credit ratings agencies regarding the country's investment status.

An application lodged by the EFF and later joined by the DA was presented before the *Constitutional Court* in February; it essentially focused on three issues: clarification of the powers of the *public protector's office* in terms of its role as a Chapter 9 institution entrenched in the constitution and being part of a legislative body accountable to parliament; the implementation of the recommendations of the public protector's report on the use of state money to upgrade the president's private residence, especially the suggestion that he unduly benefited from the renovations and should repay a reasonable portion of the money; and the protection of South Africa's status as a constitutional democracy that preserved the separation of the powers of the executive, the legislature and the judiciary. Having reserved judgement in the case in early February, the 11 sitting justices ruled on 31 March. Chief Justice Mogoeng Mogoeng announced that President Zuma had breached his constitutional oath by failing to take the remedial action recommended by the public protector to repay a portion of the money. In addition the ruling also found that parliament was in violation of its duty, since it had failed to implement the public protector's recommendation and instead set up an ad hoc committee to deliberate the findings of the report. The chief justice gave the National Treasury 60 days to determine a reasonable amount of repayment, after which the president would have 45 days to comply. The ruling was a landmark decision in that it was the first time a sitting head of state had been found to be in breach of the constitution. But the ruling was about more than Zuma "paying back the money". It was about reaching a definitive conclusion to what had become a ping-pong debate about whether the public protector's recommendations could be overridden by the results of other investigative reports, such as that of the police minister, which had sought to set aside the public protector's proposals. The decision was seen as a victory for the DA and the EFF and also gave civil society watchdog institutions such as Corruption Watch, which was also one of the plaintiffs, a renewed impetus in their work.

The ruling reaffirmed the *separation of powers* and provided an important precedent for ensuring that the role of the executive and the oversight duty of the legislature would remain independent and not complicated by the way the Nkandla issue was being manipulated to protect the president and undermine the lines of democratic accountability. Zuma gave a press conference on 1 April, at which he accepted the ruling and highlighted that the judgment "underscored the values that underpin our hard-won freedom and democracy". He thanked the court "for providing clarity" and declared that he respected the judgment and would abide by it. As he further conceded: "The matter has caused a lot of frustration and confusion, for which I apologise, on my behalf and on behalf of government." But *Zuma's press briefing* did little to alleviate the frustration and anger that was mounting, despite his attempt to accept responsibility. The question that emerged was whether Zuma had genuinely accepted liability, and the bigger issue was whether the ANC would consider recalling him, given the implications the ruling had for the party and its image. It was perhaps Zuma's nonchalance during the press briefing when he said that he had "never knowingly or deliberately set out to violate constitution" that brought into question whether he did really respect the ruling. Among opposition parties and sections of the general populace, the mood was that he should have resigned. One commentator remarked that Zuma was "preserving his own power rather than being accountable to the nation, constitution and his own party".

While the DA saw the ruling as an opportunity to initiate *impeachment proceedings* against the president, the ruling sowed more internal tensions in the ANC and pitted pro- and anti-Zuma camps against each other over whether Zuma should be recalled or not. Although he survived a motion of no confidence brought by the DA, thanks largely to the ANC's majority in the NA, this could not paper over the divisions in the party. On the one hand, there was a strong view within the party that the timing might not be conducive to an impeachment as it was a local government election year, while, on the other hand, opponents felt that Zuma might cause the party to haemorrhage electoral support. The disputes within the party continued to blight political life and informed intense discussions about the legitimacy of Zuma's administration and its implication through a plethora of networks in the capture of state resources. Protest marches took place during Freedom Day celebrations on 27 April under the banner '*Zuma Must Fall*'. ANC stalwart, Ahmed Kathrada, wrote an open letter to Zuma asking him to resign.

If the Constitutional Court ruling placed a heavy burden on Zuma, the decision by a full bench of the Pretoria High Court regarding the DA's application to have the National Prosecuting Authority (NPA) set aside its decision not to prosecute the president for fraud on the basis of evidence from the '*spy tapes*' added to his woes. On 29 April, the High Court ruled that the NPA's argument that information from the tapes could not be used to charge the president with links to a 2001 arms deal was contradictory. The NPA's 2009 decision to drop all charges had been based on the view that the prosecution was being manipulated for political ends, but the High Court noted that there were "contradictory versions of how the NPA came to decide not to prosecute Zuma". It condemned the decision as "irrational" and "inexplicable". According to the DA, the 'spy tapes' were key evidence of Zuma's involvement in the arms deal and allegedly linked him to 783 counts of corruption. In its application, the DA also wanted the 'spy tapes' to be released so that their contents could be heard.

Towards the end of May, the head of the NPA, Shaun Abrahams, announced that the NPA was going to *appeal* the High Court decision before the Supreme Court of Appeal (SCA). At the same time the Presidency issued a statement that Zuma had applied for leave to appeal the decision to the Pretoria High Court. On 24 June, the High Court in Pretoria dismissed the NPA's and Zuma's appeal applications. Zuma's legal team challenged the decision in August at the SCA. Departing from normal procedures, the SCA decided in October not to rule on the matter and instead asked Zuma's legal team to argue their case in open court. In November, Zuma's legal team filed further papers with the SCA and were given two months to file the record of the High Court's proceedings with the SCA. Regarding the NPA, the appeal against the 'spy tapes' ruling before the Constitutional Court was dismissed in October.

The Court concluded that it was not in the interest of justice to hear the matter at that stage. The DA's response to both the NPA's and Zuma's applications was that they were attempts to delay the president's appearance in court on the matter.

Parliament remained a place of unrelenting intense verbal and physical clashes whenever the president attended question and answer sessions in the NA. The EFF, in particular, sometimes buoyed by other opposition parties, continued to question the legitimacy of Zuma's presence in the parliament following two judgements by the Constitutional Court against him, seeing him as unfit to hold the office of president. The EFF's sustained efforts to make this point by raising points of order and/or disrupting the president's responses led to the party's suspension from the NA for five days in May. For ordinary South Africans and the media, such parliamentary debacles were becoming the norm but also suggested an almost broken state, with the executive holding power over the legislature.

16 June marked the 40th anniversary of the Soweto Uprising. Towards the end of the month, the Constitutional Court was again in the spotlight, this time deliberating on a case involving the Independent Electoral Commission (IEC) and defects regarding the *electoral roll*. The case stemmed from a November 2015 Constitutional Court ruling that the 2013 Tlokwe by-elections in the North West had not been free and fair. The Constitutional Court noted in its judgement that the IEC's failure to record all available voters' addresses on the national common electoral roll was inconsistent with the constitution and therefore invalidated the electoral roll. The IEC was given 18 months "to fix the defects and obtain the outstanding addresses of millions of registered voters". But despite the verdict the local government elections were to go ahead on 3 August as planned. The Court added that this did not include by-elections, for which the IEC had to have all voters' addresses on the roll.

With *local government elections* looming, the three major political parties began their campaigns by launching their election manifestos in the latter half of April. Some analysts described the ANC's electoral drive as a fight for survival, while for the official opposition DA it was about expanding its footprint beyond traditional voting constituencies and attracting black voters to its ranks. The EFF was capitalising on its success in the 2014 national elections but also demonstrating that its leadership was politically mature and could occupy the electoral space for the long haul. The EFF was aiming not to follow the trajectories of smaller opposition parties, which tended to fade relatively fast after their initial electoral appearance and relative success. But the 2016 elections were different from previous election years. This time around, the ruling party was dealing with a legitimacy crisis surrounding its president and the great unknown was what impact this would have on voter support, confidence and trust in the party. At the other end of the spectrum, there were political sensitivities regarding the candidate lists. This had been a factor in the previous local elections in 2011 and remained a contentious issue that sometimes led to political clashes over differences between candidate lists prepared by communities and those prepared by the ANC headquarters at Luthuli House. Another factor was the level of voter apathy and how political parties might be able to persuade potential voters to turn out. Levels of dissatisfaction and frustration regarding poor governance and the lack of socio-economic delivery and accountability had created a sense of cynicism about whether voting could change the situation in a country that seemed to be sliding towards dysfunction. Of course, into this mix were added first-time voters and the youth vote, which parties sought to capture.

As usual, the parties made lofty *promises to the electorate* in several common areas: efficient, effective and responsive government that would be reliable and incorruptible; job creation and enhancing skills empowerment; delivery of and equal access to quality social development services (i.e. decent and proper work, education, healthcare, water and sanitation, housing); equitable land reform; economic development that would be sustainable and inclusive; and safety and security for all South Africans. While these issues formed the broad template for what constituted election campaigning for most political parties, the difference lay in how these issues were translated into policies. The ANC stuck to its 'Better life for all, for a better Africa, a better world' catchphrase; the DA emphasised integrity and cultural diversity, while the EFF headlined the slogan 'It's now time for economic freedom' as its election motto. Corruption and better effective governance remained the most prominent issues for all parties contesting the election.

According to the IEC, the local government elections saw the highest ever recorded *voter turnout*, with over 15 m people casting their ballots. At the same time, the electoral roll had grown from 23 m in 2011 to 26 m, giving a 58.0% participation rate. This demonstrated the importance the electorate attached to the elections. The province of Gauteng registered the largest voter turnout, while in provinces such as Northern Cape and the Eastern Cape it fell by more than 2%. Three *metropolitan municipalities* (metros) were hotly contested: the Nelson Mandela Bay Municipality (Port Elizabeth), the city of Tshwane Municipality (Pretoria) and the Johannesburg Municipality, all three traditional strongholds of the ANC. The final count showed that the ANC won 54.5% of the total national votes cast, but was not able to retain control in the three key metros. This was a psychological blow for the party.

The *DA* won the city of Cape Town decisively with a two-thirds majority, and made significant inroads in other metros. Taking 27.0% of the national vote, the DA sought to snap at the heels of the ANC. In the Nelson Mandela Bay metro there was a less than 6% margin of difference between the DA and the ANC; while in Johannesburg it was just 6% and in Tshwane less than 2%. With no outright majority and hung municipalities in all three metros, the opportunity for *coalition politics* and negotiations with king makers such as the EFF became a real possibility.

The *EFF*'s performance, with more than 8% of the national vote, received mixed reactions. This being its first venture into local government elections, the leadership saw its showing at the polls as indicating a stable level of support compared with the 2014 national election, where it took 6.4% of the votes. Some commentators felt that the EFF's showing at the 2016 polls was not as impressive as in 2014, and that the party should have recorded a double-digit percentage to demonstrate its growing electoral footprint. But other commentators felt that the party's performance should be seen as strengthening its electoral base, adding that it was the party's significance as a coalition maker that made its role strategic. The leadership was clear that the EFF would not be defined as a junior partner nor would it accept being dictated to by its coalition partners regarding how it would vote for policies or take decisions. This was a clear signal from party leader Julius Malema that it was not the EFF that needed other parties but vice versa. To this end, the EFF supported the DA in Johannesburg and Tshwane metros to establish a government, but cautioned that this should not be seen as explicit backing for the DA there. The EFF warned that their vote for the DA in the two metros and in other municipalities where there was no outright winner was not aimed at establishing a ruling coalition. The party claimed that its role would be to provide checks and balances, not to endorse policies that were in contradiction to its own position.

The election also sent an important signal regarding *voter patterns and trends*. The most striking feature was the growing split between rural and urban voters. This was evidenced by the ANC retaining its electoral base in the provinces, identified as mainly rural, while in urban centres there was a notable shift away from the party. Analysts cautioned that South Africa's urbanisation had meant that urban voters had become more aware of socio-economic issues and were raising questions as to whether the ANC represented their interests. It was also suggested that, under Zuma leadership, the party had shifted its focus towards the rural elements. This caused fragmentation between those representing urban voters and those that had the backing of rural constituencies. Other analysts went even further to imply that this divide in the party was an extension of the way Zuma shaped power dynamics. The split between rural and urban voters became a pointer for how the ANC might fare in the 2019 national elections.

From September to November, South Africa's domestic landscape was shaken by stringent governance constraints. In September, the four major banks closed the accounts of Oakbay Investments, a company owned by the Gupta family on suspicion of irregularities in transactions. As a consequence, Mining Minister Mosebenzi Zwane, as part of an inter-ministerial team appointed by the president to look into the banking sector after the affair, issued a press statement announcing the establishment by a 'Cabinet Resolution' of a judicial inquiry into South Africa's *banking sector*. The government denied this while Finance Minister Gordhan contradicted the mining minister to protest that strong regulatory bodies already existed to address such an issue if it was merited. Despite being advised of the illegality of the procedure and that he was not empowered or obligated to push for an inquiry, he did not seem to be deterred. In October, Gordhan issued an affidavit revealing unusual and suspicious financial transactions by the *Gupta family*, whose accounts had been suspended by the major banks. The affidavit was produced as part of a court case in which Gordhan, as the sole applicant, was requesting the court to order that he could not interfere with the bank's decision regarding the Gupta family. According to the affidavit, Gordhan cited 72 suspicious transactions to the value of R (rand) 6.8 bn obtained from the Financial Intelligence Centre. In essence, Gordhan was asking the Court to protect him from the Guptas' pressures to intervene on their behalf. According to the investigative unit Amabungane, Gordhan's application appeared to have an additional motive "to force information about the Guptas' financial probity into the public domain".

Later, the head of the NPA, Shaun Abrahams, announced at a press briefing that the state was instituting *fraud charges against Finance Minister Gordhan* and two former South African Revenue Services (SARS) employees regarding the early retirement and re-employment of Ivan Pillay (a former deputy commissioner of SARS). The charges were based on Gordhan's approval of Pillay's early retirement request and then his reappointment on a contract basis to SARS. Legal experts noted that the charges seemed to lack legal substance that would hold up in a court of law. There was a prevailing view that this was a political witch-hunt against Gordhan, who had become a thorn in the side of the Zuma presidency. Two weeks after the charges were brought, Abrahams announced their withdrawal for lack of evidence. While Abrahams noted that the matter might be revisited at a later stage, media reports alleged that the charges were withdrawn after the NPA head had met with the president at ANC headquarters. Another speculation was that charges were withdrawn to avert protest marches planned to coincide with Gordhan's court appearance.

In mid-October, the term of *Public Protector* Thuli Madonsela came to an end. During the last weeks of her tenure, she sought to finalise her investigation into the capture of state resources. On the eve of her departure, Zuma and Minister for Cooperative Governance and Traditional Affairs Des van Rooyen sought a court order preventing her from releasing her report lest they be implicated. In November, Zuma abandoned his court application and the Pretoria High Court ordered the report to be released. Furthermore, the Court dismissed van Rooyen's application and accepted the legal bid by the EFF, the COPE, the DA and the United Democratic Movement (UDM) to prevent the release of the report.

During this legal battle, Busisiwe Mkhebane succeeded Madonsela. Mkhebane's appointment was controversial and the DA questioned her link to the State Security Agency, claimed that she lacked experience and refrained from supporting her nomination, but she took office as the *new public protector* on 17 October. The media soon questioned whether she could maintain the independence of the office as a Chapter 9 institution in maintaining democratic accountability. Other media reports asked more candidly whether Mkhebane could fill Madonsela's shoes.

The release of Madonsela's *'State Capture' report* following a court order on 2 November, caused ripple effects across the country. The report exposed the intricate levels of widespread corruption and cronyism, implicating several high-ranking officials in the Zuma cabinet as well as senior management in some state-owned enterprises. In short, it confirmed a growing concern about fraud connected to state tenders and procurement issues and political interference in state affairs by business people (the Gupta family in particular) close to the Zuma network. The report, as one media commentator remarked, had "further cleaved open the networks that have been siphoning off public funds to bless those in close proximity to the president with exorbitant wealth under the guise of transformation and empowerment". Individuals mentioned in the report included Brian Molefe, former head of the state electricity utility, Eskom, who subsequently resigned following a press briefing where he tried to defend his association with the Gupta family; the Gupta family, especially the three brothers, who were cited in the report as possibly using their political connections to influence ministers towards awarding state contracts to their business entities; and the president himself, questioning whether he had acted improperly and in violation of the Executive Ethics Code of Conduct regarding the transgressions committed by the Gupta family and others, which had sometimes been reported to him. The report was broad in its observations, noting that, if the president did not act to address these offences but behaved in such a manner as to protect personal interests, it would threaten the reputations of the ministers who had brought the issues to his attention as well as weaken the trust of ordinary South Africans in the country's democratic governance principles of accountability and transparency. The report's conclusion noted that remedial action should take the form of a *judiciary commission of inquiry* into the capture of state resources to be appointed by the president within 30 days and for the commission to be "headed solely by a judge selected by the Chief Justice who shall provide one name to the President". Given that the president had the power to appoint commissions and their heads, Zuma brought a legal challenge, arguing that the report's recommendation was in contravention of his powers as defined in the constitution. Critics pointed out that, with the president being implicated in the report, he would not be impartial in appointing the head; hence the allocation of this task to the Chief Justice.

The end of the year saw South African civil society mobilising under the banner of *'Save South Africa'* or SOS. The initiative was led by leading governance organisations such as Section 27, Corruption Watch, Lawyers for Human Rights and the Center for the Advancement of the South African Constitution and also included prominent voices from religious institutions such as the Archbishop of the Anglican Church, ANC stalwarts such as Trevor Manuel, Sipho Pityana, Cheryl Carolus, former constitutional court justice Zak Yacoob, and even CEOs of South Africa's corporate business world, who called on all South Africans to fight corruption. The SOS rallying point was around the political machinations against Finance Minister Gordhan and the need to unite behind the great symbol of the national flag and against state capture. A People's Assembly planned to coincide with Gordhan's court appearance went ahead, despite the NPA charges being dropped. In delivering the keynote address to the Assembly, Sipho Pityana labeled Zuma the "sponsor in chief of corruption" and had earlier called for the president to step down.

By December, tensions were high in the National Executive Committee (NEC) of the ANC. At a three-day meeting of the NEC towards the end of November, a *motion of no confidence in President Zuma* was tabled by Tourism Minister Derek Hanekom with the assumed support of Health Minister Aaron Motsaledi and Public Works Minister Thulas Nxesi. They made the thrust of their proposal Zuma's alleged relationship with the Gupta family and the Nkandla scandal, arguing that all this had caused confidence in the party to deteriorate and brought the ANC into disrepute. Thwarted by Zuma loyalists, the motion did not succeed, though it opened up the divisions that were taking root in the party.

As the year drew to a close, severe levels of *improper governance practices* further aggravated the domestic political situation. These included executive and financial mismanagement at the public broadcaster SABC (South African Broadcasting Company), which was investigated by a parliamentary ad hoc committee. The South African Social Development Agency, responsible for disbursing grants to at least 17 m vulnerable recipients, allegedly wasted R 1 m in dubious expenditure while the Social Development Ministry was dragging its feet in issuing a new tender for a service provider to dispense grants on its behalf. This was after the Constitutional Court had ruled three years before that the contract awarded to Cash Paymasters Service (the current service provider) was illegal. The Court had ordered the department to issue a new tender and the new service provider should have been in place by 1 April 2017.

Foreign Affairs

On 26 February, South Africa hosted the 13th *EU-SA Ministerial Political Dialogue*, which reaffirmed the strategic partnership on several significant areas of cooperation relating to trade, multilateralism and regional cooperation.

President Zuma strengthened political and economic ties with *Arab states*, visiting Saudi Arabia and the UAE at the end of March. He came under fire from the DA, who alleged that the trip was conducted partly in secret and wanted to know whether Zuma and the minister of defence and military veterans had entered into an offshore joint venture partnership with Saudi Arabia for arms production. The DA expressed their suspicion that South Africa and the Saudi Kingdom were essentially creating 'a new military industrial complex', highlighting that the joint venture was similar to the 1999 Arms Deal. At the same time, the leader of the EFF accused Zuma of taking a large sum of money from South Africa to Dubai on behalf of the Gupta family. The president rejected such claims as preposterous and defamatory, while the Gupta family also vehemently denied them.

Prime Minister Modi of *India* made his first official state visit to South Africa. Prior to the visit, speculation was rife that the controversial issue of admission to the Nuclear Supplier Group (NSG) would dominate the meeting with Zuma on 8 July. It was widely reported in Indian media that Modi had intended to use the visit to sway Pretoria to enable New Delhi to become part of the Group, which it had been trying unsuccessfully to join for several years, with China blocking its entry in recent years. Zuma affirmed South Africa's support for India's admission to the NSG. South Africa and India agreed to increase bilateral trade to $ 18 bn by 2018 and to strengthen commercial ties linked to the 'Make in India' initiative. In addition, both sides also undertook to address shared global concerns, especially in terms of strategic security issues and continual support for the reform agenda towards a more equitable, just and balanced international system. Four memoranda of understanding and agreements were signed in the areas of ICT, the establishment of grassroots innovation in science and technology, tourism, and cultural cooperation. Discussions were also held towards intensifying collaboration in defence, energy, agro-processing, human resource development, infrastructure development and science, technology and innovation. The bulk of the deliberations focused on economic cooperation and strengthening private sector investment in both markets.

The second half of the year saw a flurry of international diplomatic initiatives that impacted negatively on South Africa's *foreign policy image*. In July, Mrs Dlamini-Zuma stayed on for several further months as AU Commission chairperson following a decision by the AU to postpone the election of her successor to the next AU Summit in January 2017. In October, the minister of justice announced South Africa's *withdrawal from the ICC*. The decision seemed to be an expression of South Africa's objections to the alleged double standards operated by the Court with respect to African states. The decision seemed to have been made without following proper legislative procedure, and it raised the question of whether the Zuma government was acting in response to the 2015 debacle over Sudan's President al-Bashir or to strengthen its Africa strategy by improving its credibility on the continent. The Southern African Litigation Centre, which had brought the legal application against the government and sought a court order to arrest al-Bashir, responded to the announcement by noting that, if the legality of the decision stood, it would be sad for human rights and the international criminal system.

On 2 October, the 'Sunday Times' led with the story that the High Commissioner to Singapore was a convicted drug trafficker who had been fired from the national airline after being jailed in New York for smuggling cocaine. The article provoked debate about how this had not been picked up by national security during the vetting stage before she took up her post. It also raised questions about the way appointments to *diplomatic posts* were made, and whether the Foreign Service Bill that was under parliamentary consideration should consider a professionalised diplomatic service.

At the end of December, the DA mayor of Tshwane, Solly Msimanga, caused a diplomatic stir when he made a trip to *Taiwan*. Despite cautions from the Foreign Ministry and the ANC, Msimanga declared his visit to the Republic of China was at the invitation of his counterpart in Taipei, and he had taken the time as "personal leave and time off work to explore investment opportunities". The ANC and the government saw the visit as a violation of the 'One China policy'. Outraged by the mayor's behaviour, some in the ANC called for the mayor's passport to be revoked and believed the trip was aimed at undermining the BRICS.

In January, South Africa was re-elected to the AU's Peace and Security Council. Zuma stated that, through the Council, South Africa would continue to strengthen its *peace and security commitments* on the continent. Throughout the year, South Africa engaged in its peace building efforts in South Sudan and Lesotho. On *South Sudan*, Deputy President Cyril Ramaphosa, as Zuma's special envoy, continued his mediation attempts towards strengthening the peace process. Despite the tenuous nature of the situation, Ramaphosa hosted the South Sudanese First Vice President Tabang Deng in September. The visit focused on progress with regard to the Arusha Peace Agreement, reunification of the Sudan People's Liberation Movement (SPLM), and continued discussions towards post-conflict reconstruction and development. But a newspaper report suggested that Riek Machar, the rebel leader of the SPLA-In Opposition (SPLA-IO) faction, who had fled the fighting in August, was "being held in South Africa to stop him stirring up trouble, [according to] diplomatic and political sources". Machar's spokesman denied that the rebel leader was under any restrictions and the Foreign Ministry stressed that he was a guest of the government.

Socioeconomic Developments

The uncertainty in the political landscape increased the pressure on socio-economic development. It was a *difficult year*, which saw petrol price increases and two interest rate hikes. This placed intense burdens on household spending and consumer price inflation costs, especially on food and everyday consumer items. Allegations of *mismanagement* by the Zuma government and uncertainty in the economic policy environment saw the country facing possible credit risk downgrades, which in turn put pressure on growth trajectories. In January, two *credit rating agencies* put the government on notice. By November, despite the finance minister trying to assuage their fears, statements by Moody's and Fitch cautioned that South Africa's economic outlook had been revised to negative, even though they were leaving the bond rate at 'Baa2' and 'BBB' respectively.

At the beginning of the year, the *GDP forecast* was revised by the National Treasury from an estimated 1.7% at the time of the Medium Term Expenditure Budget Statement (MTEBS) in 2015 to 0.9%. The weaker growth prospects were a result of lower commodity prices, high borrowing costs, diminished business and investor confidence, low consumer confidence and a protracted drought. By the time the 2016 MTEBS was delivered by the finance minister on 26 October, the growth path had been revised downwards again, with the minister forecasting growth at 0.5%. During the last quarter, the economy contracted by 0.3%. Declines in mining and manufacturing were the main contributors to the economy's slowdown. The contraction of the economy in the fourth quarter also led to the *Reserve Bank* keeping interest rates unchanged. The Bank cited the consumer inflation index at 6.6% as the main the reason for their decision, although it showed signs of edging upwards according to indicators from the Statistical Agency. The Reserve Bank governor also noted that its growth forecast was at 0.4%. Therefore an increase in the Repo rate would have created added pressure to household debt.

In the third quarter, *unemployment* spiked at 27.1%, up from 26.6% recorded in the second quarter. This brought the jobless rate to its highest level in 13 years, with 5.9 m South Africans out of work. The figure was based on the standard definition used by Stats SA for people actively seeking employment. The expanded definition of unemployment, which included people who had stopped seeking work, was recorded at 36.4%. The largest job losses were recorded in the manufacturing sector, while construction and business services saw positive increases.

The level of *social protest* intensified. Strikes continued to be motivated by high levels of inequality, unemployment and lack of service delivery. The '*Fees Must Fall*' movement turned violent towards the latter part of the year. Student protests resulted in several universities being closed for weeks, which compromised the academic calendar, while infrastructure was destroyed in militant actions. Some examinations were deferred to January 2017. In addition, the student protests also raised the issue of *racism at tertiary institutions*. Clashes between students and police that unfolded across universities were described as recalling apartheid-like brutality. Some institutions employed the use of private security personnel to beef up security and students claimed they used heavy-handed tactics. In response to the fees issue, the minister for higher education and training announced that institutions would have to decide on the percentage by which fees would increase in 2017, but set a ceiling of 8%. This put more pressure on universities' financial resources. The students' protests divided the nation between those who felt that higher education should be free for all people and those who argued that costs would be too high for the state to finance.

Swaziland

Marisha Ramdeen

The Kingdom of Swaziland, ruled by King Mswati III, had been rife with political protests against undemocratic policies and police brutality for well over a decade, with concerns raised about human rights and the rule of law. Whilst the country generally fared no better within these areas, a highlight of the year was the positive ruling on the Suppression of Terrorism Act and the Subversive Activities Act, which showed signs of judicial independence. Other significant events included ongoing protests and the declaration of a state of emergency as a result of a severe drought that impacted negatively on the people and the economy.

Domestic Politics

Throughout the year, there were *protest actions* by various sectors of government services and civil society calling for salary increases, creation of employment within the health sector and improvements in working conditions. On 25 February, public sector workers marched to the capital, Mbabane, as part of a two-day strike

 | DOI 10.1163/9789004355910_054

action and delivered a petition for salary increases to the prime minister. The Swazi Trade Union Federation, TUCOSWA, which led the march, further sought to place pressure on the government to publish a salary review report. The report, intended to ensure that salaries keep up with inflation, is scheduled to be released every five years, but the last report had been published in 2004. Following the protest, the salary review report was released but caused a level of discontent as the recommendations indicated salary increases mostly for senior officials. Within the health sector, nurses petitioned against the lack of staff and the Swaziland Democratic Nurses Union called for more jobs to be created. There was approximately one nurse for every 1,000 people in Swaziland, compared with WHO recommendations of five nurses to 1,000 patients. The media, whose freedoms had been in jeopardy for many years, protested about working conditions at the king's newspaper. Members of the Media Worker's Union of Swaziland led the protest action against low wages, management intimidation and poor working conditions. The demonstration took place outside the offices of the 'Swazi Observer', as the Swaziland High Court banned the Union from holding a formal picket.

A survey undertaken by Afrobarometer found that one in three Swazis relied on the Internet for news as a result of the heavy *censorship* of Swaziland's mainstream media. Censorship also extended to higher learning institutions. The executive secretary of the Higher Education Council was quoted as saying, "The University of Swaziland teaches political studies, lectures should stick to the parameters and not go outside their domain to the detriment of the country."

A court ruling on the *Suppression of Terrorism Act* and the *Subversive Activities Act* found that sections within them were unconstitutional. The judgement concluded that provisions with regard to the definition of "sedition, subversion and terrorism and to the designation of an organisation as a terrorist entity" were "unconstitutional on the grounds that they infringed the right to freedom of expression, association and administrative justice". This judgement was the result of four separate cases initiated by political activists who had been imprisoned on charges of terrorism, sedition and subversion. For many years, these acts had been exploited to imprison any individual who spoke in support of democracy and against King Mswati III or his government. The attorney-general appealed the High Court ruling and the case was pending at year's end.

Swaziland's *human rights* record remained poor. According to the World Report released by HRW, freedom of association and assembly was particularly threatened by the excessive use of force by police. Examples included a police blockade in February that prevented TUCOSWA from marching to parliament to present a petition. In the same month, it was also reported that a Royal Swazi Police Operational Services armoured vehicle drove into a group of students protesting about delays in registration, leaving one student severely crippled. In October, police fired gunshots at students protesting about the poor quality of teaching and inferior facilities at the university. Excessive force was exercised not only by the police but also by teachers. Severe beatings in schools continued, and it was reported that there had been 4,556 cases of severe corporal punishment in the past four years. There was also a high incidence of *sexual and gender based violence*. Action for Southern Africa (ACTSA) reported that in March alone there were four brutal incidents. The Sexual Offences and Domestic Bill that was developed in 2009 to protect women's rights, was yet to be enacted by the government. Swaziland had a Gender Inequality Index of 0.557 and was ranked 150th out of 188 countries. Statistics indicated that one in three girls experienced sexual violence before the age of 18; 31% of women were HIV positive; early and forced marriage was normal and marital rape was legal.

Asian people were targeted and experienced racial discrimination. The Swaziland government initiated a *ban against Asian people* entering the Kingdom and there were incidents of Asians being evicted from their homes and banished from the area on racial grounds. A decision by the government to set up a committee to investigate immigration from Asia, mostly India and Pakistan, triggered heightened tensions. In their distrust of Asians, the police were suspected of monitoring the Muslim community by attending Friday prayers at mosques in disguise. The media supported the government's position towards Asians. The 'Times Sunday', one of the few independent newspapers, made concerted attacks on Asians in the Kingdom, declaring them to be "cheats and scoundrels". The 'Swazi Observer' was accused of misinforming the public to create support for its discrimination against Asians. For example, the newspaper indicated that "600,000 people in Swaziland are of Asian origin", while it was found that 97% of the Swazi population were African.

Foreign Affairs

In February, the *International Union of Socialist Youth*, consisting of 134 members in over 80 countries, passed a resolution at its 31st world congress that called for reforms in Swaziland to unban political parties, remove repressive legislation and introduce multi-party democracy. President of the Swaziland Youth Congress Bheki Dlamini was elected vice-president of the Union.

From 28 April to 1 May, King Mswati visited *Mozambique* to strengthen relations and cooperation. A day after the visit, a Memorandum of Understanding (MoU) was signed between the two countries for cooperation in the areas of mineral resources, energy and water resources. In addition, in May, Swaziland was one of the ten SADC countries to sign an MoU to enhance cooperation and strengthen the effective enforcement of competition law across SADC, which was described as a landmark MoU.

The international community continued to be instrumental in pushing for democratic reforms in Swaziland. ACTSA appealed to the international community to place serious pressure on the government to respects human rights and develop a genuinely democratic constitution. It warned of a protracted crisis, "unless African governments, as well as bilateral and multilateral donors vigorously and consistently engaged with the government of Swaziland so that it genuinely protects and serves all of its citizens". This call was supported by UNISON, one of the UK's largest trade unions.

In June, *SADC and the EU signed an EPA* which included Swaziland, Botswana, Lesotho, Namibia and South Africa, aimed at benefiting these countries by granting access to European markets without duties or quotas. However, Members of the European Parliament (MEPs) expressed concerns about Swaziland's human rights record. When it was put to a vote, two-thirds of MEPs endorsed Swaziland's inclusion in the Agreement, whilst the remaining third wanted Swaziland excluded.

The 104th conference of the ILO took place in June in Geneva (Switzerland) and the government of Swaziland appeared before the Committee on the Application of Standards for the violation of rights to organise, to collective bargaining and to freedom of association. However, Botswana, speaking on behalf of SADC as the Chair, indicated that there was no need for an intervention as it noted that the government of Swaziland had made progress on addressing this issue. This was the seventh consecutive time the case was discussed in the conference committee and the Kingdom had been examined 14 times, but the Botswana government again said that the Swaziland government was progressing towards implementing the convention. The Botswana Federation of Trade Unions expressed their concerns as they felt that the government of Botswana was ignoring the violation of workers' rights in Swaziland.

In 2015, King Mswati had been elected as SADC chairperson for 2016. As the chair holder, Swaziland hosted the 36th *SADC Summit* of Heads of State and Government in Lozitha on 30–31 August under the theme 'Resource Mobilisation for Investment in Sustainable Energy Infrastructure for an Inclusive SADC Industrialisation for the Prosperity of the Region'.

Socioeconomic Developments

Economic growth was projected at 1.3%, down from 1.7% in 2015. An estimated 63% of the population were living below the poverty line, and about 29% below the extreme poverty line. The HIV/AIDS prevalence of 31% of the population was one of the highest in the world and life expectancy had fallen to approximately 49 years, but there was still a population growth of 1.5%.

Ongoing drought created a severe food crisis, which resulted in a state of emergency being declared. It caused extreme water shortages, falling crop yields and the death of thousands of cattle in rural areas. According to an EU report, the drought caused by the El-Niño phenomenon resulted in the loss of more than 40,000 cattle, with more than 300,000 people facing severe food shortages. The drought also had serious repercussions on agricultural production and the economy as a whole. Maize production had fallen by 3% in 2015 and was even lower in 2016. Water rationing was imposed for the first time in history. Sugar cane harvests were hit the most, with 90% of Swaziland's sugar cane crops dependent on irrigation. Swaziland is the fourth-largest sugar producer in Africa and, with sugar accounting for almost 60% of agricultural output and 21% of GDP, the fall in production placed a severe strain on the economy. The EU continued to be the biggest market for Swazi sugar. It was estimated that E (elangeni) 2 bn was required for the next five years to address both the severe food crisis and ongoing drought.

Water restrictions impacted the education of children and put almost 197,157 students, teachers and workers nation-wide at risk of water-borne diseases and malnutrition. In response to the crisis, the government launched the National Emergency Response Mitigation and Adaptation Plan and turned to the intentional community to raise money to assist with *drought relief*. The EU, in collaboration with the Finnish Red Cross, pledged the equivalent of $ 650,000 to assist more than 21,000 people from 4,200 households with food supplies. USAID launched a drought response initiative worth approximately E 83 m.

Excessive spending and mismanagement of funds continued to make headlines. After Swaziland had appealed for E 143 m from the international community for drought relief, the government announced the intention to buy a jet plane for the king at a cost of at least E 96 m. Parliamentarians initially rejected the budget that would have approved the deal, but overturned the decision days later and agreed to pay E 200 m to China Airlines in Taiwan for an Airbus A340–300. Expenditure for the SADC Heads of State Summit was estimated at E 40 m. Approximately $ 12 m was spent on decorating the Royal Terminal Building at King Mswati Airport. The annual budget allocated 11% (approximately $ 150 m) of expenditure to security, the army, police and correctional services. The Treasury Department was accused of misappropriating funds after it was discovered that there was a shortfall of E 5.1 bn. Independent auditors feared there may have been fraud, misappropriation and embezzlement. Trade unionists called for an official inquiry into the matter.

Zambia

Edalina Rodrigues Sanches

Zambia adopted a new constitution. General elections were held. Incumbent president Edgar Lungu of the Patriotic Front (PF) polled over the 50% needed for re-election but the results were challenged by the runner-up Hakainde Hichilema, candidate of the United Party for National Development (UPND). Post-electoral violence escalated in UPND strongholds. The PF secured a majority of parliamentary seats for the first time, while the first direct elections for mayors/council chairpersons revealed a clear balance between the PF and the UPND. The referendum on a new Bill of Rights failed. Lungu's international trips intensified with the strategic goals of attracting foreign investors and strengthening bilateral relations with key partners in Africa and the Middle East. Conditions for economic growth remained tough. The electricity supply deficit continued to affect households, mining activities and other business. The currency improved and copper prices increased.

Domestic Politics

The long overdue *constitution* was finally signed into law by President Edgar Lungu at a ceremony at the National Heroes Stadium in Lusaka on 5 January. The Grand

 | DOI 10.1163/9789004355910_055

Coalition for a People-Driven Constitution boycotted the event, arguing that it was "a PF government-driven constitution". The new constitution required that a president needed to receive 50%+1 of the vote in order to win and that the vice president should be voted for by the electorate, instead of being appointed by the president. It also established a Political Parties' Fund to provide financial support to political parties with seats in the National Assembly, set a ban on tribal parties and prescribed an increase in the number of parliamentary seats, among other things.

General elections for the president, the National Assembly, local government councils and, for the first time, mayors/council chairpersons were held on 11 August. A *constitutional referendum* was held in parallel, with proposals to amend the Bill of Rights and Article 79. The elections took place under new rules. Nine presidential candidates and 13 political parties competed for votes. The presidential candidates were: Tilyenji Kaunda of the United National Independence Party (UNIP), Edith Nawakwi of the Forum for Democracy and Development (FDD), Edgar Lungu of the PF, Saviour Chishimba of the United Progressive People (UPP), Wynter Kabimba of the Rainbow Party (RP), Peter Sinkamba of the Green Party (GP), Hakainde Hichilema of the UPND, Andyford Banda of the People's Alliance for Change (PAC) and Maxwell Mwamba of the Democratic Assembly (DA). The *front runners* were Edgar Lungu and Hakainde Hichilema, who had run a close race in the previous presidential by-election held in January 2015, following the death of former president Michael Sata.

For the first time since its formation, the *Movement for Multi-Party Democracy* (MMD) did not put forward a candidate for the presidency, mainly due to a dispute between Nevers Mumba and Felix Mutati over who was the party's legitimate leader. Felix Mutati was elected leader in May, but Nevers Mumba claimed Mutati's election was illegal and continued to present himself as the legitimate MMD leader. Mutati rejected Mumba's allegations. The MMD participated in the parliamentary elections along with many of the parties already engaged in the presidential polls. Moreover, five additional parties fielded candidates for the parliamentary elections: the National Restoration Party (NAREP), the Alliance for Democracy and Development (ADD), the United Democratic Front (UDF), the Golden Progressive Party (GPP) and the Radical Revolutionary Party (RRP).

The *election campaign* took place between 16 May and 10 August. Several violent incidents compromised the integrity of the elections. A parliamentary candidate of the FDD for Namwala, Southern Province, was attacked on 17 June and a UPND rally in Lusaka was cancelled by the police on 8 July. This triggered clashes between UPND supporters and the police during which a UPND supporter was killed. As a consequence, the Electoral Commission of Zambia (ECZ) suspended campaigning in Lusaka and Namwala for ten days. The elections were also marked by the prosecution of a significant number of UPND supporters for offences related to assault, damage to property and unlawful gathering. Intermittent clashes occurred during the pre-election period and Hichilema wrote to UN Secretary-General Ban Ki-moon a few days before the polls, asking the UN to bring the participating political parties together "to sign a peace accord".

The PF, UPND and some smaller parties made their manifestos available but the campaign did not present substantive ideological differences between the parties. The *key issues* remained related to the economy, youth unemployment, poverty, education and healthcare. The country was facing the worst economic crisis in a decade, with the fall of commodity prices, the closure of several mines, the resulting unemployment of thousands of people and the energy crisis. The incumbent President Lungu focused on his government's achievements and highlighted progress in the agriculture sector and infrastructure projects such as road networks. Hichilema promised to enhance power supplies, provide free education, increase agricultural output to reduce reliance on copper and cut wasteful government spending. Personalities may have played a strong role. Lungu presented himself as candidate of all Zambians and even used the slogan 'One Zambia, One Nation' at his rallies. His incumbency also provided some advantages: Lungu featured as a man of deeds with campaign billboards highlighting the number of roads, clinics, schools and social projects his PF government had completed. Media coverage was reported to be quite biased in favour of the PF and largely excluded other parties, or only reported about them negatively.

Polling day was calm, though some disturbances were observed in the neighbourhoods of eight polling stations. Voter turnout (56.5%) was slightly higher than at the last general elections (2011). The results were announced on 15 August. In the *presidential elections*, Lungu was re-elected for a five-year term after polling 50.4% of the votes, while Hichilema came second with 47.6%. The remaining 2.0% were distributed among the other seven candidates. Of these, Andyford Banda of the PAC was the biggest surprise, coming fourth in the election, just behind Edith Nawakwi of the FDD. At the age of 35, he was the youngest candidate in the presidential race and had founded his party in July 2015. In the *parliamentary elections*, the PF won expressively and experienced the first parliamentary majority result ever (42.0% and 80 seats). The UPND came second, also improving its performance (41.7% and 58 seats). The MMD continued its downward slide, losing 52 parliamentary seats (2.7% and three seats), the FDD kept its seat (2.2% and one seat), while the ADD lost its parliamentary representation. A surprisingly high number of independent MPs (14) were elected.

Hichilema contested the result, claiming that Lungu's election had been fraudulent; he referred to numerous alleged irregularities and called for a recount. He petitioned the High Court after the Constitutional Court refused to give him more time to make a legal challenge to Lungu's re-election. Meanwhile, *post-electoral violence escalated* in many of the UPND strongholds – mainly in Southern Province – and about 300 people were arrested.

Zambia's High Court rejected the UPND's application to block Lungu's inauguration set for 13 September and he was duly sworn in as president on that day. Inonge

Wina, who in 2015 had become the first woman to hold the vice presidency, continued in office. The new *cabinet* was one of the largest ever with 29 ministers (one short of the maximum of 30 ministers allowed by the constitution and ten provincial ministers. The cabinet held its first meeting on 3 October. One of the appointments that attracted most comment was that of Felix Mutati as minister of finance. He had been a member of successive MMD governments, holding various positions, from deputy minister of finance and national planning to minister of commerce, trade and industry. Most importantly he was a known supporter of IMF and World Bank policies for Zambia.

For the first time, Zambia held direct *city and municipal elections* for councils and chairpersons of district councils. The results were quite close between the PF and the UPND. Of the 106 positions up for election, 50 PF candidates were voted in as mayors/council chairpersons and 48 from the UPND. Two independents were also elected. By-elections were held in November to assign the remaining seats. The UPND was reported to have performed well in these elections but results were not given on the ECZ website. The overall voting pattern followed that in the presidential election, with the PF taking every district in the Eastern, Luapula, Muchinga and Northern Provinces, and the UPND taking all in the Northwestern, Southern and Western regions.

Alongside the general elections, Zambians were called to vote on a *referendum* to decide whether to amend the Bill of Rights and Article 79 of the constitution, which stated that a referendum must be held to amend the article itself and the Bill of Rights. The question in the referendum was: "Do you agree to the amendment to the Constitution to enhance the Bill of Rights contained in Part III of the Constitution of Zambia and to repeal and replace Article 79 of the Constitution of Zambia?" The amendment proposed expanding Zambians' rights, namely access to food, shelter, employment and healthcare, but would also ban homosexual acts and abortion and raise the age of consent for marriage to 19. The Law Association of Zambia, TI Zambia, the Civil Society for Poverty Reduction and the Zambia Congress of Trade Unions endorsed the proposed Bill of Rights, describing it as progressive. However, many of these civil society organisations opposed the holding of the national referendum alongside the general election. They claimed that the referendum would be overshadowed by the elections and that voting would take place along partisan lines rather than on the content of the Bill. They therefore called for the matter to be addressed separately, given what was at stake. There were also requests for the translation of the Bill of Rights into local languages and fears that the scant information available to the public on the Bill of Rights would demotivate voters and affect the number of invalid votes. The referendum failed as fewer than 50% of eligible voters voted. The UPND may have played a significant role in the failure as it initially recommended its supporters to vote 'no', but later asked them to simply abstain from voting. The highest proportion of invalid/blank votes was found in UPND strongholds: Northwestern, Southern and Western Provinces.

The *media landscape* became less plural, with the government restricting the activity of several media outlets. On 21 June, the Zambia Revenue Authority (ZRA) shut down the 'Post' newspaper for alleged unpaid taxes. The opposition claimed the government was using repressive laws to restrict campaign activities and that this constituted an attack on freedom of speech and citizens' rights to access to a diversity of viewpoints and information about the main topics in the campaign. On 22 August, the Independent Broadcasting Authority suspended broadcasting licences for 'Muvi TV', 'Komboni Radio' and 'Itezhi-Tezhi Radio'. This all took place rather abruptly, justified by some broadcasters' lack of quality and citing "serious levels of inaccuracies, skewed coverage, as well as publication of unverified news items". There were allegations that 'Muvi TV', a local television station in Lusaka, had been closed for hosting the live presidential debate without President Lungu. 'Zambian Watchdog', an anti-government online newspaper website funded by UPND leader Hakainde Hichilema, continued to be under attack. Towards the end of September, first its Facebook page, then its Twitter account, and finally its website were closed down. However, the appearance of 'Zambian Watchdog Two' as well as several anti-government Facebook pages suggested the newspaper was active under different names.

Foreign Policy

International travel aimed at attracting *foreign investment* and strengthening bilateral relations remained key in foreign policy strategies. As in his previous term, Lungu was Zambia's face in the international arena, even when he was accompanied by Foreign Affairs Minister Harry Kalaba and other cabinet ministers holding key portfolios in the areas under negotiation. Travel agendas targeted strategic partners, particularly in Africa and the Middle East.

As early as 15 January, Lungu travelled to Namibia to attend the Committee of Ten (C-10) Summit of the AU on reforms at the UNSC. On 28 January, he travelled to Addis Ababa (Ethiopia) to participate in the AU's Heads of State Summit and the African Assembly Project held on 21–31 January. The theme for this year's AU Project was 'The African Year of Human Rights with Particular Focus on the Rights of Women'. This meeting was particularly important for Zambia's aspirations in the region as it won the support of 52 member states to be elected to the Peace and Security Council (PSC), the AU's decision-making body responsible for maintaining peace and security on the continent.

During February, the president made his first *European visit*. On 4 February, he travelled to Italy to meet Pope Francis, as well as the directors general of FAO and IFAD. On the 6th, he visited France, accompanied by Henry Kalaba, Minister of Commerce, Trade and Industry Margaret Mwanakatwe and Minister of Energy and Water Development Dora Siliya, to meet President François Hollande and business people. Agreements were signed between the Zambia National Broadcasting Corporation and France24, between the Schools of Mining at the University of Zambia and the University of Nantes, and between the Zambian Finance Ministry and the French Development Agency.

From 27 February to 3 March, Lungu visited *Israel* at the invitation of Prime Minister Benjamin Netanyahu. On 17 March, he started a two-day state visit to *Mozambique* to meet President Filipe Nyusi. With the inauguration of a power project in Nacala as the culmination of the visit, the main highlight was the commissioning of the supply of 100 MW of electricity from the private Karpowership docked in Nacala. On 25 April, Lungu visited *Malawi* to discuss issues surrounding climate change with his Malawian counterpart, President Peter Mutharika.

On 16–17 May, Lungu visited *Saudi Arabia* at the invitation of King Salman bin Abdulaziz Al Saud. This was praised as a landmark in the country's history. He signed a $ 20 m financing agreement for the supply of low-cost fuel. On 11 May, he joined other heads of state to attend the inauguration of Ugandan President Yoweri Kaguta Museveni. While in *Uganda*, he engaged Museveni in trade talks under the COMESA trade structures. On 4 July, he visited Uganda for a second time to attend the 40th anniversary of Operation Entebbe, the counter-terrorist hostage-rescue mission, carried out by the Israeli Defence Forces at Entebbe Airport in 1976.

Three days after being sworn in as president, Lungu participated in the 71st *UN General Assembly* in New York (16–21 September), even putting the formation of his cabinet on hold. The following month, he attended the 19th COMESA summit held on 19–20 October in Madagascar and a meeting of the ICGLR on 26 October in Angola. On 14–18 November, he attended the UN Climate Change conference in Morocco, and on 22–25 November the 4th Africa-Arab Summit in Equatorial Guinea, followed by a state visit to *Tanzania* on 27–29 November. Several agreements were signed to strengthen bilateral relations, notably to revitalise the Tanzania Zambia Railway Authority and the Tanzania Zambia Mafuta pipeline, and agreements were also concluded regarding air travel between Dar es Salaam and Lusaka, diplomatic consultations, immigration and prisons.

Lungu's last official visit of the year was to *South Africa* on 7–9 December. The visit was preceded by the signing of a Joint Commission for Cooperation between Zambia and South Africa. This was the first time that the two countries had established a permanent structured platform to periodically address issues of common interest and concern.

Lungu's foreign trips raised criticism because he was spending a considerable proportion of his working days out of the country. However, the government was quite optimistic about the outcomes of their strategy. Foreign Minister Kalaba's statements in the media stressed that "Zambia would reap from foreign relations". In fact, Lungu's travels contributed to raising the country's international profile and attracted new foreign investors by reaching out to the international community.

China remained one of Zambia's main trading partners and there were further advances to enhance bilateral ties between the two countries. During a visit by Zhang Dejiang, chairman of the Standing Committee of China's National People's Congress, on 18–22 March, there were talks aimed at increasing investment and expanding cooperation in the industry, mining and agriculture sectors.

There was some slippage with regard to relations with some *Nordic countries*. Sweden and Finland suspended all further funding to the Zambia National Farmers' Union, suggesting the union's management had mismanaged funding. Norway closed its embassy, citing economic pressures at home and Zambia's poor record in terms of economic growth and fighting of corruption.

Socioeconomic Developments

The economy remained under strain. According to World Bank and IMF estimates, annual *economic growth* stood at 3%, the lowest since 1999. This reflected broad economic trends at the regional level. The fall in commodity prices and declining Chinese demand severely affected the economies of countries across Africa. Zambia, as Africa's second-largest copper producer, relied on copper for more than 70% of its export earnings, so it was particularly hard hit. Economic performance also suffered from *domestic pressures*. Zambia had been facing a power crisis – partly due to poor rainfall – since 2015, which impacted all sectors of the economy and particularly the mining sectors, the biggest consumers of energy. Thousands of miners were dismissed in the wake of the power crisis and its effects on mining activities. Youth unemployment remained high (around 10.5% according to statements issued by Labour Minister Fackson Shamenda in January). The *cost of living* peaked. According to the Jesuit Centre for Theological Reflection (JCTR), the cost of living for Lusaka as measured by the JCTR Basic Needs Basket for an average Zambian family of five hit an all-time high of K (kwacha) 5,036.3 in the month of October.

So, unsurprisingly, the economy was a key issue in elections and was strongly highlighted in Lungu's speech on the occasion of the official opening of the first session of the 12th National Assembly on 30 September. Among many other things, he announced that the government would continue to implement *austerity measures* to stabilise the macro-economic situation, and build greater investor confidence through consistent and predictable policies. He further promised "achieving double-digit gross domestic product growth, attaining single-digit inflation rate and increasing and broadening domestic revenue collection" and sustained public debt "in order to increase the fiscal space and create room for development financing". Agriculture emerged as a key priority both in terms of diversification "away from copper and towards agriculture, livestock and fisheries" and in terms of "science and technology". Job creation through industrialisation was another important issue stressed by the president.

In early October, the government began to pave the way for an *IMF programme* by formulating an economic policy programme around four pillars. As explained by Finance Minister Mutati, the first pillar consisted of the removal of subsidies in the region of $ 1 bn, presumably on electricity, fuel and maize; the second was an increase in allocation to social safety nets, to prevent the removal of subsidies that affected the most vulnerable in society; the third was improved economic governance by making the Public Finance Act "more punitive" to address abuse of public resources; and the fourth was the restoration of budget credibility. These pillars would form the foundation for economic recovery and for future engagement with the IMF. "We shall lead the way in setting the parameters of our economic recovery and stabilisation programme," Mutati reiterated. The IMF had visited Zambia in March but had left without reaching an agreement with the government on an IMF loan programme. At that point, the IMF wanted the government to increase the prices of both electricity and fuel, and this was now included under the first pillar. At the invitation of the Zambian authorities, an IMF team led by Tsidi Tsikata visited the country on 19–31 October. The team met with Finance Minister Mutati, Bank of Zambia (BoZ) Governor Denny Kalyalya, National Development Planning Minister Lucky Mulusa, other senior government and BoZ officials, MPs, and representatives of the private sector, labour unions, civil society organisations and Zambia's development partners. The IMF's preliminary findings after the visit acknowledged huge economic challenges and promised "to support Zambia and its people as needed".

On the positive side, the annual *inflation rate* target was set at 7% and it was nearly on target in December, closing the year at 7.5%. The *kwacha*, which was one of the world's worst performing currencies in 2015, improved against other major convertible currencies on the international market. Despite late rains, the *maize* harvest increased to 2,873,052 tonnes in the 2015/16 growing season, up from 2,618,221 tonnes in 2014/15.

The government announced an increase in the *minimum wage* before the elections. They were last increased by 67% in July 2012, but the rise took a long time to implement as many sectoral factors had not been accounted for. Zambia hit the international headlines due to riots and *xenophobic attacks*. The riots started on 18 April after rumours that Rwandans were behind ritual killings in Lusaka. More than 250 people were arrested after more than 60 Rwandan-owned shops were looted in two days of violence. BBC News reported that hundreds of mainly Rwandan immigrants who own shops in the slums around the capital fled their homes after their businesses were ransacked by mobs accusing them of ritual killings.

Zimbabwe

Amin Y. Kamete

Intraparty factionalism and succession struggles within the Zimbabwe African National Union-Patriotic Front (ZANU-PF) hogged the news throughout the year. There were rumours and speculations about opposition coalitions ahead of the 2018 elections. One of the major developments was the fallout between war veterans and President Mugabe. Speculation and gossip about Mugabe's health continued unabated. While foreign relations with the usual friends remained good, there was no sign of improvement in relations with Western countries and multilateral lenders. These strained relations were characterised by arguments about 'illegal' Western sanctions and human rights abuses. The economy showed no sign of improvement, with cash shortages worsening. This gave rise to another talking point for most of the year: the controversial introduction of so-called bond notes.

Domestic Politics

The ZANU-PF *succession struggles*, which had been obvious during the party's 15th Annual People's Conference in December 2015, escalated. With the Mujuru

 | DOI 10.1163/9789004355910_056

faction almost completely purged from the party, the main factions were Team Lacoste, reportedly aligned to Vice President Emmerson Mnangagwa, and Generation 40 (G40), widely seen as being aligned to President Robert Mugabe's wife, Grace Mugabe. In the run-up to an important ZANU-PF politburo meeting, on 2 February, the 'Daily News' quoted a ZANU-PF insider as saying Mugabe was "between a rock and a hard place" as both factions had some of his most trusted lieutenants among their ranks. On 30 January, Mugabe did not take sides. Instead, he pleaded for unity in the party, pointing out that "leaders are chosen at the [party] congress". Throughout the year, groups and senior party members within ZANU-PF became embroiled in the fractious succession politics. The Zimbabwe National Liberation War Veterans Association (ZNLWVA) threatened to bar Higher Education Minister Jonathan Moyo and Saviours Kasukuwere, the national political commissar – both of the G40 faction – from attending politburo meetings. On 8 February, the ZANU-PF Women's League secretary for finance, Sarah Mahoka, a known G40 member, challenged Mnangagwa to "come out clean" about his presidential ambitions. On 10 February, at a ZANU-PF rally attended by Robert Mugabe and the two vice presidents, Mahoka rebuked Mnangagwa, warning that he risked death if he did not rein in party officials abusing his name and campaigning for him to succeed the president. The fact that Mahoka was never rebuked by the party was taken as evidence that Grace Mugabe was behind the attack on Mnangagwa. *Mnangagwa's political career* was seemingly in danger after Grace Mugabe attacked him at a rally on 12 February. In the thinly veiled attack, she accused Mnangagwa of deception and working to topple her husband, among other things. There was speculation that the politburo meeting scheduled for 10 February would be the end of *Jonathan Moyo*, who was engaged in public Twitter wars with members of Team Lacoste. However, after the meeting the G40 faction seemed to have fared better than Team Lacoste. The political careers of key Mnangagwa allies were uncertain after they appeared before the party's National Disciplinary Committee on 16 February. The most prominent casualties were outspoken War Veterans Minister Christopher Mutsvangwa and his wife.

War veterans became actively involved in the divisive succession politics. The top leadership of the veterans, including Mutsvangwa, aligned themselves to Team Lacoste. On 18 February, anti-riot police disrupted a ZNLWVA meeting in Harare. They threw tear gas canisters into the crowd, which resulted in running battles. This signalled the breakdown of the relationship between President Mugabe and the veterans. In an unprecedented move on 22 July, the ZNLWVA appeared to have ditched Mugabe, issuing a strongly-worded statement that it would no longer support him in elections. The statement pointed out that the party leadership had "dismally failed" to deal with the economic problems besetting the nation. In an apparent attack on Mugabe, the group said it noted "with concern, shock and utter dismay the entrenchment of dictatorial tendencies, personified by the president and his cohorts which have slowly devoured the values of the liberation struggle". The ZNLWVA leadership. including its spokesman, Douglas Mahiya, and secretary-general, Victor Matemadanda, were arrested on charges of undermining the president's authority. Mugabe's relationship with the war veterans did not normalise for the rest of the year.

It had become the case that factional struggles were characterised by *expulsions and suspensions of senior party members.* On 18 March, ZANU-PF's Bulawayo province suspended 19 senior members for attending a war veterans meeting addressed by Mutsvangwa and Jabulani Sibanda, the former war veterans' leader who had been expelled from the party. Among those suspended was the former Matabeleland South governor, Senator Angeline Masuku. On 6 July, Mutsvangwa and his wife were expelled from ZANU-PF. He lost his parliamentary seat on 19 July. On 3 August, ZANU-PF expelled a further nine senior members, including the four top executives of the ZNLWVA, among them Mahiya and Matemadanda. When ZANU-PF held its 16th Annual People's Congress in Masvingo on 13–18 December, it was a divided party. Moyo's Twitter wars with members of Team Lacoste showed no signs of abating. In the end, the conference, on the theme 'Moving with Zim-Asset in Peace and Unity', was an unremarkable event with no major shifts in the factional struggles. The rumoured Women's League resolution to have a women's quota reinstated, allegedly to scuttle Mnangagwa' s presidential ambitions, did not materialise. The resolution would have meant that one of the vice presidents had to be a woman. Because Phelekelezela Mphoko, the other vice president was 'safe' by virtue of being from the former Zimbabwe African People's Union (ZAPU), the proposed clause was seen as targeting Mnangagwa. On 17 December, delegates confirmed Robert Mugabe as the sole *ZANU-PF presidential candidate* for the 2018 elections.

President Mugabe's health continued to be the source of speculation and rumours. It made headlines in April after a picture in the official press showed aides helping him as he was bending over to greet mourners at a funeral. Analysts said his aides were either holding his arms to prevent him from falling on top of mourners or supporting his failing hand. In August, Mugabe left a summit of southern African leaders apparently without warning and went to Dubai. This fuelled speculation that he had been taken seriously ill, with some rumours even suggesting he may have died. In November, Mugabe's health was again in the news when a video clip showed him walking painfully across the red carpet at the COP22 climate change summit in Marrakesh (Morocco).

The *fight against corruption* became tainted with succession politics when Higher Education Minister Moyo and his deputy were accused of corruption. In July, the Zimbabwe Anti-Corruption Commission (ZACC) revealed allegations of fraud and criminal abuse of duty, including that the two had siphoned off $ 400,000 from the Zimbabwe Manpower Development Fund. In October, Moyo admitted that he used the money to finance party projects and buy bicycles for traditional leaders in his constituency. There were reports that he was being protected from arrest in what was seen as an extension of ZANU-PF's factional wars. On 2 November, Moyo handed himself over to ZACC for questioning.

The Ministry of Finance and Economic Development announced in a circular distributed to MPs on 8 March that the government was planning to start *compensating white farmers* who had been evicted during the seizure of white-owned farms at the turn of the century. Compensation would be paid for land, improvements and equipment seized by the state. Commercial Farmers' Union (CFU) chief executive officer Hendrik Oliver doubted this, saying that most CFU members were sceptical of the offer because the government had not shown any commitment to compensating them since 2000. On 15 September, Minister of Finance and Economic Development Patrick Chinamasa revealed that the government had paid nearly $ 43 m in compensation to white commercial farmers whose farms had been seized.

There was some major *industrial unrest* during the year. On 4 July, government workers went on strike over unpaid salaries. The government blamed this on the chronic cash shortage. Teachers, doctors and nurses were among the civil servants who stopped work because they had not been paid for more than a month. On 5 July, violent clashes between taxi drivers and police rocked Harare, leading to the arrest of 95 people. This coincided with the strike by doctors, teachers and nurses.

A resurgence among new *social movements* brought some life to protests, especially in urban areas. The most significant of these were #ThisFlag and #Tajamuka. The #ThisFlag movement was started in April through social media by the then little-known clergyman, *Pastor Evan Mawarire*, when he called for an end to the country's economic woes. By the second half of the year, the accidental movement had spread and become popular, especially among the youths in urban areas. On 6 July, #ThisFlag shut down Harare when it fronted a stay-away. Zimbabweans stayed at home and banks and most businesses closed operations because of the peaceful action. On 12 July, Pastor Mawarire was arrested after leading the campaign against alleged government corruption and the poor handling of the country's troubled economy. The police accused him of inciting public violence and disturbing the peace. There was an unprecedented demonstration of public support for Mawarire, with thousands of people reportedly attending his court hearing into the night of 13 July. On that day, the court freed him, ruling that the police had violated his rights. The magistrate told the packed courtroom that the decision to bring new charges against him was unconstitutional. The government apparently took Mawarire seriously, with President Mugabe himself speaking out against him on 19 July. He accused Mawarire of being foreign sponsored, calling for him to leave the country. Mawarire left the country, citing concerns about the security of his family. He ended up in the United States and stayed there for the rest of the year.

Human rights issues were mainly linked to alleged police brutality and curtailment of rights of assembly and movement. Mawarire was not the only person arrested for protesting. The most prominent cases of arrest, detention and brutality involved members of the protest group *Tajamuka-Sesijikile Campaign*. On 9 July, protest leader Promise Mkwananzi surrendered himself to police in Harare. They had been looking for him for participating in public unrest that had shut down Zimbabwe the previous week. He was facing charges related to alleged violence outside a supermarket said to be owned by Vice President Mphoko. A week after the protest, the police had reportedly arrested more than 200 people in connection with the shut down. There were reports of abductions and attempted abductions of protest leaders. On 6 July, two #Tajamuka activists, Lawrence Tembedza and Austin Nyakupinda, were allegedly abducted by suspected state security agents. Pastor Mawarire also alleged that suspected security agents had tried to abduct him but had failed.

Perhaps the most famous prisoner and symbol of the resistance and brutality was *Linda Masarira*, who was arrested on 6 July. She was detained for months in Chikurubi Maximum Security Prison, where she was reportedly locked up with dangerous male criminals. It was alleged by activists that the state was trying to make an example of her. Masarira was released on bail following a High Court judgement on 26 September. Another dogged protester who had run-ins with the state security apparatus was *Standrick Zvorwadza*, the chairman of the National Vendors Union of Zimbabwe. He was arrested at Rainbow Towers Hotel in Harare in June while protesting against Vice President Mphoko's continued stay in the hotel. He was charged with threats to commit malicious damage to property. On 18 August, Zvorwadza was admitted to hospital after heavily armed police attacked him while he was protesting at the Harare Central Police Station against alleged police ruthlessness in their treatment of vendors and prodemocracy activists.

It was a relatively quiet year in the opposition. Talks of an opposition grand coalition were perhaps the most dominant issue in *opposition politics*. On 28 April, Morgan Tsvangirai announced that the Movement for Democratic Change (MDC-T) national executive had mandated him to hold coalition negotiations with other opposition parties ahead of the 2018 elections. According to Eddie Cross, the party's secretary for local government, the MDC-T wanted any coalition to be built on two principles, "the interests of the country and the will of the people". Signalling that the talks would not be easy, Cross stated, "In the majority of cases we do not see this in our colleagues in the opposition movement." Despite pressures for an opposition coalition, there appeared to be discord on the issue within the MDC-T leadership, with some supporting it while others seemed unenthusiastic.

On 30 May, smaller opposition parties signed a coalition agreement in Harare. This marked the birth of the *Coalition of Democrats* (CODE), which was expected to field and support one candidate for president and more for other positions in elections from local government up to legislature level. The CODE signatories were the president of the Democratic Assembly for Restoration of the Economy, Gilbert Dzikiti, the president of the MDC-N, Welshman Ncube, the president of the Mavambo Khusile Dawn, Simba Makoni, the president of the Renewal Democrats, Elton Mangoma, and the president of Zimbabwe United for Democracy, Farai Mbire. Tendai Biti's People's Democratic Party and Dumiso Dambengwa's ZAPU were at the signing ceremony and gave solidarity messages, although they did not sign the agreement. MDC-T and Joice Mujuru's Zimbabwe People First did not attend. The MDC-T said they were not invited. Mujuru reportedly showed interest in the coalition but was waiting for the party's congress expected in August to give the green light to sign the agreement.

Opposition parties maintained their pressure for *electoral reforms* ahead of the 2018 elections. Operating under the National Electoral Reform Agenda (NERA) signed in December 2015, they staged several high-profile protest activities during the year. On 16 August, the NERA signatories, among them the MDC-T, resolved to take Mugabe head-on in a protest march involving more than 200,000 opposition supporters. The NERA chairperson, former presidential affairs minister Didymus Mutasa, said the planned demonstration was aimed at forcing the Zimbabwe Electoral Commission to order the army, police and other units of the state security apparatus to stay out of partisan ZANU-PF politics. Police tried to block the demonstration and NERA had to go to court to be given the go-ahead. When the event finally took place on 26 August, law enforcement agents crushed it brutally. Police continued to ban and/or suppress NERA demonstrations for the rest of the year.

After a period of speculation about his health, on 27 June, MDC-T leader, *Morgan Tsvangirai* announced that he was undergoing treatment for colon cancer in South Africa. On 15 July, following a day-long meeting with his party's executive members, he announced the appointment of two new vice presidents for the MDC-T. The two new vice-presidents, Nelson Chamisa and Ellias Mudzuri, joined Thokozani Khupe, who had held the position for several years. The move was interpreted by some – particularly ZANU-PF sympathisers – as an indication that all was not well in the MDC-T.

There were a few *by-elections* during the year, which were all boycotted by the MDC-T. In October, independent candidate Temba Mliswa, who was backed by the MDC-T and war veterans, won the Norton by-election. In November, ZANU-PF won the Chimanimani West by-election by a margin of 8,000 votes. The parties that went up against ZANU-PF were the little-known Renewal of Democrats and the National Constitutional Assembly.

Foreign Affairs

The year saw no major shift in the country's foreign relations. As before, relations with most African and Asian countries and organisations were good. There was little change in relations with OECD countries and major multilateral organisations. As expected, ZANU-PF and the government continued blaming Zimbabwe's economic woes on 'illegal' Western sanctions. On 28 January, Mugabe ended his one-year term as the *chair of the AU*. In his hour-long speech, he condemned the West's involvement in Africa's affairs. He also spoke against whites, former colonialists, Westerners, US President Barack Obama and the UN.

Zimbabwe continued to be an active and enthusiastic participant in *SADC* affairs but was not the centre of attention. Mugabe attended the 36th Heads of State and Government Summit in Mbabane (Swaziland) on 30–31 August. Zimbabwe was not on the agenda. Civil society groups had tried to force discussions on human rights abuses in Zimbabwe, citing police brutality against citizens expressing their right to demonstrate and issues regarding the use of social media to push for social justice, but they did not succeed.

While relations with most of Africa were good, relations with *Botswana* did not seem to improve. On 21 September, Reuters reported that Botswana's President Ian Khama had said Mugabe should step aside without delay and allow new leadership to emerge because Zimbabwe was dragging down the whole of southern Africa. At the end of September, Mugabe reportedly turned down an invitation by his Botswana counterpart to attend Botswana's celebrations for its 50th anniversary of Independence.

In August, Mugabe cancelled a scheduled state visit to *Ghana*, where he was to be given an award. There was confusion surrounding the cancellation and the event itself. Some reports suggested that he was angry that the hosts had also invited Morocco's King Mohammed VI. However, the Ghanaian government reportedly claimed that it had not invited Mugabe. There were also reports that Ghana's President John Mahama, who was expected to confer on Mugabe the Millennium Lifetime Achievement award, was not going to be in Accra.

Relations with *South Africa* remained friendly. On 31 October, the inaugural meeting of the South Africa–Zimbabwe Bi-National Commission started in Harare. The two countries agreed to set up a Joint Trade and Investment Committee to oversee their economic cooperation. The official opening on 2 November was co-chaired by President Jacob Zuma and President Mugabe and the two leaders also witnessed the signing of an Air Service Agreement.

Zimbabwe maintained good relations with *China*. On 3 August, China pledged $ 46 m toward the construction of a new Zimbabwean parliament building. The pledge was described as a 'gift' to Zimbabwe. It was reported that Chinese officials believed that Zimbabwe's current parliament building was too small for its lawmakers to work effectively. During the year, China opened its markets to Zimbabwean farm products. It also expanded its investments in Zimbabwe's housing and agriculture sectors, and made loans to upgrade its medical equipment in inner-city hospitals.

Zimbabwe–Russia relations remained strong. On 13 November, a delegation of Russian companies led by the deputy head of the Africa Division of the Ministry of Industry and Trade of the Russian Federation, Pavel Volosov, was in Zimbabwe and had a meeting with the government and some local companies. The two countries agreed to set up a forum to facilitate and promote trade and investments. This was hailed as evidence that economic relations between Zimbabwe and Russia were poised for strong growth.

There was no major shift in relations with the *EU*. On 15 February, following an annual review, the European Council adopted a decision extending EU restrictive measures against Zimbabwe to 20 February 2017. The measures continued to apply to President Mugabe, his wife and Zimbabwe Defence Industries. Measures against "five high ranking members of the security apparatus" would remain suspended. Significantly, "78 persons and eight entities", against whom measures had been suspended, would be removed from the list. The arms embargo would remain in place. On 9 June, the EU signed an EPA giving six SADC nations unlimited access to the economic bloc. Zimbabwe was not included.

Relations with the *United Kingdom* did not change much. The UK's goal in Zimbabwe remained "to encourage a peaceful, democratic society where the rule of law and human rights are adhered to, laying the foundations for long term sustainable development". This meant inevitable clashes with Zimbabwe, whose brand of sovereignty interpreted such statements as interference and part of a regime-change agenda. On 6 April, it was reported that the UK had taken the unusual step of blocking Mugabe's nomination for the new Zimbabwe ambassador to the UK. The man at the centre of the unusual move was Ray Ndhlukula, then deputy chief secretary in the president's office. He was said to be one of the biggest beneficiaries of Zimbabwe's controversial land reform programme.

Relations with the *US* did not improve. On 1 March, President Barack Obama extended targeted sanctions for another year, saying Mugabe's regime continued to represent "an unusual and extraordinary threat to the foreign policy of the United States". On 3 October, the US announced the lifting of sanctions on nine individuals and several companies in Zimbabwe, but Mugabe himself remained on the list

Relations with *multilateral organisations* were mixed. On 9 May, the IMF announced the completion of the 2016 Article IV Consultation Mission to Zimbabwe and the Third and Final Review of the Staff-Monitored Program (SMP). The IMF noted that economic difficulties had deepened and recommended immediate action, but also noted that the authorities in Zimbabwe had met all quantitative targets and structural benchmarks under the SMP. On 19 October, Zimbabwe cleared its arrears with the IMF as part of efforts to settle its overdue financial obligations to the institution. Towards the end of the year, Zimbabwe was frantically scrambling to secure $ 600 m from the AFDB to clear its arrears, but this was not achieved. There were indications that the World Bank was considering giving Zimbabwe $ 300 m to settle part of its arrears to the multilateral lender. However, reports suggested that the plan was thwarted due to mounting local and international pressure against the country's ambitious arrears clearance strategy.

Socioeconomic Developments

There was no let-up in the country's economic challenges during the year. *Economic indicators* did not improve much and deflationary pressures continued. Reserve Bank of Zimbabwe (RBZ) figures showed that the December consumer price index for all items was 96.2%. The annual inflation was -1.6%, compared with -2.4% in 2015. According to Economist Intelligence Unit (EIU) estimates, real GDP growth was -0.4%, a drop from 0.5% in 2015. The EIU put the nominal GDP at $ 15.5 bn, up from $ 14.4 bn in 2015. The current account balance was – $ 2.1 bn, compared with – $3.1 bn in 2015. Total international reserves dropped to $ 394 m. According to the 2017 budget statement, as at 31 October 2016, Zimbabwe's public debt stood at $ 11.2 bn or 79% of GDP. Of this $ 7.5 bn (53% of GDP), was external debt. On 4 February, the RBZ governor, John Mangudya, announced in his Monetary Policy Statement a return to *partial exchange controls.* He claimed Zimbabwe was losing $ 2 bn a year in illicit outflows.

Zimbabwe performed poorly in a number of *world ranking tables.* In the World Bank's Doing Business 2016, it was ranked 161st, four places down from 2015. The World Economic Forum's Global Competitiveness Report 2015–16 ranked Zimbabwe 125th out of 140 countries. There was some improvement in the 2016 Human Development Report, with Zimbabwe indexed at 0.516 and ranked 154th, up one place from 2015.

The country faced several *humanitarian challenges.* On 21 January, the governor of the RBZ, announced that the government had secured $ 200 m from the African-Export-Import Bank (Afreximbank) in lines of credit for grain imports. In February, Mugabe declared a state of disaster in rural areas hit by a severe drought. More than a quarter of the population faced food shortages. According to the UN Office for the Coordination of Humanitarian Affairs, the humanitarian situation deteriorated dramatically across the country. Post-harvest assessments and the July Report of the Vulnerability Assessment Committee (ZimVAC) indicated that up to 4.1 m people in rural areas would be affected by food insecurity during the peak hunger period (January–March 2017). This amounted to 42% of the rural population. In August, 2.2 m people needed urgent food assistance. The ZimVAC highlighted levels of food insecurity between 50% and 79% in 20 districts. About 4.3 m people would need water and sanitation services between September 2016 and March 2017. The nutrition situation also deteriorated. Four districts were above WHO thresholds for 'serious' or 'critical' Global Acute Malnutrition rates, and a further 16 districts were classified as 'poor'.

Harare reported several cases of *typhoid fever*, sparking fears of a major outbreak. On 25 January, the Harare City health director, said that six cases of the disease had been confirmed in the previous five days in various suburbs. In December, typhoid fever was suspected to have claimed the life of a 13-year-old girl in Mbare, Harare's oldest suburb. There were fears that it could spread to other suburbs due to persistent rains. In October, health authorities issued a *cholera and typhoid outbreak alert* in the capital due to severe water shortages. Large parts of Harare were then restricted to running water on only two days a week, and residents in both urban and rural areas turned to potentially contaminated sources of water for everyday use.

On *demographic indicators*, according to estimates, the death rate stood at 9.87 deaths per 1,000 population. Due to the deteriorating economic situation, the flow of Zimbabweans into South Africa and Botswana in search of better economic opportunities persisted. UN estimates put the net migration rate at −2.97 migrants per 1,000 population. Life expectancy for the total population was 58 years. The infant mortality rate was estimated at 38.4 deaths per 1,000 live births. The literacy rate remained above 90%, making Zimbabwe the leader in Africa.

Zimbabwe had the fifth highest *HIV* prevalence in SSA. UNAIDS figures showed that 1.4 m people were living with HIV. The prevalence rate among adults aged 15–49 was estimated at 14.7%. Adults aged 15 and over living with HIV numbered some 1.3 m, plus 77,000 children aged 14 or under. Deaths due to AIDS were estimated at 29,000. There were 450,000 orphans under 18 due to AIDS.

As in 2015, the *education and health* delivery systems continued to experience problems of staffing, equipment and funding. Health and educational personnel continued to constitute a substantial part of the brain drain. Industrial action and threats of industrial action arising out of salary disputes were a constant feature throughout the year, further compromising these sectors. Delays in paying salaries and annual bonuses did not help boost morale. Throughout the year, Lazarus Dokora, the primary and secondary school minister, generated controversy with his zeal for an endless raft of reforms. In January, it was reported that the government was fine-tuning education policies. The minister said the changes would be implemented systematically and gradually. Among his proposed reforms were the teaching of all subjects in indigenous languages and the introduction of Islam and Buddhism to the curriculum.

On 12 April, Mugabe intervened to clarify the government's position on the controversial *indigenisation law* after a spate of public disagreements between Finance Minister Patrick Chinamasa and Indigenisation Minister Patrick Zhuwao over the implementation of the legislation in the financial services sector. Mugabe complained that the conflicting positions on how to implement the country's black empowerment legislation had caused confusion to potential investors and needed to be put to rest. In a statement released by Information Minister Christopher Mushowe, Mugabe subtly backed the finance minister's conciliatory tone. Chinamasa had announced that all foreign-owned financial institutions operating in the country had managed to submit credible indigenisation plans before the 31 March deadline. He said this after Zhuwao had threatened to shut down all companies that failed to submit "credible plans" by 1 April.

In May, the RBZ announced that it would issue *bond notes* to curb the flow of money out of the country. Like the bond coins that had been introduced in 2014, the bond notes would be backed by the $ 200 m Afreximbank Nostro Support facility, which was expected to cushion the high demand for foreign exchange. RBZ Governor John Mangundya did not give a date for the introduction of the notes. There was widespread suspicion, with critics and opponents claiming this was an attempt to reintroduce the Zimbabwe dollar through the backdoor and widespread scepticism that it would bring a return to the days of hyperinflation fuelled by the collapse of the Zimbabwe dollar. Mangudya rejected these criticisms and emphasised that the introduction of the notes was only a precaution against illicit financial flows. This triggered debate, protests and litigation – most prominently a law suit brought by the former vice president, Joice Mujuru. The controversy dragged on as the issuing of the bond notes was repeatedly delayed. On 18 November, the government finally gazetted the *Reserve Bank of Zimbabwe Amendment Bill 2016* to enable the central bank and the minister of finance and economic development to issue bond notes exchangeable at par value with the US dollar. The Act was deemed to have come into force on 31 October 2016 and the RBZ rolled out the controversial bond notes on 28 November. On the same day, a High Court judgement dismissed an application by a Harare businessman challenging the legality of Statutory Instrument 133 of 2016, which backed the release of bond notes into circulation.

In November, a survey by the Confederation of Zimbabwe Industries showed that local *manufacturing sector* capacity utilisation had increased by 18% to 47.4%. Experts pointed out that the increase was mainly the outcome of distortions resulting from the closure of hundreds of companies no longer considered in a nationwide survey.

In August, the government launched *Targeted Command Agriculture*. Some 2,000 farmers were expected to benefit from the agricultural scheme, which was aimed at ensuring food self-sufficiency. The scheme was expected to target farmers near bodies of water, who could each put a minimum of 200 ha under maize cultivation. The mandate for each farmer was to produce at least 1,000 tonnes of maize. Each participating farmer was required to commit 5 tonnes per hectare towards repayment of government loans in the form of irrigation equipment, inputs and chemicals, mechanised equipment, electricity and water charges. Farmers would retain whatever they produced above the 1,000 tonnes. The programme would cost $ 500 m. Each farmer would receive $ 250,000.

On 8 December, the Finance and Economic Development Minister Patrick Chinamasa presented the *2017 national budget* with the theme 'Pushing Production Frontiers Across All Sectors of the Economy'. Chinamasa proposed a $ 4.1 bn budget. The economy was projected to grow by 1.7% in 2017. $ 2.9 bn in revenue was collected between January and October against a target of $ 3.2 bn, falling short by 9.8%. Cumulative expenditure for January to October amounted to $ 3.8 bn against a target of $ 3.3 bn, representing a $ 520 m overspend. Employment costs would account for 91% of revenue. Exports declined by 6.9% to $ 3.4 bn, against which the import bill stood at $ 5.4 bn.

www.ingramcontent.com/pod-product-compliance
Lightning Source LLC
LaVergne TN
LVHW080114011026
849160LV00013B/1103
* 9 7 8 9 0 0 4 3 5 5 9 0 3 *